Money markets

This volume is the first of its kind to present within one cover studies of twelve different money markets. It offers a comparative analysis of the money markets in major world financial centres, explaining the way they actually operate and examining the intervention techniques that central banks and monetary authorities employ within that framework.

By drawing on his extensive experience over 40 years, J. S. G. Wilson is able to place his analysis in context and trace the developments in the various money markets. In bringing all this information together, this book provides an important source of reference for those wishing to compare the recent changes in money markets throughout the world and to assess the expansion and growth of those markets in less-developed countries. It will be an essential resource for those studying financial economics and comparative banking, for financial analysts, consultants, and practitioners in banks of all kinds and financial institutions generally. This book assembles the most up-to-date information on different money markets around the world and shows exactly how they operate.

J. S. G. Wilson is Emeritus Professor of Economics and Commerce at the University of Hull. He has extensive practical experience of the workings of the money markets and, as a distinguished academic in the field, has contributed to the *New Palgrave Dictionary of Money and Finance* and the *Encyclopædia Britannica*. He is author most recently of *Banking Policy and Structure*.

Money markets

The international perspective

J. S. G. Wilson
Emeritus Professor of Economics and Commerce,
University of Hull

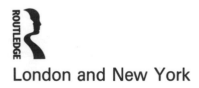

London and New York

First published 1993
by Routledge
11 New Fetter Lane, London EC4P 4EE

Simultaneously published in the USA and Canada
by Routledge
29 West 35th Street, New York, NY 10001

© 1993 J. S. G. Wilson

Typeset in English Times by
Pat and Anne Murphy, Highcliffe-on-Sea, Dorset
Printed and bound in Great Britain by
Mackays of Chatham PLC, Chatham, Kent

British Library Cataloguing-in-Publication Data
A catalogue record for this book is available from
the British Library.

ISBN 0–415–02423–4

Library of Congress Cataloging in Publication Data
Has been applied for.

ISBN 0–415–02423–4

To
BMW

Contents

List of figures and tables   ix
Preface   xi
List of abbreviations and acronyms   xvi

1 Introduction   1

2 The London money markets   7

3 Money markets in the United States of America   102

4 The money market in France   156

5 The German money market   171

6 The Italian money market   221

7 The money market in Japan   241

8 The Australian money market   267

9 The money market in Canada   297

10 The money market in Hong Kong   320

11 Money markets in India   336

12 The money market in Singapore   346

13 The South African money market   363

14 Conclusion   387

Notes   392
Index   426

Figures and tables

FIGURES

2.1 LIFFE's time zone advantage 72
5.1 Growth of the money stock M3 (a) 1989–91
    (b) 1990–2 186
5.2 Operating variables in the money market, 1990–2 194
5.3 Structure of M3 210

TABLES

2.1 International banking market size, 1983–91 22
2.2 UK government ECU Treasury bill programme:
    turnover statistics, 1988–92 32
2.3 Sterling commercial paper, October 1991 61
2.4 Risk classification of assets 94
2.5 The three categories into which exposures should
    be grouped 99
11.1 Scheduled banks in India (as on 30 June 1991) 337
12.1 Number of financial institutions in Singapore,
    1987–91 349

Preface

This book is a sister volume to my *Banking Policy and Structure: A Comparative Analysis*, published in 1986. In *Banking Policy and Structure*, I was only able to include a single chapter on 'The Role of a Money Market' (to set the scene for a consideration of intervention by central banks), but there was so much more that could have been said on the subject. Money markets is an area within the field of the comparative study of financial institutions that has been of interest to me over a long period of years. However, even within the confines of a relatively large book it has been impossible to include all the money markets which at one time or another I have had occasion to study. Hence, it is necessary to outline the basis of selection. The money markets concentrated in London and which obtain in the USA are obvious candidates for inclusion. So, too, are three markets in Western Europe – France, Germany and Italy; likewise Japan. Another group derived from my interest many years ago in 'The New Money Markets', on which I wrote an article published in *Lloyds Bank Review* in April 1962, republished in my *Monetary Policy and the Development of Money Markets* (1966). Steps were taken in the 1950s in Canada and a little earlier in South Africa to set up such markets, while in Australia during the 1950s an 'unofficial' market of quite appreciable size grew up long before the central bank began in February 1959 to provide lender of last resort facilities to 'authorized dealers' in the short-term money markets. I was also interested in Indian developments, which were later to be thwarted by *dirigisme* and ossification, from which the Indian money market has only broken out more recently. It is therefore apparent that there is a range of experience of considerable interest to countries still wishing to develop a money market *ab initio*. For all of us, too, the stories themselves are worth the telling. This explains the inclusion of chapters on Australia, Canada, India and South Africa. And in the expanding network of the economies of Asia and the Pacific, there is of course Japan and a strong case for including Singapore and Hong Kong. There were a number of other money markets that might have been included (and which I have studied), but space considerations precluded my going further. In some cases (for example Thailand), I had published a preliminary study (in September 1986), but it was not possible to keep up with subsequent developments. My friends in the countries excluded will sympathize with me in having to make a choice.

Clearly the present book could not have been written without much assistance from many people in central banks (and monetary authorities), commercial banks, and the large variety of market houses that exist in financial circles. It is difficult to express adequately – and individually – the immense help that I have received from all quarters over the years; also much courtesy and kindness. Nor should I forget – particularly in the context of arranging programmes of appointments – my friends and former colleagues on the Council of the *Société Universitaire Européenne de Recherches Financières* (SUERF), also my former students in the Bank of Japan (the so-called 'Hull Mafia') and many other personal friends elsewhere without whom on some occasions it would have been difficult to operate. To all of these I am most grateful.

Most of the markets included in this volume I have visited on a large number of occasions over a period of thirty to forty years – I have witnessed their early difficulties, but have also seen them grow and develop until they have become the mature and sophisticated complex of markets that exists today. For me, it has been a fascinating experience, which in this book I attempt to pass on to others. Moreover, there are lessons to be learnt by all of us.

My interest in the field of the comparative study of financial institutions was first stimulated when I inherited a course on Comparative Banking Institutions at the London School of Economics. It is an area of teaching and research the importance of which I have urged over an academic lifetime both on my academic colleagues and in the financial world itself. And the importance of these studies has grown considerably with the evolution of increasingly integrated communications and the spread of ideas. It is my fervent desire that both the academic world and practitioners in the financial markets will continue to see the relevance of these studies. At the same time, it has become virtually impossible for the individual researcher – in large measure because of the financial constraints – to continue in a private capacity to research in this field. I make this point in the hope that my successors will be supported by greater financial assistance both from the usual academic sources and financial institutions generally. After all, it is in the obvious interests of the latter that their activities should be understood and appreciated. Money makes the world go round, and greater understanding of its role is imperative. To press the point further, I believe new arrangements are necessary whereby scholars can be seconded to, and for a period supported by, (say) central banks and international organizations (like the International Monetary Fund, the World Bank and other regional organizations, and the Bank for International Settlements) for the specific purpose of undertaking the type of research outlined here. Moreover, if the burden – which is heavy – proves to be too much for the individual scholar, perhaps the research arms of these institutions could sponsor more team efforts, with a leading expert in the field acting as a co-ordinating editor. In this way, one could usefully supplement the excellent research publication programmes of many central banks and (though these could be accorded a wider circulation) the comparative studies sponsored by the Bank for International Settlements. Some central banks are already moving in this direction by seconding academic personnel to Institutes for Monetary and Economic Studies within the central bank concerned (as in Japan), but the idea could palpably be extended. Sometimes this kind of thing can be achieved – and very successfully – on a commercial basis, as witness the book I edited on *Managing Bank Assets and Liabilities* (1988), but that is not the usual experience for academic economists. If – as I believe – the comparative study of financial institutions is to be recognized as an important and valuable field of enquiry, it must be accorded an appropriate amount of financial support.

One of the problems of writing – and publishing – this book has been a closing-off date. For purposes of comparison, I tried to incorporate figures in most (if not all) chapters for mid-1991; in a number of cases (in particular fields) more recent figures have been included. In other instances, important new developments took place, a discussion of which I have attempted to accommodate in several Postscripts. But there are one or two additional items that deserve mention and I must do this here. For example, for many years, Hong Kong has had two note-issuing banks – the Hongkong and Shanghai Bank and the Standard Chartered Bank. In January 1993, it was announced that as from May 1994 the Bank of China would become the Colony's third note-issuing bank. This reflected China's growing role in business in Hong Kong; also the approach to the Chinese takeover in 1997 (see *Financial Times* 13/1/93). Again, in January 1993, Germany's *Deutsche Terminbörse* and the French MATIF agreed to link their markets in the most significant co-operation pact seen between exchanges. Under the agreement, members of the DTB will be able to trade the MATIF's ECU contracts, while MATIF members will have access to the DTB's important D-mark interest rate contracts. The link between the French and German markets may draw some business away from LIFFE in London, which in 1992 was Europe's most active futures exchange. The agreement offers the DTB an opportunity to increase its market share in German Bund futures trading, which is currently dominated by LIFFE with around 70 per cent of the market. The MATIF will also acquire the DTB's computerized trading system, which will be used initially for trading its ECU products. The MATIF/DTB agreement is potentially open to other exchanges of which the Netherland's European Options Exchange is believed to be the most likely candidate (see *Financial Times* 14/1/93). Towards the end of the same month in North America the decision of the directors of the Chicago Board of Trade and New York's Commodity Exchange (COMEX) agreed in principle to affiliate. Under this plan, CBOT would become the sole owner of COMEX, which has been losing volume in recent years and suffering financially. The cross-country marriage would allow COMEX to continue to trade its precious metals futures, while CBOT would maintain its separate interest rate and agricultural contracts. However, other contracts could be traded jointly, with mutual access for both memberships. Under the affiliation plan, which must be ratified by members of both exchanges, COMEX and CBOT would combine the trade clearing operations and marketing and administration activities (see *Financial Times* 26/1/93). These developments both in Europe and North America are influenced by the cost of trading less active contracts using the traditional open-cry method. It reflects, too, technological advances, which have enabled traders around the world to come together on screen-based systems, while the breakdown of barriers between markets has increased investor demand for a broader range of products. Finally, when on 4 February 1993 the Council of the Bundesbank decided to cut lombard rate by 0.50 per cent to 9 per cent and discount rate by 0.25 per cent to 8 per cent, they also decided – rather more significantly – to lower the reserve requirements imposed on the banks. It was not merely a matter of defending the European Exchange Rate Mechanism, or of attempting to calm the currency markets. Under the new measures the Bundesbank has reduced reserve requirements on time deposits and savings deposits from an average of 4.5 per cent to 2 per cent, putting German banks closer to the experience in other countries. Indeed, these days in Europe, Belgium, Denmark, Luxembourg and The Netherlands have no reserve requirements, whereas in France it is 1 per cent for most types of deposit and a nominal requirement of 0.35 per cent of eligible liabilities in the United Kingdom. It was estimated that this relaxation of German reserve requirements might result in upwards of DM 200 billion in the European money markets being deposited in future with the German banking system (because of the lower 'cost of funds' and the possibility of a rather better rate of interest now to be paid on funds deposited). It was also proposed that there should be a certain amount of restructuring of the German money market by introducing several new short-term money market instruments (see *Financial Times*, 6/7 February 1993).

It remains to thank my wife for all her help in keeping my research files over the years and in assisting in so many other ways with this book as with its predecessors. I cannot on this occasion thank a secretary or secretaries (as in the past) – I have transferred to a word processor. But I must express my appreciation to Dr Richard Walker and Mr Philip Wade of the University of Hull Computer Centre for all their assistance and advice on technical problems (especially when I got into real trouble) and for providing the bridge between my primitive material and the laser printing of the final text. I am most grateful to them both.

J. S. G. Wilson
University of Hull
England

Abbreviations and acronyms

ABSA	Amalgamated Banks of South Africa
ACSS	Automated Clearing and Settlement System
ACUs	Asian currency units
ASEAN	Association of South East Asian Nations
BDNs	Bearer Deposit Notes
BIS	Bank for International Settlements
BMTN	*bons à moyen terme négociables*
BNP	Banque Nationale de Paris
BOJ	Bank of Japan
BOTs	*buoni ordinari del Tesoro*
BSA	Building Societies Association (UK)
BSIF	*bons des institutions et sociétés financières*
BTAN	*bons du Trésor à interêts annuels*
BTF	*bons du Trésor à taux fixe*
BTPs	*buoni Tesoro poliennali*
CBC	Central Bank Council
CBOT	Chicago Board of Trade
CBRS	Canadian Bond Rating Service
CCTs	*certificati di credito Tesoro*
CDs	certificates of deposit
CDS	Canadian Depository for Securities
CEDEL	Centrale de Livraisons de Valeurs Mobilières
CGB	Canada Government Bonds
CGO	Central Gilts Office (UK)
CHIPS	Clearing House Inter-bank Payments System
CME	Chicago Mercantile Exchange
CMO	Central Moneymarkets Office (UK)
COMEX	Commodity Exchange (New York)

CPD	Corporation for Public Deposits (South Africa)
CPF	Central Provident Fund (Singapore)
CTOs	*certificati del Tesoro con opzione*
DAX	*Deutscher Aktienindex*
DBRS	Dominion Bond Rating Service (Canada)
DFHI	Discount and Finance House of India
DTB	Deutsche Terminbörse
DTCs	deposit-taking companies
EBA	Exchange Banks' Association (now HKAB)
EC	European Community
ECUs	European currency units
EMS	European Monetary System
EMU	Economic and Monetary Union
ERM	exchange rate mechanism
FDIC	Federal Deposit Insurance Corporation (US)
FIBOR	Frankfurt Inter-Bank Offered Rate
FINTRACS	Financial Transactions Recording and Clearing System
FOMC	Federal Open Market Committee (US)
FOREX	foreign exchange
FRAs	forward-rate agreements
FRNs	floating-rate notes
GDP	gross domestic product
GEMMA	Gilt-Edged Market-Makers Association (UK)
GIC	General Insurance Corporation (India)
GICs	guaranteed investment certificates
GNMA	Government National Mortgage Association (US)
GNP	gross national product
HIBOR	Hongkong Inter-Bank Offered Rate
HKAB	Hong Kong Association of Banks (formerly EBA)
IBDs	interest-bearing deposits
IBFs	international banking facilities
IBIS	Inter Banken Informations System
ICCREA	Istituto di Credito delle Casse Rurali e Artigiane
ICCRI	Istituto di Credito delle Casse di Risparmio Italiane
IFS	*institutions financières specialisées*
IMI	Istituto Mobiliare Italiano

IRI	Istituto per la Ricostruzione Industriale
LDMA	London Discount Market Association
LIBOR	London Inter-Bank Offered Rate
LIC	Life Insurance Corporation (India)
LIFFE	London International Financial Futures Exchange
LTOM	London Traded Options Market
MAS	Monetary Authority of Singapore
MATIF	Marché à Terme International de France (formerly) Marché à Terme des Instruments Financiers
MID	*Mercato telematico interbancario dei depositi*
MLR	minimum lending rate
NABARD	National Bank for Agriculture and Rural Development (India)
NCDs	negotiable certificates of deposit
NDH	National Discount House Limited (South Africa)
OATs	*obligations assimilables du Trésor*
OCBC	Oversea-Chinese Banking Corporation
OPMs	*opérateurs principaux du marché*
PAR	Prime Assets Ratio (Australia)
PIBOR	Paris Inter-Bank Offered Rate
PIC	Public Investment Commissioners (South Africa)
PN	promissory note
PRAs	purchase and resale agreements
PSBR	public sector borrowing requirement
PWLB	Public Works Loan Board (UK)
RBI	Reserve Bank of India
RITS	Registry Information Transfer System
SBI	State Bank of India
SCP	sterling commercial paper
SEC	Securities and Exchange Commission (US)
SFE	Sydney Futures Exchange
SIBOR	Singapore Inter-Bank Offered Rate
SICAV	*société d'investissement à capital variable*
SIMEX	Singapore International Monetary Exchange
SLR	statutory liquidity ratio
SPAN	standard portfolio analysis of risk
SRAs	sale and repurchase agreements
SRD	Statutory Reserve Deposit (US)

STD	Subscriber Trunk Dialling
SWIFT	Society for Worldwide International Funds Transfer
SYCOM	Sydney Computerized Overnight Market
TCN	*titres de créance négociables*
TIFFE	Tokyo International Financial Futures Exchange
UTI	Unit Trust of India
WI	when-issued

Chapter 1

Introduction

A money market may be defined as a centre in which financial institutions congregate for the purpose of dealing impersonally in monetary assets. This serves to emphasize three essential characteristics of such markets. First, the group of markets collectively described as a 'money market' is concerned to deal in a particular type of asset, the chief characteristic of which is its relative liquidity (i.e. the readiness with which it can be converted into cash without significant loss). Second, such activities tend to be concentrated in some centre (or centres) which serves (or serve) a region or area; the width of such areas may vary considerably – some money markets like London or New York have become world financial centres, or at least international in their scope; the direct influence of others may be restricted to part only of a national economy – e.g. Chicago or San Franciso in the USA, though these will tend to have links more or less strongly developed with other centres in the same economy. Indeed, with screen trading – and despite time differences in countries that are large geographically (e.g. USA, Canada, and Australia) – such markets rapidly become integrated into a national market. But in the past there have been situations which could be described as those of a 'condominium' (Sydney and Melbourne in Australia; Bombay and Calcutta in India; Toronto and Montreal in Canada; Tokyo and Osaka in Japan), though it has been the general experience that one or other will establish primacy (Sydney, Bombay, Toronto, Tokyo). Third, on a very strict definition, the relationships that characterize a money market should be impersonal in character so that competition will be relatively pure (in other words, dealings between the parties should not be governed or influenced wholly or in part by personal considerations); this is an ideal that in practice is only approximately true even in developed money markets like London and New York – over the years, more so in New York than London, the main test being the degree of competitiveness that obtains.

Perhaps the last condition can best be emphasized by offering a contrasting example. In a true money market (as also in a banking context) strictly defined, price differentials for assets of similar type (allowing for different degrees of risk and maturity) will tend to be eliminated by the interplay of supply and demand (including arbitrage). Even for similar types of assets, some differentials will no doubt continue to exist at any one point in time (this is what gives scope for arbitrage). The reason for this is that in a dynamic situation (and depending on expectations) the system of prices will be caught moving towards whatever – under current conditions – is the 'equilibrium' price. Nevertheless, such differentials as remain will not be of any great consequence, or not for any length of time. On the other hand, when credit relations become 'personalised' (and this is true both of money markets and of banking relationships generally), there may be favoured customers who are accorded special rates, because of the size or continuity of the business offered, or because the borrowing customer and his business are well and favourably known to the lender. Sometimes a loan may be granted at low rates because of mere friendship between the two parties – that is the ultimate extreme. Moreover, the reverse experience is also possible – high rates charged to borrowers who only offer small and occasional business and who may not be very well known to the lender. In fact, there is a whole spectrum of rates that relate to different degrees of risk and – subject to the impact of expectations – to different maturities. But, in addition, market imperfections (e.g. due to the personal element – the 'old boy' network – or to variations in access to information, even irrationalities) may occasion departures from the kinds of rates and credit arrangements one would expect to operate under conditions of pure or perfect competition.

Hence, it may be argued that as a description of the real world what has been suggested is much too 'pure' a view. Even when money markets in the real world are highly competitive, it is not unreasonable to expect that regularity of business, the amount of business, and trust in the individuals with whom one is dealing may give rise to a certain amount of discrimination in the matter of interest rate structures or of credit conditions. A slightly higher interest rate charged to borrowers may well be justified in terms of cost of information and allowance for risk, but as has also been indicated there may be other factors as well.

Certain other preconditions relate to the kind of economy that a money market can be expected to serve. These will already exist in countries in which a money market has grown up over the years and is now well developed, though not all 'developed' countries necessarily enjoy the services of a sophisticated money market. Hence, in countries that have only recently sought to establish money market institutions, these same preconditions must obtain.

Thus, there are certain questions that need to be asked. The first relates to the nature of the economy within which one can expect a money market to operate. For example, if it is an economy that depends for its prosperity to a large extent on exports – possibly on only one main export commodity, or at most on a small group of commodities – it is likely that the country will be very much at the mercy of its 'terms of trade' (the movement of export prices in relation to import prices); if, further, there are likely to be marked annual variations in external earnings, it may well be difficult to produce a regularly revolving fund of cash and to make available to the economy a quantum of other liquid assets on the basis of which to organize a money market. This is so much easier to ensure if an economy is already reasonably well diversified and not subject to wide seasonal swings, though holdings of foreign exchange and regulation of their expenditure by the central bank could be one means of providing a cushion against violent fluctuations in export incomes.

Second, there will need to be a minimum institutional development already present – an accepted rule of law, relative political stability, and a reasonably well developed banking and financial system. It is not only important that the managements should be experienced and already subscribe to accepted conventions of banking practice; the institutions on which a money market is to be based must also be known for their integrity. Where dealings are to be primarily in short-dated assets (with maturities of, say, up to one year), many such agreements must necessarily be based on deals entered into orally; hence integrity is a *sine qua non*. This does not mean that the existence of doubtful institutions will necessarily preclude the development of a money market, but it must impede the complete integration into a single system of the several types of banking and other monetary institutions that exist. Thus, banks and dealing houses may have to be 'licensed', 'registered', or 'approved' (though 'secondary' institutions may still operate at the fringe); again, the quality of instruments like certificates of deposit and commercial paper may have to be 'tiered'. Not all institutions and/or their paper are equally acceptable, though this can be – and is – met by credit ratings.

Third, it is reasonable to ask what purpose a money market can be expected to serve. From the point of view of the commercial banks, it should be able to provide an investment outlet for any temporarily surplus funds that may be available. If the several banks operate rather dissimilar types of business, they may well be able to accommodate each other by organizing an inter-bank call loan market; the same applies to other financial institutions, either with short-term financial surpluses or deficits (even those with mainly long-term commitments like life assurance companies or pension funds), also to non-financial corporations (in industry and commerce) with temporary surpluses or deficits of cash. On the other hand, if most business is likely to be affected by similar seasonal influences, money will be easy or tight for each institution or corporation at about the same time and the problem then becomes one that can be most easily resolved by the provision of special facilities at the central bank. Alternatively, the government may decide to 'mop up' seasonal surpluses (e.g. by issuing Treasury bills for the purpose). For this system to be attractive to the commercial banks, however, there must also be a willingness to release funds during a period of seasonal stringency, either by central bank rediscount of Treasury bills at market rates, or by means of a government switch to ways-and-means advances from the central bank (substituting an overdraft at the central bank for government borrowing on the basis of a Treasury bill issue, though ways-and-means advances may be more directly inflationary).

Hence, for a money market of some kind to exist, there must be a supply of temporarily idle cash that is seeking short-term investment in an earning asset. There must also exist a demand for temporarily available cash either by banks (and other financial institutions) for the purpose of adjusting their liquidity positions and to finance the carrying of the relevant assets in their balance sheets, or by the government, when it chooses to finance itself by adding to the floating debt or by issuing short-dated bonds. If banks and similar institutions are to employ such short-term borrowed funds with any degree of confidence, however, they must expect the supply of such funds to be reasonably regular (as must governments when they borrow against short-dated securities, such as Treasury bills and short-term bonds). In other words, there must in some sense be a revolving fund of cash. Otherwise, financial institutions in particular dare not become dependent on outside sources and must maintain their own internal liquid reserves, necessitating rather higher cash and liquidity ratios than they would otherwise need. Even so, there is in addition a case for a central bank or monetary authority to act as a lender of last resort should there be a liquidity crisis and if circumstances require it.

Whether such a revolving fund is likely to exist depends on the extent to which we are dealing with an export economy (which is the case in some degree with most economies) and on the degree of diversification of its exports, since a seasonally balanced distribution of exports will produce a continuous inflow of external earnings and of bank cash to offset the demands for cash that relate to financing the movements to the ports of the original exports and the subsequent further financing of the imports that ultimately have to be paid for from the proceeds of the exports. But sometimes even economies with quite a high degree of seasonality can nevertheless produce a sufficiently large revolving fund of cash on which to base money market development. Thus, it was somewhat surprising to find in Australia that from the beginning (i.e. during the 1950s) there were in fact moneys available to feed into a developing money market and the position has been further strengthened in more recent years by the continuing diversification of the Australian economy, where seasonality is rather less than it once was; similarly in New Zealand. In Canada, on the other hand, funds were released for use in the money market by replacing the traditional 10 per cent (and legal 5 per cent) cash ratio of the chartered banks with a legal 8 per cent minimum based on monthly averaging. In South Africa, funds were in effect transferred back from balances held in London and invested in deposits with the officially sponsored National Finance Corporation, which could then re-invest them in government paper.

If, however, an economy was relatively self-sufficient, and depended to only a minor extent on exports for its prosperity, the cash flows would be influenced for the most part by internal considerations, and the stringencies caused by lags in payments need not create any embarrassment. That is to say, if it is only the domestic economy that requires finance, the funds that accrue from borrowing and selling must remain available somewhere in the economy, even when they are passed on by spending and lending. In this context, a money market has an obvious task to perform − to seek out the funds wherever they may be and to channel them into the hands of the institutions that require them.

The difficulty may be that the market houses that could perform this function (e.g. money market dealers something like the discount houses in London) may not yet exist. There may be temporarily surplus funds in existence (e.g. in the hands of big industrial and commercial enterprises), but there may be no institutional mechansim to make available such funds for employment elsewhere in the economy; also, it is necessary to ensure that the funds can be recalled as and when required, to be replaced by other temporarily surplus funds from similar sources. There may as yet be no means of ensuring that these funds will 'revolve'.

Hence, one has found in past history that, if the prospect of making a profit out of this situation fails to attract private enterprise, there may well be a case for a public authority to take the initiative (e.g. the National Finance Corporation set up in South Africa in 1949) to provide an earning outlet for such funds as well as facilities for their withdrawal as and when required. Once the necessary stimulus has been provided, private enterprise has usually followed the lead of the authorities. On other occasions (e.g. in Canada), it has been possible (by offering concessions) to encourage private enterprise itself to supply the desired facilities, while at other times (as in Australia) it was private enterprise that forced the pace (in the 1950s) and the authorities were ultimately obliged to recognize the existence of a market and to provide it with lender-of-last-resort facilities without which no money market can approach its full potential. It is usual, too, for the monetary authorities to monitor the operations of such houses or dealers and in some form or other to 'recognize' or 'approve' them.

Chapter 2

The London money markets

The London money market has a long history.[1] It is not proposed to discuss this here, where we shall be more concerned with recent developments. For many years, the discount houses constituted the core of money market arrangements in London and, despite many important changes, they remain at the centre of market operations and retain their special relationship with the Bank of England. There used to be about twelve such houses, with a degree of minor fluctuations over the years. Latterly, there has been a degree of consolidation and there are now nine members of the London Discount Market Association.[2] They all have discount accounts with the Bank of England and these give them access to the Bank of England as lender of last resort to the banking system. To an important extent, they remain a buffer between the central bank and the commercial banks operating in and from London. Most of the discount houses have diversified and, although the majority had set up subsidiary companies to provide fee income or a less volatile source of income, the ability and desire to do this were substantially increased, particularly for the large houses, when in 1987 the Bank of England permitted the houses to work from an 80 times multiplier rather than a 40 times multiplier as previously. This enabled the houses effectively to run the same size book on half the capital previously employed. In this way, they may continue to concentrate sufficient resources on their discount house activities and this is preferred by the Bank of England, which would wish to see the discount houses' major profit centre highly sensitive to short-term monetary policy. In addition, certain big market-making firms had an interest in a discount house-type of operation – making markets also in short-term sterling instruments like bills and certificates of deposit (CDs). Until October, 1988 they did not have any relationship with the Bank of England in this respect. However, the Bank of England stood prepared to receive applications from them for counterparty status from end-October, 1988. Of the nine Association houses,[3] Union Discount Company Ltd and Gerrard & National Ltd (itself the result of a merger in June 1970 between Gerrard & Reid and the National Discount Company) are perceptibly the largest. Of the remainder, the biggest houses would include Cater Allen Ltd and Alexanders Discount plc (no longer independent, now being a subsidiary of Crédit Lyonnais of France).

Each of the houses in the Association must satisfy the Bank of England that their capitalization is adequate in relation to the Bank's tests, given the type and scale of business that a house undertakes. And the position is monitored regularly. None the less, shareholders' funds (capital and reserves) are only a small proportion of total funds employed, the remainder being borrowed primarily on a secured basis from the other financial institutions, either overnight or as 'callable fixtures' (e.g. 1 to 3 months). The bulk comes from a variety of banks in London (formerly including also licensed deposit-takers, a category that has now disappeared) and most of the remainder comes from large business corporations and building societies with surplus liquidity, and a little from overseas. In addition, the discount houses may sell assets to the Bank of England or – in certain circumstances – borrow from it. The resources of the market are then invested in commercial and other sterling bills (usually something over 40 per cent in 1990–1, with Treasury bills up to 7.4 per cent, of total sterling assets, but often much smaller),[4] bank CDs (as a rule something between 30 and 40 per cent), and building society CDs (latterly up to 6 per cent or so). British Government stock holdings are very small. Holdings of local authority bills are also very small, likewise loans to local authorities, and there are certain 'other' items. Other currency assets may at times exceed 3 per cent of the total.

Essentially, what the discount houses borrow are the temporarily surplus funds of banks and similar institutions mostly operating in or through the City of London. In an important sense, what is lent to the discount houses by these institutions represents a holding of the primary liquidity of the banking system. These institutions must keep available liquid resources adequate to meet sudden demands for cash. At the same time, they cannot afford to keep their funds idle. Hence the need for both an investment outlet and a form of investment that is highly liquid – and nothing could be much more liquid than short-term money that is formally secured.[5] In addition, there is a monetary ebb and flow – the available supply of money must be held somewhere in the system; if it has left the tills of one bank, it will generally be found in the hands of another. In other words, there is a revolving fund of money, which from time to time may be added to or subtracted from (e.g. by the authorities) but which always remains substantial, though subject of course to important seasonal movements (e.g. at holiday times and at Christmas). It is this that provides the discount houses with the bulk of their resources. Day by day, they are continuously borrowing, repaying and reborrowing, thereby keeping this revolving fund more or less fully employed.

If temporarily there is an inadequate supply (due to money leaving the commercial banking system and passing into the hands of the authorities as a result of tax payments, gilt-edged purchases by the public, increases in the note issue, payments of oil royalties, foreign exchange settlements, etc.), the Bank of England will either buy some of the assets of the discount houses or lend to them on a short-term basis, or it may be that these assets are held by the clearing banks, in which case they may sell some of them to the discount houses for onward sale to the Bank of England. The Bank of England may also offer accommodation on the basis of sale and repurchase agreements. Alternatively, if there is a surplus of money in the market, the Bank of England will sell Treasury bills to the discount market (or to the banks) in order to 'mop up' the excess. These are in the character of 'smoothing out' operations.

Apart from the sums made available from time to time by the Bank of England (for a period, and primarily by buying assets from the market or the banks), which in any event is in the nature of a marginal adjustment, the main sources of liquidity are the London clearing banks and their subsidiaries, the accepting houses, other British banks, the overseas banks, and the Scottish banks. In all, there are about 450 potential lenders to the London discount market, though there would tend to be more activity in the inter-bank market (where money is lent unsecured, whereas money lent to the discount houses is normally lent on a fully-secured basis). Of these – on the basis of money broker figures – between 300 and 400 would be lenders in the inter-bank market on a more or less regular basis. The number of really very active lenders would be very much smaller – possibly about 100 are active lenders. Perhaps 20 to 30 make two-way prices and actually trade in money.

Building societies lend to the discount houses and may be regarded as part of the inter-bank market. Non-financial corporations also lend to some extent to the discount market, especially short-dated money, but they would not be regarded as part of the inter-bank market. All the big building societies are active these days in the money markets – Halifax, Abbey National (now a bank), Nationwide Anglia, Woolwich, and National Provincial – and, because money is their business, the building societies are more important in the money markets than the large business corporations. Non-financial corporations may also borrow from the banks at market-related rates instead of by way of overdraft. To a limited extent, moneys also come to the discount houses from abroad. In these transactions, there is no minimum amount – sums vary a lot between small and large institutions, though size of loan could be reflected in rates.[6] But 'unadvised' or internal limits[7] would be applied in the inter-bank market as elsewhere. Such limits are looked at regularly and adjusted periodically.[8] However, they would not necessarily be applied rigidly, especially in the case of lending to the really big banks. The standard size of an inter-bank loan would be of the order of £5 million and a big operator or a major clearing bank would often deal in sums of £25 million or £50 million, occasionally £100 million.

These days the money markets open some time after 7.00 a.m. and certainly by 7.30 a.m. Non-financial corporations may not come in to the market until 8.30 a.m. or 9.00 a.m., but are now beginning to come in earlier. Most of the money market desks would close down by 5.30 p.m.,[9] gilt-edged transactions by 6.00 p.m. Foreign exchange transactions would normally take place between 6.30 a.m. and 6.00 p.m., but can take place at literally any time, if there is important news that impinges on the markets. Banks and money market houses (the Bank of England also) all have early morning meetings to discuss the day ahead, often with reports coming in from abroad (e.g. Tokyo).

Before they go home the night before, the clearing banks would have a good idea of what their money position was going to be for the following day. Clearing figures would be known next morning and a starting figure would be available by 9.30 a.m. or 10.00 a.m. However, dealers talk on the phone from 7.30 a.m. onwards and, as indicated, there will be an early morning meeting lasting 15 to 20 minutes. Lending or calling for the next day can begin late the previous afternoon (after 3.30 p.m. and up to 5.00 p.m.)[10] and continue from 7.30 to 8.00 a.m. the next morning.[11] Then there is a lull, with another active position around 12.00 noon.[12] It is active again from 2.00 to 2.30 p.m. Transactions in the money market tend to end at 3.00 p.m. and the position would be tidied up by 3.30 p.m., i.e. for same day business. Up to midday, the market would trade in 'period' money, after that only in overnight money. During the day, big items will be reported in (from major branches, large customers, and the like) and all the large banks have a money management team to monitor large movements of cash (whether in or out) and to report them to the money desks. Throughout the day, they can give a 'best guess', but it may be quite a bit out. They will also know what weekly, monthly, or seasonal patterns to accommodate, though the weekly and monthly patterns are less obvious than they were;[13] within the week, however, there is still the outflow on Fridays and a reverse inflow on Mondays. On the other hand, 'seasonality' has, if anything, increased – as the underlying demand for cash to pay salaries has declined. It seems that there has been an increase in the public's ability to tailor their cash holdings more exactly to holiday peaks.

The aim of the banks is not to have an overdraft at the Bank of England at the end of the day, but it does happen – not all that often but perhaps more frequently than one might suppose. The clearing banks have operational balances at the Bank of England and they try to keep on deposit what they will need. But forecasts can be wrong (e.g. big movements by the Treasury or the nationalized industries) and major transactions may not be reported to the Bank of England; clearing banks may not have operational balances great enough to cover the amounts required. The banks may also estimate inaccurately the distribution of balances amongst themselves, even if there are in fact sufficient balances in the system as a whole.[14]

In the old days, directors of discount houses wearing a top hat (now very rare) called on the senior money man at a clearing bank to borrow moneys with which to finance their book. To some extent that is still done, though most borrowing transactions would now be done from home base on the telephone. Formerly, there was a phase when some discount houses personnel kept in touch with home base by means of a walkie-talkie; nowadays a bank will have phones at its office available for the purpose of contacting home base should that be necessary. Discount house directors still call on money men at all the clearing banks, though at some not every day (except in two cases, once a week is more likely) and more for the purpose of information – keeping in touch with market conditions and to discuss interest rate expectations and possible future developments. When they are borrowing, these houses do it on the phone.[15]

THE INTER-BANK MARKET

Participation in the inter-bank market comprises the whole of the banking community (including the discount houses from time to time). It is a natural two-way market with some 540 banks as possible participants.[16] One should note, too (as we have seen), that – despite the name – non-bank institutions (e.g. the building societies) participate in this market as well. The market is served by a number of money brokers and competition is intense.[17] In an important sense, brokers tend to make the prices – they can 'make a price' within five points. The extent to which they are used varies between banks. Of the big clearers, one uses brokers extensively (80 per cent by volume compared with 20 per cent for direct deals) and others may be 25/75 or 35/65 brokers/direct. For other banks, it seems to vary from time to time.[18] Certain banks (including the larger discount houses) may take a view on inter-bank interest rates and trade in money, perhaps buying it cheap in the morning and selling it off at a better rate in the afternoon, whereas others only come into the market as and when they need to do so. Foreign banks – and especially the Japanese and American banks in London (without an established deposit base) – conduct their business with 'bought' money; this is also true of some of the small merchant bank subsidiaries. Money brokers' commissions (which would include the placing of time deposits[19] for building societies, pension funds, insurance companies, as well as big non-financial corporations like oil companies and some of the big stores, which are not part of the inter-bank market as such) are all negotiable; there is an unofficial standard but there are discounts off it for volume, and a major user gets better terms than the small and occasional user. One should note, too, that limits may be applied. Some names may be 'difficult'. Indeed, in a fast moving situation, it may not be easy to discover what one's own limits are.

In the inter-bank market, much of the money is lent overnight,[20] i.e. on a day to day basis, or at the weekend for 3 days. But quite a lot of money can also be borrowed for very short periods – even for longer periods. The main items in 'period' money would be borrowed for 1 month and 3 months, but banks may also borrow for 7 days, 15 days, or for almost any time up to 12 months. There is not much borrowing for over 12 months, but it could be for up to 5 years – that would be the longest.[21] All inter-bank money represents 'bought' or wholesale money, but it must be remembered that large sums of money are also attracted by way of large deposits through bank branches. Indeed, in calculating figures for wholesale money, banks very often include all interest-bearing deposits other than 7-day notice deposits. But large deposits – often only on an overnight basis (e.g. from large non-financial corporations) – also attract a money-market rate of interest. Since sterling is an international currency, some of this money may come in from foreign banks operating abroad. And money coming in through the branches of the clearers can be very considerable, and for some banks (e.g. the Scottish clearing banks) it can be extremely important.

Rates on inter-bank money can fluctuate not only from day to day but also within the day. They may be pretty stable some days, though certain participants reckon to do their borrowings in the mornings in the belief that rates are more steady then. On other days, rates can be quite volatile. In the past, rates could go up to high levels at the end of the day (e.g. up to 200 per cent was not unknown), but more recently that has very rarely been seen. Nevertheless, they could still go to 30 per cent or more. On the whole, however, this would only be for marginal amounts of money, even if that money was in itself expensive. As indicated, this is less likely to happen these days, since the discount houses themselves may lend money back to the banks late in the day (say, between 2.50 p.m. and 3.00 p.m., or even later) at a penalty rate, recouping themselves by borrowing late at the Bank of England. For that matter, a clearing bank could go direct to the Bank of England up to 3.00 p.m. for late accommodation by selling to it Treasury bills or local authority bills and some banks keep a stock of such bills (despite the modest rate for 'carry') for just such a purpose.

An oddity that might be briefly mentioned is that a stock exchange money broker may regularly and for technical reasons have sizeable amounts of money for on-lending into the money market (he also has a facility to borrow from the Bank of England); although this is only a minor source of funds to interested parties, it can be important at the margin.[22]

BUILDING SOCIETIES

The building societies, which have increasingly become 'near-banks', have in recent years resorted in an important way to the wholesale money market either using money brokers or doing direct deals, in this context money brokers being preferred when the market is volatile, or when the building societies need a spread, or anonymity. Building societies are generally seen – even these days – as institutions which raise savings from personal investors and then on-lend these to home buyers. Traditionally, societies did not raise funds from wholesale sources and, formerly, their only involvement with the professional money markets was through the investment of their liquid funds. However, in recent years, changes in market conditions[23] have made it both more attractive and necessary for societies also to raise money from wholesale sources,[24] and there were changes in legislation and in regulations that allowed wholesale funds to be tapped,[25] initially to the extent of up to 20 per cent of total resources raised and, from 27 November 1987 – following representations from the societies and the Building Societies Association – the Building Societies Commission and the Treasury agreed to increase the potential level of societies' wholesale funding to 40 per cent.

It was soon discovered that wholesale funding was a means of making up the shortfall of funds on the retail side and there is in fact a degree of seasonality both in terms of receipts from investors and mortgage advances. For example, when they are going to move, people tend to move house after the Easter Break. More mortgages are required for newly purchased housing. By the time the relevant arrangements are made, this results in an outflow of cash by June or July. Again, in the summer, there is a demand for funds to finance summer holidays and the inflow of funds from investors declines. Likewise when approaching Christmas. And there are quarterly outflows to meet tax payments. With major privatizations of nationalized industries, there may be emergency outflows to cover (e.g. in the context of Telecom) to meet heavy calls for new issues of shares, though this has only been a short-term phenomenon and could usually be met by temporarily running down excess liquidity.[26] Alternatively, they could go into the short-term (less than 1 year)[27] wholesale money market – e.g. issue CDs or take time deposits from the market.

As from May 1983, the building societies were permitted to pay interest gross on CDs with a minimum denomination of £50,000, provided they had a life of less than a year; also on time deposits from October 1983. This power has been used extensively. For the building societies, it is the alternative to the inter-bank market, the main source being non-financial corporations; local authorities have also been important. The average maturity is 50 days. Building society CDs are very actively traded by discount houses and banks and, indeed, the bulk would tend to be held within the banking system. Time deposits as a source of funds are slightly less attractive than CDs, because they carry a higher rate of interest, between $\frac{1}{16}$ and $\frac{1}{8}$ per cent more. Time deposits have been taken by societies of all sizes. They are also used as a means of investing (lending to the market) for purposes of short-term liquidity. When they borrow by way of time deposits, the maturity of the deposits will be based on their view of interest rates and on their need to raise money. They may also arbitrage between periods.[28] For the larger building societies, minimum amounts lent as wholesale money would be £1 million and to banks and other financial institutions £5 million, though the very biggest building societies would lend in larger amounts than that. Building societies' resort to CDs is discussed further below.

Short-term funding is used not only to cover imbalances in liquidity, but also to fund long-term lending. Because the average life of a mortgage is 7 to 8 years (i.e. a mortgage may be paid off and the money reborrowed against another property), medium-term and longer-term funding must also be undertaken. The funding base has been diversified. Not only has there been a resort to wholesale money, but negotiable bonds have been issued (e.g. by Nationwide) being unconditional obligations of an individual building society that rank alongside deposits in priority to shares and which are for over 1 year in multiples of £50,000 tradable on the Stock Exchange. In addition, there are term loans from banks (for 5 years, say) and syndicated bank loans, which are likely to be attractive to societies which do not have full access to the CD or Euro-sterling markets. Euro-bonds may be used by the large societies (for 5 years, say, or even longer).[29] Here funds are raised outside the country of the issuer and payment of interest in respect of quoted Euro-bonds may be paid gross.

NON-FINANCIAL CORPORATIONS

Quite a number of the large corporates (i.e. non-financial corporations) also have a sophisticated money-market type of operation. These would include the large oil companies (especially British Petroleum), large corporations like ICI, and a number of the major store groups. All of them would have large cash flows and some of them marked degrees of seasonality in their business, especially the store groups (e.g. in the build-up to Christmas). Oil companies have a big cash inflow in the winter months. Other major features are massive tax payments and big dividend payments twice a year. For others (e.g. ICI), diversification has resulted in a marked reduction in seasonal fluctuations. All of them would establish their money positions early each morning, but big cash movements can occur over the course of the day mainly for financial reasons, but also at times in the context of commercial activity. Some (like ICI) tend not to have a lot of short-term borrowings on a floating rate basis; they are inclined to use their own group liquidity (with overseas cash being lent to the centre). ICI also has a kind of 'in-house' bank (ICI Finance), which manages its affairs. Borrowings would be in the nature of fixed-rate, long-term debt (which can be swapped into a floating rate either in the same or another currency).

For corporates in general, short-term investment of surplus moneys is of a smaller order, but would include 'repo' bonds, where they buy with an agreement for the seller to buy the bonds back in due course; bank and building society CDs and certificate of tax deposits; commercial paper and deposits with selected banks at market-related interest rates. Most of this business is done direct, but corporates do occasionally use brokers. With a house like ICI, there may also be a currency factor to consider, when they would cover back to sterling; ICI does not tender for Treasury bills, but may very occasionally buy them from a broker, including a discount house. They also 'look at' local authority bills. In effect, they are 'looking for opportunities' – going into whatever at the time is most attractive.

BP is also centralized (each profit centre is a potential customer) – they absorb their cash surpluses and lend to other parts of the group when they need money. They also provide from the centre a range of services: foreign exchange (FOREX) which they trade around the world, forwards, options, etc., and, of course, resort to the money markets. On all counts, they have a very sophisticated operation (BP even opens like the rest of the money market at 7.30 a.m. to 7.45 a.m., with the money market business usually being done by lunchtime). They employ a banker computer package, which incorporates all the monitoring controls and systems; and they use these systems 'to make money make money'. They also trade in FOREX. If in fact they are short of money, they go into the money markets and borrow to square their books. They have standby facilities at the banks – both committed and uncommitted. (The latter may be cheaper and more convenient – e.g. overnight.) And if they have a very large payment of millions of dollars, they make the necessary provision. If they have surplus funds, they put them out very short-term with minimum credit risk and maximum liquidity (e.g. bank balances which would earn a money market rate),[30] gilts (up to 5 years' maturity), and US Treasury, German, and Japanese bonds. Limits are imposed by a management committee responsible to the board. Of money market assets, they hold CDs, not very much commercial paper (which is used more as a borrowing vehicle), and they are not interested in Treasury bills (too low a yield), nor particularly enthusiastic about local authority bills. Mostly they put money into the banking system, and trade at the short end of the gilts and Treasury markets. For the most part, they lend direct, but sometimes use brokers at the very short end. Whether they lend overnight to banks or not depends on interest rate expectations, also on their own requirements. But they would not lend for more than 1 month. They also use the short-dated swap market – dollars into sterling and back again on a day-to-day basis. And they go into futures, options, and forward-rate agreements (FRAs) to some extent. They use interest-rate and currency swaps. They have recently been particularly interested in FOREX options. They are equally as sophisticated in the capital markets in the context of long-term borrowing, but that is not our concern here. Nevertheless, we have looked at BP's experience in some detail, since it indicates the degree of sophistication that is open to a large corporation.

With the large store groups also, both the cash resources and transactions are centralized, so that effective control can be maintained. When they are in need of funds, they likewise use committed[31] and uncommitted[32] bank lines. Some have their own financial subsidiary which can issue CDs, and certain names have established sterling commercial paper programmes. Surplus moneys which would come in during the Christmas trade and at sale times can go into the inter-bank market through a financial subsidiary, usually direct (not through a broker), or at a market-related rate into a short-term bank deposit. Occasionally, they may place money with a discount house, and they may even borrow from them. Again, when placing money, they will apply limits. They may buy other corporates' commercial paper (to be held only for a short period of time) and, indeed, arbitrage against their own. Often (starting at, say, 10.00 a.m.) they will make a point of dealing in the morning only – 'afternoon rates can be very odd'. FRAs are used to some extent – they are 'very easy to understand'. The London International Financial Futures Exchange (LIFFE) market is left to the banks. Again, they have no interest in Treasury bills or local authority bonds.

It is now pertinent to look at some of the other money-market instruments in a little more detail, before considering the several means of Bank of England intervention.

BILLS OF EXCHANGE

As already indicated, an important part of the business of the discount houses is to discount – or buy – commercial bills. Indeed, it was on this type of business that the market was originally founded. Today the bills discounted include both acceptances financing foreign trade and bills that relate to the financing of domestic business. Because these transactions in some measure represent an alternative to borrowing by way of overdraft, they have at times been subject to Bank of England credit restrictions which limited their growth. Previously, there was a tendency for bill finance to increase whenever overdrafts were squeezed. But bill finance also had a role of its own and, in certain trades, resort to it was in fact traditional and customary. Now the commercial bill is once again a highly significant element in the asset structure of all discount houses and – as we shall see – the main instrument of Bank of England intervention. Commercial bills are of two kinds: bank acceptances and trade paper.[33] Both overseas and inland trade is financed by bank acceptances,[34] when, for a commission, an acceptance house or eligible bank lends its name and becomes one of the parties to the transaction. Bank acceptances (particularly eligible acceptances) are more readily saleable and the rate of discount is therefore more favourable than on trade bills, where the margin on rates is greater in proportion to the inherent risk on the bill. High rates imply partly an insurance against risk, and partly a measure of the restricted liquidity of certain bills. Throughout the period post-Second World War and up to 1971, the minimum discount rate for fine bank bills was the subject of agreement in the Discount Market Association and it is understood that the great bulk of the business was in fact done at the agreed minimum. At one time, only commercial bills relating to physical trade transactions were regarded as good, but over recent years a fair proportion of finance paper has been in circulation. In these cases, the paper may represent the financing of stocks of materials already in the hands of the user, or hire purchase sales.

Dealing in commercial bills was a highly specialized business – indeed, trade bills still require a detailed knowledge of the creditworthiness of customers in many varied trades, together with up-to-date information concerning current conditions within those trades. With bank bills, on the other hand, it is really the bank name that matters, though the discount houses still keep an eye on the drawers of the bills – if there is even a slight concern about the bank name, or about the drawer, a limit would be placed on the bills in question.

It was long the practice for the Bank of England itself to attempt to keep a watchful eye on the quality of bills being discounted in the market by regularly buying in – through its broker – samples of the bills that were currently circulating; this included both bank and trade acceptances. (It had been the practice to take these regularly from all houses in turn.) If, therefore, the market wished to sound out Bank views on a particular type of bill, some of this paper might well be included in the next sample submitted. Formerly, all bills dealt in should have two good British names,[35] one of which had to be the acceptor; the other might be the endorsement of a discount house prior to the sale of the bill, which should have no more than three months to run. After 1987, the bills of many foreign banks were granted eligibility. As at mid-1991, there were 155 'eligible' banks in London.

From time to time, the Bank of England suspended its sampling of bills. Where it was placed in a position where in any case it had to buy large quantities of eligible commercial bills (as a kind of smoothing-out operation),[36] it would make no sense also to take in samples of bills. Furthermore, after a heavy period of buying, the Bank would not wish to be in the market until their holding of bills had run down. However, once these portfolios of bills had run off, sampling would be resumed. Thus, there had been no essential change in the Bank's policy. It might be noted, too, that at that stage all these transactions would go through the Bank's broker; in the case of taking in samples of bills, the broker made all the necessary arrangements (including the negotiation of the rate), but the parcels themselves were after early 1973 delivered direct to the Bank, as are all other commercial bills. Under more recent arrangements (detailed below), the Bank of England buys in so many commercial bills – indeed, there was at one time a 'bill mountain' – that for this reason alone it no longer has need of sampling (which disappeared in 1980), though the Bank of England is still concerned to limit how much an individual bank can accept and this is monitored.[37] But subject always to the conditions of eligibility for rediscount at the Bank of England, commercial bills have now become the main basis for Bank of England intervention in the money markets.

The importance of the commercial bill has varied over the years. Latterly, there has been a very considerable increase in their use. UK bank holdings of eligible bank bills (including those of the Banking Department of the Bank of England) have fluctuated between £8.6 billion and over £10 billion from 1989 to 1991,[38] and discount house holdings have at times exceeded £8 billion over the same period, but were rather lower in 1991.[39]

THE EURO-DOLLAR MARKET

A much newer market, which developed in the late 1950s,[40] was that in Euro-dollars. These operations derived from the acceptance of dollar claim deposits by banks (chiefly in Europe and especially in London) and the lending of these claims to other customers, typically for short periods. The large increase in the supply of funds to this market consisted mainly of foreign-owned dollars as a result of a series of US balance-of-payments deficits, which caused dollars to accumulate in foreign hands. The demand came from a wide range of sources, including those who needed dollars to finance an international trade transaction and American corporations, which found the funds in this market more readily available than those that could be obtained at home, where the banks had also been heavy importers of Euro-dollar funds as they were subject under Regulation Q to a ceiling on the rates they could offer for domestic deposits. The growth of the market was also largely due to its unregulated nature (e.g. the absence for the most part of reserve requirements).[41] Moreover, Euro-dollars could be diverted to feed the domestic demand for funds in the United Kingdom. Thus, it was possible for funds to be made available to a British local authority or other domestic borrower on the basis of the borrowing of Euro-dollars. These dollars would then be sold spot for sterling, which could be lent to the local authority or other domestic borrower. At the same time, dollars would also be bought forward, so that a known amount of dollars would be available when the loan matured and the Euro-dollars that were borrowed had to be repaid. Transactions of this kind would obviously depend on the rate at which forward dollars could be bought. Hence, when the cost of a swap operation was low, foreign money could flow into the hands of domestic borrowers much more easily than when forward transactions were expensive. There are other Euro-currencies besides Euro-dollars – organized on the same set of principles – though Euro-dollars remain the most important of these. The size of the Euro-currencies market is given in Table 2.1 (according to international banking market size).

CERTIFICATES OF DEPOSIT (CDs)[42]

In order to develop further the short end of the Euro-dollar market, the First National City Bank of New York (as it then was, now Citibank) in 1966 decided to issue a dollar certificate of deposit (CD) in London similar to the ordinary US certificates of deposit issued in New York and elsewhere in the USA. The minimum amount was $25,000 and they might run for up to 5 years (longer effective terms were on occasion arranged by means of forward contracts). Once the Bank of England had given a discount house permission to open a dollar account, it became possible for it to deal in dollar CDs (but there was a delay of nearly 6 months). Certain houses were prepared to act as brokers but not as principals. Gradually, a market was built up and other US banks (as well as banks elsewhere) with a branch in London were authorized by the Bank of England to issue dollar CDs and began to do so. In the result, some of the discount houses continued to operate as brokers and others became foreign currency principals, but once a house had chosen its role it was not free to change, since as a member of the Foreign Exchange and Currency Deposit Brokers Association it might not under any circumstances be both principal and broker.

Table 2.1 International banking market size, 1983–91 (at end of period, billions of dollars)

	1983	1985	1986	1987	1988	1989	1990	1991 March	June	Sept.
GROSS CLAIMS										
Euro-currencies on residents and non-residents	**1,985**	**2,444**	**3,128**	**4,019**	**4,307**	**5,097**	**6,019**	**5,750**	**5,527**	**5,672**
On non-banks	619	745	894	1,155	1,270	1,492	1,864	1,835	1,856	1,912
On banks	1,366	1,699	2,234	2,364	3,037	3,605	4,156	3,915	3,671	3,760
In dollars	1,098	1,251	1,559	1,363	2,000	2,317	2,540	2,472	2,341	2,346
In other currencies	381	617	864	1,231	1,267	1,546	2,040	1,885	1,805	1,923
Unallocated currencies	506	576	706	925	1,040	1,234	1,440	1,392	1,381	1,403
Domestic currencies on non-residents	**573**	**693**	**903**	**1,168**	**1,233**	**1,401**	**1,559**	**1,450**	**1,409**	**1,474**
On non-banks	220	245	275	322	304	307	336	315	300	314
On banks	353	448	628	846	929	1,094	1,223	1,135	1,109	1,160
In dollars	391	402	445	460	491	536	512	496	505	500
In other currencies	182	291	458	708	742	865	1,047	955	904	974
Total	**2,558**	**3,137**	**4,031**	**5,187**	**5,540**	**6,498**	**7,579**	**7,200**	**6,936**	**7,146**
On non-banks	839	990	1,169	1,477	1,574	1,799	2,200	2,151	2,156	2,226
On banks	1,720	2,147	2,862	3,710	3,966	4,699	5,379	5,050	4,780	4,920
In dollars	1,967	2,182	2,621	3,045	3,318	3,828	4,173	4,059	3,939	3,958
In other currencies	591	955	1,410	2,142	2,222	2,670	3,406	3,142	2,997	3,187

GROSS LIABILITIES

Euro-currencies to residents and non-residents	**1,995**	**2,454**	**3,141**	**4,018**	**4,302**	**5,098**	**6,006**	**5,753**	**5,522**	**5,693**
To non-banks	452	525	638	757	811	1,159	1,440	1,428	1,406	1,455
To official monetary institutions	79	100	97	143	141	153	175	162	158	161
To banks	1,464	1,829	2,406	3,118	3,350	3,786	4,391	4,163	3,958	4,077
In dollars	1,143	1,312	1,610	1,896	2,054	2,348	2,520	2,464	2,343	2,364
In other currencies	359	591	866	1,248	1,294	1,591	2,119	1,961	1,870	1,994
Unallocated currencies	493	551	665	875	955	1,159	1,367	1,328	1,310	1,334
Domestic currencies to non-residents	**415**	**560**	**716**	**999**	**1,111**	**1,290**	**1,496**	**1,423**	**1,342**	**1,376**
To non-banks	97	132	154	186	197	252	293	274	260	272
To banks	318	429	562	813	914	1,038	1,203	1,149	1,082	1,104
In dollars	289	351	414	477	520	584	584	576	557	562
In other currencies	126	209	302	522	591	706	912	847	785	814
Total	**2,410**	**3,014**	**3,857**	**5,017**	**5,413**	**6,388**	**7,502**	**7,176**	**6,864**	**7,069**
To non-banks	549	657	792	943	1,008	1,411	1,733	1,702	1,666	1,727
To banks and official institutions	1,861	2,357	3,065	4,074	4,405	4,977	5,769	5,474	5,198	5,342
In dollars	1,898	2,162	2,597	3,049	3,308	3,815	4,095	4,013	3,861	3,886
In other currencies	512	852	1,260	1,968	2,105	2,573	3,407	3,163	3,003	3,183
Net market size	**1,240**	**1,500**	**1,790**	**2,270**	**2,450**	**2,830**	**3,445**	**3,390**	**3,260**	**3,390**

Source: Bank for International Settlements

This ruling was dropped around the spring of 1971, when all the houses with broking subsidiaries became principals in the dollar CD market and one house already in it acquired a broker.

Subsequently, a market in sterling certificates of deposit was also established. These were launched on 28 October 1968, when the Bank of England gave permission to more than forty banks in London to make such issues. These included the clearing bank subsidiaries, the merchant banks, American and other overseas banks, which issued a bearer certificate for the amount of the deposit, which receipt also indicated the rate of interest payable when the deposit matured. By 1975, the clearing banks had become the major issuers of sterling CDs. Nowadays, the CD market is split between the clearing banks, the non-clearing banks (the top names being the three largest German banks, but in this category there is in fact a whole hierarchy of names), and the building societies. On short CDs (less than 1 year), interest is paid with the principal at maturity; on longer CDs, it is paid annually. These certificates are 'negotiable', i.e. they can be bought and sold and the discount houses both hold them in portfolio and make a secondary market for them. With the effluxion of time, they can become as short as a day or two. Quotes are made on a bid and offer basis in terms of yields.

Today, the minimum size of a bank CD is £50,000 (with multiples of £10,000), but a convenient trading size is £5 million, which may be sold in parcels of £1 million × 5. This is what the clearers like to do when they are funding their book. Discount houses would probably prefer CDs in the amount of £500,000, because they can trade them better and the banks will accommodate this; in issuing CDs to bank customers, a £500,000 size would not be uncommon. Likewise, parcels of £500,000 × 10 could be put on the market. When banks are placing CDs, it tends to be 'spread around'. It is not just the discount houses to which they are issued (for trading purposes); they may also be sold direct to banks (which frequently hold other banks' CDs), building societies, other financial institutions like pension funds and insurance companies, and sometimes to non-financial corporations. Other financial intermediaries may buy in smaller amounts – e.g. for clients. Investors may telephone a bank requesting the issue of a CD, in which to place their money. Discount houses (and others) have prudential limits on all names; indeed, names will be looked at once a week, but there could also be an immediate reaction (as a result of bad news). All money brokers act as brokers in CDs (in placing or finding them). They may do this in either the primary or secondary markets. It is in the latter that one is able to disinvest (i.e. sell a CD one has been holding at whatever is its current price). Over the years, the negotiability of names has varied considerably and today names are virtually placed in three tiers. It is tradability that determines how a CD is regarded and this reflects in the rate that can be obtained; even a large and well-established clearing bank must ensure that it does not put out too much paper at any one time. Also, it may be judged that there is a greater underlying credit risk (e.g. with certain US bank names) and they will therefore be accorded a less fine rate. In circumstances like this, a discount house when approached would tend to move the rate against them.[43] The minimum maturity when first issued is 7 days (though in practice it is commonly 1 month), also 7 days for building society CDs.[44] At the long end, CDs may go out to 5 years. Or, rather than issue CDs with a life of several years, which may be less easily marketable, banks used to arrange to issue 1-year certificates in a series on the understanding that at the end of the year, as one matured, it would be replaced with another, or 'rolled over' for a further year or years. It is understood that this practice has largely died out.[45] It should be noted, too, that when a CD is sold in the secondary market, its price will of course reflect current rates, which may be very different from the rate at which it was issued. Indeed, rates are fairly flexible and are closely aligned to the rates prevailing in the inter-bank market for equivalent periods, since it is there that much of the money to carry CDs is borrowed; also, for the banks, inter-bank money represents an alternative instrument, as do time deposits placed by corporates at market-related rates. Although the discount houses deal in sterling CDs as principals, they tend to hold their CDs for only a short period of time, banks that issue them being at times either buyers or sellers. Other regular customers include investment trusts and insurance companies. It should be noted that, by September 1991, CDs and other short-term paper issued by banks in the UK approximated to £68.94 billion,[46] of which the discount houses held about £5.1 billion.[47]

Building societies may also issue CDs. Initially, there was the problem that the interest on CDs is paid gross, but societies did not have the power to pay interest in this way. Following the Phillips Report,[48] the Building Societies Association (BSA) pressed the government for societies to be permitted to pay interest gross on

CDs. In 1982, the government indicated that such a power would be included in the 1983 Finance Act. This was published on 30 March 1983, and provided for societies to have the power to pay interest gross on qualifying CDs, defined as those for £50,000 or more and for a period of less than 12 months. The first building society CD was issued (by the Nationwide Building Society) on 23 May 1983 and, within a week, 6 societies were in the market; by the end of August, 10 of the largest 11 societies had issued CDs.[49] Such issues were subject to a prudential note put out by the Chief Registrar of Building Societies on 13 May 1983. This noted a request by the BSA that Building Societies should be authorized to hold each others' CDs so as to assist in broadening the market in these instruments. The Chief Registrar accepted the validity of this, but suggested that it would be appropriate to restrict this to CDs issued by the larger societies, defined for this purpose as those with assets in excess of £2 billion. Such a power was subsequently given.[50] The figure was later reduced to £1 billion, and societies can hold other societies' issues of CDs and floating-rate notes (FRNs) (see pp. 65–6) up to a total of 2.5 per cent of the holding societies' total assets at the latest balance sheet date.[51] The Chief Registrar also stated that societies would be expected to maintain a continuing presence in the market and not to withdraw from it when interest rates shifted, and he suggested that an acceptable continuing minimum presence could be of the order of £25 million. The Chief Registrar cautioned against societies buying their own CDs and he saw little merit in a number of societies trying to raise CD finance through consortium issues. The Bank of England also gave guidance to building societies issuing CDs in London. Thus, the minimum period to maturity on issue should be 28 days; interest might be fixed or variable and should be calculated on a 365-day basis; there was no objection to CDs which incorporated an option for the issuer to repay early, provided that the terms of the option were clear to the initial and subsequent holders; there was no objection to CDs which carried no coupon and were issued at a discount, provided that this was made obvious to all parties; and it should be clear from the instrument when payments of interest or repayments would be effected in the event of the due date falling on a non-business day.

Building society CD balances grew substantially in 1983 and 1984. However, the short-term nature of CD instruments has meant that, after the initial burst of activity, the continual repayments have resulted in balances thereafter growing only modestly, though there was a significant increase in the third quarter of 1985.[52] At the end of 1984, the figures for total outstandings of the eleven largest building societies were approximately £1.8 billion, and by the end of 1987 about £3.8 billion. By the end of 1990, it had risen to £8.6 billion.

Societies employ issuing and paying agents to carry out the administration relating to CD issues. A number use the Bank of England and some use discount houses or merchant banks. Societies also use money brokers as an outlet for their CD dealings, but not as issuing and paying agents. These agents then sell the CDs on to investors like banks and non-financial corporations. Most of the large building societies deal in building society CDs and a few make prices in other building society paper. As we have seen, the smallest CD a building society can issue is £50,000, but the larger societies would not issue a CD for less than £250,000 and normally £500,000 or £1 million would be the minimum. Larger 'parcels' would be issued – as with the banks – as £1 million × 5 or £500,000 × 10. This is done because individual CDs of these sizes are more tradable. The average term is 3 months. For the building societies, funding in the CD market is cheaper than time deposits – by at least one-sixteenth of one per cent – though slightly more expensive than for the clearing banks. The lower rate is because the CD is tradable – one can always disinvest (at a price) by selling it on through the secondary market to another holder. One cannot do this with a time deposit.

TREASURY BILLS

Another security that the discount houses invest in is the Treasury bill, also the banks as one ingredient in their liquid assets for the purpose of maintaining a sufficient degree of liquidity. Depending on the emphases of government finance, there have been times when the holdings of Treasury bills within the banking system have been very large, or at least quite significant. But issues of Treasury bills have, at times, only been kept in being because the Treasury bill has long been such a useful instrument of monetary policy. In recent years, however, it has been in commercial bills that the Bank of England has operated, and at one time the Treasury bill issue all but atrophied. Thus, by August 1988, it was down to £100 million per week for 91-day bills and (with a 5-week interruption in September/October 1988) this continued until May 1989, when it was raised first to £200 million and then to £300 million until

September 1990,[53] reducing thereafter to £250 million per week until raised to £350 million per week in February 1991, and to £500 million in April. Meanwhile, issues of 182-day Treasury bills (with occasional misses) were £100 million per week from May 1989 to October 1989, raised then to £200 million per week.[54]

For many years, and prior to 1971, the ultimate decision on Treasury bill rates rested with the discount market, which every Friday tendered as a syndicate for the amount of new Treasury bills on offer. They submitted a tender at a mutually agreed price, and the total amount of their tenders was always sufficient to cover the whole amount of the bills on offer.[55]

There was at this time also an interest rate cartel, whereby the clearing banks ensured that there was:

> a set pattern of professional money rates within the framework of Bank rate and Bankers deposit rate, and the existence of substantial lines of money, from the Clearing Banks at a rate ⅛ per cent above Deposit rate, tended to ensure an average cost of money which was almost invariably below the yield obtainable on those instruments in which [the discount houses] were investing.[56]

Consistent with the changes introduced at the time of Competition and Credit Control in 1971, the syndicated bid at the Treasury bill tender was abandoned – i.e. the market would no longer tender for Treasury bills at a price agreed amongst themselves. At the same time, the Bank of England asked the market to continue to apply each week for an amount of Treasury bills sufficient to cover the amount of bills offered at the tender, when they would be prepared to continue to confine to the market their extension of last resort facilities in the form of lending or purchase of eligible paper. (It should be noted that, while there were discount brokers outside the London Discount Market Association, they continued to participate in the Treasury bill tender.) The Bank of England also stated that, when they extended last resort facilities by lending, 'they would require the houses to provide part of the collateral, up to a minimum proportion to be agreed, in the form of Treasury bills'. There was a genuine understanding that 'the market would be prepared to take up the bills if there was nobody else there to take them up'. The share to be taken up, if necessary, by each of the houses would be 'according to their capital and their size'. However, as one would expect, if houses were to undertake that bills be taken up by the market at an underwriting price, this price would necessarily be lower (i.e. the rate of discount would be higher) than for bills that were tendered for. (It was disclosed to a House of Commons Select Committee in March 1976 that the rate of interest for underwriting purposes was 'running at about 1 per cent higher than the then Treasury bill rate'.) Basically, these arrangements to underwrite the Treasury bill tender still obtain. This is confirmed in a recent paper issued by the Bank of England.[57] Nowadays, it takes the form of an agreement by the discount houses to bid for sufficient bills at the tender to cover the tender collectively. Hence the 'underwriting' takes place through a commitment to bid – the 'underwriting' price is therefore by definition the price at which houses tender for bills.

Weekly Treasury bill tenders are held on Fridays (or the last business day of the week); the Bank of England announces the amount and maturity of Treasury bills to be offered a week in advance when announcing the result of the previous week's tender. The bills on offer normally mature 91 or 182 days after their date of issue, but the Treasury Bills Act 1877 allows any maturity up to 12 months, and on occasions the Bank has offered bills with a shorter maturity than 91 days. Unlike most other countries, the bills are for issue and payment on any business day in the following week, at the option of each successful tenderer. Each tender must be for an amount not less than £50,000 and must specify the date on which the bills required are to be dated and the net amount per cent (being a multiple of half of one penny) which will be given for the amount applied for. Separate tenders must be lodged for bills of different dates. There is no restriction on who may tender for Treasury bills. Accepted tenders are allocated at the price bid. The Bank may allot less than the amount announced the previous Friday without giving any prior notice, but may not allot more than the previously announced amount. The Bank itself may tender for bills, though it would usually do this only for customers (e.g. foreign central banks). Even if a sizeable cash shortage is in prospect for the following week (as is often the case), some Treasury bills will be offered, other than in exceptional circumstances, so as to preserve a market in these bills. During a period of insufficient shortages (or in order to alleviate a future period of large prospective shortages) the weekly Treasury bill tender may be increased in size. Irrespective of its size, the Treasury bill tender is underwritten each week by the discount houses collectively. This ensures that the tender is covered.

But there is no minimum price agreed in advance between the Bank and the discount houses, and the discount houses receive no fee for undertaking the underwriting. The basis for calculating the minimum proportion of each issue for which each discount house will tender is agreed in advance between the Bank and the discount houses, taking into account the capital base of each discount house.

After the changes introduced in 1971, the discount houses also began to sell 'hot' Treasury bills to the clearing banks (i.e. the same day as bills had been taken up), really giving way to a tendency that was already in evidence and arising out of the relative shortage of Treasury bills, which were also now required by the banks as a reserve asset. Indeed, other banks were now interested in buying 'hot' bills as well, though formerly they went mainly to the clearers. The Bank of England, on the other hand, applied a penal rate to 'hot' bills offered to it to deter the market from trying to sell them to the Bank.[58] In addition to rediscounting bills acquired through the tender, the discount houses also regularly buy, at market rates, Treasury bills offered to them by 'outside' banks and other institutions. In this context, the amounts dealt in are relatively small and such bills will usually be sold subsequently to other buyers.

The discount houses still continue to hold Treasury bills for trading purposes – varying from as low as £159 million to £1,222 million in 1990–1 (monthly figures) – but there has been an increasing demand from other sectors. The clearing banks would also themselves tender for bills and they are often successful. They seem now only to go to the discount houses for bills if they are 'really desperate', or for customers. The major building societies – but not Nationwide Anglia – normally tender for large quantities of Treasury bills, often on their own behalf. Holdings of such bills assist them to satisfy the requirements of their supervisory authority. Overseas customers (both central banks and the private sector) are major purchasers. Non-financial corporations with a money-market interest do not on the whole acquire Treasury bills and hence do not tender; very occasionally, they may buy them through a broker or a discount house. Others have no interest in Treasury bills whatsoever. But there is quite a degree of overseas interest in buying short-term sterling paper like Treasury bills.

TREASURY BILLS IN EUROPEAN CURRENCY UNITS (ECUs)

In early August 1988, the UK government announced plans to repay $2.5 billion of foreign debt and to refinance part of it through the creation of a market in short-term Treasury bills denominated in ECUs (the composite currency based on a basket of eleven European currencies).[59] The move to issue UK government debt denominated in ECUs was also presented by the Treasury and the Bank of England as a step towards closer monetary co-operation with European Community partners. According to the Chancellor of the Exchequer, it would serve to widen the options for managing the UK's reserves and would establish London's position as a centre of the ECU market, which it was hoped to develop further. London, with Paris and the Benelux countries, is the main centre for the ECU financial market. It was thought that the UK's move may encourage other European governments to follow suit. The main buyers of the bills were expected to be foreign central banks and investment institutions.

The first auction by the Bank of England of ECU 900 million Treasury bills (£585 million) was in October 1988; it was heavily oversubscribed. Likewise, there was a second monthly auction of ECU 750 million. Regular issues then followed. Each tender at each yield for each maturity (several maturities were offered) must be made on a separate application form for a minimum of ECU 500,000 nominal. Tenders above this minimum must be in multiples of ECU 100,000 nominal. Tenders must be made on a yield basis (calculated on the basis of the actual number of days to maturity and a year of 360 days) rounded to two decimal places. Each application form must state the maturity date of the bills for which application is made, the yield bid, and the amount tendered for. Global and definitive bills are issued on a discount basis. Global bills are held by the Bank of England as common depository for Euroclear and Centrale de Livraisons de Valeurs Mobilières (CEDEL). Definitive bills were made available in minimum denominations of ECU 10,000. Payment and delivery is 2 days after tender. All payments are made free of withholding tax or deduction for or on account of any other UK taxes.

The Bank of England appointed twenty-nine dealers to make a market in the bills and initially much of the bidding came from dealers attempting to establish an inventory from which to trade the paper. But several dealers admitted to being less aggressive in their bidding at the second auction and it was probable that too many market-makers were appointed. Several withdrew; others were appointed later. By January 1991, there were twenty-seven dealers. On occasion, ECU Treasury bills are allotted directly to the Bank of England. These bills may be made available to market-makers through sale and repurchase transactions in order to facilitate settlement. The main investors were said to be central banks, as well as conservatively managed investment institutions and international company treasurers. Apart from the oversubscription, success was also measured by the extent to which yields on these bills were below those on equivalent maturity bank deposits (as much as $\frac{1}{4}$ per cent below the rates which banks were willing to pay for ECU deposits in London).[60] Turnover statistics are given in Table 2.2. A UK government ECU Treasury bill programme was also announced through to December 1991.

Not only did the issue of significant amounts of a new security in itself deepen the short-term market, but the creation of a lively

Table 2.2 UK government ECU Treasury bill programme: turnover statistics, 1988–92 (ECU millions)

Year	Period	Total turnover	Turnover between market-makers	Turnover of market-makers with non-market-makers
1988	Q4	6,074	3,427	2,647
1989	Q1	10,840	5,450	5,390
	Q2	12,523	6,541	5,982
	Q3	13,470	6,975	6,495
	Q4	18,004	9,527	8,477
1990	Q1	15,019	9,282	5,737
	Q2	14,528	10,111	4,417
	Q3	10,418	6,270	4,148
	Q4	9,730	6,139	3,591
1991	Q1	13,361	7,567	5,794
	Q2	13,827	8,703	5,124
	Q3	15,907	9,278	6,629
	Q4	17,686	9,765	7,921
1992	January	5,777	3,456	2,321

Note: Q = quarter
Source: Bank of England

Treasury bill market in ECUs also served to assist the ECU bond market. In addition, the issue of the new bills broadened the UK government's borrowing options. To the extent that the government did not need the money, the proceeds could be invested at a better rate in other bonds, while at the same time creating a new market for ECU paper.[61] Furthermore, because of the massive rise in official reserves that occurred in the UK (particularly after January 1987), there was a case for diversifying the currencies held as reserves. Moreover, the Bank of England during 1988 had been accumulating a basket of European currencies in order to preserve the stability of the exchange rate mechanism of the European Monetary System; the further development of the ECU tended to have a similar emphasis.

Subsequently, the UK government made its first issue of ECU bonds (by tender on 19 February 1991). This was an issue of ECU 2.5 billion $9\frac{1}{8}$ per cent bonds due in the year 2001 at a price of 100 per cent. A further ECU 250 million was subscribed to separately by the Bank of England. The issue was very successful. On 6 March 1991, a related new derivative was issued on LIFFE; eleven members were assigned to act as designated brokers for the ECU bond futures contract.[62]

LOCAL AUTHORITY SECURITIES

Local authority securities, which used to be important,[63] are now much smaller in amount, as the role of local authorities has over recent years been greatly reduced and structural changes have been imposed by the central government on their financing arrangements. Thus, until early 1990, it was the case that, every year, the Public Works Loan Board (PWLB) Commissioners – after consultation with the Treasury – would determine loan quotas for each local authority. Borrowing within these quotas was at very fine rates set by the Treasury. Additional loans might be made in specific circumstances at higher rates. At the same time – with the agreement of the Treasury – the Commissioners had been making advances at quota rates additional to the normal quotas. This was done to assist in the management of the money markets. However, it was found that local authorities – while borrowing large sums from the PWLB – were also investing very substantial sums of money with the banking sector. The combined effect of this was to reduce the size of daily banking system shortages and so cause difficulties in the Bank's management of the money markets. As a consequence, the availability of funds from the PWLB at quota rates was curtailed. As from 15 February 1990, the Commissioners were no longer prepared as a matter of course to make loans available in addition to the quotas and at quota rates, though the Commissioners were prepared to consider requests from local authorities for advances additional to normal quotas at quota rates, where these changes would cause an authority exceptional difficulties (e.g. where it faced unusually high levels of maturing debt). Non-quota loans could also be applied for but at 2 per cent more (instead of 1 per cent more) than the rate of interest on quota loans. Quota rates were also gradually to be increased so that they came to be closer to, but still below, market rates.[64]

The large discount houses still hold small amounts of local authority bills from time to time and may tender for them; local authority bonds have virtually disappeared, though there are still some in the market. The banks hold sizeable amounts of local authority securities (though much of this has been inherited from the past and it is a declining figure); they also hold a modest amount in eligible local authority bills.[65] These are still regarded as a source of liquidity. The building societies are not really interested in local authority bills, though – like the banks – they carry a declining quantum of other local authority investments. Certain non-financial corporations may 'look at' local authority bills occasionally, but it is a marginal interest. Others show no enthusiasm at all.

CENTRAL MONEYMARKETS OFFICE (CMO)[66]

For many years, transactions in negotiable instruments in the London money markets had to be settled by messenger delivery of paper securities in exchange for payment, normally in the form of cheques that would be passed through the Town Clearing. However, new settlement facilities for sterling money market transactions were introduced on 1 October 1990, whereby transfers were effected by computerized book entries instead of by physical delivery. These services were provided by the CMO. The paper handled in this way consists of bearer securities like Treasury and local authority bills, eligible and ineligible bank bills, trade bills, bank and building society CDs, and commercial paper. Initially, the several types of instrument were phased in in stages – only newly issued paper was brought into the system; as existing money market instruments matured, replacement paper was brought in and, in the context of longer maturities, arrangements were made for outstanding instruments to be brought in at a later date. By the end of 1990, most money market instruments were covered in this way. The CMO operates alongside its sister institution – the Central Gilts Office (CGO), which was set up within the Bank of England in 1986 (see p. 54).

The desirability of a book-entry transfer system had been apparent for some time, in terms both of the efficiency and security of clearing and settlement systems. These risks were well illustrated in the summer of 1990 when £292 million of Treasury bills and CDs were stolen from a City messenger in King William Street. In addition to improved security, the inauguration of CMO also increased the speed and efficiency of settlement and provided the opportunity for a greater volume of trading during the day.

Originally, forty-four institutions joined CMO as direct members. Others joined later – by mid-1991, there were sixty-six direct members.[67] A direct member has a book-entry account in CMO in its own name. It arranges for a settlement bank to make and receive payments on its behalf for instruments transferred from and to any other direct member. A large number of other firms are participating indirectly through agency arrangements. Settlement is conducted on their behalf by an agent which itself has to be a direct member and may provide similar facilities for a number of indirect participants.

CMO is a settlement system, not a dealing system. Trading continues to be done over the telephone. Once the deal has been completed, the transfer of ownership from seller to buyer and the simultaneous transmission of the payment instruction in the opposite direction are communicated over CMO's real-time computer system,[68] via terminals located in members' offices. One should note, too, that – at least for the time being – each instrument in CMO is unique and preserves its identity as a paper instrument held with CMO. Gilt-edged stock in CGO, on the other hand, is interchangeable – transactions between CGO members are settled by debiting the CGO account of the transferor and crediting that of the transferee; no stock transfer forms or paper certificates are involved. Currently, in CMO, there is no provision for the instruments to be issued and traded in purely electronic form. To achieve this would in any case require an amendment to legislation and work is in hand on the legal issues involved.

Until the end of the role of paper as evidence of ownership, instruments will still need to be prepared and brought into CMO for lodgement. The lodging member guarantees the validity of these paper instruments. Once lodged, they are immobilized in a safe-custody vault at the Bank of England, where – provided they are not subsequently sold to a non-participant – they can remain until maturity. Meanwhile a detailed description of each of the individual instruments and a record of ownership is maintained by the central computer system and can be accessed by users as appropriate.

CMO provides a comprehensive range of settlement functions. Participants in the service may: settle outright sales and purchases; settle sale and repurchase agreements; deliver securities as collateral and exchange or return collateral; receive and make presentations at maturity; and split Treasury bills, CDs, and commercial paper into smaller denominations without withdrawing the instruments. In addition, a comprehensive set of on-line terminal enquiry facilities enables the direct members to monitor their settlement positions at all times during the day. End-of-day printed reports provide comprehensive data on all aspects of business transacted – from issues of new instruments to maturities. Both settlement of primary market purchases and secondary-market sales are handled by CMO. The movement of money-market instruments as collateral will also form a significant part of settlement volumes across CMO. The discount houses, for example, use collateral to secure money-market borrowing, including that from the Bank of England during its money-market operations. Money-market instruments also move from gilt-edged market-makers or discount houses to stock-exchange money brokers as security for stock borrowing. In turn, the money brokers use such instruments to collateralize lenders of stock, which include banks, insurance companies, and pension funds.

The initial development costs were financed by the Bank of England itself. Costs of operation are covered by membership and terminal fees, transaction charges per instrument, depository charges, and a withdrawal fee. The Bank's financial objective is to break even, taking one year with another. The Bank also set up a consultative group to review the ways in which CMO might be extended and enhanced (e.g. by accepting new types of instruments) so as to continue to improve the efficiency of settlements in the London money markets.

By the end of 1990, all the relevant types of money-market

instrument (except for sterling commercial paper and CDs with maturities beyond one year) were in the system, which remained substantially unchanged, though open to enhancement as required. It is generally agreed that it works very well; it would work even better if everybody joined, at least indirectly (e.g. some of the smaller non-banking institutional firms; some small banks are also not in the CMO). At the present time, and from their point of view, these parties do not feel that the system is cost-effective, but the greater the number of participants the more cost-effective the system is likely to become.

THE GILT-EDGED MARKET

At the short end, there has long been a link between the money market proper and the market in UK government securities – gilt-edged securities or gilts. Over a period of years, for example, the discount houses fulfilled an important function as dealers in short government bonds, whether these were issued as such or – more usually – became short as they approached maturity. The market's interest in bonds, which was initially very small, seems to have gone back to the early 1920s when bills were hard to come by and money was cheap,[69] but this business could only be pursued with great circumspection because at that time the lending banks still had to be persuaded about the propriety of the business. Indeed, it was not until after the financial crisis of 1931 that the use of government bonds as security 'became recognised by the banks and countenanced by the authorities'.[70] But active official encouragement had to wait until after the Second World War, when the authorities permitted the discount houses to increase their capital so that they could deal in bonds with a much greater degree of confidence.[71] The authorities were now anxious that the discount houses should supplement the facilities in the Stock Exchange 'in those bonds, in which it is particularly important to have an active quantum, because they are near-liquid assets'[72] and as such add to the quantum of liquid instruments available to institutions like banks[73] that have regular need of such means of adjustment. To this end, the discount houses were granted jobbing facilities (for quick transfer) at the Bank of England in government bonds (at that time, of up to 5 years maturity). The authorities indicated also that the market might hold a reasonable amount of such securities and should the market wish to borrow from the Bank of England it would accept such bonds as eligible security; in this case, however, the Bank would accept as collateral for loans only bonds of up to 5 years' maturity. The bulk of the market's bond holdings were in British government short-dated stocks, but a smaller and rather less active business was also carried out in short-dated Commonwealth and British Corporation (i.e. local authority) securities.

During the post-war years of cheap money (until, say, 1951), good profits could be made from business in bonds. After 1951, however, bond prices fell as market rates and yields rose and, with the high gearing of bonds books to capital resources, the discount houses 'learned in a painful manner, how the higher level of interest rates on their low yielding bonds meant running losses, uncovered margins and erosion of inner reserves'.[74] By 1955, and despite its increased resources, the market was feeling the strain. Nevertheless, it had sufficient resources to prevent a further decline and 'justified its position as a shock-absorbing cushion for the gilt-edged market'.[75] Another authority – Wilfrid King (writing in 1962) – put the matter somewhat differently:

> the market provides in the short bond market a certain degree of shock-absorbing mechanism. We shouldn't overrate this function. There have been moments when it has attracted a great deal of attention, and when it was thought that the market provided a great shock-absorbing cushion. But this isn't true. The broad shock-absorbing system is provided by the operation of the Government departments themselves, which means the issue department of the Bank of England, which stands behind the market. Of course, when small lines of bonds are being offered on the market, then indeed the discount houses may perform an equalising function, and one big house may often operate as a true jobber. But when a clearing bank wants to sell big masses of stock, then very rarely can the discount market absorb that stock unless the authorities are standing behind it. There is however an important bond market function that the discount market does perform. It deals in short bonds, and because it is a professional dealer it can usually afford to pay a higher price for short-dated bonds than an ordinary investor can do. This means that industrial companies and others who have been holding longer stocks find that when these stocks near maturity it will pay to sell them as shorts to the discount market and then to reinvest themselves in a security more appropriate to

their own business. Hence the various stocks as they come near to maturity tend to be gathered up in the discount market – not, of course, the whole supply of them, but a fair proportion – which means that the Treasury and the Bank of England in conducting refinancing of the public debt will usually know where they can find the near-maturities. The Government broker then will be a frequent buyer of those maturities from the discount market.[76]

It was because of the possibility of difficulties of this character that there was a limit to the extent to which a discount house could invest in bonds. The ratio of bonds to published resources was of the order of 8 : 1 or 10 : 1, but it varied from house to house and could also vary from time to time. It depended on the size of the inner reserves and on the 'pattern' of the book, i.e. on the size and average length to maturity. The market was particularly vulnerable whenever there was a sharp rise in Bank rate, which would rarely have been discounted completely; this therefore resulted in a marked fall in prices. In these circumstances, it would have to choose between heavy running losses on bonds already purchased or a heavy realized loss if it was decided to sell.

At times, the business in bonds was very active; on other occasions, less so. Equally, large profits could sometimes be won; at other times, the market ran into big losses. Experience also varied as between houses, some of which were more vigorous in pursuing this business than others. Moreover, the existence of operators in short bonds prepared to absorb them, if necessary, and to undertake transactions of some size must have added:

> materially to the marketability of these bonds, so encouraging other bodies (mainly banks and other financial institutions) to hold the bonds. It is not merely a question of being able to turn the bonds readily into cash; there is also the attraction of maximizing income by being able to switch from one maturity to another as relative yields and individual requirements change.[77]

Despite its forthright statements, the change introduced in 1969 by the Bank of England and confirmed in 1971 under the terms of Competition and Credit Control was not seen by the market to be as important as in fact it turned out to be, perhaps because the Bank only referred to it as a 'modification' in their mode of operation in the gilt-edged market, which represented 'a return towards the position in the market which they occupied up to some ten years ago'. Nevertheless, it was consistent with the new policy. As the Bank pointed out:

> it is considered appropriate to accompany changes in credit control intended to allow greater freedom of competition in the banking system with lesser intervention by the authorities in the gilt-edged market so as to leave more freedom for prices to be affected by market conditions and for others to operate if they so wish.

This was further explained by the Governor of the Bank to an International Banking Conference on 28 May 1971 in Munich as not meaning that:

> we have discontinued our normal operations of selling longer-dated gilt-edged against purchases of short-dated stocks, as a technically efficient way of refinancing maturities. But it does mean that we shall not generally be prepared to buy stock outright. Thus we shall not normally be prepared to facilitate movements out of gilt-edged by the banks, even if their sales should cause the market temporarily to weaken quite sharply. These changes could, of course, mean that some gilt-edged holders may prefer to stay shorter than hitherto; but their policies will, no doubt, be influenced by the structure of rates as well as by the extent to which private institutions are stimulated to make a better market in gilt-edged than hitherto.[78]

Within this context, one would expect the development of a much more flexible policy, with the probability that there would be greater fluctuations in the prices of securities and therefore in yields and in interest rates. Both were important weapons in credit control – the prices of securities in influencing liquidity (especially when there was a possibility of sales of gilt-edged) and interest rates as influencing the cost of money. (In fact, the Bank preferred to put it slightly differently, having been forced away from Radcliffean concepts towards more monetarist views, the Chief Cashier maintaining that: 'the Bank's operations in the gilt-edged market should pay more regard to their quantitative effect on the monetary aggregates and less regard to the behaviour of interest rates'.[79] Under the new arrangements, the ability of banks – and others – 'to deal in large quantities of stock at moments of their own choosing at prices not far removed from those ruling in the market at the time would clearly be unacceptable'.[80] At the same time, in order to provide for the possibility of implementing an easy-money policy based on expansionary open market operations (since monetary restriction would not always be appropriate policy), the Bank also reserved the right to make outright purchases of stock with more than a year to run 'at their discretion and initiative'.

But for the rest, the authorities left intact the system of continuous financing and refinancing of the central government. Hence, the Bank of England continued to be buyers of near-maturing stock, sellers of tap stocks, and to engage in switching transactions, which help this process and help investors to maintain the length of their portfolios as time elapses.

There is no necessity to go over all of the story.[81] Suffice it to say that, as a result of a combination of circumstances (failure fully to appreciate that Bank of England policy had changed at a time when interest rates were trending upwards),[82] the discount houses on more than one occasion made heavy losses on their gilts business. As a consequence, the discount houses virtually moved out of gilts.

There seemed little point now in holding gilt-edged securities as an investment, though there was ample scope to make profits as a trader and this was the direction in which the discount houses turned. Moreover, with a certain lengthening out on the borrowing side, a discount house was no longer necessarily a loser when interest rates rose. This, then, was the pattern that had established itself by 1975 – a shortening of books and an emphasis on trading. On this basis, the discount houses were again making good profits. Indeed, many of them by 1975 were merely taking 'a view on the day'. The market fluctuated quite a lot, but it was possible to make money on the basis of 'informed speculation', plus a certain flair on the part of the dealer, or accurate judgement of a changing situation. Many of the discount houses were now dealing on an 'in and out' basis within the 24 hours, and this tended to be the pattern that they subsequently followed. However, when there was a strategic shift of view (as in late 1975/early 1976) taken in anticipation of a continuing fall in interest rates, the discount houses were prepared – without abandoning operations on a quick 'in and out' basis – to accept increased exposure for a limited period. But they remained very conscious of the fact that they must be 'extremely nimble' in their trading in the gilt-edged market, with a tendency to realize profits quickly and then start again, rather than to build up large paper surpluses that could so easily disappear (as in 1973).

'BIG BANG' AND THE GILTS MARKET

However, the major change in the gilts market was initiated by the 'Big Bang' of October 27, 1986. This introduced major structural changes to the market. The old order of single capacity trading, whereby in the UK there had historically been a separation of the roles of principal (jobber) and agent (broker), was swept away to be replaced by a dual-capacity system in which the two roles would be combined. On this basis, a new gilt-edged market, modelled largely on the US Treasury bond market, came into operation.

This was followed by the opening up of Stock Exchange member-ship to international and corporate entities, and this altered the face of the gilt-edged market almost beyond recognition. Many new players entered the game, and the market place shifted from the Stock Exchange floor to the telephone and the telescreen-driven operations of 'upstairs' dealing rooms. In addition, there were major alterations in the way in which gilt-edged investments were taxed. From 28 February 1986 onwards, the gross accrued interest content in the total price of a gilt-edged stock (and many other fixed-interest stocks) was treated for tax purposes as an item of income and not as capital – as it had been in the past. In addition, from 2 July 1986, capital gains tax no longer applied to these issues. In the result, there had been little less than a revolution in the gilt-edged market.[83]

In terms of structure, one has the government on one side, which uses the gilt-edged market as a means whereby a large part of the public sector deficit is funded. On the other are the investors, which comprise a wide range of individuals, corporations, and financial institutions, and for which gilt-edged stocks represent one potential investment medium. In between is the gilt-edged market, where business is conducted and where stock and money change hands.

One of the main criticisms of the old gilt-edged market was that there was not a sufficient number of jobbing firms with large enough capital resources to provide the market with the level of liquidity required.

By 1985 there were only eight jobbing firms operating in gilts. . . . Thus it was hardly surprising that when revolutionary change and the end of single capacity became inevitable the Bank of England should decide to replace the old gilt-edged market with a new sys-tem in which there would be a greater number of market-making firms and substantially increased amounts of dedicated capital.[84]

In the new market, the old separation between jobber and broker was abandoned and it was now permissible to combine the functions of principal and agent within the same firm, though not all firms wished to do so. The core of the new market was comprised of:

a number of registered market-making firms with obligations to make – on demand and in any trading conditions – continuous and effective two-way prices at which they stand committed to deal, in appropriate size as discussed in advance with the Bank of England, thereby providing continuous liquidity for the investing public. The sizes of the positions these market-makers can take are constrained by the need for each firm's aggregated position risk to be contained within certain prudential limits which are determined and monitored by the Bank. Each market-maker is required to commit an amount of dedicated capital to his gilt-edged operation and the greater this is the wider are his prudential limits.[85]

In return for obligations to make prices in this way 'in fair weather and in foul', also to submit to the prudential control of the Bank, market-makers are able to avail themselves of certain privileges which are not open to other participants in the market. These were as follows: (a) to have a direct dealing relationship with the Bank in gilt-edged securities; (b) to have, subject to the agreement of the government, exemption from Section 472(1) of the Income and Corporation Taxes Act 1970, which enables them to claim relief against tax for the full trading loss made by buying stock-cum-dividend and selling it ex-dividend in the ordinary course of business, regardless of the time interval between purchase and sale; (c) to be able to offset, for tax purposes, dividends paid by them on stock they have sold against dividends received on stock they have purchased; (d) to be able both to lend and borrow stock through approved Stock Exchange money brokers; (e) to have borrowing facilities at the Bank of England against approved security up to maximum amounts related to the market-maker's capital and reserves; and (f) to have access to the Inter-Dealer Broker (IDB) mechanism.[86] There is finally the further stipulation that all gilt-edged market-makers are required to become members of the Stock Exchange for regulatory purposes and for the maintenance of professional standards.

In the first half of 1985, the Bank of England invited applications from investment houses prepared to operate as market-makers under these conditions. This was followed by a period during which each prospective market-maker's candidature was thoroughly scrutinized before the Bank issued an initial list of twenty-nine firms to which it was prepared to award a 'franchise'. Although many of the well-known names of the old gilt-edged market were in the list, its content also reflected the emergence of new alliances between capital (mostly put up by large banks) and expertise made up of the market skills of both jobbers and brokers. This was made possible by a change in Stock Exchange rules, which after 1 March 1986 permitted 100 per cent bank ownership of a market-maker. Subsequently, one or two were non-starters; there was also some consolidation and changes of names, and ultimately six withdrawals. By mid-1991, there were eighteen gilt-edged market-makers, all were members of the Gilt-Edged Market-Makers Association (GEMMA) formed in 1985 at the instigation of the Bank of England.[87] There were also nine Stock Exchange money brokers and three inter-dealer brokers. A very important feature of the new arrangements that should be noted is that the gilt-edged market-makers do not necessarily limit their operations to market-making and transacting other firms' orders. Most of them also have trained teams of salesmen backed up by economic and technical research.

> It can be seen that there is a very high level of inter-dependence between the three essential elements of such firms. The salesmen need their market-makers' prices to be competitive in width and size, the market-makers need the salesmen to understand and, if possible, anticipate investor demands, and the whole operation needs a strong capital base and fine credit lines in order to maximise its profitability.[88]

Another change in the new gilt-edged market was the introduction of a new type of intermediary – the inter-dealer broker, which provides a means whereby market-making firms can trade with each other 'whilst maintaining anonymity. They form an inner ring to the market, matching one market-maker's bid with another's offer and vice versa. They only deal with registered gilt-edged market-makers. They do not deal with the public'.[89]

The gilt-edged market also uses the services of Stock Exchange money brokers, without which the gilt-edged market could not function efficiently. They are concerned with the business of borrowing and lending stock:

[Dealers] borrow stock in order to be able to deliver it to somebody to whom they have sold it, in order to obtain cash payment. The most usual case is that of a market-maker who has a bear book in a certain stock, but still makes a two-way market in the stock. If he then satisfies further buying orders in that stock, he will be unable to demand payment unless he can deliver stock to the buyer. This will mean that he will be out of cash which could be earning interest for him. If, however, he borrows the stock and delivers it, he will receive payment, and at some later time when his book in that stock turns round he can unwind his borrowed position. The ability of market-makers to lend and borrow stock easily is thus an essential ingredient in the general fluidity of the day-to-day market.[90]

In their everyday operations, market-makers make their money not from market-making itself, where the margin is only between bid and offer and there is no commission; they make their money from carrying a 'position'. Many market-makers run a 'front' book for the purpose of catering for customers and a 'back' book, which is the basis of their position at any time. Always there are risks, but for a good market-maker volatility is an advantage. They have to be nimble, and frequently buy and sell very quickly. The essence of position-taking is speculative and therefore highly risky. And if they are wrong, it is wise to get out; there is no point in trying to stay with it – that is when big losses are made. On the other hand, market-makers maintain that they get a lot of information as a result of their retail trading and this feeds into the running of a position. In market-making, however, what is important is not market share, but profitability.

One of the main reasons why some of the potential market-makers withdrew at an early stage, and still others after making losses, was the overcrowded scene with too many market-makers in relation to the quantum of business and the meagre profits. But that did not prevent them from trading in gilts. They are able to get very good information from the market-makers themselves (because the latter want the business) and they argue that they can achieve a better profit experience as a customer trading off the market-makers, while still restricting the risks. If one is a market-maker and customers keep taking paper from you, one has continuously to replace it. And, in any case, if on the basis of interest rate expectations, it is appropriate to take or run a position, one can always do so, whether one is a market-maker or not.

Another new feature relates to the role of the authorities. In the old market, the Bank of England operated through the Government Broker. By tradition, he was the senior partner of Mullens & Co. He was responsible for carrying through the day-to-day market activities of the authorities, which acted through the Bank of England. The operations of the Government Broker were strictly separated from Mullens' non-government business. The Government Broker had his own team consisting of himself, his deputy (another partner in Mullens), plus market-dealing staff. His team had no dealings with any other brokers (including the other part of Mullens), but dealt solely with the jobbing system. This particular system was inappropriate in the new market with its far greater number of market-makers. Tradition gave way to practical reality and the Government Broker and his team moved inside the Bank of England to become members of its gilt-edged division. Actually, the Bank of England took over the work done by Mullens in April 1986 and the work was transferred from Mullens premises to the new dealing room in the Bank at the time of Big Bang (i.e. 27 October 1986). From there a team of about a dozen staff keep in daily communication (between 8.00 a.m. and 5.00 p.m.) with the gilt-edged market-makers, dealing with them over the telephone rather than on the floor of the Stock Exchange.

The techniques employed by the Bank of England in issuing government stock on behalf of the Treasury are – with the exception of the auctions (see below) – essentially similar to what preceded Big Bang. The essence of the Bank's approach in the primary market[91] is that it aims to bring forward sufficient stock, taking one month with another, to achieve its current funding objective and in doing so to respond flexibly to demand as it is seen to emerge in different areas of the market. To this end, it makes use of a range of instruments – full-coupon conventional stocks of various maturities, convertibles, low-coupon conventionals and, after March 1981,[92] index-linked stocks. The Bank generally aims to have a variety of different types and maturities of stock on its book so that it can respond to demand where it emerges. In deciding the type of stock and maturities of new issues, the Bank has regard not only to the pattern of demand for stock, but also to cost considerations and the profile of future maturities, with the general aim, other things being equal, of trying to maintain a reasonably smooth maturity pattern and ensuring that the average life of the debt does not become unduly short.

The main approaches used by the Bank in issuing stock are, first, offers for sale by tender to the general public (including foreign investors, which have at times been an important ingredient in total demand). In this instance, new stocks (or large new tranches of existing stocks) are often issued by tender. Tenders for conventional stock normally have a minimum price, which is set in line with market prices at the time the new stock is announced. Tenders for index-linked stock normally have no minimum price, but in practice – as with tenders for conventional stocks – the Bank would not normally allot at a price below where the market was at the time the stock was announced. Both types of tender are allotted on a common price basis: all successful bidders pay a common striking price, which is the lowest price at which tenders are accepted, but higher bidders have priority in the allotment of stock. Both types of tender are effectively underwritten by the Bank of England – i.e. stock not taken up in the tender is subscribed by the Bank and is then available to it to sell 'on tap' in the secondary market. Tender offers generally involve a relatively sizeable amount of stock (perhaps £750–1,000 million in the case of a full-coupon conventional issue); to spread the impact on cash flow, the stock is often offered for subscription on a partly-paid basis. To give investors time to tender, the Bank necessarily has to allow a few days between the announcement of the stock (most frequently on Fridays) and first dealings in it in the secondary market (typically the following Thursday); but in some situations, where it was helpful to have the stock immediately available to respond to expected market demand, the Bank has on occasion issued a new stock (or tranche of an existing stock) directly to itself so that it had it available to sell immediately in the secondary market.

Second, there are 'tranchettes' of existing stocks. This approach enables the Bank to replenish its portfolio by bringing in small additional supplies of several different stocks, which are placed directly into its book where they are available for sale to the market and can be peddled out in response to demand. In this way, the Bank can respond flexibly to variations in the pattern of demand during the ordinary course of trading with minimal disturbance to market conditions. The choice between these two approaches depends on a range of considerations, including the state of the market, the state of the Bank's portfolio, and how far advanced the funding programme is in relation to the current funding objective. Consistent with its general approach, the Bank does not normally expect to sell the whole of any new issue immediately. The main purpose of new issues is rather to replenish the Bank's portfolio of stocks, so as to enable it to maintain the funding programme. The aim is to do this with the least possible disturbance to market conditions – any downwards effect on prices would generally be limited by the knowledge that the Bank does not sell stock on a falling market; and there can be occasions when new supplies of stock after a market adjustment can help the market to consolidate at a new trading level.

Exactly the same general considerations governed the Bank's approach to secondary market operations. Here the guiding principle is that the Bank does not sell stock into a falling market, but only when it is stable or rising, typically selling successive blocks of stock at progressively higher prices – the steepness of the progression depending upon its assessment of the underlying strength of market demand on the one hand and upon where the Bank stands in relation to the funding programme on the other. When the market falls, the Bank refrains from further sales and the Bank may on occasion, particularly if it judges the fall to be erratic or disorderly, and again depending upon its position in relation to the funding programme, provide some measure of market support by buying stock that is offered to it outright, normally at prices somewhat below the prevailing market price. The Bank would not resume selling until either the market recovered to its initial level or the downward price adjustment appeared to have been completed and the market showed evidence of having stabilized. Then the Bank would often re-enter the market in the first instance by selling small amounts of stock which it may hold in portfolio, other than taps or tranchettes. This would be done in order to test the market strength, though the Bank may re-enter by selling tranchettes or tap stocks, if these were bid for a sizeable amount and the Bank judged that this reflected significant investor demand. In this latter case, the Bank would tend to be somewhat more flexible in adjusting prices of tranchettes than of tap stocks.

As early as August 1986,[93] it was expected that the Bank of England would also run an experimental series of three or four gilt-edged auctions and this was confirmed when the Bank announced in mid-October that it would start discussions along these lines.[94] It outlined its broad thinking in February 1987, when it invited reactions from market participants.[95]

On the basis of comments received from market participants and further internal discussion, the Bank announced its proposals on 13 April 1987. The approximate timing of each auction was to be announced some time in advance. It would relate to a conventional short-dated (up to 7-year) stock, would be for an amount of up to £1.25 billion, and might be either fully or partly paid. The precise date and terms would be fixed having regard to the state of the funding programme and of the market at the time, but would be announced not less than 7 calendar days in advance of the auction. Decisions on further auctions would be taken in the light of experience with this first operation. Later auctions might relate to a long-dated (over 15-year) and then to a medium-dated (7–15-year) stock, in each case for an amount of up to £1 billion. The remainder of the gilt-edged funding programme would continue to be covered by the tender/tap arrangements already described.

The Bank would not sell other stock of the same type (or, in the case of a short-dated auction, any short-convertible stock) through the tap system or otherwise between the time of the announcement of the details of an auction and a period ending 28 days after the auction. It would be free to sell stock of other maturity, or other type (e.g. low-coupon or index-linked) as usual during this 'fallow' period. The Bank would not necessarily resume selling stock of the type auctioned immediately the 'fallow' period had ended and, as a matter of normal market management, would not typically expect to do so unless it were satisfied that the auction had been fully absorbed. But the Bank would be free to make such sales if it were judged to be appropriate.

Auctions would be open to applications from the public at large, subject to a minimum application of £1,000. The Bank would set no minimum price on the stock offered at the auction and would expect to allot the whole amount on offer. There would be no formal or informal underwriting arrangement for the auctions, but the Bank encouraged all gilt-edged market-makers, as part of their commitment to the market, to participate actively in the auction process. The Bank reserved the right not to allot all the stock on offer in exceptional circumstances (e.g. where the auction was covered only at an unacceptably deep discount to the prevailing market level). In that event, the Bank would take any stock not allotted into its own portfolio. The Bank would be free to sell such stock (but not other stock of that type) into the secondary market in the normal way, but during the 'fallow' period would undertake not to do so at a price below the minimum allotment price.

Auctions, at least initially, would be on a bid-price basis, in which successful bidders would be allotted stock at the price which they bid. The Bank would, as under the tender arrangements, allot stock at its absolute discretion and might decline to allot more than 25 per cent of the amount on offer to an individual bidder, if it appeared that to do so would be likely to lead to market distortion. The Bank would be prepared to accept non-competitive bids (limited to one bid per applicant) for amounts of stock up to £100,000 nominal. These would be allotted in full at the average accepted price. 'When-issued' (WI) trading (see below) would be permitted. The Bank was content that such trading might develop subject to certain conditions – in particular, the prudential supervision of the credit risk to which gilt-edged market-makers and inter-dealer brokers might become exposed. Market-makers would not be required to observe their market-making commitment in respect of the stock to be auctioned during the 'when-issued' period. The Bank proposed to publish – as soon as possible after allotments were determined – figures for the total amount of stock allotted in respect of competitive bids, the amount allotted in respect of non-competitive bids and the highest, lowest, and average price of successful competitive bids.

The first trial gilt auction was launched on 13 May 1987, when the government sold £1 billion 8 per cent gilts maturing in 1992. It was judged to be a success and was covered or subscribed for 2.3 times, though demand from both domestic and foreign institutions was modest. Dealers also participated in a WI market. This related to trading between the announcement of the precise terms of the auction and the sale itself, which gives market-makers time to build up a bank of information about the likely level of retail demand for the auction stock, to place stock in advance of the sale, and therefore to judge an accurate price for their bids at auction.[96] The second experimental auction of gilt-edged securities took place on 23 September 1987. On this occasion (to the surprise of the market) only £800 million – instead of £1 billion – was offered as a tranche of an existing stock (the Treasury 9 per cent due in the year 2008). As an existing stock, there was no difficulty in establishing price levels in WI trading, which began immediately the announcement of the issue was made on 15 September.[97] In the result, although the whole issue was sold, the retail demand was judged to be poor on this occasion and certain market-makers were left with unwanted stock.[98] The third of the experimental gilts auctions took place on 13 January 1988. The Bank of England was successful in selling £1 billion of medium-dated gilt-edged stock, the existing 8¾ per cent Treasury Loan 1997, but the bids were only 1.07 times more than the issue.

It was decided to continue with gilt auctions. Not only was the method endorsed by senior representatives of the market-makers, but it was agreed by the Treasury that the Bank should continue with auctions of gilt-edged. Auctions were not, however, expected to shoulder the main burden of the government's funding requirements in the foreseeable future and were seen rather as a useful addition to the existing funding techniques. By March 1988, it was clear that both the Bank of England and the Treasury felt it would be desirable to preserve auctions as a method of selling British government debt, but the Treasury remained opposed to the payment of underwriting fees to market-makers who bid for government stock.[99] In the result, auctions were resumed in August 1988, when the Bank of England announced the issue by auction of £750 million of short-dated gilt-edged stock. It was for an additional tranche of existing 8½ per cent Treasury stock due for redemption in 1994 and – as in earlier instances – was to be partly paid. The size of the issue was slightly smaller than expected, which probably reflected the buoyancy of government finances and the reduced need for large borrowing. The auction took place on August 10 and the stock was well covered with bids totalling 2.3 billion for the £750 million of securities on offer. It was planned to hold a further auction early in 1989, but this was cancelled, since by then the government was in substantial budget surplus.

It should be added that, at various times in between the experimental and later auctions, gilts were also offered for sale by tender. When a tender issue was undersubscribed (as in December 1987), the Bank of England took the unissued stock on to its own books and it was then reissued as a tap stock as market conditions permitted.

Another structural change which occurred in the gilts market derived from the fact that there had been a real rise in tax revenue at a time when – due to government policy – there was also a real fall in government expenditure; as a result, in 1987/8, 1988/9, and 1989/90, there were budgetary surpluses of some magnitude. And the effects were accentuated by the flow of funds into government hands as a result of the privatization of a series of government-owned or partially owned enterprises. In these circumstances, not only did the government need to borrow less; there was also a case for funding government stock by buying it in well before it matured. In addition to net repayment of debt by the government, Bank of England purchases of government stocks were disproportionately weighted towards purchases of long-dated stocks.[100] In the result, the average maturity of the government's debt continued to shorten and the gilts market to contract. Furthermore, following 'Big Bang' in October 1986, it was found that there were too many gilt-edged market-makers attempting to make a living, given the intense competition, and, in the course of the next few years, the number dropped by one-third – from 27 to 18 (the latest withdrawal being in April 1991); inter-dealer brokers (which had fallen from 4 to 2) were restored to 3 (in November 1990). The capital of the gilt-edged market-makers fell from £595 million in October 1986 to £395 million by 1990.[101] Operating losses from October 1986 to end-1989 were £202 million. Profits returned to the market in 1990 – £40 million for the year – with turnover of £4 billion a day.[102] Activity was expected to revive further as the government resumed heavy borrowing and the market was now thought to have attained a degree of stability. Moreover, according to the Bank of England: 'the absence of any withdrawals from the gilt market should not be taken to indicate that there has been any reduction in competition among the remaining firms or that they have lowered the quality of the market-making service provided to investors'.[103] Hence, after some years of difficulty due to curbs on government expenditure and budget surpluses resulting in a cutback in borrowing, the gilts market seems again to be in a relatively healthy state, with some guarantee of an adequate supply of new issues and an appropriate number of strongly capitalized dealers to take advantage of it.

Latterly, the government suffered a deteriorating fiscal position. In fact, the developing deficit was due to a combination of factors – the clear necessity to spend more money on the social services (including health) and education, poll tax relief (which came to be described as a 'black hole'), and later unemployment benefit. Then there was the advent of recession (recognized as such by September/October 1990, but increasing in severity thereafter) – this meant lower incomes and lower profits, not infrequently losses, and therefore lower income tax and corporation tax receipts, with high expenditure on unemployment benefit (as above). There was also, after August 1990 – and especially after January 1991 – the heavy extra defence costs of the Gulf Crisis and

War (offset to some extent by reimbursements from Allies). Privatization continued, but was subject at times to certain delays.

Financing the deficit was to be met by borrowing. Indeed, even prior to new issues of gilt-edged securities, the government during the summer of 1990 had resumed making direct sales of gilts to the market – since May 1990, it was estimated (by Greenwell Montagu) that the Bank of England may have quietly dribbled out £1 billion into the market.[104] In January 1991, the first conventional gilts issue[105] since August 1988 was made – £500 million of 10 per cent Conversion Stock 1996 (with a further sum of £200 million of the stock reserved for the National Debt Commissioners). This issue was subject to tender at a minimum price of 97.75 per cent. Then, at the beginning of February, three tranchettes (not subject to formal tender) totalling a further £500 million were announced – £200 million $9\frac{3}{4}$ per cent Exchequer Stock 1998, £150 million 9 per cent Conversion Stock 2000, and £150 million $9\frac{1}{2}$ per cent Conversion Stock 2004. The significance of this was that: (a) there was more stock for the market to trade – a drought that had lasted for 28 months had been broken; and (b) it assisted the Bank of England, as an 'insider trader', to manage the market.[106] It was estimated that there would be further new gilts issues in 1991/2 of £12 billion, of which £6 billion would be needed to redeem existing gilts.[107] These expectations were strengthened when another new stock – again of £500 million – carrying a rate of 10 per cent at a price of around $99\frac{15}{16}$ and maturing in 2001 was announced in February 1991.[108] At the same time, there was the danger of over-issue and, when in April 1991, an £800 million tranche of 9 per cent gilts due in 2008 was under-subscribed – and with further issues to come – the gilts market was seen (at least temporarily) to have run out of steam. None the less, the Bank of England subsequently announced that it would offer a £1.2 billion tranche of 10 per cent Conversion Stock due 1996 for auction on 24 April, which it hoped would create a 5-year benchmark. This was the first auction that the Bank of England had held since August 1988. In the result, the issue was heavily over-subscribed and was regarded as a great success.[109]

The Bank of England envisaged that the funding requirement would be met in part by a programme of auctions of gilt-edged stock to be held at intervals throughout the year. This would be combined with continuing official sales of stock by other methods, including – as appropriate – minimum price tenders, issues of packages of tranchettes, and sales in the secondary market from the

Bank's holdings of stock. By December 1991, there was evidence of a glut of issues to the market, when £500 million of bond issues were made available for trading, coming almost immediately after the creation of £1.5 billion of gilts.[110] However, the £1 billion tranche of 8½ Treasury stock due 2007, which had been over-hanging the market since its issue on 13 December 1991, was in fact disposed of before the middle of January 1992.

On the organizational side, one should note the setting up of a Central Gilts Office (CGO) with an electronic transfer system for the assured payment and delivery of gilt-edged stock. It is operated by the Bank of England. The Bank has proposed a wider participation, in order to keep down costs and expand the use of a more efficient method for the electronic transfer of gilt-edged stock.

Membership of the CGO has so far been confined to authorized gilt market-makers, Stock Exchange money brokers, inter-dealer brokers, discount houses, and the settlement banks. The Bank of England is keen to see that all others in the market, such as broker-dealers and institutional investors, benefit from the efficiency that the Office has brought to the transfer of stock. The Bank has told the CGO's current membership that it envisaged two ways in which participation could be effected: either through direct membership or by indirect membership of the CGO whereby the participant's stock is held in the nominee accounts of an existing member of the system. Large and frequent traders of gilts could be expected to apply for direct membership, while smaller players, who could not justify the expense of joining the system, could avail themselves of indirect membership.

The benefits of the CGO are that it ensures speedy delivery of stock coupled to an irrevocable commitment to pay on the same day. All transactions are conducted through a secure computer network linking members with the CGO, and the movement of stock depends upon the seller having sufficient stock available on his CGO account and the taker positively accepting an offer of stock. The banks participating in the CGO – the London and Scottish clearing banks – have given an unconditional undertaking that at the moment of transfer from seller to buyer, the buyer's bank will pay to the seller's bank on the same day. To cover the risk the buyer's bank takes on in such a transaction, the bank takes out a floating charge over stock already held in the customer's CGO account and over moneys receivable by it for any stock subsequently transferred from that account.

COMMERCIAL PAPER

Initially, the authorities announced that certain companies might issue short-term corporate bonds (1–5 years)[111] without contravening the Banking Act or the Bank of England's previously established guidelines on capital market issues. These arrangements were put in place in response to enquiries from companies about the possibility of such issues and were consistent with the view on the desirability of such an extension of corporate borrowing powers expressed in the Bank's written evidence to the Wilson Committee in 1977. The development of the Euro-note and Euro-commercial paper markets in London stimulated interest in the possibility of making even shorter-term sterling note issues as a new form of sterling money-market instrument. Previously, one-name sterling money-market instruments had been issued only by the Treasury, local authorities, banks, the former licensed deposit-takers, and building societies. Money-market instruments other than such single-name paper carried at least two names – that of the issuer and that of one other good name. The vast bulk of such paper consisted of eligible bank bills – bills drawn by a company and accepted by an eligible bank – which the Bank of England was willing to buy in its money-market operations.

Bill finance was sufficiently attractive to many borrowers to suggest that the scope for a commercial paper market seemed less in sterling than in other currencies. Nevertheless, the expressed demand for sterling commercial paper appeared to indicate that the Bank of England should not stand in the way of the development of such a market, provided that adequate investor-protection safeguards could be established. The Bank took the view that, given such a demand, unnecessary restrictions were not only undesirable in themselves but could also lead to a shift of business offshore, thereby fragmenting the London sterling market, or lead to the use of artificial devices to evade the existing restrictions.

Consequently, the powers conferred on the Treasury by the Banking Act 1979 to remove specified transactions from the definition of deposit-taking within that Act were used to allow corporate issues of sterling short-term debt, subject to certain requirements designed to provide investor protection.[112] These requirements are as follows: (i) the issuing company should be listed on the International Stock Exchange and have net assets of £50 million or more, or be the wholly-owned subsidiary, and issue under the guarantee, of such a company; (ii) issues should have an original maturity of between 7 and 364 days;[113] (iii) issues should be in denominations of £500,000 or £1 million (the minimum was subsequently reduced to £100,000); and (iv) issues must carry a statement that the issuer or its guaranteeing parent is in compliance with the International Stock Exchange Listing Rules and there has been no significant adverse change in its circumstances since information was last published in accordance with such rules. In addition, the Notice issued by the Bank of England recognized that some issuers might wish to have the paper guaranteed by a recognized bank (or at that time licensed deposit-taker) and the Regulations allowed for this, but the Bank stated that guarantees should not come from any other source except for parents of wholly-owned subsidiary issuers.

The Bank of England also recognized that issuers might wish to employ an intermediary to manage issues. Because of the uneven competitive environment that would have arisen from the different regulatory regimes applied by different supervisory authorities to different intermediaries active in the UK, management of issues was initially restricted to recognized banks and licensed deposit-takers incorporated in the UK and thus subject to the Bank's own capital adequacy and liquidity arrangements. Other prospective intermediaries were, however, able to participate, subject to arrangements agreed individually with the Bank to ensure level competition in terms of regulatory arrangements.

Issues of sterling commercial paper did not require timing consent from the Bank of England under the Control of Borrowing Order, which was suitably amended. For statistical purposes, issuers are asked to notify the Bank, at the commencement or extension of any programme, of the total amount of paper they propose to issue under that programme, and to provide monthly returns of the amount of sterling commercial paper outstanding and of issues and redemptions made since the previous return.[114] The first programmes were announced in May 1986 and were all for overseas companies, mainly the overseas financing subsidiaries of UK companies. There was initially some uncertainty about the legal position of UK companies issuing such paper without a prospectus, hence the use of overseas financing subsidiaries, but the Financial Services Act removed that uncertainty, with the result that by October 1986 new programmes for domestic issuers outnumbered those for overseas issuers, although it was not until February 1987 that this was true for the total of outstanding programmes. The main issues in the early days tended to be by property companies, since – by the nature of their business transactions – they could not resort to bank bills. The number of programmes in existence increased steadily, though not all programmes announced were activated immediately. This reflected the anticipatory behaviour of borrowers, who set up programmes as an addition to their borrowing options – to be used when market conditions were appropriate.

A relatively recent picture of the sterling commercial paper (SCP) market is given by Midland Montagu in their Sterling Commercial Paper Survey of November 1990 (the actual questionnaires were distributed in August 1990). They reported that at that time there were over 200 issuers reporting to the Bank of England. Since its inception, the SCP market has been largely investor driven in that transactions are typically initiated in response to specific investor demand identified by dealers. Although the corporate sector still dominated the SCP market in terms of numbers of investors, the share of institutional investors – pension funds, insurance companies, investment and unit trusts – had grown more rapidly. By 1990, the corporate sector accounted for about 35 per cent, but institutional investors had increased to 32 per cent (a figure which is also borne out by dealer experience in the market). On the whole, investors have found the return on SCP 'adequate'. Factors governing investor decisions were capital protection, yield pick-up, and liquidity – in that order. Average dealing sizes were up to £3 million, with only a modest number of investors accounting for individual transactions in amounts of over £10 million. Investors' individual issuer limits – where these operated[115] – were typically concentrated below £10 million. In reaching a credit decision, a credit agency rating was the most important single factor ('very important' for 79 per cent of all respondents to the survey). The other very important factors were net tangible worth (48 per cent) and name recognition and financial ratios (both 43 per cent). In a depressed economic environment, the industry sector of the issuer was also viewed as rather more important than in earlier days. Nevertheless, ratings – for the most part those of Standard & Poor and Moody's – and name familiarity were still heavily relied on. At the same time, there was a continuing appetite for unrated paper, to which, however, limits would often be applied, which is not always the case with rated paper. Lower rated paper (less than A1/P1) is also bought. Another surprise was that only 22 per cent of all respondents insisted on two formal credit ratings. It was clear, too, from the survey that SCP is a placement rather than a traded market. An overwhelming 94 per cent of investors bought SCP with the intention of holding it to maturity. None the less, 40 per cent of those same investors at some point sold SCP prior to maturity, which confirmed that liquidity is an essential feature of the market. The most typical – and obvious – reason for selling was 'need of funds'; this covered 81 per cent of those who had actually sold paper. This compared with 42 per cent who had at some time sold paper on the basis of a yield/maturity switch. Moreover, it was the dealer who played the pivotal role in providing liquidity – almost 70 per cent of paper sold was sold to the dealer from whom it was purchased and a further 16 per cent to another dealer. The liquidity offered was held to be adequate, but – according to the survey – much more important to the non-corporate investor (e.g. institutions) than to the corporates. But there would still be a preference for an active secondary market – some 62 per cent of current and potential investors would like to see such a market develop (75 per cent of non-corporate respondents). Investors tend to use more than one dealer – over one-third of actual and potential investors use four or more. Competitive pricing was often the most important consideration in choosing a dealer (indeed, dealer margins – often merely two basis points – tend to be paper thin, and dealers tend to be interested in SCP less for the returns on this form of business than, hopefully, the other types of business that they reckon to attract as a result of SCP activity). The range of issues available to individual dealers and their willingness to repurchase paper were also influential factors.

There were no data available that related to the original maturity of issues, but on average it seemed to have been very short. On the limited evidence available, it would seem that in the early days most SCP had an original maturity of between 15 and 45 days, although there were also reports of longer maturities, some out to the maximum time of 364 days.[116] This remained true until the summer of 1990, since the likelihood was that interest rates would remain at a high level; the tendency therefore was for SCP to stay very short and the average maturity became 27 to 28 days, with significant amounts at 1 to 2 weeks. In the first half of 1991, however, rates began gradually to come down, and average maturities lengthened somewhat.

On 11 January 1990, the Bank of England announced a further

broadening in the range of short-term paper issues available to certain companies without infringing the Banking Act 1987. This was made possible by the 1989 Companies Act which, in fulfilment of a commitment made in the 1989 budget, extended from 1 to 5 years the maturity of unlisted securities permitted to be issued onshore to professionals without the need for a prospectus. In order to make this extension fully effective, the exemption from the deposit-taking provisions of the Banking Act provided under the Banking Act (Exempt Transactions) Regulations for issues of commercial paper was now similarly amended. However, whereas paper up to and including 1 year continued to take the form of 'commercial paper', issues of over 1 year and up to 5 years were referred to as 'medium-term' notes. The Bank also took the opportunity to broaden the terms of the exemption to include paper issues in currencies other than sterling, including ECUs.

There is of course also a thriving secondary market in London in Euro-commercial paper and Euro-medium-term notes; the Bank wished to see this continue undisturbed. It was thought that issuers might find it convenient to have available this alternative route for issuing these forms of paper.[117]

As Table 2.3 shows, by end-October 1991, the total of outstanding SCP stood at £4,613 million. Since the inception of this form of commercial paper in May 1986, issues by a total of 235 companies have been reported to the Bank of England. Of these, 28 programmes had by October 1991 come to an end and 207 were extant. The amount outstanding was distributed by type of issuer as follows: 176 UK companies (including programmes guaranteed by overseas parent companies); 7 overseas companies (guaranteed by UK parent companies); and 24 overseas companies (other). Of the total, UK companies were responsible for £3,837 million and overseas companies (other) for £649 million. It should be noted that the data for maturities and amounts outstanding for the period from April 1990 were substantially revised following the discovery of cumulative errors in the statistical returns relating to a number of programmes.

Where guarantees are given, it has been by parent companies, though they could also be given by a recognized bank or (formerly) by a licensed deposit-taker. Most of the very largest companies have not yet made use of the market. For many of these companies, the market may be too small for them to use, given the scale of their borrowing requirements. Another important factor may be the availability to them of cheaper finance in the US and Euro-commercial paper markets – even when transaction costs have been taken into account, some major names are thought to be able to borrow dollars at around ten basis points below London Inter-Bank Bid Rate (LIBID), and Euro-commercial paper swapped into sterling can often produce a lower cost compared with straight sterling. These markets are far larger than the sterling commercial paper market and have a different perception of and appetite for short-term corporate debt.[118]

For other corporate borrowers, the choice between issuing SCP and borrowing through another means may be determined by a number of factors. For example, non-standard maturities are common in SCP issues – the issuer may have no suitable underlying transactions against which to draw eligible commercial bills (and these may be more expensive than SCP), or he may wish to go beyond the 6-month maximum maturity for eligible bills. But these are minor considerations compared with cost. The cost of issuing SCP in relation to most other borrowing techniques benefits from the absence of banking-system intermediation, which removes the margin charged by banks to cover the cost of capital and any other reserve costs required to back instruments on their balance sheets, or on which they have a contingent liability. Yet this is not sufficient to ensure that SCP costs are always the lowest. Short-term domestic finance is available through several routes – overdraft, money-market lines, eligible bills, or SCP. Overdrafts are normally the most expensive, though the most flexible, form of finance: money-market lines are priced at a margin over London Inter-Bank Offered Rate (LIBOR) – typically $\frac{1}{16}$ per cent for a major corporate. The closest price competition is between eligible bills and SCP. The cost of borrowing by way of bills is determined by the rate at which eligible bills are discounted in the market and the acceptance commission charged by eligible banks. The eligible bill rate is a money-market rate influenced by, and itself influencing, other money-market rates, while a typical commission rate might be $\frac{1}{16}$ per cent for a major borrower and $\frac{1}{8}$ per cent for a lesser one. An additional feature of the acceptance market is the use by the Bank of England of eligible bank bills in its daily money-market operations. Purchase of eligible bank (and other) bills in order to supply cash to the money-market as needed, adds to the liquidity of the bill market. Furthermore, the expansion of the Bank's list of eligible institutions has contributed to highly competitive commissions.

Table 2.3 Sterling commercial paper, October 1991

| | Programmes notified to the Bank of England* | | | |
| | Sterling paper only | | Other commercial paper/borrowing programmes with a sterling option | |
	Number	Maximum amount (£millions)	Number	Maximum amount (£millions)
Calendar month				
1991 January	1	50	—	—
February	3	400	—	—
March	1	100	1	167
April	—	—	—	—
May	2	250	1	150
June	4	475	2	412
July	—	—	—	—
August	1	400	—	—
September	—	—	—	—
October	—	—	2	574

continued overleaf

Table 2.3 Sterling commercial paper, October 1991 – (continued)

	Transactions during period		Issues, maturities and amounts outstanding (£ millions)† Outstanding at end of period			
	Issues	Maturities	Total	UK company issues	Overseas company issues (guaranteed by UK parent)	Overseas company issues (other)
Calendar quarter						
1990 Q1	14,576	13,951	4,154	3,745	235	174
Q2	14,749	13,691	5,212	4,618	253	341
Q3	16,039	15,925	5,326	4,517	282	527
Q4	11,765	13,191	3,900	3,175	71	654
1991 Q1	12,439	11,648	4,691	3,547	120	1,024
Q2	12,386	12,292	4,785	3,817	86	882
Q3	12,821	12,696	4,910	4,120	114	676
Calendar month						
1990 January	5,143	4,339	4,333	3,875	319	139
February	4,801	4,481	4,653	4,208	300	145
March	4,632	5,131	4,154	3,745	235	174
April	4,602	3,983	4,773	4,228	243	302
May	4,742	4,600	4,915	4,379	225	311
June	5,405	5,108	5,212	4,618	253	341
July	5,893	5,591	5,514	4,786	289	439
August	5,237	5,337	5,414	4,678	292	444

	Month						
	September	4,909	4,997	5,326	4,517	282	527
	October	4,793	5,047	5,072	4,222	310	540
	November	3,997	4,444	4,625	3,796	193	636
	December	2,975	3,700	3,900	3,175	71	654
1991	January	3,898	3,399	4,399	3,636	138	625
	February	4,047	3,738	4,708	3,757	152	799
	March	4,494	4,511	4,691	3,547	120	1,024
	April	4,033	4,002	4,722	3,680	94	948
	May	4,570	4,524	4,768	3,867	93	808
	June	3,783	3,766	4,785	3,817	86	882
	July	4,916	4,407	5,294	4,263	123	908
	August	3,786	3,903	5,177	4,240	123	814
	September	4,119	4,386	4,910	4,120	114	676
	October	4,485	4,782	4,613	3,837	127	649

Notes: * Amounts shown here are the total value given in letters of notification. In the case of multi-option programmes the arrangements may envisage a lower limit on the amount of the sterling commercial paper element. The values of multi-option programmes denominated in other currencies have been translated into sterling at the middle-market rates at close of business on the date of notification.

† Nominal values

It was difficult in the young sterling commercial paper (SCP) market to talk of a typical cost to an issuer – the very largest and best known issuers have been able to borrow at LIBID, but others had to pay up to twelve basis points over LIBOR (a range of twenty-five basis points).[119] In some cases, the variation reflected the presence or absence of a rating for the issuer or its programme. A good rating is now important and widens the investor base, and therefore makes placing the issue easier and reduces its cost somewhat. Some investors will not buy unrated paper. Indeed, by 1991, 85 per cent of SCP was rated. Such borrowers could obtain funds at LIBID plus three or four basis points. There was no market for the weakest credits. Even where paper is rated, investors are now much more sensitive to a company's gearing and general credit standing than was formerly the case.

Total SCP outstanding reached a peak of £5,781 million in September 1990. Thereafter there was a fall, with a significant drop in December 1990 and – as we have seen – it was down to £4,613 million by end-October 1991. However, some time before this marked falling away of the figures for outstanding SCP, there were signs of stagnation, and certain of the leading dealers had already begun to withdraw. Most blue chip companies were unlikely to notice the tightening of credit quality criteria in the SCP market, except for a modest rise in the cost of funding. But many others – and especially those labouring under a burden of heavy debt, or those (like Polly Peck) which had been incautious in their borrowing programmes – were likely to suffer, particularly where they had no back-up credit lines with their bankers. In the result, Polly Peck failed, and there were many prominent houses that were left with heavy losses on their hands. Latterly, too, losses were exacerbated by the onset of recession, which began to become evident by September/October 1990. Matters are better regulated in the United States, where only issuers carrying a rating from a recognized credit agency can use the US market; they must also maintain a standby line of credit with a bank as an added protection for holders of such paper.[120] The combination of the withdrawal of a number of dealers and investor concern over credit quality meant – at least temporarily – that the SCP market was now but a shadow of its former self.

FLOATING RATE NOTES (FRNs)

A market that is growing in importance – particularly when interest rates are rising – is that in FRNs. These are simply bonds whose coupons (interest return) vary at pre-set intervals and in line with money-market rates. Coupons are set at intervals ranging from 1 to 6 months,[121] on the basis of LIBOR – sterling issues usually being set at a margin above LIBOR of, say, plus $\frac{1}{8}$ per cent. The margin is fixed at the time the issue is announced – it is known as the 'quoted margin'. Interest accrues on an actual elapsed-day basis (normally 365 days, but every 4 years it is 366 days) and is payable in arrears on the coupon resetting date.

FRNs are issued in sizes ranging from £20 million to £500 million and with one exception (Standard Chartered Perpetual FRN) all have final maturity dates. Maturity dates vary – e.g. in the important building-society sector, the longest maturity is now 8 years and the shortest just under 1 year. Put and call options will alter the maturities in certain issues.

Subject to Bank of England approval, issues can be bought at any time. All relevant details will be published through the financial information services of Reuters and Telerate, and by telex to invitees to the underwriting and selling group. The quoted margin will be given and in some cases a fixed coupon for the first period is announced together with the closing (payment) date. In between issue announcement and closing date, an issue will be traded with a primary (closing) settlement date irrespective of the trade date. Primary settlement gives way to secondary settlement when the settlement date is subsequent to the closing date.

Sterling FRNs are traded generally on a five to twenty basis-points spread between bid and offer prices (i.e. 0.05 to 0.20 per cent). The unit of trading is £1 million, with larger sizes being available in exceptional circumstances. Prices are quoted clean of accrued interest which is added to the principal amount for calculation of the total settlement amount. There are no commissions, contract stamp, or *ad valorem* stamp duty charges when buying or selling. Whilst official trading hours are 8.30 to 12.00 and 14.00 to 16.30, trading and sales teams are often available from 8.00 to 17.30 for prices, information and opinions. All prices of major active issues are on Reuters pages, which are continuously updated throughout the day. However, due to the nature of the market, prices can change by the second. Hence, though screen prices are a good guide, 'live' dealing prices can only be given by telephone or live telex wire. Safe-custody facilities may be offered by particular houses, which means holding bonds on behalf of customers, collecting and paying coupons, and transfers of all cash on selling or maturity.

The settlement period is 7 days, with accrued interest being calculated from the last coupon reset date to settlement date. Hard copy confirmations are sent within 24 hours and settlement is effected through the two international settlement systems – 'Euroclear' (Brussels) and 'CEDEL' (Luxembourg). Other arrangements are possible, such as safe custody, direct delivery, etc. It will be appreciated that not all issues trade in the same way and that the size of trade will vary with each individual issue.

As at the end of 1990, the total outstanding value of sterling issues of FRNs was £18.7 billion.

FINANCIAL FUTURES AND OPTIONS[122]

The use made by banks and other financial institutions (also corporates with a money-market function) of financial futures and options has grown with exceptional rapidity in the last 15 years or so. They make up a most important part of the financial revolution that has changed the environment within which banks have now to operate. Financial futures and options derive from the application of the techniques of commodity futures and trade stock options to financial instruments and currencies. The collapse of the post-war Bretton Woods fixed exchange-rate system at the Smithsonian Institution meeting in 1971 gave rise to an increase in the volatility of currencies and interest rates that was to provide the essential background to the development of futures and options. Currency futures were launched in 1972 on the Chicago Mercantile Exchange, and Treasury bond futures followed 4 years later on the Chicago Board of Trade. It was only in 1982 that the London International Financial Futures Exchange (LIFFE) was established.

Futures and options are not securities, although they will typically involve the right to buy or sell specified securities at a predetermined time in the future. A futures contract is the obligation to buy or sell a security at a specified price and time. An option, on the other hand, involves the right, but not the obligation, to buy or sell at specified prices and times. In the case of American options, the option can be exercised at the specified price on any day up to the expiry date. European options, on the other hand, can only be exercised at the expiry of the option. In London, both American and European options are traded. Futures and options can either be 'exchange traded' or 'over the counter' (OTC). Futures when traded OTC are usually known as forward contracts. However, financial futures are traded on the exchange. Trading on organized markets holds considerable advantages. The contracts are usually liquid, transactions can easily be reversed, and advantage can be taken of the security of the clearing system – which is an essential part of a futures and options exchange. Prices on exchanges are formed in fiercely competitive conditions, and a market is subject to a considerable degree of regulation to ensure the protection of the customer. Prices are also widely publicized by the exchanges and public information systems. Exchange-traded instruments differ from the OTC variety in that they are in standardized amounts for the instruments concerned, and delivery or expiry is usually in a 3-month cycle. This has the advantage that it increases liquidity – more people are prepared to trade in such standarized instruments, but it means that broken days and amounts cannot be traded or hedged with precision. All exchange-traded futures and options are margined; in other words, the buyers and sellers of futures contracts and the sellers (or writers) of options – also buyers following the introduction of 'standard portfolio analysis of risk' (SPAN) margining – have to provide performance bonds, or margin, to ensure the completion of the contract. In many cases, these margins need to be topped up over time by the buyer or the seller should the price move against him. This procedure enables the clearing house to guarantee performance of all registered contracts.

There are in fact two margins: (a) an 'initial margin' – a 'bond' to support the open position based upon the perceived daily volatility, i.e. the maximum movement in 24 hours (this will vary in accordance with volatility); and (b) a 'marked to market' (i.e. daily settlement to market) or variation margin.

These instruments are employed for the purpose of hedging, or position-taking.[123] Hedging with futures or options is based on the principle that a risk to a great extent can be insulated by a futures or options position which is the reverse of the 'cash' position at risk. Thus, if a bank feared that its substantial holding of bonds was likely to decline in value because of an increase in interest rates, instead of liquidating the portfolio (any attempt at which could of itself further diminish the market price), it could sell futures contracts. The rise in interest rates would reduce the value of the cash portfolio, but the sale of futures contracts would produce profits to mitigate the losses on the cash portfolio. Similarly, should the bank wish to lock in current bond yields before receipt of funds, it can do so by buying futures contracts. Should interest rates fall, the price of futures will increase and the yields will be locked in, at least for a period. Hedging with options has advantages for some purposes over futures, and it is an important decision whether to use futures or options. Futures have the characteristic that they offer a reasonable degree of hedge protection against any price movement, whether good or bad (although basis risk may evolve from the different characteristics of the cash instrument and the nearest available derivative/hedging instrument). Options, on the other hand, can provide protection against adverse price movements but still allow the cash position to benefit from favourable price movements. However, they may initially be more expensive, due to the time and volatility components of the premium paid. The purchase of a put option can protect the cash position, should prices fall, but if prices were to increase, the loss on the options position will be limited to the premium.

Futures and options are most useful to banks in the management of their balance sheets. Banks have balance sheets that are to a large degree 'naturally hedged', with both sides of the balance sheet responding to changes in interest rates in a partially offsetting fashion. Banks' returns depend not only on the spread of rates between the assets and liabilities, but also on playing the yield curve – borrowing short at low rates and lending long at high. Banks – and other financial institutions like discount houses and market-makers – can change the risk/reward profile of the balance sheet by altering the degree to which it is naturally hedged. Thus, a bank (or other financial institution) may fear a rise in interest rates and consequently that the cost of financing the negative mismatch would increase to the detriment of its overall profitability. The solution is to hedge these net positions. The bank has the choice of using either futures or options with which to cover the risk. Banks (and others) are currently substantial users of financial futures and options. These instruments were the result of a decade of turmoil in world financial markets which produced high rates of volatility. The volatility of interest rates was closely associated with volatility in inflation and exchange rates. An important question was whether these conditions in the credit and foreign currency markets were likely to continue. Futures and options are the result of perceived volatility and in stable conditions they will not flourish. Their future depends very much on whether governments can succeed in stabilizing interest and exchange rates.

In London, LIFFE has a membership which is widely representative of the financial services industry and includes banks, stock exchange firms, commodity brokers, discount houses, market-makers, Euro-bond houses, money brokers, and experienced individual traders (frequently known as 'locals') who trade on their own account. By end-March 1991, there were 179 different members of LIFFE. This membership can be broken down into three types of shares. Thus, there were 376 A shares (these give clearing rights and allow the member to trade any of LIFFE's futures products); there were 160 B shares (these give access to all options products); and there were 376 C shares (these offer only limited access to futures products).[124] Types of membership include general clearing members, individual clearing members, non-clearing/public order members, and 'locals'. There are different levels of capital adequacy depending on the type of membership and relationship to public money. The membership is international in character and is drawn from the following parts of the world: UK 28 per cent; Continental Europe 18 per cent; USA 26 per cent; Japan 18 per cent; Others 10 per cent. Members have to meet stringent financial criteria before acceptance by the clearing house and the Exchange. Furthermore, just as members are required to deposit margin with the clearing house, so, too, must customers deposit margin with the member through which their transactions are cleared. Banks comprise the largest group of members (UK banks 11 per cent and overseas banks 31 per cent), followed by commodity brokers and dealers (which include individual traders) UK 24 per cent and overseas 13 per cent; and investment brokers and dealers – overseas 14 per cent and UK 7 per cent. As from 1 October 1988, building societies were able to seek permission to use certain 'prescribed contracts' for the purposes of reducing the risk of loss. Permission may be granted by degrees. As at mid-1991, there were no 'institutions' such as insurance companies or building societies that were members.

LIFFE was established with the approval of the Bank of England and the UK Department of Trade and Industry. Regulation of the market is overseen by the Securities and Investment Board, which itself exercises surveillance over the general conduct of all London exchanges. Day-to-day supervision, however, is the responsibility of the Board of the Exchange. The Board has the responsibility for ensuring an orderly market and the Market Supervision Department has been established to carry out this self-regulatory function. The Department monitors the financial standing of the Exchange's members and requires members to report daily their aggregate open positions in each contract. In addition, the Department is authorized to inspect a member's accounting records. The Board has power to raise margin requirements and to instruct members to close out positions in the event of a market emergency.

One of the main purposes of futures contracts in bank management is to hedge mismatches (or part of mismatches) in assets and liabilities maturities. For example, if interest-sensitive liabilities exceed interest-sensitive assets, a banker may hedge against rising interest rates by selling futures contracts in securities of similar maturity to those liabilities he is hedging. Of course, most bankers would not choose to be perfectly hedged in terms of exactly matching asset and liability maturities, since to do so would eliminate significant potential profits from taking a position on the yield curve. Again, a discount house or market-maker can trade actively in futures – trade and hedge, if necessary. Thus, if they cannot pick up stock in the cash market, they buy futures. Or if they have paper they do not want, they sell futures and get rid of it.

The contracts in which LIFFE deals can be classified in three broad categories: long-term interest rate futures and options; short-term futures and options; and stock index futures. Activity is concentrated on the interest-rate contracts. These include contracts on 3-month sterling and 3-month Euro-dollars and the four major government bond markets in the world – US T-bonds, Japanese Government bonds, UK gilts, and German Bund. Latterly, LIFFE has also traded ECU bonds and futures (which had to be relaunched in January 1992). Of these contracts, in the first half of 1991, the German Bund was the most active, but it was closely followed by short sterling; the long gilt and the Euro-mark, though much lower, were also significant. Certain options on the futures contracts exist, of which the most important are those for the German Bund and short sterling. Formerly, LIFFE had a modest volume in currency futures and options, but the bulk of this business in London was handled by the over-the-counter forward market. These have now been de-listed by LIFFE. LIFFE also trades a futures contract on the FT-SE 100 index, which complemented the options contract that was traded on the London Traded Options Market (LTOM). And there were other developments – e.g. the FT-SE Eurotrack 100 future on LIFFE with an option on LTOM and in Chicago; also the Italian government bond (BTP) future, which was most successful.

Financial futures can be traded by those who are willing to assume price risk and wish to profit from the rises and falls they expect to occur in interest rates, exchange rates, or the share index. This enables users to take a view of the trend of rates without actually having to purchase or sell the underlying currency or financial instrument. In particular, they can sell short when they feel it is likely that interest rates will rise, or a currency's value or the share index will decline. It is also possible to 'trade a spread' – one can but one month and sell another month; depending on changes in the option, they can also sell one month and buy another. Both hedgers and traders are necessary for the efficient operation of a futures market. Traders provide liquidity to the market, allowing hedgers to buy or sell in volume without difficulty. In particular cases, a futures package can be put together by banks, merchant banks, or – indeed – by certain money brokers.

Finally, one should note that one of LIFFE's chief advantages is its position between the major financial markets of the Far East and North America. Depending upon the time of year and the effect of daylight saving time in North America and British Summer Time, the gap between the end of trading in the Far East and the start of trading in Chicago can be as much as 6 hours. Figure 2.1 shows the significance of this gap and the position of LIFFE in this context.

After much discussion and some last minute hesitations, LIFFE and LTOM agreed to merge by March 1992. The main problem seems to have been to line up a sufficient number of market-makers to start trading equity options. LIFFE and the traded options market needed to recruit a critical mass of equity options market-makers for the merger to proceed.

Four of the most active firms in the underlying market – Barclays de Zoete Wedd, County NatWest, Smith New Court, and Warburg – were not prepared to act as market-makers. It was they that had pushed for a move from open outcry trading to a screen-based system, a proposal which met strong opposition from other quarters. But although they will not be involved as market-makers, these firms will act as principal traders and can contribute

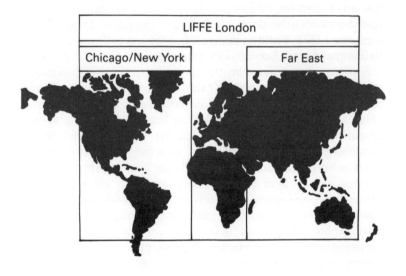

Figure 2.1 LIFFE's time zone advantage

substantial liquidity, since they hold about a dozen seats each. Each seat is equivalent to one trader on the floor. In the result, sufficient commitments were received from a nucleus of market-makers to make it possible for the merged market to continue to trade the full range of individual equity options and index options.

Six firms were prepared to act as assigned market-makers (committed to making a continuous two-way price in a particular contract) and nominated market-makers in a range of contracts (a nominated market-maker is expected to make prices on request). The six firms were J. G. Bolitho, City of London Options, Hills Independent Traders, James Capel, Kleinwort Benson, and Swiss Bank Corporation.[125]

Although not a financial future as such, brief reference should also be made to the unbundling of financial packages. Financial claims package together a number of characteristics. A 10-year fixed rate Euro-dollar bond is a package of a particular interest-rate structure (fixed rate), a specific currency (US dollars), and a certain maturity (10 years). Any of these attributes can be unpackaged and traded separately from the others. Either at the time of purchase or later, the holder could exchange the fixed interest-rate stream for floating, and the US dollar payments for another currency, keeping only the term to maturity. Alternatively, the bond could be maturity 'stripped' and sold off as a sequence of short-term instruments. It should be noted that adjustments such as these can be made without having to re-negotiate either the original loan, or its covenants. Such 'unbundling' transactions have always been possible. Modern computer technology has brought the cost of doing so within reasonable bounds. Also, financial services have in the past usually been fully integrated vertically within particular firms. Banks and savings institutions have initiated contact with the customer, made the loan, collected repayments and carried the asset. These services can be vertically 'de-integrated'. In some packages in the US, for example, origination is separated from the lending of funds, other parties insure the loans, still others undertake the loan packaging, with different firms holding the loans as trustees for the securities issue, while the servicing of customer repayments could be handled by another institution. One reason for 'unbundling' is to allow institutions to sell off part of their portfolio and 'buy in' participations in other assets, so obtaining a better spread of risks for a given balance-sheet scale. Another is to allow institutions to exploit their comparative advantages. The banks' comparative advantage may be in terms of their ability to assess credit risk and make informed selections of loans. Given the 'regulatory taxes' imposed on them and the current pressures on their capital resources, they may not be the best institutions to fund and hold assets. An arrangement by which banks originate loans and shift them 'off-balance-sheet' to other institutions may be superior to one in which the institutions that hold their assets also make the credit assessments.

BANK OF ENGLAND INTERVENTION

Prior to 1971, applications for funds by a discount house on a last-resort basis were made to the Bank of England not later than 2.30 p.m. on any business day. Where the Bank of England insisted on making accommodation available against certain eligible securities (e.g. Treasury bills, first-class bank acceptances, and

British government securities up to 5 years maturity) but only at a penal rate, it was often for 7 days. More usually, the Bank of England intervened (e.g. for 'smoothing out' purposes) through the 'special buyer' (a member of one of the small discount houses – the chairman or his deputy in Seccombe, Marshall & Campion). As agent of the Bank of England, the 'special buyer' (the Bank's broker in the discount market)[126] bought the Treasury bills, local authority bills, or eligible bank bills at pre-announced rates from individual discount houses, thereby providing them with the money they needed by 'direct assistance', or he may have operated (by buying bills again on behalf of the Bank of England) through the clearing banks, which then passed on this money as loans to the discount houses; this was known as 'made money' or 'help' ('indirect assistance').[127] In a similar way, the authorities through the 'special buyer' could mop up excess funds whenever necessary (usually by selling bills direct to the individual discount houses).

After Competition and Credit Control was introduced in September 1971, the existing conventional relationships between 'Bank rate' (the Bank of England's official discount rate) and the clearing banks' advances and deposit account rates, also the rate for 'good money' to the discount market, were discontinued. The banks now set their own base rates (which reflected movements in market rates) and to which each bank's lending rates were related. Rates charged by the clearing banks and other banks to the discount houses became much more competitive, even volatile. Then, on 13 October 1972, the Bank of England introduced its minimum lending rate (MLR) in place of Bank rate. The new rate was calculated by adding $\frac{1}{2}$ per cent to the average rate of the accepted Treasury bill tenders and rounding the result up to the nearest $\frac{1}{4}$ per cent. It could also be altered (like old Bank rate) by 'administrative decision'.

Also, some time before MLR was introduced (actually as from 22 October 1971), the Bank of England arranged an additional facility at 2.45 p.m. At the same time, the former arrangements were retained and discount houses could still go to the Bank of England up to 2.30 p.m. However, the two facilities were somewhat different both in intention and in character. When a house went to the Bank up to 2.30 p.m., it may have been 'forced into the Bank' because of a policy decision to make money short and push up interest rates. This would have been the result of a conscious decision by the Bank of England. If the Bank did not wish to do this, it could undertake 'smoothing out' operations through the 'special buyer'.

The additional facility, which was entirely at the discretion of the discount house concerned, provided for limited borrowing up to 2.45 p.m. at 7 days (or for other periods). Any such transactions were confidential between the Bank of England and the house concerned and were not reported in the press. These facilities were:

> intended to give houses time − but strictly limited time − for adjustment if fluctuations in short-term interest rates become more frequent and larger than recently; and to make a clear distinction between the use of last resort facilities for this purpose and borrowing forced on the market by the Bank, whether in the interests of smoothing out large fluctuations in money flows or as an act of monetary policy.[128]

Later, the Bank stated: 'These facilities provided a necessary but limited safety valve for the individual institutions, but on terms designed to discourage their use in preference to normal market channels. They have never formed part of the Bank's main money market operations.'[129]

On 24 November 1980, the Bank of England announced in the context of its methods of intervention in the money market that:

> it is envisaged that the Bank's intervention will place a greater emphasis on open market operations and less on discount window (lender of last resort) lending. It has been decided that these operations should continue to be conducted in the bill markets rather than through the inter-bank market, and in large part through the existing intermediaries, members of the London Discount Market Association to whom discount window facilities would remain confined.[130]

Borrowing at 2.30 p.m., which becomes public knowledge, still took place, and the Bank of England would compel it then, when it was a case of signalling that the rates on bills were not to the Bank of England's liking. It should be noted, too, that sometimes − even when a discount house had squared its book − it might borrow at the Bank of England in order to pass limited amounts of money on to the banks in the inter-bank market, where funds are unsecured, but only to the extent that houses had free security; alternatively, the banks could lodge security with the discount house against a loan.

Originally, with the introduction of Competition and Credit Control, the discount houses were required to hold a minimum of 50 per cent of their funds in public-sector debt, but experience with the 50 per cent public-sector debt ratio was not wholly satisfactory and the requirement 'tended to complicate the Bank's task of securing adequate influence over credit extended by the discount market, and produced distortions in short-term money markets'.[131]

In order to alleviate these difficulties, the public-sector debt ratio was replaced, with effect from 19 July 1973, by a multiplier, which limited the aggregate holdings of each house of assets other than those defined as public-sector assets to a maximum of 20 times its capital and reserves. The Bank of England also remained concerned that the size of each house's total business should continue to bear 'an appropriate relationship to their capital and reserves'. This multiplier (relating to a house's total business) was about 30. This was described as a 'guideline' and was essentially in the character of a prudential control, whereas the new multiplier of 20 applied to the holdings of private-sector debt was in the nature of a credit control. The overall multiplier of 30 reinforced the 20 times multiplier in restricting the creation of reserve assets through the discount market. The Bank attached considerable importance to this limit and monitored it closely. Comparable limits were imposed on discount brokers outside the London Discount Market Association and to the money trading departments of certain banks.

Although the 20 times multiplier gave the houses considerably greater flexibility in managing their books, it did not weaken the authorities' influence over credit extended by the discount market, nor represent an easing of credit control. For although the multiplier was large enough to accommodate occasional temporary movements by individual houses, it was in no sense to be regarded as a norm. Furthermore, though the obligation to hold a proportion of their assets in certain forms of public-sector debt had formally been lifted, market practices continued to require houses to include in their portfolios a substantial proportion of such assets, particularly those that provided liquidity.

A very important ingredient in Competition and Credit Control was the decision to 'restrict the extent of the Bank of England's operations in the gilt-edged market'. More particularly, the Bank would no longer be prepared to respond to requests to buy government stock outright, except in the case of stocks with one year or less to run to maturity, which stocks featured in the clearing banks' reserve assets ratio. The Bank of England reserved the right to make outright purchases of stock with more than a year to run solely at its discretion and initiative. The Bank would be prepared to undertake, at prices of its own choosing, exchanges of stock with the market, except those that unduly shortened the life of the debt; and it would be prepared to respond to bids for the sale by it of 'tap' stocks and of such other stocks held by it as it might wish to sell.

This was part of the new policy accompanying changes in credit control and which were intended to allow greater freedom of competition with a smaller degree of intervention by the authorities in the gilt-edged market 'so as to leave more freedom for prices to be affected by market conditions'. This did not mean that the Bank of England had discontinued its normal operations of selling longer-dated gilt-edged against purchases of short-dated stocks 'as a technically efficient way of refinancing maturities'. But it did mean that the Bank would 'not generally be prepared to buy stock outright'. 'Thus', they said, 'we shall not normally be prepared to facilitate movements out of gilt-edged by the banks, even if their sales should cause the market temporarily to weaken quite sharply'.

However, the discount market did not seem to appreciate the full implications of what the Bank of England had said, and the discount houses – which over a period of years had been dealers in short government bonds – went on much as before, some of them continuing to hold large amounts of government stocks either for the running yield or in the hope of making capital gains as well as providing a basis for dealing. But when in 1972 the Bank of England intervened to the disadvantage of the discount houses and then in July 1973 failed to support the market, the discount houses burnt their fingers very badly and made heavy losses.[132] As a result, some gilt-edged holders now preferred to stay shorter than hitherto and, latterly, this became true of both the discount houses and the banks. In the result, the discount market, after making some very heavy losses, became 'very much more wary' of gilt-edged, though they had now 'put their toe back in the water' and were jobbing the market 'more professionally than they had done before' (evidence to the House of Commons Select Committee in 1976). But, if there was thought to be an opportunity of capital gains because of an unexpected fall in interest rates, the discount houses (or some of them) were still prepared to chance their arm and move again (if only for a time) significantly into gilts.[133]

Under Competition and Credit Control, the clearing banks (as well as other 'statistical banks') were required to maintain a minimum of $12\frac{1}{2}$ per cent of their eligible liabilities (primarily sterling deposits of up to 2 years' maturity, including sterling CDs) in reserve assets, which consisted mainly of Treasury bills (and gilts with a life of up to 1 year) and secured money at call with the London discount market. (In practice, banks tended to move into slightly longer gilts in anticipation of their becoming reserve assets.) For the clearing banks, a balance of $1\frac{1}{2}$ per cent (included in the $12\frac{1}{2}$ per cent) had to be held in interest-free deposits with the Bank of England. (Notes and coin did not count as reserve assets, nor did Bank of England notes held as cover for notes issued by the Scottish and Northern Ireland banks in excess of their authorized, i.e. fiduciary issues.)

By 1980, the authorities already believed that the requirement to maintain a minimum $12\frac{1}{2}$ per cent reserve assets ratio was no longer necessary, and it was proposed that it should end. It was reduced to 10 per cent in early January 1981 as a step on the road, and for most of March and April it was reduced to 8 per cent for technical reasons. But it was realized that it would be necessary to have some cash requirement and it was proposed that the existing requirement ($1\frac{1}{2}$ per cent of eligible liabilities, which had to be held by the London clearing banks with the Bank of England) should be replaced by one that applied more generally. But the Special Deposit Scheme would be retained 'to guard against the possible effects of excess liquidity in the banking system as a whole'.

In the result, the minimum reserve asset ratio, including $1\frac{1}{2}$ per cent of eligible liabilities (held by the clearing banks with the Bank of England), was replaced in August 1981 by: (i) a voluntary holding of operational funds with the Bank of England by the London clearing banks ('for clearing purposes'); (ii) a uniform requirement of 0.5 per cent (later reduced to 0.45 per cent, and from 16 January 1991 to 0.4 per cent) of an institution's eligible liabilities that would be applied to all banks (and formerly to licensed deposit-takers as well),[134] with eligible liabilities averaging more than £10 million. This was the non-operational requirement and was to be set twice a year in relation to average eligible liabilities in the previous 6 months. The ratio was further reduced to 0.35 per cent on 31 January 1992.[135] In calculating eligible liabilities, inter-bank loans and secured call money placed with discount houses, money brokers, and gilt-edged jobbers in the Stock Exchange were treated as an offset. Window dressing was to be avoided, since it would be 'contrary to the objective of these agreed arrangements for any institution to reduce its eligible liabilities deliberately or artificially on reporting dates'. The Bank of England accordingly reserved the right to make spot checks.

This had implications for policy with respect to the gilt-edged market. As a consequence of abolishing the minimum reserve asset ratio requirement, the Bank of England – as from 20 August 1981 – decided to modify the basis on which it dealt in the gilt-edged market in stocks within 12 months' maturity. The Bank of England would continue to buy stock offered to it within 3 months of maturity, but at prices of its own choosing. Outright purchases of stock with more than 3 months to maturity would be solely at the Banks' discretion, though it was expected that the Bank would exercise this discretion more liberally for maturities between 3 and 12 months. In measuring and assessing the liquidity of banks, the Bank of England would take into account the resulting readier marketability of gilt-edged stocks within 12 months of maturity. As before, the Bank of England was prepared to operate in gilt-edged stock approaching maturity in order to smooth out the distortions in the money markets which would occur if the whole of each maturing stock were left in market hands and redeemed on one day. In addition, it facilitated the efficient operation of the secondary market in gilt-edged stocks. For example, it helped holders to switch into longer-dated gilts. These transactions were done through the Government Broker (who was later to disappear).

Also, as from 20 August 1981, the date when the new changes came in, all banks that were eligible acceptors were normally required to hold an average equivalent to 6 per cent of their eligible liabilities, either as secured money with discount houses or as secured call money with money brokers and gilt-edged jobbers, but the amount held in the form of secured money with a discount house was not normally to fall below 4 per cent of eligible liabilities. This was to be monitored by the Bank of England, to which banks would make monthly returns of daily figures. This money became known as 'club money'.[136] At the time, it was thought probable that this arrangement would not continue indefinitely, given the authorities' emphasis on market forces in the operation of monetary control, though it was thought that its removal would be gradual. Indeed, some of the discount houses felt that it would have been better not to have had this requirement at all. They felt that call money with a discount house would always represent such excellent liquidity for a bank that banks would deposit money with them anyway (at the right price) and thereby enable them to finance as big a bill book as they – and the Bank of England – could require.

By September 1986, 'club money' had been abolished as a monetary requirement, but for supervisory purposes banks were asked not to make significant changes in the disposition of their liquidity until new arrangements were put in place. There was a continuing discussion for some time about these matters, but there were difficulties in developing a formula that could be applied to all banks. In any case, banks continued to maintain secured funds with the discount houses – usually more than was required by the old minimum – and latterly the Bank of England has monitored the situation on an 'informal' basis for each of the individual banks.

At the same time as 'club money' had been introduced (viz., 20 August 1981) MLR had been suspended. Linked with this there were certain changes that affected discount market arrangements. It seemed that the Bank of England wished to give the money market more say in the determination of interest rates rather than themselves to impose a structure. Under the new system then introduced, short rates (say up to 7 to 14 days) were to be kept by the authorities within a range – the so-called 'unpublished band'; longer rates were to be allowed to fluctuate more freely. 'Decisions as to the band will be taken in accord with the same range of considerations as would have determined decisions about MLR, so that the new arrangements imply a change in techniques, rather than in the objectives of monetary policy'.[137] This meant scrapping the old structure of Treasury bill dealing rates, whereby the Bank of England was not only ready to lend overnight at MLR (which had now been suspended) but also to buy Treasury bills of different maturities at pre-determined levels. (Incidentally, since the Bank of England had hardly lent to the market since November 1980, MLR – though perhaps retaining a psychological influence – had virtually ceased to have any operational effect on rates.) The announcement of bill dealing rates a week ahead was one of the first things to go. The next stage – in terms of day-to-day operations – was the decision in November 1980 to shift the emphasis from lending to open market operations especially by dealing in bills. In practice, this meant primarily eligible bank bills, i.e. bankers' acceptances issued by accepting houses, the clearing banks, some Commonwealth banks, and (from August 1981) certain foreign banks. Actually, there was no deliberate decision to shift from Treasury bills to bank bills – it was really an accidental by-product of a sharp increase in the size of operations needed to balance the banking system's cash and a decline in the stock of Treasury bills available in the market to meet it.[138]

Foreign banks were allowed to join the club of eligible acceptors, provided they fulfilled certain requirements; this had the effect of greatly enlarging the bill market, making it easier for the Bank of England to supply liquidity through the purchase of bills and to influence the inter-bank market. Eligible banks are permitted to sell into the market only acceptances that comply with the Bank's regulations on the purposes for which eligible bills may be used, and with the clausing that should be used to describe the transactions. The Bank has issued periodic notices outlining these requirements.

The arrangements introduced in 1981[139] remain today essentially unchanged, so far as the mechanics of operation are concerned. On the basis of information available, the Bank of England makes known to the market simultaneously (by an announcement on a screen which will be transmitted to each of the relevant dealing rooms) its estimate of the day's position. This goes out at about 9.45 a.m. As an example, the announcement may take the form that a shortage of around q million is expected today. Among the main factors are likely to be the following:

Exchequer transactions	$\pm x$ million
(which include the effect of gilt-edged and	
Exchange Equalization Account Settlements)	
Decrease in note issue	$+ y$ million
Treasury Bills and Maturing Assistance	$- z$ million
Bankers' Balances Above/Below Target	T million

The total amount is rounded to the nearest 50. Bankers' balances are excluded if they are less than £3 million either way. The unwinding of sale and repurchase operations by the Bank would be disclosed if significant. Also, if there were early Bank of England operations, these would be put on the screen shortly afterwards. As can be expected, many of the factors (as above) will be subject to revision as the day proceeds. If by noon the overall estimate has changed greatly, the Bank of England releases a revised figure. Meanwhile, in addition to its own estimates of the market's position, the Bank of England (up to the end of 1985) would have taken into account information assembled by its broker relating to the aggregate position of the discount houses (it now does this itself within the Gilt-Edged and Money Markets Division), indications with respect to their positions from the major banks, and the state of the market as evidenced by the behaviour of short-term rates. After considering these factors, further revisions to its forecast during the morning, and any special operational objectives it has for that day, the Bank of England will decide shortly after midday whether or not it is to operate in the money market, though if the shortage is likely to be considerable, the Bank of England will have an early round and may put money out at 10.00 a.m. More generally, the Bank will make money available as 'morning assistance' about 12 noon and, if necessary, as 'afternoon assistance' about 2.00 p.m.

The banks themselves will have withdrawn any funds required from the discount houses. This they will have done before noon, though they may offer surplus funds to the houses right up to the close of business in the afternoon. (They may continue to deal for same-day settlements up to the Town Clearing, where in practice dealings cease at 3.30 p.m.) So any shortage in the system should show up by noon in the position of the discount houses. Actually, the banks may make precautionary withdrawals from the houses in the morning, some of which may turn out to be surplus to their needs later in the day. Hence, the shortage reported by the houses may be larger than the Bank's estimate. Moreover, any overall surplus is unlikely to show fully at this time. Before lunch, then, the Bank of England normally acts – if at all – only to relieve a shortage and, at this stage, its dealings with the discount houses are confined to operations in bills. The Bank informs the houses that it will consider buying bills – there is usually no distinction at this point between Treasury, local authority, and eligible bank bills – in some or all of certain maturity bands. There are four such bands: Band 1 = 1–14 days; Band 2 = 15–33 days; Band 3 = 34–63 days; and Band 4 = 64–91 days. All periods are defined in terms of the remaining, not the original, tenor of the bills. The Bank does not usually purchase outright bills with more than 3 months remaining to maturity or – in the case of eligible bank bills – within 7 days of the date of their acceptance. Furthermore, from August 1989 onwards, the Bank has confined its purchases almost entirely to Bands 1 and 2.[140]

On this basis, in response to an invitation from the Bank, each discount house may then make offers of eligible bills to the Bank. Each offer must specify the amount of bills being offered (face value); whether the bills are Treasury, local authority, or eligible bank bills; the maturity band of the bills; and the discount rate at which the bills are being offered. The Bank decides at its discretion which offers to accept and normally buys paper up to the amount of the shortage as estimated by the Bank at the best acceptable rates offered within each combination of instrument and band in which the Bank chooses to deal.[141] If offers of bills exceed the amount of the shortage, the Bank normally accepts offers of shorter rather than longer bills and offers of bills at higher rather than lower discount rates. The Bank may also distinguish among types of bills – its practice is to accept offers of Treasury bills in preference to local authority bills, and offers of local authority bills in preference to eligible bank bills. The lowest rate at which the Bank buys bills outright (the 'stop rate') may differ for different maturity bands and different types of bill. This lowest rate is not made public, but after any change in the general level of interest rates, the market is quickly able to deduce from the Bank's actions what that rate must be. The Bank may buy an amount of bills lower than the estimated shortage – for instance, if insufficient bills have been offered at acceptable rates. Although the purchase of bills in this way is commonly referred to as an 'outright' purchase, these purchases are with recourse to the seller – eligible bank bills purchased by the Bank from the discount houses are regarded by the Bank as three-name paper (the three names being those of the drawer, the acceptor, and the discount house).[142]

An alternative technique in providing the houses with money is for the Bank to invite them to enter into a sale and repurchase agreement in bills (a 'repo'), when the Bank will specify a terminal date (or dates) for the repurchase by the discount houses and the rate of discount used to calculate the proceeds of the bills. The houses then bid a rate of interest that they will pay to the Bank on the proceeds for the specified period. This rate the Bank may or may not accept. When the 'repo' is 'unwound', the houses repay the proceeds to the Bank by repurchasing the bills. The rate of interest on the proceeds is the cost to the houses of their money. In effect, the operation is similar to a secured loan for a fixed period. This technique may be chosen to enable the market position on future days to be smoothed out – e.g. a day of expected surplus could be offset by choosing it as a repurchase date. They may be

used on days of large shortage when houses are unable to sell sufficient 'outrights' to 'take out' the shortage, or where the Bank
cannot obtain the maturities it desires to purchase outright. The
Bank will usually be prepared to 'repo' bills, which because they
are not within 91 days of maturity would be ineligible for outright
purchase. Again, 'repos' may be used when the market is particularly reluctant to sell bills of certain maturities to the Bank because
of interest rate expectations. Occasionally, there may be a policy
purpose – e.g. switching between techniques to prevent a particular
rate structure from becoming too firmly entrenched. The 'repo' is
now a very useful component of the Bank's dealing techniques,
especially at times when daily shortages of over £1 billion – even £2
billion – have become quite common. In short, 'repo' transactions
have become both frequent and sizeable (e.g. £500 to £600 million
in a day).

Also, during periods of acute cash shortages in the banking
system, such as in the main tax-paying periods, the Bank of
England may undertake operations in instruments other than
eligible bills. In particular, the Bank may purchase gilt-edged stock
and certain other assets directly from banks for resale to them at a
future date. On such occasions, the Bank announces in advance
that it is offering temporary facilities to banks to take effect from a
certain date until a specified future date. The operation offers
facilities to each member of the monetary sector with eligible
liabilities in excess of a specified minimum figure for an amount up
to a specified percentage of its eligible liabilities (although for
practical reasons, the Bank imposes a minimum size on individual
transactions). The facilities are normally for sale to the Bank and
subsequent repurchase of gilt-edged stock and for the provision of
finance against promissory notes in relation to holdings of sterling
export credit and shipbuilding paper guaranteed by the Export
Credits Guarantee Department and the Department of Trade and
Industry respectively.

The transactions undertaken by the Bank of England in the
morning are made public, together with the quantities and rates for
each instrument and band. Normally, at about 2.00 p.m., the Bank
will publish any further significant revision to its estimate of the
market's position for the day. On the basis of this estimate and
other indicators, the Bank will then decide whether to invite
business from the discount houses, which may be in addition to
business transacted at the earlier session. This could involve further

operations in bills (as already described). Thus, the Bank can influence interest rates by its reactions to the offers made to it. If the Bank is content with the pattern of rates implied by these offers, it is generally prepared to accept sufficient of them to 'balance the market'. But if the rates that are offered conflict with the Bank's interest-rate objective, all or part of the offers may be rejected. If houses are then short of funds (or, indeed, at any earlier time in the day), the Bank may publish an announcement that discount houses wishing to use their borrowing facilities are invited to do so at 2.30 p.m.; on such occasions, the discount rate at which loans are made is usually published, as is the period for which loans are to be made – usually for 7 days, possibly for 14 days. There is no obligation to borrow, though the Bank will normally have engineered a situation where borrowing is likely. The limits on the size of borrowing facilities (e.g. for 'late assistance' – see below) are suspended for 2.30 p.m. lending, and the amount outstanding over the duration of the lending does not count against each discount house's borrowing facilities for late assistance on subsequent days.

Alternatively, if the Bank of England wished to maintain bank base rates at current levels, following earlier operations in bills, it could decline to operate further in the bill market that day, but would invite the discount houses to use their borrowing facilities at an unchanged rate consistent with current bank base rates (and possibly lend at 7 days, or even longer – e.g. 14 days).[143] If the Bank wishes to reduce rates it will offer to lend funds to the discount houses at a rate (say) $\frac{1}{2}$ per cent below the existing rate; this would then usually be followed by $\frac{1}{2}$ per cent reduction in clearing bank base rates and an appropriate reduction in the rate at which the Bank purchases eligible bank bills or Treasury bills. In addition and on occasion, the Bank of England may give an early morning indication of a desire to lower interest rates – e.g. when offering early assistance by buying some bills at rates (say) $\frac{1}{2}$ per cent below previously existing dealing rates. This may then be followed by a disinclination in the afternoon to invite offers of bills, but advising the discount houses that they are welcome to borrow funds at the new level; sums might then be lent at the new rate for 7 days.[144] In other words, there is a number of possible variations. By these means, the Bank of England can also give 'signals' to the money markets in order to indicate the direction of policy.

There is an additional facility at 2.45 p.m. (dating back to

October 1971, though its character has changed). It is referred to now as 'late help' or 'late assistance' and is usually repayable the next day.[145] Current arrangements for 2.45 p.m. borrowing go back to 1981, when the former 2.45 p.m. arrangements (referred to on pp. 74–5) were phased out and practice moved towards that now being described.

The Bank of England may decide to lend in the following instances.

1 When there is an isolated or unexpected shortage – possibly large – that is technical in character (e.g. an over-subscription to a new issue of government stock, or a half-yearly payment of petroleum revenue tax). In these circumstances, the Bank may not wish to relieve the shortage entirely by operations in bills, because it may cause unnecessary distortions to interest rates. It may therefore choose to lend – in which case the rate charged may be close to market rates.

2 When the Bank wishes to see very short-term interest rates higher, but believes the discount houses will not offer – or finds that they have not offered after being invited to do so – sufficient paper at high enough rates for the upward adjustment to be effected quickly through bill operations. The Bank may then decline to deal in the bill markets, or may limit its dealings, and thus force those houses that are short of cash to borrow. The Bank then sets a lending rate consistent with the higher level which it is seeking to establish in the market.

In this context, the discount houses have a right to borrow at the Bank of England – it is a 'lender of last resort' facility. Discount houses have borrowing facilities at the Bank against approved collateral up to maximum amounts related to the capital base of each house. These provide discount houses with a supplementary means of balancing their positions after the Bank's main operations in eligible bills have been concluded. Collateral acceptable to the Bank as security against this lending comprises eligible bills due after the maturity of the loan and gilt-edged stock with a residual maturity of up to 5 years. Collateral of 105 per cent in the form of eligible bills or gilt-edged stock with up to 5 years to maturity is required against lending; bills are valued at face value and gilt-edged stock is valued at the Central Gilts Office reference price. (Collateral at 108 per cent is required for bills with over 3 months to maturity.) Interest is deducted from the amount advanced, which is credited to the borrower's account at the Bank. Upon maturity of the loan the collateral is returned to the borrower in exchange for a cheque drawn on its account with the Bank.

Each discount house's facility is in two tranches, each for an amount equal to the capital base of the house concerned. Facilities are adjusted quarterly in line with changes in the capital base of each discount house, or (exceptionally) within a quarter to take account of a large specific change in capital base. Drawings on the second tranche will normally carry a higher rate of interest than those on the first tranche. The terms on which these latter facilities are available on a particular day are at the discretion of the Bank. The procedure is that, if a discount house finds itself short of funds after the Bank's main bill business has been concluded, a director of the discount house will telephone at 2.45 p.m. to request to borrow on a secured basis under its facilities. The Bank publishes the total amount of this late assistance provided to discount houses, gilt-edged market-makers and Stock Exchange money brokers (which have similar facilities related to capital size), but not the terms. Thereafter these houses may seek by telephone application to borrow further; as we have seen, such transactions are at the discretion of the Bank and usually attract increasing rates of interest. Figures relating to the latter type of transaction are not published. Prospective borrowers are invited to state the amount they wish to borrow before being told the terms on which the funds will be made available. One might note that transactions within the banking system may continue until dealing is effectively terminated by the need to present items at the Town Clearing.[146]

Again, the Bank of England may purchase from the banks at a rate of its own choosing between 2.50 p.m. and 3.00 p.m. Treasury bills or Corporation (i.e. local authority) bills, as indeed it had previously from market-makers that had a discount house type of operation with borrowing limits at the Bank of England. This also has the merit that it assists the Bank to handle shortages other than by buying commercial bills. Also – as we have indicated – discount houses may lend late in the day to banks that have need of funds in the knowledge that a discount house could reimburse itself by borrowing at the Bank of England under lender of last resort facilities. Very occasionally (e.g. when forecasts go badly wrong), the Bank of England may lend to Stock Exchange money brokers, or gilt-edged market-makers after the normal 2.45 p.m. occasion but before 3.30 p.m., but this would be very much the exception.

Nevertheless, it can happen. Indeed, clearing banks may on occasion finish up the day with an overdraft at the Bank of England.[147]

If there is a surplus of money in the market, usually the Bank of England acts only in the afternoon to absorb it. The Bank will then invite the discount houses and the clearing banks to bid for Treasury bills of one or more specified maturities for same-day settlement, but first the Bank will want to be sure that an overall surplus does exist and that any discount houses looking for funds have had full opportunity to find them. As will have been noted, the clearing banks are also included in the invitation. This is necessary, because otherwise they would be at a substantial disadvantage *vis-à-vis* the discount houses in finding an outlet for surplus funds. Indeed, it is understood that mopping up operations are more usually taken up by the banks than by the discount houses. Again, the Bank of England will use its discretion as to which bids for Treasury bills to accept, with lower rates being accepted before higher ones for bills of a particular maturity. Also, the basis for mopping up operations is Treasury bills, not eligible commercial bills, though Treasury bills may be bought when the Bank of England is making money available. Corporation (local authority) bills may also be bought at times, but mostly it is commercial bills. For one thing, there are times when too few Treasury bills are in issue. Preference for Treasury bills when mopping up is because: (a) it is easier to get the right date with a Treasury bill (new Treasury bills will be created for whatever date is required); and (b) it would be less easy to sell off private paper rather than Treasury paper. In addition, it could be a nice question as to whose private paper might be sold back to the market, especially in a market where discount houses usually endorse bills when selling them outright. There is also more work in selling commercial bills.

The operations that have been described are the principal ones undertaken by the Bank of England, and the daily timetable and procedures outlined above are now well established. But the Bank may alter its arrangements 'at any time to deal with specific temporary situations or with underlying changes in market structure'. It should also be observed that transactions within the banking system may continue for some time after the Bank has concluded its operations, if any, for the day in question. For example, the inter-bank market in overnight funds may be active until dealing is effectively terminated by the need to present items at the Town

The London money markets 89

Clearing. Moreover, only when the outcome of this clearing is known will the net money position for the day and the final positions of each of the clearing banks at the Bank of England become apparent.

THE EVOLUTION OF POLICY

Under the 1981 arrangements, the policy objectives were attained only briefly and to a limited extent. The notion of offering the market a greater say in the determination of interest rates was not new – it was a basic assumption in adopting MLR in 1972. But what was intended in 1981 was based on the premise that official market operations would normally be modest and could probably be confined to short-dated bills, with market rates on longer dated bills free to fluctuate, as would shorter rates to some extent. In practice, within months of the introduction of the new arrangements, the money market entered on a period of prolonged and heavy shortages, largely attributable to the emphasis that was placed on gilt-edged overfunding as the main means of pursuing the Government's monetary targets.

As a consequence, the Bank of England found it necessary to operate regularly in bills – and substantially in commercial bills – initially throughout the whole of the maturity range up to 91 days, and, since 1989, normally in Bands 1 and 2 (i.e. up to 33 days). In these circumstances, the rates at which the Bank showed itself willing to deal came to have much the same character as the 'official rates' that used to obtain when dealing in Treasury bills. This meant that when there was a change in the Bank's dealing rates, this represented a policy move with a fairly high profile – in effect, the Bank had become a rate-maker at all maturities in which it deals. It also meant that the market's views on interest rates came to be expressed not so much in offering bills at rates differing from the Bank's established dealing rates as in the choice of maturity of the bills being offered by the discount houses. If the houses were apprehensive that there might be an increase in rates, they would offer longer-term paper within Bands 3 or 4, in order to limit their loss if and when rates went up. However, if they anticipated that rates might fall, they would tend to retain their longer dated paper and either offer short-dated paper or none at all, relying on borrowing facilities at the Bank to square their positions. At the same time, this could give rise to the paradoxical consequence that the greater the expectation of lower interest rates the higher very short market rates might be driven. At times when for prolonged periods there has been a strong expectation of interest rate change – either upwards or downwards – there has been evidence of a kind of 'see-saw effect'. Indeed, whenever such expectations are strong, the slope of the yield curve tells the story most graphically. On other occasions (the latter half of 1988 is an example) when there were no prolonged periods of strong expectations of interest rate changes, it was difficult to judge what market sentiment actually was and the transactions undertaken probably depended more on what types and maturities of bills the houses currently had in portfolio.[148] Types of instrument might likewise be important, since the Bank of England would normally prefer Treasury bills, Corporate (or local authority) bills, and eligible commercial bills in that order. None the less, the bulk of the business done is in eligible commercial bills.

Despite all this, it remains possible for the market to generate considerable pressure for changes in the level of interest rates. In these circumstances, the mechanism foreseen in the 1981 arrangements can still operate with changes in rates occurring as a result of the Bank's accepting new rates proposed by the market. But these days it is more usual for interest rate changes to be led by the Bank of England. Partly this reflects the realities of market operations; at the same time, it also denotes an evolution in the process of policy formation. There has been a breakdown in the former relationship between monetary aggregates and nominal income. Hence, conducting monetary policy through the management of quantities – and leaving prices (interest rates) to look after themselves – has given way to a much more explicit official management of the level and structure of interest rates. The framework of such decisions was set out annually at the time of the Budget, when there was a re-statement of the government's Medium Term Financial Strategy. Operational decisions within that framework were taken as subsequent events unfolded, with the Chancellor of the Exchequer regularly consulting the Treasury and the Bank of England, which two continuously reviewed – and continue to review – the current and developing state of monetary conditions.

The Medium Term Financial Strategy was the intellectual tool resorted to by Nigel Lawson when Chancellor of the Exchequer. Working within its framework was supposed to curb inflation by limiting monetary growth and cutting budget expenditure. This strategy still exists, as is confirmed by the title to Chapter 2 of the *Financial Statement and Budget Report 1991/92* published in March 1991. After the UK pound joined the European Exchange Rate Mechanism (ERM), an alternative discipline was also provided. None the less, as part of the Medium Term Financial Strategy, the government 'is committed' to meeting its ERM obligations. Also, in terms of Norman Lamont's Budget Speech on 19 March 1991: 'Our entry into the ERM does not alter the requirement for fiscal policy to buttress monetary policy and play its part in curbing inflation'. Moreover, it was entirely consistent with the medium-term approach 'to tolerate swings in the fiscal position'.

In implementing an official decision to change the level of interest rates, it is normal nowadays for the Bank of England to publish on its Reuter and Telerate pages an invitation to discount houses wishing to make use of borrowing facilities at the Bank that day to do so at 2.30 p.m., when the rate will be x per cent; it may also be done by announcing that a different level of rates has been accepted on bills purchased. This is taken by the clearing banks to be an indication of what will be an acceptable level for base rate. After setting in chain the relevant internal procedures, this lead is usually adopted by the clearing banks with little delay, other banks adjusting their rates in sympathy. When rates are to be increased, the clearing banks seem to be quite ready to follow the lead of the Bank of England. The process may not be quite so automatic when rates are falling. Sometimes, the banks may be quite keen to lead a downward move; on other occasions, they may be a little reluctant to follow. But in the first half of 1991, such downward movements were substantially discounted before the move was made and, at times, the Bank of England found itself fighting a rearguard action (see above).

PRUDENTIAL CONTROLS AND SUPERVISION

In reorganizing market arrangements following the demise of Competition and Credit Control, the next stage was to extend prudential controls (which had already been considerably developed for the banks) to the discount houses. There had long been certain rules. For example, over many years, there had been a principal multiplier (for a long time not publicly disclosed) which established a guideline for a discount house's total book; this was set at 30 times its 'resources' (capital and reserves); and there was a subsidiary multiplier of 8 times 'resources', which was applied to a discount house's bond book. From time to time, other multipliers or controls were applied to the operations of the discount houses, for reasons other than those of prudential regulation. Thus, the credit control arrangements that lapsed in August 1981 incorporated a limit on the discount houses' holdings of certain assets; also, principally in order to conserve their capacity to operate in the sterling market, a limit of 3 times 'resources' was applied to their books in foreign currency assets when some houses entered that business.

Over recent years, a number of numerical tests had been developed for the prudential supervision of banks; most noticeably these have been concerned with capital adequacy.

> The central ingredient of that test is the assigning of risk coefficients to various classes of banking asset, so that a suitably weighted measure of each bank's exposure to risk of loss may be compared with its capital funds available to absorb losses.[149]

But the measurement devised for the generality of banks, the primary emphasis of which was on private credit risk, was not suitable for application in that form to discount houses. Nevertheless, it was apparent that a similar approach could be followed 'to categorise the degrees of risk of different assets held by Discount Houses so as to arrive at a more discriminant measure of the capital needs of a book of given size and composition' than was provided by the existing – and long-standing – multipliers. Before new arrangements were introduced, there were discussions with the London Discount Market Association, and some time was allowed for the new monetary control arrangements of August 1981 to settle down; also there were 'uncertainties over the degree of volatility of asset prices that might be experienced'. Even after the new arrangements were introduced, it was 'intended that the operation of the new system should be reviewed in the light of experience; and that it be further developed as necessary to encompass new types of activity, for example, trading in futures markets'.

The initial arrangements (set out in June 1982) were 'conceptually simple' and centred on the notion of an 'adjusted total book' which was to be limited to a fixed multiple of a house's 'capital base'. This 'adjusted total book' was calculated by assigning 'added risk weightings' to certain classes of asset and adding to the actual total book the product of the weighting and the amount of assets in each class (the 'additions'). 'Additions' attributable to the length of the maturity term of assets might be reduced if there were liabilities of corresponding maturity. In addition to the overall limit, a subsidiary limit was applied to the total net 'additions'. These arrangements had the effect that a house whose book consisted almost exclusively of low risk assets might hold a larger total book than one whose book contained higher risk assets. The actual levels set were 40 for the main multiplier and 15 for the subsidiary multiplier. Necessarily, too, the Bank of England wished to retain a degree of flexibility in administering the new system, though it was recognized that the 'exercising of such flexibility must not disturb the basis of competition within the market'. For types of risk inherent in assets held, see Table 2.4.

It is also necessary to define the capital base. This is intended to provide the best measure of a house's ability to absorb losses in its discount market operations. This means that any capital required to support other activities – whether or not they are conducted in a separate company, e.g. a subsidiary – cannot be counted a second time as part of the capital base in the money market. Subsidiaries should be adequately capitalized in their own right, or may in appropriate cases be consolidated with their discount house parent for the purpose of these measurements. The definition includes *inter alia* the amount paid up on ordinary share capital (as relating to the discount house only and not to any holding company or subsidiaries) plus items like share premium account, capital reserves, general reserves, profit and loss account, etc. From this would be deducted items like net book value of fixed assets, goodwill, book value of interests in subsidiaries and associated companies, and unsecured loans to parent company or fellow subsidiaries.

The most recent framework of prudential supervision for discount houses was laid down in October 1988.[150] Risk-taking was seen to be an essential part of a discount house's function, and the effective working of the market requires that discount houses should be as free as possible to make their own judgements about the positions they wish to run. The aim of the Bank of England's supervision was, within this framework, to ensure as far as possible that such judgements did not result in risks being taken which were disproportionate to the discount house's own funds and which would endanger its ability to meet its obligations to its counterparties. No supervisory arrangements could wholly exclude the

Table 2.4 Risk classification of assets

	Nil	$\frac{1}{2}$	1	$1\frac{1}{2}$	Added risk classes 2	4	5
Cash at bankers							
Deposits with Bank of England							
UK Treasury bills	up to 3 m.	3–9 m.	9–12 m.				
Other eligible bills	up to 3 m.	3–6 m.					
Ineligible bank bills ⎱ Trade bills[a]	up to 3 m.	3–6 m.	6–12 m.				
Other trade bills ⎱ Commercial paper[b]		up to 3 m.	1–6 m.	over 6 m.			
CDs	up to 3 m.	3–9 m.	9–18 m.	$1\frac{1}{2}$–5 y.			
Loans to banks and building societies	up to 1 m.	1–3 m.	3–6 m.	6–12 m.	1–3 y.	over 3 y.	
Other loans	to next business day		1 day to 1 month		1–3 m.		
Leases			up to 1 m.		1–3 m.	3–18 m.	over 18 m.
Fixed-rate gilts (long or short positions)[c]	up to 3 m.	3–9 m.	9–18 m.	$1\frac{1}{2}$–5 y.	5–10 y.	over 10 y.	
Other fixed-rate quoted assets	up to 3 m.	3–9 m.	9–18 m.	$1\frac{1}{2}$–5 y.	5–10 y.	over 10 y.	
Fixed-rate unquoted assets	up to 3 m.		up to 1 m.	1–6 m.	6–18 m.	over 18 m.	

Variable-rate assets issued by local authorities or government-guaranteed borrowers where rate is fixed for	up to 3 m.	3–6 m.				over 6 m.
Other variable-rate assets where rate is fixed for			up to 3 m.		3–6 m.	
Futures positions and forward commitments[d]	up to 3 m.	3–9 m.	9–18 m.	1½–5 y.	5–10 y.	over 10 y.
Deductions[e]		Fixed money 3–9 m.	9–18 m.	1½–5 y.	5–10 y. Aggregate net short open FOREX position	Equity investments (incl. pref. shares) over 10 y.

Notes:

a Trade bills which are drawn and accepted by independent names, or bear one public-sector name, or are insured.

b The Bank of England may impose a higher weight depending on the creditworthiness of the issuer.

c Where short positions in assets within a certain class exceed long positions, the added risk weight is to be applied to the short position and vice versa.

d For futures and forward commitments to purchase assets at an agreed price, the duration of the investment is taken as the period until the commitment falls due, plus the maturity of the deliverable asset. For all other purchase commitments, the duration is taken as that of the deliverable asset only.

e In addition, in calculating *basic risk*, deductions are allowed for ½ specified assets (eligible bills, government securities, CDs, deposits with and loans to banks and building societies, and sums due on margin account from LIFFE) of maturity 0–33 days; and, in the case of gilts, only the difference between the long and short position attracts *basic risk*.

m. = month(s)   y. = year(s)

risk of default, however, and it must remain the responsibility of the counterparties to satisfy themselves as to the integrity of a discount house with whom they deal.

It was further stated that the Bank requires discount houses to be separately capitalized in the UK. In addition it seeks assurances from substantial shareholders that they accept ultimate responsibility for the liabilities of the discount house. The Bank's prudential surpervision is based upon close familiarity with the management and business of each discount house, developed through quarterly bilateral discussions. It is supported by continuous assessment of the discount house's risk exposure in relation to the capital resources that it has freely available to meet losses.

Capital adequacy is of the essence of a sound and viable operation, and for discount houses this is assessed by comparing the assets of each discount house – measured in risk-adjusted terms – with its capital base.[151] For measurement purposes, assets are divided into seven classes. Four of these classes are treated as giving rise to 'added risk', which is calculated by multiplying the assets in each class by the appropriate weights. The added risk and the actual total book together comprise the adjusted total book, which must not exceed 80 times the capital base. In addition, added risk alone must not exceed 25 times capital base. These limits were to be absolute maxima and even within these the Bank reserves the right to disallow unbalanced books, but has had occasion to do so only rarely, 'conscious of the general objective of unfettered competition.'

The Bank of England detailed four main types of risk that are inherent in any assets held:

(i) *credit risk* – the risk that one or more entities will fail to discharge their liabilities, thereby impairing the value of the asset;
(ii) *position risk* – the risk of a change in the market value of the asset for other reasons (e.g. a change in interest rates);
(iii) as part of (ii), *forced sale risk* – the risk of additional loss if a supervised entity is forced to sell at short notice an asset in which the market is narrow; and
(iv) *settlement risk* – the risk that the process of exchanging money for assets will not be completed smoothly and the supervised entity will suffer some loss of value.

The assets held by discount houses carry principally risk of types (ii) and (iii), but there is also some element of credit risk in all assets, perhaps most notably trade bills or unsecured loans. Historical experience suggests that position risk increases with the term to maturity of the asset and that forced sale risk is less for holdings of gilt-edged stocks than for other marketable holdings of comparable maturity. Some degree of settlement risk is involved in all exchange of money for assets; it may be greatly reduced by the use of assured payment systems.[152]

For certain very short-term sterling assets a more favourable treatment is allowed. A deduction of a half is made against holdings of such assets with 33 days or less to run. This treatment is confined to eligible bills, government securities, CDs, deposits with and loans to banks and building societies, and sums due on margin account from LIFFE. Assets are measured at market values, consistent with the definition of capital base.[153]

Unsecured loans required to support activities conducted in a separate group company are excluded from the capital base supporting the money market activity. Where a discount house has subsidiaries, they are consolidated with their discount house parent for the purpose of these measurements. The proportion of capital that may be in the form of subordinated debt is subject to limit, discussed on a case-by-case basis and monitored continuously. The loan must be provided by a related company and the Bank of England requires the opportunity to consider its documentation beforehand. Repayment of a loan before its final maturity date (if any) is allowed only with the prior permission of the Bank.

The Bank of England allows a reduction in any added risk required because of the maturity of an asset, if it is matched by certain liabilities of comparable term. Longer term money liabilities which are totally fixed qualify for this treatment, as do short positions in the gilt market. 'Matched' long and short positions in gilts may thus be netted out in the reported assets where the relevant maturity dates are within 3 months of each other for stocks within 18 months of maturity, or within 12 months for longer stocks. Where short positions are not allowed as hedges, the added risk weighting in each risk class is applied to whichever is the larger of the long positions and the short positions in that class.

Discount houses which are active in options markets are required to calculate the 'delta value'[154] of each individual option. These delta values are aggregated for particular instruments and contract maturities and treated as a single position in the asset underlying the option contract. This position is reported and assigned an appropriate added risk weight. The difficulty of summarizing position risk exposure in a single figure is particularly acute where options are involved, and for that reason the Bank of England will look particularly closely at the detail of discount houses' positions in options, and assess the extent of their exposure to price movements in either direction. Discount houses are also required to report the margin on their combined futures and options positions. Since open positions in foreign currency can expose a discount house to exchange risk, these are included in the framework of added risk classes.

As required under the Banking Act 1987, each discount house must set out in writing to the Bank of England its policy for the monitoring of exposures to individual borrowers; this statement should normally be adopted by its board. Any subsequent changes should be discussed with the Bank before implementation. Exposures should be grouped into one of three categories (see Table 2.5 for details). All exposures in excess of 10 per cent of capital base must be reported to the Bank where they are exposures under category (c) (largely to the non-bank private sector), or under category (b) (largely banks) if more than a year in maturity. No exposures in excess of 25 per cent of capital base under either of these categories may be taken on without the Bank's prior permission, which will generally be forthcoming only in particular circumstances (see below), or otherwise in exceptional situations. In assessing 'exposures', account should be taken not only of direct claims on the borrower, but also of all contingent liabilities; and exposures to different companies in the same group should for these purposes be regarded as to a single borrower. The Bank of England reserves the right in some circumstances to deduct part or all of such large exposures from the capital base or to apply higher risk weights, though it would not normally expect to do so for exposures of less than 25 per cent of capital base.

The Bank of England is prepared to tolerate exposures in excess of 25 per cent of capital base if (i) the discount house is a subsidiary either of another institution authorized under the Banking Act, or of an overseas bank, and if there are arrangements acceptable to the Bank under which the parent bank will take over the whole exposure if problems occur or will make up any resultant dificiency in the discount house's capital; or (ii) the discount house is carrying out a lead-management function in underwriting an issue, where special arrangements may be agreed; or (iii) proper security is taken which fully covers the exposure and is in the form of British Government stock, eligible bills, or deposits held with the lender over which there is a legal right of set-off.

Table 2.5 The three categories into which exposures should be grouped

(a) Central government and specified international institutions; central banks and public sector bodies with an unconditional central government guarantee.
(b) (i) Institutions authorized under the Banking Act and overseas banks.
    (ii) Building societies.
    (iii) Stock Exchange money brokers and gilt-edged market makers.
    (iv) Contingent exposures to insurers of credit risk.
(c) All other counterparties.

The Bank of England expects discount houses to monitor their positions continuously, marking to market daily and updating the capital base to reflect any profit or loss, even if unrealized, that this revaluation shows. The multiplier limits must be observed continuously. Regular returns are required, showing the capital base and adjusted book as at close of business on the third Wednesday and last working day of every month, which must be submitted to the Bank within 7 days of the reporting date. The Bank may also ask for additional returns at any time to ensure that the multiplier limits are being observed. Large exposures returns must likewise be submitted on these dates. The returns form the basis of the supervisory process, which includes regular interviews with senior management to discuss all aspects of the discount houses' business. Discount houses are expected to provide the Bank with any information it may reasonably require in carrying out its supervision. In addition, discount houses are required to complete a number of other returns to assist the Bank in its calculation of monetary and other aggregates on weekly, monthly, or quarterly bases.

For gilt-edged market-makers, which had a dealing relationship with the Bank of England in money market instruments, the framework of their supervision was laid down in the Bank's paper on 'The future structure of the gilt-edged market' issued in April 1985. This framework was subsequently modified by the issue of market notices. On this basis, the Bank of England in October 1988 invited applications from gilt-edged market-makers wishing to establish a dealing relationship with the Bank in the sterling money market. Initially, three or four firms applied, but the position was left open for other firms to apply if they so desired. In the result, as from 13 February 1989, S. G. Warburg Discount Ltd was authorized under the Banking Act 1987 and joined the LDMA, but surrendered its banking status early in 1992; both Greenwell Montagu Gilt-Edged, a gilt-edged market-maker, and the new Warburg house (see note 3 on p. 392) now enjoyed a similar status as gilt-edged market-makers with a money market dealing relationship with the Bank of England. Apart from certain differences outlined below, the prudential supervision of these two houses was the same as that of other gilt-edged market-makers.

For example, the risk weights applied to positions held by gilt-edged market-makers were broadly similar to those applied to discount houses, taking into account the different nature of the two supervisory systems. In recognition of the role of discount houses as market-makers in bills, however, the weights applied to holdings of money market instruments with up to 3 months to maturity were lower for them than for gilt-edged market-makers. Accordingly, for gilt-edged market-makers that wished to have a money-market dealing relationship with the Bank of England, the additional risk weight of one half, which was imposed on holdings of money-market instruments of maturities less than 3 months, was reduced to one quarter. This meant that the weight applied to holdings of these instruments would be broadly the same for all the Bank's money-market dealing counterparties. The Bank expected the gilt-edged activities of a gilt-edged market-maker which had a money-market dealing relationship with the Bank normally to require the support of no more than an agreed proportion of its total capital base, in order to ensure the availability of capital to support its money-market activities. The Bank indicated that it would wish to discuss with individual prospective counterparties the determination and application of this proportion. In addition to the current supervisory reports received through the computer-linked reporting system for gilt-edged market-makers, the Bank of England would require some additional reports from a gilt-edged market-maker with which it had established a money-market dealing relationship. The reports would include a breakdown of money-market instruments by maturity band, turnover in money-market instruments, details of money-market transactions with related entities, and the profits and losses of the money-market trading operations. These reports would initially be required in paper form and mostly fortnightly.

Finally, it should be noted that when a number of years ago several 'new' money markets first began to develop in London, they were referred to as 'parallel' or 'secondary' markets. It is wrong now to do so. They have long been merely different branches of a much expanded money market that had been absorbed into a larger whole.[155] There is a sense in which one can still regard traditional discount-market arrangements as the core, but the discount houses themselves had long had footings in the 'new' markets both directly and through subsidiaries, as indeed did the clearing banks and other financial services groups (again, in some markets, through subsidiaries). Moreover, to the extent that similar institutions operate in a number of different markets, relationships between markets and their several rates of interest and yields are established and, on this basis, there is now a very high degree of integration within the complex of London's money markets.

Chapter 3

Money markets in the United States of America[1]

The most important banking and financial centre in the US is New York and it is there that money market transactions are effectively centralized. Nowhere else in the US is the financial business undertaken comparable in scope and volume. There are subsidiary money markets in other centres, of which the most important is Chicago, and San Francisco and Los Angeles are not insignificant (due in particular to the growing importance of the Japanese connection). These markets supplement the facilities offered in New York, but it is the rates and yields established there that provide the basis for dealings in the country at large. Activity in the various centres is fused into a national market in three ways. First, banks throughout the US are linked by a widespread network of correspondent relationships both with New York and with other leading centres. Second, the various dealers in securities likewise have connections across the country as well as branch offices at key points. By these means, surplus funds can be invested in a variety of short-dated assets, which can readily be sold, thereby facilitating the day-to-day adjustment by banks and others of their cash and liquid balances. Third, the transfer facilities made available by the Federal Reserve System to all depository institutions (e.g. banks, savings institutions, credit unions, etc., all of which accept deposits) greatly assist the free movement of funds throughout the whole of the US economy.

The two groups of institutions that constitute the most important elements in the New York money market – apart from the Federal Reserve authorities themselves – are the larger commercial banks and (as at January 1992) the 38 primary dealers in government securities (both bank and non-bank). The principal assets in which they operate are US government securities and securities of federal agencies, which markets – together with that in federal funds (in which non-bank government securities dealers cannot deal directly) – represent the core of the national money market. There are also subsidiary markets, such as those in commercial paper, bankers' acceptances and negotiable certificates of deposit, besides the extension of US banks as major operators into the international market for Eurodollars, which is centred for the most part in Europe. Latterly, there has also been much activity in financial futures, where Chicago is of primary importance.

MARKET FOR US GOVERNMENT SECURITIES

The intervention of the US authorities for the purpose of credit or monetary control is concentrated mainly in the highly developed US government securities market; these operations in turn have an immediate impact on the level of reserves – balances which a depository institution holds with a Federal Reserve Bank and which may be borrowed and lent; this in turn affects the supply of and demand for federal funds. Indeed, it is this latter market that provides an important initial means of spreading the effects of official monetary action throughout the banking and financial system and the economy.

Some idea of the size and composition of the market in US government securities can be derived from an analysis of the figures. Gross public debt of the Federal government at the end of 1989 was $2,976 billion. Of this amount, $1,945 billion was marketable. Excluding US government agencies and trust funds, the commercial banks and the Federal Reserve Banks were the largest groups of domestic investors, but both were lower than foreign and international investors. In recent years, state and local governments have also become important. However, with under 10 per cent of total public debt, commercial bank holdings represented a considerable decline when compared with earlier years. Foreign and international (much of it Japanese) is now the most important single holding (after US government agencies and trust funds) and fluctuates at something well over 11 per cent. For the rest, insurance companies (at about 6 per cent) are significant holders, individuals (largely non-marketable savings bonds) hold 7 per cent, and other companies 3 per cent.[2]

At the shortest end of the range of government paper are Treasury bills, issued on a discount basis with original maturities of 3, 6, and

12 months. In times past, marketable certificates of indebtedness were also issued, but they have not been issued to the public since August 1966.[3] The Treasury note has a maturity that extends from 2 to 10 years. At end-1989, outstanding issues of Treasury notes totalled $1,151.5 billion. Finally, Treasury bonds provide the instruments of long-term debt, though with the effluxion of time they, too, will qualify as short-dated securities. They carry coupons and are generally defined as having a maturity of over 10 years. At end-1989, there was a total of $348.2 billion of Treasury bonds outstanding.

Of the several kinds of government security, the Treasury bill occupied a special place in the money market. It was first introduced in December 1929, but before the Second World War the amount outstanding rarely exceeded $2.5 billion. As a result of war-time deficit finance, the Treasury bill issue increased manyfold and, in the post-war period, the amount of bills outstanding has exceeded $378 billion. The short maturity of the Treasury bill makes it much sought after for inclusion in the reserves of both financial and business corporations, as also of local governments. Moreover, the open market operations of the authorities are often carried out in this medium.

The Federal Reserve is the fiscal agent of the US Treasury, but the Treasury itself determines the coupon, maturity, and the amount of the Treasury issue. It is also responsible for its own debt management. This is undertaken by the Bureau of Public Debt. Nowadays, all marketable Treasury securities are auctioned by the Federal Reserve, except US savings bonds; the Government Account Series issued to government agencies, trust funds and accounts; and the state and local government series (the last are made up of non-marketable, dollar-denominated, and foreign currency-denominated series held by foreigners). There was quite an increase in the state and local government series in 1986, because: (1) interest rates were at a 6-year low;[4] and (2) changes were being made to the tax code and there was therefore a desire to borrow in the market before the changes took place.

The changeover to the auction technique for Treasuries came in the early 1970s – for notes and bonds as well as bills. Previously, applicants had subscribed for notes and bonds – the Treasury fixed the rate and, if an issue was oversubscribed, applicants were offered a percentage. Now the auction determines the rate at which these Treasuries are issued.[5] Also, now that so many securities are issued, the US has a very wide range of maturities out in the market – it is sufficient to provide a full yield curve; it likewise gives a lot of depth and breadth to the market, in which there is much activity.

Where monetary policy and debt management is implemented by one agency – like the Bank of Engand – one would expect there to be an interrelationship between the two. In the US, monetary policy is both framed and carried out – e.g. by way of open market operations – by the Federal Reserve independently of what the Treasury might be doing with respect to its financing and debt management. But in the US, too, there is an overlapping of the monetary effects of monetary policy and debt management (on the basis of the related money flows thereby instigated) – with a grey area between the two.

Moreover, in determining its financing arrangements, the Treasury has a degree of flexibility. This does not relate so much to the amounts that have to be raised, but the Treasury does have flexibility with regard to the maturities of notes and bonds issued and the choice between bill and coupon security issues. One constraint might be the rate at which current bonds are maturing, and it might also be noted that from 1966 to 1971 the Treasury was precluded from issuing bonds because of the $4\frac{1}{4}$ per cent ceiling on the interest rate that might be paid. Congress subsequently granted exemptions from the ceiling, which was later abolished.

Treasury auctions take place for 3-month and 6-month bills on Mondays (unless Monday is a holiday, when it would be on a Tuesday). The auction usually closes at 1.00 p.m. Eastern Time (if there are other issues in one day, it may be 12 noon).[6] In addition to 91-day and 182-day bills, there are 52 week (364-day) bills – the last are only issued every 4 weeks. All have a Thursday maturity. The tenders and the issue are made on a discount basis, the announcement of the relevant tender for 3-month and 6-month bills having been made on the previous Tuesday.[7] The announcement of the results of the 3-month and 6-month bill auctions is made about 4.00 p.m. on the same day (a Monday) on the wire from Washington. Bills won in the auction are then taken up on the following Thursday and are paid for in same-day (federal) funds. Tenders may be competitive, when any lesser amount may be awarded, or non-competitive, when the bid is not to exceed $1 million for one bidder through all sources and the rate will be at the average of accepted competitive bids. The standard form requires information about safe-keeping or delivery instructions, and payment instructions. Similary, for 2-year Treasury notes, except that here one tenders on a yield basis (to two decimal places). The Fed also tenders for Treasury bills for its own account and for customers (e.g. for foreign central banks, and/or for governments). The rate it pays is the average of accepted competitive bids.

In the US, there is no system as in London, where bills may be taken up at the tender rate on any day in the following week (thereby achieving a run of dates to suit the bank or house concerned). The US Treasury itself tends to have a rigid schedule of issue dates in order to maintain a regular pattern for the sale of its securities. At irregular intervals, there are sales of short-term obligations called cash management bills.

There is an active 'when-issued' (WI) market in Treasury bills; also in new coupon securities. Before bills are allocated, or new coupon securities are issued, dealers can trade them in advance of the allocation or issue. Pre-auction trading in the WI market is conducted on a yield basis and post-auction trading on a price basis. The WI market is said to be very important, because it sets or establishes the terms of the dealers' bids. In addition – at the time of the auction – if dealers already have a number of sales, it gives them the ability to bid aggressively.

Although the Fed tenders for Treasury bills for its own account (and for customers), it usually buys other Treasuries (notes and bonds) in the secondary market (the Fed can acquire both bills and coupon securities directly from the Treasury for its own account, but only up to the amount of maturing securities which it submits for exchange into the new issue).

In terms of maturities, it is sometimes argued that the Treasury should not issue 30-year bonds, since its issues might compete with mortgage funds. However, the savings banks and savings and loan associations in fact fund their mortgages by means of short-term funds as well as some long-term funds. On balance, it is felt that there has been no 'crowding out'. Insurance companies[8] and pension funds are the major purchasers of 30-year bonds (for some time now the Treasury has not sold a 20-year maturity). Also, because of arbitraging, a lot of 30-year bonds go to short-term investors, since one can always hedge a 30-year bond. The opportunities for arbitraging and hedging are now much greater than they were and one cannot as readily distinguish between short-term and long-term paper. In addition, the Treasury would almost certainly have to pay more to finance its debt if it did not have as wide a range of options as it currently has. Nevertheless, the Treasury is still very dependent on the bill market, despite its working very hard on developing the medium-term and long-term parts of the maturity structure. At no time do they want to have most of their eggs in one basket. It should be remembered, too, that a lot of the money that is raised has to be allocated to refund maturing debt as well as expenditure on current needs. Furthermore, the Treasury tries when making new issues to secure a run of maturities, such that not too much matures at one and the same time. Actually, when the Treasury is looking 30 years ahead, the decisions that have to be taken are often influenced to a considerable extent by current trading patterns – what the Treasury wants to ensure is a good trading market for its 30-year issues. This is very important from a debt management point of view.

THE MECHANICS OF THE MARKET[9]

It is pertinent next to look at the mechanics of the market and related Federal Reserve operations. In the USA, the Federal Reserve System is responsible for regulating the money supply, debt management being the responsibility of the Treasury. At several levels, there is effective liaison and regular consultation between the two. Within the Federal Reserve Systen, it is the Federal Open Market Committee (FOMC) which is the most important single monetary policy-making body. It is presided over by the Chairman of the System's Board of Governors, with the President of the Federal Reserve Bank of New York as its permanent Vice-Chairman; he serves on a continuous basis. Other members include the Governors of the System, and four of the Presidents of the other Federal Reserve Banks serving one year in rotation. Rotation is conducted so that each year one member is elected to the Committee by the Board of Directors of each of the following groups of Reserve Banks: (i) Boston, Philadelphia, and Richmond; (ii) Cleveland and Chicago; (iii) Atlanta, St Louis, and Dallas; and (iv) Minneapolis, Kansas City, and San Francisco. The other Presidents (who participate in the policy discussion) and a number of staff officers (who do not participate) also attend, though without votes. Staff members are selected from among the officers and employees of the Board of Governors and the Federal Reserve Banks. And a few key people will present background papers to the meetings of the Committee. Officers include: a Secretary to maintain a record of actions taken by the Committee on all questions of policy; economists to prepare and present to the Committee information regarding business and credit conditions and domestic and international economic and financial developments; General Counsel to furnish such legal advice as the Committee may require; and a Manager and Deputy Managers of the System Open Market Account to execute open market transactions and to report to the Committee on market conditions.

The law requires that meetings of the FOMC be held at least four times each year in Washington, DC, upon the call of the Chairman of the Board of Governors or at the request of any three members of the Committee. Typically, meetings are held eight times a year in the offices of the Board of Governors in Washington, according to a schedule tentatively agreed upon at the beginning of the year. If circumstances require consultation or consideration of an action between these regular meetings, members may be called upon to participate in a special meeting or telephone conference, or to vote on a recommended action by telegram or telephone. At each regular meeting, the Committee votes on the policy to be carried out during the interval between meetings; at least twice a year, the Committee also votes on certain longer-run policy objectives.

Prior to each regular meeting of the Committee, written reports from System staff on past and prospective economic and financial developments are sent to each Committee member and to nonmember Reserve Bank Presidents. Reports prepared by the management of the System Open Market Account on operations in the domestic open market and in foreign currencies since the last regular meeting are also distributed. At the meeting itself, oral reports are given by staff officers on the current and prospective business situation, on conditions in financial markets and on international financial developments. Oral reports on transactions in the System Open Market Account since the previous meeting are given by the Manager or Deputy Managers of the Account.

Following these reports, the committee members and other Reserve Bank Presidents discuss policy. Typically, each participant expresses his or her own views on the state of the economy and prospects for the future, and on the appropriate direction for monetary policy. Then each makes a more explicit recommendation for policy for the coming inter-meeting period (and for the longer term, if under consideration). Finally, the Committee develops a consensus regarding the appropriate course for policy which is incorporated in a directive to the Federal Reserve Bank of New York – the bank selected by the Committee to execute transactions for the System Open Market Account. The directive issued by the FOMC is cast in relatively specific terms so as to provide concrete guidance to the Manager in the conduct of day-to-day open market operations – e.g. the Committee's objectives for longer-term growth in certain key monetary and credit aggregates, as well as short-term operating guides for rates of growth in the monetary aggregates (as represented by M1 and M2) and associated ranges of tolerable changes in money market conditions (as represented by the federal funds rate). In fact, the FOMC sets general guidelines, with the open market desk in New York choosing the timing and the operational amounts, though in this context the New York representatives will also have taken back with them the 'feel' of the meeting.

As already indicated, the Treasury is responsible for debt management in the sense that it will itself largely decide on the types of securities to be issued and the terms on which they will be offered. It will also be responsible for refundings. In other words, it is primarily responsible for changes in the composition of federal debt. Indeed, the last time the Federal Reserve was concerned with a debt-management goal was in the early 1960s.

Meanwhile, whether from a debt-management point of view it attempts to maintain 'neutrality' or not, the Federal Reserve in its role as a central bank will be operating to influence monetary flows by undertaking transactions in the open market, which have become the main basis of quantitative credit regulation in the United States. For the most part, the Fed will deal in Treasury bills; this is also the most common medium in other countries. But the Fed may operate in other securities of longer maturity, as and when this proves to be appropriate.

If the Fed is intervening on a particular day, this will be done – as we have seen – by the Federal Reserve Bank of New York,[10] which is in charge of the System Open Market Account and which, in the matter of open market operations, acts for the Federal Reserve as a whole within a framework provided by the FOMC. This will have made a judgement of the current situation on the basis of information supplied to the meeting. It will also indicate the desired range of growth for M2 and M3 to which the reserve positions of the banks will relate. Likewise, there will be a target (within a range) for the rate on federal funds. In between meetings of the FOMC, there is a telephone conference each day between the Manager of the System Open Market Account (Domestic) in New York, occasionally one of the Governors of the Federal Reserve System, one of the Federal Reserve Bank Presidents currently serving on the FOMC, and a senior staff member of the Federal Reserve Board. A summary of these discussions is then circulated to all the Presidents of the Federal Reserve Banks. Generally speaking, this discussion is very routine – usually the participants defer to the Manager's recommendation as to what action, if any, may be appropriate that day to comply with the FOMC directive.[11] Only if there were a substantial change in underlying economic or monetary conditions not consistent with the possibilities discussed at the last FOMC meeting would there be the need for a full telephonic conference. If a vote were taken, it would be referred to in the FOMC minutes when published (on the Friday after the next meeting).

Intervention for same-day reserve effect is generally undertaken between 11.35 and 11.45 a.m., and operations for next-day delivery[12] would be initiated (if at all) in the early afternoon. Usually, operations with the primary dealers (bank and non-bank) would take the form of a repurchase agreement ('repo') if there is a temporary need to add to reserves, or a reverse 'repo' (or matched sale-purchase agreement) if there is a temporary need to drain reserves from the system. On more infrequent occasions, the Fed purchases or sells securities outright; these transactions are generally announced a day or two in advance in the afternoon. Such purchases or sales would tend to relate to needs that are basically seasonal or secular in character (i.e. if not seasonal, then associated with the growth of the economy).

When the Fed is doing 'repos', the system is to invite bids from all the dealers, giving them about 20 minutes in which to frame their offers whether for themselves or for their customers. The Fed then accepts the best rates that have been offered; the Fed takes them in order until the figure it is aiming at has been attained, though propositions occasionally fall short of the desired volume. Open market operations, which are undertaken with a view to ensuring the availability of adequate reserves, may also take the form of outright purchases. 'Repos' are aways done for cash the same day; outright purchases are done for cash the next day, even sometimes the following day. In theory, the securities wire closes at 2.30 p.m. Another alternative would be to force member banks (or other borrowers) into the Federal Reserve Banks' discount windows.[13] In the event of there being a surplus of money in the market, the Fed could intervene for the purpose of 'mopping up'. In this case, it would resort to reverse 'repos', or matched sale-purchase agreements. This arrangement goes back to 1966. The dealers act as intermediaries for commercial banks with temporarily surplus moneys that they are prepared to place against bills, subject to the Fed repurchasing them a few days later. Matched sale-purchase agreements are also done direct with the non-bank dealers, who may have a surplus cash position.

'Repos' are mostly done by the Fed overnight or over a weekend and occasionally for up to 7 days. (There is authority for doing them for up to 15 days.) In the event of an agreement for a few days, the dealer is given the option to withdraw if he could finance himself more cheaply the next day, or if he sells securities.[14]

It should be noted that effective liaison between the Fed in New York and the government securities dealers is also important, and in New York there are regular discussions of about 15 minutes between the Manager of the System Open Market Account (Domestic) – or his alternate – and the management of each of the dealing houses or dealer banks.[15]

As at 3 January 1992, there were thirty-eight primary dealers – banks, bank holding company subsidiaries, and non-bank dealers. Some dealers are owned by banks, but in varying degrees behave more like non-bank dealers (e.g. in their financing activity). In January 1992, the list of primary dealers was as follows: Bank of America NT & SA; Barclays de Zoete Wedd Securities Inc.; Bear, Stearns & Co. Inc.; BT Securities Corporation; Carroll McEntee & McGinley Incorporated; Chase Securities, Inc.; Chemical Securities, Inc.; Citicorp Securities Markets, Inc.; CRT Government Securities Ltd; Daiwa Securities America Inc.; Dean Witter Reynolds Inc.; Deutsche Bank Government Securities, Inc.; Dillon, Read & Co. Inc.; Discount Corporation of New York; Donaldson, Lufkin & Jenrette Securities Corporation; The First Boston Corporation; First Chicago Capital Markets, Inc.; Fuji Securities Inc.; Goldman, Sachs & Co.; Greenwich Capital Markets, Inc.; Harris Government Securities Inc.; Kidder, Peabody & Co., Incorporated; Aubrey G. Lanston & Co., Inc.; Lehman Government Securities, Inc.; Merrill Lynch Government Securities Inc.; J. P. Morgan Securities Inc.; Morgan Stanley & Co. Incorporated; The Nikko Securities Co. International, Inc.; Nomura Securities International, Inc.; Paine Webber Incorporated;

Prudential Securities Incorporated; Salomon Brothers Inc.; Sanwa-BGK Securities Co., L.P.; Smith Barney, Harris Upham & Co., Inc.; SBC Government Securities Inc.; UBS Securities Inc.; S. G. Warburg & Co., Inc.; and Yamaichi International (America), Inc.

Government securities dealers have three interrelated functions. First, they make two-way markets for customers and stand ready to provide a bid and ask quotation; second, they provide information, analysis, and advice to encourage transactions and customer loyalty; third, they manage their positions, speculating on market trends with a view to profiting from movements in interest rates. The extent to which they maintain an inventory will depend on their outook on interest rates. Spreads are so narrow that dealers cannot afford to maintain an inventory if – for example – rates are expected to rise.

The non-bank government securities dealers finance their positions or inventories in several ways (see p. 113). Bank dealers would be similar, except that they can also draw on the general financing operations of the bank as a whole, i.e. financing the inventory of securities would be regarded as part of the treasury function. Since the financing of a bank's dealing portfolio will have a direct impact on the overall funding position, a bank will often deal through its funding desk. In any event, there must be a close liaison between the dealing room and the funding managers, who will also have links with those in charge of the investment portfolio as such. The funding desk both employs funds and obtains them, and is in short concerned with the general availability of funds to the bank. This is estimated on the basis of all movements of funds throughout the bank. The funding desk will also seek the advice of the analysts who study the seasonal movements and, on this basis, it makes the judgement as to where reserves will be by the end of the day. For example, there is usually a definite weekly/monthly pattern and often a seasonal movement as well. One such latter influence is the low point that follows a tax date – in fact, such points come about half-way between tax dates. It need hardly be added that a much more accurate picture of these movements can now be obtained with the assistance of the computer. The funding desk has to find finance for the dealer department as for the other departments within the bank, the reserve position of the bank being adjusted by means of transactions in federal funds, in which these banks would also deal. Such adjustments would tend to be at the margin. Other techniques would be employed (e.g. purchases and/ or sales of securities or market paper) if the discrepancies were likely to be longer term. The needs of the dealer department not only change from day to day but they can vary quite a lot within one day. For this reason, policy limitations will be set for how much the trading position should be. If the dealer wishes to go over, he must get special approval. But on the whole, he must take positions within the limits laid down. In all other respects, however, the dealer department enjoys quite a high degree of autonomy.

For the most part, dealers' positions or inventories are financed by means of repurchase agreements ('repos'). This would also be true of banks, whether primary dealers or not.[16] 'Repos' may be done with non-financial corporations, states and local governments, and regional commercial banks. The cost of this form of borrowing is the lowest available to the parties concerned. One should also note that those that do 'repos' with dealers would be concerned to do business only with an approved list of dealers. To the extent that the Fed – on its own initiative – also does 'repos' with the dealers, these are likewise helpful in financing portfolios. If in the result there was a last minute acquisition of securities, or if the non-bank dealer had not yet financed the whole of its long position, it would have to go to its 'clearing bank' (one of the big money centre banks) and this loan would generally be expensive – these banks are in effect and in this context the 'lender of last resort'. And if a dealing house had too much money at the end of the day, or was acting as an intermediary for some other party with temporarily excess funds, it could lend this out by way of a reverse 'repo' – i.e. buying securities under an agreement to resell (usually this would be done overnight).

From time to time, dealers will lend securities – i.e. to a house which wishes to do a trade but which does not possess the securities of the type and/or maturity required. This kind of business may be done for a fee, or by way of a reverse 'repo' – i.e. selling securities subject to an agreement to repurchase. Obviously, too, a dealer may from time to time have to borrow securities if it lacks them in portfolio, and again this would be done by way of a 'repo'. Dealers have increasingly had to take over the business of lending securities, since the traditional sources for borrowing securities – like the insurance companies and the large money centre banks – have largely dried up. They have also become intermediaries in the borrowing of securities, as have the federal funds brokers (referred to below).

If a dealer – whether bank or non-bank – is to remain a primary reporting dealer (i.e. reporting to the Market Reports Division of the Fed in New York), it must achieve and maintain 'reasonable standards of activity'. It must also maintain an adequate capital position in order to support the amount of risk it may take on.[17] If it does not maintain reasonable standards of activity, the Fed will drop it from its list. The Federal Reserve expects primary dealers to stand ready to buy and sell Treasury securities even during adverse market conditions. By continually making markets, primary dealers maintain the very important element of liquidity for other investors in government securities. Primary dealers also add to market liquidity by virtue of their comparatively large size, which permits them to buy and sell large quantities of securities. These dealers have extensive customer networks and, as a result, can also provide information to the Federal Reserve Bank of New York and the Treasury on the amounts and types of new Treasury securities that probably will be favoured by their customers.

Comparing primary dealer firms is difficult, because of the diversity of the types of firms. For example, comparable figures for net worth for bank money market operations are not available, because bank capital is not allocated for dealer operations. As a result, bank dealers cannot be compared with non-bank dealers. But even comparing non-bank dealers with each other is difficult, since the average diversified firm registered with the Securities and Exchange Commission (SEC) has a net worth almost ten times greater than unregistered firms. In terms of transaction volume also, the top four non-bank firms account for something more than a quarter of the market, while the bottom four non-bank firms account for something less than 4 per cent.[18]

The advantage of being a primary reporting dealer[19] is largely prestige, and some investors are only willing to conduct their business with such dealers. Despite this, some dealers have been prepared to withdraw – feeling that the game was not worth the candle and that, once the volume of their government securities business fell below the standards required by the Fed, their name would quietly be dropped.[20]

In addition to primary dealers, many other firms routinely trade in US government securities. These include a mix of depository institutions, diversified securities firms, and specialty firms. Some participating firms are as large as primary dealers but have elected not to seek designation as such. Others service clients in a particular region. Still others may specialize in small transactions or odd lots. This diversity is advantageous to investors because it provides them with a greater choice of firms and services. Moreover, many banks (including some investment banks) that are not primary dealers and do not necessarily operate on a continuing basis nevertheless run trading accounts (which are kept separate from their ordinary investment portfolio) and 'make markets' in certain government securities for customers and smaller banks in their areas. Such traders would offer these facilities mainly as a service and it remains true that there is very little money in trading government securities. Indeed, the primary dealers make their money not from dealing but from taking a position and trying to outguess the market in forecasting successfully movements in interest rates. Hence, apart from maintaining a reasonable standard of activity, much of what a primary dealer undertakes is guided mainly by his interest rate expectations. To a significant extent, too, that is what often guides policy with regard to the content of bank investment portfolios.

Non-primary dealers are made up of other, usually smaller, SEC-registered firms, unregistered firms, regional banks, and others. Some of the larger non-primary dealers are larger than the smallest of the primary dealers. The trading volume of the non-primary dealers has been estimated at roughly 25 per cent of total market activity.[21] Non-primary dealers provide a variety of services to the market. Some bid actively at auctions for themselves and their customers, thereby assisting the Treasury to distribute its debt to investors. Also, by seeking out the best quotations available from primary dealers, they lower the search costs for investors. For certain securities they quote 'bid' and 'ask' prices to customers, thereby increasing liquidity in the market and providing competition to primary dealers. They provide investment consulting services to smaller investor customers, giving these customers access to the market. Non-primary dealers also represent a source of potential primary dealers once they are able and willing to meet the Federal Reserve's criteria. The total number of non-primary dealers is unknown, but may be of the order of 200 to 300. As with primary dealers, there is considerable variation in the regulatory status of non-primary dealers. Some are commercial banks, some are institutions regulated by the Securities and Exchange Commission (SEC), and some are specialist firms, or separate subsidiaries of regulated firms that operate outside the federal regulatory structure. Non-primary dealers are not subject to Federal Reserve oversight. They are not required to submit trading or financial data to the Federal Reserve (as primary dealers do daily) and are not subject to the Federal Reserve Bank of New York dealer surveillance visits. Latterly, however, under the Government Securities Act 1986, they have been subject to the oversight of the Treasury.

Then there is the role of the brokers to be considered. There are basically two types of brokers – inter-dealer brokers and retail brokers.[22] Inter-dealer brokers arrange trades between recognized market-makers (primary dealers and firms recognized by the Federal Reserve Bank of New York as aspiring to become primary dealers). Retail brokers arrange trades among all types of market participants that meet the brokers' credit criteria. Formerly, inter-dealer brokers and dealers relied on direct-wire telephone communication for the purpose of undertaking trades in the secondary market. However, during the 1970s, a more sophisticated type of electronic brokerage service appeared in the inter-dealer Treasury market. This was the result of technological change which helped to link the increased number of primary dealers and to overcome inefficiencies in dealer-to-dealer and broker-to-broker telephone communications. In rapidly changing markets, there was not enough time for dealers to learn the quotes of all the other dealers.

In 1974, automated brokerage services were offered to primary dealers in Treasury securities. Brokers providing this service came to be known as 'screen brokers' in contrast to the older 'telephone brokers'. Each primary dealer has video display screens in its offices, provided by the brokers, showing the bid and offered prices of the dealers. A dealer interested in bidding or offering can telephone the broker to offer or accept a displayed quotation. This dealer pays the quoted price plus a commission if buying, and the commission is deducted from the sale price if selling. The screen brokers offered two incentives for primary dealers to use their services. First, their services were fast. New bids and offers appeared on the screen of every dealer at the same time. Second, the usual brokerage commissions were reduced. As limited access brokers, they permit the orderly and anonymous buying and selling of Treasury securities between dealers. The bids and offers appearing on the screens are continuously updated and bid-ask spreads are very narrow. Dealers no longer need to look to one or two other dealers to make an immediate market on an issue; they look to the best quotes of between forty and fifty dealers. These quotations are currently only available to the dealers who can act on them.

The retail brokers also provide for anonymous trading among their clients. In contrast to the other brokers, however, these brokers serve as a principal by guaranteeing the execution of all trades that they arrange as an agent. The retail brokers' customer bases include, in addition to primary and aspiring primary dealers, certain non-primary dealers, regional banks, pension funds, and others whom the brokers consider to be creditworthy trading partners. These customers pay for the right to have access to the price information on the brokers' screens and to trade on the basis of that information. Other investors can see the transaction activity on these screens by subscribing to the financial information services that display it.

Lastly, there are the 'clearing banks'. Several banks act as clearing agents for the settlement of purchases and sales of government securities. A clearing bank processes the information needed to accomplish the transfer of securities from sellers to buyers and the transfer of cash from buyers to sellers, At one time, this function was performed manually, but because of the rapid growth in the market and the Federal Reserve's development of the computer-based book-entry system, clearing is now performed almost entirely by computer. Because of these computer systems, the settlement of such trades is – under normal circumstances – almost instantaneous. Every day thousands of transactions are cleared by the clearing banks, and the clearing banks assist market operations by processing transaction information that would otherwise have to be done by the Federal Reserve itself.

Formerly, the most active market was in Treasury bills, though it has declined in importance since 1984, when the average daily figures for dealer transactions were still about half the total. This was still the position – on the basis of average daily figures – in 1987, but by March 1990 it was below 30 per cent. Meanwhile 1–5 year paper had increased in importance – to 30 per cent. By comparison, dealer transactions in 5–10 year government paper was rather lower – at below 25 per cent. The Fed may also deal in federal agencies. However, for some time now, all such transactions have been limited to repurchase agreements. Although the agency market has grown considerably in size and activity over

the years, it is made up of many more individual issues and these
are generally smaller in size than issues of Treasury securities.
Hence, large market transactions in particular issues would often
be more difficult to execute than in the Treasury coupon area.
Indeed, a good deal of the trading activity in the agency market is
accounted for by the frequency of new offerings and, if the Fed
were to become involved in outright purchases and sales, this might
well result in a significant impact on prices. It might also be viewed
as an attempt to influence market conditions and such an interpretation the Fed is concerned to deny.[23] These problems can be largely
avoided by resorting to 'repos', which – except to the extent that
they affect the volume of reserves – are neutral in their effects.
Quite apart from these considerations, as a result of outright
purchases, the Fed would be faced with frequent maturities.
Treasury bills can be rolled over in the weekly auctions, but this
could not be done with agencies. Hence, there was again a preference for 'repos', which can be carried out quite impersonally.
Whether they are done or not, and in what items, depends on what
dealers are holding in inventory. The federal agencies include the
Federal Housing Administration, the Government National Mort-
gage Association, the Export–Import Bank, the Farmers' Home
Administration, the Maritime Adminstration, the Small Business
Administration, the Tennessee Valley Authority, the Washington
Metropolitan Area Transit Authority, and the Postal Service. The
federally-sponsored agencies include the Farm Credit System,
Federal Home Loan Banks, the Federal Home Loan Mortgage
Corporation, the Federal National Mortgage Association, and the
Student Loan Marketing Association. Actually, the Fed only does
'repos' in the securities of the sponsored agencies.

FEDERAL FUNDS MARKET

One of the chief purposes of a money market is to facilitate
monetary adjustment by banks and other financial institutions. To
the extent that the banks lend to the non-bank government securities dealers, they can adjust their cash positions by varying the
amounts put out either on the basis of repurchase agreements or (if
they are large New York banks) as call loans. In addition, they can
adjust their cash reserves by resort to the market for federal funds.
These are entitlements to balances with one of the twelve Federal
Reserve Banks, which with the Federal Reserve Board of Governors

in Washington comprise the central banking system of the USA. Based initially on the temporarily surplus balances of member banks of the System with the several Federal Reserve Banks, the federal funds market has latterly been extended to include virtually all depository institutions (comprehending, for example, not only banks and savings banks, but also savings and loan associations and credit unions) – since, under the Depository Institutions Deregulation and Monetary Control Act 1980 (also known as the Monetary Control Act), all these institutions were now required to hold reserves with the Federal Reserve System, and not just the member banks as was formerly the case.

The federal funds market originated in New York City, the first trades being made between several of the leading city bankers in the early summer of 1921. But it was not really until the 1950s that it developed into a national market, which was formerly used by the majority of the larger banks and which is now used by banks large and small in the US both as an outlet for surplus funds and as a source of borrowings. Federal funds, it should be noted, are immediately available to the purchaser.[24]

The development of the federal funds market during the 1950s owed much to the initiative of a New York Stock Exchange firm which acted as a broker. This was Garvin, Bantel & Co., which became Garvin GuyButler, and which set up a clearing desk to maintain regular contact both with banks having funds to sell and with prospective buyers. Today, there are five main federal funds brokers. The main brokers are Prebon Money Brokers Inc. (this used to be Mabon Nugent), Garvin GuyButler Corp., Lasser Marshall Inc., Noonan, Astley & Pearce, Inc., and Eurobrokers Inc. All the big banks use the brokers to some extent; brokers know what is going on in the market as a whole. It is much quicker very often to do business through the brokers and also easier to pick up volume. With the considerable growth in total transactions that took place in the 1950s, banks in New York and other key cities also became active as dealers in federal funds – often buying and selling more or less continuously throughout the day and without reference to their own reserve position, which was averaged over the reserve period. These banks dealt as principals and traded on both sides of the market. Latterly, big banks have tried to avoid this. It inflates the balance sheet and requires additional capital if capital adequacy is to be maintained.

The use made of brokers, which for overnight federal funds

charge a commission of 50 cents per million,[25] is most important in money market centres and particularly in New York, where it may be as high as 70–75 per cent of a bank's federal fund transactions. More commonly, it is 60 : 40 in favour of direct deals, with an emphasis on the purchasing side. Brokers tend to believe that their figures are higher – as much as 70–80 per cent of the total, though the brokers would include funds fed into regional (and other) banks, which are grossed up and often sold on through brokers. On the other hand, there are banks where 95 per cent of federal funds transactions by volume (99 per cent by tickets) would be done direct and very little goes through brokers. In the case of small correspondent banks (see below), all deals would be done direct. The World Bank in Washington, which does a lot of business in Fed funds, has direct lines, but also uses brokers, partly 'to get the feel of the market'. So do the commercial banks.

In the earlier years, the use made of the federal funds market not only varied considerably between one institution and another, but also between different parts of the country. This was attributed largely to time differences. By the early 1960s, however, banks in New Orleans and in Denver that had previously stood aloof from the market were now a regular part of it, and even quite small banks were able to use its facilities as a result of their city correspondents resorting to a collateralized loan technique. Then, in June 1963, the Comptroller of the Currency ruled that federal funds transactions were no longer subject to the borrowing and lending limits applicable to national banks,[26] though state statutes were not generally given a similar interpretation. Nevertheless, this Federal decision opened the door to the much more widespread participation by banks of all sizes in the federal funds market. As a result, though centred on New York, the market became truly nationwide.

From the late 1960s onwards, small banks were selling their federal funds to a city correspondent in their area. The latter collected funds and added them to their own positions (to some extent, the selling of federal funds by country banks took the place of keeping correspondent balances with a city bank or holding Treasury bills; entry into the federal funds market had the obvious advantage that the country bank earned interest on its money and at a good rate). Indeed, on this basis, regional areas developed their own markets – e.g. at Philadelphia, Pittsburg and Denver – and banks in these centres then fed funds into the major markets in New York and Chicago. Also, some regional and money centre banks might employ such moneys to fund their own loans and investments. Nowadays, a definite system has evolved with respect to the Fed funds transactions of the smaller banks. Both regional and money centre banks have a developed correspondent bank business. *Inter alia*, country banks and small suburban banks feed funds into the city banks and hold a 'core' balance with them in federal funds, which may be as low as $1 million and which runs on more or less continuously and to which they can add, or from which they can draw, as necessary. On some estimates, 60–80 per cent of these funds is lent on a rollover basis. But these are not defined as 'term' federal funds. This system was definitely in place by the early 1970s. Formerly, and up to the mid-1970s, the city correspondent required a small margin for this service,[27] which could involve transactions as small as $100,000 in multiples of $25,000. Today, depending on the degree of inter-bank competition in a city, the 'turn' may be shaved to $\frac{1}{16} - \frac{1}{8}$ per cent, though until recently it could on occasion be as high as $\frac{1}{4}$ per cent. On the whole, however, a city bank's interest in these transactions is not as a dealer in federal funds but reflects its interest in correspondent banking, i.e. it is done to accommodate their correspondents. For many city banks this is still regarded as an important business and one where it pays to remain competitive.

Some of the large money centre banks (especially in New York) would rarely go down as low as $100,000 or $250,000 for a direct federal funds transaction; for small banks $500,000 or $1 million would be much more common and from $1 million to $5 million would be a usual minimum for banks of any size, with median transactions being from $5 million to $10 million; there can also be really large transactions from time to time – e.g. $100 million.[28] In all cases, however, internal limits are applied (i.e. both for sales and purchases, banks apply limits to the size of transaction they will do with individual banks; these are not announced or advised – though it is easy to work them out and they are often known to brokers). Brokers may also be advised of institutions to which a bank does not wish to lend. Limits and approved lists of institutions are common for all types of money market transactions.

As well as between banks, transactions take place also with the larger savings and loan associations (though more usually with one of their central institutions – a Federal Home Loan Bank)[29] and sometimes with savings banks or large credit unions (or their 'centrals').

Money positions will be known to the various banks and other financial institutions early on a particular day, though they would have to be adjusted continuously for large transactions during the course of that day. It should be noted, too, that as part of the function of dealing in federal funds, there used to be a lot of interest arbitrage – funds were bought in to be sold out again with a spread. This was quite general, but most banks do very little of this now, since capital requirements were increased.

The bulk of federal fund lendings and borrowings are overnight – even the rolling over of a 'core' balance is technically an overnight transaction. In addition, there are term federal funds – moneys lent for (say) 1 week to 1 year. Many of the trades tend to be done for 30, 60, or 90 days. Term Fed funds in fact go back a number of years, but they have become important (say) over the past 5–10 years, though latterly with the opening up of International Banking Facilities (IBFs) Eurodollars have tended to take over much of this business. The term Fed funds market is used extensively by 'agency' banks – foreign banks that lack a deposit base and which need to buy money in (formerly, these included the Japanese banks, which now tend to use Eurodollars). Apart from the foreign banks, the market is between (as takers) big money centre banks and (as lenders) savings and loan associations, Federal Home Loan Banks, and Farm Credit Banks. Large domestic banks borrow term federal funds whenever all-in cost is less than that for CDs or Eurodollars. Some large banks trade in term federal funds; as a result of buying and selling, they often get mismatched positions and at times they may have to cover. But they regularly keep the mismatch in view. Term federal funds are also used for the general funding of the bank – they are not used just as a trading exercise. A deal of $5 million is common. The rate is fixed for the period of the term. No reserves are required against Fed funds (term or otherwise), nor any FDIC insurance, though this would be necessary with a certificate of deposit. As with overnight Fed funds, where the business is done by word of mouth, term federal funds are not secured and no note is issued – just a confirmation. With term Fed funds, it is estimated that about 90 per cent of the deals go through brokers.

Over the years, the number of banks in this market (including many small banks) has increased greatly. There is now no reason why banks anywhere should not have access to the federal funds market and, with the ready availability of correspondent relationships, small banks should not in this context have any difficulty at all. One final point should be made. The operations of the federal funds market in no way increase or decrease total member bank reserves. What the market does is to increase their availability by redistributing them, and this makes possible a fuller use of bank reserves and resources.

DAYLIGHT OVERDRAFTS

One of the phenomena that has occasioned great concern in the US in recent years – with implications *inter alia* for the markets both in US government securities and in federal funds – is the daylight overdraft. These exist in part because of market conventions for particular types of financial transactions.[30] Thus, in the markets for repurchase agreements, federal funds, Eurodollars, commercial paper, and large certificates of deposit, borrowers commonly repay funds in the morning but do not receive newly borrowed funds until later the same day. Repayments frequently occur even if a borrower renews, or rolls over, a maturing money market obligation with the same lender for an identical amount.

> Because the sum of such repayments can exceed an institution's reserve account balance, this institutional practice often creates a daylight overdraft that might last for three hours or more. A similar pattern – payments made in anticipation of funds to be received later the same day – is associated with certain types of third party payments. This pattern has evolved, in part, because depository institutions in the United States are not required, and many institutions have little incentive, to maintain positive reserve account balances during the day.[31]

Again, a convention leading to daylight overdrafts obtains in the government securities market:

> A buyer of government securities receives the accrued interest as of the originally scheduled settlement date. However, the buyer is not required to take delivery and make payment until the full amount of the securities involved in a transaction is actually delivered. When a seller fails to make timely and proper delivery of all securities in a transaction, the seller or its clearing bank typically incurs the cost of financing the securities overnight but must pass on all of the accrued interest to the buyer. Hence, a failed delivery causes the seller to lose interest for one day.

Because this interest cost increases with the size of the transaction, sellers have an incentive to build intraday securities
positions so they will be able to complete delivery of their largest
orders first. In building such positions, clearing banks make payments for securities they receive on behalf of themselves and
dealer customers. These payments result in substantial amounts
of daylight overdrafts on the reserve accounts of the clearing
banks; the overdrafts remain until securities held in position are
delivered against payment in the late morning or afternoon.[32]

It is reported that on a typical day about 1,100 depository institutions in the US incur daylight overdrafts totalling more than
$80 billion on the two large-value funds transfer systems. These
overdrafts last anywhere from several minutes to nearly all day. On
an average day, another $60 billion of overdrafts result from
transfers over the Federal Reserve's book-entry securities transfer
system.[33] There are two systems for the electronic transfer of large
dollar payments operating in the US. These are the Fedwire funds
transfer system and the Clearing House Interbank Payments
System (CHIPS). In addition, a 'book entry securities system' for
the electronic transfer of US government, agency, and other
securities operates on Fedwire.

The Federal Reserve's concern with daylight overdrafts relates to
its several roles – as a provider of payment services, as a banking
supervisor, and as a lender of last resort. Payments made on
Fedwire are final in the sense that a Federal Reserve Bank irrevoc-
ably credits the account of an institution receiving a payment once
the Reserve Bank has notified the receiver of the sender's payment
message. As a result, if the sending institution with a daylight overdraft were unable to cover the overdraft by the end of the day, the
Federal Reserve Bank would absorb any resulting loss. Fedwire
finality has the benefit of insulating the banking system as a whole
from the potential consequences of the settlement failure of the
sending institution. The Federal Reserve has also been concerned
about 'systemic risk' on private wire transfer systems – the
possibility that one institution's inability to settle could cause other
institutions to fail to settle. Originally, if an institution with a net
debit position on CHIPS was unable to settle at the end of the day,
CHIPS rules allowed for deleting from the end-of-day settlement
all payment messages involving that institution during that day.
However, deletion of payment messages might have had the effect

of creating large unanticipated changes in the net settlement positions of other participants, who in turn might have been unable to cover their recalculated settlement obligations. In the context of Federal Reserve concern with daylight overdrafts, policy was therefore directed towards the direct financial risk incurred by the Federal Reserve on Fedwire, on the one hand, and the systemic risk on private wire networks, on the other. A related concern was to ensure the effective functioning of the payments system. After several years of study by the Federal Reserve and banking industry groups, the Federal Reserve Board adopted a policy in May 1985 aimed at addressing these matters. All features of that policy were put into effect by March 1986. The Federal Deposit Insurance Corporation, the Office of the Comptroller of the Currency, the Federal Home Loan Bank Board, and the National Credit Union Administration have all supported the Federal Reserve's payments risk policy and, along with state banking supervisors, have co-operated with the Federal Reserve in administering it.

By 1987, the Federal Reserve's policy to limit risk in the payments system had three major components:

(1) all private large-dollar transfer networks obtaining Federal Reserve net settlement services required each participant to establish a limit on its net daylight exposure to each other participant ('bilateral net credit limits'); these networks also had to adopt limits on the intraday net debit positions of each participant *vis-à-vis* all other participants as a group ('network sender net debit caps');

(2) each depository institution participating in a private large-dollar transfer network or incurring daylight overdrafts on Fedwire had to establish a limit on its combined overdrafts on all large dollar networks ('cross-system sender net debit caps'); and

(3) daylight overdrafts resulting from transfers of US government and agency securities through the Federal Reserve book-entry system were exempt from sender net debit caps. And effective from 14 January 1988, the Federal Reserve established a $50 million limit for each transfer of securities processed on its book-entry system.

The Federal Reserve monitors on an *ex-post* basis the level of overdrafts of all participants in all wire systems subject to its policy, and counsels those institutions whose overdrafts exceed their cross-system limits. Also, the Federal Reserve imposes real-time controls on reserve account overdrafts of troubled institutions. Reserve Banks may ask such institutions to post collateral for daylight overdrafts and may delay Fedwire payments that would lead to overdrafts in excess of collateral values.

So far as private networks were concerned, CHIPS – which was the only private, large-dollar, wire-transfer network that received net settlement from the Federal Reserve – established bilateral credit limits in October 1984. Participants could set their limits for any dollar amount and might change these limits at any time during the business day. If a participant attempted to make a payment that would cause it to exceed a receiver's net bilateral credit limit, the CHIPS operating system automatically rejected the payment. In setting individual bilateral credit limits, CHIPS participants therefore had some incentive to monitor the creditworthiness of other participants, because of costs they might incur in a settlement failure. These costs would presumably be related to their bilateral exposures to the participant that failed to meet its settlement obligations. However, the presence of systemic risk – the chance that one participant's settlement failure could trigger such failures by other participants – implied that bilateral caps might not fully reflect all the costs of a settlement failure.

In accordance with the Federal Reserve Board's policy, CHIPS also implemented 'network sender net debit caps' in October 1985. Although the Board's policy did not stipulate a specific method for setting these caps, their purpose was to limit the aggregate amount of daylight overdrafts that any one participant could incur on an individual private network. The sum of all bilateral credit limits measured the extent to which, in the aggregate, other institutions in the network were willing to extend daylight credit to the participant whose cap was being established. However, because they were based on individually determined bilateral credit limits, the network sender net debit caps themselves might not have reflected completely the costs due to systemic risk. Then, after 4 years of discussion between interested staff at the Federal Reserve Bank of New York (in electronic payments, legal, loans and credits areas) and risk managers, operations staff and lawyers from CHIPS and the clearing banks, positive steps were taken to reduce the risk associated with a participant failing to settle at the end of a day. On 1 October 1990, CHIPS implemented new rules and procedures calculated significantly to improve the finality of the approximately

$1 trillion in payments each day that go over the private inter-bank funds transfer network. The new rules established an explicit loss-sharing arrangement and required participants to post collateral to cover their potential obligation.

The Federal Reserve was also especially concerned that its payments risk policy avoided disrupting the market for US government securities, which included issues of the US Treasury and of federal and federally sponsored agencies and certain other securities. Its policy therefore imposed no quantitative restrictions on those overdrafts resulting from book-entry transfers of such securities. This was because:

(1) The Fed of New York implemented monetary policy through transactions with primary dealers in government securities. Restrictions on book-entry overdrafts could limit the amount of trading that primary dealers would be able to conduct at a given moment and thus could hinder the timely execution of open-market operations.

(2) In operating the securities portion of the transfer system, the Federal Reserve Banks were acting on behalf of the US Treasury. In this capacity, the Federal Reserve sought to minimize the Treasury's borrowing costs by keeping transactions costs for market trading of book-entry securities as low as possible, subject to meeting objectives for monetary policy and the soundness of the financial system.

It was difficult to develop methods for reducing risk from book-entry overdrafts that would avoid disrupting the execution of monetary policy while maintaining low trading costs for market participants. The Federal Reserve therefore decided in July 1987 to continue the exemption of book-entry related overdrafts from direct quantitative limits and to examine alternatives for reducing risk due to these overdrafts. At that time, however, the Federal Reserve also amended its original policy on payments system risk to address more immediately the risks in book-entry operations. With effect from 14 January 1988, all Reserve Banks imposed a $50 million par-value limit on the size of individual transfers of book-entry government securities other than those resulting from allocations of new issues to dealers or from redemptions of maturing issues. This limit was expected to reduce incentives for position building, thereby inducing dealers to deliver securities earlier in the day and operating with lower levels of book-entry overdrafts.

Under the amended policy, the Fed of New York will monitor primary dealers, while all Reserve Banks are to monitor depository institutions in their own districts that are major users of the book-entry system. The purpose of this monitoring was to ensure that participants establish policies and follow procedures for controlling risk associated with book-entry overdrafts. If a Reserve Bank found such actions to be inadequate in controlling risk, the Reserve Bank might take steps such as requiring collateral or monitoring overdrafts in real time to limit its own risk exposure. By the first quarter of 1989, all Reserve Banks were to implement real-time monitoring of book-entry overdrafts – in which overdrafts are measured as they are created – to replace the previous system in which overdrafts were measured at a later time.[34]

Other methods for reducing payments system risk[35] might include intraday netting of payments and receipts; this would be used to reduce payment time gaps and daylight overdrafts. Funding techniques could be used to reduce daylight overdrafts – e.g. term or multi-day funds instead of overnight funds. An alternative would be rollovers and continuing contracts. Forms of pricing might be employed. Thus, the market might put a different price on over-night dollars depending on the time of day the deal was done – e.g. dollars at 8.00 a.m. are of more value to a banker than dollars at 4.00 p.m. Again, explicit fees or charges for Fedwire daylight credit might be expected to create incentives for depository institutions to reduce Fedwire overdrafts, thereby reducing direct Federal Reserve risk and contributing to economic efficiency. The establishment of liquidity reserves to cover daylight overdrafts on Fedwire, or even on private systems like CHIPS, was another possible method of reducing payments system risk and there were a number of other proposals.[36]

Although much less important than the markets in government securities and federal funds, those in bankers' acceptances, commercial paper, and negotiable certificates of deposit (CDs) also deserve mention, as does the external extension of the US markets into Eurodollars.

BANKERS' ACCEPTANCES[37]

Following the establishment of the Federal Reserve System, the authorities gave active support to the establishment of a market in bankers' acceptances. During the 1920s, it was relatively significant, but it shrank rather badly in the 1930s. After the Second World War, there was a revival in dollar volume. The market for dollar-denominated bankers' acceptances grew rapidly throughout the 1970s and into the early 1980s. The expanding dollar volume of US and world trade, and sharp increases in the price of oil and other commodities whose shipment is frequently financed with accept-ances, stimulated the growth of the market through this period. In addition, the surge in market interest rates during the late 1970s greatly increased the value of the exemption of bankers' accept-ances from reserve requirements. As a result, the proportions of US and world trade that were financed with dollar acceptances rose substantially. By the early 1980s, however, many major accepting banks were unable to accommodate further increases in demand for acceptance credit because they had reached statutory limits on the amount of acceptances they could create. As a result, regional banks and US agencies and branches of foreign banks (e.g. the Japanese and the French) were able to expand their presence in this market, but not sufficiently to keep the growth of the market from slowing or fees charged by accepting banks from rising significantly.

This restriction on supply encouraged proposals for remedial legislation and in October 1982 Congress passed the Bank Export Services Act, which effectively doubled the statutory limits on acceptances. As anticipated, immediately following passage of this legislation the volume of acceptance financing increased consider-ably and fees declined substantially as the major accepting banks attempted to regain their market share. In early 1983, however, the acceptance market began to contract; this continued until 1986. There was some recovery in 1987. Many analysts regarded the stag-nation of international trade and sharp declines in commodity prices as the primary reasons for the shrinkage of the market in bankers' acceptances. Although these factors undoubtedly played a role, the substitution of alternative sources of credit appears to have been more important. The shrinkage of the bankers' accept-ance market is symptomatic of the declining role of US banks as direct providers of short-term credit to foreign banks and multi-national non-financial corporations. Increasingly, such borrowers have obtained funding directly from domestic and foreign non-bank investors in the US commercial paper market and in the Eurodollar markets. In addition, sharp declines in market interest rates after mid-1982 reduced the cost of reserve requirements, thereby allowing bank loans to compete more actively with acceptance credit.[38]

By end-December, 1991, total US dollar acceptances amounted to $43.77 billion.[39] There had been a decline in the figures in 10 months in 1991; only in January and October had there been month-to-month increases. Of this total, acceptances financing goods stored in, or shipped between, foreign countries – known as third-country trade acceptances – amounted to $16.2 billion. US import acceptances totalled $12.84 billion, while acceptances created to finance US exports were $10.35 billion. Acceptances to finance the shipment and storage of goods within the US (which would need to be secured by a warehouse receipt) were $4.38 billion. Sales by issuing banks in that month reached $12.74 billion, of which $7.26 billion was sold to dealers in the open market and $5.48 billion was sold directly to banks' customers. At that time, too, banks held in their portfolios $9.35 billion of their own acceptances as well as $1.67 billion of the outstanding obligations of other issuers. About 71.4 per cent of total acceptances is generated in the New York Federal Reserve district and 63.6 per cent of the remainder in the San Francisco district. Next in order of importance is Chicago.

Bankers' acceptances in the US are trade related. If they are not, they are ineligible at the Federal Reserve for a collateralized advance – the Federal Reserve have discontinued rediscounting assets. Hence they can come in all sorts of odd amounts. However, for trading purposes, bankers' acceptances are often broken up, for example, into amounts of $1 million, $250,000, and a 'tail'. Banks may also trade them down to $500,000. Frequently, they are put together as 'packages' (where one can get a bunch of similar dates), when a median figure for a package would be $5 million, which means that some 'blocks' of acceptances could be larger (e.g. $7.5 million). Odd amounts give rise to 'tails', which are accommodated in a separate document. They may be held in portfolio by a bank until maturity, or sold retail to small businesses with money to invest, or to a wealthy individual, or the odd amounts may be pooled, when a bank would sell a participation in the pool (with the customer receiving a participation certificate). To meet the needs of customers, a bank may also buy in other banks' acceptances and place them in the retail market. As already indicated, more bankers' acceptances are sold to dealers in the open market than are sold direct to investors – if one wants to move quickly, one goes through a dealer – but a number of banks now have a big staff marketing their paper direct and prefer this to operating through a dealer. The most frequent original maturity – or tenor – for a banker's acceptance is 90 days. Eligible acceptances must have an original maturity of 6 months or less.

The principal investors are institutions – money market mutual funds, trust departments, state and local governments, insurance companies and other corporations, pension funds, foreign central banks, and commercial banks. Smaller denomination acceptances may be placed directly with individuals by the accepting bank.

Some acceptances do not arise from the shipment or storage of goods. For example, a firm may draw a draft on its bank for acceptance in order to borrow funds for working capital purposes. Such acceptances are termed 'finance bills'. This paper – if accepted by a reputable bank – is marketable at least to some extent (even though it is not eligible) because it has a good bank name on it. It is reported, however, that today few ineligible acceptances trade in the secondary market.

COMMERCIAL PAPER

Much larger than the market in bankers' acceptances is that in commercial paper – at 1 January 1992, total commercial paper outstanding amounted to $526.8 billion. This paper consists of short-term unsecured promissory notes of industrial, commercial, utility and financial borrowers, which is placed on the market either through dealers or direct. It is generally sold on a discounted basis[40] to institutional investors. It is viewed by them as a high-quality instrument, and this is based either on the creditworthiness of the issuer or on the credit backing of an insurance company or bank. Included in commercial paper is 'finance paper', much of which is placed direct by large finance companies (like GMAC and CIT) and latterly also by some of the conglomerates. The paper of non-financial companies would be mainly placed through dealers, but some of its would be placed direct.[41]

Commercial paper notes, which are issued in bearer form, are exempt from SEC registration and prospectus requirements, provided they are issued under one of the exemptions listed in the Securities Act of 1933. The most frequently used exemption is Section 3(a)(3), whereby commercial paper can be used to finance 'current transactions' such as working capital requirements. Commercial paper can be issued on an overnight basis and the longest permissible maturity is 270 days: the norm is probably

15–45 days and the median 30 days. It remains a physical delivery instrument. Under a second exemption – Section 4(2) – issuers are also employing commercial paper for longer-term purposes. (The use of Master Notes will be referred to later.) Commercial paper is being used, too, in conjunction with such products as financial futures and foreign exchange to capitalize further on its relatively low costs. Towards the latter part of 1986, for example, there was the 'universal commercial paper' introduced by Goldman Sachs. This is issued in the US and sold to US investors, but denominated in a foreign currency. Goldman Sachs then synthetically creates an equivalent dollar-denominated instrument through the FOREX market, converting the proceeds of the borrowing back into dollars for the company concerned. This intricate package means that US companies can borrow in dollars but attract a different stable of investors who wish to have non-dollar debt. Goldman Sachs arranged its first universal commercial paper programme in 1986 and subsequently did about twenty similar deals with a volume of about $4 billion in 1987. There are currently about 1,700 commercial paper issuers, not all of whom are active at any one time either selling their notes directly or through a commercial paper dealer.

For 1 January 1992, the amount of commercial paper out-standing in the US was $526.8 billion. Of this, $402.3 billion related to financial companies,[42] $221.1 billion being placed through dealers and $181.1 billion being placed directly. Non-financial companies[43] (where the paper would be placed mainly by dealers) accounted for $124.5 billion. Bank-related paper is a component of financial company paper and in the US is normally issued by bank holding companies, often being sold off as its agent by the lead bank in the group. The proceeds may be 'downstreamed' to the bank, or used to finance subsidiary companies (e.g. finance, leasing, and factoring companies). Foreign banks also issue commercial paper in the US. It is sometimes said that paper placed directly is slightly cheaper than paper placed through dealers, but dealers can at times issue commercial paper at better rates than direct issuers; also dealers have the advantage that they have a whole range of paper on offer and therefore it can be more economical to satisfy one's needs on the basis of a single phone call.

The chief advantage of commercial paper financing is its low cost – both on the basis of interest cost and also when associated fees (e.g. the rating fee and the cost of liquidity back-up by way of bank lines or a revolving credit) have been added to calculate the all-in cost. It has generally been lower than bank lending rates (e.g. LIBOR plus a margin, or a rate based on 'cost of funds' – CDs or federal funds). There is also a financing flexibility: an organization with large, complex, or rapidly changing funding needs will certainly have established bank credit lines; the commercial paper market provides it with direct access to an alternative funding source and a variety of institutional investors; it can be used in addition to, or in place of, bank lines of credit, depending on relative costs. Furthermore, a company can tailor its paper issuance and maturity dates to its own – or customers' – expected cash requirements. And the market's operational efficiency makes it possible to respond to unexpected needs very rapidly. Finally, it establishes a 'market presence' among institutional investors and other debt and equity market participants. Buyers of commercial paper include bank trust departments, other financial institutions, pension funds, insurance companies, and corporations. The issuing process also involves establishment of commercial paper ratings by one or more debt rating agencies. Establishment of a long-term debt rating is also simpler for a firm with established paper ratings.

At the same time, the impact of commercial paper on bank lending will in some quarters be regarded as a major disadvantage. In other words, competition from the issue of commercial paper has pushed the banks' corporate lending to lower levels, despite the introduction of a certain amount of short-term 'cost of funds' lending. Loss of interest income has led the banks to seek fee income to an increasing extent and latterly (see p. 135) they have begun to move into the field of underwriting and placing commercial paper as well.

By 1991, there were some sixteen dealers responding to the regular survey of commercial paper conducted by the Federal Reserve Bank of New York (and involved domestically). Of these, Merrill Lynch (which bought A. G. Becker, the former Chicago firm, from Paribas) and Goldman Sachs are the largest, with Lehmans a close third and First Boston somewhat smaller. The first three would do 70–75 per cent of the dealer business. And the dealers as a whole would do between 50 per cent and 55 per cent of total commercial paper business. The business done by the new bank dealers is small – the cost of entry is high and the margins very thin; the interest of the banks in this business is largely to create and maintain relationships with customers. Indeed, the advantage to the dealers generally of being in this business is largely the other business they attract in bonds and equities, since the margins on commercial paper are small. They also undertake other types of financing business. The dealers operate as principals – not as brokers – but inventory only represents a small percentage of the total outstanding for a particular firm (e.g. not much more than 1 per cent). Indeed, much of this is its own paper which has been bought back from investors wishing to disinvest (whether temporarily or not). The secondary market is very small. On the whole, paper is bought to be held and can always be tailored to meet the customers' needs. So far as the dealer is concerned, the paper may be disposed of the same day, or it may stay in inventory for 4 or 5 days. The minimum size of an issue would be $100,000, though this is very rarely seen, and most transactions are for $5 million (5 × $1 million to provide market flexibility).

Although commercial paper is used primarily for short-term finance, there are ways in which the maturity may be extended and accommodation be provided more or less semi-permanently. Thus, the paper may be 'rolled over' on a floating rate basis, the rate being revised (say) every 30 days. Resort to *Master Notes* is another way of extending the availability of accommodation. Such a Note may state that the issuer of commercial paper can borrow for a minimum of (say) $1 million up to (say) $25 million; it will also indicate a basis for pricing – e.g. whether the pricing is based on overnight rates, or whether it varies from week to week; indeed, it may be fixed for any period of time up to 180 days. In this case, the paper would be interest-bearing and would be issued direct. Master Notes may be used when a lender has fluctuating amounts of excess money available. They were originally set up to meet the needs of trust companies and the trust departments of banks, which regularly put together odd amounts and gross them up for investment purposes. For example, a direct issuer like GMAC may approach a number of trust departments of banks, or a trust company subsidiary, with a view to them investing short-term a flow of small sums within the framework of a Master Note. Moneys from various trust accounts can be invested in this way; typically the daily fluctuations in the total outstanding are small. For the issuer, Master Notes provide a dependable source of funds and reduce bookkeeping costs, though the rate paid may be slightly higher than on short-term commercial paper. Hence, issuers tend to limit the amount taken in under Master Notes – which would typically be well below half of their total outstandings.[44] Master Notes would normally be reviewed annually. A somewhat similar instrument is the *Discount Note* issued by federal agencies and the World Bank, which qualify as quality paper. In this case, the World Bank is in direct competition with the federal agencies. The World Bank issues through a syndicate of five dealers – they do not really need the money; they do it to keep their hand in (just in case long-term money becomes difficult to obtain); the proceeds would be invested immediately in federal funds with a small spread. They have geared themselves to the Discount Note market, because they get better rates than on commercial paper. Maturities are from 5 to 360 days, with better rates obtainable in the 60–90 day area, where they operate. Issues are now done on a book-entry basis.

Reference has already been made to the emergence of the banks as underwriters and placers of commercial paper. The first bank to attempt to embark on this type of activity was Bankers Trust in New York. Then, in February 1986, a US Federal Court in Washington issued a permanent injunction preventing Bankers Trust from distributing commercial paper to take effect on 1 March of that year. This came after a Federal Court ruling that Bankers Trust's commercial paper activities – previously permitted by the Federal Reserve – violated Federal law – only Federal Congress could allow banks to operate in the US commercial paper market. The case went to appeal. Later, in December 1986, the Federal Reserve Board gave Bankers Trust permission to sell commercial paper through a subsidiary – Bankers Trust Commercial Corporation. This would take over the commercial paper placement activities of Bankers Trust. The Fed said that placement of commercial paper did not constitute 'underwriting' as defined by the Glass-Steagal Act, which separates investment from commercial banking, because no public offerings were involved in commercial paper placement, but it limited its share of the total dealer-placed commercial paper market to 5 per cent (since revised to 10 per cent), provided also that underwriting revenues (including commercial paper business) did not make up more than 5 per cent of Bankers Trust Commercial Corporation's total revenues. So that even if the Glass-Steagal Act applied, the banks would not be engaging 'principally' in the underwriting of securities. (For further developments, see below.) By end-April 1987, after much deliberation, the Fed approved applications by J. P. Morgan, Citicorp, and Bankers Trust to underwrite and deal in commercial paper, mortgage-backed securities and municipal revenue bonds. The Fed had already permitted Bankers Trust and Chase Manhattan to begin selling commercial paper and the latest approvals meant that the commercial banks now had the power to enter the commercial paper market.

Subsequently, the US Supreme Court, without comment, left intact a US Appeal Court decision (of December 1986) that banks may place commercial paper, although it did not rule on the controversial question of whether they were permitted to underwrite commercial paper. This was the subject of a separate lawsuit before the courts. The Supreme Court decision ended an 8-year legal battle, which began when the Securities Industry Association (the main trade association of Wall Street's investment banks) challenged a decision by Bankers Trust to enter the rapidly growing US commercial paper business. Bankers Trust and other money centre banks interested in this field were thus enabled to continue to operate as before, i.e. placing commercial paper as an agent and for a commission. But in August 1987 the Senate Banking Committee slapped a moratorium on aspiring banks, the intention being to prevent any extension of bank powers for a year, while the case was studied. In June 1988, the US Supreme Court left intact a Federal Appeals Court ruling that the Federal Reserve Board had correctly interpreted the Glass-Steagal Act in granting approval for Bankers Trust Corporation subsidiaries to underwrite various securities, including commercial paper.

Later still,[45] bank holding company subsidiaries were authorized *inter alia* to underwrite and deal in 'bank-ineligible securities' (which includes commercial paper) – consistent with Section 20 of the Glass-Steagal Act – up to a revenue limit of 10 per cent (previously 5 per cent) of total revenues. In addition to the revenue limitation, the Federal Reserve Board had established a number of prudential limitations on the conduct of this activity and these were continued. The Board made it clear, however, that its approval extended only to the ineligible securities underwriting and dealing activities previously approved for individual bank holding companies and did not expand the types of securities any applicant had previously received authority to underwrite and deal in.

Although things have changed greatly in the commercial paper market since its origins in the nineteenth century, when paper was said often to be bought 'by the inch' (i.e. on the basis of a certain quantity without reference to the names), it is still not a homogeneous market – there is both a large number of names and a wide range of creditworthiness reflected in the rating of this paper. A-1 names have been greatly reduced since the early 1980s, when a number were downgraded and those that remained tended to be 'cash-rich' and not in need of finance. Yet 85 per cent of the remaining names would today be rated A-1 (Standard & Poor) or P-1 (Moody's), and the other 15 per cent would still be good companies. Overall, therefore, the quality of commercial paper is very good. It is known that one firm sells unrated paper, but this is an exception and the amount is small. Because of competition for the business, the spread is very tight and margins are thin. The difference between A-1/P-1 paper and A-2/P-2 paper is about 10 basis points.

Highly rated companies that do issue commercial paper include: industrial corporations like Merck and AT&T; leading retailers (to finance inventories); oil companies (to smooth out their cash flows); and a lot of foreign companies (since commercial paper represents a cheaper source of finance).[46] Foreign banks likewise resort to the US commercial paper market as an alternative source of funds. They use it to finance their own portfolio, or to arbitrage it back into the inter-bank market (Federal funds in the US, or their own inter-bank markets at home, into which they could swap). These would include a number of West European banks, but not yet the Japanese. English and Swiss banks are leading names in the commercial paper market. Other interested parties are the Australians, the Indians, the Spaniards, and the Italians. The Scottish clearing banks do not use it.

Although the dealers in no way guarantee the commercial paper they sell, the leading dealers are concerned only to place quality paper and they would be prepared to make a bid for any paper coming back (provided it was its own). This arrangement explains why the secondary market is so thin – investors have no need to sell on the open market.

Investors in commercial paper are (in order of importance): the mutual funds; the money-market funds; bank trust departments and trust companies (which used to be the most important source of demand for commercial paper); insurance companies (when they are very liquid); states, cities, and municipalities; other corporations (including very often medium-sized companies); and, sometimes, savings and loan associations. One leading dealer sells to over 5,000 investors over the course of a year, though 80 per cent of the paper would be held by a hard core of some 400 investors.

Hence, it is not a very large pool. Years ago, a significant demand for commercial paper came through city correspondents for the smaller country banks (to offset the seasonal low in their loan portfolios).[47] This is no longer so, and today they use their city correspondents as a means of entering the federal funds market (see pp. 120–1). The only major bank demand in recent years has been from bank trust departments and trust banks, though (as borrowers) bank holding companies also use this market to quite an extent.

Euro-Notes – an alternative to Euro-commercial paper – have also been issued through a tender panel syndicate and were dealt with primarily in London. Initially, such Notes did not require to be rated and therefore did not need credit back-up lines from banks. Hence, they avoided having to pay a rating fee. Latterly, they were required to be rated and therefore must also have arranged the kind of back-up lines that apply to domestic paper. But the market was confined to only the most creditworthy of corporations and lacked the flexibility of domestic paper. Euro-Notes have also tended to give way to Euro-commercial paper on the basis of an on-going issue. Tender panels turned out to be too unwieldy. In any case, the arrangements for Euro-commercial paper already resembled those for domestic commercial paper, since the former likewise required the setting up of back-up lines and resort to a rating agency. This is generally true even for the very good names, the cost being offset by the finer rate they are accorded. Euro-commercial paper may be issued overnight (one day) right out to 12 months (though some programmes only go out to 9 months).

NEGOTIABLE CERTIFICATES OF DEPOSIT

The market for NCDs is much less active than in the 1970s; the NCD is also of diminished importance. This general view is supported by an inspection of bank annual reports; for those banks that publish figures for CDs, there is – on the whole – evidence of a decline in importance over recent years, and this would probably be seen to be even greater if the smaller non-negotiable CDs (e.g. those approximating $100,000 or less) were excluded. This evidence is also supported by dealer figures (averages of transactions) since 1984.[48] The main reason for this was the deregulation of consumer deposits (and the introduction of money market deposit accounts) that resulted in many banks being much less dependent on wholesale funding. An ancillary reason related to the Continental Illinois and related crises of 1982−3; as a result of these, some of the large banks lost their prime credit rating and the market became less homogeneous (i.e. it was not the same instrument that was now being traded across the market, as when there were ten large banks with prime names all trading their paper on equal terms); with less homogeneity, the instrument traded less well and was less liquid; the market became 'tiered' (good names and less good names); this was reflected, too, in a winding down of dealer positions, some of the leading houses now only dealing occasionally in CDs. Again, because of this 'tiering', less creditworthy banks faced the necessity of a 'premium' on their paper (i.e. having to pay a higher rate); as a result they tended to withdraw from funding by way of CDs; not unreasonably, they preferred to use sources of funds that only required rates comparable with other banks. Finally, a number of banks that would have resorted to CDs in the past now regarded the funds so attracted as 'hot money' unlikely to stay with them if it was needed. More of them came to depend on a stable core of deposits, supported by time deposits and collateralized public deposits. 'Investor' and 'consumer' retail CDs, which represented cheaper money, also became relatively more important and were a reliable source of funds. Moreover, they carried no reserve requirements. [49] These are more like time deposits, non-negotiable and registered in a name, whereas the large wholesale negotiable CDs are issued to bearer. What is left of the wholesale CD market has become very much a quality market and this has been assisted by Moody's rating bank CDs (and other senior debt obligations) as from January 1986, though dealers would already have required a premium on less creditworthy CDs and this would have cheapened the relevant names. Besides CDs, the Moody's service also covered inter-bank placements, bankers' acceptances, and obligations to deliver foreign exchange. It was intended to assist investors − corporate treasurers, central banks, pension funds, money market funds, and even bank money market desks themselves − to assess relative credit risks. It also helped corporations and other bank customers in assessing the value of back-up lines of credit and other bank commitments.

The NCD goes back to February 1961, when the First National City Bank of New York (today's Citibank) introduced its so-called 'negotiable' time certificate of deposit, offered to corporate customers and intended to appeal especially to them by reason of its marketability. The other major money market banks in New York and elsewhere soon followed suit, some with more enthusiasm than others. But it soon became well established and a secondary market was developed, so that a holder could sell his CD in order to disinvest. About 90 per cent of large CDs are made out to bearer. Partly they are issued for funding purposes, but equally important (perhaps these days more important) they are issued to meet customers' needs (e.g. as an investment outlet for a corporation with temporarily surplus funds available). CDs can be issued for as little as $100,000, retail CDs sometimes for smaller amounts, though these are non-negotiable. But the effective minimum for market purposes is $1 million and a typical transaction would be for $5 million, in a block made up of $5 \times 1 million to ensure both marketability and flexibility. To meet customers' requirements, CDs may be tailored both as to size and to maturity. The common maturities would be 30, 60, or 90 days, but they can be shorter or longer (e.g. 7 days to 7 years). There is no real market for CDs over 6 months. CDs over 18 months are not subject to reserve requirements.

For the most part, banks issue wholesale CDs direct, substantially to their own customers. Alternatively, they post rates to indicate what they are offering. Perhaps 90 per cent of NCDs are issued direct, with (say) 10 per cent being placed through dealers. A dealer (or a broker – see below) could be particularly useful: for example, if a bank were attempting a less usual type of transaction (like issuing a floating rate CD), or if a bank wished to raise large amounts, or to match and fund quickly a particular asset.

There seems today to be less enthusiasm for holding other banks' CDs and this is reflected in activity in the secondary market. Some banks do hold other banks' CDs, but more would hold them for trading only[50] (rather than as a liquid investment) or buy them in for customer's account. In the secondary market, where the minimum trade would be $1 million, 90 per cent of the business would be done by dealers[51] and 10 per cent would be done direct. As we have already indicated, the secondary market for CDs is no longer as strong or as active as it was – there is less homogeneity and therefore less liquidity. None the less, there are still strong names to be found in the market, and purchasers protect themselves in any case by applying limits to the amount of a single name that they will buy.

Foreign banks – e.g. Bank of Tokyo and the Canadian banks –

issue Yankee CDs, often with a slight premium and they may be traded. Yankee CDs are defined as dollar-denominated CDs issued by foreign banks in the domestic market through branches or agencies established there.

Customers for NCDs still include money market funds (though less so than formerly), to some extent other banks (including regional and smaller banks), bank trust departments, corporations, pension funds, public bodies, even individuals.

RESORT TO EURODOLLARS

When NCDs were first issued, the rates that might be paid were subject to the ceilings that were applicable by the Federal Reserve under Regulation Q. As interest rates rose (especially after 1965) the ceilings became increasingly unrealistic and, at the rates that could be paid, CDs were no longer a competitive means of raising funds. Gradually, the number of existing CDs ran off and there was a significant fall in the supply of CDs to the market. However, when (as a matter of policy) the Fed raised the ceiling (as in January 1970 for the longest maturity deposits), or interest rates came down to levels that could be accommodated within the ceilings, there was a tendency for the CD market to revive. But it was the difficulty of attracting funds by issuing CDs that encouraged large banks (as well as a number of others) to enter the Eurodollar market. The growth in the use made of Eurodollars increased steadily,[52] reflecting the interaction of rising demand for bank credit in the US, the reduced availability of bank reserves after late 1968, and the maintenance of ceilings on time deposit interest rates under Regulation Q. Interest rates on newly issued NCDs reached the permissible ceiling under Regulation Q during the final weeks of 1968.[53] From then until about the end of July 1969, banks increased their borrowings of Eurodollars with particular rapidity in an effort to meet both the rising customer demand for credit and the run-off of maturing CDs. At times in 1968–9, US banks' borrowings of Eurodollars were also increased by speculative flows of funds out of certain European currencies.

Regulation Q ceilings were ended in 1970 for 3 months CDs equal to or less than $100,000 and gradually for other maturities. None the less, FDIC premia and reserve requirements for CDs continued to make Eurodollars relatively more attractive. But the ending of Regulation Q ceilings reduced the volatility in deposit levels.

Eurodollars are interest-earning dollar deposits in banks outside the US; they include deposits in foreign branches of US banks. A bank accepting a Eurodollar deposit receives, in settlement of the transaction, a dollar balance with a bank in the US, whereas a bank making a Eurodollar deposit or loan (other than an advance by a US bank branch to its own head office) completes the transaction with a transfer from its US bank balance. A bank abroad may take Eurodollar deposits from non-banks (i.e. from individuals, corporations, or other non-banking institutions) in its own country or elsewhere. The depositor may have obtained dollars through a current or capital account transaction settled in dollars, or by purchase on the foreign exchange market. A bank may take Eurodollars also by deposit or by loan from other commercial banks. The lending bank may be redepositing funds which it has itself obtained through Eurodollar transactions; or it may be using dollars purchased on the foreign exchange market (or by special arrangement directly from its central bank) because it wished to switch out of assets in its domestic currency or in some third currency. A bank that acquires Eurodollar deposits may lend dollars to business enterprises in its own country or another country, either to finance dollar payments or for conversion into another currency. A bank may itself switch out of dollars into another currency via foreign exchange market transactions (generally covered by forward purchases of dollars). Or it may lend dollars to other banks (including foreign branches of US banks, which in turn may lend either outside the US or to head offices in the US). It was in this last context that funds were sucked in from the Eurodollar market to finance domestic lending by US banks. Eurodollar deposits were used as a substitute for other financial resources and particularly for time deposits in domestic currency. Nor was it necessary for an American bank to have a branch abroad. It was possible for a bank to approach one of the dealers, who would act as an intermediary in obtaining Eurodollars through a broker in London.

From its very beginnings, the Eurodollar market was centred on London, largely because for many years it was the world's major financial centre. Latterly, a number of other centres have been developed, since it was to become a worldwide market, trading round the clock. Singapore and Hong Kong soon became important centres in Asia and the Pacific – trading in so-called 'Asian' dollars – though their role remained secondary. Until liberalization began in earnest in the second half of the 1980s, Tokyo remained of limited importance, though Japanese banks have long been important participants in the Euro-markets. In due course, however, it is probable that Tokyo will supplant both Singapore and Hong Kong. Sydney in Australia is unlikely to become a major centre.

Despite London's other attractions – notably its expertise, wide range of facilities, and flexible arrangements – UK corporate taxation has operated as something of a deterrent, although no withholding taxes are imposed on interest paid by banks to non-resident depositors. Largely to avoid corporate taxation, 'booking centres' were developed in places that offered favourable tax treatment of profits – the most important being Bahrain in the Middle East and Nassau and Grand Cayman in the Caribbean.

Banks that operate branches in these centers book there loans negotiated and made in London, New York, or elsewhere. They fund these loans either by having their branch buy money in its own name in the Eurodollar market or by funding the operation with dollars purchased in the name of their London branch. Nassau and Grand Cayman offer one important advantage over Bahrain; they are in the same time zone as New York and only one hour ahead of Chicago. Thus it is easy for management in U.S. money market banks to direct their operations in these centers during normal working hours.[54]

After London, New York is the second most important Euro-market centre. For a number of years, New York has been an active centre in Eurodollars (Euros) trading. Then, when International Banking Facilities (IBFs) were introduced in December 1981, it became possible for New York banks to accept Euro-deposits. Before that, New York banks and the New York branches set up by major foreign banks were – and remain – active takers of Euros in the name of a Nassau or Grand Cayman branch. Again, there was – and is – active arbitraging between Euro and domestic dollars. In addition, many of the largest banks in the US direct worldwide Euro operations from New York. As a result, New York as a Euro centre has gradually increased in importance in relation to London.

The general pattern of operations is for banks to borrow in Euro-currencies for on-lending to domestic borrowers in the same Euro-currency; in due course, the loan must be repaid in the relevant Euro-currency; the borrowing customer usually carries the exchange risk, though he may cover himself by buying forward. Sometimes, a bank may hedge the exchange risk and charge the customer in its pricing. Provision for customers' needs would be done to a considerable extent by regional banks in the US. The large banks – primarily based in New York and Chicago, but also elsewhere in the US – would mostly operate in these markets for the purpose of funds management, Eurodollars and domestic dollars being fully interchangeable, or fungible. There is no currency risk; it is just a matter of price, though if Eurodollars are used domestically they are subject to reserve requirements.[55] It is rare for a large bank not to use the Eurodollar market at all. Quite often a bank will operate through its IBF. Euro-currency funding usually relates to Euro-currency lending (this is also true of funds management); likewise when borrowing and lending is off-shore. Not infrequently, there is funding from a combination of domestic sources and Euro-currencies (mostly Eurodollars). Also, if there is a shortage of Euro-currency and a surplus of domestic money (some US banks can be quite liquid), there may be a transfer of resources to foreign branches in order to put funds out as Euro-deposits, though this would depend on relative interest rates. From time to time, swap operations (whether in currencies or in maturities) may be undertaken. Much use can be made of interest rates futures, especially on the basis of the Eurodollar contract in order to manage interest rate exposure. In effect, the interest rate and currency swaps markets are concerned to make bets about the yield curve – either the course of interest rates or the relative movement in exchange rates. Swaps in currencies have deepened the market and, in essence, the demand for long-term accommodation has made for a deepening of the foreign exchange markets. Transactions can now go out beyond 12 months and one can arbitrage the capital markets as well because of swaps. There is quite a lot of arbitrage undertaken in New York. Much of Euro-currency borrowing and lending is on an overnight basis and arbitraging is reflected in the similarity of rates between overnight Euros and federal funds. There is a constant reference between the two rates and funding is based on the cheapest rate available – from whatever source. There is also a relationship between the rates on Euro-dollar and US CDs (e.g. for 3 and 6 months).[56]

For the large banks – and some of the regionals – round-the-world trading is common, based on New York, London, and an Asian centre. Very often deals are done through brokers, though some banks prefer direct deals, and in fact there would be a mix. In size, transactions would range from $10 to $100 million, with $10 to $25 million on average. All banks would operate limits on the size of transaction with an individual bank or corporation, whether buying or selling. Some banks close out their book daily. Clearly, there are risks involved, but one might question whether banks always fully understand the nature of the risk being undertaken. There need not be a risk on price, because it can be hedged, but there is a credit risk (hence resort to limits), also a settlement risk as well (as witness the Herstatt bank failure in West Germany). For a long time, the Federal Reserve (and other central bank authorities) were concerned about the growth of the Euro-currency markets, but they have learnt to live with this phenomenon and the extent of the exposure in these markets.

FINANCIAL FUTURES

In addition to the instruments already considered, there has been much activity in interest rate futures – most banks of any size are involved and some also trade in them.[57] Financial futures, or interest rate futures,[58] describe futures contracts based on financial instruments where there is an inverse relationship between prices and yields. As with all futures contracts, financial futures represent a firm commitment to buy or sell a specific commodity or financial instrument, during a specified month, at a price established through open outcry in a central, regulated market-place. Futures contracts are standardized. Unlike the cash market, where coupon rate, maturity, issuer, price, quantity and other information must be explicitly stated, buying or selling a futures contract is limited to one variable – price. Thus, futures contracts allow ease of quotation and trading. The contract terms themselves may be reviewed and revised as necessary to reflect changes in the market-place. Financial futures are based on the principle that interest rates – the cost of credit – can be viewed in the same way as the price of other commodities, and that certain kinds of institutions need a means of protecting themselves from volatile interest rates. Just as with futures in soybeans or silver, US Treasury bond and Eurodollar futures represent a viable market for transferring the risk of price volatility.

Briefly, a futures contract specifies that the seller of the contract will deliver whatever item the contract is for to the buyer at some future date at some fixed price. That is the theory and in fact there is a significant amount of delivery, but often a buyer of a futures contract will close out his position before the contract matures by making an offsetting sale of the same contract, a seller by making an offsetting purchase, the reason being that people enter into futures contracts either to offset risk on a long or short position in a 'commodity', i.e. to hedge that position by taking a temporary equal and offsetting position in futures, or to speculate on a change in the price of the 'commodity', or a change in price spreads. The users of financial futures include money- and bond-market dealers (which involves a number of the big banks), pension funds, corporations, insurance companies, etc.; also arbitrageurs and speculators ('without the liquidity they give the market, there would be no market'). Interest rate futures contracts were first introduced by the Chicago Board of Trade (CBOT) in 1975 in the form of a contract in the Government National Mortgage Association (GNMA) mortgage-backed securities. The Chicago Mercantile Exchange (CME) had introduced the first financial futures in 1972 when it began trading currency futures. Subsequently, additional futures contracts were introduced based on US Treasury bonds, certificate delivery GNMA, and US Treasury notes, followed by US Treasury bills, 3-months Eurodollars, 1-month LIBOR, and a number of major foreign currency contracts. The contract that initially took off was that in bill futures, the volume of which rose rapidly and dramatically. More recently, it was the CME 3-month Eurodollar future that became the dominant short-term rate contract. But as long-term rates have become increasingly important, the Treasury bond contract has become the world's most actively traded financial future. Latterly, New York has provided similar facilities, but is much less important. The CBOT also has its own Clearing Corporation, originally established in 1925, since when there has never been a financial loss due to default on a CBOT futures contract. The clearing corporation settles the account of each member firm at the end of each trading day, precisely matching each of the day's purchases and sales, collecting all losses and paying all profits.

On 6 May 1982, the CME began trading options on S&P 500 futures and by late 1982, other US exchanges were allowed to trade options on futures contracts. These new option contracts gave the option holder the right, but not the obligation, to buy or sell a futures contract at a specified price until a fixed future date. In the financial field, this extended to gold and silver futures, foreign currencies, debt instruments, and stock indices. The chief distinction between an option contract and either a futures or a forward contract lies in the obligation of the contract holder. Both futures and forward contracts obligate the buyer (long) to purchase and take delivery of the underlying instrument or commodity, if the contract is held to expiration. To do otherwise is to default on the contract. The buyer of an option, however, is not legally obliged to take any further action over the life of the contract once the option has been purchased. If the option is not exercised at or prior to expiration, the option seller or writer (short) is also freed of all contractual obligations.[59] In addition to the heavily traded Euro-dollar contract, currency futures are also important on the CME.

In recent years, exchanges and banks have developed a variety of new financial instruments designed to give customers the option to buy or sell foreign currencies. Exchanges in Amsterdam, Montreal, Asia, and Philadelphia opened trading in standardized options on foreign currencies in late 1982. Banks responded by resurrecting an old practice of writing tailor-made foreign currency options for their customers. And in January 1984, the CME opened trading in an option on its DM futures contract. Indeed, it offers trading in options on all its currency futures products. They have also introduced cross-rate futures contracts.

Traders have been able to use options on foreign currencies in addition to forward and futures contracts to manage their exchange rate risk. These options may allow traders to profit from favourable exchange rate changes while limiting the risks of adverse movements. Because they convey the right, but not the obligation, to buy or sell a foreign currency, options can be used to hedge transactions that are not certain to occur. Continued volatility in exchange rates and growth in international trade will ensure a demand for currency options. Exchange options and over-the-counter bank options are likely to co-exist for some time because they are different instruments and appeal to different customers. Typically the dealer in OTC options will offset his risk on the exchange. Customers often use both exchange and off-exchange. Many exchange options, however, are close substitutes for each other. The experience with futures markets suggests that not all options will prosper and that traders will increasingly give their business to the market able to offer the greatest liquidity and ease of execution.[60]

Banks also set up and trade in interest rate swaps. An interest rate swap is an exchange of differing interest payments at regular intervals between participants in the transaction. A classic 'coupon' or 'plain vanilla' swap is a financial transaction in which a stream of fixed-rate interest payments is exchanged for a stream of floating-rate interest payments in the same currency. There are also 'basis' swaps, which swap floating-rate interest payments priced on one basis (e.g. LIBOR) with another (e.g. US prime or commercial paper rates). In a 'cross-currency' swap (frequently referred to simply as a 'currency' swap) the parties exchange interest payments in one currency for those in another currency. In contrast to interest-rate swaps, where interest is calculated on the basis of a notional principal amount but no exchange of principal actually takes place, cross-currency swaps usually involve a final exchange of principal and sometimes also an initial exchange of principal (although the spot foreign exchange market might be used instead). Liabilities can be swapped on a fixed/fixed basis or on a floating/floating basis. Finally, cross-currency interest-rate swaps combine interest-rate and cross-currency swaps. These exchanges work on the principle of the 'gains from trade'. An interest-rate swap may take place between highly rated and lower rated entities, if there are quality spread differentials between the floating-rate loan market and the fixed-rate bond market large enough to cover the documentation and intermediation/broking costs involved. Each party raises funds on the market where it has a comparative advantage and then trades with the assistance of an intermediary. A cross-currency swap may be due to differences in the risk assessment of borrowers in markets for fund-raising in different currencies. For example, a US firm wanting DM funding but unknown in the German capital market, and a German firm seeking US dollar borrowings, but little known in the US, can each borrow in their home currency and swap the interest and principal at an agreed exchange rate.[61] In this context, too, one should note that the CBOT has now introduced 3-year and 5-year interest rate swap futures and options (see *CBOT Swap Futures, The Reference Guide* (1991)).

HOURS OF OPERATION[62]

Not only do markets trade right across the US; they have now become virtually worldwide, traversing a number of time zones right around the clock – New York, London, Singapore/Hong Kong/Tokyo, and back to New York. Trading in the Eurodollar contract would begin at 7.30 a.m. New York time, which means that staff should be there by 7.20 a.m. Actually, some people may start at 4.00 a.m. to talk to London (just a couple of people); others come in from 6.00 to 8.00 a.m. and they remain active until 5.00 p.m. (most banks close at 5.00 p.m.). But from 7.00 p.m. to 10 or 11 p.m., some people need to be available to talk to Singapore and the Far East. If people come in at 4.00 a.m., they leave early – about 3.00 p.m.

On the domestic scene, for overnight Fed funds, operations would begin at 8.00 a.m. New York time and run on until 6.30 p.m. Staff can also be kept late by computer problems, whether at the Fed or at a commercial bank, and sometimes staff can be much later. It is not uncommon for them to be at the office until 8.00 or 9.00 p.m. Already in New York – particularly with international markets in mind – consideration is being given to working towards a regular shift system based on either a 16- or a 24-hour day. For example, there may be a regular day shift, followed by a 'swing' shift (3.00 p.m. to 11.00 p.m.), and a 'graveyard' shift (after 11.00 p.m. until about 6.00 a.m.).

Despite the growth of a number of new markets, the most relevant markets remain those in government securities and federal funds, and it is through these that idle money in the US is mobilized and distributed across the country as a whole. In this context, full use is made of correspondent relationships, and both the banks and the dealers attempt to tap every possible source of funds. The intensity of this search for new sources of money has had the effect of binding together much more closely the various parts of the financial mechanism and has made it much more sensitive to Federal Reserve action. Finally, certain of the money centre banks provide 'lender of last resort' assistance, though it is rather expensive, to non-bank government securities dealers in urgent need of funds to balance their books at the end of a day. Whether they actively participate in all these markets or not, both the banks and the dealers will also be influenced by the dealings of their customers in other related markets. By switching their activities from one market to another in response to changing rate relationships, the operations of the banks, the dealers, and their customers tend to produce a rate structure consistent with the available supply of money, the credit 'climate', and the current preferences of investors. By these means also, the money market is effectively integrated both at the centre, over the country as a whole, and, indeed, with the European and Asian markets as well.

POSTSCRIPT

Following the Salomon Brothers bond trading scandal revealed in August 1991, the authorities decided to take a close look at the arrangements obtaining in the government securities market.[63]

Inquiries by the Federal Reserve Bank of New York also resulted in several reports being submitted by the firm in question over the period September through December 1991. These related to (1) the sweeping changes in management and management structure that were put in place following the disclosures made by the firm in August 1991; (2) the major changes in internal control procedures and compliance systems that were put in place over the period in question; (3) various estimates of the profits associated with the auctions in which irregularities had been acknowledged by the firm; and (4) further details regarding the firm's financing activities in certain of the Treasury issues. Where relevant, all such materials were made available to the Securities and Exchange Commission and to the US Attorney.[64]

In his Statement on the Joint Report on the Government Securities Market, E. Gerald Corrigan, President of the Federal Reserve Bank of New York, considered the future of the primary dealer system. While he agreed that change was needed, the complete dismantling of this system – including the responsibility of dealers to make markets for Fed open market operations and to participate meaningfully in Treasury auctions – would not have been a prudent step. Second, partly because the existing approach has been viewed as conferring special status on dealer firms carrying with it elements of 'franchise' value, and partly because of fairness and equity considerations, it was important to provide for a more 'open' system of primary dealers. This was accomplished by the elimination of the so-called 1 per cent market share requirement and the use of straightforward and objective capital standards for eligibility as a primary dealer. Together the changes will substantially increase the potential number of firms that can become primary dealers. Third, partly because of 'moral hazard' considerations and partly because of legal and regulatory realities, it was important that the Federal Reserve Bank of New York did *not* regulate the primary dealer firms. For this reason, the Fed proceeded to disband the Bank's *dealer* surveillance unit. Fourth, and obviously, it was necessary to clarify the reasons and the conditions under which the New York Fed would alter its relationships with a primary dealer firm.

Under the new administrative procedures, there are three independent sets of circumstances under which that might occur:

(1) a dealer firm's status will be altered if a firm fails to meet its responsibilities to make reasonable markets for Fed open market operations, or it fails to participate meaningfully in Treasury auctions, or it fails to meet its responsibilities to provide the Fed with meaningful market intelligence over time. To the extent that a firm's dealer status is altered for any or all of these reasons, that action by the Fed will reflect considerations relating to the business relationship alone and will carry no implication as to the creditworthiness, financial strength, or managerial competence of the firm;

(2) a dealer firm's status will be altered if its capital falls below the relevant capital standards and it does not, in the eyes of its primary federal regulator, have a credible plan to restore such capital in a reasonable period of time; and

(3) a dealer firm's status will be altered if the firm is convicted of a felony under US law or pleads guilty or *nolo contendere* to a felony under US law for activities directly or indirectly related to its business relationships with the Federal Reserve.

This should create powerful incentives for a firm – when faced with wrongdoing by individual employees – to take immediate and strong actions to root out the source of the problem so as to minimize the risk to that firm. While major elements in the changes in the administration of the relationships with primary dealers began to take place immediately, the full benefits of these changes would only occur as the automation of Treasury auctions and Fed open market operations take place and as the other changes contemplated by the Joint Report take hold. Over time, however, the automation efforts are likely to prove particularly important.

The design work for the automation of the competitive bidding portion of Treasury auctions based on existing auction techniques had been under way for some time and should be completed late in 1992. The software for the automation of the auctions is not particularly difficult to develop. The difficult aspects of this task relate more to its communications system – particularly as the number and nature of prospective direct participants in the auctions change. But what makes this automation effort especially difficult is the need to build into the computer systems and the communication system a very high level of operational integrity, as well as multiple levels of back-up for various contingencies. If the Treasury were to decide to move to a different auction technique (see below), the strategy would be to enhance the system currently being developed to accommodate both types of auctions. This would not, however, delay the planned implementation of automated procedures for the current auction by the end of 1992.

The full automation of Fed open market operations will be a more complex and time-consuming task, especially since it is impossible to pre-judge with any precision the number, location, and other characteristics of potential counterparties for such operations. Moreover the operating systems and communication systems associated with this effort must be integrated with a number of other highly complex automated systems, including the Fed's existing money and securities transfer systems. Because of this, an extraordinary high level of reliability and integrity will be needed.

There has also been discussion of US auction techniques in the government securities markets. Because Treasury auctions are not as yet automated, it has been impossible to place all potential competitive bidders in Treasury auctions in direct communication at the same time. As a result, the Treasury has used a sealed-bid auction rather than an 'open' auction – in which bidding is public and competing bidders can respond. In addition, different bidders currently pay different prices for the same security, based on their bids. These multiple-price awards result in what is sometimes referred to as the 'winner's curse' – the highest bidder 'wins' the auction by paying the highest price only to find that the price paid is higher than the consensus price as reflected in the market. Because bidders are aware of this 'curse', they tend to shade their bids below the maximum they are actually willing to pay.

The other type of sealed-bid auction that some commentators have argued would produce superior results for the Treasury is the uniform-price, sealed-bid auction, sometimes called a 'Dutch' auction. In this type of auction, all bidders whose tenders are accepted pay the same price for a given security. This price is the lowest of the accepted prices bid (or the highest of the accepted yields). As a result, some of the bidders whose tenders are accepted pay a lower price than they actually bid. At first glance, this approach might appear to produce lower revenue, since money appears to be 'left on the table'. On the other hand, participants in a uniform-price, sealed-bid auction can be expected to bid higher prices than they would in a multiple-price, sealed-bid auction, since there is no 'winner's curse', i.e. they do not run the risk of paying a higher price than others whose tenders are accepted. The expected revenue effects of uniform price auction versus current US practice turns on whether the revenue generated from increased demand in uniform-price, sealed-bid auctions is greater than the revenue that is apparently foregone due to the difference between prices bid and prices paid.

Quite apart from revenue considerations, a perceived advantage of a uniform-price, sealed-bid auction is that it would eliminate much of the need for pooling information to gauge the market consensus. Thus, the incentive for bidding through dealers would be lessened. It is argued that this would broaden auction participation and encourage a wider range of investors to bid directly for their own account rather than through primary dealers. This should lead to less concentration of ownership of securities awarded at auction.

During 1973 and 1974, the Treasury conducted six uniform-price, sealed-bid auctions. The results of this experiment were inconclusive. In the August 1973 uniform-price auction of 20-year bonds, tenders received from the public were not sufficient to sell the entire issue. However, the failure of this auction appears to have been unrelated to the auction technique actually chosen.

But there is an alternative. Irrespective of whether the single-price, sealed-bid auction would prove superior to the current practice, the Agencies believe that there is an auction technique that may be superior to both the types of sealed-bid auction techniques already discussed. This is an ascending-price, open-auction system, which will be feasible for the first time once the auctions are automated. Auction theory suggests that, generally speaking, Treasury revenue would not suffer – and indeed might increase – in the switch to an open, ascending-price system.

In this type of auction, registered dealers and other major market participants would have terminals that are connected by telephone line (with appropriate security) to a central computer.[65] The auction would begin with the Treasury announcing an opening yield above the yield at which the security is quoted in 'when-issued' (WI) trading. All interested parties would then immediately submit tenders electronically for the quantity of securities they would be willing to purchase at that yield. Once all the bids were submitted, the resulting total volume of bids at this high yield would be announced; presumably, the issue would be over-subscribed after the first round, since the yield quoted would be higher than the WI yield. The yield would then be reduced, perhaps by one basis point, and the bidding process repeated. Bidding would proceed in successive rounds – perhaps at 10-minute intervals – with decreasing yields until the volume demanded was smaller than the size of the issue. All participants who bid at that closing yield would receive awards, but at the next higher yield. That is to say the Treasury would sell all of the issues at the last rate that covered the auction, making full awards to those that bid below the selling rate. Those who bid in the next-to-last round, but did not bid at the last round, would receive pro-rated awards at the same yield.

From the viewpoint of a bidder, this decreasing sequence of yields lessens the risk to participants of bidding too low a yield for the securities. Even if an investor had a much higher valuation of the securities than other bidders, the bidding would stop before the yield moved downward very far, as other bidders dropped out of the bidding. The open nature of the bidding, plus the single-price outcome, should eliminate the 'winner's curse'. Furthermore, the public exposure of the volume of bids provides information about other bidders' valuation of the securities, perhaps augmenting overall demand.

An open auction system also allows participants to react to surprise bids, thereby turning market forces against attempts at market manipulation. Entities attempting to corner this type of auction are effectively forced to disclose their intentions to their competitors, as they continually bid as the Treasury lowers the yield. This allows those not party to the attempted market manipulation – particularly those holding short positions from WI trading – to bid along with those trying to corner the issue. Hence, the would-be market manipulators may either fail to corner the security, or at the very least find it a more expensive proposition.

By way of contrast, in a sealed-bid auction – of either the multiple- or single-price variety – the price reaction comes at the announcement of surprising awards, when dealers may realize that they are caught short and react. In a real-time open auction, that reaction occurs when the bidding is still open; hence the Treasury garners part of the profits of any attempted corner.

The Agencies believe that the new type of auction now being considered – in combination with other recommendations of the Joint Report – has the potential for reducing the incentives for market participants to engage in manipulation, and would also provide assurances to market participants that they are not seriously disadvantaged in participating in Treasury auctions. The Treasury intends to discuss the proposed new form of auction with market participants, academic experts, and others, and welcomes the views of all interested parties.

See also Vincent Reinhart: 'An Analysis of Potential Treasury Auction Techniques' in *Federal Reserve Bulletin*, June 1992, pp. 403–13, in which the academic literature on auctions is reviewed. The more important references in the literature are listed at the end of the article.

Chapter 4

The money market in France

In December 1985, new money-market arrangements were introduced in France,[1] the first major change in this field since June 1967.[2]

There were now to be two markets: The first was the inter-bank market (*le marché interbancaire*), which comprehended three groups of institutions:

(a) the *établissements de crédit* – the big banks (*les grands établissements*), the regional and local banks, the mutual and co-operative banks (e.g. the Crédit Agricole), the savings banks, the *caisses de crédit municipal*, the *sociétés financières*, and specialized institutions like the *maisons de réescompte* and *banques de trésorerie* (the last are usually small subsidiaries of large banks and, being small, able to adopt flexible policies), and various other specialized institutions (like the Crédit National and the Crédit Foncier) – as at 31 December 1990, there was a total of 1,865 such firms in France (metropolitan and overseas) plus 20 in Monaco;

(b) belonging to this market was a group of five institutions comprising the Bank of France, *le Trésor public* (the State Treasury), the Caisse de Dépôts et Consignations, and the two central bank institutions for overseas territories (e.g. in the French *départements d'outre mer*), but not the financial services of the Post Office; and

(c) 162 *maisons de titres* (houses dealing in securities), plus one in Monaco.

These constituted the 'professional' operators in the money market. Other institutions that were previously included in the inter-bank market were phased out progressively; these included the insurance companies, pension funds, stockbrokers, and unit trusts. Hence, in total there were 2,027 separate institutions in this market (1,865 + 162).

The second market was a 'new' short-term market in negotiable securities, which was open to all comers, including all those qualified to participate in the inter-bank market, industrial and commercial corporations with treasury requirements to accommodate, insurance companies and mutual funds, also wealthy individuals. In particular, it comprehended all money market operations between banks and other parties, and between the other parties themselves. It covered short-term bonds, negotiable instruments like certificates of deposit, commercial paper, *bons du Trésor* or Treasury bills, and the bonds of the *institutions financières specialisées* (*IFS*), the first such issue being made on 20 January 1986.

MONEY MARKET INSTRUMENTS

Before proceeding further, it is pertinent to describe briefly the several money market instruments that are available for investment and trading.

From a money market point of view, the types of government paper that are relevant in France are the *bons du Trésor à taux fixe* (*BTF*), which are Treasury bills issued with a maturity of less than 1 year on a discount basis, and the *bons du Trésor à interêts annuels* (*BTAN*), which are Treasury notes with annual interest which may have a maturity of between 1 and 7 years − so far they have only been issued with maturities of 2 and 5 years; they carry a fixed rate coupon with the yield varying in accordance with movements in market prices. Technically, the *bons du Trésor sur formules* issued on tap still exist, but there is only a nominal amount outstanding held primarily by households, because of their low denominations. They are not a money market instrument. The *BTF*, which are issued on the basis of a weekly auction − maturities are usually 3, 6, or 12 months − are issued in large denominations and are therefore held by banks, big corporations and money market funds (in the last case, indirectly by small firms and households). *BTAN* are issued once a month. Both *BTF* and *BTAN* are held in accounts with the Bank of France.

Issues of *bons du Trésor* have increased greatly. By mid-1991, *bons du Trésor* (except for *bons sur formules*) in issue totalled

Ffr 565.3 milliards.[3] All *bons du Trésor* are held in current account (*comptes courants*) at the Bank of France – they have no physical existence, being merely figures in the computer at the Bank of France. About 80 per cent of the *bons du Trésor* issued are bought by banks. There is a developed secondary market in them, where about fifteen brokers[4] quote prices; they also operate through an inter-dealer broker system[5] comparable to those which are in place in London and New York. This market is also used by banks when they fail at the auction to get the *bons du Trésor* that they want.

When *BTF* are auctioned, tenderers put in a range of prices for each auction in descending order of magnitude (to two decimal places) – the Treasury accepts the highest bids (i.e. the lowest yields). The relevant form on which the banks apply carries the number of the account of the subscriber. The coming auction is advised in advance on a Tuesday, with the auction taking place on the following Monday. On the Monday (before 3.00 p.m.), the banks submit their bids to the Treasury, though brokers will have estimated what the various prices will be for the several maturities and have worked out a *fourchette de prix*, or range of prices. The banks decide upon which prices to bid.[6] Bids may be put in direct to the Treasury, or through a broker, which will make no charge – it is a service furnished gratis.

Brokers (of which there are about ten that are active) make their profits from commissions as a broker in the secondary market for *bons du Trésor*, where there are discounts for volume (the big banks because of the size of their transactions pay less than the smaller banks). The broker's job is to establish a price between buyer and seller, on which they will agree. On a normal day in the secondary market, turnover is of the order of Ffr 10 milliards, but it may go up to Ffr 15 milliards. But there are quiet days as well and turnover may be as low as Ffr 5 milliards. The market opens around 9.00 a.m. and runs through to 6.00 p.m. every working day.[7]

Certificates of deposit, whether in French francs or in foreign currencies, could be issued by banks as from 1 March 1985. Reserve requirements apply – originally 3 per cent of liabilities but since 16 October 1990, $\frac{1}{2}$ per cent. Initially, the minimum amount that could be issued was Ffr 10 million; the minimum now is Ffr 1 million,[8] with maturities of from 10 days to 7 years (originally, the maturities for French francs ranged from 6 months to 5 years, and from 2 years to 5 years for CDs in foreign currencies including

ECUs). They are issued at a fixed or variable rate by banks, mainly to non-financial corporations. By mid-1991, some Ffr 1,005.3 milliards of CDs were in issue. There is only a very thin secondary market, though certain banks are prepared to offer two-way prices.

The first issue of commercial paper (*billets de trésorerie*) in France was on 18 December 1985.[9] It serves a similar purpose to the long-established use of commercial paper in the USA. The minimum size at issue was Ffr 5 million (reduced in 1988 to Ffr 1 million). Issues may be for from 10 days to 7 years. In practice, issues are for less than 6 months. It is issued at a fixed rate. The banks provide back-up lines of credit (no less than 95 per cent of the outstanding paper) and the big banks are the main intermediaries, money market intermediaries in this context being only of marginal importance.[10] Mainly established non-financial corporations issue such paper. A rating is compulsory for any issue of more than 2 years. A credit agency was set up with the assistance of the Crédit National in April 1986. In all, there are now four such agencies. By mid-1991, some Ffr 168.8 milliards of commercial paper had been issued. Again, there is virtually no secondary market, but it is purchased readily by other non-financial corporations and by institutional investors like insurance companies and pension funds, also unit trusts (*société d'investissement à capital variable – SICAV*).

One might also mention the securities issued by specialized financial institutions like the Crédit National, the Crédit Foncier, regional development agencies, and the Comptoir des Entrepreneurs – the *bons des institutions et sociétés financières (BISF)*. These have been available since December 1985. They have maturities of from 10 days to 7 years, the minimum amount is Ffr 1 million; they may attract a fixed or variable rate; and they may be held in custody at the Bank of France. Although initially the several money market instruments had maturities (maximum and minimum) which varied somewhat they have now all come into line and range from 10 days to 7 years.

On the external side, French banks have a very active interest in Eurodollars. Following the relaxation of market rules from the beginning of 1987,[11] there has also been a steady development of the Euro-franc market, especially for bonds. Euro-currency operations (primarily Eurodollar, but including the Euro-franc) tend to be centred on London, though some business is also done in Brussels and Geneva. There is less and less done in Euro-sterling.

Swaps are often effected between foreign and domestic books within a bank. Interest rate swaps are also common.

THE INTER-BANK MONEY MARKET

The core of money market activity in France is the inter-bank market in balances with the Bank of France, much of it being done through brokers but some of it direct between banks. Loans may be made unsecured (*en blanc*), when no paper is delivered. If a loan is collateralized, it would be an *en pension* transaction. Being central bank money, it is available the same day. French banks have to maintain certain reserves against their several kinds of deposit liabilities and it is therefore necessary to manage carefully a bank's money position over the course of the day and with a view to maintaining an appropriate average over the month.

The *réserves obligatoires* as imposed by the Bank of France are a very relevant element in controlling bank liquidity.[12] Such reserves apply to virtually all resident deposit liabilities with a maturity of less than 2 years.[13] *Opérations de réméré* are also covered, a *réméré* being the sale of a security with an *option* to repurchase the security. Since August 1987, reserves have been calculated on the basis of an average daily figure from the 16th of one month to the 15th of the next month. Over this period, banks can either run above or below their requirement so long as they maintain that requirement on an average over the whole month. How they manage their money over this period will depend on the liquidity of the market and related interest rates, also on their own expectations with regard to interest rates. In other words, a bank may take a position with regard to interest rates.

The day will usually begin about 8.30 a.m. with an exchange of information between the leading banks. All relevant information is centralized in the hands of a bank's Treasury, including for banks with widespread branch networks figures from their numerous local branches *en province*. This is necessary since the branches of big banks *en province* would conduct their inter-bank business through the local branches of the Bank of France. For the big banks, the information relating to their total deposits with the Bank of France would be supplemented by details of big movements of money from their own branches. Furthermore, large corporation customers would be expected over the course of the day to advise any big movements of money that were contemplated, whether in or out of their account. In the case of a term deposit, the corporation concerned would give notice. Generally speaking, a bank would know its position fairly certainly by 3.00 p.m., but activity may go on until 5.00 p.m. or 5.30 p.m. Actually, the inter-bank market is most active from 8.30 a.m. to noon, and again from 3.00 p.m. to 5.00 p.m. Should the banks have surplus money, which they do not wish to lend out inter-bank, they may buy commercial bills or *bons du Trésor*, but not very much in CDs. Sometimes, in the big banks, the bank Treasury is also responsible for the bank's bond portfolio, where operations will tend to reflect both the bank's own needs and its expectations with regard to interest rates.

On the basis of their money positions at the end of the day, the banks used to have a morning 'fixing' of the interest rate on day-to-day money, which provided the basis for other rates. The fixing took place for overnight/day-to-day money from 8.30 a.m. to 9.30 a.m., when the Bank of France itself might provide money to assist the positions of the banks. Once the fixing had been made for day-to-day money, the banks would lend and borrow money for the longer maturities, the longest being 12 years, though the market was very thin beyond 5 years.

It will be apparent that this system of 'fixing' had its disadvantages. It took place early in the day on the basis of estimates that could not possibly foresee developments that might eventuate later in the day with related fluctuations in liquidity. It also failed to take into account differences in the creditworthiness of borrowers, though to some extent this could be accommodated by applying internal limits to such borrowers. Finally, the 'fixing' tended to result in a certain rigidity of rates.[14]

The 'fixing' disappeared after 1 December 1986. Thereafter there was a wider variation of rates over the course of the day. But since the rate determined at the 'fixing' had formerly been a point of reference for other rates – some of them long-term – the Bank of France now decided to calculate a weighted average of operations in day-to-day money on a daily basis, and this is announced the following day at the end of the morning. Clearly, because of existing institutional arrangements, some kind of reference point had to be retained.

As already indicated, the inter-bank money market is limited to banks and to banking-type institutions like the Caisse des Dépôts et Consignations, the Crédit National, the Crédit Foncier, etc. Of the

2,048 relevant institutions (including Monaco), however, only 200 to 230 would be active, and 26 have qualified as *opérateurs principaux du marché* (*OPM*), chosen among the candidates as the most active in the inter-bank market by reason of their size or specialization. Expertise and a minimum capital are also relevant. It is through these institutions, too, that the Bank of France would for the most part operate when intervening in the market.

As we have seen, the commodity dealt in in the inter-bank market is balances at the Bank of France. There are no clearing house funds in France; in other words, all clearings are effected through accounts at the Bank of France. This is as true of longer-dated money (whatever its maturity) as of day-to-day money. Also, a large number of inter-bank transactions go through brokers (many of whom are brokers in other instruments as well as money,[15] of which there are 32 that are recognized, some 10 of them being really active. The big banks would use several brokers. The bulk of the transactions would be secured – say, 95 per cent – resorting to the French *en pension* arrangements (which are in the nature of a sale and repurchase agreement); only about 5 per cent would be *en blanc* (unsecured). The basis of the *en pension* transaction is mostly *effets privés*, i.e. not government paper. Where *effets privés* are accepted *en pension* they are not transferred physically from the borrowing bank to the lending bank – they remain in the dossier of the borrowing bank (*effets sous dossier*). Only a memorandum of entitlement is exchanged. No particular maturity is 'normal', but it is usually less than 3 months (it could be longer); the average maturity would be less than 1 month.[16]

The bulk of the money lent and borrowed would be overnight (i.e. day-to-day), but deals are also done in 'period' money. Thus, money may be borrowed (again *en pension*) for several days, or a week, or indeed for any period up to 12 months. For the really big banks, inter-bank loans would be unsecured (*en blanc*); otherwise loans for up to 12 months would be done *en pension*. The most common periods – apart from overnight – are 1 to 2 weeks, 1 to 3 months, 6 months, and 12 months. For over 12 months' money, banks would buy a CD or a *bon du Trésor* from another bank.

In the inter-bank market, banks will tend to be borrowers on one occasion and lenders on another, depending on movements in their liquidity, though on the whole they will tend to be net borrowers (which means that the Bank of France will have to put money into the market – see below). Only the Caisse des Dépôts et

Consignations is almost always a net lender – it still has large liquid funds to deploy; this also used to be true of the Caisse Nationale du Crédit Agricole, but this is less true today as it has developed a very sizeable lending business of its own and is now virtually a large commercial bank with a greatly expanded level of business, and is itself in great need of funds to deploy. It tends to borrow on a day-to-day basis, but is a lender at term. One should remember, too, that the former *maisons de réescompte* are part of the inter-bank market; they borrow and lend and, indeed, as with any other bank, often 'take a position' in money, which brokers may not do. The former *maisons de réescompte* operate as '*banques de trésorerie*' and arbitrage in much the same way as the money market room of a big bank.[17] Indeed, the big banks have their own *banques de trésorerie* as subsidiaries, which being smaller than the parent bank can be more flexible.

THE GOVERNMENT BOND MARKET

Because, at the short end, the market for French Government bonds impinges on the money market, reference must also be made to the changes that have occurred in this sector as well. About the beginning of 1987, a number of innovations were introduced. At the end of 1986, the French Ministry of Finance named thirteen primary dealers.[18] By end-1991, there were fifteen. These were expected to maintain competent teams of dealers and to quote two-way prices whatever market conditions might develop; otherwise they would have to face the wrath of the authorities and the probability of being de-listed. Spreads between buying and selling prices narrowed significantly as a wave of reforms was implemented – in order to deregulate the system and greatly to reduce previously existing rigidities. The primary dealers were also to keep the Treasury informed on market developments, take a regular part in the placing of government debt, and – as indicated – make continuous two-way prices across the full range of government securities, including both Treasury bills and government bonds.

The primary dealers were selected on the basis of their activity in the government debt markets over the previous 3 or 4 months, as well as on their technical skills. Banks which had taken an 'intellectual' lead in the development of the Paris financial markets (such as the creation of the new financial futures exchange, or MATIF) were also favoured. In addition, the French Treasury wished to achieve a range of skills in the market and chose four smaller operators which in its judgement had the capacity to develop. At the same time, a minimum capital requirement was stipulated. As well as the four leading commercial banks (Banque Nationale de Paris, Crédit Lyonnais, Société Générale, and Crédit Commercial de France), the two major investment banks (Paribas and Indosuez), and semi-public institutions like the Caisse des Dépôts et Consignations and the Crédit Agricole, two of them (the Banque d'Escompte and the Caisse de Gestion Mobilière) belonged to the group of traditional discount houses with an expertise in the bill market but little previous exposure to government bonds. One was a foreign bank (Banque Morgan) which had long had a base in Paris. By December 1987, an inter-dealer broker to assist in ensuring market liquidity had been set up (jointly owned by the primary dealers), when the dealers could also begin to borrow and lend stock amongst themselves.

The French government debt market (including *bons du Trésor*) has increased dramatically in size over the past 5 years or so, and now dominates the fixed-interest markets as a whole. Some bank instruments are in fact quoted not on an absolute basis, but as a spread over the rate on *bons du Trésor*. In the bond market, government debt accounts for about 30 per cent of outstanding issues, but for as much as two-thirds of turnover. Bonds are issued with maturities of 7 to 30 years on the first Thursday of the month, using the same auction method as with *bons du Trésor*. In this context, the primary dealers have an advantage over other financial institutions, since they have a limited access to 'non-competitive bids'. Besides bidding for government securities in competition with other institutions, they are entitled to receive 20 per cent of the amount they bid for at the average price of the last three auctions. Very soon the dealers making prices through the Reuters, Telerate, and other screen systems were generating nearly half of the Ffr 40 milliards of transactions in French government bonds each week, and this hold on the market has continued to grow – primary dealers now handling from 75 to 80 per cent of the transactions on the primary market for Treasury paper and from 70 to 75 per cent of the total on the secondary market, though rising yields – and capital losses – created some problems. The object of these and related developments is to make Paris the premier financing centre in Continental Europe.

FINANCIAL FUTURES – THE MATIF

Meanwhile, the *Marché à Terme des Instruments Financiers* (the MATIF) had been set up in February 1986.[19] It is now called the *Marché à Terme International de France* (and still the MATIF). Trading started on the basis of a Ffr 500,000 nominal 10-year 10 per cent state bond futures contract, and turnover grew dramatically. Then came a short contract based on a 13-week Treasury bill; this was established in June 1986 but never really took off. In Paris – unlike the early days of LIFFE in London – speculation was a central element behind activity and this complemented the hedging and covering business provided by bond dealers. In line with the brisk start to business, the number of floor members of the futures market grew quickly. These included 20 stockbroking firms and 53 banks and financial institutions, including the Caisse de Dépôts et Consignations.[20] However, only five banks – Banque d'Escompte, Banque Nationale de Paris, Paribas, Crédit Lyonnais, and Société Générale – played a really active role in the early stages. Others preferred to wait and see. By mid-1991, there were 146 members dealing with financial derivatives, and growth had been such that the Clearing House of MATIF had to move to new premises. Within the first year, daily volume in the notional long-term contract averaged well over 15,000 contracts a day, with trading peaks of over 40,000 contracts. Indeed, this long-bond contract became the price to watch in the French bond market.

Within a year, further contracts were introduced – one was a private index called OMF 50 (on 21 July 1988).[21] An option on its main long-bond contract was also introduced by MATIF (on 20 August 1988). It was said that the private contract seemed to be more liquid than the official one.

In July 1988, the margin on Treasury bond futures was cut from 5 per cent to 4 per cent of the 10-year bond contract's face value – Ffr 500,000 – to reduce the margin in cash terms from Ffr 25,000 to Ffr 20,000. Subsequently (August 1988), in order to counter emerging competition, the MATIF introduced a new stock index future open only to clearing members of the MATIF. The contract was based on the recently launched CAC 40 index. This was followed by a new short-term interest rate contract (September 1988) based on the Paris inter-bank 3-month offered rate (PIBOR 3-month) calculated daily by the French Banks' Association and already traded over the counter since June 1987. It was expected largely to displace the existing Paris futures exchange contract on Treasury bills, which had not proved to be a success.

In October 1990, MATIF launched a new ECU bond futures product. After March 1991, activity expanded greatly, contracts being framed to include most issues of ECU bonds by sovereign states and supranational institutions with maturities of from 6 to 10 years. MATIF claimed that by July 1991 its average daily volume amounted to 75 per cent of world trading of these contracts. The success of ECU bond futures was said to derive from a combination of factors – high quality, homogeneous underlying instruments, and dynamic market-makers (BNP, Crédit Lyonnais, Banque San Paolo, and Société Générale) thereby providing a high degree of market liquidity and the growing importance of ECU bond issues.

As will be apparent, the MATIF now has much the same range of instruments as Chicago, New York, and London. There is also considerable rivalry between MATIF and LIFFE in London.

INTERVENTION BY THE BANK OF FRANCE

Bank of France intervention in the money markets may take three forms: (1) a procedure whereby the Bank of France invites tenders for central bank money from the banks (*l'appel d'offres*); (2) the provision of similar accommodation on the basis of a *pension* (sale and repurchase agreement); and (3) on the basis of outright purchases (or sales) of government securities on the open market.

(1) Making money available in response to tenders for funds is the means most commonly employed in supplying central bank funds to the inter-bank money market. As a matter of history, this means of intervention assumed importance once the Bank of France discontinued its discount function. The first lending operations against *bons du Trésor* and *effets privés éligibles* took place in 1969. And it was on 21 June 1973 that the first invitation to banks to tender for funds (*l'appel d'offres*) was made. But the latter innovation was originally associated with an outright purchase of securities; later it became an *en pension* transaction. At the time the Bank of France was buying short-term securities outright, it would hold them in its portfolio until maturity – there was no secondary market. With a *pension* the Bank of France would hold 'title' only during the duration of the *pension*.

In terms of the reform of 1 December 1986, accommodation was made available following an invitation from the Bank of France to tender for central bank money (the technique of *l'appel d'offres*). *Pension* transactions are preferred.[22] Moreover, there was to be no delivery of the relevant securities (unless the central bank should require it); the transaction would merely be evidenced by a document for the total amount involved (by *billets globaux de mobilisation*). Non-delivery of *effets privés* saved much mechanical labour. Actually, not all *effets privés* were eligible. For the big banks, with a large commercial business, holdings of *effets privés* are large and a most convenient basis for *en pension* transactions; smaller banks would generally only have *bons du Trésor* as a basis, the borrowing bank having the discretion as to which kind of paper to employ. It should be noted, too, that there is no physical delivery of *bons du Trésor* – they are merely held as figures on a computer at the Bank of France, the *bons du Trésor* being transferred from the account of the borrower to the credit of the Bank of France account on the computer.

Nowadays, the Bank of France admits the paper of any firm with a good Bank of France rating (this is done through the branches of the Bank of France where the bulk of this business is undertaken), paper being graded for quality between 1 and 5.

The procedure in the present context is for the Bank of France to invite the *établissements de credit* and the specialized financial institutions (i.e. those institutions that operate in the inter-bank market) to indicate the amounts of money they desire to borrow from the Bank of France and the rate of interest they are prepared to pay for it. This information is passed to the Bank of France through the *opérateurs principaux du marché (OPMs)*, which assemble the details (without fee) before passing it on to the Bank of France for processing and consideration as a whole. The Bank of France – at its discretion – then decides on the rate at which it will provide funds to the banks and the proportion of the total requests that will be accommodated. Usually the submissions made by the banks will represent a range of amounts and of rates; the amount the Bank of France will be intending to grant will generally be much lower and the interest rate chosen will depend on the level stipulated by the Bank of France. The Bank of France response to a tender for funds would usually be given at 2.00 p.m. (on Mondays, normally at 1.30 p.m., because Treasury bill bids need to be processed) on the basis of submissions to the Bank of France normally made between 10.00 a.m. and 12.30 p.m.

In 1990, the Bank of France introduced a somewhat new type of contract – the *pension livrée* – which was considered to be safer than the ordinary *pension*,[23] or the *réméré*, which was popular in the market. The *pension livrée* is a combination of an outright purchase and a sale forward, both transactions being concluded at the same time and for the same amount of capital. As collateral, the Bank of France accepts either Treasury bills or Treasury notes, but not so far *obligations assimilables du Trésor* (or *OAT*). It also accepts bank credit paper[24] where banks have granted credit to companies or firms which have obtained a good rating from the Bank of France. The assets (Treasury bills or Treasury notes) or the titles to the bank credits are transferred to the Bank of France for the duration of the combined contracts. At the end of its term – in general, 2 weeks – the assets or the title to the bank credit are transferred back to the bank concerned when it repays its debt (capital and interest).

(2) *Pensions* for a short period of days were introduced on 5 January 1971, though previously accommodation had been made available *en pension* for 1 and 3 months against *bons du Trésor*, bonds of the Crédit Foncier de France, and *effets privés éligibles* – this procedure was suspended several times and finally abandoned in March 1980. *Pensions à 7 jours* were used to quite a considerable extent between 1982 and 1984 at a time when the day-to-day rate in the inter-bank market was highly volatile. Subsequently, this technique was not in use until the reform of 1 December 1986, after which they were reactivated as 'same-day money'. As a rule, the *pensions à 7 jours* money was made available at a rate about $\frac{1}{2}$ per cent higher than the money for which banks tendered by *l'appel d'offres*. Since the summer of 1988, applications for *pensions* at the initiative of the bank concerned[25] may be for 5 to 10 days (instead of for 7 days) and the rate may be $\frac{1}{2}$ to 1 per cent higher than the rate on *l'appel d'offres*. Clearly, banks would be interested in such money when the day-to-day rate in the inter-bank market is higher than such Bank of France money and the banks believe it is likely to remain so for some days. For this reason, the inter-bank rate for day-to-day money is not likely very often, nor for very long, to be above the rate on *pensions à 5–10 jours*. In general, the inter-bank rate tends to be somewhere between the two Bank of France rates discussed above; hence these rates are often referred to as '*taux directeurs*'.

However, although less important in 1990/1 than (say) 5 years or so before, the main way of making money available to the market is still by way of *l'appel d'offres*. None the less, money by way of *pensions à 5–10 jours* is now resorted to much more than it used to be. Both kinds of money are made available *en pension*. Because *l'appel d'offres* is the main way of making money available to the market, its rate becomes the key intervention rate in the money market – the *taux d'intervention* – and it is therefore the rate that is watched; when it changes, it is clear that there has been a policy adjustment. It would usually be accompanied by a related change in the rate for *pensions à 5–10 jours*. It will also tend to be followed by a change in bank base lending rates. Sometimes, to protect the franc, the significant change may be in the 5–10-day *pension* rate.[26] At other times, these rates are lowered, albeit cautiously.[27]

(3) Since December 1986, the Bank of France has also been prepared to operate in the open market with a view to influencing bank liquidity – it does this by purchases and sales of Treasury bills and Treasury notes at market prices on the secondary market. When Treasury paper is purchased, the Bank of France may either re-sell it or hold it until maturity. If the Bank of France is purchasing in the open market, this will tend to push rates down in the inter-bank market and, if it is selling, rates are likely to go up. Consistent with this, if there is excess liquidity and some 'mopping up' is in order – which tends to be rare – the Bank of France will sell *bons du Trésor*.[28] By way of contrast to the two other methods of operation, in the case of open-market activity, policy is implemented by way of outright purchases or sales – not by way of a *pension*.

If the main emphasis was to be on open-market operations of this kind, it would require a large market in Treasury paper. There has been a significant growth in such paper in recent years in France, and the government securities market as a basis of open-market operations is now used much more extensively – during the latter part of 1991 possibly amounting to 25–30 per cent of global refinancing.

POSTSCRIPT

A new instrument – *bons à moyen terme négociables* (or *BMTN*) – has been instituted in France and was first issued on the markets in 1992.[29] The *BMTN* are another kind of *titres de créance négociables* (*TCN*), a category that also includes the certificate of deposit (CD) issued by banks and the commercial paper (*billets de trésorerie*) issued by industrial and commercial firms. The minimum maturity of *BMTN* is 1 year. There is no upper limit. At the short end, it represents a money-market instrument. They may be issued by banks or by firms, in French francs or in a foreign currency. But now no commercial paper can be issued with a maturity of more than 1 year (previously issues might be for from 10 days to 7 years; in practice, issues were for less than 6 months) and no CD for more than 1 (or 2) years (previously for 10 days to 7 years).

Hence, the choice now open to banks is either to issue CDs for less than 1 year combined with issues of *BMTN* with maturities from 1 year and upwards, or CDs for up to 2 years and *BMTN* for 2 years or more. In a sense, *BMTN* are a substitute for commercial paper and CDs. All issuers of *BMTN* must be rated compulsorily (for creditworthiness), whereas no rating is necessary for issuing CDs of 2 years or less. It is understood that certain small and medium-sized banks were reluctant to be rated.

Chapter 5

The German money market

Once the German banking system had re-established itself after the Second World War (say, by 1958),[1] a familiar pattern began to emerge, viz a 'hybrid' system,[2] made up at end-1990 of three big banks (together with their Berlin subsidiaries), some 192 regional and 'other' banks[3] – 34 of them with a monthly volume of business of DM 100 million to DM 250 million, 54 with a volume of business of DM 1 billion to DM 5 billion, and 24 at DM 5 billion and over; 60 branches of foreign banks (of various sizes); and 83 private banks organized in the form of a sole proprietorship or partnership. Then come the 11 regional giro institutions (all of which are large) and 771 savings banks, the vast majority with a volume of business of over DM 100 million and 34 with business of over DM 5 billion. There are 4 regional institutions of credit co-operatives (all of them large) – these include the Deutsche Genossenschaftsbank – and 3,392 credit co-operatives, of which the bulk of the business volume lies between DM 25 million to DM 250 million (3 of them are large). There are 36 mortgage banks – 27 private and 9 public (27 are large). Banks with special functions number 18, postal giro and postal savings bank offices 16, and building and loan associations 32 (19 private and 13 public).[4]

As at end-June 1991, deposits and borrowing from non-banks for the commercial banks represented 22.4 per cent of the total for all categories of banks (lending to non-banks 29.8 per cent), with big banks at 11.0 per cent (lending 10.4 per cent), regional banks 9.9 per cent (lending 17.3 per cent), unincorporated private banks about 1.2 per cent each side, and foreign bank branches even smaller. The business of the important savings-bank sector is large – 33.4 per cent of deposits and borrowing from non-banks (lending

21.4 per cent), regional giro institutions being a further 6.5 per cent (lending 12.7 per cent). Credit co-operatives had deposits of 19.6 per cent (lending 14.6 per cent), and mortgage banks 10.5 per cent (lending 17 per cent). Of the several types of banks, the largest in order of size were: Deutsche Bank; Dresdner Bank; Commerzbank; Westdeutsche Landes Bank Girozentrale; Bayerische Vereinsbank; Bayerische Hypotheken- und Wechsel-Bank; Bayerische Landesbank Girozentrale; Deutsche Genossenschaftsbank; Norddeutsche Landesbank Girozentrale; and Hessische Landesbank Girozentrale.

THE INTER-BANK MONEY MARKET

The core of the money market in Germany is comprised of inter-bank dealings in central bank balances held at the Landeszentralbanken (which are grouped under the Deutsche Bundesbank in a federal system similar to the Federal Reserve System in the United States) – the market is similar to the market in federal funds in the US. Thus, the inter-bank money market enables domestic credit institutions to make available to others (mainly banks) their excess central bank balances, or – where necessary – to borrow (or buy) such balances in order to add to one's own liquidity. Although they are not part of the money market, non-banks (especially large companies) may also put deposits with the big banks at money-market rates (minus the cost of required minimum reserves). This followed the de-control of interest rates in 1967. The centre of the market is in Frankfurt, but dealings may well feed in from Dusseldorf, Hamburg, Munich, Mainz, and Berlin. And, indeed, the money market is countrywide. The big lenders in the market are certain of the savings banks and their Girozentralen, where deposits and borrowing from non-banks may exceed their lending to non-banks. To some extent, too, whether one is lending or not will depend on seasonal factors. Big banks may borrow or lend and are in the market more or less regularly (on balance they would be lenders);[5] small banks (e.g. most regional banks, the private banks, and foreign bank branches) tend to be regular borrowers.

Basic to establishing what excess balances may or may not be available are the minimum reserves required of commercial banks, savings banks, and other credit institutions by the Deutsche Bundesbank. The required ratios are announced from time to time, but on the whole are not varied all that often.[6] The last change was made on 1 February 1987. At the beginning of a month, the liquidity position of credit institutions is always relatively unclear, if only because the minimum reserve requirement which the credit institutions have to meet on a daily average basis over the current month is not known in the first half of the month. The requirement is calculated from the average of the credit institutions' liabilities subject to reserve requirements during the last 2 weeks of the preceding month and the first 2 weeks of the current month. It is not until the second half of the month, when the credit institutions know what their minimum reserve requirement is for that month, that they can really assess their liquidity position. Moreover, the banks' central bank balances often fluctuate sharply owing to unforeseen market factors (such as foreign exchange movements or public sector cash transactions).[7]

Although minimum reserves only have to be maintained on average over the course of a month,[8] the liquidity of banks and other credit institutions can fluctuate from day-to-day, though to an important extent the Bundesbank will intervene with short-term assistance measures in the open market to iron out any sharp swings in liquidity. Clearly, banks (and similar institutions) will wish to establish what their current liquidity position is as early in the working day as possible. All the big 'universal' banks[9] have a large number of branches throughout the country, with branches in different parts of the country reporting in to a central point; these regional or district centres, which are on-line to Frankfurt, then feed information into the main money desk there and keep it up to date throughout the day (e.g. in respect of large movements of cash whether in or out due to the operations of large corporations).[10] The central money desk will begin to explore the situation about 8.30 a.m., but it may not be too sure of its cash position by 9.00 a.m., even by 10.00 a.m. and – as indicated – the situation can in fact remain fluid over the rest of the working day. None the less, an experienced team of money market personnel can usually get the 'feel' of how the situation is developing. The starting point will be the minimum reserve requirement from which will be deducted cash held in the branches (e.g. for transactions and clearing purposes). The daily calculation will be supported by regular forecasting,[11] judgements as to what the Bundesbank is doing, and allowance for anticipated large movements – due, for example, to large tax payments,[12] or payments in connection with a big underwriting issue. They may also be influenced by interest rate expectations. The incidence of weekends and month-ends is likewise relevant.

So far as the big Landesbanken Gironzentralen are concerned, the situation is a little different. Not only are the large Girozentralen universal banks and highly active in the money markets in their own right, but they are also the central institutions of the savings banks, where only the largest savings banks would deal directly in the money market. For the rest, the associated savings banks are not obliged to tell the Girozentrale what they intend to do and, where the savings banks operate in the money market through their Girozentrale, money can come in or go out over the course of the entire working day.

The bulk of the money dealt in in the inter-bank market is *Tagesgeld*. Either the money will be called each day, or – if allowed to run on – the rate (and/or the amount) will be re-negotiated. Such moneys are normally lent unsecured, though borrowers are subject to limits, which are not disclosed to them. On the other hand, it is not difficult to determine what one's borrowing limits actually are. The emphasis on day-to-day money is because of the need of money for adjustment purposes. Occasionally, too, there are placements of money for a period – for 1, 2, or 3 months up to (say) 12 months. The normal period would be 1–3 months. Such activity enables banks to offset foreseeable disequilibria in liquidity (e.g. shortages on major tax payment dates); the placing of such money may also be influenced by interest rate expectations. In addition, the Deutsche Genossenschaftsbank (the central bank of the Volksbanken) is a lender of period money, and the savings banks with a lot of fixed deposits also tend to lend period money to their central institutions. There may also be inter-bank deposits – e.g. up to 30 days, with fixed deposits of 3–6 months.

Money brokers are not used by the big banks and other large credit institutions in the domestic inter-bank market,[13] the reason being that the bank money market people know each other well, integrity is high and 'a man's word is his bond'. In the Euro-markets, however, brokers are of some importance, though a lot of deals are also done direct. It should be noted, too, that certain banks will use the Euro-currency markets instead of the domestic inter-bank market, if rates are significantly more favourable. Also Euro-funds are in 30-day months and, if it is a 31-day month, banks can buy Eurodollars and swap them into DMs and gain the use of them for an extra day. On the whole, however, the big German banks are lenders in the Eurodollar market. All deals between banks are done on the telephone. Frankfurt is the main centre − where the bulk of the business is done, but the market is countrywide − with banks in Dusseldorf, Hamburg, Mainz, Munich, and Berlin dealing in Frankfurt, or indeed between themselves. There was usually no confirmation by Telex − transactions were normally confirmed a day later on the computer print-out. But now the banks resort to SWIFT (Society for Worldwide International Funds Transfer), and deals are confirmed instantaneously and automatically.

The minimum size of an inter-bank money market transaction might be − for a small bank − DM 1 million. More normally, it would be DM 5 million, and − for a large bank − DM 100 million would be quite common. Amounts could go up to DM 1 billion − it all depends on the size of the bank and on its needs of liquidity; also on the size of potential lenders. So far as the market as a whole is concerned, it is difficult to estimate size, but reports suggest that daily turnover in the inter-bank money market may vary between a minimum of DM 20 billion up to a maximum of perhaps DM 50 billion.[14]

The market would open between 8.30 a.m. and 9.00 a.m., the domestic market being linked to the Euro-markets, which also start up about then. Operations continue until 12.00 noon or 12.30 p.m., but they may run on until later − it depends on the liquidity positions of the several banks. The busiest time is 10.00 a.m. until 11.15 a.m. Normally, the market closes at 12.00 noon, but (e.g. in the last days of the month) the closing time can be extended (usually up to 3.00 p.m.),[15] provided the relevant Landeszentralbank (these are affiliates of the Bundesbank) remains open. After that time, the banks would have to apply for a lombard loan (see pp. 192−5).

Before 10.00 a.m., banks are looking at their cash position and considering rates. By 9.30 a.m. a rate may be emerging but there may be no reliable rate until (say) 10.15 a.m. On this basis, the Bundesbank then decides what it will do. It is less easy to get quotations after 11.30 a.m., when the market goes to lunch. However, foreign banks have begun to come in late with a heavy volume of transactions,[16] and this comes into the inter-bank clearing (the last being at 2.00 p.m.). Foreign banks can get big movements in liquidity late in the day and the inter-bank market may be active until 2.30 p.m., even 2.45 p.m. Usually, the Bundesbank goes into the market about 10.30 a.m. and would certainly have completed its operations by 11.00 a.m. If foreign banks cannot borrow in the inter-bank market later in the day, they will have to go into lombard; such borrowing would usually be up to 1.30 p.m., but could be as late as necessary (e.g. as late as 4.30 p.m.). But foreign banks would prefer to borrow in the market. When the Bundesbank is less willing to help – is even being 'difficult' – this may be done to edge rates up. Whether the Bundesbank is prepared to transfer funds from one bank to another late in the day is at their discretion. If the Bundesbank remains closed, a bank may either have to sit on excess money, or – if short – take up a lombard loan (as we have seen). By varying its attitudes, the Bundesbank is able to give a 'signal'. None the less, banks will always get the liquidity they require; the question is only – at what rate?

MONEY MARKET INSTRUMENTS

Although very important in facilitating adjustments in bank (and other credit institution) liquidity, the inter-bank money market in central bank balances requires to be supported by the existence of, and trading in, other money market instruments – i.e. in money market paper. In Germany, these include Treasury bills, Treasury discount paper (known in Germany as *U-Schätze*),[17] prime acceptances (or *Wechsel*), and the resort to repurchase agreements by the Bundesbank on the basis of securities and bills (see below). Dealing in money market paper is mainly between the Bundesbank, on the one hand, and the several groups of credit institutions, on the other. Transactions in money market paper also take place between the Bundesbank and certain public bodies – especially the Federal Post Office, the ERP Special Fund, and (formerly) the social security funds.

During the period before 1967, when interest rates were controlled, business enterprises and private individuals were not allowed to acquire money market paper. They invested their liquid funds or funds that they did not need for a time almost exclusively in sight, time or savings deposits with the banks. However, in the years following the decontrol of interest rates the Bundesbank, in cooperation with the Federal Ministry of Finance, tried to make money market paper attractive to these groups of investors as well. There has so far been very little dealing in money market paper between banks or between banks and non-banks, in other words without the participation of the

Bundesbank. The interest rates in the market for money market paper are therefore determined by the Bundesbank in close accord with the situation in the money market. The Bundesbank sets the conditions on which it will sell money market paper (or purchase it before maturity). Of course, the volume of sales and purchases does not depend solely on whether and with what offers the Bundesbank is 'in the market'; it also depends on the extent to which the other market participants take up these offers. Altogether, the possibilities open to the Bundesbank for controlling bank liquidity through 'discreet' open market operations would appear to be very limited. Its interventions in the money market often have a signal effect stemming from the interest rates quoted to the banks.[18]

Money market paper is created initially by the borrowing of public bodies such as the Federal Government, the Federal Railways, the Federal Post Office, and the Länder Governments (i.e. provincial or state governments). The Federal Government or other public authorities, acting in conjunction with the Bundesbank, issue Treasury bills and Treasury discount paper to provide short-term financing for part of the public borrowing requirement. The paper created in this way is also known as *'financing' paper* – to distinguish it from the mobilization and liquidity paper discussed below. Treasury discount paper is discounted like Treasury bills. A distinction must be drawn between the paper which is included in the Bundesbank's 'money market regulating arrangements' – and is therefore accepted at any time by the central bank in return for central bank balances – and 'N paper',[19] which in principle is not repurchased by the Bundesbank before maturity. Hence, the issue of financing paper leads to an increase in bank liquidity – in the sense of easier access by banks to additional central bank balances, but only if this paper is included in the Bundesbank's market regulating arrangements and is purchased by banks. Conversely, a decline in the amount of such paper outstanding will diminish bank liquidity. In the past, the only paper sold to banks has been paper without repurchasing commitment, which carries a higher interest rate to compensate for its lower degree of liquidity. This is because the Bundesbank has been trying to prevent the banks from gaining 'quasi-automatic' access to the supply of central bank balances, which would have been possible through premature resales of market regulation paper. For years now, the banks have held no paper included in the money market regulating arrangements. The Bundesbank fixes selling rates (it used to fix repurchase rates as well) for Treasury bills and Treasury rediscount paper and varies these according to developments in the market and its own monetary policy aims. Treasury discount paper of the public sector, which is not included in the money market regulating arrangements, is also offered under the tender procedure.

In addition to the money market paper created to meet the public sector borrowing requirement, such paper also comes into being on the initiative of the Bundesbank. To enable the Bundesbank to sell Treasury bills and Treasury discount paper for open market policy purposes and irrespective of the public authorities need for finance, Section 42 of the Bundesbank Act states that the Bundesbank may request the Federal Government to convert all or part of equalization claims of around DM 8 billion it holds on the Federal Government (as a result of the currency reform of 1948) into Treasury bills or Treasury discount paper. Paper created in this way is known as *mobilization paper*. The Bundesbank is liable to the Federal Government for meeting all obligations arising from mobilization paper. In reality, therefore, it constitutes issues of the Bundesbank and not of the Federal Government. To enable the Bundesbank to issue Treasury bills and Treasury discount paper beyond the amount of the equalization claim, the Stability and Growth Act 1967 added a clause to the Bundesbank Act (Section 42a) according to which – if mobilization paper has already been put into circulation to the amount of the equalization claim – the Federal Government must supply the Bundesbank on request with further Treasury bills and Treasury discount paper up to a maximum amount of DM 8 billion. This is referred to in the Act as *liquidity paper*. The proceeds of the issue may only be used to redeem the paper on or before maturity. For a number of years, mobilization and liquidity paper included in the money market regulating arrangements has only been sold to non-residents and the Federal Post Office (on the basis of particular investment regulations). As a result, the banks no longer have any non-regulated paper ('N-paper'). To absorb short-term surplus liquidity in the banking system, however, the Bundesbank also offers Treasury bills from time to time, usually with a maturity of 3 days; these cannot be sold before maturity. This is done mainly to prevent the rate for day-to-day money from dropping too much during the monthly minimum reserve periods. The amount of mobilization and liquidity paper outstanding is shown in the Bundesbank's Weekly Return and Balance Sheet on the liabilities side.[20]

As already indicated, dealings in Treasury bills are usually between the Bundesbank and the banks (and other credit institutions). Although there may be occasional sales and purchases between banks, there is no general secondary market in Treasury bills in Germany. But – as we shall see – Treasury bills are an important basis for Bundesbank open market operations (e.g. as a basis for repurchase agreements, or a Bundesbank sale to absorb surplus funds). Since March 1980, there has been a tender (or auction) for Treasury bills – it may be a 'volume tender', where the interest rate is prescribed and the banks tender for the quantity that they want, the amount actually allocated being pro rata in relation to the quantities bid for. With an 'interest rate tender', the Bundesbank stipulates a minimum offering rate and the banks may tender at rates above that with a view to winning whatever amounts they are aiming at. They tender for what they want, usually at a range of prices – if they are unlucky, they may get nothing. Allocation is on the basis of price.

Another type of money market paper is the prime acceptance, or *Wechsel*. Prime acceptances are used to finance the movement of goods (exports and imports, but domestically as well) and have long been rediscountable at the Bundesbank up to specified quotas, also in open market operations to regulate the money market (in which case they do not count against the rediscount quotas). In this context, however, there is an upper limit. They become eligible once they have a maturity of no more than 90 days. If a bank has already exhausted its quota, it will have to go to the money market for its additional discounts or obtain accommodation from the central bank, i.e. borrow against government securities lodged in safe custody with the Bundesbank. So far as the customer is concerned, *Wechsel* are discounted at market rates up to an agreed line of credit, which is reconsidered every 3 or 6 months. Nowadays and for some years past, *Wechsel* have been much less important. As far back as 1973, *Wechsel* (or bills discounted) only represented 4 per cent of total lending to non-banks; loans of up to 1 year were then 18.8 per cent of the total. For end-June 1991, the relevant figures were 2.16 per cent and 17.38 per cent.

For many years, the Bundesbank also bought and sold *Wechsel* only through Privatdiskont-AG, which in turn dealt in suitable bankers' acceptances with the banks (and other credit institutions).

This was in addition to being rediscounted at the Bundesbank within the discount quotas. This has now ceased. On 7 September 1989, the Central Bank Council decided to phase out as from 1990, by way of:

a structural adjustment, certain special facilities available to the banks for foreign trade financing (including limit B of the Export Credit Company and the ceiling of Privatdiskont AG). To compensate for the loss of liquidity, it was at the same time decided to increase the 'regular' rediscount quotas by DM 5 billion. The increase became effective as early as November 2, 1989.[21]

Resort to Privatdiskont, which was owned by the several banks, was a vestigial remain and only continued to exist over the years for historical reasons, and was a cheap source of finance.[22]

In Germany, it has been the practice of large corporations to keep their surplus liquid funds in the form of large deposits with the banks, when a market-related rate of interest would be paid (after allowing for the cost of maintaining required minimum reserves). The market for 'wholesale money', or large deposits from customers, is very flexible and very competitive. It was a development favoured by the foreign banks when they began to buy in wholesale moneys for short periods – large sums bought from customers for 3, 4, or 5 days, whereas the minimum period for a time deposit is 30 days. An obvious question was: Why were *negotiable certificates of deposit* not introduced for this purpose? In early 1985, the Bundesbank looked into the possibility of permitting the issue of DM certificates of deposit (CDs), but at that time decided not to proceed. The view taken then was that CDs, as bearer bonds issued by the banks, would not fall under minimum reserve regulations, while time deposits – their close competitors – were covered by the rules.

Not only did this look unfair – it threatened to drive a gaping hole through the minimum reserve instrument. Already the Bundesbank had noticed that some banks were issuing more short-dated bonds with maturities of around a year as a 'subtitute' for time deposits and thus escaping minimum reserves.

The Bundesbank mulled over the issue for months and finally took its decision [in December 1985]. CDs would be allowed after all, but they would fall under minimum reserves, along with bearer and order bonds with maturities of less than two years, which had hitherto not been covered by the rules.

The central bank concluded that it had the power to take this step under section 16 of the Bundesbank law – but it at once ran into trouble, above all from public sector banks which rely heavily on short-term bond issues for their refinancing.[23]

In addition, a turnover tax,[24] which made CDs unattractive, was applied, and – despite an issue by Morgan Guaranty – CDs did not take off and no market for them developed. The German banks still seem to prefer to attract money by way of large deposits, on which they pay market-related rates. This seems to be the facility favoured by both the banks and the large corporations. If the latter wish to disinvest prior to maturity, the bank would make a loan against the security of the deposit; it would insist that the latter be held to date of maturity. Reserve requirements of course apply.

Following a regulatory change at the beginning of 1991, *commercial paper* has begun to be issued in Germany. This has helped to fill an important gap in the range of DM investment instruments. The prospect of the abolition of stock exchange turnover tax, together with the removal of cumbersome official approval procedures for new securities issues, persuaded Deutsche Bank in December 1990 to announce a first programme of DM 500 million for Daimler-Benz. Latterly, J. P. Morgan, as well as other German institutions, have also begun to participate. By the end of October 1991, some 20 facilities totalling DM 13.6 billion had been signed, with outstandings amounting to over DM 8 billion, showing that the bulk of the programmes were being actively used.[25] By far the largest is the DM 5 billion facility for Treuhand (which is in charge of the privatization of state industry in the former DDR of eastern Germany), with the other borrowers almost exclusively German household names. The first foreign entrant – Alcatel of France – also announced a programme, and other foreign names were expected to follow. Investor interest has been strong. Some companies have tapped the market themselves in order to invest the proceeds in higher yielding commercial paper carrying other less popular names. Investment funds with short-term liquidity (most of the paper being for maturities of under 3 months) have provided another outlet. An unexpected source of interest came from municipalities in eastern Germany, which were temporarily flush with cash (because of transfers from the west) that they had failed to convert speedily into investment projects. Indeed, the appetite for paper initially drove yields down to levels at which they were unlikely to be sustained. Hence, in the early days, institutional investors opted to seek better rates elsewhere. However, in the longer run, it will be necessary to attract foreign buyers also, if the market is to develop a steady investor base. So far only one programme (Volkswagen A.G.) carries a credit rating – German companies have traditionally been reluctant to acknowledge the need for them. In the longer run, however, they may well become necessary, especially if foreign buyers are to be drawn into the market.[26]

One of the criticisms one hears in money market circles in Germany relates to the dearth of money market instruments through the agency of which the Bundesbank can operate. It may also have impeded the development of a more sophisticated money market. In this context, therefore, some interest was expressed in a domestic market issue by the Bundesbahn (Federal Railways) of *DM floating-rate notes* on the basis of a US-style auction (i.e. what people in most other countries regard as a normal type of competitive auction); this issue was in March 1990 and was the first such auction of public-authority debt in Germany. The auction was held by the Bundesbank and was for 10-year paper, with an option for the borrower to call the issue after 2 years. It carried a coupon of 20 basis points below the 3-month London Inter-Bank Offered Rate (LIBOR). The issue was a success and attracted DM 2 billion, which was in line with expectations. In June 1990, a further issue of DM 2 billion was made by way of sale through the Frankfurt Stock Exchange.[27] Subsequent issues were to be made at Frankfurt rates (FIBOR). The Bundesbahn issue was seen as an important step forward in the liberalization of Germany's capital markets. Also, following the Federal Railways' move, similar issues were made on behalf of the Federal Government and the Bundespost. But more important from our point of view, this new issue of floating rate notes was seen as a significant advance in the development of the domestic money market. Furthermore, floating rate notes could be used as part of the basis for repurchase agreements with the Bundesbank.[28]

As from May 1991, *Treasury notes* (or *Bundesschatzanweisungen*) were issued on the basis of a US-style price auction on a regular 2-monthly basis. They complemented the 5-year *Bundesobligationen* issued on a tap basis and the longer term *Bund* issues placed in the market, partly via a consortium and partly by auction. Earlier the Bundesbank had initiated important modernizations in the technicalities of the government borrowing programme, including the introduction of the part auction process for 10-year paper. These measures were given an added urgency by the flood of new debt burdening the market in the course of German unification.[29] The development of *Bund* futures on LIFFE in London and on the Deutsche Terminbörse in Frankfurt also assisted the rapid expansion of cash trading in the German bond market.[30]

FINANCIAL FUTURES AND OPTIONS – DEUTSCHE TERMINBÖRSE (DTB)

The Deutsche Terminbörse (DTB) was opened on 26 January 1990. Initially, it traded options on fourteen blue-chip German stocks. This was done in order to test products of largely domestic appeal that were not yet listed on rival derivatives exchanges.[31] Trading was reported to have got off to a brisk start.[32]

It was expected that the futures contracts would be launched in September 1990. These were to include a contract on the DAX blue-chip equity index and another on 10-year government bonds (*Bunds*), the latter was very similar to the successful contract launched on LIFFE in London in September 1988. The German version was introduced in November 1990. None the less, despite the good start, the approach was cautious. Initially, there was a $3\frac{1}{2}$ months' simulation phase on the basis of a new market-making system, though the DTB is more than a derivatives exchange. The Germans sidestepped the disputes in other centres over the merits of pit versus electronic trading. DTB was always to be automated, as the only solution to the problem in a decentralized country. It was only a matter of time before the stock market (which was divided – very unequally – into eight exchanges) was forced to follow suit, and *Inter Banken Informations System* (*IBIS*), the embryo stock price reporting system, was seen as a prelude to centralized electronic trading (at least for leading stocks and bonds).

By June 1990, the DTB planned to add 5 products to its range of options on 14 leading equities. By August 1991, a further options contract on the *Bund* was introduced and there was an additional option on the DAX index of 30 blue-chip stocks. The latter was expected to appeal to retail as well as to institutional investors.[33]

DTB started with a complement of 53 members. The big banks set up sizeable new departments – 50 people at Deutsche Bank, more than 40 at Dresdner, and 70 at Commerzbank. Only Deutsche and Dresdner were committed to make markets in all 14 options. Commerzbank decided to make markets in 10; Deutsche Genossenschaftsbank and a local Frankfurt broker in 6. Other commitments were smaller. Foreign institutions were on the whole notable by their absence. Yet, in several cases, it was as much reservations about the initial success of the options business – particularly given the handicaps of a not always liquid cash market and large bid– offer spreads (plus generous commissions) and an embryo stock borrowing programme – that deterred greater numbers from joining.

The only major further development up to the end of 1991 related to the *Bund* futures contract. First, transaction fees on *Bund* futures contract trading were removed. And then, in November, there was some discussion that market-makers on the DTB – notably Deutsche Bank, Dresdner Bank, Commerzbank, and J. P. Morgan – might commit themselves to trading a minimum daily volume of contracts. Although it was not clear whether this had in fact been agreed, there was nevertheless a significant transfer of *Bund* futures business from LIFFE in London to the DTB in Frankfurt.[34]

CENTRAL BANK INTERVENTION

Monetary targeting

According to the Bundesbank Act and the central bank's own understanding of its role, the basic aim and direction of monetary policy are unequivocal: in the interaction of all the entities responsible for economic policy, the Deutsche Bundesbank has the particular task of safeguarding the currency by regulating the amount of money in circulation and of credit supplied to the economy. By keeping purchasing power stable and the money supply under control, the central bank in a market economy at the same time creates the monetary conditions for maintaining a high level of employment over the longer term, with adequate economic growth.[35]

In this context, and over a number of years, the Bundesbank has set itself a monetary target, which in a sense provides a focus for policy. It first set an annual monetary target and made it known in advance in December 1974. In principle, it has adhered to this practice ever since, though at various times the target has been formulated in different ways.[36] There is no point in attempting to cover the whole story back to the early years.[37] Suffice it to say that, in line with international practice, the Bundesbank has defined various concepts of money stock both in the broader and the narrower sense. Thus, M1 = currency and sight deposits of domestic non-banks with domestic banks; M2 = M1 plus time deposits of domestic non-banks for less than 4 years; M3 = M2 plus savings deposits of domestic non-banks at statutory notice. One might note, too, that central bank money stock was equated to currency held by non-banks plus required minimum reserves held against banks' domestic liabilities (calculated at constant reserve ratios), but excluding bank bonds subject to minimum reserve requirements. M1, M2, and M3 are calculated from banking statistics on the basis of end-of-month figures. Latterly (from 1988 onwards), the Bundesbank has targeted M3, because of the disproportionately increased weighting of money in circulation in the central bank money stock.[38]

In every year since 1975, the Bundesbank has derived its target for the money stock from 'its views on the economic trend envisaged in the year concerned'. The monetary target has always been based on an overall economic projection which has been discussed with the Federal Government, and the key variables have been fixed 'according to normative criteria'. More specifically, the main variables to be taken into account are: (a) the expected growth in the production potential; and (b) the rise in prices. Self-corrective factors in the economy:

> contribute to an increase in the 'velocity of circulation' of money during an upswing as the utilisation of the production potential also rises, while it declines in a downswing as utilisation falls. In principle, therefore, the growth in the money stock should vary less than the development of production since purely cyclical fluctuations in the degree of utilisation and the 'velocity of circulation' tend to neutralise each other in their effect on the demand for money in the economy. The changes in the 'velocity of circulation' of money do not, however, simply reflect the business cycle; changes in the demand for money mirroring a general trend and structural factors may also play a part.[39]

(a) 1989–91

a Target and movement to date (R)

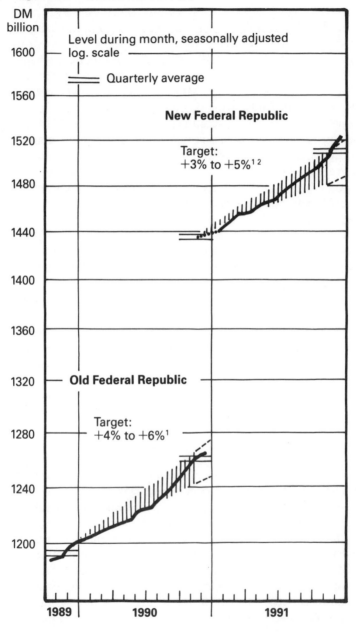

(b) 1990—2

Figure 5.1   Growth of the money stock M3* (a) 1989—91 (b) 1990—2

b Target and movement to date

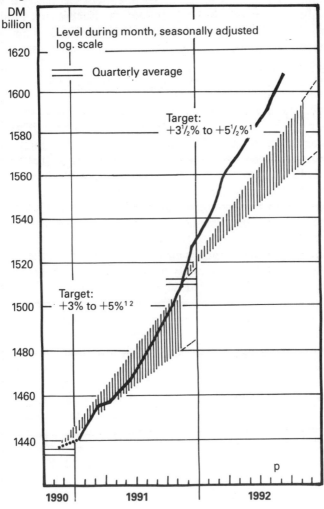

Notes: * Average of 5 bank-week return days, end-of-month levels included with a weight of 50 per cent
[1] Between the fourth quarter of the preceding year and the fourth quarter of the current year
[2] In accordance with the adjustment of the monetary target in July 1991

Source: Deutsche Bundesbank

Since unification of East and West Germany, account has also had to be taken of the strong expansion of the money stock M3 in the wake of the currency conversion. This was being curbed by more rapid monetary adjustment processes in eastern Germany. It was primarily this situation which prompted the Bundesbank to alter the target range of M3 growth from 4–6 per cent to 3–5 per cent for the entire currency area of the DM.[40] This was subsequently increased to $3\frac{1}{2}$–$5\frac{1}{2}$ per cent.[41]

Also, since the mid-1970s, the Bundesbank has regularly employed an econometric model of the economy of the Federal Republic of Germany as a basis for macro-economic analyses. Over the years, the model has been further refined and adjusted to changing structural and development factors. In the preparation of the monetary target, the econometric model can be of great assistance, though its potential applications are much wider than that. In addition, it is appreciated that monetary and fiscal policy measures, like other economic policy decisions, generally exercise their full effects with a time-lag – sometimes a considerable one (it may be as long as 3 years). 'In other words, the consequences of economic and monetary policy measures extend far into the future, while short-run effects are rarely to be observed, so that there is a tendency to be disappointed about the effectiveness of these measures.' However, an econometric model is a formal instrument, which enables the interrelationships between economic developments and political measures to be recorded and revealed in a consistent overall picture. But an econometric model can provide only a simplified representation of complex economic relations. Hence, sources of uncertainty in a forecast can be estimated, but not eliminated. Parallel to the econometric forecasts, the Bundesbank also elaborates non-econometric predictions, and the results of the two forecasting methods are subjected to mutual checks. The remaining uncertainties are one reason why economic policy decisions cannot simply be derived from the forecasts.[42]

Within this framework, the monetary target can only operate as a guideline. At the same time, it is a recognition of the view that money matters, and that there is a relationship between money and prices. Some years ago, the target was met by resorting to the 'corridor concept':[43] for example, the target for the growth of the central bank money stock was set in 1986 to lie between 3.5 to 5.5 per cent and, in 1987, to between 3 and 6 per cent. In M3 terms, in 1988, a target was set at from 3 to 6 per cent growth.[44] The use of a 'corridor' was first and foremost 'intended to give monetary policy over the course of a year scope for reacting to unexpected disruptions to economic activity, prices and exchange rates without jeopardising the credibility of monetary targeting'.[45] Also, a certain discretionary room for manoeuvre in monetary policy is often very necessary to take account of short-term irregularities in the way in which financial markets function. But a corridor has not always been laid down and, in 1989, the target was set at 'about' 5 per cent. In any event, the Bundesbank has always operated monetary targets in a flexible manner – not month by month (when the target may well be exceeded), but over the course of the year. In addition, the Bundesbank tends to favour a forward strategy, believing that there is always a time-lag between the occurrence of monetary indiscipline and the development of inflationary price rises, though it is not always easy to sell this view to a public which may be more concerned with levels of employment. Thus, after it had lowered the 1991 monetary target from a corridor of 4–6 per cent to that of 3–5 per cent on the occasion of its annual review in July – supported in mid-August by a rise in its discount and lombard rates by 1 per cent (to 7.5 per cent) and $\frac{1}{4}$ per cent ($9\frac{1}{4}$ per cent) respectively – it reaffirmed this policy stance on 5 December 1991, when the Central Bank Council adopted the same monetary target for 1992.[46]

The Bundesbank also keeps its eye on the exchange rate. If there is a feeling that a misalignment of the exchange rate has had an adverse effect on prices, the Bundesbank would attempt to reassert monetary discipline and move closer to the target. Furthermore, there is now the complication that the DM is generally regarded as a reserve currency – the problem being that, if one is successful in keeping the volume of money relatively stable, there is a tendency to attract inflows of money from abroad with an obvious impact within the domestic economy.

Minimum reserve requirements

Although variation of minimum reserve requirements is a means of central banking intervention, the level at which the ratios have been set provides in an important sense the framework within which the authorities have to operate in terms of their regular market intervention with a view to influencing the liquidity of the banking system and, indeed, of the economy as a whole.

Required minimum reserves were first introduced in Germany[47] when the Bank Deutscher Länder was established in 1948. The intention was from the start to provide the central bank with a flexible and effective instrument as a basis for liquidity policy. In earlier years, the minimum reserves were revised with relative frequency. Latterly,[48] this has been less true and, indeed, the last change was made on 1 February 1987. That is why one might well regard such minima as providing the liquidity framework within which the authorities – and the banks (and other credit institutions) – now operate.

The relevant regulations are based on Section 16 of the Bundesbank Act, which states that the Bundesbank may require banks to hold a specific percentage of their liabilities arising from sight deposits, time deposits, and savings deposits as well as from short- and medium-term borrowing (other than their liabilities to other banks themselves subject to reserve requirements). The percentages set by the Bank may not exceed 30 for sight liabilities, 20 for time liabilities, and 10 for savings deposits. However, the Bank may set a percentage of up to 100 for liabilities to non-residents. Within these limits, the Bundesbank may set the percentages at different levels, especially for individual groups of banks, on the basis of general considerations, and may exclude certain liabilities from the calculation.[49]

REFINANCING POLICY

'Refinancing' generally means lending by the Bundesbank to the credit institutions through the purchase of bills (rediscounting) and the granting of loans against collateral (lombard loans). According to Section 15 of the Bundesbank Act, the aim of refinancing is to influence the amount of money in circulation and of credit granted. Interest rates are 'the main action parameters' of refinancing policy. But under the same section of the Act, there is also the possibility of Bundesbank restrictions on refinancing that are of a qualitative or quantitative character. The individual banks have no general right to refinancing facilities under the Act. The provision of rediscount and lombard credit by the Bundesbank to the banks is dependent on the general monetary situation. Also, the particular circumstances of the institution seeking credit may likewise be taken into account. And the provision of lombard credit at the ruling lombard rate not only can be limited quantitatively; it can even be suspended altogether for monetary policy reasons.

Rediscount policy

Section 19 of the Bundesbank Act gives the Deutsche Bundesbank the right to buy from and sell to banks trade bills and Treasury bills of the Federal and Länder governments and the Federal Special Funds (the Federal Railways, the Federal Post Office, the Equalization of Burdens Fund, and the ERP Special Fund) at a rate which it sets for itself (the discount rate), provided that the bills satisfy the conditions specified in the Act. The Act only lays down the minimum requirements for rediscountable bills. They must be backed by three parties known to be solvent; they must fall due within 3 months of purchase; and they should be good trade bills. In its credit policy regulations introduced in 1977, the Bundesbank has defined in greater detail the requirements for the purchase of bills. According to these regulations, only parties whose financial position can be adequately assessed (e.g. on the basis of annual accounts) can be regarded as 'known to be solvent'. The trade bills purchased by the Bundesbank are those drawn between enterprises and/or the self-employed on the basis of deliveries of goods or services. Of major importance for liquidity policy is the possibility of limiting the total amount of rediscount credit available to the banks by establishing global rediscount quotas. All bills rediscounted at the Bundesbank and not yet due are counted against these rediscount quotas. Formerly, there could be special rediscount lines for particular bills – e.g. certain promissory notes to finance business with the German Democratic Republic.

The total amount of the rediscount quotas is fixed by the Central Bank Council. For the distribution of this total among the individual credit institutions the Bundesbank introduced a uniform method of calculation in 1974 to enable a 'standard quota' to be computed for each bank according to objective criteria. An institution's liable capital forms the basis for this computation. The acquisition of a major participation in another credit institution which already has a discount quota generally brings a corresponding cut in the quota. In addition, the particular business structure of the institution is taken into account through a structural component calculated from the share of shorter-term lending to nonbanks in the total volume of business. Moreover, since mid-1978, the extent to which the credit institution holds bills which can be rediscounted within the quota is also taken into consideration. Finally, the procedure includes a multiplier which is uniform for all credit institutions and is determined according to the total amount of the rediscount quotas fixed by the Central Bank Council. After the standard quotas have been calculated in this way, the rediscount quota for each credit institution is fixed individually. Due regard is also paid to whether the bank is observing the Principles of the Federal Banking Supervisory Office concerning Capital and Liquidity, and whether its conduct of business is otherwise beyond reproach. The quotas fixed generally apply for 1 year.

In the past, the rediscount quotas fixed were often generally reduced or increased according to the requirements of monetary policy. More recently, one or two revisions of discount quotas were made – as 'technical adjustments' to bank liquidity – e.g. a DM 5 billion increase effective 2 November 1988 to enable the banks to replace part of the large volume of repurchase agreements outstanding with comparatively inexpensive bill-based borrowing; again, there was a DM 5 billion increase effective 2 November 1989, when the supplementary rediscount ceiling at Privatdiskont was being phased out. Also, following monetary union between the Federal Republic of Germany and the German Democratic Republic on 1 July 1990, the Deutsche Bundesbank granted the GDR banks – initially on the basis of their individual balance sheet totals – 'refinancing quotas' totalling just over DM 25 billion with effect from 1 July. These quotas could be utilized (at the discount rate) by submitting bank promissory notes.[50] Quotas have on occasion also been reduced.

The rate at which bills (*Wechsel*) are rediscounted at the Bundesbank within the quotas is discount rate. The Bundesbank Act does not lay down maximum or minimum levels for the discount rate. The Bundesbank can therefore act with complete autonomy in setting the rate and can adjust it to meet current monetary policy requirements.[51] The rate applies uniformly to all bills presented for rediscount at the Bundesbank. It is generally also applied to cash advances to the public sector within the statutory ceilings.

Lombard policy

Under Section 19(1)3 of the Bundesbank Act, the Deutsche Bundesbank may also grant the credit institutions loans at interest against the collateral of certain securities and Debt Register claims. Such loans are known as lombard loans. They may not be extended for longer than 3 months. In principle, the Bundesbank can grant lombard loans against: (a) bills (including Treasury bills) which meet the conditions for rediscount; (b) Treasury discount paper (*U-Schätze*) maturing within 1 year; (c) bonds and Debt Register claims of the Federal Government, a Land Government, or a Federal Special Fund; (d) other bonds and Debt Register claims specified by the Bundesbank; and (e) equalization claims entered in the Debt Register. The limit up to which credit may be granted differs according to the type of collateral. The paper listed under (a) is eligible for a loan of up to 90 per cent of its nominal value and all the other paper for a loan of up to 75 per cent of its market or nominal value. In principle, the Bundesbank only grants lombard loans to bridge temporary liquidity needs on the part of a credit institution and if the purpose of the loan is acceptable.[52] The rate for lombard loans[53] has so far always been above the discount rate, an indication of the fact that lombard loans are designed to be for special purposes. For example, banks might be forced to draw quite heavily on lombard loans towards the end of a month in order to adjust liquidity, though – if the Bundesbank has been restrictive – the banks may be pushed to draw funds in this way at a very early date in a particular month (e.g. in July 1988, when there was a persistent tendency for money market rates to tighten).[54] Again, since the banks may take up lombard loans at their discretion in advance of a probable rise in lombard rates, they may borrow heavily in this way (as in December 1988),[55] but – after a rise in the lombard rate on 20 January 1989 and in order to get lombard borrowing down to much lower levels – the Bundesbank could come in (as it did then) and offer 1-month securities repurchase agreements, initially as a volume tender at a fixed rate of 5 per cent. This was done immediately after the raising of the lombard rate. Thereafter, the banks' lombard borrowing remained almost constantly at its usual low level.[56] Also, when securities repurchase transactions were put on a more market-related basis in the autumn of 1988, the banks showed: 'a growing tendency to draw comparatively heavily on lombard loans in periods when interest rates in the money market were rising temporarily, and sometimes for purely "speculative" reasons, even though they were not experiencing any liquidity squeeze.' This trend was due to the fact:

> that the banks quickly discounted any suddenly emerging market expectations of adjustments to the Bundesbank's 'key interest rates' by adjusting their bidding rates for securities repurchase

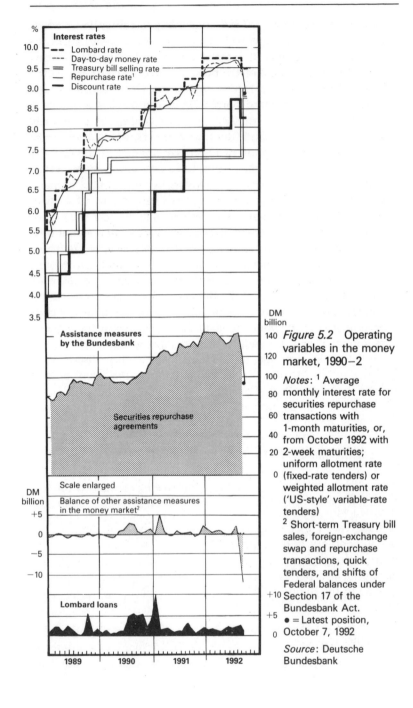

Figure 5.2 Operating variables in the money market, 1990−2

Notes: [1] Average monthly interest rate for securities repurchase transactions with 1-month maturities, or, from October 1992 with 2-week maturities; uniform allotment rate (fixed-rate tenders) or weighted allotment rate ('US-style' variable-rate tenders)

[2] Short-term Treasury bill sales, foreign-exchange swap and repurchase transactions, quick tenders, and shifts of Federal balances under Section 17 of the Bundesbank Act.

● = Latest position, October 7, 1992

Source: Deutsche Bundesbank

agreements accordingly. This can give rise to a situation in which recourse to the lombard facility may sometimes seem attractive not only on grounds of interest rate speculation, but – when market rates and most of the rates tendered reach or exceed the level of the lombard rate – ultimately also because of the increased cost. Lombard borrowing of this kind is at variance with the exceptional nature of this facility, which is intended only for meeting peak needs; it does not necessarily, however, cause any permanent disruption of the money market as the Bundesbank can prevent an undesirable 'liquidity glut' in the money market in particular by reducing the volume of subsequent securities repurchase agreements accordingly. Quite apart from this, unfulfilled expectations of further interest rate rises often make speculative lombard borrowing appear unrewarding in retrospect because the call money rates may ease later on. Thus, after the heavy lombard borrowing in February and early March [1989], the amount of lombard loans outstanding dropped relatively quickly again to a mere DM 0.3 billion in April (on a monthly average).There were indications of a similar trend at the beginning of June when lombard borrowing manifestly returned to normal after some spells of excessive borrowing in May.[57]

Resort to lombard credits by the German commercial banks fluctuates from time to time – there was a sharp rise in October 1989 – but it usually drops back quite quickly to lower levels. However, after 1 July 1990, when GDR banks could also draw on the lombard loan facility at the Bundesbank (on the basis of promissory notes), there was a significant rise in lombard loans, which continued – more or less on a plateau – until September 1990, when there was a sharp fall.[58] But this was followed by a marked rise thereafter to a peak early in 1991. More normal conditions then returned with small use being made of the facility into the first half of that year. This was associated with the raising of the lombard rate in February 1991 'to correct the distortion of the shorter-term interest rate pattern and thus regain scope for tight money market management'. Before that, the call money rate and the rates applied to the Bundesbank's securities repurchase agreements had been running virtually at, or slightly above, the level of the lombard rate (of 8.5 per cent at the time), and 'this had encouraged heavy and rather unpredictable lombard borrowing by the banks'.[59]

OPEN MARKET OPERATIONS

The Bundesbank first engaged in open market operations in the money market in 1955. Until the beginning of the 1970s, efforts were concentrated mainly on offering the credit institutions opportunities for investing their surplus liquidity in interest-bearing assets, largely as a result of what were at times extremely heavy inflows of funds from abroad. These open market operations were all with the credit institutions and were in mobilization paper, which was included in the Bundesbank's money market regulating arrangements. In August 1958, the volume of mobilization paper outstanding reached a temporary peak – at more than DM 7 billion. During the 1960s, these operations again receded somewhat, the main reason being that – under the system of fixed exchange rates and after the transition to full convertibility as from the beginning of 1959 – the credit institutions were no longer obliged to hold their secondary liquid reserves in domestic investments and they began to acquire an increasing amount of short-term foreign assets as well. At the same time, the Bundesbank was anxious to encourage the banks to hold foreign-exchange reserves. Subsequently, during the expansive monetary phase of 1967–8, very little mobilization paper was sold to the banks, so that the money market was kept liquid and a downward trend in interest rates was encouraged.

As from July 1970, greater quantities of mobilization paper were sold once more to the banks. When the scope for such sales was exhausted at the beginning of 1971, liquidity paper was issued for the first time. In mid-1971, the Bundesbank also began to include non-banks in open market operations in money market paper, offering Bundesbank discount paper (standardized *U-Schätze* which could not be returned before maturity) to private investors as well. At the end of 1973, the outstanding amount of mobilization and liquidity paper amounted to some DM 10 billion (of which some DM 7.7 billion had been placed with non-banks – mainly the social security funds and the Post Office). The Bundesbank has sold the banks no further mobilization or liquidity paper covered by its money market regulating arrangements since the spring of 1975. By the end of 1977, the volume of mobilization and liquidity paper outstanding had dropped to DM 5.4 billion. But there was a renewed and very strong rise in the following year (to DM 14.7 billion in mid-November 1978) as the Bundesbank absorbed part of the massive inflows of liquidity from abroad at that time by selling non-returnable money market paper. At the end of December 1981, the total amount of mobilization and liquidity paper in circulation was about DM 5 billion – it was held by foreign central banks and the Post Office. At that date, no such paper was placed with the banks, since the Bundesbank had repurchased prematurely the remaining paper in the banks' portfolios by the spring of 1980 to compensate for outflows of foreign exchange.

Repurchase agreements

A big change in the emphasis of open market operations was initiated in June 1979, when the Bundesbank began to develop such transactions on the basis of repurchase agreements against fixed-interest securities already eligible as collateral for lombard loans (see above). This type of operation grew especially fast in 1985, when it began to be used very regularly – even more so after May 1988. Transactions of this nature had been effected against domestic bills since April 1973. Now this facility was being extended to fixed-interest securities as a means of making central bank balances available for a limited period. For monetary policy purposes, this procedure had the advantage over an outright purchase of financial assets of being reversible after a short period. Such transactions also had the advantage over refinancing policy measures of always leaving the initiative with the Bundesbank; moreover, the terms – maturity, rate structure, and total amount – could be varied according to the current liquidity situation. After March 1980, the 'volume tender' (with a prescribed interest rate) or the 'interest rate tender' (when only a minimum offering rate is fixed) proved to be very successful. Transactions under repurchase agreements in fixed-interest securities have the further advantage over outright purchases that they do not directly affect prices in the bond market. They therefore only serve to regulate the money market. It is from there that their repercussive effects spread to exercise an influence on the capital market.

Resort to repurchase agreements against fixed-interest securities has now become the main means in Germany of making central bank balances available to the banking system. By 1986 and 1987, it represented quite a significant input of funds, especially compared with lombard loans, which were quite small, though marginally of importance from time to time. However, after May 1988, resort to repurchase agreements increased markedly in importance and it is now clearly the main means of market intervention by the Bundesbank. Over the same period, though at a much lower level, greater use was also made of lombard loans (see above).[60]

It may be instructive to look in more detail at recent experience of the resort to repurchase agreements. For example, after May 1988, the Bundesbank sought to pursue a markedly less expansionary monetary policy. The day-to-day money rate began to rise, also the repurchase rate, and this was consolidated by increases in discount rate, the selling rate for Treasury bills, and lombard rate (see Figure 5.2). With temporary hesitations, all these rates were to go on climbing until well into 1991. Over this period, beginning about May 1988, the Bundesbank was encouraging a slight tightening of short-term money market rates as part of its money market management, by slightly reducing its ongoing provision of liquidity relative to the sharp rise in the banks' liquidity needs. The rate applied to securities repurchase agreements, all of which were offered as volume tenders until the end of August 1988, was raised from 3.25 per cent to 4.25 per cent in a number of steps. In addition, the Bundesbank increased the discount rate from 2.50 per cent to 3.00 per cent with effect from July 1, and the lombard rate from 4.50 per cent to 5.00 per cent with effect from July 29. The further raising of the discount rate – from 3.00 per cent to 3.50 per cent as from 26 August – consolidated the rise in market rates that had occurred in the meantime. On the other hand, the Bundesbank facilitated the 'entering' of the August reserve period by adding to liquidity through short-term foreign exchange swaps (see p. 205) and by introducing a 'fourth' monthly securities repurchase agreements programme. In this way, recourse to the lombard facility was kept within fairly narrow limits. The call money rate ran initially just below the lombard rate, but it fell markedly in the last bank-week of August 1988. In the light of the high 'plateau' of repurchase agreements outstanding and the additional requirements of funds to be expected in September, which is a 'major' tax-payment month, the Bundesbank at the beginning of that month supplied the banks with longer-term funds through an interest-rate tender with a 2-month maturity; this was done in conjunction with a regular volume tender with an unchanged fixed rate of 4.25 per cent and a maturity of 1 month. For the first time, the Bundesbank used a flexible allotment procedure which gave the banks a greater say in determining the interest rate they would be charged. In contrast to the previous practice for interest rate tenders, the Bundesbank did not prescribe a minimum bidding rate, and it made allotments not on the basis of a uniform interest rate (the so-called 'Dutch' allotment procedure), but – beginning with the highest tender rates – on the basis of the individual bidding rates of the banks (what the Germans call the 'American' allotment procedure). About DM 12 billion was allotted for 2 months under the interest-rate-tender tranche, with accepted bids ranging from 4.50 per cent to 5.15 per cent.

Use of the 'US-style' allotment method for securities repurchase agreements was a technical innovation.[61] By resorting to this method – in contrast to the 'Dutch' allotment procedure or a volume tender – banks had to pay exactly what they bid for their funds rather than an average computed on the basis of all bids. The repurchase rates that the banks had to pay were thus more in line with money-market conditions, as perceived by the individual banks bidding for funds. The new more market-related method was first tested in September 1988 upon the issue of longer-term tranches; since the end of October 1988, it has also been applied to securities repurchase transactions with the standard 1-month maturity. All the rates tendered by banks in bids allotted by the Bundesbank were above the previously applied fixed rate of 4.25 per cent and thus approached more closely to the ruling money market rates.

In its ongoing provision of liquidity, the Bundesbank relied primarily on revolving securities repurchase agreements between September and November 1988, following some temporary recourse to lombard borrowing in the summer months. In addition, it resorted to some very short-term assistance measures for 'fine tuning' the money market. For instance, in September, when liquidity was reduced not only as a result of the 'major' tax payment date, but also because of exceptionally heavy Federal Government market borrowing, additional funds were provided by means of shifts of Federal balances to the banking system (under Section 17 of the Bundesbank Act). Again, at the end of November, when heavy pressure was building up in the market, the Bundesbank for the first time gave the banking system short-term assistance by means of short-dated (4-day) securities repurchase agreements. This new 'quick tender' was primarily directed at banks that were particularly active in the money market and which were able to pass on speedily the funds obtained from the Bundesbank. Accordingly, the period for winding up such deals – with announcement, bidding, allotment and crediting all taking place witin a few hours – was comparatively short. This was to become a permanent addition to the armoury of Bundesbank money-market operations.

The objective implied by the monetary target for 1989 – viz. of restraining monetary growth – prompted the Bundesbank slightly to tighten monetary policy around the turn of the year. In December 1988, it initially abstained from easing the pressures that were building up in the money market (as is usual in December) and raised the lombard rate from 5.00 per cent to 5.50 per cent with effect from 16 December. After money-market rates had started to edge upwards in the ensuing period, the Bundesbank – in line with similar measures taken in other industrial countries – raised the discount and lombard rates by half a per cent each to 4.00 per cent and 6.00 per cent respectively, with effect from 20 January 1989. In December, too, some banks had been relying heavily on lombard borrowing from the Bundesbank, especially in anticipation of the raising of the lombard rate. To prompt a stabilization of interest-rate expectations in the money market, and thereby also to encourage a rapid decline in recourse to the lombard facility on interest-cost grounds, the Bundesbank offered 1-month securities repurchase agreements, initially in the form of a volume tender at a fixed rate of 5.00 per cent; this was done immediately after raising the lombard rate. Thereafter, the banks' lombard borrowing remained almost consistently at its usual low level and the call money rate was mostly below the lombard rate (of 5.50 per cent) until well into January 1989. When the Bundesbank resumed the 'US-style' interest rate tenders in mid-January, allocations in the tender were mainly below the new lombard rate of 6.00 per cent, or approached it only in isolated cases. Around the turn of the year, liquidity policy measures as part of ongoing money market management were virtually confined to the usual revolving securities repurchase agreements. It was only at the end of January 1989 that some liquidity was temporarily siphoned off through short-term foreign exchange repurchase agreements with banks when – because of the very low Federal government borrowing through a Treasury paper tender – a considerable and unexpected liquidity glut emerged in the money market.

After the discount rate and lombard rate increases in January 1989, the Bundesbank 'followed a steadying strategy' in its money-market management. Moreover, it saw no reason to yield to what it regarded as at times exaggerated financial-market speculation on a further rise in interest rates in Germany. Later in the period, it became evident, however, that the pace of monetary expansion was still quite rapid and that the upward movement in costs and prices was threatening to become rather stronger than had originally been expected. The Central Bank Council of the Bundesbank therefore decided to raise the discount and lombard rates by $\frac{1}{2}$ per cent each – to 4.50 per cent and 6.50 per cent respectively, with effect from 21 April 1989. This resulted in a moderate increase in the short-term money market rates.

The chief instrument used for the ongoing provision of central bank balances was revolving securities repurchase agreements, with one of the five monthly tenders being of 2-months maturity and the remaining four tenders of 1-month maturity. To ease the pressure that built up in the money market at the turn of each month, when the trend in bank liquidity is occasionally difficult to foresee, the Bundesbank resorted in addition to very short-term assistance measures. At the end of February 1989, when the banks' minimum reserve requirements turned out to be appreciably higher than had generally been expected, the Bundesbank provided additional funds through a 'quick tender' (a securities repurchase agreement running for a few days only). When the opposite situation arose at the end of March, it mopped up temporary excess liquidity in the money market by selling Treasury bills to the banking system. Through 'US-style' interest rate tenders (allotment in the order of the bids beginning with the highest rates tendered), the Bundesbank continued its policy of applying to the individual securities repurchase agreements allotment rates, which – based on the individual banks' bidding rates – came as close as possible to market rates. Only in March 1989 did it temporarily offer volume tenders (with a fixed allotment rate) in order to counteract an undesirable tightening of money-market rates and to discourage banks from large-scale lombard borrowing.

In the summer months of 1989, the Bundesbank maintained what it called its 'basic monetary policy stance'; this was geared to containing monetary expansion and to stabilizing the level of prices over the longer term. Since by mid-year the pressures of mounting cyclical demand and external factors were exacerbating the risks to future price and cost trends, the Bundesbank raised its interest rates further. When reviewing and confirming the 1989 monetary target, the Central Bank Council raised the discount and lombard rates by

$\frac{1}{2}$ per cent each to 5 per cent and 7 per cent respectively, with effect from 30 June. By taking such action, the Bundesbank made it clear that for the remainder of the year it intended 'to keep monetary growth as moderate as possible and to work towards the stabilisation of the domestic and external purchasing power of the Deutsche Mark'.

Following these interest-rate policy measures, the Bundesbank assisted the banks by offering repurchase agreements (initially for 1 month) in the form of volume tenders at a fixed-interest rate of 6.60 per cent. In the wake of the measures adopted at the end of June 1989, interest rates at the short end of the money market went up. By way of contrast, longer-term rates (3 months and over) tended to follow the temporary easing (and subsequent tightening) of conditions in the domestic capital market as well as international interest-rate and dollar-exchange-rate movements. It made little difference when in August the Bundesbank reverted to interest-rate tenders for its securities repurchase agreements. The allotment rates were only slightly above those applied to the preceding volume tenders. Overall longer-term money market rates edged up only marginally between the end of June and the beginning of September. Since other European central banks followed this raising of interest rates by the Bundesbank, the level of interest rates in Germany (also that in Japan) continued to be at the bottom end of the international interest-rate range.

For its current provision of central bank balances in this period, the Bundesbank relied almost exclusively on the instrument of revolving securities repurchase agreements. In view of the large volume of these transactions, the stock of which now averaged DM 96 billion, some of the funds provided in this way were at rather longer term. As from July 1989, the Bundesbank concluded 2-month securities repurchase agreements – along with the usual 1-month agreements – not only at the beginning of the month, but also in mid-month. The banks increasingly reduced their use of the lombard facility during this period. There was also little need for very short-term assistance measures in the summer months – only at the end of August was a temporary slump in money market rates arrested by sales to the banks of very short-term Treasury bills. In this context, the Treasury bill selling rate – which in effect represents the lower limit to the call money rate – was raised from 5.50 per cent to 6.00 per cent with effect from 29 August 1989.

During the autumn of 1989, Bundesbank monetary policy

remained geared 'to the objective of counteracting at an early stage any overheating of the economy and any emergence of inflationary pressures'. To this end, it was considered appropriate to raise money market rates further. With effect from 6 October 1989, the discount and lombard rates of the Bundesbank were put up by 1 per cent each to 6 per cent and 8 per cent respectively. Prior to that (on 7 September) – as we have seen – the Central Bank Council 'by way of a structural adjustment' had phased out certain facilities available to the banks for foreign-trade financing, and the loss of liquidity was compensated by an increase in the 'regular' rediscount quotas by DM 5 billion, an increase that became effective on 2 November 1989.

To make it easier for the money market to adjust to the new key interest rates, the Bundesbank switched to a fixed rate for its 1-month securities repurchase agreements offered as part of its ongoing money-market management, following interest-rate decisions already referred to, and the repurchase rate was set at 7.30 per cent. Longer-term repurchase agreements continued to be in the form of interest-rate tenders. But the call money rate did not deviate very much from the new lombard rate during October, and longer inter-bank rates tightened further. The main reason for this was probably that – in anticipation of the lombard rate increase – the banks had drawn very heavily on the lombard facility at the Bundesbank (DM 38 billion at the peak). As a consequence, they secured well in advance (and on an unusually large scale) the funds they needed to meet minimum reserve requirements – which are based on daily averages of the calendar month. This resulted in a comparatively low level of reserves for the remainder of the month, which apparently caused problems for the daily liquidity management of some banks and there was a certain amount of tension in the money market. This did not ease until November, when there was a decline in the call money rate.

Revolving securities repurchase agreements remained the main channel for the current provision of funds to the banking system between September and November 1989 (apart from the major role played by lombard loans in October). In November, with the rapid utilization of the higher rediscount quotas by the banks, the amount outstanding under open market operations fell appreciably (to an average of DM 92.5 billion). In December, this amount was to climb again to DM 101.9 billion. The Bundesbank offered very short-term assistance only on isolated occasions during this period (e.g. in October, when it shifted Federal funds into the money market on a daily basis under Section 17 of the Bundesbank Act); in November, it mopped up temporary excess liquidity in the market by means of sales of short-term Treasury bills. In this connection, the selling rate was raised from 6.50 per cent to 7.00 per cent with effect from November 17, in order to prevent an unduly marked easing of call money rates.

Reference has already been made to action in February 1991 to correct the distortion of the shorter-term, interest-rate pattern – and its implications for the level of the lombard rate (then 8.5 per cent), which encouraged heavy and rather unpredictable lombard borrowing at that time. The Bundesbank now underlined its intention of eliminating distortions in the interest-rate pattern in the money market by its simultaneous transition to fixed-rate tenders for 1-month securities repurchase agreements – the initial rate was 8.5 per cent. By April 1991, however, it had increased the rate to 8.6 per cent, thus bringing it more into line with comparable current market rates. As we have seen (see p. 189), this tight monetary policy stance was reinforced by an increase both in discount rate and lombard rate (in mid-August 1991) and the extension into 1992 of a lower corridor for the monetary target. There was also a $\frac{1}{2}$ per cent increase in interest rates in December 1991, with discount rate rising to 8 per cent and lombard rate to 9.75 per cent.[62]

'FINE-TUNING'

Now that resort to repurchase agreements (as described above) has taken over as the main method whereby an appropriate quantum of liquidity is made available to the system, 'fine-tuning' relates only to the other techniques of short-term intervention – measures principally employed to neutralize temporary fluctuations in bank liquidity (any impact on money market rates to be 'discreet', i.e. not liable to provoke unwelcome signal effects). If we exclude the main operation on the basis of repurchase agreements, the measures that have been employed as a means of fine-tuning include: *foreign exchange swaps* (normally DM against US dollars) – it may do this whether it wishes to put money into the system or, conversely, to withdraw it (see below); alternatively, it may do a *foreign exchange repurchase agreement* (again, see below); another technique of 'mopping up' is the *sale of short-dated Treasury bills*;

or (to put funds into the system, or to withdraw them) the Bundesbank can shift the funds of Federal government accounts[63] as deposits either to (or from) the banking system in accordance with Section 17 of the Bundesbank Act.[64]

A more recent example of 'fine-tuning' was the *resort to 'quick tenders'* in February 1989 (at a time when the banks' minimum reserve requirements turned out to be appreciably higher than had generally been expected); additional funds were then provided through securities repurchase agreements running for a few days only. Subsequently, 'quick tenders' became recognized as a useful additional instrument for purposes of fine-tuning. All of these measures referred to here are in the nature of 'smoothing-out' operations.

These several types of measures have been referred to already in the wider context of money market management (and especially in the section on securities repurchase agreements), so they need little further elaboration. But it may be appropriate to say something more about *foreign exchange swaps*. In a swap transaction, the Bundesbank buys (or sells) foreign exchange spot and at the same time sells (or buys) it back forward. A swap transaction is therefore a combination of a spot and a forward transaction and the rate quoted − the swap rate − is the equivalent of an interest rate. In contrast to earlier swap policy measures (e.g. to counteract speculative foreign exchange flows), the foreign exchange swap transactions the Bundesbank has engaged in since 1979 have only served the purposes of fine-tuning the money market. If the Bundesbank buys dollars from the banks in a swap transaction, it is in fact providing them with central bank balances for a specific period. Conversely, if it sells dollars to the banks in a swap deal, it is taking liquidity out of the money market for a specific length of time. All these transactions are carried out at the ruling market rates. Generally speaking, they do not exercise a direct influence on the exchange rate in addition to their effect on liquidity.

In order to achieve a temporary absorption of liquidity, the Bundesbank has also concluded *foreign exchange transactions under repurchase agreements* with the credit institutions; it has done this since the summer of 1979. In these transactions a 'claim to delivery' of specific foreign assets held by the Bundesbank is transferred to the banks for a limited period. A foreign exchange transaction under repurchase agreement has the same effect on liquidity as a swap transaction in which dollars are sold spot to the credit institutions – the banks' deposits at the central bank are reduced. But whereas a contractive swap transaction also lowers the Bundesbank's net foreign assets, a foreign exchange transaction under repurchase agreement leaves these unchanged – only the Bundesbank's liabilities to credit institutions arising from repurchase obligations will increase; in other words, there has been no reduction in the Bundesbank's balance sheet, only an exchange of liabilities. As far as their significance for money market policy is concerned, foreign exchange swap and repurchase transactions are analogous to repurchase transactions in securities and bills; they have the same effect as reversible open market operations.

OPEN MARKET OPERATIONS IN LONG-TERM SECURITIES

For the most part, the Bundesbank, which first conducted open market operations in bonds in mid-1967, has engaged in major open market operations in long-term securities only sporadically; even then it has restricted its activities to sales and purchases of public bonds. But such open market transactions in bonds have not yet resulted in the Bundesbank holding considerable amounts of public bonds for any period of time. At end-July 1991, bonds and interest-bearing Treasury paper of Federal and Länder governments held by the Bundesbank on its balance sheet totalled DM 3.072 billion, and holdings of this paper have tended to decline since October 1990. Bundesbank holdings of similar paper of the Federal Railways and Federal Post Office has latterly been DM 935 million. It is argued that, if the central bank were to build up a sizeable portfolio of long-term public paper, this could easily give rise to the suspicion that the primary aim was to facilitate the financing of the public sector deficit, even if that motive were not in fact of any significance. Moreover, the Bundesbank has always applied very strict standards to intervention of this nature, since any heavier commitment by the central bank in the bond market might arouse the false impression that the movement of interest rates in that market was largely the outcome of monetary policy measures and hence was the Bundesbank's responsibility. In fact, the long-term interest rate is predominantly determined by market forces which the Bundesbank cannot influence, or at best can only influence indirectly, such as interest rate movements abroad and inflationary expectations.[65] For the rest, it is pointed out that, even in countries in which open market policy has traditionally been at the centre of monetary policy measures, outright purchases of long-term paper by the central bank are not as important as is often assumed. The open market operations of the US Federal Reserve System – for instance, those which serve purely monetary policy purposes – are virtually limited to very short-term transactions under repurchase agreements.[66]

Although the choice of techniques employed in central bank operations – and their combination – will vary from time to time, there would seem to have been, beginning about 1980 in Germany: (1) a change in the emphasis of policy, such that there was less immediate impact on interest rates and more on liquidity (with, of course, interest-rate effects); and (2) the evolution of a more coherent pattern of intervention, the main burden of liquidity adjustment now being borne by repurchase agreements, though supplemented in the short term by 'fine-tuning'.

Interest rates in the markets used to depend most obviously on adjustments to, and the signal effects of, movements in Bundesbank discount and lombard rates. Although changes in these rates are still made (if only to recognize a shift which may already have taken place in and through the markets), there was during the 1980s a gradual changeover to a greater emphasis on influencing liquidity by resorting to repurchase agreements (beginning in March 1982 and – by the spring of 1985 – becoming the main basis of intervention) in order to ensure that the minimum reserve requirements of credit institutions were maintained. These days the rate on repurchase agreements has the most immediate impact on market rates, though the Treasury bill selling rate (when Treasury paper is sold to 'mop-up' excess funds) will provide a floor below which rates will not be allowed to fall; the lombard rate, on the other hand, will provide an effective ceiling, since lombard loans usually represent expensive money and will therefore tend to be a last resort (see Figure 5.2). Usually, such loans are overnight, or at most for a few days. The day-to-day rate will fluctuate as a rule within these two limits and may at times be quite volatile – even within the day – depending on whether the Bundesbank is tightening liquidity, maintaining it, or making it more readily available. (If banks cannot get the money they need, they will go mainly into lombard and that will of itself push up rates.)

As we have seen, repurchase agreements may be tendered for

by volume (with a fixed rate) or by way of an interest rate tender. Nevertheless, the rate set by repurchase agreement accommodation will also be the basis for money market rates, though with a ceiling and floor as indicated above. This system is supplemented by refinancing policy (primarily through the agency of rediscount quotas, but supported by lombard loans) and by 'fine-tuning' measures: foreign exchange swaps (for a few days); the day-to-day placement with (or withdrawal from) the banks of government deposits (Section 17 of the Bundesbank Act), and the 'quick tenders' (providing accommodation for only a few days) introduced in February 1989. And the framework within which these operations are conducted is determined, on the one hand, by the minimum reserve ratios that are set for credit institutions from time to time and, on the other, by the levels of discount rate and lombard rate that are laid down. This seems now to be the established pattern of central bank intervention in Germany.

POSTSCRIPT

Following the tight monetary stance emphasized in December 1991 by the Bundesbank, when discount rate was raised to 8 per cent and lombard rate to $9\frac{3}{4}$ per cent, the necessity for continuing such a policy was reinforced by fiscal considerations. The trend in public-sector budgets was fairly favourable at the beginning of 1992. During the first quarter of that year, the Federal Government deficit amounted to DM 11 billion as against DM 33 billion in the same period of the previous year. The strong improvement owed something to the fact that at the start of 1991 sizeable funds had been provided to help finance the costs of the Gulf War, as well as for eastern Germany. The tax increases which took effect in mid-1991 also made themselves felt. In 1992, however, the detrimental factors associated with the high and still rising transfers for the economic integration of eastern Germany again increased in importance. In particular, social security funds were to deteriorate considerably, because pension funds payments in the new Federal Länder had risen sharply with the adoption of the west German pension law. In addition, the 1-year solidarity surcharge on income taxes was abolished in mid-1992. Against this background, it was anticipated that the deficit of the public authorities (including the social security funds) would rise to between DM 120 billion and DM 130 billion in 1992; in 1991 the figure was roughly DM 110 billion. The fiscal policy benchmarks submitted by the Federal Government in May 1992 and the statement by the Financial Planning Council at the beginning of June outlined a strategy which was intended to cut back significantly the public-sector deficits – to 2 per cent of nominal GNP – by 1996. The target was ambitious, but it could be achieved if the Federal Government and the governments of the West German Länder (also the local authorities) adhered to strict spending discipline.

On the monetary front, the growth of the money stock gave rise to some anxiety. The target for M3 (for the structure of M3, see Figure 5.3) had been set at between $3\frac{1}{2}$ and $5\frac{1}{2}$ per cent, but by April 1992, M3 had exceeded its level of the fourth quarter of 1991 with a seasonally adjusted annual rate of about 9 per cent (see Figure 5.1b). To some extent the rise in M3 was artificial. As is usual in periods of high short-term interest rates, monetary growth continued to focus on short-term time deposits, mainly to the detriment of non-interest or low-interest-bearing money components. But, in addition, because of a degree of stagnation in the capital market and, owing to the inverse interest-rate pattern, the evidence suggests that funds planned for long-term investment were being 'parked' in time accounts. Furthermore, there was renewed discussion about future taxation of interest income and that was also likely to foster the move into short-term investments. There was likewise a sharp rise in currency in circulation. Moreover, so far as this was discernible, the money stock in eastern Germany was growing more rapidly than in the west. Since the higher income and transaction volumes in the east were often based on transfers from the west (and not on higher output), the implementation of monetary policy had to allow for some accommodation of the associated higher demand for money, especially as the strong monetary expansion in eastern Germany should actually have been offset by compensatory contractionary effects in western Germany. The evidence suggests that the underlying trend in monetary expansion was still in excess of the medium-term requirements of monetary stability, even if special factors were taken into account.

As a result of the strong expansion of money and credit and on account of greater uncertainty about fiscal and wage policies, also the future taxation of interest income, interest rates on the capital market and at the long end of the money market rose somewhat in the spring. The temporary weakness of the Deutsche Mark on the foreign exchange markets and the increase in US capital market

Quarterly averages, seasonally adjusted

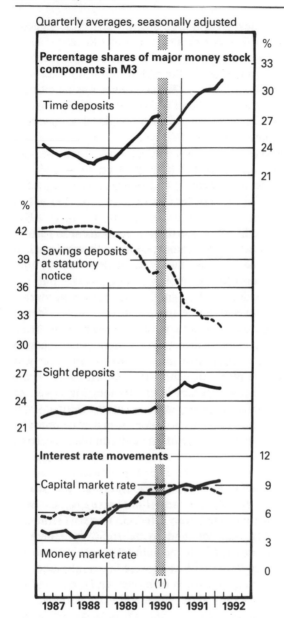

Figure 5.3 Structure of M3

Notes: (1) = German monetary union

Source: Deutsche Bundesbank

rates worked in the same direction. There was a corresponding rise in the rates on the Bundesbank's securities repurchase agreements, which were still being offered as 'US-style' variable-rate tenders. The day-to-day money rate drew slightly closer to the lombard rate, without causing problems for the Bundesbank's money market management. Here the emphasis was still on securities repurchase agreements. The rates applied went up, the banks' bidding rates providing an up-to-date picture of both the current market situation and current market expectations. Prevailing rates of 1-month repurchase agreements rose from 9.4 to 9.65 per cent between February and May. The day-to-day money rate also settled down at this level by mid-May, its differential against the lombard rate thus having narrowed almost continuously since the beginning of 1992. It was not until the second half of May, when tensions produced by the labour disputes eased and when (contrary to widespread fears) the pace of monetary expansion did *not* accelerate further, that there was a slight relaxation of conditions in the domestic financial markets. Actually assistance by way of securities repurchase agreements (as rates rose) declined somewhat (see Figure 5.2).

From time to time, such action was supplemented by shifts of Federal balances pursuant to Section 17 of the Bundesbank Act, in order (at short notice) to steady the movement of interest rates in the day-to-day money market. In the last 10 days of May, on the other hand, the Bundesbank mopped up a temporary excess of liquidity through foreign exchange repurchase agreements in order to counteract a sharp fall in the day-to-day money market rates.[67]

By mid-July, it was clear that the Bundesbank would be forced to take further action. There were no signs that the then current high level of German interest rates was damping down the rate of growth in money supply. There was evidence, too, that government subsidized credits to assist in rebuilding eastern Germany were being diverted to expenditure on consumption. At the same time, the Deutsche Mark remained strong. Some form of tightening of credit was expected as a signal that the Bundesbank was taking seriously the 9 per cent increase in M3 for 1992, well beyond the range of the $3\frac{1}{2}-5\frac{1}{2}$ per cent target. In this context, it was felt that the huge public subsidies flowing from west to east to finance the costs of German unification had blunted the edge of monetary policy. Subsidies had made a large part of this investment insensitive to interest-rate charges. As we have seen, M3 had been artificially inflated when high short-term interest rates attracted savings from longer-term investments. This was accentuated by uncertainty over the government's plans to tax savings income; this caused further funds to pile up in high-yielding short-term deposits. In addition, there was the build-up of DM assets in eastern Europe. Moreover, though it was domestic circumstances that were most pressing (including credit expansion by the banks to finance the purchase of property, which supported the inflationary tendencies), the German authorities could not be unmindful of the effects of high interest rates on their European partners within the exchange rate mechanism (ERM). Likewise – and most delicate of all – there was the impact that Bundesbank tightening of credit might have on acceptance of the Maastricht Treaty and on economic and monetary union (EMU).

In the result, on 16 July 1992, the Bundesbank Council raised its discount rate by $\frac{3}{4}$ per cent to $8\frac{3}{4}$ per cent, but elected for the time being to keep unchanged at $9\frac{3}{4}$ per cent its lombard rate, changes in which are regarded as having a greater impact on the money markets and are also of more importance internationally than changes in its discount rate. The latter does influence some domestic consumer and business borrowing costs (see pp. 191–2); it is also likely to operate as a signal and to have a psychological effect. According to the President of the Bundesbank (Mr Helmut Schlesinger), the action taken 'mainly had domestic targets in mind, namely reducing the rise of the money supply in its present magnitude'.[68] So far as immediate international reactions were concerned, only Italy raised its official central bank discount rate from 13 per cent to $13\frac{3}{4}$ per cent, and the Bank of Italy's short-term interest rates on funds advanced to commercial banks by $\frac{3}{4}$ per cent to $15\frac{1}{4}$ per cent. In some quarters, there was a certain amount of discussion of possible devaluation (e.g. of sterling), but this view was resisted. At the same time, one could not rule out the possibility that the Bundesbank would in due course also lift its key lombard rate and that at some future date there would be a revaluation of the Deutsche Mark and a realignment of other European currencies within the ERM.

On Monday, 20 July 1992,[69] there was a heavy slide in equity markets – in the USA and Tokyo as well as in Europe (even the DAX index on the Frankfurt Bourse fell steeply). This occurred despite strong intervention in the foreign exchange markets by a number of central banks – led by the US Federal Reserve and the Deutsche Bundesbank – when US dollars were bought for Deutsche

Marks to reduce strains in the European exchange rate mechansism caused by the German currency's recent strong rise. It was clear, too, that there was a persistent feeling that interest rates were likely to be pushed higher. In fact, during the following weeks, there was no further change in the official German interest rates and no realignment of currencies within the ERM. Indeed, on two occasions, positive statements were made rejecting realignment at least for the time being. On 28 August, European Community finance ministers ruled out a realignment of the European Monetary System's exchange rate mechanism after a tense day on the currency markets in which the EMS suffered its most severe strain in five years. The statement was co-ordinated by Mr Norman Lamont, the UK Chancellor of the Exchequer, in his capacity as current president of the European council of finance ministers. On 3 September, as a support operation, the UK Government announced that it would borrow the equivalent of Ecu 10 billion in D-Marks and a range of other foreign currencies, using the funds to support sterling in the foreign exchange market and to fund government spending.[70] Then, over the weekend 4 to 6 September in Bath, European Community governments strongly reaffirmed existing exchange rates within the EMS and this was supported by a pledge from the Bundesbank that it would not increase its interest rates 'in present circumstances'.[71]

Yet it was clear that all was not well. The UK authorities were already staking large amounts of borrowed money to shore up the wilting sterling exchange rate. Two of the Nordic countries with unofficial links with the European Monetary System – Finland and Sweden – were facing difficulties with their currencies. The Finnish marka was floated off its link to the EMS hybrid currency, the Ecu. The marka immediately sank by some 13 per cent against the D-Mark, and then a desperate battle began in Sweden to save the krona, involving at one stage overnight interest rates of 75 per cent. Within the EC proper the greatest pressure had been on the Italian lira. Interest rates were raised sharply, taking the margin over D-Mark rates for 3 months deposits up to about 10 percentage points. Meanwhile, the Italian government was seeking emergency powers to tackle that country's economic crisis, the immediate trigger for all this being the approach of the French referendum on the Maastricht Treaty. The crack in the ERM proper came with the devaluation by 7 per cent of the Italian lira within the ERM. This was to be followed by cuts in the Bundesbank's leading interest rates the following day (i.e. on 14 September). In the result, the Bundesbank decided to cut lombard rate only by 0.25 per cent to 9.5 per cent, discount rate by 0.5 per cent to 8.25 per cent; also the more significant repo rate – more significant from a market point of view – was to be pushed down from 9.7 per cent to 9.2 per cent at the next fixed tender at the current week's securities repurchase operation. This was calculated to ease foreign exchange pressures and to keep rates below the lombard emergency funding rate, since it is the money market rate which defines the problem on the foreign exchange market, not the lombard rate. From a German point of view, there was the problem of the huge inflow of D-Marks as a result of Bundesbank interventions on the foreign exchange markets of Europe. Clearly, this had major implications for German M3 and quite obviously the target of 3.5 to 5.5 per cent would not be achieved in 1992, though it remained the medium-term objective. Elsewhere in Europe there was disappointment in the modest reduction in German rates – largely dictated by domestic considerations – though it was euphemistically accepted as 'a first step'.

The day of reckoning for the pound sterling came on 16 September, 1992.[72] Trading started in the City at 0700 with the pound close to its floor of 2.7780 in the ERM. At 0900 the Bank of England disbursed about £1 billion in its first wave of intervention, but this action failed to lift sterling off the floor. At 0930, the Bundesbank and the Bank of France intervened to support sterling; they were to spend around £2 billion during the day. After consultations with the Prime Minister, Minimum Lending Rate[73] was re-introduced and set at 12 per cent (an increase in basic rates of 2 per cent). Bank base rates followed. This was about 11.00 hours. At Noon, the Bank of England spent a further £3 billion in the attempt to support sterling, but by 13.00 hours sterling had fallen below its ERM floor. By 14.15 the Treasury had announced that MLR was to be increased to 15 per cent the following day. The policy remained 'to take whatever measures are necessary to maintain sterling's parity within the Exchange Rate Mechanism.' During the afternoon, the Bank of England was to spend a further £3 billion in attempting to provide support for sterling, with overnight sterling rates being quoted at 100 per cent by 14.15. At 17.00 hours the markets closed with the pound at DM 2.75. At 17.15, the pound was suspended as a member of the ERM. The proposed increase in MLR to 15 per cent was cancelled. The pound fell to 2.7260. For obvious reasons, the FT stock exchange index also fell heavily during the day. Furthermore, the announcement that sterling's membership was being 'suspended' in the exchange rate mechanism amounted to an acknowledgement at Westminster that the pound was in effect being devalued against the D-Mark. Meanwhile, the Spanish peseta had been devalued within the ERM by 5 per cent and the over-valued lira had been suspended from ERM membership.

But there was more to come the next day, when the 2 per cent rise in MLR to 12 per cent was cancelled and base rates were restored to 10 per cent. During the following days, sterling continued to fall to lower levels against the D-Mark and there could be no question of considering re-entry to the ERM until the pound had settled down to what could be regarded as a sustainable rate.

It is an open question whether or not earlier action by the UK and Italy could have saved the situation. For example, in a British context, there could have been a much earlier and more modest increase in interest rates *vis-à-vis* German rates, even if the Germans – faced as they were with problems arising from reunification and their own budgetary deficits – felt unable to reduce their rates to any significant extent. Alternatively, or possibly contemporaneously, an orderly realignment of exchange rates within the ERM might have been achieved. In reality, the ERM was always intended to accommodate a limited flexibility and, indeed, in its earlier years, had agreed to a number of realignments of exchange rates as between member countries. It was only in more recent times that virtual fixity of exchange rates had become the rule. Unfortunately, in the UK months of inactivity in terms of positive economic policy had left the British economy in a parlous condition – a low rate of inflation certainly, but a deepening recession, increasing unemployment, a massive balance of payments deficit, and negative growth. It was not just a question of declining to give the economy a 'kick-start'. Some more generally positive measures, e.g. restoration or a building up of the infrastructure leading to a revival of the construction industry, would have provided a badly needed stimulus to employment. Investment could have been further encouraged by tax allowances. Despite the debt overhang, a reduction in unemployment and greater security for those in work might well have led to some increase in consumer expenditure and thereby have contributed to further employment. In Italy, it was largely a question of persistent and increasing budgetary deficits, which had accumulated over many years, partially obscured by a high savings ratio in the private sector, plus a whole range of structural problems that was the trouble. The point is that both these economies were extremely vulnerable to external shocks or uncertainties (like the French referendum on Maastricht). It was this very vulnerability that produced the successive waves of speculation that led to the crises in the currency markets.

In the wake of the speculative attacks on the pound sterling, other currencies – like the Irish punt, the Danish krona, and the Portuguese escudo – also came in for speculative pressure. Then Ireland and Portugal followed Spain in temporarily re-imposing exchange controls on capital movements as a defensive measure. Interest rates were also raised. Indeed, because of the build-up of these pressures, it was no great surprise when the attack moved to the French franc, partly motivated by the narrow Yes vote in the French referendum on Maastricht (*le petit oui*) on Sunday 20 September 1992. Initially, France and Germany – the two strongest remaining members of the ERM – mounted a concerted effort to 'talk up' the French franc as it tended to fall on the currency markets following the Maastricht vote. But central banks were forced to intervene to support several of the currencies in the ERM, including the French franc, which, despite the fundamental strength of the French economy, closed two days after the vote barely half a centime above its floor in the ERM after a day of turmoil on the foreign exchanges. And it is clear that, without the massive intervention of the Bundesbank the following day, the French franc must have fallen. It was only the very considerable German support that saved it. In addition, a joint statement was made by the Bank of France, the Bundesbank, the French Finance Ministry, and the Finance Ministry in Bonn declaring that there was no justification for a change in the franc's parity. France, for its part, and combined with its own intervention, pushed its short-term money market interest rates sharply higher.

In Germany, by August 1992, the broad indicator M3 had advanced at an annual rate of 9 per cent, with bank lending still expanding quite rapidly, whereas – as we have seen – the Bundes-bank's own ambitious target was to hold that growth within a range of 3.5 to 5.5 per cent. Officially, this remained the objective. More-over, only if money supply could be reined back significantly could a further reduction in German interest rates be contemplated. The money supply was already inflated by the extensive intervention in the foreign exchange markets, when the pound sterling and the lira came under pressure. The situation was further exacerbated when the Bundesbank intervened heavily to save the French franc from devaluation, thereby sending the German domestic money supply figures even more beyond the 1992 target range despite money market operations to mop up liquidity. These took the form of cancelling on several occasions the weekly provision of securities repurchase agreements with the Bundesbank. As we have seen, the commercial banks in Germany use these repos as a form of refinancing. In addition, in order to absorb even more liquidity, the Bundesbank made use of Treasury bill offers and currency repos to banks sometimes for a number of days running. Indeed, questions now came to be asked as to whether the Bundesbank should relax its adherence to M3 at a time of such unprecedented turbulence in the foreign exchange markets, complicated as it had been by the manifold strains of German re-unification. Would it not be advisable, for example, to relate to a wider range of economic variables, including asset prices and also to consider M0 (cash and demand deposits) as a supplementary targeting basis? It is not unknown for well-tried monetary aggregates, given a change in the economic and financial environment, to become less reliable as a policy objective.

What of the future? It is probably unwise to attempt to look too far ahead. On the basis of current expectations, it would appear that there could be no question of the pound sterling – or for that matter the Italian lira – rejoining the ERM until these currencies have established a rate of exchange *vis-à-vis* the D-Mark that has stabilized at what would seem to be a sustainable level. The effective devaluation of sterling gave a temporary stimulus to the UK economy (by encouraging exports at a more competitive rate of exchange and curtailing imports, thereby assisting with the balance of payments deficit). This – supported by other measures – could be expected to begin to lift the UK economy out of the deep recession into which it had been allowed to slip. There was also much talk of cuts in UK interest rates and on 22 September base rate was reduced to 9 per cent (not a cut in MLR on this occasion, but as a result of the normal invitation by the Bank of England to the discount houses wishing to use their borrowing facilities to do so at the rate of 9 per cent). This was followed by some reduction in rates on mortgages and on National Savings. The latter was expected to assist the building societies in attracting funds. But were interest rates to be cut further – even dramatically to much lower levels –

or, in defence of the sterling exchange rate, were they to be maintained at (say) a level within the range of 7 to 9 per cent?

The highly respected economist James Meade,[74] felt that 'For the present, while we are outside the ERM, we should by stages reduce significantly the rate of interest, and leave the pound free to find its own level in the foreign-exchange markets.' These measures should help to 'ease the overhang of mortgage and other debt, both by reducing the interest payments on such debt and by raising the value of houses and other real assets.' The intention was also 'to promote investment in the capital equipment of our run-down industries; . . . to encourage exports and discourage imports through the greater competitiveness due to a no longer over-valued currency, thus reducing our huge balance of payments deficit; . . . to encourage a revival in output and employment through the increase in the demand for our products, not so much for consumption purposes as for the restoration of our domestic productive capacity and the reduction of our excessive reliance on imports; . . . [and] to achieve such recovery by means which do not add to government expenditure, but by means which would decrease our excessive budget deficit by the reduction in the cost of support for the unemployed.'

The obvious danger, as Meade also pointed out, was 'the possible adverse effect on the rate of inflation of money wage rates and prices.' In order to set a limit, he advocated a moderate target for the rate of growth with fiscal measures calculated to contain it (e.g. a rise in the rate of income tax, in addition to the avoidance of 'unnecessary' government expenditure). This would also help to reduce 'our excessive budget deficit'. At a more difficult level, he also advocated 'radical measures to limit the rate of rise in money wage rates and prices so as to ensure that increased money expenditures on goods and services lead to increased output and employment, rather than to an increase in the money costs and prices of the existing output.' He believed that 'this last requirement – to deal with inflation on the supply side by control of money costs, as well as on the demand side by control of money expenditures – is far and away the most important and difficult of our economic problems and, in order to avoid intolerable adverse effects on the distribution of income, requires much more radical and unfamiliar changes in our institutions than is generally recognised.' He concluded that the adoption of these measures 'is in no way incompatible with our rejoining a suitable ERM-type of European monetary institution. But some period of independence would be needed for the working out of the effect of these measures to indicate at what sort of foreign-exchange rate we should initially rejoin the system.'

Personally, I would feel that there is less to be gained from cutting rates of interests to a relatively low level – witness the experience of the recession in the USA, where rates were pushed down to very low levels, but with little effect. Very high rates held high for long periods of time may virtually 'cause' a recession; low rates do not necessarily put the economy into reverse. What is needed – in my judgment – is a lowering of interest rates (say, to a range of 7 to 9 per cent for base rates), strongly supported by the positive encouragement of investment by fiscal means (tax allowances) and badly needed public expenditure on the infrastructure (e.g. projects relating to transport, schools, hospitals, housing, or prisons). There should follow greater consumption expenditure, further investment, and a gradual increase in employment. It is not intended that this should be rushed and lead to what is feared as the inevitable boom. Indeed, one would hope that the target would continue to be 'low' inflation, but certainly not zero inflation, also that attempts to reduce public expenditure would not be too Draconian. Once the economy begins to recover, there could be moderate tax increases in order to offset the growth in public expenditure. So far as monetary policy was concerned, it might relate not merely to the rate of growth of 'narrow' money (M0) but also to 'broad' money (M3), asset prices, and the exchange rate. An evaluation of such indicators would become a basis for determining variations in interest rates.

That leaves open the question of what to do about the ERM. After sterling had been suspended from the ERM, UK membership was 'put on indefinite hold'. As already indicated, re-entry could only be at a rate of exchange (against the D-Mark) that had both stabilized and which one could fairly confidently predict would be sustainable. Almost certainly, such a rate would have to be renegotiated with other members of the ERM. There may in the interim have been some realignment within the ERM of other rates of exchange. But for the UK to benefit from resumed ERM membership, it would be necessary for it to make tangible progress in restoring the economy to a fundamentally healthy position with an ability to maintain that situation. And that is not something that can be achieved overnight. At the same time, one cannot expect full recovery to be achieved in the short term and there may be a case for more flexible arrangements within the ERM than in the years before the emergence of the September 1992 crisis (e.g. in terms of more frequent realignments of rates of exchange – not excluding sterling – at least until the system settles down). Basically, what one is hoping for is a greater degree of 'convergence' of member economies. Nor should such action be long delayed. This is not entirely to ignore political aspects of the problem. Clearly the UK cannot isolate itself from Europe and 'go it alone', and there must be some accommodation (e.g. on Maastricht) with fellow members of the European Community.

Note: For 'The latest exchange rate realignments in the European Monetary System and the interest rate policy decisions of the Bundesbank', see Deutsche Bundesbank, *Monthly Report*, October 1992, pp. 14–16.

Chapter 6

The Italian money market

As a background to this study of the Italian money market, it is first necessary to outline the structure of the Italian banking and financial system. At first glance, this appears to be rather complicated, but there are certain main banking sectors into which the several groups of institutions can be divided and this makes the task of description somewhat easier. A basic feature of the Italian banking system is a clear-cut division between commercial banks, granting almost exclusively short-term loans, and special credit institutions, operating in the medium- and long-term sectors. The Italian commercial banks (*aziende di credito*), which for all categories numbered 1,064 at the end of 1990, with 17,721 offices, virtually fall into seven categories. First, there are the public law banks (*istituti di credito di diritto pubblico*), six in all, of which the largest are the Banca Nazionale del Lavoro, Istituto Bancario S. Paolo di Torino, and Banco di Napoli; these banks are either fully owned by the state or owned by foundations; at the end of 1990, they had 2,449 offices. They themselves own and control a network of special credit institutions called 'sections', which operate in specialized fields of credit (e.g. industry, real estate, foreign trade, etc.), but which are in effect merged with the bank itself. Second, there are the banks of 'national interest' (*banche d'interesse nazionale*), of which there are three – Banca Commerciale Italiana, Credito Italiano, and Banco di Roma (with 1,459 offices at end 1990) – and which are controlled by the Istituto per la Ricostruzione Industriale (IRI), the major industrial state-owned holding company.[1] Third, there were 106 ordinary credit banks (*banche di credito ordinario*), of which there were 3,981 offices at end-1990, and which are privately-owned joint stock companies, or otherwise incorporated institutions. These tend to be rather smaller in size than those listed above: the most important are the Banca Nazionale dell' Agricoltura, the Banco di Santo Spirito, and the Istituto Bancario Italiano. Fourth, and excluded from the ordinary credit bank figures, there were 37 foreign banks (50 offices), the opening of branches being regulated by the Bank of Italy; such branches are restricted in number (indeed, they are mostly unit banks) and this means that their deposit base is limited and they therefore have to fund their operations with wholesale money; otherwise, there is no discrimination against foreign banks. Foreign banks may also have a number of para-banking operations as do the Italian banks themselves – e.g. a finance company (for consumer credit), leasing and factoring companies, and merchant banking. Fifth, there are the savings banks and first-class pledge banks (*casse di risparmio e monti di credito su pegno di 1° categoria*) 82 in all with 4,689 offices; in Italy, these are also important. Several are large and have spread out beyond their own geographic areas; they are mainly devoted to the collection of small savings, but now the larger ones also engage in general banking business and operate at the national level. Nevertheless, there is still an emphasis on long-term lending partly based on the issue of bonds through their medium- and long-term credit sections – mortgages, loans to agriculture, and public works loans; they have a central clearing house called Istituto di Credito delle Casse di Risparmio Italiane (ICCRI) and an Association (Associazione fra le Casse di Risparmio Italiane). In total, savings banks attract 28.4 per cent of Italian deposits. The co-operative institutions form the final two categories – on the one hand, there are the people's banks (*banche popolari co-operative*), of which there were 108 (in 1990) with 3,290 offices, and which come under a special law (there are special national and special individual statutes); these are in effect commercial banks. On the other hand, there were 715 rural and artisan banks (*casse rurali e artigiane e monti di credito su pegno de 2° categoria*) with 1,792 offices (this movement was inspired by the Raiffeisen idea – co-operative societies set up to cater for groups of small agriculturalists and artisans as common members of each *cassa*, with a central credit institute in Rome called Istituto di Credito delle Casse Rurali e Artigiane (ICCREA). There are also a number of special credit institutions, which can both borrow and lend at medium- and long-term – e.g. for building and construction, shipbuilding, the development of tourism, lending to companies at medium-term, lending to finance the purchase of equipment, etc.

Like the special credit sections of the public law banks and the savings banks, they borrow by issuing bonds or special certificates of deposit (minimum maturity is 18 months, but they may go out to 5 years). Special credit institutions' certificates of deposit (CDs) are not subject to reserve requirements.

Despite the existence of the Istituto Mobiliare Italiano (IMI), a public body founded in 1931, there was a growing need after the Second World War for industrial finance in Italy, both to provide the capital to support the growth of the economy and, as part of this process, to finance the introduction of modern technologies and the development of new industrial ventures. It was the latter that made necessary the provision of new financing channels. There were two phases in the process of this development: initially, it had a sectoral character; this merged into a second phase, where there was a more geographical orientation. During the first phase, new institutions were set up by the different categories of banks. During the second, numerous regional institutes were created on the initiative of the state and with the participation of local banks. But because of the limited amount of own resources at the disposal of these new bodies, a financing institute (Mediocredito Centrale) was set up in 1952 with the task of refinancing these bodies and reducing the cost of financing the medium-sized and small firms and, subsequently, the related export credits. At the same time, the Artigiancassa was allocated tasks similar to those set for the Mediocredito Centrale, but related to credits effected in favour of artisan enterprises by the banks empowered to do so. The funds of the refinancing institutes are provided by the Italian Treasury, but owing to the paucity of is endowment fund, the intervention of the refinancing institute has mainly taken the form of interest subsidies, granted as an alternative to or in conjunction with rediscounting. In more recent years, the Mediocredito Centrale has raised funds on the market by means of bond issues, the proceeds of which have been advanced to the regional institutes; it has thereby become their financing centre. In addition, Mediocredito Centrale obtains loans from the European Investment Bank. Nowadays, too, several of the regional institutes issue bonds directly through the market.

MONEY MARKET INSTRUMENTS

In Italy, there is a relatively small number of money market instruments available as a means of undertaking appropriate operations, whether by market participants themselves or for purposes of intervention by the country's central bank – the Bank of Italy. The bulk of the relevant paper is issued by the Government of Italy (i.e. by the Treasury through the Bank of Italy). The most important short-term instruments in the money market are *Buoni Ordinari del Tesoro* (*BOTs*), which are Treasury bills – these are sold at a discount and are issued to bearer. There are also *Certificati di Credito Tesoro* (*CCTs*) – they are floating rate Treasury debt instruments. The interest rate is based on the average of the yield of 1-year Treasury bills as determined at the time of the auctions; by 1990, their maturity was for 7 years; and they are issued twice a month (at the beginning and at mid-month).

GOVERNMENT PAPER[2]

BOTs are issued in maturities of 3, 6, and 12 months by auction twice a month – on the nearest working days to the 15th and at the end of the month, the latter being consistently the larger issue of the two.[3] Formerly, there was a legal obligation such that the Bank of Italy was required to buy them when they were offered to it (thereby ensuring their liquidity) – in other words, the Bank of Italy was the residual purchaser. But, in 1981, there was a 'divorce' between the Treasury and the Bank of Italy as a result of which there is now no obligation on the part of the Bank of Italy to underwrite the Treasury bill tender. The Bank of Italy is free to subscribe should it desire to do so and has a duty to regulate the liquidity of the economy (see below). It now has a much greater freedom of action, though from time to time it may feel it is necessary to support the market by taking up more Treasury paper than it might desire. However, it remains true that the Bank of Italy is now much more autonomous *vis-à-vis* the Treasury than it once was.

As already indicated, the Treasury bill auction takes place twice a month – in the middle and at the end of the month, when the issue tends to be rather larger. The auction is announced a week ahead. Each maturity is offered at these auctions. What is offered – and taken up – depends on interest rate expectations, also on customers' requirements. But there may be other considerations, as in June, when 6-month bills are very popular, since they will mature at the end of the year in December, when it is imperative to have money available for balance sheet purposes. If rates are likely to fall, there will be a demand for the longer-dated bills in order to 'lock in' at the higher rates. *BOTs* are in denominations of L 5 million up to L 50 billion (they may also be figures on a computer, in which case they could be very large). The Treasury has a preference for the longer maturities, which enables them to manage their cash flow more easily. When the Bank of Italy tenders for its own account, it takes up the bills at the price it bids, provided this price is higher than the 'stop-out price'. When the price it bids is as high as the stop-out price, the amount of bills the central bank receives is a residual with respect to the bills taken up by the market. Whenever the bid price of the Bank of Italy is lower than the stop-out price it does not obtain any bills. All other financial institutions may tender – banks of all kinds and other types of financial institutions, including stockbrokers. They have a need to secure bills for their own treasury and/or inventory requirements (e.g. to sell them on to their customers – they are important retailers of bills). Banks use them to absorb liquidity at the margin and – at times when loan demand is low – they resort to them as a substitute asset.

Bids have to be in by 12.00 noon on the day of the tender and the results are announced on the Reuters screen by 5.00–5.30 p.m. on the same day for the mid-month auction[4] (the day after for the auction at the end of the month). Settlement for Treasury bills won in the auction takes place 5–7 days later than the day of the auction – the settlement date is the basis for the date of maturity.

On 30 March 1984, the Bank of Italy designated as 'market-makers' a list of the ten most important banks in Italy (as at end-1991, the figure was twenty-two). These banks were obliged at each auction (on the basis of market share)[5] to buy a fixed minimum proportion of the amount of each issue and to be prepared to absorb this amount at a price of their own choosing. In effect, the Bank of Italy asked the market-makers to underwrite issues of *BOTs*, originally to the extent of 60 per cent, latterly 65 per cent.[6] On the other hand, part of an issue may remain unallocated (e.g. if rates bid were inordinately high). What is allocated is always at the discretion of the authorities.

From January 1985, to avoid the drying up of liquidity in the banking system, each of the market-makers could also borrow from the Bank of Italy, subject to certain conditions. Let us assume that the Treasury is offering amounts of *BOTs* as follows: 3-month *BOTs*, L 5,000 billion; 6-month *BOTs*, L 8,000 billion; and 12-month *BOTs*, L 10,000 billion. Let us also assume that the quota or 'belt' (*cintura*) of a particular bank – on the basis of market share (as above) – is 10 per cent of the issue; the 'belt' for that bank would be L 500 billion + L 800 billion + L 1,000 billion, or a total of L 2,300 billion. Let us assume further that the additional purchases of *BOTs* (for own account, not for customers) were respectively L 100 billion, zero, and L 100 billion; that bank could then borrow from the Bank of Italy up to L 200 billion. But if a bank did not cover the full quota or 'belt', it could be financed by the Bank of Italy only for the total exceeding the 'belt' and for the maturity that actually exceeds the quota. Compare, for example, Case A with Case B (the 'belt' is shown in the first column of A).

	Case A			*Case B*		
3-month	500 + 100 =	600		500 + 400 =	900	
6-month	800 + 0 =	800		800 + 0 =	800	
12-month	1,000 + 100 =	1,100		800 + 0 =	800	
	2,300	200	2,500	2,100	400	2,500

Under example A, the bank could borrow up to L 200 billion (as stated). But in example B, with the 'belt' at L 2,300 billion, the bank can only be financed for L 200 billion (2,500 − 2,300) and for 3-month bills, despite bidding for an extra L 400 billion on the 3-month bill. The sum of the market shares (as indicated by the Bank of Italy) for the twenty-two market-makers should represent a minimum of 65 per cent of the market (the *cintura* or 'belt'). This accommodation from the Bank of Italy that is referred to here is made available (under a short-term line of credit) by way of a loan or advance from the Bank of Italy. Usually, repayment is made within 3−5 days (for mid-month tenders) and for up to 11 days[7] (for end-of-month tenders); the rate applied is normally the average subscription rate.

CCTs – or Treasury certificates – are longer-dated paper than *BOTs*. Latterly (since March 1991), they have been issued with a maturity of 7 years. Issues are regularly made twice a month. *CCTs* have been issued by way of an auction since July 1990. (The allocation is made in the decreasing order of prices bid until all securities are allocated. The price corresponding to the last bid received represents the allotment price for all bidders.) In the secondary market, where they are traded in large quantities, a sale (net of accrued interest) will be negotiated at a price. To this must be added accrued interest. This is calculated on the basis of a 360-day year. In calculating accrued interest, each calendar month is considered to be 30 days from and including the day from which interest is to accrue up to and including the value date of the transaction. For example, if the entitlement begins on 1 January and the settlement day is 31 May, the calculation will be 150 days of accrued interest.

Buoni Tesoro Poliennali (*BTPs*) are Treasury bonds. They have maturities of 5, 7, and 10 years with a fixed coupon. With lower inflation and decreases in interest rates (and in consequence the opportunity of capital gains), they are now of increasing importance.[8] They tend to be purchased mainly by banks and institutional investors,[9] and are traded on the secondary screen market, where they amount to almost 70 per cent of the bonds traded. The calculations on which transactions are based are the same as for Treasury certificates. It should be noted, too, that from September 1991 futures on the 10-year, fixed-rate bond (and from October 1991 options on futures) have been traded both on LIFFE and MATIF.[10]

Of the other types of government securities, Treasury bills and certificates denominated in ECUs deserve a mention. The former have been issued monthly by auction since October 1987 with maturities of 1 year; the latter carry maturities of 5 years; normally they are issued every quarter (in 1991, both for *BTEs* and *CTEs*, the Treasury only made an issue when a reimbursement had to be effected). The 1-year bills are not quoted on the stock exchange, but the longer-term certificates are so listed both in Italy and in Luxembourg. Institutional investors, many of which are non-resident, hold large amounts of these securities, since each issue amounts to ECUs 700 million to 1,000 million, thereby offering a good measure of liquidity. Moreover, the Treasury bills in ECUs are virtually the only ECU-denominated securities with a maturity of 1 year.[11]

The securities with maturities of 1 year or less – Treasury bills in lire and ECUs – are not physically printed, except at the request of subscribers. Ownership is established through accounts in the name of holders with the Bank of Italy. Securities with maturities over 1 year are printed, but do not usually circulate in material form, except in the case of small transactions between private savers when they request it. Almost 90 per cent of the bills, certificates and bonds in circulation are deposited with the Bank of Italy's central system for handling securities, which is directly linked with the clearing houses, thereby enabling the settlement of transactions in these securities to be effected rapidly and efficiently.

In December 1988, Treasury option certificates (*Certificati del Tesoro con Opzione*, or *CTOs*) were issued for the first time with the aim of lengthening the average life of the public debt and to match investors' preferences. *CTOs* are 6-year, fixed-rate bonds carrying a 'put' option for investors (European-style option) which entitles the holder to request the reimbursement of the certificates at a certain moment in their life (e.g. at the end of the third year). They are offered by the uniform-price auction technique (as with *CCTs* – see above). The new instrument represented the first example of a 'retractable bond' in Italy – it would be particularly attractive to investors with declining interest-rate expectations. The first issue of the new certificates was not very successful, because of intial problems in evaluating the financial characteristics of the new bonds; in placing the following issues more stress was laid on their interest to institutional investors, which could better evaluate the option.[12]

It is also worth mentioning that, as from November 1989 for *CCTs* and as from February 1990 for *CTOs* and *BTPs*, these instruments are now issued in *tranches*, i.e. an instrument with the same characteristics (e.g. yield and maturity) is issued in several 'slices', thereby enhancing the liquidity of the several secondary markets in these instruments.

Formerly, issues of government paper were free of tax, whereas deposits (including inter-bank deposits) were subject to a withholding tax of 30 per cent, which obviously discriminated in favour of government paper. Latterly (dating from 19 September 1986), all government bonds (including *BOTs* and *CCTs*) were subject to a tax of $6\frac{1}{4}$ per cent. In September 1987, this tax was raised to $12\frac{1}{2}$ per cent. However, since deposits (including negotiable certificates of deposit) were subject to a withholding tax of 25 per cent (later raised to 30 per cent on up to 12-month paper), there was still a clear discrimination in favour of government paper.[13] Nevertheless, the tax had the effect of forcing down net yields, despite some increase in the nominal gross yields. The 30 per cent withholding tax on interest from domestic inter-bank deposits was abolished by Decree No. 47 of 1 February 1992.

NEGOTIABLE CERTIFICATES OF DEPOSIT[14]

Italy introduced CDs in 1983. It is understood that the Bank of Italy encouraged the issue of CDs in order to increase the proportion of time liabilities in the Italian banks' deposit structure. It also created a new money market instrument. The most obvious reason for holding CDs is said to be fiscal. It is a bearer instrument (though there are some exceptions to this) and if, for example, a holder were to die, it could be passed on to bearer. This is not the case with a bank deposit. But in a country with a high savings ratio – though for the private sector it had fallen from about 30 per cent of disposable income to 25 per cent by 1989[15] – large deposits remain an important ingredient in the banks' structure of liabilities. As evidence of a deposit, however, CDs attract the same reserve requirements as other deposits. On the other hand, such reserves are paid a rate of interest and the rate is higher on the reserves that relate to CDs.

The banks issued a large amount of CDs in 1983 and 1984, when rates were rising. Then rates fell and were not regarded as sufficiently high to attract financial institutions and corporations, which preferred *BOTs* and *CCTs*. Also, the minimum maturity was 6 months, which was not really short enough for a monetary instrument, especially when there was virtually no secondary market. Hence, at that time, issues of CDs were only absorbed by households, which tended to hold them to maturity. The minimum size was L 1 million and the average size L 10 million mainly held by households, which also held *BOTs*. As indicated above, these enjoy a tax advantage over deposits of all kinds; there are also active secondary markets for *BOTs* and *CCTs*, especially the latter. At that time, too, the same rates were paid whatever the size of the CD. Then, in order to encourage a demand from corporations, banks were allowed to issue 3-month CDs and to pay rates related to the size of the CD – a higher rate being paid on CDs of L 1 billion and more. And, despite the fact that (on the basis of a gentleman's agreement) a bank may not take back its own CDs, they could be absorbed by a subsidiary within the same bank group. It was hoped that these changes would lead to the development of a secondary market. Initially, this was very thin and only obtained for large denominations in CDs.

Again, in 1988 and 1989, there was a very rapid growth in CDs, both for banks and – to a lesser extent – for special credit institutions. At that time, there was only a slow growth in current and savings account deposits and this led banks to boost their promotion of CDs, primarily through appropriate interest-rate policies. As a result, the after-tax return on bank CDs, which now benefited from more favourable tax treatment as compared with current accounts, was kept constantly above the rate of inflation and close to the yield available on Treasury bills. In particular, the investment of household savings was substantially attracted to CDs. So far as special credit institutions were concerned, CDs have been an important fund-raising instrument for some time as an alternative to bond issues. The long maturities of bonds issued by these institutions means that demand is weak in periods of uncertain expectations. The maturities of the CDs issued by special credit institutions can vary between 18 and 60 months, and the main issues made by industrial credit institutions have maturities of between 18 and 24 months. In addition, the CDs of special credit institutions are an effective means of diversifying portfolios, since rapid innovation has led to the development of a wide range of instruments, which may be bearer, or registered, of fixed or variable amount, with fixed or floating rates, and with coupons or discounts.[16]

Following the establishment of a Euro-lire securities market in 1985, with gross annual issues of L 4,700 billion by 1989, the Bank of Italy – in 1990 – authorized the issue of Euro-lire CDs to foreign branches of Italian banks operating in London.[17]

BANKERS' ACCEPTANCES

Bankers' acceptances were first introduced in Italy in 1976. They were regarded as a successful monetary instrument until a with-holding tax was imposed on interest deriving from them in 1981. In fact, they were quite important at the time that credit ceilings were imposed on bank loans,[18] since resort to them was a means of evading the ceilings, and there was a rapid growth in the figures for bankers' acceptances in 1980 and 1981. But in 1981, the amount of bankers' acceptances that could be issued by an individual bank was restricted to two-fifths of capital and reserves,[19] and special credit institutions could not negotiate bankers' acceptances for more than one-quarter of capital and reserves. They have now virtually disappeared.

COMMERCIAL PAPER

Euro-commercial paper may be issued by overseas branches of Italian commercial banks, which are also responsible for other Euro-currency transactions. The attraction of Euro-deposits[20] (for 30 to 45 days) can be important (e.g. for financing Italian exports and imports). Although a bank may not issue Euro-commercial paper, it may buy it and place it with institutional investors – e.g. insurance companies.

Lira commercial paper was introduced in 1982, but the amounts issued have been small. In any event, Italian commercial paper is not on the US model. Italian commercial paper is based on an exchange of letters between the parties backed by a bank guarantee to the buyer of the letter, who will receive interest. There may also be a promissory note (PN) or 'acceptance', which passes to the buyer – the PN bears the signature of the bank, which provides the back-up line to the party (e.g. a firm or corporation) which is the borrower. This type of activity is favoured in particular by the Italian branches of foreign banks, seeking out new kinds of paper to replace the fall in loan demand. The paper is taken up by private investors and there is a small secondary market.

REPURCHASE AGREEMENTS

Resort to *repurchase agreements* ('repos') and *reverse 'repos'* (where paper is bought – to absorb funds – under an agreement to resell at a specified future date) has become an important means in Italy of managing bank assets and liabilities and in order to ensure adequate bank liquidity.[21] The arrangements are based on Article 10 of a Bill No. 70 of 14 March 1988, which became Law No. 154 of 13 May 1988. In Italy, a 'repo' takes the form of a combination of linked contracts. In other words, a 'repo' consists of selling 'spot' a certain quantity of securities, while at the same time purchasing 'forward' an equal quantity of securities of the same kind. In practice, bonds or money market instruments are used as a basis for this type of operation, generally for a period of 1–3 months. Other types of securities could also be involved. The 'spot' price is fixed by calculating the market value of the security and the relevant interest rate; the 'forward' price is determined by capitalizing the 'spot' price on the basis of the interest rate agreed between the parties.

This technique can be employed between banks lending and borrowing in the inter-bank market, by banks lending to or borrowing from their customers on the basis of money market instruments, or by the Bank of Italy in its open market operations (see below).

Of direct relevance to the development of the money market is the resort to 'repos' by banks and other credit institutions as an extension of the inter-bank market. It is in effect an alternative method of inter-bank lending and borrowing, but on a secured basis. For example, a bank with excess funds can purchase 'spot' securities from a bank in need of money and sell 'forward', as at a future date, an equivalent amount of similar securities; if a bank has need of funds, it can sell securities 'spot' and buy back 'forward' an equivalent amount of similar securities as at a specified date. In these cases, resort to this technique is a means of adjusting liquidity, but there may also be a speculative element in order to take advantage of any difference that exists – or which it is anticipated may exist – between the inter-bank money market rate and the rate implied by a 'repo' transaction. This may well be the case where dynamic management of a bank's treasury is a favoured policy.

An extension of these arrangements to a bank's own customers merely represents a widening of the resort to a money-market technique. In other contexts, large non-financial corporations often have a money-market arm and even smaller corporations may have access to money (or investments) at market-related rates. The same is true of 'repos'. In addition, 'repos' can be used as a means of financing the holdings in a bank's own portfolio as well as providing an outlet for customers' temporarily excess funds. Up to 1982, 'repo' transactions as a means of raising additional funds from bank customers were exempt from mandatory reserve requirements. When this exemption was abolished in 1982, there was a significant contraction in the number of these operations carried out by banks. In order to evade required cash reserves against 'repos', some banks put these transactions through a finance company in which they had a capital interest. As a result, it had been difficult to estimate the size of the 'repo' market as a whole, but it was thought to be of the order of L 100,000 billion in 1990.[22]

The 'repo' market seems to be used primarily to attract funds from customers at rates somewhat higher than the returns on traditional deposits; this market is also used to assist in 'window-dressing' the balance sheet towards the end of the financial year. However, in May 1991, when the reserve requirement for net currency borrowings was reduced to zero, the requirement was also abolished for 'repos'. Temporary sales of securities to bank customers – on a 'repo' basis – were expected to represent an attractive alternative to the issue of CDs as a means of seeking additional funds, the advantage being that such funds could be raised for periods materially shorter than by CDs, thereby assisting banks to manage their liabilities more flexibly. From the bank's point of view, there may be less flexibility in financing – by way of 'repos' – its securities portfolio, since the requirements of the customer (in terms of the period of a short-dated investment) is likely to be the main criterion. But this is not likely to be a major worry, since there will tend to be a continuous turnover of funds. The minimum size for a 'repo' transaction ranges from L 50 million to L 100 million.

The range of securities that may provide a basis for such 'repo' operations has now been extended to include not only the most common types of government paper, but any public or private securities in ECU and other currencies. It seems that in Italy there is a preference for securities with a short residual life, but that is not a necessary condition – a security of any maturity can be employed as a basis for a 'repo' transaction, provided only that its maturity is longer than that of the 'repo' transaction itself. In addition, following the currency liberalization process, non-financial corporations are increasingly resorting to currency 'repos' as an alternative to buying currency bonds with an equal residual life.[23]

THE INTER-BANK MONEY MARKET

As is the case with many money markets that have lacked a full range of monetary instruments, the inter-bank market in short-term money is very important in Italy, especially as a means of marginal adjustment. Before approaching such a market, however, it is necessary for a bank to establish its cash position for that day. The large banks in Italy, with branch networks that traverse the country, have the most obvious problem, which can be resolved in two ways – by sophisticated computer programmes and on-line branches and/or by forecasting and the development of projections, again assisted by computer installations. A number of banks have their own models for forecasting the liquidity of the whole system and the results are sent in to a private research institute (PROMETEIA), which also receives information from individual banks as to their liquidity positions for the following day; these are then summated to provide another basis of calculation of total system liquidity. It is these two sources of information that provide the basis for the estimate of system liquidity that appears daily on MID screens. The Bank of Italy also provides some *ex post* information (e.g. the average level of total reserves).

During the day, large amounts of cash – whether in or out – would be reported in to the treasury of the bank (e.g. from branches) as they occur. The 'difficult' figures are usually those for outflows. But the objective is to establish on a reasonably reliable basis the bank's cash position as early as possible in the day. For banks in the MID system (an automated system employed in the inter-bank deposits market), trading begins in mid-morning and ends from 4.00 p.m. to 4.30 p.m. – the most active period is usually between 2.00 p.m. and 4.00 p.m. Transactions after 4.00 p.m. – and until 5.00 p.m. (when the Bank of Italy stops accepting payments) – are nevertheless for value the same day; this market is very thin.

So far as a seasonal movement is concerned, that seems to relate to tax payments in May and November – in May, one must pay the balance of tax due from the year before; one must also pay the 40 per cent of 98 per cent[24] of expected income for the current year; and in November one has to pay the 60 per cent of 98 per cent of expected income for the current year.

Reserve requirements imposed by the Bank of Italy on the commercial banks must be adjusted monthly, the basis of required reserves for the present month being the average of deposit liabilities over the preceding month. As a rule, the only time that the reserve requirement payment is likely to give rise to concern is in February – the February calculation of deposits (relating to figures between December and January) is heavier than January (based on the variation of deposits between November and December). This is because of the interest paid on deposits that customers tend to hold in their current accounts for almost the whole of January. Banks may utilize up to 5 per cent of their stock of reserves that is due for the maintenance period (on average). If at the end of the maintenance period, a bank's effective average stock of reserves is less than the reserve due, the bank concerned would pay on the difference a rate equivalent to discount rate + 5 percentage points (e.g. if discount rate was 11.5 per cent, the bank would pay on the difference 16.5 per cent). If the average stock of reserves is in excess of the requirement, the Bank of Italy would pay the bank concerned on the amount of the excess a rate of 0.5 per cent. Hence, tightness in the inter-bank market can now be accommodated more readily and short-term rates in this market are much less volatile, indeed more stable, though they can be higher on days when large payments are being made to the Treasury. They may also vary quite a lot – up or down – in the last two days of the maintenance period, when banks establish whether they are over or under the average reserve figure for the period.

There may also be some increase in bank liabilities – and therefore in bank cash – at the end of the year associated with 'window-dressing' of bank balance sheets, though this is a practice that is now of decreasing importance. This is followed by a shortage at the beginning of the year. More general seasonal movements (e.g. those relating to agriculture) do not apply to the large banks with branches throughout Italy, as a result of which fluctuations in cash tend to even out. In any event, commercial banks – though they lend to some extent to this sector do not seem to lend very large amounts to agriculture, which depends for the greater part of its needs on other specialist lenders.

Even less clear cut is the emphasis on lending and/or borrowing institutions within the banking community. The big banks would tend to be net borrowers in the inter-bank market, but on any day they are most likely to feature as both borrowers and lenders. Institutions that were formerly highly liquid – such as savings banks and *banche popolari* (people's banks) – seem now to be less so (especially most of the larger savings banks) as they tend to move more into general commercial banking business and to move away from their more specific savings function. But this is not true of the central institution of the co-operative banks – ICCREA – which is a net lender. Small banks, which in Italy have traditionally had special relationships with large bank correspondents (rather similar to US experience), still tend to leave their surplus cash with the large commercial banks at interest, though it is said that some of them are now becoming much more sophisticated and are beginning to shop around for better rates, even to enter the inter-bank money market direct.[25] The loan business of small banks is also tending to grow as the smaller firms that they serve themselves grow in size. None the less, small banks can still be net lenders.

Again, at the other extreme, a large specialized institution like IMI, which is primarily a medium-term and long-term lender substantially funded by the issue of bonds (mainly issued on the foreign market), may be a significant lender at discrete intervals (e.g. it may be heavily in funds – at least for a short period – after making a new issue of bonds). In other words, in managing its cash flow and when it is flush with money, it may well lend in the inter-bank market. It has done this since the early 1980s. The alternative is a large number of inter-bank, medium-sized time deposits with many Italian banks, well spread around. On occasion, if it does not borrow from the banks (e.g. by way of overdraft), or from abroad (allied to a currency swap), IMI may be temporarily short of funds and may be a borrower in the inter-bank market – in either case, due to a mismatch in the flow of funds. However, since IMI is technically not a bank, where 'inter-bank' funds have been placed as a deposit by IMI and are in the hands of a bank at the end of a month, reserve requirements will apply to that bank as with deposits proper.

Foreign banks, on the other hand, are likely to remain net borrowers, since they lack a developed local branch network through which to attract a significant volume of deposits in relation to their loans/investment portfolios. This is a common phenomenon in a number of countries.

Interest rate expectations also enter into it – when interest rates are tending to fall, banks will tend to lock themselves into securities like *BOTs* in order to benefit from currently higher rates than might be obtainable in the future. In these circumstances, banks will become less liquid and may borrow in the inter-bank market to adjust their positions. The inflow of savings into banks is also influenced by the purchase by individuals of *BOTs* and *CCTs* – and this is now a significant element in the investment of household savings.

Within the inter-bank money market, there are two markets – one for overnight money and the other for call money. The overnight market, where money is borrowed one morning to be repaid the following morning, only goes back to April 1982 and was much smaller than the call money market, and, being smaller, overnight rates tended to be much more volatile – it was primarily used for marginal adjustments to bank cash; hence, small movements in money at that time reflected more directly in rates. Latterly, the overnight market has expanded significantly (greatly assisted as from February 1992 by the abolition of the 30 per cent tax on interest from domestic inter-bank deposits) and – as we have seen – there were other factors in inducing greater stability in rates (see p. 235). In terms of flows, the overnight market probably accounts for more than three-quarters of the funds traded between banks (but it represents only about 2 per cent of the stock of inter-bank deposits). Some of the deals may be done in the morning, even though rates may be higher than later in the day (they could also be high late in the day, if 'special situations' are likely to emerge). Foreign banks tend to pay more than the domestic banks.

There is some trading on the call money market (which goes back to the 1960s). Technically, call money refers to a transaction that takes place 2 days after quotation; repayment requires 48 hours' notice. It used to be a very 'cosy' market – a small number of banks dealing between themselves and rates then tended to be indicative only, deals subsequently being done on the telephone at rates above or below those that appeared on the screen. Nowadays, banks trade deposits of all kinds on MID (e.g. both overnight and time deposits), but not call money. There are in fact certain banks that quote rates for call money on MID, but there is no screen trading. So far as trades in deposits are concerned, these pass into the 'memory' of the system and, at the end of the day, MID can supply information relating to the volume of deposits traded and the average rate for any maturity. If there is a quotation, but no trades (as would be the case with call money), the rate will be shown as 'not available'. The implication is that trades in call money are done on the telephone. The total amount of call money is still considerable, but, as a result of the resort to the MID system, time deposits are becoming more and more important.

The minimum size for the pricing of an inter-bank money market transaction is L 3 billion. Frequently, transactions are in the range of L 10 to L 20 billion – they could be for as much as L 50 billion, even more. All inter-bank money market loans are unsecured, though all banks would operate internal limits on the amounts they would lend to particular parties, but such limits may be flexible, especially for the big banks, which know each other well.

No brokers operate today in the inter-bank market. All deals are done direct. Brokers are active in the context of Euro-currency transactions and FOREX, though much of this business is also done directly between banks. (They may also be used for *BOT* and

CCT transactions in the secondary markets.) There are about 15 brokers in Milan (where the main markets are) and about 5–7 in Rome.

INTERVENTION BY THE BANK OF ITALY

The Bank of Italy began using 'repos' in December 1979. Initially, the terms of the 'repo' operation were decided by the Bank of Italy itself. In more recent years, beginning in 1981, the Bank of Italy has been increasingly active in money market operations, which are now based on a competitive auction. The Bank is in the market virtually every day either by way of making funds available on the basis of 'repos' (the purchase of securities by the Bank of Italy – largely *BTPs* and *CCTs* – subject to a parallel contract to sell back such securities after a certain period), or, if it is necessary to absorb funds, by way of reverse 'repos' (the sale of securities subject to a parallel contract to repurchase them after a specified period). First thing in the morning, the Bank of Italy will establish what interest rates are being quoted. It will know from its own data what the overall shortage (or surplus) is likely to be in the money market. If there is a shortage, the Bank of Italy then announces a figure on Reuters and invites bids from the banks for funds, but for the banks that are successful in their bids the periods and the amounts of the 'repos' on offer are at the discretion of the Head of the Discount Department at the Bank of Italy. If there is an excess of liquidity, a 'mopping up' operation (on the basis of *BTPs*, *CCTs*, and *CTOs*, even *BOTs*) may be in order, when the Bank of Italy will undertake reverse 'repos' (as above). The relevant period for these transactions would usually be for up to 14 days (often for 6 or 10 days). 'Repos' for longer than that are less usual. The maximum is laid down as 120 days, but the effective maximum is 1 month to 45 days. In this context, the external factor may be important – if the lira is in trouble, the first thing the Bank of Italy will do is to reduce liquidity by selling securities (subject to a reverse 'repo') usually for 1 month. Sometimes this is done for a shorter period – e.g. 15 days – but not for less than 15 days.

The amount that the Bank of Italy has on offer for 'repos' is normally put on the screen from 8.30 a.m. to 9.00 a.m. Banks have to put in their bids by 10.00 a.m. Usually, they would get their answer by 11.00 a.m., or at the latest by noon. Reverse 'repos' would be announced in the same way. If a bank missed out on a 'repo' it would have to look for money in the inter-bank market (probably overnight), which could be expensive, or it could apply to the Bank of Italy for an advance at discount rate (see below). The first 'repos' done by the Bank of Italy were in December 1979, but now it is an established – and, indeed, the main – technique of intervention. Furthermore, 'repos' are frequently allowed to mature about the same time as a Treasury bill auction. As a result, banks will be put in funds at a time when they will usually wish to take up bills.

If a bank fails to obtain funds from the Bank of Italy by way of a 'repo' and finds money in the overnight market too expensive, it may apply for an advance/loan from the Bank of Italy at discount rate. Formerly, this rate was proposed by the Governor of the Bank of Italy, but fixed by the Treasury (not by the Ministry of Finance). Discount rate had to be set by government decree. Normally, there was agreement between the Governor of the Bank of Italy and the Minister of the Treasury at a time when a change in discount rate was being considered. If the Governor had reason to believe that the Treasury was not likely to change the rate, he would not make a proposal. And the Treasury for its part could not change the rate without a proposal. Then, in July 1991, a project law was presented in order to give the Bank of Italy freedom directly to vary the discount rate. This law was finally approved in early 1992 prior to the dissolution of Parliament in preparation for a general election.[26] There continue to be ongoing discussions between the Bank and the Treasury about such matters and effective liaison between the parties.

Generally speaking, it will be the objective of the Bank of Italy so to organize the release of funds through the agency of 'repos' that resort to the discount window will not be necessary. Some banks would use the discount window only rarely; other banks more often. However, the amount to be lent and the period of the loan is at the discretion of the Bank of Italy. Formerly, going to the discount window too often was strongly discouraged by the application of a system of penalty rates. But this system was abolished in May 1991. All banks now pay the same rate, but for reasons relating to the control of bank liquidity the Bank of Italy can decide (as it did on November 26, 1991) to raise the rate actually applied – in that case by $\frac{1}{2}$ per cent. It is understood that this could be done up to a ceiling of discount rate + 1.75 per cent. The deadline for borrowing at the Bank of Italy is 12.00 noon, but usually any necessary arrangements have been made long before that. All banks have a line of credit at the Bank of Italy (to which discount rate would apply); if they wish to exceed that line, they may apply for additional accommodation, but there is no guarantee that they will get it.

Finally, the Bank of Italy may make outright purchases or sales of government securities. If the Bank of Italy intends to operate in the market, it will come into the market about 9.30 a.m., but there is no fixed time. It will do this through a broker, but the market knows it is the Bank of Italy that is purchasing (or selling) the relevant securities. The market is advised of the Bank's pricing and it makes bids for securities it wishes to buy, the objective still being to regulate the liquidity of the banking system. Clearly, the Bank of Italy's pricing announcements – supported by outright purchases or sales of government securities – will also have an influence on the structure of interest rates.

Chapter 7

The money market in Japan

Of the institutions that go to form the Japanese money market complex, the most central to the basic market processes are the banks: as at end-1990, 12 city and 64 regional banks, the 3 long-term credit banks, 7 trust banks, 82 foreign banks, the 68 secondary regional banks, formerly the *sogo* (mutual) co-operatives, and the central institutions for the co-operatives – the Shoko Chukin Bank (the central bank for commercial and industrial co-operatives) and the Norin Chukin Bank (the central co-operative bank for agriculture and fisheries and their federations of agricultural credit co-operatives). In addition, there are 495 credit associations (*shinyo-kinko* – abbreviated to *shinkin*) and 455 credit co-operatives (*shinyo-kumiai*), which are regional financial institutions that cater mainly for smaller enterprises. There are also insurance companies – life and non-life – and 210 securities companies, of which 4 are large. Finally, there are a number of government financial institutions: 2 banks (the Japan Development Bank and the Export–Import Bank of Japan) and 10 finance corporations (*koko*), which supplement the activities of the private financial institutions in a variety of fields – e.g. regional development finance, the finance of housing, and the financing of smaller enterprises. There are also over 23,000 units within the Post Office, which operate like the branches of a financial institution. Nor should one overlook the 6 Tanshi houses (or brokers), which assist in providing links between the several categories of institutions.[1]

There is a variety of instruments employed in the various markets within the money market complex – call money, bills of exchange (including bank-guaranteed export and import bills), negotiable certificates of deposit (NCDs), Finance bills and short-dated government securities, commercial paper, and Euro-currencies.

There are also *gensaki* transactions (sale and repurchase agreements) in government securities, NCDs, and commercial paper, as well as swaps out of foreign currencies and Euro-currencies into Japanese yen. Sometimes, the money is put (e.g. by medium-sized firms) into foreign currencies by way of time deposits with swaps (*gaika yokin*).

The markets in which these several instruments are traded comprehend the following: the inter-bank yen call money market; the bill discount market; the market in NCDs; an active secondary market in commercial paper; the *gensaki* market; the Tokyo-dollar call market; and the offshore market. Originally, the inter-bank call money market and the bill discount market were the only money markets in Japan. These markets were regulated by the Bank of Japan (BOJ). Then 'open' markets (in *gensaki* and NCDs) were established i.e., although still under the indirect influence of the BOJ, they were open to a wide range of institutions – banks, securities companies, and non-financial institutions (corporations and manufacturers), sometimes individuals (wealthy persons). Latterly, market practice in the call money market and the bill discount market, which was rather restrictive, had begun to be liberalized in the sense that interest rates were freer. There also remained some degree of regulation even in the 'open' market – e.g. in the terms and conditions of the instruments, but not of interest rates. For example, for NCDs, there was a minimum amount of Y 50 million (originally Y 500 million); formerly, too, there were terms of 3 to 6 months, now it was 2 weeks to 24 months. But regulation was not the only criterion; these several markets catered for instruments of different maturities – call money was overnight to 7 days; bills for 1 to 3 months; NCDs for 2 weeks to 24 months; and commercial paper for 2 weeks to 9 months.

With *gensaki*, there were much the same considerations, but use of the instrument emerged rather more naturally. The minimum trading amount tends to be Y 100 million, but there is no convention as to term – such transactions can be for a period as short as a few days to a week – but there are tax problems, since securities transaction tax relates to amount and not to term. Hence, it is relatively uneconomic to undertake short trades; nevertheless, quite a large number of them take place. In fact, the contract period in the *gensaki* market may range from only a few days up to 1 year, though most contracts are arranged for a period of 6 months or less.

Again, 'regulation' of the markets is not now the right word to employ – it is rather a matter of BOJ 'influence'. This influence is exerted by operations in the call money and bill discount markets. Formerly, the BOJ might also have 'suggested' to the Tanshi houses (brokers) the level of rates that it wished to emerge, though this tended to be supported by BOJ operations in the markets. The element of 'suggestion' has now disappeared. Also, with greater liberalization, there has been much more fluctuation in rates even within the same trading day. An increasing number of interest rates ceased to be regulated, though Japan's international commitments to co-ordinate interest-rate policies had made it more difficult for the BOJ to raise the official discount rate if it was to choke off perceived threats of inflation. Discount rate,[2] which after February 1987 was for a long time held at 2.5 per cent, was raised from May 1989 to August 1990 in a number of steps to 6 per cent. In July 1991, it became necessary to lower rates slightly in view of a degree of recession and loss of confidence in the economy. In September, BOJ also injected liquidity into the market to put downward pressure on short-term interest rates. Nevertheless, it has been necessary to decouple the official discount rate from market interest rates, and BOJ turned instead to influencing rates in the short-term money and inter-bank markets, which were now much broader than they were until the early 1980s. Previously, the principal open market instrument was the *gensaki*. After November 1988, BOJ set about deregulating these markets and creating more instruments to provide it with greater operational influence (see below).

It is appropriate now to look in detail at the several markets.

INTER-BANK CALL MONEY MARKET

In the inter-bank call money market, which goes back many years (to 1902),[3] money was lent and borrowed overnight, for periods of up to 7 days, or at call for up to 7 days. Terms of 2 or 3 weeks were introduced in August 1985, with terms of 1 to 6 months on uncollateralized call transactions in November 1988 and terms of 7 months to 1 year on uncollateralized call transactions in April 1989. Participants are confined to financial institutions. Lenders include the long-term credit banks, regional banks, the trust banks, Norin Chukin Bank (the central institution for the agricultural co-operatives) and Zenshiren Bank (the central institution of the credit associations), also their affiliates, some *shinkin* money, sometimes a city bank when liquid. Securities houses, too, occasionally have a surplus, also their trust fund subsidiaries and the investment trusts. Borrowers are mainly city banks and some of the regional banks. There are also foreign banks in the call money market, some of which (though their number is limited) are quite active (maybe twenty or thirty are really active). They are mostly borrowers, but occasionally they lend when they have a surplus of liquidity. They are also active in the bills-discounting market and may likewise sell NCDs. Moreover, as banks have developed their assets and liabilities management, they have also begun to undertake interest-rate arbitrage and may borrow in order to lend on at a more favourable rate, as do the foreign banks. Latterly, the call money market has become more active and rates fluctuate more even within the day. In addition, there is a seasonal movement in the money market (e.g. a seasonal outflow of cash in early December to pay workers' bonuses and corporation taxes). Banks in some areas also need less money in the summer, partly because of the local tax inflow, which adds to bank deposits (many regional banks act for their local governments). Apart from December, there is a shortage of cash in March and September, especially for the city banks, whereas banks are highly liquid in April and May.

Moneys are normally lent through brokers called Tanshi houses.[4] In the inter-bank collaterized market, the Tanshi houses pool the moneys and lend them out to whomever seeks to borrow. Hence, in this context, they are dealers – e.g. they borrow money from the regional banks and lend it on to the city banks. Large lenders would usually divide their money between the several houses. Formerly, commission was the difference between bid and offer (as set by the brokers) and amounted to $\frac{1}{16}$ per cent across the board. Where loans are secured (on the basis of government bonds or corporate bills), collateral, which is exchanged through the broker, usually takes the form of 'alternative certificates', which are issued by the BOJ against the government bonds surrendered by the borrower to the BOJ; the certificate is passed on by the Tanshi house to the lending institution together with a promissory note representing the amount lent. The certificate gives the details of the security actually held against the loan at BOJ. So far as the lender is concerned, however, it is 'no name' security – only the Tanshi houses know who is the borrower. There is always a margin – e.g. for every Y 1 million lent, the collateral will tend to be Y 1.1 million. The lenders cannot operate 'internal' lending limits with respect to borrowers in this market (since they do not know their names) – the 'limit' is the amount of collateral that a bank actually has. Since July 1985, there has also been an unsecured inter-bank market. In this market Tanshi houses act only as brokers, and lenders place 'internal' lending limits on borrowers just as in the Euro-money markets. The bulk of the inter-bank business is done in Tokyo, with a little also in Osaka and Nagoya (where certain Tanshi houses have their head offices, even though most of their business would be done in Tokyo). BOJ monitors both the inter-bank call and bill discount money markets; the rates are interrelated and changes in one market affect other markets. Hence, if BOJ intervenes – as it does from time to time in the bill discount market by buying and selling bills with a view to keeping rates fairly stable – this will also influence the inter-bank call market, where rates otherwise depend on the supply and demand for short-term money. Formerly, BOJ may at times have 'suggested' to the Tanshi houses that a certain level of rates on call money was desirable. Such 'suggestions' tended to be followed by BOJ action in the markets, where – depending on circumstances – funds might either be made available or if there was an excess they would be 'mopped up'.[5]

The market opens at 9.00 a.m., when there is an early morning exchange of information about rates on unsecured call money – this information was passed on to BOJ by the Tanshi houses. About 9.30 a.m., after consultation with the Tanshi houses, a rate was decided on in the market for 1–6-day call money. Usually, the rate on secured call money was $\frac{5}{32}$ per cent below that on unsecured money. Then in December 1990, trading practice changed to a competitive offer–bid system. Previously, the rates which had been set daily at about 10.00 a.m. local time remained the same throughout the day. Interest rates are now determined by market forces in response to the best bid and offer. On the whole, BOJ would be content to follow the trend of the market, but if it believes rates are out of line, it may intervene. For example, if it feels rates are too high, it will enter the market either to buy bills or to lend money. On the whole, however, rates are now much more market-oriented. City banks have also been encouraged by BOJ to operate in the uncollateralized call money market.

There is an adjustment transaction to cover withdrawal of bank notes at 9.00 a.m. Hence, the banks know what their position is first thing in the morning. At 1.00 p.m. there is a clearing – settlement being at 3.00 p.m. But banks must handle transfers until 4.30 p.m. in anticipation of the 9.00 a.m. adjustment transaction the next morning. Physical exchange of cheques has decreased; it is now largely done on a computer basis.[6] There is now no business on Saturdays. On working days, intra-day loans may be made either in the morning or the afternoon. Banks have an account with the BOJ, through which they can make transfers to and from other institutions, and this account must never go into debit. To avoid this – when a bank is already low in cash and has debits to pay off to another bank – banks may have to borrow money for half a day, sometimes in the morning before the 1.00 p.m. clearing (when it must be repaid) or, more generally, in the afternoon before the 3.00 p.m. clearing. Money borrowed in the afternoon must be repaid by the end of the day – by 3.00 p.m. Such loans are quite common. Borrowers tend to be city banks and big regional banks (though the latter are usually lenders). Intra-day loans also go through a Tanshi house. Overnight money can be borrowed at any time of the day, to be repaid by 1.00 p.m. on the next day. If a bank has difficulty in borrowing overnight in the call money market, it may borrow from BOJ, but BOJ may only lend for an extended period. At the end of the day, every bank must be in credit at BOJ and be in a position to maintain its minimum reserve requirement (usually slightly more). If the balance is small, that bank will try to borrow funds next morning. Alternatively, if a bank is likely to be short, it will borrow overnight – just before 3.00 p.m.

It might be noted that small regional banks without an office in Tokyo would tend to be lenders and, to this end, would telephone a Tanshi house, and not use a city bank as correspondent. However, in cities like Kobe or Sapporo, even in Tokyo, a small bank may deposit with a large bank, and the large bank may in turn put moneys out in the money market partly on this basis; that is fairly common.

THE BILL DISCOUNT MARKET

Until May 1971, the short-term money market in Japan consisted mainly of the inter-bank call money market (in yen) and the *gensaki* market (see pp. 250–2); the latter had begun to grow rapidly in the early 1970s. As early as 1919,[7] various unsuccessful attempts had been made to develop a bill-discount market (i.e., an open market in bills of exchange). By 1971, the call market had become less short-term – by now perhaps 80 per cent of call loans outstanding consisted of over-month-end money instead of truly short-term loans. Also, BOJ was finding it more difficult to carry out open market operations – it had been resorting mainly to government and government-guaranteed bonds and there was a need to supplement these with a new instrument such as bills of exchange. Hence, in May 1971, the market was split into a relatively short-term call money market and a longer-term market – the bill discount market – which could accommodate over-month-end transactions.

The bill-discount market was formally established on 20 May 1971 by the money-market brokers who had long been active in operating the call-money market. The market was deliberately designed to include maturities over month-end and up to a maximum of four months. Since its establishment, the market has operated in Tokyo, Osaka, and Nagoya. Of the three cities, Tokyo predominates.[8]

The bill discount market is also confined to financial institutions. If a bank has excess money, it will buy bills; if it needs funds, it will sell them. Transactions always go through the Tanshi houses, in which other financial institutions hold shares, but which operate independently. Commission is again $\frac{1}{16}$ per cent – the difference between 'bid' and 'asked' at the time of the discount – though for very large amounts there could be a volume discount. All markets are interrelated and operations in one market will affect other markets within the money market complex, and – as has been indicated – BOJ monitors both the call money market and the bill-discount market, in which it also intervenes from time to time by purchasing or selling bills (a 'smoothing out' type of operation). The bill discount market is a 'medium-term' market, with bill maturities of 1 week to 1 year (as a result of the liberalization of the markets in April 1989). Rates are generally lower than on uncollateralized call money.

Before proceeding further, it is pertinent to indicate how the paper is originated. When a bank lends to a company, it takes a promissory note (PN); if it wishes to discount (i.e. sell) this paper, the bank draws a covering bill of exchange with a Tanshi house as payee; the amount of the PN must be the same or greater than the amount of the bill of exchange. Likewise, the maturity of the collateral paper must normally be the same or longer than that of the bill of exchange (it is possible to vary the latter with the consent of the buyer). Sometimes – though not usually – a bill of exchange may 'cover' two or three PNs (there might even be five) but in all cases they must have maturities that exceed that of the bill of exchange. Occasionally, PNs are traded a number of times in the secondary market. All bills-discounted transactions go through a Tanshi house.

The main buyers of bills (i.e. lenders) are the trust banks (over 40 per cent of the total) – for their trust accounts. Norin Chukin Bank (the central institution of the agricultural co-operatives) and Zenshiren Bank (the central institution of the credit associations), which were formerly very important, are still significant buyers, but now relatively much less so. Other lenders include the long-term credit banks (buying and selling in order to arbitrage interest rates), the savings and co-operative institutions (other than Norin Chukin and Zenshiren Banks), the regional banks[9] (including the smaller ones), and the foreign banks (buying and selling largely for the purpose of interest rate arbitrage), though they are of minor importance. Borrowing by selling bills is done mainly by the city banks. Clearly, in these cases, whether one is a buyer or a seller, one knows who is the other party.

For bill discounts, the clearance of transactions takes place at the 1.00 p.m. clearing. Most of the lending is done by then, but it could take place up to 3.00 p.m. Final payment of bills at maturity must be at a 1.00 p.m. clearing. Payment is on due date – there are no days of grace in Japan.

Bill discounts cover a range of periods of from 7 days to 1 year. The inter-bank call money transactions are also for up to 1 year. But the *gensaki* and NCD markets (see below) are used for a wider range of periods, which overlap the terms of bill discounts and inter-bank call money. For short periods, the CD *gensaki* may be resorted to, since thereby one can overcome the tax problems of both the NCD and the short-dated *gensaki* against bonds.

Before considering the role of BOJ in this context, it is pertinent to say a word about the Tanshi houses. If one wishes to purchase a bill, one places an order with a Tanshi house and these orders are distributed between the sellers of bills – the takers of funds (mainly the city banks). When bills are discounted, the bank concerned will usually accept without question the distribution allocated to it, since it is necessary for the borrowing banks to maintain good relations with the Tanshi houses, which are left to bring the parties together at the market rate. The bulk of the transactions is carried out in Tokyo, with minor amounts in Osaka and Nagoya.

It is the function of the Tanshi houses to act as the eyes and ears of BOJ and to pass on to them details of market conditions. As already indicated, BOJ itself may intervene in the bill market to make money available (by buying bills at market rates), smoothing out any acute shortages; it tends to do this in order to avoid lending direct to the city banks, though this is a possibility. Such transactions do not go through a Tanshi house. Ten of the twelve city banks have a credit line with BOJ, but it must not be abused. Sometimes, BOJ lent to the Tanshi houses and they lent it on, but it was much easier for BOJ to buy bills through the Tanshi houses. When money is lent by BOJ to the banks, it may be lent overnight (in effect that means for 2 days), but usually funds are lent by BOJ for 1 or 2 weeks, with funds normally being rolled over every 2 weeks. On the whole, this will not suit the banks. Hence it is better all round for BOJ to take the initiative and to stand prepared to buy bills from the banks through the Tanshi houses. If, nevertheless, a bank remained desperately short of funds despite bidding a higher rate and funds still did not 'come out', it would go to the Euro-currency market. Indeed, this tends to be quite a regular experience. On the other hand, if BOJ is 'mopping up' (because of excess liquidity in the banking system), it will request the city banks to repay any BOJ loans to them and, if necessary, would sell them Finance bills (say 30–60-day bills).[10]

In June 1985, a yen-denominated bankers' acceptance market was opened in Japan as part of the United States–Japanese agreements on internationalization of the Tokyo capital markets. Such paper was trade related. An exporter presented a yen-denominated trade draft to a Japanese bank, which the bank accepted and sold on into the secondary market. Over the first few months, the market grew to a peak of Y 70 billion in outstanding balances. However, funding costs and the banks' spreads turned out to be higher than for conventional trade financing, and a number of large potential users (e.g. steel and oil traders) did not in fact resort to bankers' acceptances.[11] After April 1986, securities dealers were permitted to participate as intermediaries in this market, but the market just did not take off and figures dropped virtually to zero.

THE *GENSAKI* MARKET

Gensaki transactions,[12] which are based on a sale and repurchase agreement, first developed in the late 1940s, when the securities companies found that they required cash funds on a short-term basis. To meet their needs, they sold bonds out of portfolio 'on a conditional basis and then repurchased them later'. The difference between the selling and the repurchase price is the main determinant of the yield on the transaction. Initially, bonds were sold to agricultural financial institutions – especially to those that experienced seasonal inflows of cash. Subsequently – in the second half of the 1960s – the commercial banks began to participate in the market when they needed funds during periods of monetary restraint. Interest rates were rising, and, to avoid capital losses, the banks sold bonds in the *gensaki* market to raise the necessary funds, buying time until market conditions improved. But – as already indicated – *gensaki* transactions did not really take off until the 1970s, at the end of which there were certain relaxations: banks could now lend in both the *gensaki* and call money markets (Spring 1981) and non-residents could participate in *gensaki* after May 1979.

On the selling side (i.e. borrowing), the important participants are the bond dealers followed by 'other financial institutions' and, to a much smaller extent, the life and non-life insurance companies, city and trust banks. On the purchasing side (i.e., lending) – apart from bond dealers and 'others' – 'other financial institutions', trust banks, and business corporations are the most important.[13] But the relative importance of the several categories does, of course, change from time to time. In general, the securities companies tend to dominate the market on the borrowing side and the non-financial business corporations and trust banks (sometimes the bond dealers) on the lending side. Banks operating in the *gensaki* market (e.g. as a service to their customers) were formerly subject to a limit imposed by BOJ. This limit was abolished in April 1980.

All transactions in the market are normally arranged through the securities companies, which often act as brokers and are then responsible for screening the creditworthiness of the relevant paper. Sometimes, the banks may arrange *gensaki* transactions direct. Because such transactions tend to be short-term and also because detailed documentation is involved, most of the bonds and debentures traded in the *gensaki* market are kept in the vaults of the

securities companies. This is particularly true of registered bonds
and for short-term transactions of 10 days or less. In lieu of actual
transfer of the bond, bond custody certificates or letters of
guarantee are used:

> For each *gensaki* transaction, written contracts must be
> exchanged between the parties. After all conditions are accepted
> by both parties, two contract notes are prepared, and each party
> signs both notes. Each party thus holds one original copy of the
> agreement.[14]

There are in fact three basic types of *gensaki* transaction:

> The first is a one-sided trade (*jiko gensaki*) which usually
> involved the securities companies selling securities from their
> portfolio to a customer. The second is a matched trade (*itaku
> gensaki*) where the transaction is between two customers with the
> securities company acting simultaneously as buyer and as seller
> of the securities being transacted. The third is a transaction
> between, say, Customer A and Customer B, with the securities
> company merely acting as a broker.[15]

The instruments on which *gensaki* transactions are based include
government bonds and government-guaranteed bonds, municipal
and public corporation securities, also bank debentures, even
sometimes industrial bonds or debentures other than convertible
bonds (rather seldom in the case of debentures, because the market
is limited). Formerly, *gensaki* was based primarily on government
bonds. *Gensaki* is also now done against NCDs (to avoid security
transactions tax) and commercial paper (in the latter context, there
is a lot of overnight and 2–3-day *gensaki* business). Indeed,
commercial paper is now the dominant instrument on which
gensaki is based, followed by NCDs and government bonds. Some
transactions are done against Finance bills sold by BOJ to the
market. These bills can then be used (e.g. by a large securities
house) as a basis for a *gensaki* transaction, the big advantage being
that there is no transfer tax to pay. If government bonds are used,
there is a transfer tax of 0.03 per cent (for dealing accounts 0.01 per
cent). The large securities houses may also do *gensaki* transactions
with European central banks in order that the latter may invest
their foreign exchange reserves, which are based on US dollars. Yen
may be swapped against US dollars, since European central banks
hold few yen but have more in dollars. The dollars are then put

out on a *gensaki* basis for 1 or 2 days, or for any period up to 1 month.

It should be noted that the *gensaki* market is now smaller than it used to be, both relatively and to a lesser extent in absolute terms. Formerly, securities houses financed their portfolios with *gensaki* transactions and still do so. In addition, they would do this to purchase further securities, if prices are expected to rise, when they would hope to make a capital gain. But they also use them to accommodate clients – e.g. such transactions may be done for banks against their bonds or offered as a service to business corporations that have temporarily surplus funds to absorb. At the same time, the securities houses have to finance their own positions, and *gensaki* remains one of the most important ways in which they finance their inventory.[16] One reason why *gensaki* transactions against bonds have decreased, at least in relative importance, is because of the introduction of NCDs and commercial paper (see below).

Banks also do *gensaki* and offer the *gensaki* rate to their customers. But sometimes the securities houses may for a very short time need money at almost any price and will offer very high rates, taking away the business from the banks.

There are a number of reasons why participants in the *gensaki* market may sell bonds on a repurchase basis. The most common is probably to obtain temporarily available liquid funds, but it may be to arbitrage and make a profit (e.g. by borrowing in the *gensaki* market and investing the proceeds in the call money or bill-discount market). Again, it may be the means of delaying a final sale of bonds in the expectation that these could be sold outright later on at a higher price. Or bonds may be sold in the *gensaki* market in order to acquire funds to buy additional bonds on a long-term basis, but without having to sell outright bonds already held. Alternatively, buying bonds in the *gensaki* market may be a means of securing higher yields than in other sectors of the money market, or on short-term time deposits. Bonds may also be bought temporarily (in the *gensaki* market) with the intention of using the repurchase proceeds later to buy bonds on a long-term basis when the price (hopefully) is lower, or to hedge (or 'balance') a portfolio by selling long-term bonds against repurchase agreements and buying bonds short-term in the *gensaki* market.

NEGOTIABLE CERTIFICATES OF DEPOSIT (NCDs)

The Japanese market for yen-dominated NCDs was established on 16 May 1979. They began to be issued rather slowly but grew quite rapidly after June 1980. By the end of 1989, the figure was well over Y 21 trillion, though by end-1990 it had fallen to less than Y 19 trillion. The minimum size was initially set at Y 500 million; it was progressively reduced to Y 50 million by April 1988. The typical size for large takers would be Y 500 million, but the tendency is to break this up into 5 × Y 100 million for marketing purposes. Interest rates on NCDs are determined by market forces and are unregulated,[17] but every week BOJ announces the average rate for the past week and, on this basis, the rate for money market certificates is set.[18]

Some NCD transactions go through the Tanshi houses, but some are done direct. Probably the amount going through the Tanshi houses is falling at least relatively. But there are two good reasons for continuing to go through these houses: (1) very large amounts can be placed with a Tanshi house at one go, and it has the expertise to place these NCDs around the market without much delay; and (2) if a bank finds that rates are going up, it can again place a large quantum of NCDs with the Tanshi houses, moving quickly before rates rise even higher. All the large banks have subsidiary companies, through which they issue NCDs. They are primary dealers and sometimes also operate in the secondary market. They likewise undertake CD *gensaki* transactions. From 1 June 1985, securities houses were also permitted to do this. City banks may issue their NCDs directly to customers and sometimes to Tanshi houses; some may be sold to a bank's subsidiary company, which acts as a dealer. There are perhaps twenty or thirty of these subsidiary companies. Some of the regional banks have subsidiary companies as well. Banks apply internal limits to the amounts of other banks' CDs that they will hold, and other banks do the same to them.

Formerly, the Ministry of Finance set a limit on the total amount of the banks' NCD issues (it was initially 10 per cent of net worth and was progressively raised to 300 per cent in April 1987). This limit has since been abolished (in October 1987). In addition, by April 1988, the term had been widened progressively from 3 to 6 months to from 2 weeks to 2 years.

As already indicated, Tanshi houses may hold CDs, financing these holdings on the basis of own capital. But the positions they carry are not so large – they buy and sell CDs in the secondary market and hold them only briefly. Indeed, a bank may either issue a CD directly to a non-financial corporation or to a Tanshi house, and technically the latter passes it on into the secondary market,[19] though really it is more in the nature of a primary CD. Transactions of *gensaki* CDs may also be done through a Tanshi house.

There is a withholding tax on NCDs. The last holder of the CD is responsible for payment of this tax and the tax has to be paid on interest earned for the whole period of the NCD. When CDs change hands in the secondary market, tax due as at that date is reflected in the price. But, to avoid paying tax, banks may sell before maturity to non-taxpaying bodies like schools, charities, and religious institutions. They do this with some success.

As one would expect, when NCDs were first issued, they tended to replace time deposits, the main customers being the non-financial corporations. Occasionally, they may be issued to financial institutions and a bank may hold the CDs of another bank. Although the minimum size is now Y 50 million, as already indicated, a trade might well be for Y 500 million; at the same time, the amount of a typical trade is tending to become smaller. Moreover, individuals can and do buy NCDs and they might well be interested in the smaller amounts.

As already noted, in addition to *gensaki* proper, *gensakis* are also done in NCDs. It was in January 1981 that a modest beginning was made in trading in NCDs for short periods on the basis of repurchase agreements. The growth in the secondary market for NCDs, which expanded rapidly after the summer of 1981, also attracted funds that would otherwise have gone into the *gensaki* market proper. Much of the rise in volume in the NCD secondary market represented *gensaki* trading in NCDs for short periods and, in fact, it is frequently in the nature of interest arbitrage. These operations are primarily undertaken by banks and Tanshi houses. The principal reason for the shift away from *gensaki* proper was that NCD *gensakis* were free of taxation, whereas *gensaki* proper was subject to a tax on each transaction, based on the principal amount of the bond. In the secondary market, CDs are mostly traded in the form of *gensaki*. But the effective rate will reflect the current rates on CDs. None the less, the banker–customer relationship can affect the rate that is negotiated. In Japan, however, the rates on NCDs are very similar between banks, whereas in Europe and the USA the rate on a CD will depend on the creditworthiness of the bank concerned. BOJ monitors these transactions very closely, but does not in fact apply limits.

The CD *gensaki* is done mainly with non-financial corporations to meet the needs of customers – e.g. to provide an investment outlet for temporarily surplus funds. CD *gensakis* are done for 7–30 days, and the CDs are therefore tied up for that period. On the other hand, if a corporation buys a CD outright, it can sell it on the secondary market if it wishes to disinvest. It should be noted that when a bank does a CD *gensaki*, the item appears on both sides of the balance sheet.

When NCDs are issued, they are not issued to bearer but are registered. In order to transfer domestic CDs, the seller has to notify the issuing bank in writing that a sale is being effected with another party and this notice has to be stamped by a notary public, evidencing the date of the transaction. The reason for this cumbrous procedure is that if NCDs were in bearer form, legally the NCD would constitute a security and it could be argued that it would not then be legally possible for a bank to undertake such transactions.

TREASURY AND FINANCE BILLS

It was the practice of the Japanese government to issue short-term government bills (latterly called Finance bills) whenever there was a need for the government to cover a temporary shortage of cash funds.[20] But, unlike the United States, where a relatively large amount of Treasury bills always remains outstanding, the amount outstanding of what were originally called Treasury bills in the Japanese market fluctuated sharply from month to month and, at times, all of the bills were redeemed and none was left outstanding.[21] Then, in the spring of 1981, BOJ began selling such bills (at a time when there were quite a number of highly liquid industrial and commercial companies with funds to invest) with a view to developing a market in these bills. Initially, BOJ attempted to sell these bills through the Tanshi houses to the banks[22] and securities houses, with the possibility that the market might be used at some time in the future for the purpose of open-market operations. None the less, the Ministry of Finance was reluctant to see the over-rapid resort to such bills, because of the danger of rising rates of interest. By April 1985, the rate was still quite low – and when BOJ sold to the public, it did so at a loss in order to underwrite the experiment.

At the same time, the bill rate was still regulated and was determined by the Ministry of Finance in consultation with BOJ – which did, however, take into account other rates. Hence, the bill rate was to a certain extent market-related. It also bore a loose relationship to BOJ discount rate (about $\frac{1}{8}$ per cent below).

The name of the instrument was changed from Treasury bill to Finance bill in 1986. These bills were for periods of 59 to 63 days. Very few were sold to the public, and the unsold portion (which was fairly large) was underwritten by BOJ – the bills being issued 'on tap' at a low fixed rate to the central bank, as were the previously existing Treasury bills.

New Treasury bills were introduced in February 1986. These were now issued on a tender basis of 6 months or more. They were primarily employed as a means of facilitating the redemption of long-term bonds. Sometimes, Treasury bills are issued with maturities of 3 months and are held by city banks. They can then be bought up by BOJ if – and when – it wishes to provide liquidity to the market.

The total figure for Finance bills outstanding is very much larger than that for Treasury bills – Y 22 trillion compared with Y 4 trillion, with the Finance bills being rolled over as they mature. It is understood that BOJ would prefer a rate on Finance bills that is closer to market rates, but so far negotiations with the Ministry of Finance under this head have not been successful. It is understood further that Treasury bill financing, which is very small, may be expanded – with the possibility that it may be employed in the future as a basis for money market operations.

COMMERCIAL PAPER

In November 1987, Japan launched a commercial paper market and it proceeded to grow steadily to over Y 15.7 trillion by the end of 1990. By 1990, the number of companies permitted by the Ministry of Finance to issue paper was about 150. There were about 70 top-tier groups allowed to issue paper without a back-up line of credit from a leading bank. The Long-Term Credit Bank of Japan has been the largest underwriter in this market. The reason for the rapid growth of commercial paper is *zaitech*, the business of investing corporate funds in financial markets. Although there have been losses, the bulk of *zaitech* has always been concerned with making relatively safe investments in the money markets. Companies exploited their high creditworthiness to raise funds cheaply in one market and re-invest them in another where yields were higher.

This safety-first policy was reinforced when the prices of equities plunged in October 1987. This set the scene for the commercial paper market, which saw the light of day in the gloom of November. Banks and securities companies then swung into action offering cut-price rates to companies to tempt them into using the new market. Risk-free returns of almost 0.5 per cent could be made by issuing paper at 3.9 to 4.0 per cent and putting the money on deposit at 4.4 per cent. On this basis, some underwriters were losing money on issues of commercial paper in the early days. After that, under-writers were forced to pay more attention to margin than to market share and the returns available to the *zaitech* players shrank to from 0.1 to 0.2 per cent. Nevertheless, this was still attractive enough to issuers. At that time, dealers estimated that some 70 per cent of the issues were used to raise money for *zaitech* – among the largest issuers were companies which were previously among the most aggressive *zaitech* investors in the securities and money markets.[23]

As the number of companies permitted to use the market grew, commercial paper also became a more popular source of commercial funding, reducing the *zaitech* element to perhaps 50 per cent. Again, in order to meet new international standards for capital adequacy, banks had to raise the proportion of capital to total assets, and commercial paper was seen as a flexible way of reducing bank loan books, since commercial paper could be sold by the bank to an investing institution. A secondary market has also developed – small at first – but receiving a boost when, in May 1989, the BOJ started to buy commercial paper as a means of widening the range of instruments it employed in its money market operations. In this context, BOJ buys overnight on a 'repo' basis commercial paper through the Tanshi houses, which themselves will have bought it on a 'repo' basis from market participants endorsing the relevant commercial paper before it passes into the hands of BOJ.

TOKYO DOLLAR AND OFFSHORE MARKETS

A less central activity in the complex of Japanese money markets has been the Tokyo dollar call market. This was originally set up on 17 April 1972, when operations were being carried out by 41 banks (18 Japanese and 23 foreign). But in the first 2 or 3 years it was not very active. Up to 1975, the Japanese banks were takers of US dollars; after 1975, the market became much more active and banks operated sometimes on one side, sometimes on the other. By the end of 1989, there were some 150 Japanese banks and 82 foreign banks with branches in Japan operating in the market, which was supported by 8 brokers. There were also 9 foreign trust banks – subsidiaries of foreign banks. Foreign banks outside Japan could (after February 1985) operate in this market through brokers. It was really the domestic market for transactions in foreign currencies – mainly US dollars (more than 90 per cent of total business). Initially, currencies were not lent for more than 6 months; latterly, there was no definite rule, but there were very few transactions for over 1 year. Apart from overnight, a typical period was 3 or 6 months. Overnight was most common. Withholding tax was not applied to this market, since it was a call and not a deposit market. Again, Tanshi houses might act as brokers; if they had a subsidiary, this business would be done through the subsidiary. If not, it would go through the Tanshi house's foreign department. Commission was of the order of $\frac{1}{50}$ per cent whatever the amount.[24] The banks set internal limits on these transactions, which were unsecured; in this way, they could both restrict and diversify their risks.

In order to adjust their short-term foreign exchange funding, these banks might lend or borrow short-term dollar funds. The suppliers of funds were the large Japanese banks and the foreign banks with branches in Japan; the borrowers were trust banks, local banks, and other small banks. The annual turnover was of the order of US\$ 1,870 billion in 1990 and the outstanding balance was estimated at US\$ 110 billion. The Tokyo market was a facility for Japanese banks to adjust their positions, trading between banks in dollars held in Japan itself. The main business in currency deposits (dollars for the most part) was done by overseas branches of Japanese banks on behalf of Tokyo.

In the foreign exchange market, the big banks bought and sold foreign exchange to adjust the imbalances in their exchange positions that arose out of transactions with clients. For example, they might sell dollars from London for yen; they could also buy dollars for yen. The main participants in this market were – and remain – the large banks, the foreign banks, a number of brokers (including the Tanshi houses), and the Foreign Exchange Fund Special Account operated by BOJ. They could also do swaps in the foreign exchange market, and the link between the foreign exchange and the domestic money markets (including the Tokyo dollar call market) was the swap from US dollars into yen; at the end of the swap, it was reversed – back from yen into dollars. In recent years, however, the foreign exchange market in Japan has broadened considerably. The Tokyo market used to be dominated by the yen–dollar trade. But by 1988/89, cross-currency transactions had increased substantially in inter-bank trading and there are days when trading in other currencies exceeds yen–dollar trading. Indeed, between 1986 and 1988, trading in currencies other than the dollar grew from US$ 600 billion to US$ 1,600 billion.[25]

In December 1986, Japan established an offshore market, which is parallel to the dollar call market. It grew rapidly, supported largely by the short-term funding needs of the Japanese banks. To some extent, the authorities' resolve to stimulate the domestic short-term money markets threatened to hamper the development of Japan's offshore market. But this was offset by the setting up in Tokyo of two new financial futures markets (see pp. 261–2). These provided opportunities for hedging and arbitrage, and promised to add a new dimension to offshore activity. Since 1987, Japan's offshore market has seen a remarkable surge of activity with external assets reaching over US$ 605 billion by the end of 1989. This places it well above New York's International Banking Facilities (IBFs),[26] which had comparable external assets of US$ 302 billion by 1990, although Japan is still far behind the offshore market in London.

The bulk of the activity on Japan's offshore market has in the past come from banks seeking short-term funding. The role of the offshore market as an inter-bank lending market for short-term needs was greatly enhanced by the limited scope of the domestic markets. The Japanese authorities have also kept a tight rein on seepage from offshore accounts into the domestic market, limiting the flow to 5 per cent of a bank's average balance of transactions with non-residents in the previous month. Nevertheless, banks have been able to bring more of their offshore funds into their onshore accounts by using inter-office swaps.

As the liberalization of Japan's markets has gathered pace, the authorities have taken concrete steps to encourage the development of a fully functional domestic market for short-term funding. The liberalization of interest rates in November 1988 on 3-month bills, for example, tended to rob the offshore market of its major role as a short-term lending market. On the other hand, the continued strength of the offshore market has been greatly assisted by an increase in arbitrage between domestic-bill interest rates and offshore rates. Also, while the offshore market's role as a source of short-term funding tended to shrink with the increased deregulation of the domestic markets, the setting up of interest-rate and currency-futures markets' in Tokyo assisted in keeping offshore activity alive and well by offering investors more opportunities for hedging and arbitrage between their cash yen accounts on the offshore market and Euro-yen futures. In addition, Euro-yen futures will offer a much needed hedging tool for yen positions during Tokyo hours and this will be an added attraction for holding offshore yen accounts. In fact, the offshore market has remained very active.

DEREGULATION OF THE MONEY MARKETS

Since November 1988, there have been a number of reforms that have radically modified short-term money markets in Japan. Thus, in November 1988, BOJ decided to expand the scope of the discount bill market by shortening maturities to less than 1 month. The BOJ now allowed trading in 1–3-week bills. Again, it changed the longest maturity in the unsecured call market from 3 weeks to 6 months. This could be presented by BOJ as a sympathetic response to complaints by foreign banks that liberalization of the short-term money markets was squeezing them out of the unsecured call loan market. This market is their main source of funds in Japan since they lack a local deposit-taking base, having few, if any, branches. Nevertheless, BOJ's main objective was to encourage funds that had flowed to the less heavily regulated Euro-yen market to return to the domestic market. As a result, the inter-bank market revived somewhat. BOJ also started using 1–3-week bills and commercial paper in its own buying operations, which had traditionally involved transactions in 2-month discount bills. Buying operations which resorted to instruments with shorter maturities allowed the central bank to operate with more mobility and flexibility.

To increase the bill market's liquidity, BOJ from January 1989 eased both the trading rules and restrictions that hampered banks from arbitraging between short-term and long-term interest rates (such as limits on the amounts of funds they could take from the unsecured call market and ceilings on holdings of CDs; until January 1989, the average monthly balance of holdings of CDs was limited). An earlier step to increase the size of the short-term money markets had been to launch (in November 1987) a market in yen commercial paper. Latterly, the range of allowable maturities was enlarged from 1 to 6 months to anything between 2 weeks and 9 months. Indeed, from April 1990, BOJ allowed trading in maturities of 7 months to 1 year in the unsecured call market, also in the bill discount market. Decoupling of the official discount rate proceeded further with the introduction of a new short-term prime rate for loans by the commercial banks to their best customers. Short-term prime had previously been set by adding a margin to the official discount rate. Now the banks could calculate a new rate from an average of four sets of interest rates (CDs, demand deposits, small- and large-lot time deposits, and interbank money) weighted to reflect the banks' sources of funds.

FINANCIAL FUTURES AND OPTIONS

Trading in financial futures began in Tokyo in October 1985 on the basis of a 10-year government bond future. This was followed by trading in 20-year government bond futures in July 1988; T-bond futures trading began in December 1989 – on the Tokyo Stock Exchange (TSE) – and 3-month Euro-yen interest rate futures (on the new financial futures exchange in Tokyo) in June 1989. Meanwhile, starting in June 1987, trading in stock futures 50 had begun on the Osaka Stock Exchange. In June 1989, the Osaka Stock Exchange started trading Nikkei 225 index options and, in October 1989, the Tokyo Stock Exchange commenced trading its Topix stock index options. Osaka's lead with the Nikkei futures gave it an edge *vis-à-vis* Tokyo with its put and call options on the index. Indeed, even the Nagoya Stock Exchange's option at times rivalled the Topix option in terms of average daily trade (e.g. in January 1990). The Nagoya contract is based on an index of the leading twenty-five Stock Exchange issues.

These new instruments provided Japanese investors with much needed means of hedging against adverse movements in the stock, money, and currency markets. They also marked a further step in the internationalization of Japan's capital markets and of futures trading as a whole. However, despite the introduction of these new futures, the markets on which they are traded remain regulated in a number of important respects. Of these constraints, the most significant was the rejection of the original proposal by the Financial

System Research Council to establish a single unified futures exchange with free competition between financial institutions. Instead of this, equity-based products were traded on the existing stock markets, while currency and money market products were traded separately on the Tokyo International Financial Futures Exchange (or TIFFE). As a result, the dichotomy between securities firms and banks continued to apply. Securities houses were barred from trading currency options, since the execution of options rights involved the handling of cash currency transactions and therefore contravened the banks' valuable monopoly of FOREX business. Similarly, banks were barred from broking stock index futures and options.

While the two stock exchanges in Tokyo and Osaka provided means of share hedging and speculation (with, in addition, a bond futures option introduced on the TSE in May 1990), the new products on TIFFE, by way of contrast, helped to satisfy the increasing need of Japan's financial institutions to hedge interest rates and currencies. In recent years, interest rate risk has risen, as deregulation of the domestic money market has resulted in the rapid growth of assets subject to floating rates and an increase in the role of market-related instruments in the raising of bank funds. As for currencies, the heavy exchange losses that were suffered from time to time by Japanese financial institutions, and the increasing use of foreign currency for short-term transactions, similarly increased exposure to risk.[27]

On TIFFE, three contracts are on offer – a 3-month Euro-yen interest rate future, a 3-month Euro-dollar future, and a yen/US dollar currency future. Only the Euro-yen contract has established a significant trading interest. The difficulty with the contracts traded through TIFFE are said to be twofold. First, there is the fact that the bulk of trading is 'proprietary' – i.e. it is carried out directly by market participants and affiliated companies; this accounts for an estimated 90 per cent or more of the total number of contracts traded. Second, there is the absolute concentration on near-dated contracts, with little or no interest in longer dates. The opening hours are too limited and there are too few contracts. There are also complaints about the semi-automatic trading system.[28]

TANSHI HOUSES

Reference has been made from time to time to the brokers, or Tanshi houses. To some extent, they act as principals, but they are brokers rather than dealers. They are six in number, of which four are larger than the others: they are mostly based in Tokyo; two have their head offices in Osaka (although the bulk of their business would be in Tokyo) and one in Nagoya. Basically, they are independent of other financial institutions.[29] Some of them have subsidiaries (e.g., to undertake foreign exchange broking).[30] Call money (subject to some direct deals) and bill discount transactions go through the Tanshi houses – the return is $\frac{1}{16}$ per cent (the difference between bid and offer). For uncollateralized call loans, it is $\frac{1}{50}$ per cent.[31] Intra-day loans also go through the Tanshi houses. Most of these houses carry a portfolio of NCDs on the basis of own capital, but their positions are not large. Tanshi houses may also hold positions in commercial paper; and carry small amounts of equities as an investment, or hold National Bonds as a reserve. Banks sometimes sell NCDs to the Tanshi houses, which may themselves undertake CD *gensaki*.[32] The BOJ places Finance bills through the Tanshi houses for on-selling to banks and their customers. Only one acts as a broker in the Tokyo dollar market; five other houses have established a joint venture as foreign exchange brokers. Virtually all banks use them – even small local banks. The Tanshi houses do not act as brokers in the *gensaki* market. To the extent that there is a brokerage function there, it is performed by the securities houses. But perhaps the most important function of the Tanshi houses (e.g., in passing on information about market conditions) is to act as the eyes and ears of the BOJ. And BOJ can exert a direct influence by buying bills through the Tanshi houses, which it does when insufficient funds are available elsewhere.

In the context of the inter-bank call money market, there was thought to be some 'administrative guidance' by the authorities, prompting foreign and Japanese banks to use the Tanshi houses as their intermediaries in preference to direct deals. Meanwhile, BOJ had argued that 'it gives no guidance and imposes no restrictions on direct dealing'. It was acknowledged that there had been some concern expressed by foreign governments and institutions relating to the reform of the financial system and – on behalf of BOJ – it was stated that:

We appreciate people using the tanshi, but that does not mean we don't want to see people in the market dealing on a direct basis. We have become more and more sensitive to foreign banks' needs. I think we have come to put a little more international consideration into money market activities.[33]

At the same time, it was likely that some foreign banks – although they were quite capable of handling the paper work that accompanies direct dealing in Japan – would continue to use the Tanshi houses as a matter of convenience. None the less, it was anticipated that city, regional, and agricultural banks in Japan would change over gradually – 'in a series of steps' – to direct dealing.[34]

BANK OF JAPAN INTERVENTION

Finally, a word may be said about BOJ operations. As we have seen, BOJ has for some years now been less concerned to regulate money markets and more concerned to exercise influence. This is exerted primarily by way of operations in the call money and bill markets, but latterly it has also operated in other instruments as well (e.g., commercial paper and NCDs). BOJ no longer suggests to the Tanshi houses a level of rates (e.g. on call money) that it feels is desirable and may wish to see maintained, and – with a greater emphasis on liberalization – rates have become more volatile. In the bill market, BOJ can exert a more direct influence. This is done by buying bills through the Tanshi houses. Day by day the participants in the market will be monitoring the cash situation (e.g. trying to estimate whether tax payments are likely to result in tight money); they also try to establish what BOJ may decide to do and they will take some sort of view as to how interest rates will tend to move; also, from August 1989, BOJ has published daily certain information about the supply of and demand for funds in the short-term markets and about its own operations. Meanwhile, BOJ will be estimating the net balance that will be required each day. If it is likely that money will be short, BOJ may either be willing to buy bills from the market through the Tanshi houses, or to lend money to the banks. The path that will be chosen is entirely at the discretion of BOJ. If it decides to lend (against eligible securities), it will do so just before 3.00 p.m. Eligible securities include National Bonds, government-guaranteed bonds, local-authority bonds, bank debentures, and some blue chip bonds (e.g. private electricity companies with good names). When BOJ lends, it is against security which is held in safe custody at BOJ and ownership is transferred between the parties by BOJ (some holdings, e.g. registered bonds, are computerized; otherwise, actual paper is transferred at BOJ from one party to another – in effect, from one pigeon-hole to another.)

Minimum reserves have to be based on a reserve accounting period that begins on the 16th of one month and ends on the 15th of the following month. When adjustments are necessary, to some extent these will be effected by the operations of the banks themselves. None the less, BOJ also has to act such that all banks can maintain their average balances over the month and, if money is needed, BOJ can buy bills from or lend money to the banks. If bills have been bought, they will mature on a certain day, when funds will be absorbed by BOJ. Moreover, this may be done deliberately to offset seasonal surpluses. On the other hand, if BOJ has lent to the banks – and it wishes to withdraw funds – it may request repayment of loans by the borrowing banks. Usually, BOJ loans (which may be 'overnight' or, in effect, for 2 days) are for 2 weeks, but they may either be rolled over (the money is re-lent), or the loan may be called in early. More recently, BOJ has sold Finance bills in order to mop up excess liquidity. These are sold to the market at a market rate, which would tend to be higher than the low fixed rate when issued; BOJ therefore sells at a loss.

Because of the Japanese Government's policy of favouring a budget surplus, it is disinclined to issue Treasury bills in large amounts, and resort to Finance bills for open market operations is limited so long as the Ministry of Finance insists on their issue at below market rates. Hence, there has been a shortage of paper on the basis of which to conduct such operations.[35] To overcome this difficulty, BOJ has more recently resorted to transactions based on NCDs and commercial paper. There is no market in domestic bankers' acceptances in Japan. Moreover, limitations on the negotiability of NCDs makes them less than ideal as an instrument for open market operations and, despite its varying quality, BOJ has favoured greater use of commercial paper for this purpose.

To some extent, the objectives of BOJ were achieved by buying commercial paper through the Tanshi houses (in order to put funds out into the market). Then, in March 1986, it put money out on the basis of NCDs. It did this by making loans to Tanshi houses, which moneys could be used to buy NCDs; hitherto, these houses had not been permitted to employ loans from BOJ for any other purpose than making placements in the call money market. Next, in December 1987, BOJ started purchasing long-term government bonds under repurchase agreements (in the form of *gensaki*) in order to adjust the liquidity level in the market for bank reserves.[36] Likewise against commercial paper in May 1989. When a commercial paper operation is announced, the Tanshi houses collect commercial paper from banks and securities houses under repurchase agreements and the BOJ buys it through the Tanshi houses with their endorsements. This greatly enhanced the ways in which BOJ could supply funds to the market. Reverse 'repos' were also employed (as from January 1986) in order to 'mop up' funds that were in over-supply. All these operations may be done overnight. In these several ways, BOJ operations have come to resemble rather more those of the Federal Reserve Bank of New York. After November 1988, BOJ had already sought to plug maturity gaps in the short-term markets, but use of the 'repo' gives it maximum flexibility.

These moves have been calculated to permit the BOJ to focus the maturity of its open market operations towards the short end of the maturity spectrum, concentrating on maturity of up to 3 weeks, whereas previously the focus had been out to 3 months. As a Bank of Japan official has explained:

> Speculation on the path of future interest rates starts in the two-to three-month area, while in the shorter-term markets there is much smaller pressure of expectations. We can now leave the market to decide the level of the three-month bill.[37]

In other words, the emphasis is now on short rates and, in particular, on the overnight call rate, where it would seem that BOJ has for some time now attempted to aim at a kind of 'target' and operated at the short end to achieve this.

Chapter 8

The Australian money market[1]

It is useful to look first at the early history of the Australian money market, since much of what exists today derives from that experience.[2] Prior to the 1950s, the means of investing money for short periods in Australia were rather limited. The traditional outlet was the 'fixed deposit' accepted by the trading banks for terms of 3 to 24 months. However, during the 1950s, the rates paid on such deposits had ceased to be competitive with alternative outlets, such as the issue of short-term debenture stock and unsecured notes by finance companies. This latter facility began to be offered (soon by other enterprises as well) about 1950, but trustees and public authorities were unable to employ this technique because of legislative restrictions. Hence, a means had to be devised to meet the needs of investors who wanted the security of government paper, but whose funds were unlikely to be available long enough to justify an outright purchase. Also government securities with only a few months to maturity were not normally available in large amounts. This need was met by the 'buy-back' facilities that certain stock and share brokers in Sydney and Melbourne were prepared to offer their customers. Moreover, by selling securities subject to an agreement to repurchase, as well as the more normal borrowing of funds at short-term, these brokers were able to build up quite sizeable portfolios. The big disadvantage of this system was the absence of a true lender of last resort, which could assure ultimate liquidity in the event of need. At that stage, stockbrokers for the most part could only fall back on their facilities with the trading banks,[3] but it was unreasonable to regard these as always and necessarily available.

It was not until February 1959, by which time there already existed a market of quite appreciable size, that the central bank –

still then the Commonwealth Bank of Australia, but from January 1960 the Reserve Bank of Australia – began to provide formal lender of last resort facilities to 'authorized dealers' in the short-term money market. At all times, dealer companies had to be ready and able to engage in the buying and selling of money market securities. The other point to note is that with the emergence of 'authorized dealers' an 'official' money market was established, and operations which fell outside official dealings became the basis of an 'unofficial' market.

TREASURY NOTES

For some time, there remained something of a shortage of securities with a sufficient range of maturity dates to accommodate seasonal variations in liquidity. The range of available securities was widened to some extent with the issue in November 1959 of 3-month seasonal Treasury notes, which were rediscountable at the central bank. These were originally issued fortnightly, but latterly on a daily basis during the flush period of the year from about September to March. They had to be redeemed by the end of each financial year (June 30) and no new issue could therefore be made after March 31 until the following September. Then, as from 16 July 1962, the Federal Government began to issue, in minimum amounts of A$ 10,000, also at a rate of discount and on a continuous basis, 3-month Treasury notes – which were likewise rediscountable at the Reserve Bank. These replaced seasonal Treasury notes. The attraction of the Treasury note was further enhanced by the introduction of a 26-weeks maturity in July 1967. Its issue price was varied from time to time and became the barometer of short-term money market rates. As a result of these changes, the Treasury bill disappeared from trading-bank balance sheets (about July 1962), and they now came to be held entirely by the Reserve Bank itself. After 1959, too, the dealers were able to supplement their supplies of securities by purchases from the Reserve Bank, which became a significant source. Since there were no brokerage or similar charges on these transactions, rate competition had full play.

OFFICIAL MONEY MARKET DEALERS

The eight official dealers operating in mid-1991 were as follows: All-States Discount Limited; Colonial Mutual Discount Company

Limited; FBA (Discount) Ltd; F.R. Australian Discount Limited; Potter Warburg Discount Limited; Rothschild Australia Discount Limited; Schroders Australia Discount Limited; and Short Term Discount Limited. Since May 1981, all dealers transact with and report to the Sydney, NSW office of the Reserve Bank of Australia.

Originally, there were two main types of houses: (1) those who were money dealers – these traded in money, and with the money that they borrowed they purchased securities and 'sat on them'; and (2) traders in securities, who regarded everything in their portfolio as being available for sale and who were in the market to buy anything on offer – in both cases at a price. Some houses tried to establish a balance between the two types of business.

Currently, dealers are active traders of Commonwealth government securities. However, a large part of these trades are conducted with the Reserve Bank. On average, dealers turn over their assets twice in a 3-day period. Indeed, 30 per cent of all turnover in the Commonwealth government securities market (including repurchase agreements) is undertaken by dealers. Certain of the official dealers are active participants in professional bill dealing. Authorized dealers – the official market – are still restricted in the securities that they can hold and the ratios that they have to maintain between capital and total holdings and between their several types of assets. Thus, they can only hold assets the weighted value[4] of which does not exceed thirty-three times total shareholders' funds, though they may not wish to hold as much as that. This is the multiplier or 'gearing maximum', which imposes a limit to the permissible figure for the total book. At this ratio, a house could have (say) a 3 per cent fall in the value of its assets and this would be covered by shareholders' funds.

Also, from February 1990, they may not hold more than 50 per cent of the maximum gearing limit in non-Commonwealth securities (previously, it was 30 per cent). Although there is no direct limit on repurchase transactions, 'repo' transactions outstanding at the end of each day are included in the calculation of dealers' gearing levels. At times, this may constrain dealers' use of these instruments. Within the 50 per cent referred to, the most important items would be bank bills (bank accepted or endorsed) and negotiable certificates of deposit (NCDs), which are regarded as an asset that in terms of liquidity is virtually interchangeable with bank bills. Also, up to $2\frac{1}{2}$ per cent within the 50 per cent could be held in almost anything else – e.g. non-bank bills of firms of good standing.

Before July 1982, authorized dealers' holdings of non-government securities had been more strictly regulated.

For some time, no specific minimum capital was required, though the Reserve Bank monitored closely the current capital provisions of all the official houses. Latterly, a minimum capital (shareholders' funds) has been required and, since May 1989, this has been set at A$ 10 million. The minimum size of transaction on the official market is now A$ 50,000 for loans and purchases or sales of notes, and A$ 100,000 for bonds.

An important privilege accorded to the authorized dealers was lender of last resort facilities at the central bank. This has now been replaced by end-of-day repurchase agreements. There was no limit to the length of stock that could be used for the line of credit, but any such loans had to be secured by Commonwealth government paper and were at a rate determined by the Reserve Bank. Only licensed trading banks and authorized dealers have accounts at the Reserve Bank and can therefore provide payments in exchange settlement funds or same day money (bank cheque funds are only available the next day). All loans from the banks to the official dealers must be in exchange settlement funds.[5] These loans are always secured and, if secured by appropriate Commonwealth securities, will constitute a 'prime asset' and qualify for inclusion in the trading and savings banks' Prime Assets Ratio. Although loans from banks to dealers must be in exchange settlement funds, bank cheque funds may be borrowed from other players (e.g. non-financial corporations). Also, purchases or sales of assets – even when transactions are between banks and official dealers – are settled with bank cheque funds. Indeed, repurchase agreements allow a dealer actively to participate in the daily bank cheque market and banks can supplement their cash requirements by borrowing on 'repo' from the authorized dealers in a formal market. Dealers have been permitted to enter into repurchase agreements with the Reserve Bank since August 1984. Repurchase agreements with other parties have been permitted since August 1986.

The Reserve Bank requires dealers to give security cover to lenders. To facilitate this, it operates a money market system for dealers' Commonwealth government securities and issues acknowledgement forms at branches to dealers against securities held in nominated accounts at Sydney and Melbourne branches. The forms acknowledge, for the benefit of dealers' clients, that the Bank is holding stated securities on account of the dealer.

Some of the official dealers in the money market are also included in the nineteen market-makers in government bonds; these are listed as 'reporting' bond dealers and are committed to active trading in the secondary market. All of them (including the several stockbroking firms in the list) trade directly with the Reserve Bank. Of this group, the authorized dealers were permitted to deal directly with the Reserve Bank in government bonds of less than 1 year to maturity. Except for the banks, other reporting dealers have direct access to the central bank (by rediscounting) only in the context of bonds of more than 1 year to maturity. Since the late 1960s, at the discretion of the Reserve Bank, banks also have been permitted to deal directly with it in bonds with less than 3 months to maturity. Such transactions are often much cheaper for the banks than rediscounting Treasury notes. Other categories of financial institutions have to deal through an intermediary when trading with the Reserve Bank.

DAYLIGHT OVERDRAFTS

With continuous trading in funds and securities, it often happens that a dealer will have arranged to repay funds before receiving the moneys from new borrowing. Funds to replace those that have been repaid may be due, but not until later in the day. In the meantime, the first loan has to be repaid. To overcome this difficulty (which also exists in other money markets – e.g. the USA and Canada), the Reserve Bank permits the authorized dealers to run an unsecured 'daylight overdraft' in funds and securities (subject to agreed limits). This assists the market to operate smoothly. (The need for such an overdraft reflects the fact that nearly all of the dealers' assets will be committed.) But the dealers' accounts with the Reserve Bank must be in credit by the close of the day's trading. Under the 'daylight overdraft' facility, the Reserve Bank will also issue a dealer with acknowledgement forms in excess of holdings throughout the trading day (i.e. lend securities) to facilitate settlements, provided the deficit is covered on an Australian-wide basis by the end of the day. The daylight overdraft facility is used by the dealers less frequently than in the past because most large transactions between the banks and dealers are now settled directly on Reserve Bank premises.

BORROWING ARRANGEMENTS

It is appropriate to turn now to the borrowing arrangements within the money market, where all of the official dealers also have an 'unofficial' arm, which thereby forms part of the unofficial money market, where the so-called 'money market corporations', or merchant banks, are prominent, though by no means all would undertake unofficial money market operations. By mid-1991, there were about 100 operational money market groups. The unofficial market would also comprehend certain of the finance houses. When the official market was first set up, there was a tendency for the market houses to borrow moneys from a limited range of clients, where relationships were often on a somewhat personal basis; the rates did not always fluctuate to the same extent as the market and were less flexible. On the other hand, houses that from the first were primarily dependent on bank money were more impersonal in their relationships and paid more competitive rates. Over the years, operations have become increasingly competitive and sophisticated. In the official market, the houses depend to a very large extent on overnight money (borrowed one day and repaid before 11.00 a.m. the next day).[6] These loans are all secured (and margin is often required) and, if secured by Commonwealth securities, they will qualify as part of the liquid base of the trading and savings banks (PAR). The small remainder would be almost entirely 7-day fixed money and the rest at 24-hour call (the latter is lent for 7 days, subject at the end of the period to 24-hour call).[7] If it were to run on, the rate would be adjusted. There may be a little 'fixed term' money secured by semi-governments and bank bills. Whatever their predilections, it is said that the official dealers cannot compete with the banks and the unofficial market for term money, most of which would be obtained against an NCD. The bulk of the official market's money would come from the banks. The banks bulk up bank cheque funds, which become exchange settlement funds the following day. As a result, the banks lend to dealers in large amounts, this being their most convenient option, though 'other' (mostly non-financial corporations) can also be quite significant.[8] 'Other' would be lent in bank cheque (i.e. next day) funds.[9] In fact, the banks only hold small balances in their exchange settlement accounts in order to minimize opportunity costs (exchange settlement balances do not earn interest). Inter-dealer loans are also made. Nor must one overlook the facilities available at the Reserve Bank – rediscount of Treasury notes, and Reserve Bank repurchase agreements.[10]

UNOFFICIAL MONEY MARKET

As already indicated, all authorized dealers also have an unofficial arm, with transactions in the two markets often being effected by the same dealer from the same desk, though of course with separate books. The advantage to the authorized dealer of having a foot in the unofficial market is that he gets a 'feel' of the availability of funds.[11] The unofficial houses borrow money from the same sources – though in bank cheque funds (next day money) – from the trading banks, the merchant banks, the corporates (both large and small), and (in a slightly different way) from the building societies. Most unofficial money is unsecured (whether bank or non-bank); if secured, a margin would be required.[12] Because the unofficial houses can invest in a wider range of money market instruments (carrying higher yields than on Commonwealth paper), and without limit, they can afford to pay higher rates on moneys borrowed; these rates also cover the higher degree of risk. Compared with the official market, and allowing for the fact that loans are in bank cheque (i.e. next day) funds, there is less emphasis on the use of overnight money (though some houses may borrow specifically at 24-hour call) and more emphasis on 7-day money (subject thereafter to 24-hour call), and, to a lesser extent, on term money – effectively out to 6 months and with no restrictions as to size. They also raise money by way of 'buy-backs' (the sale of securities for a short period, subject to an agreement to repurchase); this happens to suit some customers, such as the building societies, which often prefer buy-backs – even overnight, likewise for 7 days or longer, a favourite basis being bank-accepted bills. In the official market, they could deposit money overnight on a secured basis with an authorized dealer. Corporates also sometimes prefer to lend money to unofficial money-market houses by way of buy-backs instead of lending moneys in the normal way.

Alternatively, these houses may borrow some of their money off-shore;[13] where this is in foreign currency (e.g. Eurodollars), they may take a view on exchange rates and take a position for a certain period, letting it run. Or they may prefer to swap out of (say) US dollars into Australian dollars, buying forward cover, in which case there would be no exchange rate exposure. But they may run an interest rate exposure, borrowing (say) at 6 months and lending money on at 3 months (e.g. if they expect rates to rise).

As we have seen, requirements with regard to the asset structure of the official dealers are somewhat restrictive – only up to 50 per cent of the gearing limit being permitted in non-Commonwealth government securities; the remainder in Commonwealth government securities. Because of the high degree of freedom that the unofficial houses enjoy, and which permits of a more flexible investment policy, one finds a completely different mix of assets in the unofficial market – and this is reflected in higher yields. Thus, if the unofficial houses so desire, they can carry a larger portfolio than that imposed on official houses and there is no obligation to hold Commonwealth paper. Hence, one finds the unofficial houses very interested in holding bank bills (bank-accepted or bank-endorsed) as an interest-bearing asset. Moreover, the yield on bank-endorsed bills will usually be 5 to 10 cents higher than for bank accepted bills. Non-bank bills (i.e. accepted by a financial intermediary that is not a bank – e.g. money market corporations) would carry an even higher yield. The unofficial houses can also be quite interested in promissory notes (P-notes or PNs) – the Australian form of one-name commercial paper. Where P-notes are issued by a leading corporate with an A1 rating, the house holding them will enjoy both a good return and liquidity. Unlike bank bills, however, PNs are not homogeneous instruments with respect to credit risk, though in aggregate there is a reasonable turnover in the market.

USE OF BROKERS

On the whole, transactions in the form of money-market loans are done direct and not through a money broker. Enquiries reveal that 'almost all' of such transactions effected by the official dealers and the trading banks are done direct. Indeed, both for cash and in the short-dated securities markets, professional screen dealing is very important. Where brokers are used in a money transaction, it is said to be 'not to any extent', or 'very rarely' – e.g. where there is a specific requirement to be met. Sometimes money comes in – more particularly in the unofficial market – through money brokers from small corporates (from whom it may be cheaper).[14] Although professional participants actively discourage it, one or two of the large corporates also may from time to time – when it suits them – resort to money brokers, of which there may be some half-dozen. Where brokers do have a role is in the bill market (and especially in the bank-bill forward market), in the placement of NCDs (which may also be done as a broking function by the merchant banks), in placing P-notes, and in FOREX, where about 33 per cent of FOREX business goes through the seven brokers. However, in the placing of money market instruments, it would be more usual for market houses and banks to be approached by a broker than the other way round. On the other hand, a corporate may approach a broker from time to time to contact a number of small people, who on the whole may not get such a good deal from the merchant banks, though from the corporate's point of view it is cheap money, some of which sticks. Of the broking firms that cover the whole range of business, four would be large and with international connections.

INTER-BANK MARKET

As well as lending to the official and unofficial markets, the banks also lend between themselves in the inter-bank market. Inter-bank transactions may be in exchange settlement funds, or in bank cheque (i.e. next day) funds. Most loans in inter-bank exchange settlement funds are overnight and the bulk of transactions is completed by 10.00 a.m.[15] Again, transactions would usually be effected direct between the parties and are largely unsecured. This business would usually be done early in order to assist in squaring exchange settlement positions. But not all transactions are 11.00 a.m. call money; some (usually in bank cheque funds) are 7 day money and, indeed, they may be for up to 30 days, certainly less than 6 months.[16] Also some transactions may be done later in the afternoon (for the next day), if funds were suddenly in surplus, or alternatively very tight.

Then there was the influx of fifteen foreign banks in 1985,[17] and five new domestic banks were also established. Despite the efforts of some of them to build up a retail base, they lacked the same access to deposits that the established Australian trading banks enjoyed and there was some further development of the inter-bank market in Australia, as a result of the need of such banks to fund themselves – sometimes to a significant extent – in the wholesale market. Strictly speaking, the inter-bank market is between banks only. Merchant banks are participants in the bank cheque (next day) funds market.

THE ROLE OF THE CORPORATES

So far as corporates are concerned, they used to accommodate each other to a considerable extent through the agency of the inter-company market,[18] but this is less common now, since the fully-drawn advance has tended to take over from the more flexible over-draft, when corporates could borrow from their bankers and lend it out to other corporates – so-called 'interest arbitrage'. Also, the large corporates – e.g. BHP, CRA, CSR, and Coles-Myer – now-adays themselves run a sophisticated money-market operation, often through a financial subsidiary; they generally lend to, and borrow from, the unofficial market,[19] but they also lend to the trading banks on an 11.00 a.m. call basis, or as 7-day money (subject thereafter to 24-hour call). These moneys may be secured or unsecured – it depends on the creditworthiness of the borrower, for whom they will also have internal (or undisclosed) limits up to which they will lend to particular borrowers. If they have moneys over, they may also lend to the official market, but only in bank cheque funds. When borrowing themselves, they may do a 'repo',[20] and the purchase of bank bills is a way of absorbing funds. Certain of these corporates that sell heavily overseas also have FOREX to manage, and may put funds out in overseas centres like New York and London – centres in which they also borrow. Because of their size, the large corporates receive a number of approaches from bankers abroad, which offer both facilities and services. In their own time zone, they can use Singapore, Hong Kong, or Tokyo. Funds are brought back as necessary, or sold off if there is an opportunity to sell currency at a favourable exchange rate. Certain corporates (like CSR) still have a seasonal movement in their over-seas funds (in the case of CSR because of seasonal sugar exports to the northern hemisphere). Should it be required, it is also possible to fund in offshore centres and to swap into Australian dollars, with forward cover. But firms with a seasonal need (like CSR) may likewise borrow on the domestic market – overnight or for 7 days – or issue P-notes on an unsecured basis. And, when flush with funds, they may lend (either secured or unsecured) overnight, at 7 days, or for a term. Alternatively, they may buy bills or NCDs. Internal limits may apply to NCDs and also to P-notes (PNs). In addition, transactions are effected with other corporates and, when dealing with small corporates, they may well use the services of a broker.

MONEY MARKET INSTRUMENTS

It is appropriate next to look in more detail at the various assets in which the official and unofficial markets invest their resources. Reference has already been made to Treasury bills and Treasury notes. Although, technically, external Treasury bills could still be re-introduced, they disappeared from the statistics in 1983.[21] In Australia, they were never important from a money market point of view.

Treasury notes

So far as Treasury notes were concerned – as we have seen – these were established by the early 1960s. They are short-term securities issued through its agent – the Reserve Bank of Australia – by the Federal Government. Treasury notes were first made regularly available in 1962, initially only in a maturity of 13 weeks. A 26-week maturity was introduced in 1967. The composition of Treasury note holders varies throughout the year.[22] They are held primarily by banks other than the Reserve Bank (67 per cent in May 1991 of total Treasury notes in issue); the holdings of authorized money market dealers vary, but in 1990/91 the highest monthly holding represented less than 12 per cent of the total. Reserve Bank holdings also fluctuate quite a lot.[23] For the most part, and apart from some offshore investors (since they are free of withholding tax), notes are not regarded very favourably by other investors – even by certain of the building societies – since the return is not thought to be attractive.

Treasury note auctions

Originally, Treasury notes were made available on a daily basis through the 'tap' by the Reserve Bank at a rate set by the Bank; this was varied from time to time and it became the barometer for movements in short-term money market rates. Clearly, in the interests of developing a more flexible structure of money market rates, there was a case for moving to a Treasury note auction, or tender. Indeed, the present author pressed for this privately for a number of years both within the Reserve Bank and the Commonwealth Treasury, and publicly advocated it as early as March 1973 as a means of achieving even greater rate flexibility.[24] However, from December 1979, Treasury notes have been issued by means of a regular (usually weekly) tender. It is only possible to tender if a party is 'registered' for the purpose. The tender is competitive, with rates being determined in the market. Bids are on the basis of yield (to two decimal places), not price, but the notes sell at a discount from face value. The Reserve Bank conducts the Treasury note tender as part of its role as agent for the Commonwealth Treasury. Until recently (see below), only 13-week and 26-week notes (3 and 6 months) were issued, and these remain the main instruments. Treasury note tenders are announced at 12 noon (Eastern Standard Time) on Tuesdays. Bids are due by 12.30 p.m. the next day (Wednesday) and must be lodged in the tender box at any Australian branch of the Reserve Bank. The results are announced later the same day at 2.00 p.m., with details of the average yield at which the notes were sold and the range of accepted bids. The Federal Treasurer reserves the right to accept bids for the full amount of the tender or any part thereof and to reject any bid or part thereof. If the Reserve Bank wishes itself to acquire Treasury notes, it will announce in advance what it will take up (this is in addition to the amount offered for public tender); these notes are then taken up at the weighted average issue yield(s) announced for the relevant tender. When the Reserve Bank takes up Treasury notes, this is done in order to secure a supply of notes to sell at a future date as a means of regulating liquidity. Each bid must be for a minimum parcel of A$ 100,000 face value and in multiples of A$ 5,000 face value thereafter. Notes may be paid for on any day of the following week (as also in London) – i.e., in the case of Australia from the Thursday after the tender to the close of business the following Wednesday – and the Reserve Bank provides daily information as to how many notes remain to be paid for from a tender. This privilege of spreading purchases over the following week enables the market to obtain a range of maturities. When the notes are paid for, they are transferred to the stock account of the purchaser at the Reserve Bank.

In the early days, there was a kind of 'talk around' amongst the dealers, but there is very little of this now. Within a house, of course, there will be a discussion between senior management and their dealers in order to judge what to bid.

In November 1991, it was announced that a new 5-week Treasury note would be issued to supplement existing note maturities. It was argued that a 5-week note would enhance the flexibility of cash balance management, both because of its shorter duration and because it will mature in a different part of the monthly cash cycle from when it is issued. The new 5-week note is subject to the regular tender arrangements. The first 5-week Treasury note was issued at the tender on 13 November 1991.

It is expected that the authorized dealers will always tender – it is regarded as part of their function. Indeed, there is an understanding that they will always cover the tender. What they would be required to take up – if necessary – depends on their own capital and reserves in relation to the total capitalization for all houses (which is advised to them). Usually the dealers will tender at a range of rates. The authorized dealers do not now carry large stocks of Treasury notes to trade. They only carry stocks to speculate on Reserve Bank purchasing requirements. For the most part, banks also bid keenly at Treasury note auctions – they need the notes to meet their PAR requirements and, as already noted, the banks are the largest holders of Treasury notes.

Treasury note tenders over the last several years have varied from A$ 200 million to A$ 700 million (13-week notes), and from A$ 100 million to A$ 500 million (for 26-week notes). For classification by holder,[25] it will be seen that banks are the most important holders, though one must not forget that for the smaller holdings of the authorized dealers turnover would be high. One might note, too, that the banks may have real difficulty in buying Treasury notes, if the Reserve Bank has not been selling them for some time. Sometimes, this leads to PAR stock shortages.[26]

Commonwealth government bonds

In addition to a liquid asset like Treasury notes, money market houses will also hold short-dated – even somewhat longer-dated – Commonwealth government bonds, the actual maturity composition of the portfolio being largely determined by interest-rate expectations and cash-flow requirements. This is true also of the trading banks, savings and merchant banks, building societies, and the larger corporations. Following the successful introduction of a tender system for Treasury notes in December 1979, a similar system was set up for Commonwealth bonds in August 1982, where yields in the tenders tended to reflect prevailing conditions in the secondary markets. Anybody who registered with the Reserve Bank could tender for bonds. Unlike the Treasury note tenders, those for

Commonwealth bonds were less frequent and not at regular dates. In this context, however, there was latterly a shrinkage in the supply of Commonwealth government securities, due to the Federal Government running a large budget surplus, as a result of which there was for a time no need for borrowing. Indeed, at the end of 1989, there was a reverse bond tender to retire Federal Government domestic debt.[27]

As with Treasury notes, the Reserve Bank bought stock in the bond tenders from time to time, taking them up at the average yields that resulted from the competitive bidding. It did this in order to maintain its portfolio of Commonwealth securities, which it employed from time to time in the course of managing the liquidity of the economy.

Formerly, the bond market in Australia consisted mostly of the captive primary market, where bonds were issued to those who had to buy bonds for ratio purposes – i.e., banks, life offices, super-annuation funds, and authorized money-market dealers. The secondary market, where bonds are traded, was rather thin. Latterly, this changed, and the secondary market acquired far greater depth – partly because of the tender system, which allowed interest rates to be determined by the market and partly because institutions trading bonds developed a more active and sophis-ticated approach to the managing of a bond portfolio. In addition, there were very significant offshore holdings of Commonwealth bonds, partly as a result of deregulation and the need of overseas portfolio managers to diversify their portfolios. Another factor was the resort to bond futures contracts, which allowed operators to hedge positions. The Treasury note market also expanded, due to high interest rates and the absence of withholding tax, which likewise stimulated overseas interest.

Semi-government and local authority securities

Semi-government and local authority securities are also held by a variety of financial institutions, as they give a better yield than Commonwealth securities. State banks regard themselves as subject to an unwritten convention to take up such securities when issued by authorities in their own state. Funds are borrowed by such parties largely to finance capital works, such as roads, bridges, etc., or to provide electricity, gas, and water supplies. Until the 1970s, semi-government authorities raised the money they required directly from institutions like savings banks and life offices. During the 1970s, the increasing demand for funds meant larger loans, and the issuers began to tap the household as well as the institutional market. The first of the new public loans was the fully underwritten A\$ 200 million Telecom issue in 1976. Thereafter, until the early 1980s, such loans were underwritten and marketed by syndicates of brokers, merchant banks, and banks. More recently, in order to streamline such borrowings, central borrowing authorities have been formed in the states to concentrate much of this borrowing in the hands of a single borrowing authority, thereby achieving greater order and reduced costs, though certain of the large borrowers in a state (e.g. the electricity authorities) have remained independent. Also, many semi-government loans are now raised by selling securities to institutional investors and professional trading houses. It is understood that a large part of these issues take the form of private placements. These placements can be made either directly with large investors or via the dealing panel for each authority. The amount of funds semi-governments may borrow each year is for the most part allocated to the states by the Australian Loan Council.[28] In addition to these state authorities, there are Commonwealth entities like Telecom Australia, which borrow on public markets in the same way as the state authorities. To some extent, these semi-government borrowers may also now borrow in markets overseas.

Bank bills

As an alternative to the overdraft, which was for long employed as the main means of bank lending in Australia, there is bill finance. In 1965,[29] banks were authorized to undertake additional commercial bill activity in order to test and explore the real demand for this form of financing. Simultaneously, the authorized dealers were granted permission to deal in commercial bills, which had been accepted or endorsed by a trading bank, and to hold a proportion of their portfolios in bills of this type. For middle-sized to larger companies, an integrated financial package may be arranged – with the several parts of a corporation's requirements being met by over-draft, a fully-drawn advance, and bills (bank acceptances or an acceptance discount line)[30] with terms (usances) of 3 and 6 months. In adddition, merchant banks make accommodation available to large corporations in the form of non-bank bills against a rollover facility. These bills may be subsequently upgraded by bank endorsement. Banks were also involved in the development of a letter-of-credit market, and in the underwriting of promissory note issues by larger companies and various statutory authorities.[31]

There are three ways in which banks can facilitate financing through bills: (1) acceptance, where the bank accepts a bill for a customer who then on-sells into the market to obtain the required funds; (2) acceptance/discount, where the bank accepts the bill, purchases it from the customer and then (usually) rediscounts it into the market (sometimes these bills can be held on balance sheet); and (3) endorsement, where a bank lends its name to an existing non-bank bill to improve its credit quality and facilitate rediscounting in the market.[32] One might note, too, that it is a convention in the market that bank bills are accepted by banks. Bills that are only endorsed by banks cannot be delivered in settlement of futures contracts, nor can they be traded on the screens without being clearly distinguished. The majority of bank bills may be bought initially by banks and other financial institutions, but 'other' investors (e.g. corporates) constitute by far the largest of end-holders – 70 per cent of the total in April 1991.[33]

In Australia, very few bills are trade-related; the bulk – over 90 per cent – would be accommodation or finance bills, i.e. not for value received. This is reflected in the fact that the bulk of them is in round amounts, with a minimum of (say) A\$ 100,000, but commonly sold in the market in parcels of A\$ 500,000. However, banks will accept bills for odd days and in odd amounts for small customer names. Small bills would be parcelled up into larger amounts before being sold. When buying bills, some banks apply internal limits to the names concerned, though the names of large banks are usually excepted. With the influx of a number of new banks after 1985, the application of internal limits has become more common. Usances (or the terms to maturity) are commonly 30, 90, or 180 days; bank bills are not usually drawn for maturities longer than 185 days.[34] Formerly, if bills passed through the market a number of times, they came to carry numerous endorsements and, if there ceased to be room for them on the bill itself, they could be carried on an annexed piece of paper called an allonge. It is now possible to endorse a bill, or to elect not to do so, and most would not now be endorsed as most of the paper traded by major trading banks is settled electronically through Austraclear.

Austraclear operates a computer (real-time) system for storing money-market securities in safe custody and recording and settling transactions involving these securities. The Austraclear computer system known as FINTRACS (Financial Transactions Recording and Clearing System) is widely used in Australia (with depositories located in major financial centres) by banks, the official dealers, merchant banks, insurance companies, semi-government authorities, and other financial institutions. The system allows for the settlement of transactions in bank bills, bank endorsed bills, non-bank bills, NCDs, PNs, and semi-government, fixed-interest securities. It also caters for the recording and settlement of forward trades of securities, forward interest rate transactions, and cash transfers. Initially, the Reserve Bank was not part of the system, but in conjunction with Austraclear it developed a parallel system for the electronic settlement of Commonwealth Government securities transactions – RITS (Registry Information Transfer System), which became operational in August 1991. But manual settlement continued to be offered in parallel.

A trade bill is where a supplier provides goods on extended credit and the buyer accepts the bill, which can then be discounted, or – if the supplier prefers it – it can be held. If discounted by a bank, a trade bill would normally be held in portfolio;[35] they rarely come on to the market. Bank bills (especially bank-accepted bills), on the other hand, because they are readily marketable, are highly regarded as a liquid asset – indeed, after Commonwealth paper they are a preferred liquid asset (they are also more remunerative). There is an active secondary market in bank bills.

The heyday of bank bill usage was the 1980s; after 1985, figures positively exploded.[36] In the earlier years, this was associated with the quantitative restrictions on bank lending, since it was a ready means of evasion. Growth in the figures only ran out of steam at the end of the 1980s, but has since been maintained at a high level. Apart from the removal of restrictions on bank lending, this was because of a change in statutory reserve deposit (SRD) regulations in 1988, also the lifting of the interest rates paid on non-callable deposits – when SRDs only paid 5 per cent, bills were a substantially cheaper financing method. At the same time, there was a dramatic surge in NCDs.

Certificates of deposit

Bank negotiable certificates of deposit were introduced in Australia in March 1969, but their original introduction proved to be only moderately successful, mainly because of the ceiling on interest rates that then obtained. NCDs were also liable to stamp duty. Subsequently, this was abolished and replaced by a broader financial transactions tax. CDs were freed from all interest rate controls in September 1973. For a time, the amounts attracted against the issue of CDs were small and their significance was really only marginal, the banks resorting to them mainly when their liquidity was threatened and they needed an urgent addition to their funds. In other words, issues of CDs (minimum size of A$ 50,000) were then used primarily for topping up a bank's liquidity. By April 1991, though subject to some variation from month to month, CDs outstanding totalled A$ 30 billion, compared with total fixed deposits of around A$ 78 billion and current account deposits not bearing interest of about A$ 14 billion for all banks.[37]

Some banks may still regard the issue of CDs as a basis of marginal adjustment, but the larger banks now seem to see them increasingly as a means of sustaining a desired level of funding. Resort to CDs, which are issued to bearer, became much more important with the establishment of quite an active secondary market, CDs being regarded as a liquid asset comparable to – indeed, interchangeable with – bank bills, rates being similar to bank-accepted bill rates. They may be issued for periods ranging as short as a few days right out to several years.[38] Usually, 1 day to 180–185 days is the range. CDs are actively traded in the market; hence, one can readily disinvest. Banks hold other banks' CDs as a liquid asset, as do authorized dealers, and a whole range of other financial institutions and investors (including corporates and wealthy individuals). As already noted, the minimum size is A$ 50,000,[39] but it is normal to issue them in parcels of A$ 5 million, even A$ 20 million to A$ 30 million, often in pieces of A$ 500,000 or A$ 1 million. Another aspect of marketability is a good bank name on the CD, though all banks – even the four major banks – will have limits on their liabilities imposed by lenders. With the entry of new banks after 1985, these limits were significantly tightened up. It should be noted, too, that a bank NCD is totally different from other NCDs (e.g. as issued by merchant banks), because of different levels of risk.

We have noted that CDs and bank bills are largely interchangeable instruments; there is also a forward market – i.e. buying now for delivery at a future date – with bills and CDs deliverable in that market on an interchangeable basis. The forward market relates, too, to the bank-bill futures contract and to forward-rate agreements (FRAs) giving rise to arbitrage opportunities.

Another source of money (no longer subject to a maximum interest rate) are large market-oriented deposits (in amounts of over A\$ 250,000), where rates are negotiable, though less volatile than on CDs. 'Big' deposits may be accepted for unrestricted terms. Merchant banks have also issued CDs as a means of raising funds, but they are less attractive than trading banks CDs and, indeed, are more like a P-note (see below). Although there is no legal restriction, building societies prefer not to issue CDs. Borrowing against CDs denominated in foreign currency became possible after December 1983, when exchange controls were virtually abandoned. However, it remains true that time deposits provide a more stable pool of money than CDs.

Promissory notes (PNs) or P-notes

One-name paper emerged in the Australian market in the early 1970s. It is in promissory-note form and is generally referred to as a P-note. It is equivalent to what is described as 'commercial paper' in other countries. It is a convenient way of raising money used by both corporate and public-sector authorities (like Telecom Australia and the Australian Wheat Board). Quite a lot of paper of all maturities is also issued by semi-government borrowing authorities. PNs are now issued by over one hundred private-sector companies and some twenty-five public-sector authorities. P-notes are usually issued in maturities of 30, 60, 90, 120, or 180 days, but facilities to issue may be granted for up to 3 years on a rollover basis. Such notes would tend to be held to maturity. P-notes are covered by the Australian Bills of Exchange Act. A P-note must be signed by the party making the promise, must be for a specific sum of money, and must specify the time for repayment. These promissory notes are instruments in bearer form, transferable by delivery, and do not require endorsement when sold in the market. The notes are issued at a discount from face value, redeemable at par on maturity. Large issues may be underwritten by a bank (including a merchant bank) or syndicate and sold by attracting competitive bids from a tender panel of buyers. There are also private placements. Other large corporates approach the market directly. They are generally priced at a margin above the bank-bill rate of a corresponding maturity. Moreover, if desired, borrowings can be tailored to a specific maturity. Less well-known names may secure the backing of a letter of credit, issued under a trust deed and confirmed by an Australian trading bank. This has been the means of further extending the market – which, however, has had its ups and downs (latterly, it has been about 20 per cent of the size of the bill market).

In the early 1980s, a number of banks attempted to develop business with the corporates – e.g. by underwriting PNs, which began to trade like bank paper. Margins were cut very fine and banks tended to make losses. PNs were not really very popular. It is now possible that they may be resuscitated. Because of capital adequacy requirements, PNs are not likely to be held by banks, but they may be held by other corporates (a variant of an inter-company market), though by mid-1991 they were not all that important. The major banks are now very selective as to what PNs they will underwrite and attempt to place any such PNs privately with end-investors.

THE FOREIGN EXCHANGE MARKET

A word must also be said about the foreign exchange (FOREX) markets. The Australian trading banks and merchant banks had already moved some years ago towards a 24-hour coverage of their FOREX positions. Nowadays, however, Sydney positions are more likely to be passed direct to London rather than through Asia. From London, operations may pass to New York and – towards the end of the 24 hours – finally to the US west coast. Prior to October 1983, the Australian banks were not permitted to hold open FOREX positions overnight, although in effect this could be overcome by using overseas offices to generate trading. Between end-October 1983 and the floating of the Australian dollar in December, banks were permitted to hold net forward positions within limits approved by the Reserve Bank. After December 1983 (and the virtual end of exchange control), the Reserve Bank allowed banks and authorized FOREX traders to hold open FOREX positions overnight, subject to Reserve Bank oversight, and this stimulated 24-hour FOREX activity.

In the Australian FOREX market there are twenty-seven

authorized FOREX dealers – banks and non-banks – which make prices and trade currencies professionally; transactions between them account for about 33 per cent of gross market turnover; transactions with banks (at 50 per cent) are higher; they provide facilities through overseas branch networks to enable local institutions to manage their foreign currency exposures, particularly in third currencies; the remaining 17 per cent involved transactions with customers, almost all residents in Australia. There are also foreign exchange brokers – intermediaries who bring together various principals in the market (and who are paid a commission). They are involved in close to one-third of all transactions.

Many transactions are spot transactions (deals which must normally be settled within 2 working days of being arranged) – about 49 per cent of gross turnover; swaps (mostly short-dated) were about 45 per cent and forwards around 5 per cent. Trading in foreign currency options and futures has been a relatively minor activity; contracts with more than 2 working days to maturity (other than forwards, which also have more than 2 days to maturity) account for the balance. The average size of transaction is around A$ 7 million, but larger amounts are common. The forward market is 'deep' out to 12 months; transactions beyond 1 year were insignificant.

So far as currency composition is concerned, the bulk of the activity in the market involves the Australian dollar. Gross dollar turnover in Australia[40] averaged US$ 23.3 billion over the 12 months to end-April 1991; after adjusting for double-counting, daily turnover averaged US$ 18.5 billion. Australian dollar trading was about 44 per cent of gross turnover, US dollar against Deutschemark 18 per cent, US dollar against Japanese yen 14 per cent, and US dollar against sterling 9 per cent. Gross currency trading, involving neither the US dollar nor the Australian dollar, was only 3 per cent of the total.

The Australian FOREX market is relatively concentrated. The top ten dealers accounted for about 60 per cent of gross turnover and the top twenty for almost 80 per cent. The pattern of concentration is very similar in trading between Australian and US dollars, but differs for some third currencies (e.g. around 55 per cent of Japanese yen trading in Australia was accounted for by the top ten yen dealers, but the comparable figure for trading in Swiss francs and New Zealand dollars was around 80 per cent).

Most dealers are not significant position-takers, preferring to avoid currency risk. Corporate players are the real position-takers.

On average, only about 23 per cent[41] of the net open overnight position limits set by the Reserve Bank is used, though of course some dealers will use more of their available limits than others, but on the whole they are not big risk-takers. At the same time, the market has become much more competitive in recent years, with inter-bank dealing spreads averaging around seven points most of the time, with the spread largely dependent on the size of the transaction. The time zone has been of considerable benefit to the growth of the market. The Australian market, centred as it is in Sydney and Melbourne, enjoys an advantage over other markets in the Asia/Pacific region – as the early and late parts of the trading day overlap with late New York and early European trading respectively. The Australian market can thus bridge effectively the world's two largest FOREX markets. Markets on the west coast of the United States seem to have lost volume, with trading passing from New York to Australia. There also seems to be increased liquidity in the New York market during their afternoon. At the same time, there is an increased volume of trading between the Australian market and Tokyo.

The Reserve Bank requires dealers to maintain certain conditions. Thus, it sets a minimum level for shareholders' funds; it looks for a competent and experienced dealing team and evidence of prudent internal controls; it also requires a dealer to keep its end-of-day open position within an agreed limit (both direct exposures against the Australian dollar and third currency exposures). So far as its attitude to market intervention is concerned, it does not try to dictate what the exchange rate should be to try to keep it at a particular level; it attempts to help the market deal with heavy pressures from time to time and to foster general market stability; following severe disturbances, its aim is to help the market find an acceptable rate and to test whether sharp rate movements are well based.[42]

FINANCIAL FUTURES AND OPTIONS

As with certain other exchanges that now deal with financial futures (e.g. Chicago Board of Trade), Sydney also began as a market in commodity futures. As such, it began operating in May 1960 as the Sydney Greasy Wool Futures Exchange, and wool[43] remained the only commodity future traded until the introduction of the live cattle futures in July 1975. The first non-pastoral commodity that was introduced was gold in April 1978. The name was changed to the Sydney Futures Exchange (SFE) in 1972. The first of the financial futures came in October 1979 with the 90-day bank-bill futures contract. The SFE began trading currencies in March 1980, with US dollar and yen futures contracts, the choice being determined by two factors – most of Australia's trade is denominated in US dollars and the bulk of that trade is with Japan. The yen contract, however, was suspended in 1981, because of a disappointingly low level of activity. Sterling was introduced in 1980, but was suspended in early 1982. The US dollar contract was delisted in 1987 and replaced by the A$/US$ futures contract in February 1988. The new FX contract had its face value in Australian (not US) dollars. Next came a contract based on the Stock Exchange all-ordinaries index introduced in February 1983; a 2-year Commonwealth bond contract was traded from February 1984 and this was followed in December 1984 by a contract based on a 10-year Commonwealth bond. Then, from early in 1985, options were available on all financial futures contracts. And in October 1986, the SFE began trading a US Treasury bond contract listed jointly with LIFFE (in London) and which was fully fungible (i.e., investors were able to open positions in one exchange and close them in the other). This was later suspended. Meanwhile, a 3-months Eurodollar interest-rate futures contract was introduced from end-October 1986 (later also suspended). In May 1988, a 3-year Treasury bond contract was introduced. The 5-year semi-government bond futures contract was delisted in March 1990 and replaced by new 5- and 10-year semi-government bond futures and options contracts in October 1990. On the gold contract, there was a link with COMEX in New York (subsequently discontinued).

One should note that the SFE offers different classes of membership. On October 18, 1990, there were 29 floor members, 118 full associate members, 104 market associate members, 18 introducing broker associated members, and 71 local members, including 41 leased local memberships. These classes of membership have different rights. Floor members have full voting rights, are members of the clearing house, and can trade on the floor in their own right and on behalf of clients. Local members are the only other members permitted to trade on the floor. Local members do not represent clients but trade on their own account. Their trades are cleared through a floor member. None of the three types of associate member (full, market, and introducing broker) trade directly on the floor. Full associate members and introducing broker associate members may deal on their own behalf or on behalf of clients; however, only full associate members may hold client funds. Market associate members are not permitted to trade on behalf of clients. While trading is conducted through a floor member, all three types of associate members are eligible to have their own accounts with the clearing house. All members who are permitted to represent clients must be licensed under the futures industry code. In addition, any director or employee of the member firm who is advising clients must be registered with the SFE as a registered representative.

So far, most of the interest has focused on domestic financial futures contracts for 90-day bank accepted bills and 10-year Australian Treasury bonds, and – for a time – on a contract based on the all-ordinaries share price index. The 2-year bond contract did not take off and was replaced by the 3-year contract, which did relatively well. All the major banks – including the state banks – use financial futures actively and have seats on the exchange, as do money-market houses (sometimes through a subsidiary). Some Australian banks have seats on LIFFE in London. Certain of the big building societies are also interested in financial futures and use them as a basis for hedging on interest rates. There is also currency hedging and interest rate swaps. From the start, progress was good, with an emphasis on consolidation of the expansion achieved, though there was a feeling that overseas interest in the SFE was unlikely to develop fully until there were more 'locals' on the exchange – individuals physically located on the floor of the exchange, who trade on their own account. This is important, because speculators and 'locals' add to market liquidity and depth – both contribute to the market through their willingness to take on short-term positions, which add to market activity. And speculators are attracted to a market if prices get out of line with the physical commodity in the 'real' world and there is an opportunity for profit. Contracts that did well included the 90-day bank-bill contract and the 10-year Australian Treasury bond contract; likewise options on bank-bill futures and on the 10-year bond contract. A further strong contribution came from the new 3-year bond futures contract. However, the contract based on the all-ordinaries share price index showed the opposite trend, as did the related options contract. In both cases, this was a direct result of the stock market crash in 1987. Subsequently, there was some recovery.

The SFE has now moved to new quarters, trebling the size of its trading floor, currently one of the most technologically advanced in the world.[44] Nevertheless, the SFE has been more successful with domestic futures than on the international front. This has been reflected in the revision of working hours (which had previously been extended in an attempt to provide an international triple-exchange overlap); current trading floor hours are 8.30 a.m. (the earliest) to 4.30 p.m. (the latest), which no longer overlap with Chicago and London. In November 1989, the problem of hours was addressed through the introduction of an after-hours electronic dealing facility known as SYCOM (Sydney Computerized Overnight Market). Initially, trading hours for SYCOM were 4.45 p.m. to midnight (Sydney time), but with the intention that these be expanded, right through to the following morning. SYCOM trades 10-year Australian Treasury bonds and futures on bank bills, the all-ordinaries index, and semi-government bonds; it also trades 3-year bond futures.

INTERVENTION BY THE RESERVE BANK

The Reserve Bank has a variety of techniques whereby it can influence the liquidity of the banking system and the economy, whether through the money market in the narrow sense or by operating in financial markets across a wider spectrum. It does this by means of open market operations – buying or selling securities in the open market either outright or through repurchase agreements, thereby either adding to or subtracting from the funds available to the banking and financial system. The central bank can also inject cash into the domestic system by buying foreign currency in exchange for Australian dollars. To drain funds from the system – or to 'mop up' excess cash – it can sell short-dated government securities to the market (e.g. selling securities of less than 12 months to maturity to the authorized dealers). It would tailor the maturities of the securities offered for sale to coincide with its projections for times of tighter money. So far as price is concerned, the authorized dealers would come into the Reserve Bank by 10.00 a.m. with their bids for whatever the Reserve Bank was willing to sell. The Reserve Bank then considers the bids (or offers) made in the light of the volume of business it wishes to transact that day and accepts those most favourable to it. Dealing is usually completed by 10.30 a.m., each dealer being told individually whether he has been successful or not. The transactions would then be completed with the Registry. The Bank's transactions with the reporting bond dealers are less frequent and are conducted separately – normally between 11.00 a.m. and 11.30 a.m. At 11.00 a.m., they will have been told what the Reserve Bank is doing, but not necessarily every day. The reporting bond dealers have no facility at the Reserve Bank other than direct dealing access.[45] The Reserve Bank also provides weekly – on the Reuters and Telerate screens – a commentary on the cash effects of transactions like settlements for Treasury notes and bonds, and any 'repos' between the Reserve Bank and the authorized dealers. The Reserve Bank continues to monitor market conditions throughout the day and may enter the market again, if conditions warrant.

Another technique for 'mopping up', which more recently has been revived, is the acceptance occasionally by the Reserve Bank from the trading banks of interest-bearing deposits (IBDs). The banks will put forward such a proposal for consideration by the Reserve Bank and ask whether the Bank could be interested in doing it. Such IBDs are only accepted by the Reserve Bank for short periods.

The Reserve Bank provides the system each day with the relevant figures at 9.30 a.m. – on the Reuters and Telerate screens (and through a press release). This provides the money market with the estimated cash position. The central bank also notes any settlements outstanding from Treasury note or bond tenders and states its dealing intentions for the day (e.g. what the Reserve Bank will be doing with the authorized dealers in Treasury notes and 'repos'). It also states the level of rediscount rate (if there is any change, this will be the first notice of such a change). In deciding on its operations, the Reserve Bank takes into account not only the opening cash position of the market but also the many other factors which might affect market conditions on that day, such as possible settlements of Treasury note and bond tenders, the repayment of 'repos', pressures in the bank cheque (unofficial) market, and the outlook for the days ahead.

In addition, the Reserve Bank will have looked ahead on the basis of regular forecasting in order to establish the emerging trends (whether money will be plentiful or whether it will be tight). When one gets to the day in question, it will be an actual figure, including what has gone into the overnight clearing. They know what the money position is at the start of the day and this is the money market information that they provide. They are then ready to undertake sales or purchases of short-dated government paper, or to do 'repos', with the latter becoming increasingly important.

However, the operations of the Reserve Bank do not always offset completely the surplus or shortage of funds as indicated by the cash position in the money market. Any remaining surplus or deficit is dealt with by the market in one of several ways. The market may – through the operations of the authorized dealers – shift funds to the next day, or borrow from the next day. And this is usually the main mechanism through which the final squaring of the books for the day takes place. If the market is very short of funds, the shortage may be overcome by rediscounting Treasury notes, or by late-in-the-day balancing operations undertaken by the Reserve Bank, the chosen method being end-of-day repurchase agreements, or 'repos'. Usually, a 7-day fixed borrowing commitment will be imposed, though in fact the term may vary quite dramatically. The rate itself is determined by the Reserve Bank on application and is set at 2.30 p.m. on the basis of: liquidity within the market; a need not to encourage a volatile interest-rate environment (which could be occasioned by the dealer creating large volumes of additional liquidity); and the efforts made by the dealer to square off – i.e. it is expected that all reasonable efforts have been made to obtain funds in the market. In other words – as formerly with the lender of last resort facility – there is still a line of credit available to dealers, but the basis of the facility has changed (from loans to repurchase agreements).

Over the years, there has been much talk about the use made of open-market operations based on the Reserve Bank's own portfolio of government securities or holdings of foreign exchange, though after the floating of the Australian dollar in December 1983 the Reserve Bank's declared intention was only a minimal intervention in foreign exchange. However, the Bank trades in the market for FOREX to service its customers, to smooth large transactions through the market, and to test movements of exchange rates. In general terms – according to the Reserve Bank – it seeks essentially to provide a steadying influence in the market, particularly when there is a pervasion of uncertainty. It does not seek to achieve or maintain a particular exchange rate, rather to ensure that movements in the exchange rate are well based. In this context, attention is paid to a number of factors – including the US dollar/Australian dollar rate and the trade-weighted index,[46] but it is not the intention – as has sometimes been suggested – to 'target' the latter. If the Bank buys foreign currencies in exchange for Australian dollars, it adds to the supply of local currency and therefore to the pool of domestic cash. Alternatively, if the Bank were to sell foreign currency in exchange for Australian dollars, this would reduce the supply of cash.

Open market operations – in the sense of trading in securities with dealers – have existed since authorized dealers were established in 1959. They became important for the purposes of monetary management after the floating of the Australian dollar in December 1983. From August 1984 onwards, resort to open market operations has been supplemented to an important extent by the use of repurchase agreements (or 'repos'). They are carried out between the Reserve Bank and the authorized dealers and are particularly useful when there is a shortage of the precise maturities that the Bank requires. This procedure also provides additional flexibility in the Bank's management of liquidity, since securities of virtually any maturity can be employed for the purpose. By means of a 'repo', the Reserve Bank can buy securities from the dealers when cash is tight, subject to the securities being repurchased by the same dealers on a specified date at a price agreed at the time of the initial purchase. When there is a temporary surplus of cash, the Reserve Bank can sell 'repos' – i.e., sell securities to dealers subject to their resale to the Bank at a specified date and at a predetermined price. 'Repos' are carried out at the Reserve Bank's discretion. The arrangements make a significant contribution to the Reserve Bank's ability to smooth out fluctuations in liquidity. 'Repos' may be done for a few days, or even longer. They can therefore be trimmed to cover whatever period of cash shortage (or cash surplus) is judged to require offsetting action.

It should be noted that the bulk of open market operations[47] (and of 'repos') would be undertaken for the purpose of 'smoothing out' fluctuations in liquidity, but they may also reflect a change in the emphasis of monetary policy. The latter (since January 1990) is now explicitly announced by the Reserve Bank.

Debt management, too, has monetary effects, and there is a fine line to be drawn between action prompted by a change in monetary policy and what results from debt management as such. Hence, action under either head needs to be integrated with the other, such that overall policy is consistent. In Australia, the Reserve Bank shares with the Commonwealth Treasury responsibility for the Federal Government's debt programme. In other words, it is necessary to tailor the government's borrowing to mesh with any requirements of deficit financing and to dovetail this with a longer-term borrowing strategy. Within this framework, the Reserve Bank also has to consider short-term liquidity management, such that (say) the demands of selling a large quantum of Commonwealth bonds in order to fund a deficit are not exaggerated in their effects by a contemporaneous funding in the non-government sector of an outflow of cash to meet tax payments. Moreover, since the Australian dollar was floated in December 1983, the authorities have been able to smooth out more easily erratic movements in the availability of cash and therefore of interest rates.

CONCLUSION

On the basis of a recent statistical study,[48] the asset growth of the authorized dealers and their size in relation to money market corporations (as an index to the size of the unofficial market) has not changed significantly since 1985, though the rate of growth of bank assets has been rather greater. At the same time, it is important to note that the unofficial market has always been very much larger than the official market.

But there is little risk of the official dealers disappearing. They are too useful to the Reserve Bank as a means of undertaking the day-to-day management of liquidity in the economy as a whole. To this end, the Reserve Bank entered the market as required and, in recent years, has traded on most days – buying and selling Commonwealth government securities in the physical market both outright and through repurchase agreements ('repos'). Latterly, the situation changed somewhat as a result of large Federal Government budget surpluses, which began to erode the supply of Commonwealth government securities in which the official houses substantially dealt. Since the Federal Government had no need to borrow domestically (it also paid off some external debt), there was a drying up of new bond auctions. In addition to which, in December 1989, there was a reverse bond tender, i.e. the buying back of government bonds. There were no more reverse bond tenders, but there was considerable further consolidation of the stock of Treasury bonds through operations of the Reserve Bank. Consolidation continued in 1991. The Reserve Bank also considered possible changes to its operating methods. There was an increasing resort to repurchase agreements. This enabled the market to trade in long-term bonds without requiring the buyers of bonds under 'repo' to assume the capital risks (which are large for long-term securities) associated with changes in yields. Nevertheless, despite the resort to 'repos', there was a danger – if large fiscal surpluses were maintained over the long term – that by the mid-1990s the supply of bonds might become extremely limited. Because of this, both the Federal Government and the Reserve Bank explored the possibility of dealing in private-sector securities, even to issue central bank paper, as a basis of open market operations. Resort to debentures, P-notes, or CDs had an advantage over movements in deposits with the central bank, since they could be traded in secondary markets. In the result, because of the impact of recession, the Australian Government cut its budget surplus forecast for 1990/91 from A$ 8.1 billion to A$ 1.7 billion. The revision meant the PSBR was likely to be around A$ 7 billion for the financial year to the end of June, compared with a budget forecast of zero. Beginning in April 1991, the government was also forced back to the bond market for the first time since July 1989. It was thought that it would probably raise up to A$ 3.5 billion in 1991 and A$ 5 billion the following year. It was further stated that Federal Government debt would remain steady over the two-year period. Previously, it had forecast a repayment.[49] Hence, it was unlikely that the feared shortage of government paper would now develop and there was therefore no need to consider resort to private paper as a substitute.

Chapter 9

The money market in Canada[1]

Canada provides one of the leading examples of a country in which the development of a money market was officially encouraged and assisted. In particular, the Canadian experience emphasizes what can be achieved in quite a short space of years, given the necessary underlying conditions that favour the emergence of such a market, plus the support both of the government and of the central bank.

Although the establishment of a money market in Canada is essentially a post-Second World War phenomenon, one of the essential steps was taken as far back as 1934 (which was the year before the Bank of Canada opened for business), when arrangements were first made to sell Treasury bills by tender. Gradually, both the number of issues and the total volume outstanding were increased, though trading in Treasury bills was at that stage largely between the chartered banks and the Bank of Canada. Dealers may have done a little business in bills, but only on a commission basis for customers. In pre-war days, they never carried inventories.

It was during the Second World War that dealers began to take Treasury bills more seriously and only towards the end of the war that they even thought of carrying a small inventory. The big step forward came in January 1953, with the introduction of a weekly tender (previously it had been once every 2 weeks) and the granting of 'limits' to certain dealers by the Bank of Canada. This permitted them to secure accommodation on the basis of a sale of short-dated government securities (including but not confined to Treasury bills), subject to an agreement to repurchase within a specified period of time and at rates cheaper than those charged by the chartered banks. By this means, it was hoped to increase non-bank holdings of Treasury bills, to build up dealer experience of the relevant techniques, and to broaden the market for Treasury bills and short-term government bonds.

By April 1954, the Bank of Canada felt that the dealers were ready for the next step. The way was prepared by a revision of the Bank Act in 1954 that replaced the traditional 10 per cent (and legal 5 per cent) cash ratio with a legal 8 per cent minimum based on monthly averaging. This made it easier for the banks to adjust their cash positions and also freed a large volume of reserves for lending to dealers on a day-to-day basis, in amounts and at rates that enabled the latter to carry inventory at a profit. From the banks' point of view, day-to-day loans were a highly liquid earning asset, which facilitated the fullest possible employment of their funds, since they were committed for no more than a day at a time.

In order to encourage the dealers (or 'jobbers') to carry as principals as much inventory as was consistent with the available supply of day-to-day money, and as a means of underwriting the experiment, the Bank of Canada stood prepared to act as the lender of last resort. Not being specifically authorized to lend to dealers, the Bank arranged to make accommodation available to certain dealers as a privilege – up to negotiated limits – on the basis of a purchase and resale (PRA) agreement, whenever it proved impossible to raise sufficient money elsewhere with which to carry inventory; the cost of this accommodation being calculated as the difference between the prices at purchase and resale. Initially, the cost of the PRA facility was lower than the cost of call money from the banks.

In the early days, the dealers' chief difficulty was to find customers for the bills they carried in inventory. But gradually they established retail outlets by selling bills to business corporations (often on a 'buy-back' basis, in some cases terminable by either party on demand). They were further assisted by the Bank of Canada's wire transfer arrangements that ensured speedy delivery of securities at whichever of the Bank's nine agencies (i.e. branches) might be stipulated and, if necessary, in separate parcels.

After February 1957, it was also possible to borrow securities from the Bank of Canada.[2] The chartered banks, too, were tending to use the dealers to an increasing extent, in order to sell or buy money market assets with appropriate maturities. At the same time, since the banks remained in the Treasury bill tender, often they could adjust their bill portfolios without resorting to the dealers – simply by varying their intake of new bills. Moreover, a big barrier to the stimulation of dealer interest was partially removed when the chartered banks first reduced and, in March 1957, modified the over-certification charge made on 'daylight overdrafts', thereby encouraging an increase in the turnover of loanable funds. Although it no longer applied to certain money market transactions (there were now 'free' over-certification arrangements when a day-to-day loan was moved from one bank to another, provided the original lending bank called the loan), this charge was still levied on other transactions. Moreover, the chartered banks, despite the arguments of the dealers, were never likely to give it up altogether (because it added to their profits). Over the years the dealers have learnt to live with it and latterly it has no longer been regarded as quite the important matter it once was. By the end of the 1980s, dealers paid fees at a flat rate for specified daylight overdraft limits. Dealers could not function without such overdrafts and the banks require to be compensated for the degree of risk exposure.

There were originally sixteen dealers in the market, of which seven or eight were regarded as really important,[3] though some of the other dealers were strong in particular aspects of money-market business. The leading houses, on the other hand, were active over the full range of money-market transactions. There has been much restructuring over more recent years and some changes in ownership, with the chartered banks themselves taking up participations in certain of these firms. By late 1991 there were eight money-market jobbers,[4] and the Bank of Canada recognized fifty-two primary distributors. Another important change that has taken place over the years was the increase in the relative importance of Toronto as a money-market centre. Montreal has remained active, but of rather less importance than in earlier years. However, by the mid-1980s, there was some recovery in Montreal's position. None the less, Toronto remains the main money-market centre in Canada. Vancouver in British Columbia, far out to the west, is also of some importance; 'western' accounts – such as the Province of British Columbia – are handled by Vancouver offices, but Vancouver trades on Toronto time.[5] Communications are good both between the Bank of Canada offices themselves and between them and the market houses – the market as a whole has become fully integrated. The Bank of Canada is engaged in continuous communication with money-market dealers throughout the day (e.g. to discuss market conditions, expectations, inventory size and holdings of certain securities, bank cash positions, levels of commercial paper trading, and so on).

TREASURY BILLS

In terms of market activity, Treasury bill transactions have varied from time to time in the degree of their market significance. Latterly, they have been the most important single-market instrument. As has been indicated, there has been a Treasury bill tender since 1934, and tender arrangements for Treasury bills have remained substantially similar over the years and have become very much a matter of routine. On the basis of figures for mid-1991, the tender for 91-day Treasury bills was C$ 3,900 million (it had been as high as C$ 4,000 million), for 182-day bills it was C$ 1,600 million (with a high of C$ 2,000 million), and for 1-year bills it was C$ 1,200 million (also the high). The Bank of Canada, the chartered banks, and investment dealers eligible to act as primary distributors may all tender for Treasury bills, the main ultimate holders being the chartered banks, the Bank of Canada, mortgage loan companies, trust companies, investment funds, and investment dealers. There are also the Crown Corporations (e.g. Federal Business Development Bank, Export Development Corporation, Canadian Wheat Board and Canada Post) and corporates. The banks, in fact, tender very competitively – with the dealers being the primary purchasers of the bills issued. (Actually, the percentage of the tender that goes to the dealers can vary quite a lot, depending on market sentiment.)

Government of Canada Treasury bills are issued in bearer form in denominations of C$ 1,000, C$ 5,000, C$ 25,000, C$ 100,000 and C$ 1 million (the smaller amounts in order to cater for a retail demand,[6] money market trades would only be in C$ 500,000 or C$ 1 million pieces). They are redeemed at maturity at any agency of the Bank of Canada. Each tender submitted shall be for the amount of C$ 1,000 or multiples thereof and shall state the price per hundred dollars to not more than three places of decimals. Tenders may be submitted directly to the Bank of Canada in Ottawa on the official application form,[7] or through CN/CP Telecommunications DIALCOM electronic mail service. Each money-market jobber may bid for a specific percentage of each tender in each term. The Bank of Canada puts in a competitive bid for the bills it gets. For this reason, the Bank of Canada is able to exert some influence on price. The Bank may also tender for customers (e.g. other central banks and the World Bank). The Minister of Finance reserves the right to accept or reject any (or all) tenders, whether in whole or in part, including without limitation the right to accept less than the total of any amount called. The normal auction day is now the Tuesday, results being announced as before by the Bank of Canada on the DIALCOM system, and those submitting tenders may thereby confirm their acceptance or rejection, in whole or in part.

There are also cash management tenders of Treasury bills; these began on 24 October 1968 – they became more frequent after October 1983. These tenders are called periodically when government cash balances are low; the call for tender and issue date may be other than the standard routine; the term is usually 21 to 31 days.

The date of issue and settlement has recenty been changed, though there was a 1-year transition period before the regular Treasury bill auction date and settlement date were actually moved to new dates. Thus, beginning with the 28 November 1991 scheduled auction, all tenders of 1-year Treasury bills were dated to mature on Thursdays instead of Fridays. Similarly, 6 months later, starting on 28 May 1992, all tenders of 6-month bills were also dated to mature on Thursdays. Finally, beginning 27 August 1992, all 3-month tenders were dated to mature on Thursdays. Regular weekly auctions of Treasury bills on the proposed new schedule were to begin with the 24 November 1992 tender. The change to a 2-day interval from the previous 1 day between auction and delivery provided the investment community with more time for distribution and back office processing of new Treasury bill issues.

In the case of banks, payment shall be made by means of: clearing house settlements negotiable through the local clearing house; drafts of, or cheques drawn upon, members of the Canadian Payments Association that are banks subject to the Bank Act or the Quebec Savings Bank Act, and other members which clear directly, including members that have a group clearer. In the case of investment dealers eligible to act as primary distributors, a payment shall be made by means of drafts of, or certified cheques drawn on, members of the Canadian Payments Association as already noted. All such settlements shall be made payable to the Receiver General for Canada. Payment for and delivery of the bills may be made at any agency of the Bank of Canada. Provincial Treasury bill tenders (and their allotment) have been on various days.[8]

Prior to a tender of Canada Treasury bills, there used to be a 'talk around' among the investment dealers, but this has now gone. However, there are informal discussions with the Bank of Canada. The Bank is said to be 'a good listener',[9] and thereby gets a feel of how the dealers might bid. Results are released about 2.00 p.m. Eastern Standard Time on the day of the tender and, in the 'after market', the dealers might well sell the bulk of their bills to a whole range of investors (but mostly to non-banks), only retaining in inventory the remainder. If a bank – or a dealer – misses at the tender, but still wants bills (e.g. for trading purposes, or for customers),[10] requirements will be bought in the secondary market. Furthermore, in the 'when issued' (or WI) market, dealers will generally start to trade for the following week's tender in the afternoon after the current tender. This is a very active market and it is important because it gives the trader an opportunity to anticipate markets without putting up hard cash. It also provides some sort of idea of what will happen at the next tender and, by trading next week's bills in the WI market, it may be the means of avoiding the borrowing of securities.[11]

CANADA BONDS

Excluding Treasury bills and Canada savings bonds, Government of Canada bonds outstanding as of the end of June 1991 were C\$ 150.8 billion. These are marketable bonds and are normally issued in the most receptive segment of the market, with the government usually borrowing heavily to meet deficits on expenditure. New issues normally take the form of a package of two or more securities. So far as the banks and the investment dealers are concerned, holdings of Government of Canada bonds are much less important and, from a money market point of view, only bonds with maturities of less than 3 years are relevant. When there is an issue, the Bank of Canada may announce a rate that is fairly close to market rates, or there may be an auction, when only dealers and banks may tender, on the basis of which the Bank of Canada will allocate the bonds.

BANKERS' ACCEPTANCES

A word may also be said about bankers' acceptances, which go back to June 1962, though they only became a significant factor in

the money market in mid-1965. In Canada, all bankers' acceptances are now finance or accommodation paper – i.e., they are no
longer trade related.[12] In effect, firms borrow in this way to fund
themselves. What one is selling is the bank's name – its acceptance
of the risk. When they are dealt in in the secondary market, there
are no endorsements. The minimum size is C$ 100,000, but effect-
ively the trading minimum is C$ 1 million, to which may be added a
number of C$ 100,000 pieces. Trading is often done in C$ 5 million
pieces. Generally, the size of a block of bankers' acceptances will
be under C$ 100 million in the Canadian market. Most transactions
are done direct when dealing in bankers' acceptances. The bulk of
the business is in 30-day paper, though it may go out to 12 months.
Indeed, there can be long-term bankers' acceptances that go out to
5 years, but these are rare. About 98 per cent could be for 1 year or
less, and 90 per cent for 30 days or less.

It is said to be a not very profitable business – with very thin
margins. The banks are very competitive and charge low stamping
(acceptance) fees. What is actually charged depends on the credit
quality of the drawer. From the customer's point of view, however,
bankers' acceptances are very popular and – like commercial paper
(see below) – resort to them has eaten into the banks' loan business.
There is a large and active secondary market and the banks themselves invest in bankers' acceptances.

BEARER DEPOSIT NOTES (BDNs)

Certificates of deposit may be issued in Canada, but they are
normally non-negotiable and registered in a name. If sold, they have
to be re-registered in the new name.[13] In this context – though its
importance varies from time to time – the bearer deposit note
(BDN)[14] – which is bearer in form, sold at a discount, and negotiable
– appears to fill the role of a negotiable CD in Canada. Except for
the foreign banks, however – which lack a developed deposit base –
wholesale money proper tends to be a very low percentage of total
resources. At times when corporate loan demand is at low levels and
the chartered banks are highly liquid, there is little resort to BDNs,
since the banks have no need of extra funding; also – so far as the
big Canadian chartered banks are concerned – the bulk of their
resources would derive from retail deposits through their branch
networks, or as large corporate deposits (semi-wholesale money)
also lodged at their branches. These are their 'core' resources.

BDNs were first issued about 1965. In the very early stages, a number of corporations and individuals that traditionally had large low-interest demand deposits with the banks shifted these into chartered bank paper in order to obtain the higher rates of return and, at the time, these new instruments and the relatively high rates available seem to have made potential market customers more aware of the scope for investing short-term funds in other forms as well, thereby accelerating the general development of the money market. Although dealers bought up chartered bank paper for inventory and borrowed against it, there was never more than a fairly good trading market in it. This was the basis of the BDN. The minimum size is again C$ 100,000, but for trading purposes C$ 1 million is the effective minimum. On the whole, BDNs tend to be issued for very short periods – often for less than 30 days – even though BDNs and time deposit receipts (TDRs) are primarily used as funding instruments.

In recent years, resort to BDNs seems to have been in decline. There has been a shift in short-term corporate-credit demand in favour of bankers' acceptances and commercial paper, which are funded directly in the market. This – combined with weaker credit-market demand generally – has resulted in a decline in the whole-sale deposit growth of the banks.

GUARANTEED INVESTMENT CERTIFICATES (GICs)

Guaranteed investment certificates (GICs) are issued by trust companies and the mortgage affiliates of the chartered banks. They are often transferable, and a secondary market has developed amongst dealers with large retail customer bases; they are primarily a retail instrument. Bids for them can be sorted out by the dealers, banks, and trust companies. Generally speaking, they would be for 1–5 years, but some may be as short as 30 days.

COMMERCIAL PAPER

Commercial paper also deserves mention in any survey of money market instruments. Canadian finance companies raise a substantial percentage of their cash requirements by borrowing against the issue of commercial paper in the money market and several have money desks. The proceeds are used primarily for financing the distribution of a wide range of durable consumer goods. In addition, a limited number of large Canadian manufacturing and merchandising corporations have formed their own sales finance subsidiaries. Arrangements vary, and the short-term promissory notes that are issued may be secured, unsecured, and/or guaranteed by a parent organization. Such paper will be given a rating by the Dominion Bond Rating Service (DBRS) or the Canadian Bond Rating Service (CBRS). The short-term notes of many of these companies are legal investments for banks, life insurance, and trust companies. Investment may be for terms ranging from demand up to 5 years, even longer. There is a large secondary market in commercial paper maturing in 1 year or less for all DBRS rated issues, also for CBRS-rated paper.

Prime commercial paper consisting of unsecured promissory notes issued in minimum denominations of C$ 100,000 (and often in multiples thereof) is also issued by some of the larger Canadian corporations (also by the Canadian subsidiaries of US corporations). The notes are backed by the general credit of the issuing corporation. Sometimes, where these are subsidiaries of US companies, the paper is issued with the guarantee of the US company. As in the USA, such paper may also be supported by a back-up line of credit for which a bank will charge a fee. There has been a big growth in this market in recent years, both in the number of issuers and in the amounts that are issued. There are now about 150 companies in Canada that issue commercial paper. Some corporations issue their paper direct (e.g. GMAC and Ford) – they name how much they are offering and invite tenders.[15] Others will issue their commercial paper through a dealer, a group of dealers, or a dealer/bank group and pay them a commission – there may be no need to assume a liability; the dealers purchase the paper outright as principals. Trading is mainly in the new issue market. As in the USA, there is no real secondary market, though a large dealer – for a good customer – may, if necessary, be prepared to buy back commercial paper, which would be absorbed temporarily in its portfolio.

Commercial paper tends to be issued for terms of 1 day to 1 year, depending on both market conditions and the cash-flow requirements of borrowers. Normally, issuers post rates for 1–3 months or 4–12 months. Short-term needs may also be met by a repurchase agreement ('repo') against a Treasury bill, such 'repos' being made more to meet a customer's need than as a funding operation. In many cases, the issue of commercial paper has become the major means whereby a corporation in Canada will raise working capital, with the banks losing loan business to the investor community.

THE INTER-BANK MARKET

For the big chartered banks in Canada, with their nationwide networks of branches, management of their day-to-day money positions is never likely to be easy, even in the new system with zero reserve requirements, the framework of which went into effect on 18 November 1991. Previous arrangements were to be phased out over a 2-year period. The underlying objective of the new system for implementing monetary policy is to permit the Bank of Canada to exercise a degree of influence over very short-term interest rates similar to that of the system that was current. The new system would require a direct clearer, which has to take a secured overdraft loan to avoid a negative settlement position at the Bank of Canada, to offset the overdraft loan – either with an excess balance at the Bank of Canada on some other day during the same calculation period,[16] or with an advance (at Bank rate) equal to the difference between total overdraft loans and total excess balances over the calculation period, or to pay a fee in lieu of such an advance. Given the costs thus associated with both holdings of clearing balances and overdrafts from the Bank of Canada, the direct clearers would be induced to take prompt action in the money markets to position themselves to try to avoid such outcomes. (With zero reserve requirements, a direct clearer would typically aim for a settlement balance near zero when its cumulative position was near zero.) Hence the Bank of Canada's actions to increase or reduce the quantity of settlement balances available to direct clearers would lead the direct clearers to adjust their positions and would thereby produce movements in very short-term interest rates in the direction desired.

To establish the money position in North America, the banks' money desks begin work at about 7.30 a.m. (earlier – local time – on the west coast).[17] The initial money position for the day would be established by 8.00 or 8.30 a.m. – the cut-off time for the clearing being 12.30 a.m. (i.e. the night before). The cash position is known by 4.00 a.m., but the Bank of Canada draw-down (or re-deposit) only by 8.30 a.m. Information with respect to large movements of cash would be fed in by the big corporations throughout the day. Indeed, banks would have direct lines with a number of their corporate customers. The Bank of Canada also keys in information relating to the state of the Receiver-General's account (i.e. government moneys) – this will have been estimated in advance and adjusted later, if necessary.

For those chartered banks that use Euro-currencies to an important extent and which run a global book, trading will be around the clock from Tokyo and Hong Kong to Singapore, Frankfurt, London, New York, and Chicago. Hence, for a big bank, major changes in available resources will tend to result from movements on the international side of the bank's business. However, so far as domestic cash is concerned, virtually all their major branches are 'on-line' and large cash movements (whether in or out) are advised promptly. There are also seasonal factors to consider.

Apart from buying money market instruments (with a view to absorbing cash), the chartered banks may lend to, or (if short of cash, call loans from) the investment dealers, or lend to/borrow from other banks. The latter relates to the inter-bank market, where inter-bank funds may trade all day for same-day value. The inter-bank market first developed in the 1970s, when it was a cosy market between the large chartered banks. These inter-bank loans were made direct – i.e. without resorting to brokers. The big change came in the early 1980s, when the Schedule B banks as they then were) came into the market (e.g. foreign bank subsidiaries set up in Canada to compete with the old established chartered banks). There were also several smaller regional chartered banks established in western Canada. Foreign banks, with parents in London or New York, were accustomed to using a developed and active inter-bank market (in New York, the federal funds market). Both they and some of the smaller regional banks lacked a sizeable deposit base and therefore regularly required to fund themselves quite substantially by buying wholesale money in the inter-bank market. Not only were they more dependent on an inter-bank market than the old established chartered banks, but they were also more used to resorting to money brokers. Because, on the whole, they were more liquid, the big chartered banks were mainly lenders in this market (often being approached by foreign banks through a broker), though the chartered banks would also resort to the inter-bank market, if necessary, to make a marginal adjustment to their own cash. Internal (or undisclosed) limits are applied to all counterparties, but perhaps more flexibly to the large banks and more strictly to the smaller chartered and foreign banks. Prior to 1981, the inter-bank market dealt primarily in overnight money and was used by the major banks. Foreign banks may also borrow overnight, or for 7 days, but also for longer periods (e.g., up to 3 months). Money is lent unsecured but may be subject to limits (see above).

The main inter-bank market is in Toronto (some business is likewise done in Montreal); there is also a subsidiary market in Vancouver on the West Coast. Banks there come into Toronto between 6.00 and 8.00 a.m. Vancouver time and there may be a second busy period later in the morning (which would be afternoon Toronto time). And in Vancouver some money may come in through their bankers from corporate accounts in the east looking for an outlet late in the day. There may also be some afternoon activity deriving from local sources in Vancouver. To some extent, Calgary has a similar experience.

INTERNATIONAL PAPER

From the early 1970s onwards, the area in which the Canadian banks most obviously expanded their market activity related to international paper and there was a marked extension of the Canadian money market beyond its own borders. Thus, the Canadian chartered banks not only had large volumes of US dollar deposits on their books; their New York agencies could also actively seek out dollar deposits in the USA, provided these deposits represented obligations of their respective Canadian head offices. This rapidly became an expanding business, because US lenders – both corporate and institutional – often found that fixed-term US dollar deposits with Candian banks offered higher yields than equivalent domestic transactions. Moreover, when issued in Canada and purchased by Americans, these deposits were not subject either to the 15 per cent Canadian non-resident withholding tax nor to the US interest equalization tax[18] and, when purchased by Canadians, the 15 per cent US non-resident withholding tax did not apply.

Again, under certain conditions, the chartered banks could offer the short-term investor holding Canadian dollars attractive rates on 'swapped' deposits. This was known as a 'bank swap'. It was non-liquid and consisted essentially of a US dollar deposit with the Canadian investor enjoying protection from exchange rate fluctuations. The 15 per cent US withholding tax did not apply. To obtain a rate equivalent to a bank swap deposit, the investor with Canadian dollars would first have to convert them into US dollars, so that he could create the deposit, and – in order to obtain protection against the risk of exchange rate fluctuations during the life of the investment – simultaneous arrangements would have to be made to convert the US proceeds back into Canadian dollars at the pre-determined maturity date. The double conversion process was known as a 'swap' or 'hedge', and took place at the outset. The exchange rates at which these two simultaneous transactions would take place formed an integral part of the all-in yield of the investment. In practice, the Canadian banks quoted an all-in yield (in terms of Canadian dollars), which included both the US dollar deposit rate and the effect of the swap, so that the prospective investor was able to avoid going through the step by step process just described. Quoted rates could vary widely, depending on the term required, current forward exchange rates, and the chartered bank concerned. A similar transaction could be done in reverse.

In addition, Canadian organizations may, under certain specified conditions, invest in Eurodollar negotiable certificates of deposit denominated in US dollars. These CDs will be issued by the London branch of a Canadian chartered bank, or a US bank, and are subject to the laws of the UK. They are issued in bearer form, with interest accruing on a 360-day basis. While these CDs are not redeemable prior to maturity, a substantial secondary market in London assures their liquidity, subject of course to the market conditions obtaining there from time to time. Payment at settlement or at maturity is typically done in London.

Dealers likewise have their contacts with other markets. For example, a lot of Canadian commercial paper is sold in the USA, fully hedged, on the dealer's recommendation. They also have European clients and some of the dealers have established contacts with the large English clearing (and other) banks, as well as with the merchant banks, which from time to time themselves may hold Canadian paper.

FINANCIAL FUTURES

Of more recent growth is the use of interest-rate futures and interest-rate swaps. There are active markets in these in both Toronto and Montreal. A number of risk-management products is provided primarily to manage the impact of interest-rate volatility on the cost of operations. Thus, there is an active over-the-counter market in Canada in forward-rate agreements (FRAs), interest-rate swaps, bond and swap options, and interest-rate caps.[19] In terms of exchange traded products, the most important is the Montreal Stock Exchange Canada bond futures contract (CGB), which has been fairly slow to take off; it appears that some Canadian institutions use the Chicago Board of Trade US Treasury bond futures to hedge their positions. There is also a bankers' acceptance futures contract, which trades on the Montreal Stock Exchange.

THE ROLE OF THE INVESTMENT DEALERS

We have now discussed in some detail the several sectors of the Canadian money market and the instruments in which the dealers operate or upon the use of which they advise. Although in some respects they act more as brokers than as principals, the dealers by definition carry an inventory and, although only the largest dealers would operate over the whole field, all dealers in the market will have some inventory to finance. Since capital and reserves provide no more than a basis for their operations, the bulk of what they require must be borrowed. It is proposed first to summarize the position with regard to inventory and then to consider the sources of their borrowings.

Because Government of Canada Treasury bills, commercial paper, and – to a lesser extent – bankers' acceptances, are significant instruments in the money market, they will also be the object of investment dealer activity, though one must also mention trust and mortgage loan company obligations. In general terms, Treasury bills probably constitute about half the market, with about a quarter relating to bankers' acceptances. Commercial paper may not feature very largely in dealer inventories, but there is a large primary market for commercial paper with maturities of up to 1 year. Dealer holdings of Canada bonds with maturities of 3 years or less are small, as also are holdings of Provincial Treasury bills, which are issued by a number of provinces; they are bid for by banks and dealers.[20]

All the money market dealers would be expected to tender regularly – and aggressively – for Treasury bills, and the Bank of Canada monitors their activity in this field. As with similar instruments in the USA, large amounts of Canada Treasury bills are sold on to non-residents, with US dealers also selling them on to non-American buyers, including the Japanese, though the latter are more interested in Canadian bonds than in Treasury bills.

So far as bankers' acceptances are concerned, the maturities that the money market dealers prefer to buy for inventory depend on the current yield curve, the time of year, and rate projections – dealers will not wish to hold all maturities at all times. The bankers' acceptances held would relate less to the blue-chip companies (which would tend to issue commercial paper) than to mid-sized concerns,[21] which have their paper 'stamped' by a chartered bank (largely by the five major banks),[22] in order to ensure the marketability of that paper, the creditworthiness of the customer being reflected in the 'stamping fee' charged. None the less, competition from the foreign banks has driven this down in recent years. Although, being accommodation paper, bankers' acceptances are usually in round amounts, some small broken amounts are occasionally seen (and may be trade-related); these can most easily be placed with a retail customer. Liquidity can be provided by the willingness of the dealer to buy back any such paper – at market rates – should this be necessary. One reason for the popularity of bankers' acceptances is the interest that the banks have in pushing them – in order to retain contact with their customers as a substitute for corporate loans, this being perhaps the main reason why there has been so much competition with regard to 'stamping fees'.

Similar in importance to bankers' acceptances have been the issues of commercial paper. There are now about 150 rated issuers of commercial paper in Canada and a number of major issuers of finance paper (like GMAC and Ford). Commercial paper may also be issued by companies that are less than fully blue chip (but with a capital of – say – C$ 100 million or more) provided they carry adequate back-up lines of credit from a reputable chartered bank. Some small companies are supported by a guarantee from a parent corporation. The issue of commercial paper has become a major means whereby large corporations in Canada now finance their working capital requirements and it has eaten heavily into the corporate lending figures of the chartered banks. Depending on market conditions (which may fluctuate daily or seasonally), the dealers may bid for paper, sometimes selling it out of inventory after only a short period of time; on other occasions, dealers (and banks) may hold blocks of commercial paper to maturity, if there is a positive carry, or if perhaps they are quite unable to sell it.

Whenever the chartered banks have been highly liquid, the issue of BDNs has been much less important than when more funding has been required (e.g. to meet an increased demand for credit). Guaranteed investment certificates (GICs) – with a minimum period of 1 year out to 5 years – may be sold by investment dealers as an agent of a trust company, but they are only tradable to a limited extent. For the rest, investment dealers (and banks) would be active in arranging swapped deposits[23] maturing in 1 month to 1 year, when there is a lack of product to any specific term, or where the swapped deposit rate is superior to that offered by any domestic instrument.[24]

For dealing purposes, the markets would open about 8.30 a.m. Eastern Standard Time, most of the trading being done in the morning. It is very active until 10.30 a.m., but tapers off by noon. In the afternoon, the dealers will effect the relevant deliveries and seek to resolve any associated difficulties (e.g., where necessary, by doing a lieu delivery – i.e. substituting securities – or, alternatively, by issue of a letter of undertaking to deliver). In the context of hours, one should note that Toronto, Ottawa, and Montreal are all in the same time zone. However, Vancouver is 3 hours behind; Calgary and Edmonton 2 hours behind; Winnipeg 1 hour behind. Dealers also have to arrange business on the east coast and the Maritimes, which may be $1\frac{1}{2}$ hours (depending on daylight saving arrangements) ahead of Toronto time.

It is now necessary to consider how the dealers' business – and, in particular, their inventories – is financed. When the Canadian money market was first set up in the 1950s – as we have seen – the primary source of finance was the day-to-day loan introduced in 1954. It is overnight and for 1 day only; designated collateral is Government of Canada Treasury bills and short-dated Canadas (i.e. with maturities of less than 3 years). This remained true until 1967 when special-call loans were offered by the chartered banks. These (and other short loans) steadily increased in importance, subject to some fluctuation from time to time. Latterly, it has been call loans from the chartered banks that provide rate leadership, but off-street lenders do the bulk of the business (e.g. non-financial corporations) – about two-thirds of the inventory of non-bank jobbers is financed with off-street money. Day-to-day money is still made available by the chartered banks, but the amounts are small.

Day-to-day loans (or day loans) are fully secured against the security of Government of Canada Treasury bills, or direct and

guaranteed bonds of up to 3 years maturity. Day loans are renegotiated each day and are extended unless called, wholly or in
part, by the bank or the dealer on any business day, provided notice
is given before noon Eastern Standard Time, or on the following
day if the call is made after noon. If there is no call before noon,
the loan is automatically renewed for a further day. When a day
loan is made, settlement will be effected with the delivery of
collateral securities to the lender, or his designated depository.
Often delivery is made after 5.00 p.m. One should note, too, that
accommodation at the central bank plus day loans may not exceed
a dealer's line of credit with the Bank of Canada.

The 'special call loan' market was initiated by the chartered
banks in 1967 in order to achieve more flexible cash management.
Previously, the traditional means of adjustment in primary and
cash reserves had been day loans and Treasury bills, but the
demand for day loans and/or the supply of Treasury bills of
specific maturities were not always adequate to absorb large
amounts quickly. Then, with the introduction of an averaging
period for bank reserves beginning in January 1969, frequent
adjustment in the banks' cash reserve positions became more necessary and this contributed to a greater use of special call loans as a
tool of cash management. The term 'special call loan' applies to a
loan made by a bank to an investment dealer to finance its
inventory where the acceptable collateral is less restricted than it
would be for a day loan, though it can be called in a similar way,
whereas an ordinary call loan can be pledged against virtually any
collateral and called by the lender at short notice (in practice, they
are considered to be collateral loans with a little longer period to
maturity than their name implies). In other words, they are not as
liquid as day loans or special call loans. Rates on special call loans
are frequently higher than on day loans, but lower than on call
loans.[25]

But the reason why call loans of all kinds have now become the
established way of lending to investment dealers to enable them to
carry their inventory is that it is a convenient means of lending both
from the banks' and the dealers' points of view. Banks now lend to
dealers up to internal limits, and often – once internal limits have
been reached – lenders will do 'repos' instead of a straight call loan.
On his side, each dealer has a call-loan desk to negotiate the
amounts and the rates for such loans. All these bank loans are
made direct – i.e. not through brokers.

It should be noted, too, that in the call loan market (in its broadest sense) moneys may be lent not only by banks (whose relative share has been declining), but much more so by trust companies, provinces, municipalities, oil companies and other corporates (which may also borrow), life insurance companies, pension funds and, in this wider sense, some business may go through brokers.[26] Investment dealers remain the main borrowers – though what they borrow from banks is less than it was. At times, however, they may also borrow marginal amounts of money from the banks at the end of the day by way of overdraft (but this is expensive).

In the USA, repurchase agreements are used extensively by the government securities dealers to finance the carrying of inventory. In Canada these arrangements are not so well developed, but the practice of resorting to standardized 'repos' is increasing. 'Repos' have been used more for the purpose of accommodating a customer's needs. Thus corporates may buy securities one day for re-sale the following day in order to absorb surplus cash overnight. (Banks likewise might do a 'repo' for a corporate against a Treasury bill to accommodate them.)

Most investment dealers have a considerable stock-retailing operation. The retail clients of such houses maintain 'margin accounts', which result in considerable client balances[27] being left with the dealing house, on which balances a competitive rate of interest is paid. In addition to the firm's capital, such accounts provide a large money base with which to carry inventory; it is only after this has been absorbed that such firms need to attract call money. An investment dealer with a large corporate parent may have part of the proceeds of commercial paper issued by the parent come downstream for use in financing inventory. Alternatively, the house itself may issue commercial paper in its own name.

To some extent, too, the investment dealers may raise finance with which to assist in carrying inventory by borrowing abroad (e.g., in the USA). If on a fully-hedged basis, this would involve an overnight loan in US dollars at a fixed rate, and the sale of US dollars for Canadian dollars today matched by a sale of Canadian dollars to purchase US dollars tomorrow. This is a North-bound swap: it is a two-part transaction with the US party investing in Canada; and the process may be reversed as a South-bound swap, when a Canadian house wishes to invest in the USA.

Lastly, though we shall be more concerned with this in the next section, certain authorized dealers may borrow against approved collateral and within their line of credit at the Bank of Canada; they may also be accommodated by special 'repo' (see below).

BANK OF CANADA INTERVENTION

As central bank, the Bank of Canada has responsibility for monetary policy, in the context of which it operates directly and day by day in the overnight and other short-term areas of the money market. The effects of action taken there filter through to the rest of the financial system, and from there into the 'real economy'. In addition, the Bank of Canada is the fiscal agent for the Government of Canada, which it advises and for which it conducts borrowing operations. In recent years, the government has made considerable use of the money market both as a regular source of financing – building up a substantial stock of debt in Treasury bills – and for the purpose of bridging temporary short-falls of cash. The government's cash balances are held at the direct clearing institutions,[28] in the form of either term[29] or demand[30] deposits. In addition, a small amount is held at the Bank of Canada.

The primary tool of implementing monetary policy is cash management. By altering the quantity of clearing balances available to the direct clearers, the bank of Canada can exert a noticeable influence on short-term rates. The mechanism through which the Bank alters the clearing balances is the drawdown/redeposit technique. This involves the transfer of Government of Canada deposits between the government's account at the Bank of Canada and its accounts at the direct clearers. A drawdown refers to a transfer of deposits to the Bank from the direct clearers, effectively draining the supply of available cash balances. A redeposit is just the opposite – a transfer from the Bank to the direct clearers (i.e. an injection of balances).

Each morning – at around 8.30 a.m. – the transfer occurs through the Automated Clearing and Settlement System (ACSS) and is read by each direct clearer via computer. The direct clearers, which share in the demand balances, watch this number carefully, since it is the last piece of information that the cash manager requires to calculate the closing position for the previous day. The drawdown or redeposit is determined by the Bank of Canada after the close of business each day and implemented the following morning on a back-dated basis. Each evening the Bank of Canada analyses the amount of reserves demanded by the banks and adjusts the supply relative to that demanded level. If it wishes overnight rates to fall, it supplies more than the banks appear to be demanding; if it wishes rates to rise, it supplies less. The drawndown/redeposit transaction, as it completes each direct clearer's daily position, will also tell them whether or not they are in an overdraft situation. More importantly, from the point of view of the monetary policy perspective, each cash manager will compare the actual system drawdown or redeposit to his own forecast and make a judgement as to whether there might have been a shift in the Bank of Canada's short-run stance. Then the cash manager and trader colleagues together respond accordingly in the money market.

The drawdown or redeposit of government balances enables the Bank of Canada to control the amount of settlement balances or reserves in the banking system on a daily basis. Each day the government and the Bank are engaged in a multitude of transactions with the direct clearers, such as regular government receipts and disbursements as well as the Bank of Canada's domestic and exchange market intervention. These transactions may lead to an undesirable contraction or expansion of the level of reserves in the system. Therefore the Bank uses the drawdown and redeposit mechanism, first to neutralize the effects of these cash flows and then, second, to affect the level of reserves consistent with the Bank of Canada's monetary policy objective.

In 1985, the Bank of Canada started to use the 'special PRA' (or 'special repo'). Regular purchase and re-sale agreements (PRAs) could be done at Bank rate and at the discretion of the investment dealer, who could 'back out' if he could obtain funds elsewhere. 'Special repos' are at the discretion of the Bank of Canada. They are normally overnight (except at weekends, when they are repayable on the following business day). In this case, if dealers have committed themselves, they cannot 'back out'. Special PRAs were done to offset the occasional upward rate movements that occurred in the overnight market. It was also a means of ensuring that the relevant moneys got through to the investment dealers and were not held up in the hands of the banks. In this case, if it was desired to put money out (and dealers could collectively clearly demonstrate a 'need' of funds), Government of Canada securities up to 3 years maturity (but usually Treasury bills) would be purchased by the Bank of Canada, the transaction being reversed by re-sale one day later, except at weekends – see above. By this means, the Bank of

Canada was able 'more directly and immediately' to influence the overnight rate. With experience, the Bank began to see benefits in using these transactions 'to ease undue upward rate pressures on a more regular basis'. Usually, such transactions are effected in the morning, with the process typically wrapped up by noon.

More recently, the Bank of Canada also began to carry out SRAs – sales (e.g. of Treasury bills) with an agreement to repurchase – where excess liquidity required to be 'mopped up'. Typically, SRAs were done just with the banks. This, too, has come into more frequent use 'to counter excessive rate pressures in a downward direction'. Unlike the traditional PRAs, where application to the Bank of Canada was at the discretion of the dealers, the Bank set the rate, the amount, and the timing of both the special PRAs and the SRAs. Although this has meant a higher profile for the Bank of Canada in the overnight market, this has been accepted as a necessity if the Bank is to signal its intentions efficiently.

However, while greater emphasis has been placed on transactions with a 1-day term and on a repurchase/re-sale basis, the Bank of Canada has not abandoned the use of outright purchase and sale of Treasury bills. But they have tended to reserve such transactions:

> for occasions when our actions in the overnight market appear to require special reinforcement. These transactions with the market, whether for cash or in trade for other treasury bills, generally are undertaken to indicate more directly that the interest-rate movements of the day are proceeding farther and faster than seems appropriate.

In these several ways, while not attempting to dictate the level of interest rates, the Bank of Canada 'can, does, and will continue to exercise leadership', though it is recognized that, if the Bank's actions 'do not prove to chart a credible course, then they will have no lasting effect on interest rate levels. This is true even in the shorter-term area of the market, where [the Bank's] influence is the most direct and the least tempered by market expectations'.

Again, the Bank's activities may be complicated by 'the inevitable and important interaction' between the money market and the FOREX market. Indeed, to influence the money market is virtually to affect the FOREX market as well. Hence, both levels of interest rates and the exchange value of the Canadian dollar must be seen as elements in the way monetary policy is transmitted. 'And since events in either the money or exchange market can easily trigger a response in the other market, we may find at times a combined shift occurring in these markets that we view as too extreme.' This might well happen in periods of volatile exchange rates, when at times the Bank of Canada has had to be:

> very watchful to ensure that in seeking a change in interest rates, we do not trigger an exaggerated movement in the exchange rate. On other occasions we have had the difficulty of coping with developments in the exchange market that have set in motion pressures on interest rates. Earlier in the 1980s, there were several instances when a sharply weakening dollar forced short-term interest rates higher than we, at least, felt should have been completely necessary in the circumstances.[31]

All these decisions are based on what is virtually a continuous monitoring of economic and financial data. The Bank of Canada itself releases weekly financial statistics every Friday at 2.00 p.m. These are very complete (and include the Bank of Canada balance sheet) and are as up-to-date as possible. (Board Minutes are published with a 5–6 week lag – after the next Board meeting.) In addition, there are the periodic speeches made by the Governor of the Bank of Canada[32] and by other senior officials. Always, too, dealers (and others) are able to call regularly to see senior officials at the Bank of Canada. The discussions are sometimes frank and the questions, it is said, have become increasingly sophisticated.

Furthermore, the efficiency of the market has been greatly increased by the speed of communication and processing, which – as we shall see – will soon be further developed. Moreover, the money market is now both broad and deep,[33] which greatly assists the transmission of the impact effects of central bank policies; it also facilitates its role as a fiscal agent and has enabled it to handle more easily the record amount of Government of Canada Treasury bill offerings and the increase of over one-quarter in the stock of bills during 1988/89. By mid-1991, the stock of Treasury bills stood at C$ 144.3 billion, up 20 per cent from the end of 1989.[34] It would have been more difficult, too, to accommodate smoothly the large swings in bill offerings from one week to the next and the issue at short notice of cash management bills, which have resulted from the tighter management in recent years of government cash balances.

Reference was made earlier to further innovations that are being contemplated and which will assist in increasing the existing efficiency of the financial markets in Canada. Thus, the Canadian payments system appears to be evolving towards a situation where paper cheques settled on the existing basis will co-exist with a large-value electronic payments system with same-day settlement. It was thought that the increase in the use of the large-value payments system would be gradual and that there would be no abrupt switching away from certified cheques for large value transactions. Eventually, as the electronic payments system comes to absorb a major share of the total value of payment flows in the system, more restructuring of the settlement process will become necessary.

In addition, a new system to clear and settle money market transactions is being developed by the Canadian Depository for Securities (CDS). This project has drawn on joint resources from the banking, trust-company, and investment-dealer industries; the Bank of Canada has also been involved. When the system is operational, all major money-market instruments will be immobilized in the custody of the CDS. Transactions will be settled instantaneously by book-entry transfers of securities in the computer-based accounts of the CDS against a net payment to or from the CDS at the end of the day. However, before the shift to this new way of settling money market transactins can occur, the Bank of Canada and other participants will need to be satisfied that risks associated with settling transactions in this new system have been identified and that appropriate safeguards have been developed.

Finally, as Governor Crow has also pointed out, interest rates and exchange rates are not the goals of monetary policy. The 'basic objective is using monetary policy to secure moderate monetary expansion, thereby contributing to broad price stability as an important condition for sustained economic progress'.

NOTE   Beginning on 24 November 1992, the normal auction day for Government of Canada Treasury bills was changed from Thursday to Tuesday. Concurrent with this change the normal settlement date for the bill auctions was shifted to Thursday from Friday. As a consequence, the weekly Bank rate setting, which is based on the 3-months Treasury bill average yield at the auction, was also to be announced on Tuesdays commencing on 24 November 1992.

Chapter 10

The money market in Hong Kong

In one form or another, Hong Kong has operated a three-tiered financial structure since 1982. Thus, at end-September 1991, there were 162 licensed banks (excluding BCCHK Limited, which was placed in provisional liquidation in July 1991), 50 restricted licence banks, and 162 deposit-taking companies (there had been a significant decrease in the figure for the last group, since some companies that were inactive in the deposit-taking business voluntarily revoked their registration at the end of the grace period for meeting the new minimum paid-up capital requirements). These requirements dated from 10 March 1991 and were to ensure that only institutions of substance were to be entrusted with public savings. The minimum capital requirements for locally incorporated licensed banks, restricted-licence banks, and deposit-taking companies were raised from HK$ 100 million, HK$ 75 million, and HK$ 10 million to HK$ 150 million, HK$ 100 million, and HK$ 25 million respectively. Power to implement such arrangements and, indeed, the general supervision of banking and financial institutions in Hong Kong is granted to the Commissioner of Banking and Monetary Affairs under the Banking Ordinance, as amended.[1]

An important element in banking is the maintenance of sufficient liquidity to meet obligations as they fall due. It is often a lack of liquidity that precipitates the failure of the less soundly run institutions. Liquidity for licensed banks, restricted-licence banks, and deposit-taking companies has been set at 25 per cent[2] of 'liquefiable assets' (e.g. cash, short-term loans repayable within 1 month, certain export bills, government guaranteed securities, and other negotiable paper) in relation to qualifying liabilities (the net balance of '1-month liabilities').

As from 12 January 1981, the former Exchange Banks'

Association (EBA) was replaced by a new statutory body – the Hong Kong Association of Banks (HKAB). The HKAB took over the functions of the EBA in fixing interest rates for deposits and setting rules in respect of certain banking services and the charges to be levied for them. The chairmanship of the HKAB's committee rotates between the two note-issuing banks – the Hongkong and Shanghai Banking Corporation and Standard Chartered Bank. Nine of the twelve places on the committee are filled by election and the other three are allocated in perpetuity to the Bank of China and the two note-issuing banks. Formerly, interest rates were fixed for two groups of banks. In January 1991, the two-tier categorization of banks was ended with the publication of the amended HKAB Rules on Interest Rates and Deposit Charges.

There is no central bank in Hong Kong, but certain quasi-central banking functions (such as issuing bank notes, administering the clearing mechanism, serving as the government's banker) have in fact been performed by the two leading banks – the Hongkong and Shanghai Banking Corporation and the Standard Chartered Bank.

Of the total value of currency issue, the commercial bank issue normally accounts for over 90 per cent, the government issue being confined to subsidiary coins and commemorative gold coins only. Issue of bank notes is backed by certificates of indebtedness issued by the Exchange Fund against payment in US dollars at the fixed rate of HK\$ 7.80 = US\$ 1.00 by the two note-issuing banks to the Exchange Fund. This Fund was set up by the government in 1935, when Hong Kong abandoned the silver standard and adopted the sterling exchange standard. In addition to receiving the proceeds of all bank-note issues and the government's own coin issues, the Exchange Fund is also funded by moneys representing the major part of the government's fiscal surpluses and the fund's own net earnings on its assets.

On the monetary side, in late 1976, the post of Secretary of Monetary Affairs was created to replace the former post of Accountant-General. The Secretary for Monetary Affairs heads the Monetary Affairs Branch, which carries out the government's monetary policies and manages the Exchange Fund and its foreign-exchange operations. Under the overall direction of the Financial Secretary, the Secretary for Monetary Affairs and the Banking Commissioner exercise control over and supervision of Hong Kong's banking and monetary sector.

In addition to the banks and the deposit-taking companies

(DTCs), other financial institutions include the Hong Kong Building and Loans Agency Ltd, which is a quoted public company in which the Government of Hong Kong is a shareholder and guarantor against default. This company provides mortgage finance at reasonable rates of interest to prospective owner-occupiers of flats in the middle income group; it is run on commercial lines. The Export Credit Insurance Corporation is a public corporation which functions as a credit insurer and protects exporters against the risk of non-payment by overseas buyers. It is also run on commercial lines. However, the activities of these two quasi-governmental financial institutions are not significant in terms of the volume of funding provided compared with those of the private commercial banks and deposit-taking companies.

There are two main money markets in Hong Kong: the inter-bank market in Hong Kong dollars (which will be described in detail in the next section) and the market in foreign exchange (FOREX) – which, together with the Asian dollar market, foreign currency deposits and swaps, will be considered in a later section.

THE INTER-BANK MARKET

The inter-bank market in Hong Kong dollars may be in overnight money (which is quite large), in money for 1 or 2 months, and for 1–6 months (the demand for money for 1 month is quite sizeable, but it is not so large at 6 months). Very occasionally, money is lent for 12 months, but this is rare. All loans are unsecured. Hence, it is necessary to apply 'internal limits' to borrowers, referred to in Hong Kong as 'money market dealing lines' between the licensed banks and the large deposit-taking companies which are participants in the market. Generally speaking, the lenders in this market are the British note-issuing banks – the Hongkong and Shanghai Banking Corporation, which is in fact domiciled in Hong Kong, and Standard Chartered Bank – and the Chinese banks, the most important of which from this point of view would be the highly cohesive group of thirteen banks headed by the Bank of China and controlled by the People's Republic of China, but operating in Hong Kong just like any other commercial bank; other important Chinese banks are Hang Seng Bank, since 1965 a subsidiary of the Hongkong and Shanghai Banking Corporation, and the Bank of East Asia. Altogether there would be ten to twelve big banking groups that would usually be lenders. For the most part, borrowers are non-British foreign banks (especially where they are wholesale banks) and DTCs without a substantial local deposit base, though several of the foreign banks now have something of a retail business. However, such banks also do a lot of financing offshore. Many of the foreign bank branches service the region from Hong Kong – from Thailand to Indonesia, even Australia and New Zealand. In this context, the Japanese banks have been very active players.

The DTCs which operate in the money market tend to be the large ones, but even some of the smaller ones try to get in and, if such a company has a large bank presence in its capital, they may be able to obtain a line of credit more easily. There are also one or two large corporations (e.g. Hong Kong Land and Jardines), which in effect have access to inter-bank facilities; their financial controllers are known to the banks' dealers, also to the DTC dealers, and these corporations borrow money from the banks and DTCs at inter-bank rates. Big banks like Hongkong and Shanghai and Standard Chartered will be in and out of the market more or less continuously – both lending and borrowing, thereby helping to make the market; regular lenders like the Bank of China group will also occasionally borrow; likewise the American banks, which tend to be borrowers, may at times lend; Japanese banks tend to be persistently net takers. When foreign banks become temporary lenders, it is usually where they have strong 'parents' and have brought in from overseas amounts of Euro- or Asian dollars, which are swapped into Hong Kong dollars and may therefore be available in the short-term for lending on the inter-bank money market.

As one would expect, the large local banks (including in this category the Hongkong and Shanghai Banking Corporation, Standard Chartered, and Bank of China), although they are primarily lenders, would obtain a very good rate if borrowing. Moreover, the inter-bank market is now rather more active than it was some years ago, and money market rates – especially up to 1 month – can fluctuate quite considerably, even within the day.

All the large banks have sophisticated computer-based installations, with which both to establish their money position first thing in the morning (even the night before) and to monitor it throughout the day. Where necessary (e.g. where not all the branches are on-line), branches would telephone in large transactions taking place during the day. Quick and reliable reporting is essential, since – in a situation where customers are extremely sensitive to changes in interest rates – funds can be quickly switched from one type of investment to another. For the Hongkong and Shanghai Banking Corporation, all branches are computer-based – everything is on-line. They also have 'large transactions reporting terminals', and 'reporting limits' are set for deposits, foreign exchange, money market transactions, and foreign currency deposits. Everything locks in to the system. With a computer programme, too, the balance of deposits can be quickly updated. Moreover, in some of the smaller banks, which may none the less be very sophisticated, large transactions (e.g. a large loan done at money-market rates) do not go through the branches, but are concentrated in the hands of the central treasury. Settlement may be through a branch.

As in most economies, movements in government accounts are as important in Hong Kong as elsewhere. The Government maintains accounts with a number of banks in Hong Kong, but mainly with the Hongkong and Shanghai Banking Corporation. (The Government uses about ten of the larger banks in Hong Kong.)[3] If moneys are withdrawn by taxation, government balances go up at the Hongkong and Shanghai Banking Corporation (and at other banks), and these moneys would tend to be lent out in the money market. Hence the importance of watching the Hongkong and Shanghai to get a feel of what is likely to happen in terms of the quantity of money available and its impact on interest rates. Again, if the Government is a net spender over a period, bank customers will be flush with funds, deposits will increase, and more funds will be available for bank lending; the tendency will be for interest rates to decline. Meanwhile, short-term surpluses or deficits of funds will have been evened out between the banks through the money market. The banks are obliged to pay interest to the Government on these accounts – even on current accounts, though this is not true for the ordinary current accounts of the general public.

In Hong Kong, there is a General Revenue Account at the Treasury, with government moneys flowing in and out – revenue and expenditure. Surpluses are paid into the Exchange Fund against the issue of debt certificates, which are interest-bearing and are liabilities of the Exchange Fund. Other liabilities are certificates of indebtedness issued to the note issuing banks (Hongkong and Shanghai and Standard Chartered) against their note issues, which are bank liabilities. These certificates are not interest-bearing. To obtain these certificates of indebtedness, the note-issuing banks have to pay moneys to the Exchange Fund, which moneys offset their note issues. They used to pay these moneys in Hong Kong dollars, but after 17 October 1983 they were obliged to pay over US dollars at a rate of HK$ 7.8 to the US dollar, receiving in exchange a non-interest-bearing certificate of indebtedness from the Exchange Fund. Moneys received by the Exchange Fund are invested in US dollars, sterling, yen, and European currencies; their assets tend to be very liquid, with a concentration in US dollar assets (largely because of the exchange link with the US dollar). None the less, the Fund resorts to a basket of currencies for investment purposes. The Government holds foreign-currency deposits both with banks in Hong Kong and with banks outside Hong Kong (through the Exchange Fund).

For 'smoothing out' purposes, the resources of the Exchange Fund could be used in the money market – e.g. to stabilize the exchange value of the Hong Kong dollar. The Government could also make its views known to the Hong Kong Association of Banks at its weekly meetings with them. However, in Hong Kong, the authorities for long believed that a freely adjusting system was best – there was no need for a mopping up of liquidity as such, and interest rates and FOREX rates would adjust – though there were rigidities in the system (e.g. the cartel fixing domestic interest rates). But if Hong Kong interest rates were lower than US interest rates, there would be a movement of funds into US dollars with effects on interest rates in Hong Kong. Since the introduction of the accounting arrangements of July 1988, the Exchange Fund has taken up the additional central banking role of being the ultimate provider of liquidity in the inter-bank market. By taking action under these arrangements, it is now much better placed to influence inter-bank liquidity and interest rates, and to maintain exchange rate stability within the framework of the linked exchange rate system. Liquidity is now influenced by adjusting net credit balances with the Exchange Fund. Although the Exchange Fund may be lending in the inter-bank market throughout the day at money market rates, it may also lend (when necessary) late in the afternoon (4.15 to 4.45 p.m.) to banks in urgent need of funds (the rate is determined by the Government). So, although there is still no central bank, there is now a lender of last resort and a kind of 'monetary authority'. (See also 'Postscript' at end of this chapter.)

A question that it is relevant to ask is whether there is any degree of seasonality in money market activity in Hong Kong. There used to be a big demand for money for (say) 4–6 weeks before the

Chinese New Year. At such times there was formerly a big physical demand for cash. Now seasonal fluctuations seem to be rather muted. Exports build up in the autumn (October), when there tends to be greater liquidity and there is an increased demand for consumer goods at Christmas. On the whole, however, and despite large outflows of cash at holiday times, the banks take Christmas, Easter, and the summer holidays in their stride. December tends to be a quiet month, when the foreign exchange dealers in particular seem to go on holiday and their 'number twos' do not take positions while they are away. Alternatively, it is said that those who have had a good year rest on their laurels until after the holidays; those that have done badly are disinclined to take any further risks until the year is over. More generally, there is now a much larger number of banks in Hong Kong, which borrow in foreign currencies quite as much as in Hong Kong dollars; wealth is also much more diversified. But most important is the fact that the banks are now positioning themselves much better, especially with regard to cash management, borrowing US dollars rather than Hong Kong dollars when necessary. The demand for the note issue seems to be more stable. Nowadays, financial stringency seems to be dictated more by political tension and the general economic situation – events worldwide rather than by local factors. The exchange link with the US dollar has likewise led to greater exchange rate stability, but probably more volatility in interest rates.

Daily operations in the inter-bank money market begin about 8.30 a.m.,[4] although the Hongkong and Shanghai Banking Corporation with its 250 Hong Kong branches will know its money position by 7.30 a.m. and quotations will have been obtainable from the money brokers by 8.00 a.m. Most of the business is done between 8.30 a.m. and 11.30 a.m., especially in overnight money, which may represent 80 per cent of the total. It is thinner in the afternoon. Only if there is an urgent need of money will it be taken then, and usually what is done in the afternoon (after 2.00 p.m.) is done for the next day. For 'period' money (1 month and over) the bulk of the business is done by 11.30 a.m. There is a staggered close, the market winding down from 4.00 p.m. onwards. There is no real money market business on Saturdays, though banks sometimes get calls from the half dozen or so customers 'with Saturday income'. FOREX transactions are almost non-existent on Saturdays, though there may be a little business from time to time. The market is not required to be open on Saturdays.

It remains to indicate the extent to which brokers are employed in the inter-bank market. There are ten brokers in all, who are full members of the brokers' association and specializing in money market and FOREX (one specialises as a deposit broker; all the others do FOREX and business in Hong Kong dollars). Of the ten brokers, three or four are more active than the others. But money market deals are also done direct between banks. Practice depends to some extent on the style of the bank – some prefer doing business through brokers; others think it is too slow. Not infrequently, a bank will start the day going through brokers to get the feel of the market and then do the rest of its business by way of direct deals. It is difficult to estimate where the balance of business lies. But in volume (as opposed to number of transactions), it is probably of the order of 60 per cent through brokers and 40 per cent direct.

MONEY MARKET INSTRUMENTS

What other money market instruments are available in Hong Kong? Some reference must be made in this context to negotiable certificates of deposit (NCDs), to wholesale and foreign currency deposits, and to commercial paper. No Treasury bills have been issued in Hong Kong, but latterly there have been issues of Exchange Fund Bills.

NCDs were first introduced in 1973, but activity in this market did not really take off until the beginning of the 1980s. The effective minimum is now HK$ 500,000. NCDs may also be issued in US dollars. Indeed, foreign currency CDs tend to grow faster than Hong Kong dollar CDs – customers tend to move into them when there is likely to be a depreciation in the Hong Kong dollar. Yet NCDs have never really taken off as a major instrument in Hong Kong, and the secondary market in NCDs is very small indeed – there being only a few good names. There are no true brokers in placing NCDs or in stimulating secondary-market activity, though certain merchant banks (DTCs) attempt to play that role to a certain extent.

There are also wholesale deposits. These are for more than HK$ 500,000 and are still important. Amounts of HK$ 100,000 to HK$ 500,000 would come in through branches. Over HK$ 500,000, banks can bid at more than HKAB rates. They can do this for periods of up to 3 months. None of these large customer deposits is an NCD. Such transactions would be undertaken by a bank's treasury – they are for large amounts and are short term and therefore attract a good money market rate. It is easier to raise big money this way than by way of tranches of NCDs, because the paper market in Hong Kong is still very undeveloped. Wholesale deposits have long been used as part of the banks' 'gapping' strategy – filling from this source any gaps that occur.

Another alternative instrument has been foreign-currency deposits in Hong Kong; they have been growing at a very high rate during the last few years. As a result, about half the deposits in the local monetary system are now denominated in foreign currencies, mainly in US dollars, compared with only 18 per cent in 1981. This rapid and continuing increase, compared with the relatively slow rise in Hong Kong dollar deposits during the same period, caused concern in certain quarters. The trend is sometimes seen as evidence of a weakening of confidence in the Hong Kong dollar, that the increased popularity of foreign-currency deposits may eventually jeopardize the viability of the local currency. However, the rapid growth in foreign-currency deposits is largely a reflection of Hong Kong's increasing role as a financial centre, changes in tax laws on interest earnings, and the greater sophistication of local residents in managing their assets. The process gathered momentum in early 1982, when the 15 per cent withholding tax on foreign-currency deposits was abolished. Before that, Singapore had a considerable advantage.

By about 1983, there were the beginnings in Hong Kong of a resort to commercial paper as a means of corporate funding – not on the American model as an unsecured note but on the basis of batches of discounted bills of exchange. The rate was based on Hong Kong Inter-Bank Offered Rate (HIBOR), plus a spread varying between 0.1 and 0.5 per cent. It is usually issued on a tender basis either through a merchant bank (DTC) or the merchant-banking division of a licensed bank. Commercial paper can only be issued by a first-class corporation (e.g. the Mass Transit Railway) and the lending is 'clean', i.e. unsecured. By 1986, the total of outstanding issues was starting to grow, and resort to commercial paper in Hong Kong was becoming more fashionable. The paper itself tends to be rather short-term (1–3 months), but it is normally 'rolled over' for up to 3–4 years. Activity in the secondary market has been rather limited, as most of the issues tend to be locked up by investors as a long-term investment and are seldom traded.

Because the Hong Kong Government favours a conservative fiscal policy, there was for many years very little issue of government paper and no Treasury bill issue at all. Such government paper as had been issued was held by financial institutions (including banks) as one of the specified liquid assets required by the authorities and there was no active trading in this paper. Institutions held to maturity what they acquired. None the less, some of the banks would have liked to see the issue of a short-term instrument like a Treasury bill, which could have been used as a basis for regulating the liquidity situation in the economy. Then, in mid-March 1990, an Exchange Fund Bills programme was launched. The Exchange Fund was first set up in 1935 and was gradually extended until it held the bulk of the Government's financial assets, including foreign reserves. Its statutory role is to influence the exchange value of the Hong Kong dollar, which is pegged at HK$ 7.80 to the US dollar. For Exchange Fund Bills, the minimum denomination was HK$ 500,000, initially with a maturity of 91 days. Tenders were held weekly (on Tuesdays). From October 1990, 182-day Exchange Fund Bills were issued and on February 26, 1991, a programme for 364-day bills was also launched. Tenders for these bills were to be held once every 4 weeks. Exchange Fund Bills are issued solely for the purpose of monetary policy. They cannot be used for financing government expenditure or fiscal deficits. In this respect, they differ from Treasury bills issued elsewhere. Exchange Fund Bills represent debt for the account of the Exchange Fund; the funds borrowed are not available for the general purposes of government finance. Exchange Fund operations have been described as follows:

> With the launching of the Exchange Fund Bills programme in mid-March 1990, the Exchange Fund operates more frequently in the local money market. Under normal circumstances, the operations are either for the purpose of relieving a shortage of liquidity arising from a take-up of Exchange Fund Bills or to mop up surplus liquidity arising from a redemption of these bills. But if the need arises, the Exchange Fund may, through under-or over-compensating the effect of the issue or redemption of Exchange Fund Bills, or through buying or selling these bills in the secondary market, produce a level of interbank liquidity that is appropriate for ensuring exchange rate stability.[5]

On March 6, 1991, the Financial Secretary also announced in the 1991/92 Budget Speech that it was his intention further to develop the government debt market by a modest programme of short-term bonds denominated in Hong Kong dollars. Bonds were to be issued under the Loans Ordinance (Cap. 61) and the proceeds were to be credited to the Capital Works Reserve Fund or the Capital Investment Fund for the financing of capital expenditure, subject to the necessary resolutions being passed by the Legislative Council from time to time. Pursuant to Section 5 of the Loans Ordinance (Cap. 61), any sum borrowed under the Ordinance and all interest or charges thereon were to be charged upon, and would be payable out of, the general revenues and assets of Hong Kong.

In the first instance, bonds of 2 years to maturity were to be issued normally at quarterly intervals, or at such time as the Financial Secretary might determine. The ceiling for the amount to be borrowed under this bond programme was to be determined by a Resolution passed by the Legislative Council. In addition to the 2-year bonds, bonds of other maturities might be offered from time to time at the discretion of the Financial Secretary. The specific amounts and maturities of bonds on offer at each tender were to be announced at least 4 business days in advance.[6] The Hong Kong Government bond programme was introduced in November 1991. The proceeds could be used to finance capital expenditure.

In June 1991, it was also announced that Hong Kong intended to enter the international bond market in the final 3 months of 1991 with an issue of about HK$ 500 million maturing in 2 or 3 years. The Government would test the market for about a year before deciding whether to launch 5–7 year bonds. These would need approval from China because they would mature after the UK relinquished sovereignty in 1997. The plan is designed to expand Hong Kong's role as a financial centre by developing a debt market. It will also help finance government spending (e.g. on a new international airport). It is hoped that the value issued will be sufficient to provide the basis of a secondary market.[7]

FINANCIAL FUTURES

Hong Kong has also experimented with futures. The Hong Kong Commodity Exchange (now known as the Hong Kong Futures Exchange) was established in 1977. It operates commodity futures markets of cotton (no trading has taken place in recent years), sugar, soybeans, and gold, in addition to the Hang Seng Stock Exchange Index Futures.

Following a sharp fall on Wall Street on 16 October 1987, the Hang Seng Index fell by more than 400 points on 19 October. This was followed by a record fall of over 500 points in New York later that same day after the Hong Kong market had closed. On 20 October, the General Committee of the Stock Exchange unanimously decided to suspend trading for 4 days to enable all outstanding transactions to be settled in accordance with the trading rules of the Exchange. Following the Stock Exchange decision to suspend trading, the Hong Kong Futures Exchange also suspended trading for the same period. The sharp fall in the Hang Seng Index on 19 October and the expected further crash on the re-opening of the Stock Exchange, pointed to the possibility of defaults by those investors who had gone long in the Hang Seng Futures market. This raised serious doubts as to whether the Hong Kong Futures Guarantee Corporation, which guarantees payment on all contracts executed on the Futures Exchange, would be able to meet its obligations.

If the Guarantee Corporation were to collapse, the Futures Exchange would not be able to operate, or re-open. There were close links with the Futures Exchange, which provided a hedging device for physical holdings of shares by mainly international investors. If the Futures Exchange were unable to re-open, the hedging device would be lost and shareholders would dump stocks, further depressing the market.

A rescue package was put together on 25 October 1987. The main element of the package was a credit facility of HK$ 2 billion to the Guarantee Corporation, of which HK$ 500 million was provided by the Guarantee Corporation's six shareholders and HK$ 500 million by a number of members of the Futures Exchange. The remaining HK$ 1 billion was provided by the Exchange Fund on a last-in-first-out basis. When the stock market was re-opened on 26 October, the Hang Seng Index plunged 1,120 points and another credit facility of HK$ 2 billion was extended to the Guarantee Corporation. Of this HK$ 2 billion, HK$ 1 billion was provided by the Government through the Exchange Fund, and the remaining HK$ 1 billion by the Hongkong and Shanghai Bank, the Standard Chartered Bank, and the Bank of China. The second facility was never utilized. As a result of the support operation, the system remained intact, and both the stock and futures markets subsequently returned to orderly trading.

Wide ranging structural and operational reforms were introduced, including guarantee and clearing corporations. This was achieved under the guidance of a Canadian from Winnipeg – Mr Douglas Ford – but he failed to expand the business of the exchange and was replaced by Mr Gary Knight, a US options specialist from Chicago. The main product of the exchange relates to futures on the local Hang Seng Stock Exchange Index, but business is slow. There is also only limited trading in soybeans, sugar, and gold. In order to boost business, in July 1991, the exchange introduced the first of a series of contracts based on sub-indices of the Hang Seng Stock Market Index. But interest-rate and currencies futures have been slow in developing.[8]

FOREIGN EXCHANGE MARKET

The other main money market sector in Hong Kong – certainly as important as the inter-bank market – is the foreign exchange market (FOREX) and, related to this, the Asian dollar market. In the FOREX market, much of the business is done through brokers – and especially the international brokers like Astley and Pearce, and Marshalls, which regularly provide prices for Tokyo and Singapore and, later in the day, for London and New York. Brokers are used because on the whole the rates that can be obtained are better. Some local brokers will act as an intermediary for transactions between HK dollars and US dollars, but not for other currencies.

The foreign exchange market is a completely free market; even the nominal exchange control on sterling area transactions had been terminated as far back as 1 January 1973. Virtually all the licensed banks and the larger DTCs offer foreign-exchange facilities. In addition, there are many authorized foreign-exchange dealers and money changers that buy and sell foreign currencies. Very approximately, it is said that the normal daily volume of such transactions in Hong Kong is about US$ 50 billion, of which the US$–DM and US$–Yen contracts are the most actively traded.

Currency swaps are also commonly employed. Banks in Hong Kong buy US dollars with HK dollars and sell forward (say, for 3 months). The banks may then use the US dollars for on-lending to customers who have need of US dollars. Alternatively, spot US dollars may be sold for HK dollars, and forward cover may be arranged to avoid the exchange risk; only an interest rate risk will then be involved. Currency swaps may likewise be done on a syndicated basis – for 12 months up to 9 years. Such swaps are sometimes more fashionable than on other occasions. One might note, too, that not always do banks switch spot to forward, especially in the short term; banks do quite often take a risk on the exchange rate.

Again, a swap mechanism exists in the inter-bank market, through which the non-British foreign banks and DTCs may obtain HK dollar funds by selling US dollars with an agreement to repurchase them at a fixed price at a future date. The price reflects the market deposit rate and the associated risks involved. This is also a means of providing a link between the inter-bank market and the FOREX market. It is greatly facilitated by the complete absence of exchange control and the liberal policy attitude of the Government towards the financial sector and the economy. There is complete freedom in the movement of funds both into and out of the territory and at all times. Indeed, Hong Kong's approach to financial development differs from that of Singapore in that Hong Kong relies basically on the spontaneous initiatives of the private sector. The Government merely provides the general framework within which the financial processes operate.

Hong Kong, Tokyo, and Singapore markets all open about the same time – 8.00 a.m. in Hong Kong and 9.00 a.m. in Tokyo – so that the three centres are virtually in the same time zone, and banks and DTCs can either come to the market for money in Hong Kong, or in Singapore, or in Tokyo. London opens at 3.30 p.m. to 4.30 p.m. local Hong Kong time and Hong Kong banks can either telephone London direct or go through brokers (which many of them do). This business lasts until 5.00 p.m. to 6.00 p.m. In the evening – local time 7.30 p.m. to 8.30 p.m. – the New York market opens and business begins again. The FOREX market is not open on Saturdays, though there may be occasional transactions of HK dollars against US dollars for settlement on the Monday.

It remains to consider Hong Kong's role in the Asian dollar market, which derived from the Eurodollar market that grew up in the 1950s based on the acceptance of dollar-claim deposits by banks (mostly in Europe) and the lending of these claims to other customers, usually for short periods. The development of this market (then largely based in London) was stimulated by non-resident convertibility of sterling, which came at the end of 1958 (non-residents could exchange European currencies without restriction into dollars). Similar operations also came to be carried out in claims to non-European currencies. The concept of an Asian dollar market had been under consideration since the early 1960s, when it was recognized that US dollar and other currency holdings of residents in Asia could be pooled and used more effectively. It dates from 1968 when the Singapore government decided to abolish withholding tax on interest paid to non-residents on their foreign-currency deposits with approved banks. This move attracted borrowers and lenders of US dollars and other foreign currencies to form the nucleus of the market. Asian dollar-type transactions were also undertaken in Tokyo and Hong Kong, but the Asian dollar market came to be most closely associated with Singapore, where its development was fostered by the authorities who created an environment conducive to its growth.

Singapore undoubtedly stole a march on Hong Kong in 1968 in abolishing withholding tax on interest paid to non-residents on their offshore deposits. Hong Kong did not abolish a similar tax until March 1982. Once that had been done, Hong Kong – with its absence of exchange control – greatly expanded its Asian dollar operations. It is true that in 1978 a new tax of 17 per cent had been introduced and applied to the net offshore earnings of financial institutions based in Hong Kong and obtained without the substantial intervention of a branch elsewhere, but although the tax attracted some protests from the banking community it did not produce the dire consequences predicted by its opponents. After an initial decline, offshore loans arranged in Hong Kong resumed their rapid trend upwards. With effect from 1 April 1984, the locality of the business carried on, rather than the physical location of the moneys lent, was used to determine the true territorial source of interest income accruing to businesses. As a result, sums received or accruing by way of interest to businesses carried on in Hong Kong were now chargeable to profits tax, irrespective of the currency in which the transactions were denominated and notwithstanding that the moneys in respect of which the interest was received or accrued was made available to borrowers outside Hong Kong.

Through the agency of the Asian dollar market, funds are raised for offshore lending, a lot of which is done in the Pacific area – e.g. South East Asia, the People's Republic of China, Korea, Australia, and New Zealand, mostly to governments and government agencies, but also to some big private companies; loans are also 'booked' in South America and in Eastern Europe, but the main area is the

Pacific. Some loans are made by individual banks; but others are syndicated – loans are made by a number of banks acting in concert and led by a *chef de file* or 'lead bank'. Banks also fund themselves in US dollars – the Japanese banks in particular are mainly takers of money – and these moneys can either be on-lent as US dollars or swapped into HK dollars for lending in Hong Kong. Whether a bank uses domestic dollars and/or Euro- or Asian dollars for its funding – on an interchangeable basis – depends on expectations with regard to interest rates and foreign-exchange rates. Much the same is true where there is a 'matching' of borrowing and lending transactions.

POSTSCRIPT

A further development of the arrangements referred to at p. 325 was the opening – as from 8 June 1992 – of a discount window to be administered by the Office of the Exchange Fund. It is referred to as the 'liquidity adjustment facility' and will enable banks to make late adjustments to their liquidity positions. Overnight funds are normally provided to banks through repurchase agreements against their holdings of exchange fund bills and Hong Kong government bonds. The Director of the Office of the Exchange Fund has also been given power to make unsecured loans, though necessarily subject to scrutiny of a bank's liquidity experience and its prudence over time. The discount window is open from 4.00 p.m. to 5.00 p.m. on weekdays and from 11.30 a.m. to noon on Saturdays to allow banks to correct undesired shortages or excesses of liquidity. However, the facility is not to be regarded as a substitute for prudent liquidity management and banks are therefore not expected to make use of the liquidity adjustment facility on a regular basis. To encourage prudence, the bid and offered rates were initially set each day at a 2 percentage point spread – i.e. a wide spread that would penalize banks if they made frequent use of the facility. Banks can also lend moneys to the Exchange Fund through this facility whenever – late in the day – they hold an excess of funds.[9]

Chapter 11

Money markets in India[1]

In India, all the larger commercial banks have been nationalized. The State Bank of India (SBI) still has a small number of private shareholders (about 7 per cent of its shares are held by private individuals) as do four of the seven associated banks (the other three are fully owned by SBI). Public-sector commercial banks include the fourteen large commercial banks nationalized in 1969 and the six commercial banks nationalized in 1980. These (with the SBI Group) account for over 90 per cent of aggregate deposits of all commercial banks in India. Hence, the remaining banks must be small.

The regional rural banks were set up under the Regional Rural Bank Act 1975 to provide institutional credit to rural people; they are mostly sponsored by one or other of the nationalized commercial banks and have increased rapidly in number over recent years. In particular, they have served to increase the flow of credit to small borrowers in rural areas. They have a specified area of operations – usually limited to one or more districts; staff are recruited locally.

Scheduled banks are banks included in the second schedule of the Reserve Bank of India Act (see Table 11.1) and having paid-up capital and reserves of not less than Rs 5 lakhs = Rs 500,000. The rate of exchange (February 1991) was approximately Rs 50 = £1 sterling. Non-scheduled commercial banks numbered three. The total number of banks in India (at mid-1991) was 298.

In addition, the community is served by a network of co-operative banks – at end-August 1990 there were 28 State co-operative banks (of which 14 were scheduled banks), 338 central co-operative banks, and 1,392 primary co-operative banks (as at end-1990), of which 14 were scheduled urban co-operative banks. The basis of this superstructure was 87,305 primary agricultural credit societies

Table 11.1   Scheduled banks in India (as on 30 June 1991)

State Bank of India Group	8
Other public sector scheduled commercial banks	20
Foreign banks	24
Other scheduled commercial banks	19
Scheduled State co-operative banks	14
Scheduled urban co-operative banks	14
Regional rural banks	196

Source: Reserve Bank of India

and 28,807 primary non-agricultural credit societies (as at June 1989). These institutions mainly provide short-term credit. The medium- and long-term credit institutions in the co-operative sector comprise central land development banks and about 900 primary land development banks. These banks are supplemented – particularly in South India – first, by *chit funds*, which accept and pay interest on monthly deposits against which it is only possible to draw by way of loan (money can also be borrowed against fixed assets) and, second, by *nidhis*, which are mutual loan societies which have developed into semi-banking institutions, but which only deal with their member shareholders.

In India, there is also still a large but unknown number of indigenous bankers and moneylenders, who – particularly in the rural parts of India – continue to provide part of the available banking and quasi-banking services. However, initially in the form of the 'social' control of banking and then with the nationalization of the largest Indian commercial banks, the commercial banks accelerated the opening of more branches in rural and semi-rural areas in order to complement the facilities already offered by the SBI (and its associated banks) and by the co-operatives.

THE INTER-BANK MONEY MARKET

The core of the Indian money market structure is the inter-bank call money market, which is centralized primarily in Bombay, but with sub-markets in Delhi, Madras, and Calcutta. All the major banks have large networks of branches. Information about the cash/deposit position is fed into regional and zonal offices and through these into Bombay; there is also a certain amount of forecasting with respect to required cash reserves (since 4 May 1991 an incremental cash reserve ratio – 10 per cent of the increase in net demand and time liabilities over the level as of 3-May 1991 – was added to the then existing 15 per cent of net demand and time liabilities). The statutory liquidity ratio (SLR) is based on the position a fortnight earlier. On the whole, both the big banks and the smaller ones know their position for the day either the night before or early next morning (say, by 10.00 a.m.), but because movements of funds can be quite large during the course of a day, adjustments have to be effected virtually up to the time the market closes.

The Discount and Finance House of India (DFHI), which began operations on 25 April 1988, acts as a market-maker, and to a certain extent as a broker in the inter-bank market. Its head office is in Bombay with regional offices in Calcutta, Madras, Delhi, Ahmedabad, and Bangalore.

Institutions permitted to participate in the inter-bank market for call loans and money at notice are all the scheduled commercial banks, the co-operative banks, and the DFHI. Certain other parties – including the leading non-bank financial institutions and a number of the large mutual funds – are permitted to participate in this market only as lenders.

In order to widen the call/notice money market, also the bills rediscounting market, it was decided in 1991 to provide access to these markets – as lenders – of those institutions able to provide evidence to the Reserve Bank of bulk lendable resources (with a minimum size of operations of Rs 20 crores[2] per transaction, such transactions only to be permitted through the DFHI. It was necessary, too, to give an undertaking that such potential lenders had no outstanding borrowings from the banking system.

There used to be a ceiling on interest rates in the inter-bank market. This was abandoned as from 1 May 1989 'with a view to greater transparency and flexibility'. In line with this change, interest rate ceilings on inter-bank term money, the discounting of commercial bills, and inter-bank participations without risk were also withdrawn.

If banks wish to borrow at the Reserve Bank of India (RBI), they would normally do this by 2.45 p.m. – they have a limit up to which they can borrow at any time. This would be at Bank rate. Formerly, they also enjoyed various refinance facilities (e.g. refinance against 182-day Treasury bills, standby and discretionary finance, and food credit finance); as from 9 October 1991, these have now been withdrawn. In the event of any mopping up being required, the RBI could increase the minimum reserve cash requirement (if semipermanent action needed to be taken), or banks could themselves 'mop up' by putting moneys into Treasury bills.

For many years, the major lender was the SBI – its figures used to represent upwards of 50 per cent of the market. Latterly, the dominant lender has been the Unit Trust of India (UTI). Other significant lenders are the Life Insurance Corporation (LIC) and the General Insurance Corporation of India (GIC). The North Indian banks based on Delhi – even the small ones – are lenders (this is a surplus area) and, although the South of India is a deficit area, two of the big banks with head offices in Madras are for the most part also lenders. Very often, banks with head offices other than in Bombay will do the bulk of their lending in Bombay and banks with head offices elsewhere will usually do their borrowing in Bombay through their main branch there.

Although by no means as pronounced as it once was, there is still a busy season in India (e.g. in tea, jute, and sugar), but the economy is becoming more diversified (with the increased import- ance of industries like engineering and pharmaceuticals) and the effects increasingly diffused. The busy season lasts from November to April, when there is a return flow of government funds (e.g. in the form of government grants). There is still financial stringency (e.g. in March), which is probably felt more in Calcutta, but it is no longer an acute situation. Also, because of faster communications, money flows readily from one sector to another (even if rates in Bombay still tend to be lower than in Calcutta).

In the inter-bank money market, one finds that, although it varies from time to time and from bank to bank, more than half the money is lent overnight and the remainder at call (for up to 14 days), though in the latter case, too, the money may be lent virtually overnight since the rate will be reconsidered each day and the loan runs on until it is called. At the end of 14 days, moneys must be repaid before being reborrowed. Usually, such moneys run on for 2 or 3 days with a maximum of 1 week. All inter-bank money loans are unsecured, but they are subject to internal limits, i.e. limits are not communicated to the borrowing banks. The resort to limits is not just a matter of spreading the risk. The main lenders also have to supply funds to so many banks and resort to limits is one way of spreading the money around. Unsatisfied customers can then try somebody else.

THE BILL DISCOUNT MARKET

A leading alternative to the inter-bank money market is the bill discount market, where bills can be rediscounted up to lines granted to individual banks usually by the specialized institutions. This is usually more expensive than inter-bank money. Steps have also been taken to encourage greater use of bill finance (e.g. by creating usance promissory notes on the basis of genuine trade bills already rediscounted, remitting stamp duty on these derivative usance promissory notes and on short-dated usance bills of exchange, and restricting cash credits and overdrafts).

The bill discount market is regularly in use. Most banks – large and small – are participants, including the foreign banks (which in any event because of restrictions on branches lack an adequate deposit base). First-class paper is rediscounted with specialist institutions (e.g. LIC, GIC, and UTI) that often have large pools of money available that they wish to invest short-term. The documents do not change hands and are held by the borrowing bank to the order of the lending institution, which is given a declaration or certificate that the relevant bills are held to its order by the rediscounting bank.

TREASURY BILLS

For a long time, Treasury bills did not play a significant role in Indian money market arrangements. Although there had previously been a weekly auction, from 12 July 1965 onwards 3-month Treasury bills were not issued by auction or tender, but sold on tap at administered rates, which since 1974 had been unchanged at 4.6 per cent. These were rediscountable without limit at the RBI. Practice tended to be for banks to place in Treasury bills any large amounts of unexpectedly temporarily available funds for which no obvious alternative existed (e.g. an excess of reserve balances at the end of a reserve period). However, from 28 October 1986, a 182-day Treasury bill was introduced on the basis of a monthly (after June 1988 a fortnightly) auction, but without any rediscounting facilities at the RBI. The new instrument provides an alternative avenue for short-term investments and it was the intention that an active secondary market be developed in the course of time. In the result, major participants in the auction were the Indian public-sector banks, the foreign banks, the National Bank for Agriculture and Rural Development (NABARD), DFHI, and the Deposit Insurance and Credit Guarantee Corporation, but business corporations and individuals might also apply. On the other hand, LIC, GIC, and UTI were not active in the primary market for 182-day Treasury bills (3-month Treasury bills continued to be issued on tap and at an administered rate).

Much of the credit for the success of the 182-day Treasury bill tender must go to the developing role of the DFHI as marketmaker. Its main objective was to facilitate the smoothing out of short-term liquidity imbalances and to assist in the creation of a more active money market by integrating its various segments. To this end, it maintained a close relationship with the RBI, the commercial banks, and other Indian financial institutions. In the context of Treasury bills, it participated actively in the primary auctions but also traded in the secondary market by quoting two-way prices with fine spreads. As a result of its dealings in these bills, the DFHI has come to play a vital role in developing a secondary market in this instrument. Also, since April 1988, and up to certain limits, the RBI has extended a refinance facility to the DFHI against the collateral of 182-day Treasury bills. In addition, there is now a further refinance facility against commercial bills and derivative usance promissory notes with unexpired usances not exceeding 90 days. By end-1991, DFHI could borrow from RBI up to an overall limit of Rs 1,500 crores. By varying the quantum and the rate of interest on refinance to the DFHI, the RBI has also been able to transmit signals to the short-term money market.

GOVERNMENT BONDS

Unfortunately, there is not much of a secondary market in government bonds. Some switches are done in search of better deals, but for the most part these represent the substitution of new government securities at higher rates for old securities that are absorbed by the RBI and virtually disappear from the market. Switches may also be done by institutions other than the RBI. Furthermore, regular switches into new securities may be a means of 'gradualizing' the associated depreciation. The only real utility of government securities from a bank liquidity point of view (apart from eligibility in the statutory liquidity ratio) was as a basis for repurchase agreements, but these have now been restricted.

OTHER MONEY MARKET INSTRUMENTS

In more recent years, a number of other money market instruments have been introduced. Thus, the negotiable certificate of deposit (NCD) was introduced in March 1989 to be issued by scheduled commercial banks (other than the regional rural banks) for maturities of not less than 3 months or for more than 1 year. These were transferable by endorsement and delivery, but only after 45 days from date of issue. There was little activity in the secondary market. Such CDs tend to be held to maturity. Again, subject to eligibility criteria and a credit rating, commercial paper (on the American model) could be issued from 1 January 1990 for maturities of 3–6 months. There is a small secondary market. The issue of 'inter-bank participations' with risk sharing also exists, but the amounts are not large.

THE FOREIGN EXCHANGE MARKET

It is appropriate to consider next within the framework of Indian money market arrangements the foreign exchange market, where FOREX brokers operate and are important. There are about sixteen active FOREX brokers in Bombay. Brokers also operate in other smaller centres such as Calcutta, Delhi, Madras, Cochin, Bangalore, and Ahmedabad. The total is fifty to fifty-five operating across India (some are in more than one centre). Of these, only ten firms are in the first category. The rest are small or medium-sized. Commissions are fixed on the basis of value by the Foreign Exchange Association of India and on the recommendation of RBI, which imposes guidelines. (Brokerage rates were revised downwards on 1 July 1991, when the rupee was devalued.)

The main means of communication between markets in India is by teleprinter and STD. Markets are also linked by telex connections and brokers have direct lines to all the banks. There are also Reuters monitor screens. The Bombay market opens at 9.10 a.m., when the RBI announces the rupee/sterling rate on the basis of which all the other rates are calculated. Operations continue until around 4.00 p.m. There is only a very thin market after that, with a limited amount of activity up to 7.00 p.m. by way of purchases abroad (e.g. in London or New York). Some banks also deal in immigrant remittances up to 5.00 or 6.00 p.m. with banks coming in from overseas. There is no business on Saturdays, when the 'back-up' work has to be done.

In earlier years, only the British exchange banks undertook FOREX transactions. Subsequently, Bank of India, Central Bank of India, and SBI entered the market. By mid-1991, there were 76 banks that had been authorized to deal in the FOREX market, of which 28 were public sector banks, 3 were large co-operative banks, and 26 foreign banks (British, US, Japanese and West German, also French, Dutch, Canadian, and Middle East). There were also 19 Indian private sector banks. By 1991, commercial business was transacted in an approximate ratio of 65 : 35 Indian banks to foreign banks, with SBI handling about 70 per cent of the commercial business done by Indian banks. On the other hand, FOREX trading tends to be in the ratio of 30 : 70 Indian banks to foreign banks. Communications have improved and they tend to be very good internationally. The Indian FOREX market has become increasingly sophisticated over the years since 1984 and – even though volume is restricted – dealers have developed an expertise comparable with other markets around the world.

THE INDIGENOUS INSTITUTIONS

Before proceeding further, a word should be said about the indigenous institutions. Reference has already been made to chit funds and nidhis. These are not important for the money market as such, though they do absorb funds (as does the inter-company market) that might otherwise have fed into the banking system. A more obvious money market institution is the *Multani shroff*. Formerly, and indeed into the 1960s and the early 1970s, the Multani shroff lent money to customers by discounting a hundi (which was originally in promissory note form) and then, after endorsement and by arrangement through a hundi broker, rediscounted with a scheduled bank up to limits agreed upon. Usually, the Multani had limits with several banks, the most important of these being the SBI, the Bank of India, and the Central Bank of India, but there were others. In this way, the Multani acted as an intermediary between the joint stock banks and the small trader – about whose creditworthiness the banks would not have any detailed information. In the Multani community today, hundis are not trade related; they represent finance or accommodation paper. The hundis are now drawn in bill of exchange form (accepted by the person who owes the money, though they may be payable to a third party). Nevertheless, they are still called a hundi. Over more recent years, limits for the rediscounting of hundis were no longer available from some banks and at other banks had been greatly reduced (certainly in real terms). By the mid-1980s, Multani limits for the rediscount of hundis had completely disappeared at SBI and other public-sector banks. However, the Multani shroff still operates and discounts hundis for small and medium-sized, even big traders, also for medium-sized industry. In fact, their coverage of economic activity is fairly extensive. Under an amendment to the banking law, the taking of deposits is now considerably restricted and has greatly hampered other shroffs, who continue to survive as commission agents. In accord with the new situation, the Multanis no longer accept deposits from the public – only from friends – and their trading is now based on their own capital (which they have increased by ploughing back profits, thereby offsetting the virtual withdrawal of bank finance). It was maintained that the Multanis still had sufficient capital resources to continue in business and discounting hundis would remain a significant part of their business. As well as Bombay, Multanis operate in a small way in Calcutta and Madras, but do not operate at all in Delhi. Multani shroffs are also active in financing the movement to the ports of crops from up-country areas (e.g. in central and southern India), though the competition from the wide-ranging branch network of the public sector and other banks must over the years have eaten greatly into their business. So far the Multanis have survived as part of the indigenous sector – the amount of lending against hundis has been maintained (capital has been increased to offset the loss of rediscount limits at the banks) – but it is rare these days to meet a young Multani. Most of their sons are tending to go into the professions, or technological employment, or other forms of business. One would expect therefore the Multani shroff gradually to disappear and in real terms their lending role is already tending to decline.

FURTHER DEVELOPMENT OF THE MONEY MARKET

In considering ways in which the Indian money markets might be developed further, there was first the question of the lopsidedness of the call money market, because of the presence of dominant lenders (formerly the SBI, latterly the UTI). The SBI for many years dominated the Indian banking scene. The extent to which it operated as banker for public-sector accounts provided it regularly – allowing for some ebb and flow – with huge amounts of cash, whereas the majority of other public-sector banks tended to be net borrowers. Now the UTI – which collects vast sums of money for the purpose of more permanent investment (like LIC, NABARD, and the Industrial Development Bank of India) – is a heavy and regular lender in the inter-bank call money market and inevitably dominates on the supply side. To some extent, as we have already seen, the position has been relieved by opening up the inter-bank money market to a wider range of lenders. Another way in which to achieve a greater degree of balance both in banking business and in the availability of deposits and cash could be to spread around among the other public-sector banks a high proportion of the public-sector moneys, with medium-sized public-sector accounts going to the less large public-sector banks. It is understood that this is already beginning to happen, but the process could certainly be accelerated. Better balance between banks could also be achieved by a number of mergers, such that there might be a reduction in the number of public sector banks from twenty-eight to, say, about eight (excluding banks in the SBI Group). Initially, this may make for less activity in the inter-bank market, since there would tend to be more offsetting of balances within individual institutions, but this would tend to be accompanied by a better balance of business between banks. Moreover, if 'black money' (arising out of unde-clared incomes that evade tax) was reduced in quantity (it is said to represent 18 per cent to 21 per cent of GDP) and the inter-company market in deposits became less important, more money would flow into and through the banking system resulting in a much higher degree of integration and a consolidation of markets.

Furthermore, if a complex of money markets were to emerge along these lines with a wide range of participants and a broader market comprehending a large number of types of instruments, possibly even a market greatly expanded in volume, there would be a strong case for restoring the money broker to his former role and 'approving' several brokers in addition to the DFHI. But above all there would need to be a progressive and considerable improvement in communications. At the same time, it is one thing to perceive the direction that changes should take; there needs also to be a will to change and that there now seems to be.

Chapter 12

The money market in Singapore

Because of its geographic position – and for many years – Singapore has served as an entrepôt for its region, and banks played a key role in financing the growing volume of regional trade that passed through its port. The entrepôt factor may be less true today, but it is still important. Almost inevitably, the development of financial markets and institutions owed much to the role of Singapore as an international trading centre. Latterly, too, with independence in 1965, the financial sector in Singapore also played an important part in stimulating the growth of local industry. On these bases, a strategy was developed to establish Singapore as an international financial centre.

MONETARY AUTHORITIES

To this end, the Monetary Authority of Singapore (MAS) was established and began operations on 1 January 1971. It is responsible for formulating and implementing Singapore's monetary and exchange rate policies. Under various legislative provisions, it also regulates and monitors the activities of institutions in the financial sector. It acts as banker to and financial agent of the Government. In this context, it manages the public debt and acts for the Government in issuing all government securities. It conducts regular auctions of Treasury bills and other government securities, other participants being the banks, the government securities dealers, and the public. It is authorized to buy, sell, discount, and rediscount Treasury bills, government securities, bills of exchange, and other securities. It also provides rediscounting facilities for export and pre-export bills. It provides banking facilities to commercial banks and finance companies, which maintain current account balances with MAS partly to satisfy statutory minimum cash requirements (from 21 May 1987 the minimum liquid assets ratio was reduced from 20 per cent to 18 per cent. In the new liquidity structure, there is no tiering of liquid assets); the banks' current accounts are also used for the daily settlement of net balances between banks as a result of the centralized clearing of cheques, remittances, and government securities transactions. Finance companies maintain accounts with MAS for the sole purpose of meeting their statutory minimum cash requirements, which are regularly adjusted for changes in their deposit liabilities. So far as the issue of currency is concerned (notes and coin), this is entrusted to a separate currency board – The Board of Commissioners of Currency of Singapore – the Singapore dollar being 100 per cent backed by external assets.

As already indicated, MAS is responsible for the formulation and implementation of monetary and exchange-rate policies. The conduct of monetary policy in Singapore is constrained by the openness of the economy and its considerable network of international financial linkages, which result in a high degree of capital mobility and a close relationship between domestic and foreign interest rates. Hence, the policy emphasis, particularly in the 1980s, has been on the exchange rate, rather than on the domestic money supply, or on interest rates.

Exchange-rate policy is formulated with the primary objective of maintaining domestic price stability. The Singapore dollar is monitored in terms of a basket of currencies of Singapore's major trading partners and allowed to float within a broad band. MAS intervenes in the foreign exchange market:

> to maintain the currency basket within the band, to counter excessive speculation and to smooth out sharp day-to-day fluctuations. Intervention is done mainly through the purchase or sale of US dollars. Traditionally, the Singapore dollar has been underpinned by strong capital inflows and the high domestic savings rate generated by budgetary surpluses and net contributions to the Central Provident Fund.[1]

To complement its exchange rate policy, MAS conducts money-market operations to ensure there is an appropriate level of liquidity in the banking system. The instruments used are mainly foreign exchange swaps and overnight loans (often made on the basis of repurchase agreements – 'repos'). MAS can also influence liquidity and interest rates by varying the net amount of Treasury bills auctioned weekly. A larger issue may be introduced to mop up excess liquidity and, conversely, a smaller issue will be introduced when an easier monetary policy is desired. With the issue of government securities at market rates and the development of a more active secondary market in goverment securities after May 1987, MAS now has an additional instrument on the basis of which to conduct monetary policy.

FINANCIAL INSTITUTIONS

Commercial banking in Singapore goes back to 1840, when the Union Bank of Calcutta was established. It was soon followed by banks from other countries – the UK, the Netherlands, France, and the US. These banks were primarily concerned with international banking and concentrated on providing documentary services and short-term finance related to imports and exports (including re-exports). The first local bank set up specifically to serve the needs of local businessmen came in 1903, but it had its difficulties and was liquidated in 1913. However, other local banking entrepreneurs followed, the oldest of these banks (and still in existence) being the Four Seas Communications Bank. Other local banks set up in 1912–19 were amalgamated in 1932 to form the present Oversea-Chinese Banking Corporation (OCBC). Local banks provided services complementary to those of the foreign banks, on which local businessmen and traders depended for their foreign exchange transactions. At the same time, foreign banks received deposits from local banks which collected domestic savings and deposits from the local community. More banks were established after World War II to assist in financing the reconstruction and rehabilitation of the economy. From the 1970s onwards, after the banking sector had been liberalized, many foreign banks began setting up in Singapore. Between 1970 and mid-1991, the number of foreign banks, primarily branches of large banks, increased from 25 to 122; at the same date, there were 135 commercial banks in Singapore, of which 13 were local. Table 12.1 shows the number of financial institutions in Singapore between 1987 and 1991.

Commercial banks in Singapore are licensed under the Banking Act. There are three different categories of banks: full licence banks, restricted licence banks, and offshore licence banks. All three categories of banks may apply for special approval to set up separate bookkeeping units known as Asian currency units (ACUs) in order to operate in the Asian dollar market. The distinction between them relates to the various restrictions on their domestic banking business conducted through domestic banking units.

Table 12.1 Number of financial institutions in Singapore

	June 1987	June 1988	June 1989	June 1990	June 1991
Commercial banks	134	133	138	136	135
Local*	13	13	13	13	13
Foreign	121	120	125	123	122
Full banks	23	22	22	22	22
Restricted banks	14	14	14	14	14
Offshore banks	84	84	89	87	86
Banking offices including head offices/main offices	396	407	413	421	429
Merchant banks	59	62	67	68	74
Finance companies	31	31	28	28	27
Stockbroking companies	40	45	52	59	65
Local companies	24	24	25	26	26
Foreign companies	16	21	27	33	39
Investment advisers	14	27	49	66	84
Insurance companies	100	101	115	127	136
International money brokers	8	8	8	8	7
Simex members	72	79	80	78	74
Corporate clearing members	30	35	36	38	37
Corporate non-clearing members	42	44	44	40	37

Note: *All local banks are full banks
Source: Monetary Authority of Singapore

Banks with restricted licences may engage in the whole range of domestic banking business as for the full licence banks, except that they cannot operate savings accounts or accept fixed deposits of less than S$ 250,000 (or its equivalent) per deposit from non-bank customers; also, they cannot open any sub-branches in Singapore. Offshore banking licences were created in recognition of the scope for more operators in the Asian dollar market and to strengthen further the financial linkages with international banks abroad. In addition to the restrictions on restricted licence banks, offshore licence banks may not accept any interest-bearing deposits from resident non-bank customers and are currently subject to a limit of S$ 50 million on total credit facilities extended to resident non-bank customers. The first offshore licence bank was established in 1973; as at mid-1991, there were eighty-six such banks.

There are also merchant banks, first established in Singapore in the early 1970s. As a group, merchant banks are not homogeneous and their areas of operation are influenced by the interests of their shareholders and their expertise in various fields. Their activities include offshore banking, corporate finance, underwriting of share and bond issues, mergers and acquisitions, portfolio investment management, management consultancy, and other fee-based activities. Generally, their activities tend to complement those of the commercial banks. At mid-1991, there were 74 merchant banks in Singapore.

Finance companies go back further. The majority were established in the 1950s to undertake the small-scale financing in which the banks were not interested. This included instalment credit for motor vehicles and consumer durables, and mortgage loans for housing. At the time, finance companies were not regulated or licensed. With the growth in their activities, concern developed over the lack of proper control and protection for depositors. As a consequence, the Finance Companies Act 1967 was passed and only finance companies granted licences were now permitted to operate. Several of the smaller companies merged, while some – unable to meet the capital requirements and other provisions – ceased operations. When the Act came into effect in January 1968, there were thirty-six finance companies. By mid-1991, there were twenty-seven.

THE MONEY MARKET

Originally, the domestic money market in Singapore was comprised of two interrelated markets – the inter-bank market and the discount market. The discount market as such really derived from the establishment of discount houses in September 1971,[2] and was where short-term money market instruments were issued, traded and discounted. The instruments included Treasury bills, Singapore dollar negotiable certificates of deposit (S$NCDs), bills of exchange, short-term commercial paper, and short-dated government securities. The major participants were banks, discount houses, money brokers, and the MAS. When the government securities market was restructured in May 1987, the discount houses ceased to exist and the 'discount market' – what was left of it – became a much more diffuse affair, with the several groups of financial institutions (but primarily the banks) as its participants, with some dealings in bills discounted, S$NCDs, and commercial paper. However, secondary markets in these items tend to be small and, for the most part, such paper would usually be held to maturity. Now the division of the domestic money market is between the inter-bank market and the government securities market (which would include also dealings in Treasury bills). However, the changeover was less than it might seem, since in the days of the discount houses, Treasury bills were their most important asset (over 46 per cent of the total at end-1985) and government securities over 20 per cent. Thus two-thirds of their assets consisted of government paper.[3]

The inter-bank market is in Singapore dollars only – the Asian dollar market and floating rate Asian dollar certificates of deposit are completely separate. The inter-bank market pre-dates the establishment of the discount houses in 1972 and also their predecessors, but at that stage the inter-bank market was not very well developed and operated largely on an 'old boy' basis. Today it is highly active with funds placed on an overnight basis, or for 1 week or longer, usually up to 12 months. Its participants include banks of all kinds, though merchant banks tend to be borrowers and usually pay a premium when borrowing inter-bank. Otherwise, local banks are largely lenders, while the foreign banks, particularly those with restrictions on their deposit collection, are frequent borrowers. Finance houses may lend to banks, but if a bank lends to a finance house, this is not an inter-bank transaction. Practice varies somewhat between banks, but in most cases banks tend to employ the services of money brokers in effecting both borrowing and lending transactions. Nevertheless, direct deals between the banks are done from time to time. These may come in, for example, as telex enquiries at the end of the day. Loans between banks are unsecured, but internal limits would be applied by one bank on loans to another, the limits reflecting degrees of creditworthiness.

In May 1987, as has been indicated, the government securities market was restructured. It was now modelled on the US Treasury bond market. Traditionally, in Singapore, government securities had a large primary market, but a relatively inactive secondary market. Originally, government securities carried interest rates set by the government. And, prior to July 1975, bank interest rates had themselves been determined by a cartel system, with prime lending and deposit rates agreed to by all banks.[4] After July 1975, with the introduction of S$NCDs that carried market-determined interest rates, banks were free to quote their own prime lending and deposit rates. Subsequently, all interest rates were liberalized. In addition, with the removal of the last vestiges of exchange control in 1978, domestic interest rates became more sensitive to movements in international interest rates. Then, in 1985, as part of its efforts to develop the financial sector, MAS embarked on a scheme to make the government securities market more active. Legislative amendments were passed to enable the Government to issue book entry (scripless) Singapore government securities on a regular basis and to restructure the market by introducing a new distribution network of government securities dealers, who were to be 'primary dealers'.

There were three major objectives for developing the government securities market: (a) to provide investors with another liquid investment alternative carrying no risk of default; (b) to establish a liquid secondary market which would serve as a benchmark for developing a corporate debt securities market; and (c) to encourage the development of skills relating to fixed-income securities and to broaden the spectrum of financial services available in Singapore. Under the scheme, the Government makes regular issues of varying amounts of securities which are auctioned to the public through primary dealers and carry market-determined interest rates. Investors can submit competitive bids or non-competitive bids through a primary dealer. Non-competitive bids are limited to S$ 500,000 per person and are allotted at the weighted average price and yield of the successful competitive bids. Government securities dealers now number seven; five are primary dealer divisions within a bank. These dealers replaced discount houses as market-makers in government securities.[5] The dealers are committed to making two-way quotes in all government securities and to ensuring liquidity in the market under all conditions. They are also required to apply for new issues of government securities in amounts corresponding to their share of turnover in the secondary market. All government securities dealers are approved by the MAS; they and the banks must, in addition to maintaining a cash settlement account with MAS, operate two other securities accounts – one for their own holdings and the other for their customers' holdings. All transactions of government securities involve only book entries in the accounting records. The timing, size, and maturities of government securities issues are influenced by market conditions, the investment needs of the Central Provident Fund, and the demands of financial institutions. There is a regular schedule of 2- and 5-year issues to meet the demands of financial institutions and the public. The Government continues to issue long-dated bonds primarily to cater for the needs of the CPF.

Treasury bills and all other government securities issues are auctioned. As indicated, the approved government securities dealers – the primary dealers – apply to subscribe to a new issue in proportion to their share of the market. They are subject to MAS guidelines and dealer activities are monitored regularly to ensure compliance. All other applications – whether for institutions or their customers – must go through a primary dealer (e.g. for non-dealer banks, or for a corporation, or a member of the public). The same system applies both to Treasury bills and to government bonds. The MAS may also apply from time to time for new issues (Treasury bills or bonds), but for domestic purposes only; these bids do not go through a primary dealer. The auctions for 91-day Treasury bills are weekly. For 182-day and 364-day Treasury bills, or for 2- and 5-year notes, there is usually a monthly auction by rotation for each of these categories, which will participate every fourth month – i.e. there will normally be three issues per annum for each of these categories in rotation. So far, MAS has always allocated the full amount of an issue. Except for issues to the Central Provident Fund (CPF), bond issues are not common. Issues to the CPF depend on their requirements and are done by way of a private placement at a rate pegged to savings and fixed deposit rates.

The primary dealers tender regularly and for significant amounts. As has been noted, they are required to apply for new issues of government securities in amounts corresponding to their share of turnover in the secondary market. Indeed, although there is no formal arrangement, it is understood that they will in effect underwrite the issues that come to the primary market. So far as their general business is concerned, all the primary dealers are required to submit regular returns to the MAS, which also monitors their activities. In addition, following the changes of May 1987, a Market Committee with representatives from financial institutions was formed to provide MAS with feedback on market conditions. When there were discount houses, they used to meet at MAS once a week on Thursday afternoons. Now the primary dealers meet there when there are matters to discuss and which concern the MAS, the primary dealers and the market. But at any time MAS may call up a primary dealer to ask them what they have done or are doing. Informal contacts of this kind are more or less an everyday occurrence.

Open market operations are employed with a view to influencing the liquidity of the system. As has been indicated, in this context the MAS resorts mainly to foreign-exchange swaps and overnight loans. The latter are often done on the basis of repurchase agreements ('repos'), where – to put money out – MAS would purchase securities under an agreement to re-sell to the primary dealers on an agreed date. If liquidity is to be absorbed, securities would be sold by MAS to the primary dealers and repurchased (say) the following day – a reverse 'repo'. Alternatively, MAS could sell them Treasury bills with a very short maturity. 'Repos' are much more important than outright purchases and sales by MAS. 'Repos' as a basis for open market operations would usually be overnight transactions (i.e. reversed the next day) and are done at market-related rates. Similarly, though nowadays they are resorted to less than 'repos', a swap out of (say) US dollars into Singapore dollars will add to domestic liquidity; a swap out of Singapore dollars into US dollars (or any other foreign currency) will reduce domestic liquidity and – as with 'repos' – both of these transactions can be reversed. They would usually be done with banks rather than with non-bank primary dealers. One might note, too, that while the rediscounting of export bills by MAS is not used primarily as a monetary instrument, it does affect liquidity.

One might also note that – following US experience – the usual (and main) way of financing primary dealer portfolios (or inventories) is by means of 'repos' (these are the cheapest source of finance available; they are also the most flexible) – they are usually done overnight, or (as a 'term repo') have a maturity of only a few days, but could be for up to one month.[6] The emphasis on 'repos' is reflected in the balance sheet of a primary dealer – assets are comprised of a portfolio of government paper; these are financed to a small extent by the firm's capital, but for the most part by 'repos'. Where a primary dealer operation represents part of a bank's business, the bank would not make a specific allocation of capital to the primary dealer function (theoretically one could call on the total capital funds of the bank as a whole).

The profits of a primary dealer are made largely by taking a 'position' (in its portfolio) on the basis of the firm's view of future movements in interest rates, which in Singapore – though they are much more flexible than they used to be – are not as volatile as in London or New York.[7] Where a financial institution – a bank or finance company – lends money by way of a 'repo' to a primary dealer, the amount involved will qualify as part of its liquidity requirement.

There are also active secondary markets for Treasury bills and government notes and bonds. Operators in these markets range more widely than the approved government securities dealers – the primary dealers – and include several of the non-dealer banks, which do not enjoy the same privileges as a primary dealer (such as the right to tender for new issues), but which offer two-way quotes in the secondary market; necessarily, the paper that they buy from the primary markets must be obtained through a primary dealer, who can tender direct. Clearly, too, the secondary markets are open to all financial institutions, non-financial corporations, and the general public.

Certain of these other institutions – mostly banks – may be approved by MAS as 'same-day dealers'; they operate for customer account, but can only participate in the auctions by submitting a bid through a primary dealer – the spread between bid and offer being 5 cents per S$ 100.

THE FOREIGN EXCHANGE MARKET

Until the early 1970s, the foreign exchange market in Singapore was rudimentary. Activity was confined largely to banks squaring their FOREX positions that resulted from dealings with non-bank customers. The then prevailing cartel system of exchange-rate quotation inhibited competition and stifled initiative and innovation in the market. With government support and the admission of foreign banks and international money brokers[8] in the 1970s, the foreign exchange market began to expand rapidly. The floating of the Singapore dollar and the abolition of cartel exchange rate quotations in 1973 provided further impetus to the development of the market. Over time, the scope of FOREX activities has expanded to cover spot and forward transactions as well as arbitrage operations in all currencies. Participants in the foreign exchange market include commercial banks, Asian Currency Units, merchant banks, international money brokers, central banks, and non-bank customers.

An important factor contributing to the development of the Singapore foreign exchange market is its time-zone advantage. In the morning, FOREX dealers and brokers in Singapore are able to deal with their counterparts in South East Asia, Japan, Australia and New Zealand. In addition, institutions in the US pass their overnight orders to branches or correspondents in Singapore to be executed in the morning. In the afternoon, dealers are able to enter into transactions with the Middle East and Europe. Activity has also been boosted by the development of financial futures trading in Singapore and the operations of a 'night shift' by several institutions. It has also benefited from a spillover from the growth in Tokyo's FOREX turnover following the liberalization of Japan's financial markets. Certain currencies tend to dominate the foreign exchange market in Singapore. Until June 1972, the pound sterling (to which the Singapore dollar was pegged) was the most widely traded currency. Following the switch to the US dollar as the intervention currency, the US dollar became predominant in the FOREX market. It is the currency against which all other currencies are quoted and from which other cross-rates are computed. The share of third currency transactions remains fairly small. Approximately 55 per cent of all trades were spot transactions. Swap transactions would amount to another 42 per cent, the remainder being accounted for by outright forward transactions.

MAS together with representatives from banks and money brokers continually reviews the development of the FOREX market. Practices adopted by participants are also monitored to promote higher standards of conduct among dealers and brokers. Also, the Singapore Foreign Exchange Market Committee (formed in March 1986) monitors the development of the market, and takes measures to encourage its continued growth and to enhance its stature and maintain its reputation; it also discusses technical issues and recommends standards where appropriate. With their consent, it may arbitrate in disputes between market participants and at all times serves as a channel for information and dialogue between them.

ASIAN DOLLAR MARKET

Much of Singapore's growth as an international financial centre is a reflection of the rapid growth of the Asian dollar market, which is the Asian counterpart of the Eurodollar market largely based in London. The Asian dollar market is an international money and capital market in foreign currencies. The major currencies transacted are the US dollar, the Deutschmark, Japanese yen, pound sterling, and Swiss franc. In the early 1960s, it was recognized that

US dollar and other foreign currency holdings of residents in Asia could be pooled and utilized more productively. There was growing confidence that – given appropriate support and incentives – a market similar to the Eurodollar market could be developed. As a site for this offshore market, Singapore offered several advantages. These included a sound financial infrastructure, an excellent communications network, a stable government, and a geographic location with a time-zone advantage. Transactions with Europe, the rest of the Far East, and the South West Pacific are possible within the same trading day.

To allow for better domestic monetary control, any financial institution seeking approval to operate in the Asian dollar market is required to set up a separate bookkeeping unit for such transactions. The unit designated as an Asian Currency Unit (ACU) is permitted to accept deposits from and lend to other ACUs, authorized banks, and non-residents in all currencies other than the Singapore dollar. Transactions with residents were initially subject to various restrictions, but these restrictions were removed with the liberalization of exchange control in June 1978. All restricted (14) and offshore (86) banks have approval to operate ACUs; 25 full banks (local and foreign), 73 merchant banks, and 1 investment institution also operated ACUs – the figures are for mid-1991.

The structure of the Asian dollar market closely resembles that of the Eurodollar market. Transactions are predominantly inter-bank, though transactions with non-bank customers may also be significant. This reflects the role of Singapore as a funding centre for the international activities of banks and as a base for interest arbitrage between financial centres and for the deployment of surplus funds. Inter-bank activites have been facilitated by the presence of eight international money brokers. The parallel development of the foreign exchange market has also provided important support.

Asian dollar credits are mainly short- and medium-term. Maturities tend to be for 1, 3, and 6 months and usually do not exceed 5 years; this reflects the large inter-bank sector. Dealings in longer-term loans, although they are increasing, are still small in relation to the overall size of the market. Over the years, the extension of credit in the form of syndicated credit facilities has become more important.

Asian dollar credits share many features with Euro-credits. They are usually provided on a 3-month or 6-month rollover basis and carry floating interest rates pegged either to the Singapore Inter-Bank Offered Rate (SIBOR) or to LIBOR in London. In the early years, LIBOR was preferred by both banks and non-bank customers. In recent years, it has tended to be SIBOR, with the ACUs quoting interest rates based on their assessment of market conditions each morning before the London market begins operations. While ACU quotes are influenced by London's closing rate for the previous day, SIBOR also influences LIBOR when the London market opens later in the day. And, in the course of the day, the flow of funds between the two centres tends to bring about a convergence of the two rates.

In line with international trends, the maturity of Asian dollar credits has shown a tendency to increase; this has been due to the greater liquidity of banks and the larger amount of loans to governments for financing either balance of payments deficits or development projects. ACUs have also been able to increase the size and maturity of their credits partly through increased participation in loan syndications. While the maturities of their assets and liabilities are fairly closely matched, ACUs perform a certain amount of maturity transformation or 'gapping' operations. Usually, however, they have to observe limits imposed by their head offices on gapping operations as well as on currency and country exposures. Although the US dollar predominates, over twenty foreign currencies are dealt with in the Asian dollar market, increasing interest being shown in the Japanese yen and the Deutschmark.

Financial institutions participating in the Asian dollar market come from the Association of South East Asian Nations (ASEAN) countries,[9] Hong Kong, Japan, other parts of Asia, Western Europe, the United States, Australia, and the Middle East. For the most part, the suppliers of funds are from Hong Kong, ASEAN countries, and Europe, while the users include Australia, the ASEAN countries, and Hong Kong.

In the early years, more than half the liabilities of the ACUs was in the form of non-bank deposits. In 1970, for example, non-bank deposits accounted for 63 per cent of the total, while inter-bank funds comprised about 36 per cent. Since then inter-bank funds have rapidly become dominant. By mid-1991, inter-bank funds constituted 79 per cent of liabilities, while non-bank deposits accounted for only 18 per cent.[10]

Non-bank depositors are mainly private individuals and multi-national corporations with foreign currency funds from sources such as trade and income from investments abroad. Regional central banks also deposit some of their official foreign exchange reserves in the Asian dollar market. The bulk of non-bank deposits is from non-residents.

On the assets side, the pattern was somewhat different. While inter-bank lending was dominant (and is still well over half), an increasing proportion of total lending has been channelled to non-bank users. Until 1970, loans to non-bank customers amounted to less than 5 per cent of total assets. At mid-1991, 36 per cent of ACU funds were lent to non-bank customers, while 55 per cent went to banks abroad and other ACUs.[11] The non-bank borrowers include multinational corporations, securities firms, resident companies engaged in the export trades, and foreign governments which need funds to finance development projects or to meet liquidity requirements.

Reflecting the worldwide trend towards securitization, there has been a shift towards fee-based and capital-market activities, and financial institutions have increasingly undertaken the managing and underwriting of debt securities. At the same time, there has emerged a number of new financial instruments. In the Asian dollar market, these include revolving underwriting facilities, floating rate notes, note issuance facilities, and Asian commercial paper.

There is also an Asian dollar bond market, but this is concerned to raise medium- and long-term capital. Borrowers are mainly from the Asia-Pacific countries and comprise banks (including development banks), multinational companies, and governments. In recent years, Japanese institutions have been very active as issuers and managers. Most Asian dollar bonds are denominated in US dollars. Besides straight bond issues, floating rate notes, convertible bonds, and bonds with warrants are also issued.

A number of tax incentives have also assisted in the development of the Asian dollar market. The first major tax concession granted to encourage its development was the waiving of withholding tax on deposit interest earned by non-residents in 1968. Other fiscal incentives have since been given to encourage banks to bring their offshore activities to Singapore. There have also been tax exemptions on interest received by non-residents on approved Asian dollar bonds, exemptions from estate duty on non-residents' deposits with ACUs and holdings of approved Asian dollar bonds and US$ NCDs. On other activities, there have been concessionary rates of tax and tax-exemption schemes (e.g. in 1983 to promote offshore loan syndication activities and for fund management). With the growing importance of trading in international securities, tax incentives were introduced in March 1987 to encourage the trading of foreign securities in Singapore. From 1988, there was exemption from stamp duty on these transactions.[12]

The MAS regulates and supervises activities in the Asian dollar market. ACUs are governed by the provisions of the Banking Act and the terms and conditions laid down from time to time by the MAS, to which monthly statements and other returns have to be submitted. Although ACUs are governed by the Banking Act, they are exempted from some of its provisions – such as the statutory liquidity requirements and the maintenance of minimum cash balances with MAS. The initial 20 per cent statutory liquidity ratio for ACUs was abolished in 1972 to bring the Asian dollar market into line with the Eurodollar market. After June 1978, following the liberalization of exchange control, ACUs have been permitted to accept time and call deposits from and make loans to both residents and non-residents, provided the transactions are in foreign currencies. ACUs may transact with other ACUs and with banks in and outside Singapore. Other activities that ACUs may engage in include investments in securities denominated in foreign currencies, dealings in foreign currencies, and FOREX trans-actions. They may also open and advise letters of credit and discount bills, and issue guarantees for any customer provided they are denominated in foreign currencies. The activities of the ACUs are constrained by the maximum size of their assets/liabilities as stipulated by MAS, though book size may be revised on application to MAS.

FINANCIAL FUTURES

Interest in establishing a financial futures market in Singapore began in the early 1980s. Apart from Australia (with its 90-day bank bill futures contract in October 1979), there were at that time no financial futures markets in the area, and the establishment of a market in Singapore was expected to facilitate round-the-clock trading in financial futures. Moreover, as an international financial centre, Singapore needed to provide a market for investors to hedge against interest and exchange risks.

To ensure a sufficient volume of transactions and liquidity, a linkage with a major US exchange was sought. Negotiations were commenced with the Chicago Mercantile Exchange (CME) and an agreement was reached in June 1984. A 'mutual offset' system was established, which would enable a position opened in one exchange to be transferred to, offset, or cancelled out in the other without having to pay additional margin in the second exchange. This was intended to reduce trading costs and extend the trading period because of the time difference between Singapore and Chicago.

Since an institutional set-up for gold futures trading was already in place, the Gold Exchange of Singapore was chosen as the site to establish financial futures trading. To reflect its expanded role, the exchange was renamed the Singapore International Monetary Exchange (SIMEX) in December 1983.[13]

In view of CME's success, it was chosen as a model for SIMEX, which adopted the CME's open outcry trading, gross margining,[14] record keeping, market surveillance, and common bond systems. Under the common bond system, all clearing members of SIMEX jointly and severally guarantee all contracts traded on SIMEX. The clearing members thus assume the liabilities of the buyers and sellers in the market – i.e. each member becomes a 'buyer to every seller' and a 'seller to every buyer'. This ensures that all contracts are honoured.

There are four categories of membership in SIMEX – corporate clearing, corporate non-clearing, commercial associate, and individual non-clearing. Clearing members are corporations with a minimum paid-up capital of S$ 2 million. They are also required to maintain a minimum adjusted net capital of S$ 4 million, or 10 per cent of customer funds, whichever is higher. They are shareholders of SIMEX and are subject to the common bond system. Individual non-clearing membership includes trading permit holders. Corporate non-clearing members are not subject to the common bond system, but have to put their trades through a clearing member. Both clearing and non-clearing corporate members have to acquire at least three seats in SIMEX. Commercial associates, who can deal only for their related or associated companies, need purchase only one seat. Individual members also require one seat or a trading permit. They can act either as floor traders or brokers. At mid-1991, there were 37 corporate clearing, 37 corporate non-clearing, 12 commercial associate, and 458 individual non-clearing members.

To develop the new market, a number of incentives were offered. SIMEX and its members were granted a 10-year tax exemption from March 1984 on income derived from futures activities in SIMEX. In addition, a concessionary 10 per cent tax rate was granted on the income of corporate members arising from transactions with non-residents, ACUs and other SIMEX members, also to individual members' income derived from trading on SIMEX. In 1987, interest paid by members of SIMEX to non-residents on margin deposits for gold and financial futures transactions was exempted from withholding tax. So, too, was interest paid by SIMEX members for Loco-London gold transactions.

So far as recent experience goes, SIMEX traded a total of 5.72 million contracts in 1990 compared with 6.27 million in the previous year. The decline was associated with a global decline in Eurodollar activity. Despite the decline, the SIMEX Eurodollar market increased its share of the total figure for the sixth consecutive year (to 8.8 per cent). For the first half of 1991, SIMEX traded 2.62 million contracts, a rise of 6 per cent over the same period in the preceding year. The most outstanding contract during this period in 1991 was the Euro-yen contract, which saw its market share rise from 5.3 per cent in 1990 to 7.8 per cent in the first half of 1991. The Eurodollar interest rate contract also performed well, but not currency futures contracts – in yen, DMs, and sterling. Other relatively successful contracts include the High Sulphur Fuel Oil, the Nikkei Stock Average, and – to some extent – the new Euro-mark 3-month interest rate future (identical to the one offered by LIFFE in London).

Thus, over the years since its inception, SIMEX has performed a useful function as an international risk management and trading centre. In 1990, for example, 71 per cent of customer trades were international in origin – coming primarily from Japan, the USA, Europe, and from the rest of the Asia-Pacific area.

Chapter 13

The South African money market[1]

Prior to the passing of the Deposit-taking Institutions Act (No. 94 of 1990), which was applicable as from 1 February 1991 (and was supported by appropriate Regulations), there were 25 commercial banks, 27 general banks, 11 merchant banks, and 4 discount houses. All of these were now classified as 'deposit-taking institutions'. There was no longer a distinction between the various functional groups of financial institutions, but the Act did not apply to the Reserve Bank, the Land Bank, the Corporation for Public Deposits, the Public Investment Corporation, and mutual building societies.

Following a number of discussions – in 1990 and 1991 – with a view to reorganizing the South African banking and financial scene, a new financial group emerged amalgamating the interests of what had been the United Building Society (which by then had already opted to be a bank), the Allied Building Society (which had also demutualized and bought the French Merchant Bank, to become the Allied Bank), Volkskas (which had exchanged shares with what was in 1987 the United Building Society), and Sage Financial Services – this now became the Amalgamated Banks of South Africa (ABSA).[2] The other big banking groups comprised the Standard Bank of South Africa (now South African-owned), First National Bank (formerly Barclays and now owned by Anglo-American Corporation), which in turn bought the South African interests of Citibank, and, finally, the result of a merger between Nedbank and the South African Permanent Building Society, setting up NEDCOR as the holding company of Nedperm Bank, which has two divisions – Nedbank and the South African Permanent Building Society.

A Land and Agricultural Bank (the Land Bank) had been

established in 1912. It provides various types of farm credit – mortgage loans to assist in the purchase of fixed property, charge loans to finance improvements to property (e.g. irrigation or electricity), and short-term loans to meet seasonal requirements. From a money market point of view, its significance is that it issues bills, call bonds, and promissory notes.

ORIGINS OF A MONEY MARKET

In South Africa, a short-term money market was established in the years after the Second World War. A National Finance Corporation (NFC) had been set up in 1949 with capital subscribed both by the private financial institutions and the Reserve Bank, the Board reflecting this shareholder interest but also including a Treasury representative. The Governor of the Reserve Bank was Chairman.

By establishing this institution, the authorities hoped, first, to reduce the large volume of short-term central bank advances to the government and, second, to provide an outlet for some of the large current-account balances that appeared to be available but which were not being invested in Treasury bills or other government stocks. These moneys might now be placed on deposit with the NFC, which would then invest them in government paper. Initially, the liquidity of the NFC was guaranteed by the Reserve Bank.[3]

In the first instance, it was excess domestic current account balances (e.g. those of the big corporations) that it was attempted to tap, though the banks also placed money on deposit. To cushion the banks against the immediate effects of this transfer of funds, their required minimum cash reserves were temporarily reduced. For a time, bank deposits with the NFC tended to fluctuate quite considerably, even though cash reserves were often well above the required minimum, but from 1953 onwards excess balances were steadily reduced.

Latterly, the evidence suggested that the banks had been using both NFC facilities and the call money market with increasing freedom as a means of adjusting their cash positions. Moreover, the NFC's own total deposit liabilities became much less volatile as a result of compensating movements in the balances of other depositors, which included the big mining houses.

When the NFC was first launched, there were many who were decidedly critical of its proposed role. It was regarded very much as an adjunct of the Reserve Bank, which in a sense it was, and there was a tendency to think of it as little more than an engine for siphoning off surplus short-term funds for the purpose of expenditure by the government. That would seem to have been far too uncharitable an interpretation and the setting up of the NFC should more properly be regarded as an experiment that broke new ground and pointed the way to the development of a true money market.

In particular, the successful operations of the NFC in due course encouraged private enterprise to take the plunge in expanding money market facilities, when towards the end of 1955 Union Acceptances Limited was set up to develop an acceptance and discounting business. Two years later, the discount business was transferred to a separate company, with the original institution acting as managers for the new discount house, the latter's business being modelled on the London practice of borrowing money at call in order to finance a portfolio of commercial and Treasury bills and of short-dated government bonds. In addition, it stood prepared to retail bills to institutions seeking investment for temporarily surplus funds. The success of these two houses attracted other companies into the field, such as the Central Finance and Acceptance Corporation, the Accepting Bank for Industry, and the Philip Hill Acceptance Company. Finally, a separate discount house was established, specifically to take over the discount business formerly undertaken by these three merchant banks.

On the official side, too, important changes had been taking place. In June 1958, Treasury bill rates that had been 'administered' (though changed periodically with some reference to market conditions at home and abroad) became subject to a competitive weekly tender, with the NFC's call money rate fluctuating in sympathy, thereby imparting for the first time a measure of true flexibility to the rate structure. Subsequently, in 1960, the Reserve Bank also freed the prices of short-dated bonds, thus encouraging an expansion in discount-house bond dealings. Further, by withdrawing its undertaking to sell and discount Treasury bills at preferential rates, the Reserve Bank clearly indicated that the money market was now to be the main source of bills and the place where they could be converted into cash. But the Reserve Bank also began to develop a closer liaison with market houses, which it was prepared to help at times of severe strain, and 'smoothing out' operations became more frequent. The NFC, which had become virtually a sub-department of the Reserve Bank, was phased out in 1984 – in respect of deposits of short-term funds arising in the public sector[4] and was replaced by the Corporation for Public Deposits (CPD), which combined the functions of the NFC and the former Public Debt Commissioners (the Public Investment Corporation since 1984). The CPD has come to play an important role in money market relationships.

SEASONAL FACTORS

In the ordinary course of things, one would expect there to be fluctuations – sometimes sharp and sudden – in bank liquidity and from time to time either the need for (or surpluses in) money. Also one might expect movements in bank liquidity because of the incidence of seasonal factors, though these may now be less pronounced than was the case in the past. Thus, in South Africa, the harvesting of primary products – e.g. maize and wool, fruits and wine – has less of an impact now than in the days when the economy was less diversified. Gold production has been declining and it is now a less important ingredient in GDP than was formerly the case.[5] Indeed, these days – apart from the increase in notes in circulation over Christmas and the summer holidays for about 5 weeks each year – it is the exigencies of public finance that exert the most influence. Thus, there are large inflows of taxes – and therefore tightness in the money markets – in February and August, when there are major payments of taxes by the mining houses (e.g. for gold, though gold production now represents only 8.7 per cent of GDP). Other mining taxes come in May and November. This has to be offset by the Reserve Bank making more money available. As we have seen, primary products – i.e. mining, agriculture, and forestry (which only represent 16 per cent of GDP) – are no longer important as a source of seasonal fluctuations.

On the other hand, money comes on to the market beginning in April,[6] and again six months later in October, as a result of heavy government expenditure in those months. The financial year commences on 1 April, and heavy government expenditure runs on into June. Both in the earlier and later periods, there is an impact on the money markets. To a certain extent, the maize crop also plays a role (with the season sometimes moving from March/April to June, or even August, if there are late rains). None of the other crops is so important. At times of monetary inflow, the Reserve Bank will operate to offset the related effects by 'mopping up' excess liquidity.

More generally, the most noticeable shortages in the money market occur at month-ends (and for a few days thereafter). But one of the big unknowns in terms of monetary effects is Reserve Bank intervention in the foreign exchange market, which interventions do not seem to have any periodicity and do tend to upset money market calculations. Flows can be very large and there is no predictable pattern. Obviously, when the Reserve Bank is buying currency, it injects Rands into the money market. This can be offset by forward contracts and swaps – there is in fact a fairly active spot and forward market between the banks, with the Reserve Bank coming in when banks are unable to balance their transactions. At times, too, the Reserve Bank may be a net seller of FOREX in the forward markets, and day by day there can be an impact of forward transactions entered into 1 month or even 12 months ago.

MANAGING BANK MONEY POSITIONS

In South Africa, all the large banks have widespread networks of branches and agencies, and – as elsewhere – this can complicate the estimation of a bank's money position over the course of the day. The first estimation of a bank's money position will be known the previous evening, and by 7.30 a.m. on the day they will have had a preliminary computer run; the books will be tidied up and the clearing effected with other banks by 8.30 a.m. All the banks will monitor their cash positions over the course of the day with information coming in – for the big banks – from about fifty clearing centres,[7] which could account for 80 per cent of the daily turnover. In addition, any big money flows (e.g. if big use is made of an overdraft facility) will be reported in whatever the size of the branch. And there will be a cash monitoring desk in the bank's dealing room.

Quite apart from the reserve assets requirements imposed by the Reserve Bank – a cash ratio of 4 per cent of short-term liabilities and 20 per cent (including the 4 per cent) of short-term liabilities for the liquid assets[8] ratio – individual banks may also have their own internal rules with respect to the liquidity they wish to maintain and which is employed as a basis of adjustment. Assets will also be ranked as having different degrees of liquidity.

THE INTER-BANK MONEY MARKET

It is in the inter-bank market that one sees which banks have money
to lend and which banks are in need of money. Primarily, it is a
market between banks; mining houses have always been regarded
as part of this market; building societies were on the periphery, but
now the largest of them have become banks and/or are associated
with banks and hence are now an integral part of the market. If the
banks need more money than they can get in the inter-bank market,
they can approach the Reserve Bank through the discount window.
Hence, the constituent members of the inter-bank money market
are the Reserve Bank, the large deposit-taking institutions (including the discount houses), and the mining houses. Funds come from
the mining houses and − to a lesser extent − from the insurance
companies, which are both net lenders, also still from banks that
were formerly building societies; the large commercial banks would
tend to be net borrowers, but they may also lend from time to time.
Indeed, whether as lenders or borrowers, a bank − or mining house
− may be one way or the other for a period as long as 10 weeks.
What were general banks (e.g. finance houses) were not constituent
members of the inter-bank market, but they were frequently members of a group with a commercial bank that was. The part played
by corporates in this context will be considered below.

The market deals in call money; usually, this is placed overnight
and called the next day, when the rate and/or the amount may be
renegotiated. Over a weekend, or at month-ends, money may be
lent for 2 or 3 days. It may be for 7 days at a month-end. The
longest term in the inter-bank market would be 30 days. Typically,
money is lent unsecured. Exceptionally, certain of the small banks
may be asked for some security. But all loans would be subject to
limits, which tend to be unadvised (though it is not difficult to
establish what those limits are). On the whole, deals are done direct
and not through money brokers − the business is not big enough to
attract brokers in money, though brokers commonly operate in the
FOREX market.

The minimum size of transaction is R 500,000 to R 1 million.
More generally, deals would be in the R 5−10 million range; R 20
million would be not uncommon and amounts could go up to R 50
million (or more) on occasion. The median may be of the order of
R 5 million. Turnover would average R 400 million to R 500
million a day and could go up to R 1 billion plus (including both
lending and borrowing).

So far as hours of operation are concerned, desks would open up from 7.00 a.m. to 7.30 a.m. The clearing with other banks will be effected between 8.00 a.m. and 8.30 a.m., after which they begin to deal in the inter-bank market. If there is any difficulty, funds will be provided by the Reserve Bank (see pp. 383–4). If loans are to be called, it must be done by 8.30 a.m. Generally speaking, the busy period would be from 8.30 a.m. to 12.30 p.m. (with peaks between 8.30 a.m. and 9.30 a.m. and at noon, even 3.00 p.m.). The market closes at 3.30 p.m., or 3.45 p.m., but after 3.30 p.m. transactions would be done for next day's date – though not very often.

THE ROLE OF THE CORPORATES

The corporates are not part of the inter-bank market. But – depending on cash flow – they may at times have funds to put out and, on other occasions, themselves require short-term assistance.[9] If banks take money from a corporate, it will be in the form of a deposit, but – if the amount is large – the rate paid will relate to money market rates (with some allowance for the cost of maintaining required reserves). On the other hand, if a corporate is in need of short-term accommodation, a bank would make this available in the form of a 'cash loan' and, for a large corporation, the rate would tend to be below the Prime overdraft rate and much more related to money market rates.[10] Whether it is a deposit or a 'cash loan', such transactions may often be done on an overnight basis. In some cases, a bank may act as a broker – putting a corporation with funds to lend in touch with a corporate that desires to borrow. This is where the banks are said to be getting into the 'grey market'. There is also a 'grey market' proper, where corporates lend and borrow between themselves (as in an inter-company market)[11] – often within the same group of companies – and without the intermediation of a bank. When deals are done between independent corporations, resort may be made to a money broker.[12]

THE CONTRIBUTION OF THE DISCOUNT HOUSES

There were four discount houses in South Africa – excluding the National Finance Corporation of South Africa (established in 1949, the operations of which have now been phased out altogether). The discount houses proper were the Discount House of South Africa Limited (established in 1957), the National Discount

House (NDH) of South Africa Limited (1961), the Interbank Discount House Limited (1972), and the Securities Discount House Limited (1985). The first and the last were larger than the others. Latterly, NDH, Interbank, and Securities Discount all fell within the Sechold group. Strictly speaking, therefore, there were now two discount house groups, although the three in the Sechold group all operated quite independently. The traditional business of a discount house was to provide an outlet for the short-term funds of the banking system and to invest these moneys in a range of relatively risk-free, mainly short-term, negotiable securities.[13] As we shall see, there has been a change of emphasis in recent years. Whereas, previously, discount houses enjoyed a special relationship with the Reserve Bank in terms of communication and accommodation, these privileges have now been bestowed on all deposit-taking institutions.

In order to finance their portfolios of Treasury and Land Bank bills, trade bills, promissory notes (PNs) and acceptances, negotiable certificates of deposit (NCDs), government stock, Land Bank debentures, stocks of local authorities and public corporations, and bills of and loans to public corporations, as well as 'other assets',[14] the discount houses borrow or raise money from a variety of sources. Formerly, significant (and sometimes large) amounts of money were lent by the Corporation for Public Deposits (including prior to March 1984 deposits received from the so-called 'pooled funds' administered by the former Public Debt Commissioners) but there were no such moneys in 1988 and very little in 1989 (because the CPD invested more money in Land Bank bills). Commercial banks tended to be an important and regular source of funds – though it could vary quite a lot – with the merchant banks also regular lenders to the discount houses, but on the whole at a much lower level. The building societies could be very important lenders and the amounts were often much higher (especially after mid-1988) than those from the commercial banks. Mining houses likewise were known to be a source of funds; they were included under 'other' and, on that basis, did not seem to be very important.[15] Although the figures varied from time to time, the important portfolio items were, on the one hand, trade bills, PNs and acceptances and, on the other, government stock. Treasury bill holdings varied a lot, holdings of NCDs less so.[16]

So far as dealings in government stocks are concerned, there are no formally recognized market-makers in South Africa, but the merchant banks and, to a lesser exent, the discount houses, made markets in specified government stocks. More recently, the Reserve Bank has actively traded in government stocks to enhance their marketability. Also, by 1991, government debt in the form of forty-four loans had been consolidated into only four loans, and maturities were scheduled to coincide with important tax payment dates. About the same time, there was a scrapping of prescribed investments whereby certain institutions were required to invest a proportion of their funds in specified tradable instruments. This has greatly simplified this market.

Normally, the discount houses operated as principals and for their own account, but – sometimes – they acted as a broker when banks were looking for cash, or when insurance companies or pension funds wished to do business in the money market, or were investing in the capital market (e.g. by buying government stock).

Previously, the discount houses assisted the banks by doing re-purchase agreements ('repos') for them (e.g. overnight) and – when the discount houses did not have enough money of their own – knew that they could go to the Reserve Bank. Either (1) they could buy ineligible assets from the banks and rediscount eligible assets with the Reserve Bank, or (2) they could buy – by way of a 'repo' (as above) – eligible assets from the banks and sell on those eligible assets to the Reserve Bank. Nowadays, all banks can either rediscount eligible assets or negotiate overnight loans with the Reserve Bank.

Moneys lent by the commercial banks to the discount houses were for the most part in the form of 'call money', though in practice it was really lent overnight and repaid the next day, when the rate and/or the amount could be renegotiated. Mining houses tended to lend in the same way and call money rates were the most important ingredient in the discount houses' cost of funds. Sometimes call money could be placed for a number of days, but rather rarely. 'Fixed deposits' might also be made; these could vary for periods of from a few days to a few months with a maximum of (say) 6 months. Moneys placed with the discount houses were always fully secured with – as a matter of practice – a margin of from 1.02 per cent to 1.05 per cent. The usual security was Treasury bills and short-dated gilts (government stocks) – about 90 per cent of loans to the discount houses were secured by 'liquid assets' such as these, and 10 per cent by non-liquid assets (such as NCDs). Borrowings and repayments were all arranged on the telephone.

Some lenders insisted on the physical delivery of the security. Others were prepared to have it assigned to them by the discount house and held 'in-house' (i.e. it was merely moved from one pigeon-hole to another), or securities could be held as a 'pool' in safe custody at the Reserve Bank, when the lenders received a 'chit' detailing the security that had been transferred. This was also the case when the security was held 'in-house'. And in all cases the amount of the loan could be confirmed by a broker's note.

But the discount houses could not borrow without limit. They were subject to a multiplier of fifty times their capital and published reserves. This was the limit for total borrowings. However, the amount so calculated did not include unmatched 'repos' – e.g. if a Treasury bill had a maturity of 90 days and it was sold, on a 'repo' basis, for 80 days, then this was 'unmatched'. Similarly, if a discount house did a 'carry', which was really a re-sale agreement – e.g. if a discount house 'carried' securities for another party for a certain period and sold that 'carry' on (on the basis of a 'repo') for less than the period of its life, again it was 'unmatched'. Matched 'repos' were of course included.

Individual lenders might also apply 'limits' on loans to a discount house. But in any case a bank usually spread the money it wished to put out among the several discount houses, as would a large mining house when it had a lot of money to place. In fact, and for the larger discount houses, it was a question of only being limited by the amount (and quality) of the security they had available.

Where moneys were made available by building societies – and, indeed, by some of the corporates – this would be done on the basis of a repurchase agreement, or 'repo', and in fact it had become common for discount houses to reckon to finance a considerable part of their portfolios on this basis. This was consistent with the changing emphasis of their business. The traditional business of a discount house was the simple financing and holding of a portfolio, profits being based on the difference between two sets of interest rates. None the less, there was also a regular retailing of the types of instruments held. Latterly – in South Africa as elsewhere – discount houses have become traders in government securities and other money market instruments. This has involved taking a view on interest rates and, where appropriate, maintaining a 'position'. Profits now depended more on trading a 'book' and on the differences between prices. This requires a greater degree of nimbleness and moving in and out of the market. This was the big change that took place some years ago and, within the respective groups, the discount houses for some time still tended to emphasize this type of business; in due course the discount houses completed the change-over to become trading houses in terms of the new Deposit-taking Institutions Act.[17]

Nowadays, the discount houses and other deposit-taking institutions may borrow at the Reserve Bank and, at times when any of these institutions are very liquid, the Reserve Bank is available to sell assets back to the market during the trading day in order to absorb cash. Although they will be operating throughout the trading day, buying and/or selling short-dated credit instruments, raising or 'losing' money (i.e. borrowing or lending), much of the business will be done mainly between 2.00 p.m. and 3.00 p.m. The market closes at 3.30 p.m., but institutions may remain open for business until 4.30 p.m. Indeed, staff may stay until 5.00 p.m. for the gold-fixing in London.

Although the discount houses are less important these days as channels of communication between the Reserve Bank and the banking system, a relationship is still maintained between the discount houses and the Reserve Bank – in that the discount houses report their positions daily to the Reserve Bank in the morning after the inter-bank clearing. Even more important is the now greatly widened monthly meeting between the Treasurers of banks, building societies, discount houses and merchant banks and the Reserve Bank. The Governor and the three Deputy Governors attend, together with the Reserve Bank's financial specialists, the Bank's economist, and the Registrar of Deposit-Taking Institutions. This has replaced the former meeting between the old-style discount houses and the Reserve Bank. There is, as formerly, a freely flowing discussion – the Reserve Bank can put forward views that it wishes to discuss with these institutions and the latter can raise issues of interest to themselves and thereby invite Reserve Bank reactions. Both sides find the meetings extremely useful.

TREASURY BILLS

The total outstanding figure for marketable Treasury bills varies quite a lot from time to time, also within the year, though this form of debt seems to be high in the period from May to August/September each year. At such times, a significant quantum seems to be absorbed by the Reserve Bank and, latterly, by the commercial banks (sometimes by the Public Investment Commissioners). On the basis of end-of-month figures, the deposit-taking institutions can at times be very light holders of Treasury bills. In 1988 and 1989, there were times when they held none – the various institutions invested in other assets because they offered better returns. The link between the rate on Treasury bills and the Bank rate (which was for some time non-market related) encouraged a lack of interest in Treasury bills. Similarly with the commercial banks – an active demand in 1987, very little in 1988, and a return of interest May to July 1989; also from May 1990 onwards in 1990/91. The general banks display some interest, but (except in 1990) not the merchant banks. Until 1990/91, building societies were only modest holders and the bulk of non-central bank demand usually comes from 'other holders' which includes the Public Investment Commissioners (PIC). There is no non-resident interest. Since mid-July 1990 to end-June 1991, the total outstanding figure for marketable Treasury bills varied from a low of R 1,479 million in February 1991 to a high of R 4,596 million at end-June 1991.[18]

There has been a weekly Treasury bill tender in South Africa since 1958. The amount of the offer is announced on the Thursday about 2.30 p.m. The tender has to be in by 10.00 a.m. the next day – Friday – and the results (the amount accepted and the average rate) are announced on the Reuters screen the same day at 12.00 noon. If they are successful in the tender, the party concerned can take up their bills on any day in the following week, provided it is a business day. If they so desire, they can choose a day when bills mature. This is also a means whereby a more continuous series of maturities can be achieved. Since July 1990, the average weekly tender has been of the order of R 140 million.

The main participants in the tender are the discount houses, some banks and building societies, and private financial institutions; the PIC does not tender (it buys Treasury bills direct from the Reserve Bank), but the CPD does. So far as the old-style discount houses were concerned, there was no cartel and no obligation to underwrite the issue – though *de facto* their tenders would normally cover it, and the larger discount houses felt they had a moral responsibility to tender. Since the Reserve Bank puts in its own tender after it has seen the other tenders, it is in a position to influence the results and may be instrumental in moving the rate either way (i.e. it can put in a high price and push the rate down, or increase the amount of the tender with the implication that the price will be lower and the rate will be pushed up).

Anybody can tender. It is merely necessary to fill in the relevant form and lodge it with the Reserve Bank. The minimum size of Treasury bill is R 100,000, and they are issued in bearer form. The Reserve Bank also holds tenders for special Treasury bills – these 'little taps' are usually for minimum amounts of R 1 million, and only regular tenderers may participate. Tap bills are issued at the latest tender rate. Tenders are submitted by telephone. Special tender bills may be issued with a tenor (or maturity) other than 91 days, but not for longer than 1 year. Special Treasury bills with more flexible maturities have largely replaced tax bills, which were usually issued to coincide with specific tax dates. In addition, the scheduled maturities of public debt have reduced the need for tax bills.

Until the early 1980s, the secondary market in Treasury bills was very limited, largely because the yields tended to be unattractive to private-sector institutions, and this still remains substantially true. But with the transition from a liquid-assets to a cash-reserve system, so far as institutional requirements are concerned, Treasury bills (and similar assets) are not as likely to be held semi-permanently (in other words, due to an artificial demand) and are now free to come on to the market; as a result, activity in the secondary market for Treasury bills has expanded somewhat, though it is still likely to be rather thin. The discount houses quote buying prices for all maturities and denominations of Treasury bills, and selling prices when they have such bills in portfolio.

LAND BANK BILLS

Land Bank bills[19] are issued by tender primarily to finance the short-term advances of the Land Bank. For this reason, changes in the amounts outstanding tend to reflect crop seasons. Since mid-1984, Land Bank bills have been offered by way of a weekly tender conducted by the Reserve Bank on behalf of the Land Bank. Land Bank bills are issued in bearer form and in denominations of R 10 million, R 5 million, R 1 million, and R 500,000. Prior to 1982, Land Bank bills were held mainly by the Reserve Bank and the National Finance Corporation. For brief periods between 1965 and 1973, such bills were held by discount houses when sold to them by the Reserve Bank for the purpose of absorbing surplus funds. Since

1982, and especially since the introduction of tenders for Land Bank bills in mid-1984, the range of holders has widened to include all financial institutions, the mining houses, and certain public and private corporations. The amount offered each week has varied from R 10 million to R 100 million, and the amount outstanding – though it has fluctuated markedly – was of the order of R 2,780 million in 1990 and R 2,500 million in 1991.

The Land Bank bills tender is on Mondays. Hence, if tenderers miss out at the Treasury bill tender on the Friday, they can have a second bite at the cherry on the Monday. There is also a relationship between the yields on Treasury bills and on Land Bank bills. The usual spread of twenty basis points between Treasury bills and Land Bank bills is the result of an agreement between the Land Bank and those investing in their paper.

There is a secondary market. Since the introduction of tenders for Land Bank bills, discount houses have been prepared to quote buying and selling prices and a secondary market in these bills has grown rapidly. Sales by the discount houses have been as high as R 390 million in 1 month.

BANKERS' ACCEPTANCES

A banker's acceptance[20] is a bill of exchange drawn on and accepted by a bank. It is a simple instrument of high quality and can be negotiated in a secondary market. The typical size of a banker's acceptance is R 1 million, a size which is convenient from a trading point of view. It will usually be issued under a Letter of Credit (a facility that relates to total turnover),[21] and will indicate the type of industry or commerce it purports to finance. Because such finance relates to turnover, it is not strictly trade-related. Hence, the vast majority of bankers' acceptances are issued in even amounts, which may be as small as R 100,000 or R 250,000. It is an instrument greatly preferred by banks as both liquid and offering a reasonable return. But they would swap into other banks' acceptances, not hold their own. The broken amount – or the 'tail' – which derives from the financing of a complete series of bankers' acceptances transactions, would either be held (after discount) in portfolio, or (with other bits and pieces) it may be traded in a 'parcel' for which there will be some demand from modest investors, who would hold the parcel to maturity.[22] A 90-day maturity (or tenor) is most common.

There are also 'project bills' – sometimes called 'capital project bills' or 'prescribed bills' (because they used to be a prescribed asset for pension funds and life offices). These bills may be used to finance public corporations or municipalities (which use a 'bridging bond'). There is also an overnight market in these bills – taking surplus balances from one municipality and placing it overnight with another that has need of funds.

Bankers' acceptances are traded in a secondary market, though discount houses place limits on the names (of the accepting banks) that are on the acceptances that they will endorse. In the secondary market it is the discount houses that are the main market-makers; it is an active market and comprehends both (1) 'liquid' bankers' acceptances (where the underlying transaction is of a self-liquidating nature such as the movement of goods) and which are not drawn for longer than 120 days, and (2) 'non-liquid' bills which generally represent accommodation paper (non-trade-related) and may be drawn for any period. A discount house may be active in both and sometimes be more active in the non-liquid acceptances, which tend to go to insurance companies and pension funds. In fact, this has become a very big and active market. Liquid bankers' acceptances transactions may be effected on the basis of a repurchase agreement (or 'repo'); for non-liquid acceptances, transactions are always in the form of an outright purchase/sale. Resort to 'buybacks' (or 'repos') for transactions in liquid acceptances greatly increases the scope of the market, since such transactions are off-balance-sheet.

NEGOTIABLE CERTIFICATES OF DEPOSIT (NCDs)

In South Africa, NCDs go back to July 1964. They may be issued for periods of up to 5 years. When issued for a period of less than 1 year, interest is payable at the end of the period. When issued for longer than 1 year, interest may be payable either at the end of the period, or 6-monthly in arrears, usually the latter. Of the banks, there are only about eight regular issuers of NCDs; others would be occasional issuers. Since August 1983, building societies have also been permitted to issue NCDs for periods of 1 to 5 years. For both banks and building societies, the authorities used to require that the total amount of NCDs issued might not exceed 40 per cent of deposit and debenture liabilities, and issues of NCDs of up to 2 years might not exceed 20 per cent of deposits. This requirement ceased to apply after 1 February 1991. The main purpose of NCD issues is to raise wholesale money. Not all banks are regarded as prime risks and those that are regarded as less creditworthy may have to pay interest at a rate of up to 1 per cent more than for prime banks. The typical (and median) denomination is R 1 million; R 500,000 is also common, and the minimum size would be R 100,000. Although, for real marketability, a size of R 1 million is preferred. NCDs for R 5 million also circulate. Some commercial banks will issue smaller denominations in the name of a depositor in order to cater for retail clients. Normally, NCDs are issued in bearer form (95 per cent of the total), occasionally in the name of the original depositor, though transferable by open endorsement. The normal maturity – and the bulk of the trading – would be in 12 months CDs and the minimum period 3 months. Very few would be for longer than 3 years.

In addition to issuing NCDs to customers, banks (and building societies) will issue them to discount houses, which in this market virtually act as brokers and place them through the market – the demand comes from other banks (of all kinds), mining houses, insurance companies, pension funds, corporates, unit trusts, trust funds, municipal authorities, public enterprises, even individuals. Packages of R 20 million could be placed in the market (usually as R 1 million × 20, or R 5 million × 4) and packages may go up to R 50 million, but in a case like that they would not go into the secondary market, but would be issued to be held. Discount houses will also operate limits on NCDs issued, such that they monitor the amounts that individual banks have in issue (similarly with building societies).

So far as the secondary market is concerned, it has been described both as 'developed' and 'very active'; in fact, it can be 'quirky' – there is either a 'drought' or a 'flood'; indeed, one day it will be 'alive' and the next day it can be 'stone dead'; as one commentator put it, 'it is inclined to come and go'. Many would argue that it is not big enough – there are not enough players. In addition, while the demand to hold an NCD clearly postulates an availability of surplus funds, interest-rate expectations are also likely to be important. The level of rates would of course depend on market conditions, but if the market is tight and rates go up, the differentials in rates for prime and less creditworthy risks will widen. In a flush market, on the other hand, rates will fall and differentials will narrow. In the secondary market, transactions would be effected direct – on the basis of screen trading – not through brokers. When NCDs are issued to the discount houses, they 'would move them on very quickly'. If NCDs go through the hands of a discount house, they would be endorsed by the discount house, not by the seller. One should note, too, that, although NCDs are subject to stamp duty on issue, they are exempted from such duty when traded in the secondary market.

RESALE AND REPURCHASE AGREEMENTS[23]

A convenient way of raising money, or of financing a portfolio, is to sell a security or credit instrument under an agreement to repurchase it after a defined interval of time. It is a very flexible technique – it can be done for any period and on the basis of virtually any security or instrument, provided such instrument has a maturity at least as long as the tenor of the agreement. In a South African context, the basis can be Treasury bills, Land Bank bills or debentures, government securities (or gilts), NCDs, bankers' acceptances, or promissory notes (PNs, where these have been dis-counted for customers). The cost of a 'repo' is the difference between two prices – at sale and repurchase – the difference reflecting current rates of interest. Technically, they may be done for any period (within the remaining maturity of the security or instrument) – 3 months would be common. Not many are done for a period of days – the minimum period would be over the month's end. In the markets, one does not see the reverse 'repo', though these could be done by the Reserve Bank, if the money market was in surplus – something that has not occurred all that often.

Sometimes, 'repos' are used specifically for the purpose of financing the carrying of a portfolio (e.g. in order to assist a bank in carrying its portfolio of gilts), or by the discount houses when not borrowing from banks, mining houses, or building societies (e.g. when borrowing from corporates). Such accommodation can be arranged for any period and against a whole range of securities. In other contexts, resort to 'repos' may be seen as part of a normal funding operation. The chief advantages of resort to this procedure is to benefit from changes in interest rate differentials and promoting the mobility of funds within financial markets.

Repurchase agreement

This relates to the obtaining of money (which shall be deemed to have been so obtained by way of a loan) through the sale of an asset to any other person subject to an agreement in terms of which the seller undertakes to purchase from the buyer at a future date the asset so sold or any other asset issued by the issuer, and which have been so issued subject to the same conditions regarding term, interest rate, and price as the asset so sold.

Resale agreement

This relates to the provision of money (which money shall be deemed to have been so provided by way of a loan) through the purchase of an asset from any other person subject to an agreement in terms of which the buyer undertakes to sell to the seller at a future date the asset so purchased or any other asset issued by the issuer, and which have been so issued subject to the same conditions regarding term, interest rate, and price as the asset so purchased.

COMMERCIAL PAPER

Although not formalized on the American model, there were already the beginnings of something like commercial paper in South Africa prior to the issue of guidelines for issues of debentures and commercial paper by the Reserve Bank in November 1990. Thus, one of the merchant banks had developed a note instrument based on a signed PN made out in favour of the bank. These PNs were then discounted in the market or sold on to one of the bank's own customers, the latter procedure becoming more and more common. This was done off-balance-sheet. The PNs were kept in safe custody; if the customer needed his money, the bank would repurchase them; in effect, the bank made a book in PNs. But because the bank was prepared to hold its own paper and to buy back paper from which a customer wished to disinvest, there was little chance of developing a secondary market (though this is not unusual with commercial paper). Latterly, the PNs were made payable to bearer and did not need a bank endorsement on them. None the less, there are still customers who preferred a bank name on this paper. In any event, most of the big companies, which were sufficiently creditworthy to borrow on the basis of commercial paper, were themselves associated with a large group within which members could borrow at need from other members of the group. Because of this, some of the conditions favourable to the development of commercial paper proper were already present.

Under the guidelines referred to above, it was noted that the issue of debentures was already a well-established practice in South African financial markets, but to ensure there was no circumvention of prudential regulation it was provided that debentures issued in terms of the Companies Act and commercial paper which complied with the guidelines would be exempt from the Deposit-taking Institutions Act. The guidelines covered such matters as:

(1) Issuers (companies with a net asset value of R 100 million and certain subsidiaries of a holding company).
(2) Minimum amounts – if listed on the Johannesburg Stock Exchange – to be issued and transferable in amounts of R 500,000 to R 2 million; if unlisted, to be issued in units of more than R 2 million; in the latter case, the issue would only be to registered financial institutions.
(3) Period (initially for a period shorter than 24 months and a renewal period shorter than 12 months).
(4) There were also requirements as to disclosure – whether the specific issue is listed; whether the funds to be subscribed in terms of the issue are embarked for a specific project; whether the commercial paper or debentures offered are to be secured or unsecured; and whether the issuer's latest audited financial statements (a copy of which is to be attached to such offer) deviate in any material respects from the financial position of the issuer at the date of the offer for subscription of commercial paper or debentures. Furthermore, nothing in these disclosures should be construed as relieving the issuer from any other disclosure obligations in terms of the Companies Act, or any other statute or regulation, or the common law.

In January 1992, the Reserve Bank issued Regulations requiring institutions to report to it holdings of commercial paper. At the time of writing, no official statistics had been published.

FOREIGN EXCHANGE

All the major banks operate in the foreign exchange market, where the Reserve Bank has appointed twenty-nine authorized FOREX dealers. Both spot and forward transactions are undertaken – for the banks' own accounts and for customers. In the FOREX market, resort to brokers is common, but is not universal – quite a number of direct deals are also made. In addition, currency swaps may be done by the banks for their own account or for customers. Some of the big banks operate an integrated money market desk – domestic and foreign; others prefer to separate them.

The banks form the natural intermediary between foreign exchange supply and demand. The main task of a bank's foreign exchange department is to enable its commercial or financial customers to convert assets held in one currency into funds in another currency. This conversion can take the form of a 'spot' transaction or a 'forward' operation. Banking activities in the foreign exchange field tend inevitably to establish a uniform price range for a particular currency throughout the financial centres of the world. If at a given moment the market râte in one centre deviates too far from the average, the balance will soon be restored through arbitrage, which is the process of taking advantage of price differences in different centres. It can be seen that foreign exchange business acts as a very important regulator in a free monetary system.[24]

CENTRAL BANK INTERVENTION

In South Africa – as in so many other countries – the authorities imposed on the banks (including the merchant banks and the general banks) a cash reserve requirement. Until recently, this was in addition to cash in their vaults, tills, and automated teller machines in the form of bank notes and coin – these being their working balances. Vault cash is now included in the required cash reserve. Current provisions are imposed under the Deposit-taking Institutions Act (and related Regulations).[25] This was set at 4 per cent of short-term liabilities to the public (excluding short-term loans under repurchase agreements; short-term deposits pledged for loans granted; short-term amounts owing to the reporting institution by another deposit-taking institution or by a mutual building society, as well as credit balances originating from a clearing house settlement and an amount equal to 50 per cent of the average daily amount of remittances in transit).[26]

Given the necessity to maintain balances as above, such holdings will require adjustment from time to time – if only in absolute terms. In this context, the banks can either call money from, or place money with, the discount houses or – through the inter-bank market – make adjustments by calling funds from, or placing funds with, other banks. To the extent that deposit-taking institutions are still short of funds after having sought to adjust their positions, they will have to apply to the Reserve Bank for refinancing. At the same time, it has been policy to keep the banks (and other deposit-taking institutions) persistently slightly short of cash in order to ensure that the Reserve Bank remains more or less fully in control of the situation.

When there is a shortage of funds, the Reserve Bank will first try to identify the reasons for the shortage (e.g. it may be as a result of payment of taxes to the Government). Government balances will primarily be held by the Corporation for Public Deposits (CPD) and the Reserve Bank (in consultation with the Exchequer) may then put into the market a certain proportion of CPD funds. The Exchequer will welcome this, since they will not have to sacrifice interest on funds they cannot immediately utilize. These funds would be placed in the market at a money-market-related rate (which when funds were short would tend to be above Bank rate) – formerly, there was a distribution formula based on the capital and reserves of the discount houses (i.e. the size of each discount house determined the share each got of the money put out). However, when the banks were relatively liquid, it was less easy to place CPD funds except at lower rates of interest, which might well be below Bank rate, with the CPD rate being the more strategic rate. For this reason, a rate tender was introduced as from 1 April 1987, with the funds being made available for bidding both by the discount houses and the clearing banks. But the amounts became so large that the Reserve Bank's rediscount assistance proved to be of minor importance. Bank rate was consequently no longer seen as the effective cost of rediscount accommodation – the rate for CPD call deposits unofficially having been a more important monetary policy instrument. The Reserve Bank therefore decided to correct this misconception and to restore Bank rate to its original degree of importance.

Traditionally, the most obvious instrument of refinancing was to resort to the discount window, and this technique is still used in South Africa. Formerly, this facility might be availed of either by the discount houses or by the banks themselves – the discount houses often on-lending to the banks. Nowadays, the banks approach the Reserve Bank directly – preferential accommodation to the discount houses ceased on 23 February 1989.[27]

Nowadays, the Reserve Bank has to decide on the amount that will be put out to tender and the amount that it is willing to lend through the discount window, the objective being to keep the market in balance, with the tender rate being just below what would have to be paid through the discount window (i.e. Bank rate).

There are two ways in which refinancing at the discount window may be made available:

(1) through the rediscounting of Treasury bills, Land Bank bills, and liquid bankers' acceptances. When Treasury bills are rediscounted, this is done at Bank rate (as at mid-1991, this was 17 per cent). The remaining rediscount rates are higher than the Bank rate by specified and fixed margins (as at that date, Land Bank bills carried a rate of 17.15 per cent and bankers' acceptances 17.5 per cent);

(2) through the extension of overnight loans against the security of Treasury bills or short-term government stock, Land Bank bills, bankers' acceptances, and gilt- and semi-gilt-edged securities. The overnight borrowing rates when pledging securities in the four kinds of collateral applying to them and up to 105 per cent of the amount borrowed were somewhat higher than Bank rate – as at mid-1991, they were respectively 19.5, 19.75, 20.25, and 21.5 per cent.

The Reserve Bank may also resort to repurchase agreements ('repos') whereby it buys securities (e.g. Treasury bills, Land Bank bills, or government securities – gilts), if it wishes to make money available, under an agreement within a specified period, to sell those securities back to the accommodated party.[28] The 'repo' method has the advantage of being based on securities of almost any maturity and of making money available for any required period, though normally Reserve Bank 'repos' would only provide accommodation for a short period (e.g. overnight or for a few days). This was a technique that was much used when the Reserve Bank wished to be accommodating, but it has been used very little since January, 1990. In practice, a 'reverse repo' may also be done (a sale by the Reserve Bank of securities under an agreement to repurchase) in order to 'mop up' excess liquidity, but it is more usual for the Reserve Bank to sell short-dated Treasury bills to the market for this purpose.[29] Alternatively, special Treasury bills (as above) may be sold to the banks, to mature when the surplus liquidity was likely to disappear.

In these several ways, the Reserve Bank is able to influence the level of interest rates[30] – mainly by influencing the total quantum of cash in the market (either by injecting cash, or 'mopping up' any surplus). Primarily, the Reserve Bank is able to influence short-term rates; it does not have all that much influence on long-term rates in the capital market. On the whole, the Reserve Bank's objective has been to keep the banks persistently slightly short of cash and thereby to force the banks (and other deposit-taking institutions) to become regular borrowers.

Open market operations, in the sense of outright purchases or sales of government securities, is another possibility. On the whole, however, these are usually part of a funding operation and they are mostly concerned with debt management. But, when selling securities, the Reserve Bank attempts to place them in the market during periods of high liquidity; because of this, there is necessarily also a monetary effect. For open market operations proper, purchases and sales would tend to be in terms of short-dated instruments – Treasury bills, Land Bank bills, and bankers' acceptances.

The other important aspect of open market activity is the operations of the foreign desk at the Reserve Bank[31] – the buying and selling of US dollars in the market, also undertaking dollar swaps to influence the market. Because of the existence of exchange control, South Africa lacks the same 'openness' of most countries with similar economies. None the less, there is normally a good supply of dollars coming in against the sale of gold and in payment for diamonds and other minerals (in 1986, it was coal). Other exporters are required to sell their dollars back to the authorized FOREX dealers within 7 days. Within the Reserve Bank, attempts have been made to co-ordinate external action with domestic money market policy and there is a short meeting every morning between the FOREX and money market staff for this purpose. The heads of these departments also meet with the Governors on a weekly basis to determine policy for the coming week and, indeed, to look ahead to the following month. So far as exchange rate management is concerned, the system is one of managed floating, the main purpose of operations in the FOREX market being to stabilize the exchange rate value of the Rand. At the same time, its impact on money market management has to be taken into account and vice versa.

POSTSCRIPT

Towards the end of March 1992, the South African Reserve Bank announced its decision to intervene in the Financial Rand market with a view to making South Africa a more attractive investment proposition for foreigners by reducing currency risk. Traditionally, the market had been very volatile, with a thin volume of trading. The Reserve Bank was now to intervene by buying and selling the Financial Rand against US dollars. The Financial Rand represents a fixed pool of investment currency for foreigners. It was introduced in 1985 at the time of the country's debt standstill in order to protect the balance of payments, the reasoning being that foreign holders of South African equities should be treated on the same terms as those who had lent money to the country, which had then been blocked by the standstill.

The Governor of the Reserve Bank Bank (Mr Chris Stals) stated that intervention should have five main advantages:

1 The total supply of Financial Rand would reduce if – as expected – the Reserve Bank proved to be a net purchaser.
2 The Reserve Bank's intervention should narrow the discount between the Commercial and Financial Rand.
3 The market should enjoy a greater degree of stability.
4 The application of gold and foreign exchange reserves would provide an additional means for the Reserve Bank to control domestic liquidity.
5 Foreign creditors with claims within the debt standstill net would be able to sell the balances indirectly to the Reserve Bank through authorized dealers in foreign exchange.

There were also implications for the money market (as was explained by the Deputy Governor, Mr Jaap Meijer). There had been a marked improvement in the country's balance of payments position in the first 9 months of 1991. This led to an easing of liquidity in the money markets such that the Reserve Bank had had to struggle to maintain an adequate shortage. It would be useful to have this additional instrument with which to regulate liquidity, even though the amounts involved would probably be fairly small when compared with monthly movements in reserves.[32]

Chapter 14

Conclusion

In conclusion, let us turn briefly to summarize some of the institutional detail. Defined in a narrow sense, the term 'money market' can be applied to that group of related markets which deals in assets of relative liquidity. The most obvious of these assets is call money, frequently lent overnight or for a short period of time (usually for a few days – up to 1 week). 'Call money' (more often than not overnight money) is the most liquid of assets other than cash. The lender has the right virtually to demand immediate repayment. Ordinarily, call money markets serve the purpose of ensuring employment for temporarily surplus cash and, in the banking system as a whole, there will usually exist a 'revolving fund' of such cash, much of which is borrowed one day, repaid the next, and often then reborrowed. Money may be lent or borrowed either direct between the parties or through money brokers in an inter-bank market, though in some centres (e.g. in Germany) there is a disinclination to use brokers. The extent to which brokers are used will vary between banks – some banks prefer for the most part to deal with other banks direct; others feel that dealing through brokers – with their knowledge of the market and their access to the fullest possible information – is likely to be more efficient. Certainly, where the market is volatile and banks may need a large volume of money fairly quickly, resort to brokers is more probable. In quieter times, large balances can be built up gradually and direct deals are likely to be more common.

Virtually all of the money dealt in is 'same day' money, though loans made late in the day may well be for tomorrow's date. In London – and in many other markets – it is surplus commercial bank balances that are lent. In the USA, it is commercial bank (and other financial institutional) balances at a Federal Reserve Bank that are traded. (There are twelve Federal Reserve Banks, and these – together with the Federal Reserve Board – constitute the central banking system of the United States.) These balances are lent and borrowed in the federal funds market (which is national in scope, but based in New York); they are traded both by commercial banks and other financial institutions like the larger savings and loan associations, sometimes a savings bank or a large credit union, but more generally through central institutions like a Federal Home Loan Bank or a credit union 'central'. This is the form that the inter-bank money market takes in the United States. Likewise, it is commercial bank balances at the central bank that are traded in France and Germany. Indeed, in France and Germany, also in Italy, the inter-bank market is virtually the core of the money market. It is normal for all inter-bank money-market loans to be unsecured, though all banks would operate internal limits on the amounts they would lend to particular parties (for the big banks, such limits may well be flexible).

Of the money-market instruments proper that are traded, an important group consists of Treasury bills (invented in England by Walter Bagehot in 1876/7), Treasury notes, and short-dated government bonds. Usually such issues, which are common to most countries, are arranged by the central bank in the country concerned as agent of the Treasury or Ministry of Finance. Being government paper (and therefore government guaranteed), such issues are normally relatively free of risk and generally provide the 'floor' to rates in the money market. Such securities are employed by governments as short-term borrowing instruments. Issues of Treasury bills and government bonds are usually subject to a competitive tender or auction, with allocations going to the highest bidders (i.e. those paying the highest prices, or offering the lowest rate or yield); sometimes they may be issued through the 'tap' – i.e. directly at an 'administered' rate.

Another important money market instrument is the bill of exchange, banker's acceptance, or eligible bank bill – the *Wechsel* (in Germany), and (in France) *effets privés*. The quality of such paper (making it eligible for central bank rediscount or purchase) depends on the good name of the acceptor – usually a leading bank or accepting house – and of other signatures to it (e.g. of another bank or discount house). There are also rights of recourse. Hence, it is readily tradable and therefore highly liquid paper; it is likewise a profitable short-term investment. Trade bills also exist, but, because they do not carry the name of an accepting bank, they are much less liquid.

Again, there are negotiable certificates of deposit (NCDs or CDs), first issued in the USA in 1961, but now common in a large number of countries (a certificate is issued to bearer as evidence of receipt of a deposit usually for a standard amount, or its multiple, which certificate may be sold in a secondary market if the holder wishes to disinvest). In some cases, there are certain restrictions on transferability (as in Japan) and this will inhibit the extent to which a secondary market can be developed.

Commercial paper on the US model is now a common instrument in a number of countries; elsewhere a local variation may be employed. Such paper is essentially an IOU, which may be issued by banks and holding companies, though it is mostly issued by industrial and commercial corporations (ideally it carries a credit rating and may be backed by a line of bank credit; it is not usually traded in a secondary market, but normally held to maturity, which can be but a few days).

In recent years, repurchase agreements ('repos') – or 'buy-backs' – have become increasingly important both as a means of providing the finance to carry a bank's or security dealer's investment portfolio, or inventory, and as a basis for providing temporary central bank accommodation. Very frequently, they are offered overnight, or for a few days, but may be renewed. In France, they are known as *pensions*, and in Japan as *gensaki*. 'Repos' provide the means whereby (if funds are required) paper is sold subject to an agreement to repurchase after a stated period (usually a few days), or a 'reverse repo', where paper is purchased subject to an agreement to resell, in circumstances where it is desired to absorb funds.

Nor should one neglect the Eurodollars and other Eurocurrencies, which may be bought and sold, and the Asian counterparts, dealt in – for example – in the Asian Dollar market largely based in Singapore. Japan perhaps more than other countries resorts to both the Eurodollar and the Asian dollar markets. These have grown rapidly, since the inception of the Eurodollar market in the late 1950s and the Asian dollar market in the late 1960s. Transactions take place between banks that issue and accept deposits in currencies other than those of the country in which the bank is located. The market is wholesale in character and almost totally exempt from national regulation, though this has been considered from time to time. If a bank has no immediate use for an incoming Euro-currency or Asian currency deposit, it may lend that deposit in an inter-bank market. It operates on a name basis and, since loans are unsecured, banks normally impose credit limits on other bank participants. The markets are intensely competitive. In addition, an increasing number of markets now deal in 'derivatives' such as financial futures, options, and swaps.

Finally, in relation to money markets, it is necessary to offer a brief word on central bank intervention. Central banks – in making money available to the banking system – often buy paper (e.g. eligible bank bills by the Bank of England, or, up to specified quotas, *Wechsel* by the Bundesbank in Germany), or lend against it (as do the US Federal Reserve banks direct to the commercial banks through the Fed's discount windows); in other cases – and this is now quite common – central banks will employ 'repos' (repurchase agreements) for the purpose of putting money into the system; on this basis, it is possible to resort to any form of acceptable paper and of any maturity greater than the maturity of the loan (including long-term government bonds); it is common for central banks, too, to invite commercial banks to submit bids for money in order to encourage the operation of market forces. The central bank accepts the best bids that have been offered. If it is a question of absorbing, or 'mopping up', excess liquidity, a central bank can either sell paper (usually Treasury bills) or employ the technique of the 'reverse repo' (a matched sale-purchase agreement) with a maturity perhaps of only a few days. In New York, the Federal Reserve Bank would usually resort to 'repos' with the government securities dealers (bank and non-bank), when funds are being made available ('reverse repos' where funds are being absorbed). In London also, in order to complement transactions in bills, 'repos' are resorted to by the Bank of England quite frequently and can be for large amounts; they are used especially where it is desired to target with precision forthcoming surpluses. This technique also enables the Bank to 'capture' longer-dated bills without buying them outright.

By its operations in the money market, a central bank can edge interest rates up or down. If it wishes to give a signal that there should be a shift in rates to a new level, it can elect to lend at either a higher or a lower Bank rate, or discount rate. Other rates will fall into line. Sometimes, a limited amount of 'emergency' credit can be made available (e.g. the lombard credits in Germany, or by forcing banks into the Bank of England to borrow at a penalty rate and probably for a minimum period). Central banks may also employ foreign exchange swaps for the purpose either of adding to or withdrawing money from the banking system. To a lesser extent, some central banks may employ the placement with or the withdrawal from commercial banks of government balances as a means of influencing liquidity in the economy. More generally, open market operations (as above) may be employed, to offset the effects of government additions to liquidity (as a result of government expenditure) or the withdrawal of funds by government action (e.g. as at tax dates, or when major issues of government securities are made).

We have noted that a money market can be defined in a narrow sense; sometimes (though this is less true now) very narrowly indeed, as used to be the case in London where the money market was regarded as deriving primarily from the market relationships between the discount houses and the commercial banks. Nevertheless, such an emphasis – where it occurs – must not blind us to the fact that at the very least the term should be applied to the whole complex of related markets in short-term and liquid assets in which banks and other financial institutions deal. Indeed, not infrequently, the term is also applied in a wider and looser context. In its broader connotations, it may be taken to encompass the whole complex of financial institutions – and their inter-relationships – which in varying degrees act together to satisfy the monetary needs of a community, and sometimes such institutions are scattered spatially over a wide area. Increasingly, too, assisted by screen trading and highly developed communications, there are links between money markets throughout the world.

Notes

CHAPTER 2

1 See W. T. C. King, *History of the London Discount Market* (1936); Gillett Brothers Discount Company Limited, *The Bill on London* (first edition, 1952 and subsequent editions); the Institute of Bankers, *The London Discount Market Today* (1962, as revised 1969); R. S. Sayers, *Gilletts in the London Money Market 1867–1967* (1968); W. M. Scammell, *The London Discount Market* (1968); Cater Ryder & Co, Ltd, *Cater Ryder 1816–1966: Discount Bankers* (With Additional History, 1966–1971) (1971); E. R. Shaw, *The London Money Market* (1975); Malcolm Craig, *The Sterling Money Markets* (1976); J. S. G. Wilson, *The London Money Markets* (1976 and 1989); and George and Pamela Cleaver, *The Union Discount – A Centenary Album* (1985).

2 There are seven discount houses (which are authorized banks); two of the nine are 'hybrids' – a combined discount house and gilt-edged market-maker.

3 Alexanders Discount plc; Cater Allen Ltd; Clive Discount Company Ltd; Gerrard & National Ltd; King & Shaxson Ltd; Seccombe, Marshall & Campion plc; Union Discount Company Ltd (all authorized under the Banking Act 1987); and Greenwell Montagu Gilt-Edged and S. G. Warburg, Akroyd, Rowe and Pitman, Mullens (Gilt-Edged) Ltd (gilt-edged market-makers). Of these, Union Discount Coy, Gerrard & National, Cater Allen, and King & Shaxson remain independent. (S. G. Warburg, Akroyd, Rowe and Pitman, Mullens (Gilt-Edged) Ltd ceased its discount house operations at the end of September 1992.)

4 In the past, holdings of Treasury bills have been much higher, depending on the needs of government finance. In any case, a large proportion of Treasury bills are held outside the hands of the discount houses, mostly in other banks, building societies, and overseas.

5 Of secured money placed by banks in the United Kingdom, the bulk goes into the discount market, which really has no serious competitors for secured money.

6 For an inter-bank loan, the effective minimum would be £500,000 or £1 million. Typical loans would be £5 million, £10 million, or £15 million.

7 On the international side, limits are sometimes advised. And if a

participant is really active, they would in any case get to know what their limits are.

8 At the very least, they would be subject to an annual review.

9 'It dies a death around about 5.30 p.m.' But if there is a base rate change, or other developments, as in New York, business may run on until after 6.00 p.m., even very rarely to 8.00 p.m. Same-day dealing always ends at 3.00 to 3.30 p.m.

10 For transactions in CDs, commercial bills, Treasury bills, etc., if such items were to be delivered the same day, the transaction would usually have to be done by 12 noon.

11 The market for wholesale money now opens about 7.30 a.m. (it used to be 9.00 a.m.).

12 Noon is the cut-off time for calling back call money, but trading can go on for same-day settlement until 3.30 p.m.

13 A much lower proportion of salaries is now paid in cash and the intra-month pattern now seems to be less prominent than it was.

14 The Bank of England now puts on the screen at the beginning of each day a figure for the previous day's bank balances (but only if it is more than £3 million either way).

15 Note that the discount houses these days no longer have a 'money book'; it is now a 'page' on the computer. And for the purpose of maintaining records of daily activity a computer print-out will be retained for a period of 6 years (Statute of Limitations).

16 These are the 'authorized institutions', of which there were 537 in December 1990. Formerly, under previous legislation, the figures were divided between banks and licensed deposit-takers (there were about 280 of the latter and around 300 recognized banks).

17 Brokers, of course, serve more than the inter-bank deposit market – indeed, 60 per cent of broker activity relates to foreign exchange, and foreign currency deposits to 25 per cent, sterling deposits to less than 10 per cent. In the past 2 years or so, there has been a marked increase in business in forward-rate agreements, over-the-counter options, and swaps. See 'The role of brokers in the London money markets', Bank of England *Quarterly Bulletin*, May 1990, pp. 221ff.

18 It is said that when one deals through brokers one really wants to do the deal. When operating direct, one or the other party may not actually want to do the deal. Brokers are at their busiest when banks need to operate in a hurry, i.e. in a fast-moving market. In a quiet market, one can build up positions gradually by direct deals.

19 There may also be broking in CDs both in the primary and secondary markets; this is really just another aspect of the business in deposits.

20 It may be 80 per cent or more of total turnover. But it must be remembered that in calculating this statistic, overnight money is turned over every day; 1-month money, for example, is only turned over once in the month, and similarly for other 'period' money.

21 The rate actually quoted is for 5-year CDs. The inter-bank trading market is up to 1 year. But a lot can be done by way of interest rate swaps or futures.

22 See Cazenove Money Brokers, *Money Broking – A Service to the Market Place* (no date).

23 Formerly, money market rates were seen to be very volatile and, on average, they would have cost more (in the 1960s and 1970s) than retail funds and, at times, substantially more. Retail funds are still cheaper than wholesale, but the supply is obviously limited and the difference in cost has declined. Due to the growth of external competition, the building societies' interest rate cartel had also been abandoned, and this gave building societies greater flexibility. There was also a greater demand for funds by them.

24 Building societies now face significant competition for mortgage lending from institutions that fund such lending from the wholesale market. This may cause the mortgage rate to become more market-related in the future with a closer correlation between it and (say) 3-month LIBOR.

25 Building Societies Association *Bulletin*, No. 44, October 1985, pp. 7–15.

26 Formerly, the minimum was 7.5 per cent of total funds, but – following the Building Societies Act 1986 – there is now no minimum liquidity ratio. However, it remains the responsibility of societies' boards to ensure that they have sufficient liquidity (and that they satisfy the Building Societies Commission). There is a maximum limit of $33\frac{1}{3}$ per cent imposed by the Act to ensure that societies continue with their traditional business.

27 Often less than 1 month.

28 When they lend, which may also be to a discount house, it is usually unsecured – as in the inter-bank market proper – and they likewise apply 'unadvised' or internal limits to their borrowers. The Building Societies (Liquid Assets) Regulations 1987, which came into force on 1 October 1987, do not stipulate any limit. However, for purposes of prudential supervision, the building societies are expected to operate a minimum limit of 10 per cent of counter-party shareholders' funds, or 10 per cent of free reserves, whichever is the less.

29 These can either be floating-rate notes or, if fixed, be converted back into a floating-rate instrument by an interest-rate swap. They can also issue currency bonds, when they could do a currency swap as well.

30 They may sometimes lend to discount houses on a secured basis.

31 These may be put out to tender to get the lowest price available. Money is usually for 1 week, or 1 month, but may be overnight.

32 Uncommitted lines usually relate to overnight money, though uncommitted period lines also exist.

33 Trade bills are drawn on one trader by another against actual trade transactions. It is two-name paper (drawer and acceptor), but there is no bank name. They have declined in relative importance over the last 10 years or so, but there is still at least some £700 million (mid-1991) in the market. Most of the trade bill business is done by Alexanders and Union.

34 And some are finance paper, i.e. not based on a trade transaction in physical goods.

35 In this context, the London branch of certain Commonwealth banks might count as British.

36 E.g. when there was an acute shortage of Treasury bills.

37 The last sample taken was in March 1980. Prior to that it had become an adjunct to credit control (in monitoring the extent to which hire purchase and instalment credit were being financed through bills). The need for sampling was also greatly reduced by greater emphasis on bill purchases created by the new form of official market operations in 1981. Banks' total amounts of bill acceptances are monitored through their regular monthly balance sheet reports, which are required for more general statistical and supervisory purposes.

38 Bank of England *Quarterly Bulletins*, Table 3.1.

39 Ibid., Table 4.

40 For a summary of its early history and its definition, see Daniel R. Kane, *The Eurodollar Market and the Years of Crisis* (1983), pp. 1–3 and 127–131.

41 The main exception was the 'marginal reserve requirement' imposed by the Federal Reserve Board in the US in 1979–80. See J. S. G. Wilson, *Banking Policy and Structure: A Comparative Analysis* (1986), pp. 419–20.

42 For further details, see British Bankers' Association, *Certificates of Deposit on the London Market* (August 1987).

43 Formerly, there was a forward market in sterling CDs, which reached a peak in 1971/2. It began to disappear after mid-1973 as a consequence of the secondary banking crisis. Isolated forward deals did occur from time to time, but in effect the market ceased to exist (see Wilson, *The London Money Markets* (1976), pp. 48–9).

44 Clearly, whatever the initial situation, as a CD approaches maturity, it can again become as short as a few days.

45 An obvious reason for this could be where a CD has been sold in a secondary market and the bank may not find it easy to persuade the subsequent holder to agree to a rollover.

46 Bank of England *Quarterly Bulletin*, Table 3.1.

47 Ibid., Table 4.

48 The Phillips Report was drawn up by a working group chaired by Brian Phillips of the Nationwide Building Society and reporting in August 1980.

49 See BSA *Bulletin*, No. 44, October 1985, pp. 8 and 10.

50 For further details, see ibid., pp. 10–11.

51 See The Building Societies (Liquid Assets) Regulations 1987.

52 BSA *Bulletin*, No. 44, p. 11.

53 See Bank of England *Quarterly Bulletin*, Table 9.2.

54 For further details, see Wilson *The London Money Markets* (1976), pp. 29–31 and notes.

55 P. J. Lee quoted in Wilson, *The London Money Markets* (1976), p. 31.

56 *Bank of England Operations in the Sterling Money Market: The Extension of the Bank of England's Dealing Relationships in the Sterling Money Market*, October 1988, pp. 2 and 17.

57 Ibid., October 1988.

58 Formerly, the Bank of England declined to buy Treasury bills unless they had been held for 7 days. This requirement has never been removed altogether.

59 The ECU was officially introduced in March 1979 to replace the European Unit of Account, which had been established in 1975. The ECU serves as the basis for determining exchange rate parities and as a reserve asset and means of settlement in the European Monetary System (EMS). The ECU is valued on the basis of specified amounts of the currencies of eleven member states of the European Community (Luxembourg is not included). The details need not concern us here. The basis may be changed by the Community and this may include changes in the components. The EMS provides for re-examination every 5 years of the weights of the currencies in the basket (or on request, if the weight of any currency has changed by 25 per cent) and for the inclusion of currencies of new member states of the European Community. The last revision was in September 1989.

60 See *Financial Times* 12/10/88 and 9/11/88.

61 Or the money might be channelled by the Bank of England to the Bank for International Settlements (BIS) as a deposit, when the BIS might invest it in the money markets around the world.

62 See *Financial Times* 12/2/91. It was pointed out that brokers are used for contracts which need some support, but do not need prices to be made the whole time. On the other hand, the MATIF in France, which launched the first ECU bond futures contract in October 1990, took the opposite view that market-makers were required because the underlying cash market had not yet matured sufficiently.

63 For a survey of the local authority market as it once was, see Wilson, *The London Money Markets* (1976), pp. 37ff.

64 See HM Treasury press release 15/2/90.

65 See Bank of England *Quarterly Bulletins*.

66 For greater detail, see 'Central Moneymarkets Office' in Bank of England *Quarterly Bulletin*, November 1990, pp. 514ff.

67 The institutions that have joined CMO include all the discount houses (the main market-makers in bills), the Stock Exchange money brokers (the intermediaries for collateralized stock borrowing and lending) and the major banks that issue and trade actively in CDs. Eighteen members announced their intention to provide agency facilities; others confined their offer of these facilities to their existing clients (ibid., pp. 516–17).

68 i.e. one which is continuously updated with current information (and immediately carries out users' instructions) as distinct from being based on historical data.

69 Sayers, *Gilletts*, p. 101. But, as Sayers also points out, Gilletts had been dabbling in bonds in the nineteenth century; this was possibly true of some of the other houses as well.

70 H. F. Goodson, Institute of Bankers, *The London Discount Market Today* (London, 1962, as revised 1969), p. 39.

71 See Sayers, *Gilletts*, p. 142.

72 Radcliffe Committee *Minutes of Evidence*, Q. 531, p. 32.

73 Large industrial and commercial companies were also interested.

74 Goodson, loc. cit., p. 40.

75 Ibid.

76 Wilfred King, Institute of Bankers, *The London Discount Market Today*, p. 14.

77 Radcliffe Committee *Report*, para. 174, p. 62.

78 See *Competition and Credit Control*, being articles reprinted from the Bank of England *Quarterly Bulletin*, 1971 and 1973, pp. 5, 6, and 9.

79 Chief Cashier in ibid., p. 17.

80 Ibid., p. 18.

81 For further details relating to this period, see Wilson, *The London Money Markets* (1989), pp. 36–40.

82 See ibid., pp. 39–40.

83 See The Stock Exchange Notice, 'The choice of a new dealing system for gilt-edged securities', and Bank of England, *The Future Structure of the Gilt-edged Market*, November 1984 and April 1985. Also, Patrick Phillips, *Inside the New Gilt-edged Market* (2nd edition, 1987).

84 Phillips, op. cit. pp. 12–13.

85 Ibid.

86 Ibid.

87 The original list and their make-up is given by Phillips, op. cit. pp. 14–15. By April 1991, the list included Aitken Campbell (Gilts) Limited; Barclays de Zoete Wedd Gilts Limited; Baring Sterling Bonds; BT Gilts Limited; CSFB (GILTS) Limited; Daiwa Europe (Gilts) Limited; Gerrard & National Securities Limited; Goldman Sachs Government Securities (U.K.) Limited; Greenwell Montagu Gilt-Edged; James Capel Gilts Limited; J. P. Morgan Sterling Securities Ltd; Kleinwort Benson Gilts Limited; Lehman Brothers Gilts Limited; NatWest Gilts Limited; Nomura Gilts Limited; Salomon Brothers UK Limited; S. G. Warburg, Akroyd, Rowe & Pitman, Mullens (Gilt-Edged) Ltd; and UBS Phillips & Drew Gilts Limited.

88 Phillips, op. cit. p. 15.

89 Ibid. There were six firms (there are now three), all carefully vetted by the Bank of England. These are Garban Gilts Limited; Williams, Cooke, Lott & Kissack Limited; and Cantor Fitzgerald (Gilts) Limited.

90 Phillips, op. cit. p. 16.

91 See Bank of England *Quarterly Bulletin*, December 1986, pp. 569ff.

92 Initially, only for pension funds, but generally available by 1982.

93 See *Financial Times*, 26/8/86.

94 See *Financial Times*, 15/10/86.

95 See *Financial Times*, 14/2/87.

96 See *Financial Times*, 14/5/87.

97 See *Financial Times*, 16/9/87.

98 *Financial Times*, 28/9/87.

99 *Financial Times*, 25/3/88.

100 See J. S. G. Wilson, *The London Money Markets* (1989), p. 56; also Chart 1 in Bank of England *Quarterly Bulletin*, February 1991, p. 49.

101 Bank of England *Quarterly Bulletin*, February 1991, Table B, p. 50.

102 According to the Bank of England, the six largest market-makers in

gilt-edged have over 60 per cent of the business in terms of gilts turnover. See ibid., Chart 5, p. 51.

103 Ibid., p. 50.
104 See *The Independent*, 19/1/91.
105 An indexed gilt was sold in October 1988.
106 See *The Independent* and *Daily Telegraph* for 19/1/91.
107 *Financial Times*, 19/1/91.
108 See *Financial Times*, 16/2/91.
109 See *Financial Times*, 11/4/91, 15/4/91, 17/4/91, and 25/4/91. See also *The Independent*, 25/4/91.
110 See *Financial Times*, 2/12/91 and 7/1/92.
111 See Bank of England Notice, 19/3/85.
112 See Bank of England Notice, 29/4/86.
113 A period of 364 days is less than 1 year; hence interest can be paid gross.
114 For these and other details, see 'The early development of the sterling commercial paper market' in Bank of England *Quarterly Bulletin*, November 1987, pp. 527ff.
115 Approaching two-thirds of institutional investors had no upper limit for investing in SCP.
116 Bank of England *Quarterly Bulletin*, November 1987, p. 528.
117 See Bank of England, *Quarterly Bulletin*, February 1990, p. 36.
118 See 'Commercial paper markets', Bank of England *Quarterly Bulletin*, February 1987, pp. 46–53.
119 But with a heavy concentration in the range Bid + 4 to Offered.
120 See Stephen Fidler in *Financial Times*, 23/10/90.
121 In 1990/91, the vast majority had a period of 3 months.
122 For further details, see Robert Miller, 'Risk control for banks: the use of financial futures and options' in J. S. G. Wilson (editor), *Managing Bank Assets and Liabilities* (1988).
123 Futures and options are useful for taking positions at much less capital cost than would be needed for the underlying instrument, because of the lower credit risk involved.
124 The C shares in issue are mostly held by members who also hold A and B shares. C shares or permits allow one trader into certain specified pits where the exchange wishes to encourage liquidity – C permits are cheaper to own because of this restriction and are valid for the futures pits (not options), though excluding short sterling, long gilt, Euro-dollar, and US Treasury bond contracts.
125 See *Financial Times*, and *The Independent* 15/1/92.
126 Seccombes ceased to be the Bank's broker from the beginning of January 1986.
127 Indirect assistance, or indirect help, was referred to in the 1967 edition of R. S. Sayers, *Modern Banking*. Some time thereafter the term seems to have dropped out of use. However, I am advised by Mr Peter Lee, formerly of Union Discount, that the purchase of bills by the Bank of England from the clearing banks – generally because the discount houses did not have the maturities required by the Bank – with the express intention that these moneys should be on-lent to the

money market 'certainly still occurred during the years of Competition and Credit Control, though somewhat infrequently', and it may no longer have been termed 'indirect help'. Today, the term is no longer used.

128 *Competition and Credit Control 1971–74*, p. 15. The quote is from the text of part of a Sykes Memorial Lecture given by the Chief Cashier to the Institute of Bankers on November 10, 1971.

129 Bank of England *Quarterly Bulletin*, March 1982, p. 87.

130 Bank of England *Quarterly Bulletin*, December 1980, p. 428.

131 For example, the requirement that a house should hold 50 per cent of its funds in certain forms of public-sector debt placed a premium on these public-sector assets, particularly those such as Treasury and local-authority bills which were bought by the Bank of England when providing assistance to the market. For more details, see J. S. G. Wilson, 'An experiment in competition and credit control – the U.K. experience post-1971', *Geld en onderneming* (Leyden, 1976), as reprinted by SUERF, p. 13.

132 The situation was complicated by the fact that the discount houses had been observing the 50 per cent public-sector-debt ratio, and therefore had virtually had to hold gilts. This requirement was now removed somewhat suddenly instead of being phased out more gradually, and at a time when MLR was being increased quite substantially.

133 Under new multiplier arrangements (see p. 96), there were now limitations imposed by the added risk weightings.

134 These have now ceased to exist.

135 'The purpose of the cash ratio scheme is to provide resources and income to the Bank; it is of no relevance to the day-to-day management of the money market since the deposits placed with the Bank are fixed for some months at a time (the period will be six months when the scheme is fully established).' Bank of England *Quarterly Bulletin*, March 1982, p. 89. Latterly, the Bank of England had less need for the ratio at such a level – with the considerable explosion in the size of bank balance sheets; hence the reductions indicated in the text.

136 The 'club money' pool was of the order of £3,000 million; market holdings were (say) £5,500 million. Much of the balance would have come from secured bank loans to the discount houses over and above the 6 per cent 'club money', as well as from business corporations.

137 See Bank of England *Quarterly Bulletin*, September 1981, p. 312.

138 Ibid., June 1982, p. 181.

139 See 'The role of the Bank of England in the money market', Bank of England *Quarterly Bulletin*, March 1982, pp. 86ff.

140 This can be checked in *Financial Times* Money Market Reports.

141 Unless the Bank wishes to keep the market short of money in order to emphasize its view on interest rates (see p. 84–5).

142 *Bank of England Operations in the Sterling Money Market: The Extension of the Bank of England's Dealing Relationships in the Sterling Money Market*, October 1988, paras. 16 and 17, pp. 15–16.

143 For examples, see *Financial Times* Money Market Reports 4/11/90,

and 19/12/90. See also reports in *Financial Times*, 16/2/91, 2/3/91, 9/3/91, and 27/4/91.

144 Ibid., 13/4/91.

145 It is not always repaid the next day; repayment may be put into a day when there is going to be a surplus, or it may be a penalty for too much late borrowing.

146 See *Bank of England Operations in the Sterling Money Market*, October 1988, p. 18.

147 See R. O. Close in J. S. G. Wilson (editor), *Managing Bank Assets and Liabilities*, pp. 121–6 and especially p. 122.

148 The day to day details – together with the rates at which business is done – can be assembled by inspection of the daily Money Market Reports in, for example, *Financial Times*.

149 Release by Bank of England on 'Discount house multipliers', June 1982.

150 See *Bank of England Operations in the Sterling Money Market*.

151 In this context, it should be noted that the European Commission has accorded discount houses a 'temporary' exemption from the requirements of Council Directive No. L 386/15 of 18 December 1989 on a solvency ratio for credit institutions. See Article 1, para. 4. Subject to certain provisions, this relates to 'any credit institution specializing in the inter-bank and public-debt markets and fulfilling, together with the central bank, the institutional function of banking-system liquidity regulator' where 'its main activity consists of acting as intermediary between the central bank of its Member State and the banking system' and 'the competent authority applies adequate systems of supervision and control of its credit, interest-rate and market risks'.

152 The risk classification of assets is shown in Table 2.4 on pp. 94–5.

153 As laid down by the Bank of England in *Bank of England Operations in the Sterling Money Market*.

154 The amount of the underlying instrument that the option carries the right to buy or sell multiplied by the probability of the option being exercised.

155 See J. S. G. Wilson, *The London Money Markets* (1976), and integration had already taken place before then.

CHAPTER 3

1 For a more detailed coverage of the subject, see Marcia Stigum, *The Money Market* (revised edition, 1983, and third edition 1990); see also Ann-Marie Meulendyke, *U.S. Monetary Policy and Financial Markets*, Federal Reserve Bank of New York, 1989.

2 These figures should be treated with some reserve, since ownership data for investors other than US government agencies, the Federal Reserve, and foreign governments are not reliable.

3 Non-marketable certificates of indebtedness can be issued to trust accounts.

4 See Board of Governors of the Federal Reserve System, *1989 Historical Chart Book*, pp. 96–7.

5 Unlike bills, notes and bonds pay separate interest every 6 months. They carry a fixed interest payment – the coupon rate – and hence are called coupon securities. The coupon rate is established at auction. Bidding on coupon issues is based on yields, not prices. After an issue has been awarded at auction, the Treasury establishes a fixed coupon, which generally is rounded down to the nearest eighth of 1 per cent, based on the weighted average of the accepted competitive yields.

6 The system with regard to the submission of tenders is for the form to be filled in in blank and to be taken down to the Fed in New York by a representative of the dealing firm, who – after a phone call from base just before 1.00 p.m. (or whatever is the relevant time) – fills in the figures and lodges the completed form in the box where the bids must be deposited. The Fed maintains a bank of telephones nearby for the purpose. Normally, a dealer will tender over a range of bids and amounts. One might note that the World Bank tenders by wire from Washington.

7 Auctions of the 52-week bill are announced on the Friday prior to the auction and the auction itself is held one week before the bill is issued (i.e. on a Thursday).

8 Japanese insurance companies were big buyers in the 1980s.

9 In this context, see US General Accounting Office, *U.S. Treasury Securities – The Market's Structure, Risks and Regulation* (August 1986); *U.S. Government Securities – Dealer Views on Market Operations and Federal Reserve Oversight* (September 1986); *U.S. Government Securities – The Federal Reserve Response Regarding its Market-Making Standard* (April 1987); and *U.S. Government Securities – An Examination of Views Expressed about Access to Brokers' Services* (December 1987).

10 Prior to 1935, the individual Reserve Banks had some latitude to engage independently in open market operations. But the last transaction outside New York occurred prior to 1930.

11 There are often several possible actions that would be consistent with the directive.

12 Temporary transactions – e.g. by way of 'repos' – are for same day delivery; outright transactions are for next day or for two days-forward delivery.

13 See J. S. G. Wilson, *Banking Policy and Structure* (1986), pp. 405–7.

14 On occasion, the desk at the Fed has fixed the term of the 'repo' and not allowed early withdrawal.

15 There are two to four meetings each day and at the end of 3 weeks the Federal Reserve managers will have met with all the dealers.

16 For a careful consideration of the use made of repurchase agreements, see Sheila L. Tschinkel and her colleagues in Federal Reserve Bank of Atlanta, *Economic Review*, September 1985. *Inter alia*, this review of these arrangements was concerned with safety. Investors, including public authorities and depository institutions, suffered financial losses when firms dealing in repurchase agreements using government

securities failed. Repurchase agreements (or 'repos') have been used extensively in the money market for many years now by investors seeking to earn a return on idle cash and by institutions needing to raise funds on a short-term basis. Meanwhile, although each failure has had its own distinct characteristics, some common elements have been evident. Had certain procedures been followed by all parties, losses could have been prevented, or at least limited. In particular, it is desirable that the parties abide by a master 'repo' contract, evaluate collateral carefully, establish control over collateral, and monitor the value of collateral and interest accruals during the term of a 'repo', making margin calls when necessary. Prudent management practices can go a long way toward preventing fraud. It is largely a matter of education in safe methods of doing business, and the Federal Reserve System attempted this in a nationwide series of workshops beginning in 1985.

17 Primary dealers serve two crucial functions: they help distribute the Treasury debt and they stand ready to 'make markets', or buy and sell securities for customers. Their selection by the Fed as counterparties revolves around their ability to fulfil these two functions. Besides their ability to meet the needs of the Fed, criteria for being a primary dealer include: volume of activity and participation in Treasury auctions; breadth of customer base; ability and commitment to buy and sell securities for customers even when market conditions are unfavourable; financial strength; depth of experience of management; and commitment to filling this role over the long term.

18 *U.S. Treasury Securities – The Market's Structure, Risks, and Regulation* (August 1986), p. 23.

19 Daily financial information reported by the primary dealers to the Federal Reserve usually consists of transactions and positions in: (i) Treasury bills, notes, and bonds; (ii) federal agency securities; (iii) futures, forward positions, and options in Treasury and agency securities; and (iv) other money market instruments, including investments in bankers' acceptances, CDs, and commercial paper. Financing of positions through repurchase agreements is also reported daily.

20 Some dealers have been surprised to discover the extent of the risks involved and the potential losses with which they might be faced.

21 See *U.S. Treasury Securities – The Market's Structure, Risks, and Regulation* (August 1986), p. 23.

22 These firms provide only brokering services, i.e. they conduct only matched transactions and do not take positions for their own account. They are different from primary and non-primary dealers, who may also perform a broker function, when they conduct matching transactions between customers.

23 Actually, during the 1970s, the Fed did buy agency issues outright and built up a portfolio, which is now rolled over as various issues mature. When the Fed did buy outright, it was constrained by guidelines designed to avoid the possible influences just referred to.

24 The pioneering work in the study of this market was undertaken by the late Parker B. Willis of the Federal Reserve Bank of Boston, see his

Federal Funds Market – Its Origin and Development, originally published in 1957 and running to a fifth edition in 1972. In addition, reference may be made to *The Federal Funds Market – A Study by a Federal Reserve System Committee*, Board of Governors of the Federal Reserve System, May 1959; also Dorothy M. Nichols, *Trading in Federal Funds (Findings of a Three-Year Survey)*, Board of Governors of the Federal Reserve System, September 1965; Parker B. Willis, *A Study of the Market for Federal Funds*, prepared for the Steering Committee for the Fundamental Reappraisal of the Discount Mechanism appointed by the Board of Governors of the Federal Reserve System, March 1967; J. S. G. Wilson, 'Money markets in the United States of America', Banca Nazionale del Lavoro *Quarterly Review*, December 1970; and Marcia Stigum, *The Money Market* (revised edition 1983, third edition 1990).

25 For very big 'plays', the commission may be slightly reduced. There is some price competition.

26 See Nichols, op. cit., pp. 4n and 28.

27 It used to be of the order of half a per cent.

28 It should be noted that brokers rarely go under $10 million (occasionally $1 million might be done as an odd lot).

29 Federal Home Loan Banks bundle up the excess reserves of member institutions and sell them in the brokers' market.

30 See 'Daylight overdrafts and payments system risk', *Federal Reserve Bulletin*, November 1987.

31 Ibid., p. 840. See also: Board of Governors of Federal Reserve System, 'Daylight overdraft policy', *Federal Register*, vol. 50, No. 99; Federal Reserve Bank of New York, 'Reducing risks on large-dollar wire transfer systems – new daylight overdraft policy' (effective 27 March 1986), Circular No. 9868, 31 May 1985; 'Proposed changes in the payments system risk reduction program' (28 June 1989), Circular No. 10301; 'Payments system risk reduction program' (18 June 1990), Circular No. 10353; and 'Policy statements regarding daylight overdrafts', *Federal Register*, 31 May 1990, vol. 55, No. 105, pp. 22087–98.

32 *Federal Reserve Bulletin*, November 1987, p. 840.

33 Ibid.

34 For experience with the policy of payments risk, see *Federal Reserve Bulletin*, November 1987, pp. 845–9.

35 See ibid., pp. 850–2.

36 See Federal Reserve Bank of New York, Circular No. 10301, 20/6/89, pp. 3–5.

37 A banker's acceptance is a time draft drawn on a bank, usually to finance the shipment or temporary storage of goods. By 'accepting' the draft, the bank makes an unconditional promise to pay the holder of the draft a stated amount at a specified date. Thus, the bank effectively substitutes its own credit for that of a borrower and in the process creates a negotiable instrument that may be freely traded. The market is highly liquid and is supported by about thirty dealers and a dozen brokers.

38 See 'Recent developments in the bankers acceptance market', *Federal Reserve Bulletin*, January 1986.

39 See Federal Reserve Bank of New York, *Monthly Survey*, 7/2/92.
40 A small proportion is interest-bearing, but there would be no more than 10 per cent of this in the dealer market.
41 With directly placed paper, it is usual for the maturities to be tailor-made, but the issuer is also 'willing to pick it up at any time', i.e. it is redeemable.
42 Financial companies are institutions engaged primarily in activities such as (but not limited to): commercial, savings, and mortgage banking; sales, personal, and mortgage financing; factoring, finance leasing, and other business lending; insurance underwriting; and other investment activities.
43 Non-financial companies include public utilities and firms primarily engaged in activities such as communications, construction, manufacturing, mining, wholesale and retail trade, transportation, and services.
44 See also Marcia Stigum, *The Money Market* (revised edition), pp. 644–5, where reference is made to A and B Notes, which distinguish between moneys lent more or less semi-permanently and moneys which are available on demand.
45 See Order of the Board of Governors of the Federal Reserve System, effective 21 September 1989, and Federal Reserve Bank of New York Circular no. 10314, 24 October 1989.
46 Most of them would swap the proceeds into local currencies, though some of them would have dollar needs of their own.
47 See J. S. G. Wilson, *Banking Policy and Structure*, pp. 100–1.
48 See *Federal Reserve Bulletins*.
49 Retail CDs may carry an interest rate $\frac{1}{8}$ per cent less than wholesale CDs, and the fact that there are no reserve requirements is worth another $\frac{1}{4}$ per cent.
50 They may also trade Eurodollar CDs. These resemble domestic CDs except that, instead of being the liability of a domestic bank, they are the liability of the London branch of a US bank, of a British bank, or of some other foreign bank with a branch in London. See Marcia Stigum, *The Money Market* (revised edition, 1983), p. 37 and pp. 550ff.
51 Brokers also exist, see Stigum (revised edition), pp. 544–5.

Brokers are actively used by CD traders for the same reasons they are used by traders in governments – they provide anonymity and speedy communication with other dealers. Also, a dealer may be able to do a large volume in the brokers market, which would be difficult to do direct.

52 See J. S. G. Wilson, 'Money markets in the United States of America', Banca Nazionale del Lavoro *Quarterly Review*, December 1970.
53 Of itself, Regulation Q provided a powerful incentive for holding dollar deposits abroad.
54 Marcia Stigum, *The Money Market* (revised edition), p. 140. For a fuller coverage, see Stigum, pp. 129ff.
55 There is a 3 per cent reserve requirement on net borrowings of Eurodollars by home office. Many banks have long-term placements abroad that allow non-reservable borrowings of short-term Eurodollars.

56 For further consideration, see Stigum, *The Money Market* (revised edition), pp. 592ff.

57 It is said that over 1,000 banks out of something over the 13,000 in the US are active in financial futures.

58 Note that with interest rate futures involving Treasury bills, notes and bonds, there may still be physical delivery of a debt instrument. The Chicago Board of Trade has also introduced a cash-settled 2-year Treasury note in addition to physical delivery. The contract is set up such that the instrument has to be of a certain maturity – e.g. a bond with at least 15 years to maturity, or a Treasury bill with 13 weeks to maturity. Trading starts up approximately 18 months before delivery (though one can really go out 2 to 3 years), i.e. trading begins before an actual instrument exists. One might also mention that new contracts are produced from time to time – some become established; others fail and disappear.

59 See G. D. Koppenhaver, 'Futures options and their use by financial intermediaries', Federal Reserve Bank of Chicago, *Economic Perspectives*, January/February 1986, pp. 18ff.

60 See Brian Gendreau, 'New markets in foreign currency options', Federal Reserve Bank of Philadelphia, *Business Review*, July/August 1984, pp. 3ff.

61 See also M. K. Lewis in J. S. G. Wilson (ed.), *Managing Bank Assets and Liabilities*, Euromoney 1988, pp. 171–2.

62 Hours of operation reflect supply and demand, and brokers' hours influence when trading is active. Obviously the OTC markets can only trade when there are people there to do it.

63 See *Joint Report on the Government Securities Market* (Department of the Treasury, Securities and Exchange Commission, and the Board of Governors of the Federal Reserve System), January 1992.

64 See also E. Gerald Corrigan, 'Changes in the government securities market' in Federal Reserve Bank of New York, *Quarterly Review*, Winter 1991–92, Volume 16, Number 4, pp. 6–11, being Statement before the Committee on Banking, Finance, and Urban Affairs and the Subcommittee on Domestic Monetary Policy of the House of Representatives, 6 February 1992.

65 Those not pre-registered could appear at their local Federal Reserve Bank with sufficient documentation and acceptable payment arrangements to be included in the auction through a computer hookup provided at the Bank.

CHAPTER 4

1 See *Règlement no. 85–17 du Comité de la réglementation bancaire* signed on 17 December 1985 by the Minister of Economy and Finance.

2 *Décision de caractère général*, no. 67–10 taken by Conseil national du crédit on 28 June 1967.

3 See Bank of France *Bulletin Trimestriel*, No. 79, September 1991, Table 6.

4 These are the *spécialistes en valeurs du Trésor*, who participate in the auction (the primary market) and are expected to quote realistic prices on the secondary market, where they will also be active.

5 This is a system where prices and quantities are put on a screen by the broker on behalf of the party that is quoting. Such prices and quantities are firm quotes.

6 Big institutions would use their own judgement; small banks may find it easier to seek guidance from a broker.

7 Exceptionally, it may be later.

8 Corporations are said to like the Ffr 5 million size, but transactions may often be for from Ffr 5 to 20 million.

9 See F.-J. Credot, in *Banque*, June 1986 and P. L. Bordenave, H. de Boysson, and M. Konczaty in *Banque* for August/September 1986.

10 BNP, Société Générale, and Crédit Lyonnais handling about two-thirds of the issues, and BNP, Société Générale, Crédit Lyonnais, Paribas, and the Banque Française du Commerce Extérieur more than three-quarters – see *Banque*, no. 464, August/September 1986, p. 735.

11 See *Financial Times*, 5/11/86.

12 They were revised in October 1990. See *Financial Times*, 17/10/90. *Inter alia*, banks were now allowed to include their holdings of notes as part of their compulsory reserves.

13 There are certain exceptions; see Banque de France, *Le système des réserves obligatoires*. Note d'information no. 77 (1), April 1988, p. 7.

14 See A. Icard, *'La réforme du marché interbancaire'*, *Banque*, January 1987, p. 78.

15 These *courtiers* are also described as *agents des marchés interbancaires (AMI)*. They do not always operate in foreign exchange (FOREX).

16 *Effets privés* may be trade-related or finance paper; both kinds of paper are employed.

17 Both might go 'short' or 'long' depending on interest rate expectations. Thus, banks may borrow and lend at the same time, but for different maturities.

18 See 'The big bond road show', *The Banker* (London), August 1987, pp. 70–2.

19 For greater detail, see Francine Roure, *Les Mécanismes du MATIF*, Paris 1988.

20 The remainder tend to be *groupements* of diverse interests that join forces to operate on the MATIF.

21 OMF 50 was launched by OMF, which was a French subsidiary of OMS (Option Market Sweden). Then several of the big banks – Crédit Commercial de France, Banque Nationale de Paris, Paribas, and Société Générale – also became shareholders of OMF, as did a broker Finacor. In 1990, a sizeable share in OMF was bought by MATIF itself.

22 It should be noted that *pensions* may be employed by the Bank of France either for lending money to or borrowing from the system, but for the most part the Bank of France would be lending money.

23 The *pension livrée* may also be used by the commercial banks themselves.

24 When there is no physical delivery of the relevant paper.

25 Up to the amount of the collateral they have available, they can choose both the amount and – within the stated limits – the number of days, provided they will pay the rate.

26 For example, see *Financial Times*, 31/12/86.

27 See *Financial Times*, 10/3/87, 26/1/88, 1/11/90, and 19/11/91.

28 Another type of 'mopping up' operation is when the Bank of France has borrowed *en pension* – just for a day, the transaction being reversed the following day.

29 The relevant official texts were Article 19 of the Law 91–716 of 26/7/91 followed by Decree No. 92–137 of 13/2/92, implemented by a Text issued by the *Comité de la réglementation bancaire* No. 92–03.

CHAPTER 5

1 A summary of the earlier history of German banking is available elsewhere – see J. S. G. Wilson, *Banking Policy and Structure: A Comparative Analysis*, 1986, pp. 151ff.

2 See ibid., pp. 134ff.

3 Including private bankers, whose business is not organized in the form of a sole proprietorship or partnership.

4 See *Monthly Report* of the Deutsche Bundesbank, August 1991, Table 25 – on the basis of size of balance sheet and published off-balance sheet items (e.g. contingent liabilities like acceptances).

5 However, unlike the 'money market banks' used to do in the US, for the most part the German banks do not trade in central bank balances, buying and selling on the basis of a narrow margin. The German banks are really concerned with managing their liquidity – if they have a surplus, they dispose of it; if they need funds, they buy them in.

6 See Table in *Monthly Reports* of the Deutsche Bundesbank: IV Minimum Reserves – 1. Reserve Ratios.

7 See *The Deutsche Bundesbank: Its Monetary Policy Instruments and Functions*, third edition, 1989, p. 28.

8 The required minimum reserves for any specific month are calculated by applying the minimum reserve ratios fixed by the Bundesbank to the average amount of liabilities subject to reserve requirements which a credit institution holds. This amount can be calculated by the banks either from the levels at the close of the business days and non-business days from the 16th of the preceding month to the 15th of the current month; or from the levels on the 23rd and the last day of the preceding month and the 7th and 15th of the current month. However, in certain cases, calculation according to the levels on the above-mentioned bank week return days can be partly or wholly excluded for individual banks.

9 Their business is not limited to commercial or investment banking or brokerage activities. They are in a position to provide all banking services – loans, traditional banking services, investment banking, trading in securities for own or customer's account, as well as cross-

border transactions through their own branches abroad or banking correspondents.

10 The large 'universal' banks grant big lines of credit to major corporations, so that they can draw large amounts at short notice, but such banks would also have funds lent out at different maturities, so that funds will mature at regular intervals and thereby provide a continuing inflow of cash.

11 All morning there will be an exchange of information between all the relevant departments in the bank.

12 Tax payments are spread throughout the year, but heavy payments occur at various dates in March, June, September, and December. Smaller and medium-sized levies occur in the other months.

13 It is said that foreign banks – and the smaller German banks – may use money brokers from time to time.

14 In this context, for details of the amount of minimum required reserves by category of credit institution, one might refer to Table IV (c) in Deutsche Bundesbank *Monthly Reports*.

15 Sometimes later. On the last day of the month, a lot of banks are short of money, with the Deutsche Bundesbank and certain of the Landeszentralbanken possibly remaining open to about 4.00 p.m. depending on local circumstances.

16 Due to FOREX activity, and especially DM/US$ turnover.

17 *Unverzinslich* – i.e. non-interest-bearing, but discountable securities.

18 *The Deutsche Bundesbank*, 1989, pp. 29–30.

19 I.e. *Nicht reguliert*.

20 See *The Deutsche Bundesbank*, 1989, pp. 30–1.

21 See *Monthly Report* of the Deutsche Bundesbank, December 1989, p. 10.

22 Privatdiskont AG was set up in 1963 as a successor institution serving the Berlin private discount market in bankers' acceptances. It was not really a success and the Bundesbank kept a close eye on the situation. Since it was difficult to find a buyer for paper sold to Privatdiskont, Privatdiskont's discounts found their way to the Bundesbank – in effect, this facility represented an additional rediscount quota and, in January 1987, when discount quotas were reduced, the Bundesbank also reduced the ceiling on Privatdiskont rediscounts.

23 See *Financial Times*, 1/5/86.

24 This has now disappeared.

25 By February 1992, the total value of programmes amounted to DM 25 billion and it was anticipated that the figure would rise to DM 40 billion by the end of 1992. Of this, half was expected to be issued and outstanding in the market place. See *Financial Times*, 24/2/92.

26 See *Financial Times Series: Part 7 – European Finance and Investment – Germany*, 17/7/91.

27 See *Financial Times*, 7/6/90.

28 See *Financial Times*, 3/3/90, 6/3/90, and 7/6/90.

29 See *Financial Times*, 16/5/91.

30 See *Financial Times*, 4/5/90.

31 See Katherine Campbell in *Financial Times*, 26/1/90.

32 Ibid., 29/1/90.
33 See *Financial Times*, 12/6/90 and 16/8/91.
34 See *Financial Times*, 11/11/91.
35 *The Deutsche Bundesbank*, 1989, p. 81.
36 Ibid., p. 95.
37 It is adequately documented in ibid., pp. 81ff.
38 See ibid., pp. 87–95.
39 See ibid., p. 98.
40 See Deutsche Bundesbank *Monthly Report*, July 1991, pp. 14–17.
41 See *Monthly Report*, March 1992, p. 5.
42 These models are discussed from time to time in *Monthly Reports* of the Deutsche Bundesbank, the latest reference to the matter being in May 1989, pp. 27ff.
43 *The Deutsche Bundesbank*, second edition, 1982, pp. 86–7.
44 *Monthly Report*, August 1988, p. 6.
45 *The Deutsche Bundesbank*, 1982, p. 86.
46 See *Monthly Report*, December 1991, pp. 8–10.
47 The Banking Act of 1934 did contain a provision stating that the banks should keep a certain percentage – which the Act did not specify – of their deposits covered by balances at the central bank. But this was a regulation of principle only, which was designed less as a monetary policy measure than to ensure that the banks had adequate liquidity to cover their customers' deposits. Nor was the regulation ever implemented.
48 See Table IV.1 in *Monthly Reports*.
49 For further details, see *The Deutsche Bundesbank*, 1989, pp. 56–65.
50 See Deutsche Bundesbank *Monthly Report*, September 1990, p. 11.
51 For a summary of the variations over the years, see Table V.1 in *Monthly Reports*.
52 For a summary of past experience, see *The Deutsche Bundesbank*, 1989, pp. 48–51.
53 See Table V.1 in *Monthly Reports*.
54 See *Monthly Report*, September 1988, p. 10.
55 See *Monthly Report*, February 1989, p. 10. Also in October 1989, see *Monthly Report*, December 1989, p. 10.
56 Ibid.
57 *Monthly Report*, June 1989, pp. 9–10.
58 In view of the uncertainties about the liquidity-holding pattern of banks in East Germany, the Bundesbank allowed the banks to meet a comparatively large part of their short-term liquidity needs through lombard borrowing. See Deutsche Bundesbank *Monthly Report*, December 1990, p. 11.
59 *Monthly Report*, June 1991, p. 11.
60 See *Monthly Reports*, September 1988, p. 10 and December 1989, p. 10. For the rates that applied to the several types of short-term money market operations, see *Monthly Reports*, Tables V 2, 3, and 4.
61 See *Monthly Report*, December 1988, pp. 12–13.
62 See *Monthly Reports*, June 1991, p. 11, December 1991, pp. 8–10, and January 1992, p. 15. Central bank operations during the period of the

later 1980s and the beginning of the 1990s have been considered in some detail in order to demonstrate the interrelation in the use of the several instruments available to the Bundesbank, also the flexible ways in which they have been deployed. The story is based on material derived from the *Monthly Reports* of the Deutsche Bundesbank over the relevant period.

63 Länder governments are offered quotas so that they can shift funds without referring to the Bundesbank and they therefore have freedom to deploy their funds themselves as long as they remain within their quotas.

64 Of course, this instrument of monetary policy cannot be used without restriction. Public funds can only be moved into the banking system if they are available in sufficient quantities and for the period considered necessary. Generally speaking, therefore, deposit policy can only be used for very short-term money market management, in fact from day to day. Moreover, the funds can only be moved with the approval of the public authorities, though as a rule these authorities would agree on grounds of profitability, since their deposits with commercial banks carry the usual interest rates, while no interest at all is payable on the accounts maintained by public authorities with the central bank. See *The Deutsche Bundesbank*, 1989, pp. 75–6.

65 See *The Deutsche Bundesbank*, 1989, pp. 72–4.

66 See ibid., p. 73.

67 For an extended discussion, see Deutsche Bundesbank, *Monthly Report*, June 1992, pp. 8–16.

68 See *Financial Times*, 17/7/92.

69 See *Financial Times*, 21/7/92.

70 A week later, it was announced that Sweden had also arranged an Ecu 8 billion syndicated credit as part of the central bank's Ecu 16 billion programme to bolster the Krona and – supported by a regime of high interest rates (the marginal lending rate at the central bank was pushed up to 500 per cent to check currency speculation) – to crush rumours that the Swedish currency was about to be devalued. In due course, these very high marginal overnight lending rates were considerably reduced in a cautious adjustment to a 'more normal interest rate level'.

71 See *Financial Times*, 29/8/92, 30/8/92 and 7/9/92.

72 See *Financial Times*, *passim*, 17/9/92.

73 The Bank of England had ceased to announce MLR in 1981, when it introduced a new system for day-to-day market operations. Although seemingly abandoning MLR, the Bank retained the right in appropriate circumstances to announce in advance the MLR which, for a short period ahead, it would apply in any lending to the London discount houses. Previously, MLR had in fact been reintroduced for one day in January 1985, also at 12 per cent but up from a level of 10.5 per cent, when the Bank of England was trying to prop up a pound moving close to parity with the US dollar.

74 See his letter to *The Independent* 29/9/92. For the political limitations to Professor Meade's programme, see letter from Professor Lord Desai, also in *The Independent* 1/10/92.

CHAPTER 6

1 In January 1992, it was announced that Banco di Roma (until then controlled by IRI, the state holding company) would become part of a
three-way banking merger with Cassa di Risparmio di Roma and Banco
di Santo Spirito, the new product to become Banca di Roma. IRI would
then hold 35 per cent of the capital of the holding company controlling
the three banks. It is understood that IRI may in due course reduce its
holding further by floating at least part of its own shareholding in the
new concern.

2 For a summary of the Italian government securities market, see Banca
Commerciale Italiana, *The Italian Economy: Monetary Trends*, No.
42, October 1990. For BTP (Treasury bond) futures and options on
MATIF and LIFFE, see Editoriale Lavoro, *Basic Statistics on the
Italian Economy*, No. 11, November 1991, p. 3. LIFFE also planned to
introduce a futures contract on the 3-month Euro-lire interest rate on
12 May 1992. See *Financial Times*, 6/2/92.

3 The average amounts of the Treasury bill auctions are L 13,000 to
L 15,000 billion for mid-month and L 35,000 to L 40,000 billion for the
end of the month.

4 The precise dates of the auctions (for *CCTs*, *BTPs*, and *CTOs* as well)
are usually the dates that coincide with the maturity dates of any securities that are to be repaid. For long-term securities, settlement dates may
be different, with accrued interest being paid in addition to the auction
price as necessary. As almost all bonds are now issued in *tranches*,
sometimes many days of accrued interest have to be paid (possibly up to
3 months).

5 Market share of deposits plus estimates of BOT holdings of customers.
The calculation is made by the Bank of Italy.

6 Market-makers are required to participate to the extent of 65 per cent
of the issue; they do not necessarily have to take up the whole of the 65
per cent.

7 Often the period is much shorter.

8 They represent almost 45 per cent of outstanding public debt.

9 BTPs with maturities of 7 and 10 years are also of interest to foreign
institutional investors.

10 The Italian telematic market was also planning to launch Treasury bond
futures and options in the spring of 1992, while an over-the-counter
futures market was already growing. See Editoriale Lavoro, *Basic
Statistics on the Italian Economy*, November 1991, p. 3.

11 The exception is a non-government issue.

12 See EUROMOBILIARE, *Investing in Italian Government Bonds: A
Handbook*, September 1989, pp. 40–1.

13 The withholding tax on CDs was set at < 12 months = 30 per cent; ≥
12 months and < 18 months = 25 per cent; and ≥ 18 months = 12.5
per cent.

14 For a very useful survey of the role of bank CDs in Italy, see Banca
Commerciale Italiana, *The Italian Economy: Monetary Trends*, No.
44, July 1991.

15 This is offset by a negative rate of -5 per cent in the public sector, giving a net 20 per cent.

16 See Editoriale Lavoro, *Basic Statistics on the Italian Economy*, No. 6, June 1989.

17 See Editoriale Lavoro, 'New expansion for the Euro-lire market', in *Basic Statistics on the Italian Economy*, No. 5, May 1990, p. 3.

18 Credit ceilings were imposed from 1973 to 1983, when they were discontinued. They were temporarily restored from March 1986 to September 1986 and from September 1987 to March 1988.

19 On the basis of the Bank of Italy's definition – net worth plus contingency and some other funds, minus doubtful loans and losses, minus own shares in portfolio.

20 Brokers are used to a considerable extent for Euro-deposits at least by number of transactions, though the big transactions would be done direct.

21 See 'Repos as an instrument for managing banks' liquidity and liabilities', Editoriale Lavoro, *Basic Statistics on the Italian Economy*, No. 9, September 1991, pp. 2–5.

22 Ibid.

23 There can be tax advantages. See ibid., p. 5.

24 This was changed from 95 per cent in November 1991.

25 At the same time, big banks still have 'gentlemen's agreements' with small banks – as a result of which, when the market is flush with funds, the big banks are still under an obligation to absorb money from the small banks, whether the big banks want it or not. At such times, big banks can be excessively liquid. On the other hand, when money is tight, the big banks could depend (less so now) on an inflow of money from the small banks that had a special relationship with them.

26 See Law No. 82 of 7 February 1992, effective from 29 February 1992.

CHAPTER 7

1 See The Bank of Japan, *Economic Statistics Annuals*.

2 It is fixed by a seven-man board. This is comprised of one representative from the Ministry of Finance (no vote), one from the Economic Planning Agency (no vote), four representatives of major economic sectors – like agriculture and industry (two votes) and the city and regional banks (two votes). The Governor of the Bank of Japan, who also has a vote, is by tradition the Chairman. Hence, there are five voting members.

3 See Robert F. Emery, *The Japanese Money Market* (Lexington, 1984, p. 41).

4 Sometimes, deals are done direct in the inter-bank market (see pp. 263–4); bill discounts always go through a Tanshi house, which acts as a broker.

5 Before April 1979, it was maintained that BOJ 'regulated' rates through the Tanshi houses; after that, the Tanshi houses were free to fix their own rates.

6 The BOJ has set up a Bank of Japan Financial Network System (BOJ-NET) to process transactions data between the BOJ and financial institutions through its on-line network. The BOJ began developing BOJ-NET in 1982 when the basic design was first discussed. After completion of various tests, on-line processing in the funds transfer service through BOJ accounts was introduced in October 1988, followed by the foreign exchange/yen settlement service in March 1989, and the JGB (Japanese government bond) service in May 1990. See Bank of Japan, *BOJ-NET – Its Role and Functions in the Japanese Payment System*, Special Paper No. 200, March 1991.

7 See Emery, op. cit., p. 29.

8 Ibid.

9 One such bank advised the author that 70 per cent of its lending was in the form of bills purchased, mostly of 3-months maturity or less, though they preferred 3-months bills in order to obtain a higher rate of return.

10 The BOJ carries a large portfolio of Finance bills, which are equivalent to short-term Treasury bills in other countries; Finance bills are underwriten by BOJ. Almost all Finance bills are issued to finance government requirements on a 'tap' basis, not by tender.

11 See *Financial Times*, 6/6/86.

12 As Emery (op. cit., p. 55) explains:

> The name *gensaki* derives from the fact that both a present and a future transaction must occur in carrying out a complete transaction in this market. Thus, the word *gensaki* comes from two Chinese characters meaning 'present' (*gen*) and 'future' (*saki*).

13 See The Bank of Japan, *Economic Statistics Annual* 1990, Table 93.

14 Emery, p. 58.

15 Ibid., p. 56.

16 For a large securities house, financing inventory may be as high as 80 per cent of total *gensaki*; the other 20 per cent would be to service clients, though some transactions may in fact do both.

17 When the banks began to issue CDs, there was a rise in interest rates and therefore in funding costs. As for time deposits, reserve requirements also have to be held against CDs.

18 Money market certificates are similar to NCDs. They have been issued from April 1985 onwards. They tend to be smaller in the amount per instrument than for NCDs and attract rates of interest that are about three-quarters of a per cent lower (for maturities within 1 year), and half a per cent lower (for maturities of over 1 year and within 2 years).

19 The return for this service would be the difference between two prices; what that difference was would depend on the skill of the Tanshi house (e.g. in forecasting interest rates and placing the CD in the secondary market).

20 See Emery, p. 86.

21 Ibid.

22 The commission earned by the Tanshi houses as a difference between bid and offer was close to $\frac{1}{16}$ per cent – it could vary slightly depending on the remaining term of the bill.

23 See Stefan Wagstyl, *Financial Times*, 2/12/88.
24 For very large amounts, there could be a volume discount.
25 See Michiyo Nakamoto in *Financial Times*, 25/5/89.
26 For a description of these facilities in the USA, see J. S. G. Wilson, *Banking Policy and Structure*, pp. 107–9.
27 See John Ridding in *Financial Times*, 13/3/89.
28 See *The Banker* (London), March 1990, pp. 8–11.
29 The capital of the Tanshi houses is partially held by other financial institutions (e.g., by city and long-term credit banks), but it will be well distributed between the several institutions concerned and done in consultation with BOJ. The biggest shareholder can only hold 2 per cent of the capital of a Tanshi house and usually it is less – (say) 1 per cent. This avoids conflicts of interest.
30 In this context (broking in foreign exchange and foreign currency deposits), a Tanshi house may have a joint venture – e.g., with a money broker in London – but the majority interest would be held by the Tanshi house itself. The intention is to maintain contact with other financial markets in international centres.
31 In these contexts, the Tanshi houses act as a principal – hence the difference is between bid and offer.
32 From June 1985, securities houses could do this as well.
33 Quoted by Robert Thomson from Tokyo in *Financial Times*, 8/12/89.
34 Ibid.
35 This is not an unique experience. Something similar happened in the United Kingdom (see pp. 51–2) and in Australia (see pp. 295–6).
36 Prior to December 1987, BOJ's purchases of long-term government bonds had been confined to outright purchases made for the purpose of meeting an increase in the demand for money in line with long-run economic growth, not for the purpose of short-run 'fine-tuning' in the money market.
37 Quoted by Stephen Fidler in *Financial Times Supplement* on 'Japanese financial markets', 15/3/90. (See contribution on short-term money markets.) See also K. Osugi, 'Japan's experience of financial deregulation since 1984 in an international perspective', Bank for International Settlements *Economic Papers*, No. 26, January 1990.

CHAPTER 8

1 For relatively recent treatments of this subject, see Edna Carew, *Fast Money – The Money Market in Australia* (1983), *Fast Money 2* (1985), and *Fast Money 3 – The Financial Markets in Australia* (1991). See also Gerry Forster 'Reserve Bank money market operations', *The Australian Banker*, August 1986; I. J. Macfarlane, 'Open market operations since the float', being paper presented to the Victorian branch of the Economic Society in Melbourne, 26 November 1986 and reprinted in Reserve Bank of Australia *Bulletin*, December 1986; Michael Dotsey, 'Open market operations in Australia: a U.S. perspective', Reserve Bank of Australia Research Discussion Paper 8702, May 1987; R.

Battellino and I. J. Macfarlane, 'Research report: open market operations – some international comparisons', Reserve Bank of Australia *Bulletin*, December 1987; D. J. Juttner, 'Money markets and monetary policy implementation', *Economic Papers*, volume 1, no. 4, December 1988; M. J. Phillips, 'A central banking triptych', Reserve Bank of Australia *Bulletin*, October 1989; 'The Reserve Bank's domestic market operations, Reserve Bank of Australia *Bulletin*, December 1990; 'Authorised short-term money market dealers', Reserve Bank of Australia *Bulletin*, June 1991; and – for general background – Parliament of the Commonwealth of Australia, The House of Representatives Standing Committee on Finance and Public Administration, *A Pocket Full of Change – Banking and Deregulation*, November 1991.

2 See also J. S. G. Wilson, 'The Australian money market' in Banca Nazionale del Lavoro, *Quarterly Review*, March 1973, pp. 46ff and in the same *Review*, June 1990, pp. 179ff.

3 There was also a limited amount of dealing between buy-back brokers and the old Commonwealth Bank of Australia (which at that time also acted as the central bank).

4 For example, assets with maturity categories of 0–3 months were weighted at 0.6; 3–6 months 0.8; 6–12 months 1.0; 1–2 years 1.5; 2–5 years 2.5; 5–8 years 3.5; and more than 8 years to maturity 4.25.

5 Banks are not permitted to lend to or call funds from dealers by using bank cheques. And banks may not borrow from the authorized dealers. Even though technically the banks cannot lend bank cheque funds to the official dealers, they can and do lend to the dealers' finance or property companies, which in turn lend bank cheque funds to the official or authorized dealers.

6 While no precise figures are available, overnight money still constitutes a large part of borrowings in both the official and unofficial markets.

7 Official dealers tend to borrow overnight. Banks may wish to lend for 7 days, but dealers may not oblige because of uncertain market conditions and volatility of rates. But official dealers also borrow from other parties (corporates and even individuals) and it may not suit such parties to lend overnight.

8 See Reserve Bank *Bulletins*, Table C.3.

9 One might note, too, that the level of authorized dealer involvement in the unofficial market can greatly affect the unofficial cash rates. In periods of tight liquidity, it is not unusual for the authorized dealers to be heavy borrowers of bank cheque funds (since exchange settlement balances are relatively low), thereby exerting upward pressure on both cash markets.

10 Treasury note rediscounting is available to any holder of Treasury notes of less than 91 days to maturity. However, only banks and authorized dealers can obtain same day funds through rediscounting. End-of-day repurchase agreements are only available to official dealers.

11 The unofficial arm is invariably small and only occasionally is used for funding purposes, normally to transfer unofficial funds from a bank. Official dealers can borrow unofficial funds from any lender, except a

bank, and the unofficial arm has no role to play in this matter. In fact, most official dealers try to play one market off against the other in order to lower their cost of funds.

12 Some lenders always require security and may insist on Commonwealth paper, or bank accepted bills.

13 If they do, they have to take into account withholding tax (where it applies).

14 They would tend to get a market-related deposit rate.

15 Times referred to are Eastern Standard Time, the bulk of the business being done in Sydney and Melbourne. Perth in Western Australia is 2 hours behind the eastern states, but – with daylight-saving time – the difference can be 3 hours. The period of most activity in Perth (local time) is 7.00 a.m. to 12 noon (in winter) and 6.00 a.m. to 12 noon (in summer). The money markets in Australia in fact operate nationwide; in effect, it is a telephone market.

16 Both balance-sheet and statutory-reserve-deposit (SRD) considerations deterred the development of a term cash market – i.e. major banks were not prepared to raise funds which attracted SRDs to on-lend them to another bank, which transactions were SRD exempt. They would have preferred to trade in and out of cash positions. SRDs were replaced in 1988 by non-callable deposit accounts, on which a relatively low rate of interest was paid.

17 The Australian Government announced in February 1985 that sixteen new banks, with varying degrees of foreign ownership, had been invited to establish operations in Australia. Of the sixteen invited, fifteen established domestic banking operations.

18 See Wilson (1973), pp. 62–5, and Carew (1983), pp. 18–19.

19 Corporates that are primarily borrowers may – if they have a cash surplus – merely pay off debt (a zero cash policy).

20 In this case, selling securities under an agreement to repurchase.

21 However, internal Treasury bills are issued from time to time to facilitate public-sector financing objectives. (See 'Government securities on issue at 30 June 1989', Budget-related Paper No. 1, p. 5).

22 See Table E.4 in Reserve Bank *Bulletins*.

23 Trading banks hold Treasury notes primarily to meet PAR, but partly to assist liquidity management (through the medium of rediscounting or by taking up Treasury notes). Authorized dealers hold them in order to satisfy their obligation to trade short-term Commonwealth Government securities.

24 See Wilson (1973), p. 68. It was understood at the time that the opposition came from within the Federal Treasury; it is known that there were also critical voices within the Reserve Bank, but it is almost certain that the Treasury was the major stumbling block.

25 See Reserve Bank *Bulletins*, Table E.9.

26 For details of PAR, see J. S. G. Wilson, *Banking Policy and Structure: A Comparative Analysis*, pp. 430–1.

27 Originally, the authorized money-market dealers and several stock-broking firms were regarded as specialist bond traders, partly because of their ability to trade directly with the Reserve Bank. Then a list of

twenty-one reporting bond dealers was announced in December 1984, the system coming into effect on 1 January 1985. There are now nineteen – drawn from certain of the authorized dealers and trading banks, some merchant banks, certain stockbrokers, two of the largest life assurance societies, and a number of other houses.

28 The Loan Council was established under the Financial Agreement of 1927 to co-ordinate Commonwealth and state government borrowings. Semi-government and local government authorities were brought under the Loan Council on the basis of a gentlemen's agreement in 1936. By the early 1980s, however, the Loan Council was exercising increasingly less influence under the gentlemen's agreement over the totality of authority borrowings. This reflected extensive use of non-conventional financing techniques, such as financial leasing and similar forms of borrowing, which were outside the scope of the agreement. The decision in June 1982 to exclude domestic borrowings by electricity authorities from Loan Council control for a trial period of 3 years further reduced Loan Council influence on authority borrowings. These developments culminated in the gentlemen's agreement being suspended at the 21 June 1984 Loan Council meeting and the 'global approach' being adopted on a trial basis for 1984/5. The objective of the global approach was to broaden the scope of Loan Council oversight of authority borrowings by bringing within voluntarily agreed limits all forms of borrowings by Commonwealth and state semi-government and local authorities, government-owned companies and trusts. The global approach also allows for the publication of timely information on total borrowings by Commonwealth and state authorities.

29 Previously, in Australia, commercial bills had been held within the banking system.

30 Against which a customer can draw bills and discount them in the market.

31 See J. S. G. Wilson, 'The Australian money market' (1973), pp. 55–56.

32 Bank endorsed bills are said to be much less common and would be dealt in more in the unofficial market. They cost 5 to 10 cents more than bank accepted bills, depending on interest rates.

33 See Table B.12 in Reserve Bank *Bulletin*, June 1991.

34 With the introduction of financial futures (see pp. 288–91), bills tend to be drawn to approximate the next date for the related futures contract and these would tend to be the most liquid maturities.

35 The small number of trade-related bank bills would also tend to stay in portfolio.

36 See Reserve Bank *Bulletin*, Table B.10, December 1990.

37 See Reserve Bank of Australia Bulletin, Table B.2, June 1991.

38 Customers' needs are also a factor in determining the maturity of CDs issued.

39 CDs for maturities of 185 days or less attract a lower rate of 'financial transactions' duty, a tax that is applied on a state-by-state basis (except in Queensland).

40 For purposes of international comparison these items are measured in US dollars.

41 Since the definition was amended in July 1989.
42 See Reserve Bank *Bulletin*, December 1988.
43 Currently, the contract is virtually dormant.
44 See *Financial Times*, 31/1/89.
45 Except that the reporting dealers can avail themselves of the Treasury note rediscount facility as can any other holder of Treasury notes.
46 This appears every working day on the Reuters screen at 9.00 a.m., 12 noon, and 4.00 p.m. The method for calculating the trade weighted index is revised each year.
47 Including purchase of short Commonwealth bonds from the trading banks (e.g. bonds within 3 months of maturity).
48 See Table 1 at p. 23 in 'Authorised short term money market dealers', Reserve Bank of Australia *Bulletin*, June 1991.
49 See *Financial Times*, 23/2/91.

CHAPTER 9

1 For an outline of the origins and early history of this market, see: J. S. G. Wilson, 'The Canadian money market experiment', in Banca Nazionale del Lavoro *Quarterly Review*, March 1958; and J. S. G. Wilson, 'The money market in Canada', in Banca Nazionale del Lavoro *Quarterly Review*, June 1972. For a more recent study, see S. Sarpkaya, *The Money Market in Canada*, 3rd edition (1984). See also George S. Watts: 'The Bank of Canada in 1953 and 1954: A further stage in the evolution of central banking in Canada', *Bank of Canada Review*, January 1976; 'The evolution of bankers' acceptances in Canada', *Bank of Canada Review*, October 1981; 'Overnight financing in Canada: special call loans', *Bank of Canada Review*, May 1983; 'Revision to the reserves regulations: introducing weighted averaging', *Bank of Canada Review*, September 1983; 'The interbank deposit market in Canada', *Bank of Canada Review*, February 1986; 'The market for Government of Canada treasury bills', *Bank of Canada Review*, December 1987. See also speeches by John W. Crow, Governor of the Bank of Canada: 'Buy-back techniques in the conduct of monetary policy', to the Toronto Money Market Association on 26 April 1989, in *Bank of Canada Review*, July 1989; and 'Clearing and settlement of financial transactions: a perspective from the Bank of Canada', to the Eighth Annual Cash and Treasury Management Conference, Toronto, Ontario, on 7 November 1990. See also Bank of Canada: press release on 'Targets for reducing inflation and reaching price stability in Canada', 26 February 1991; 'The implementation of monetary policy in a system with zero reserve requirements', being Discussion Paper No. 3 as revised 6 September 1991; and 'Bank of Canada operations in the money market and the new framework for implementation of monetary policy', being presentation by Donna Howard to Ninth Annual TMAC Conference, Edmonton, Alberta, 1 October 1991.
2 After the chartered banks entered the field of securities lending, the Bank of Canada withdrew these services.

3 At that stage the big dealers included: A.E. Ames & Company Limited; Dominion Securities Corporation Limited; Fry Mills Spence & Company Limited; Greenshields Incorporated; Harris & Partners Limited; Nesbitt Thomson Securities Limited; Merrill Lynch; Royal Securities Limited; and Wood Gundy Limited.

4 These were: Burns Fry Ltd; Scotia McLeod Inc.; Wood Gundy Inc.; Richardson Greenshields of Canada Ltd; Midland Doherty Ltd; Levesque Beaubien Inc.; RBC Dominion Securities Inc.; and Nesbitt Thomson Deacon Inc.

5 One might note that a large number of western accounts are commercial paper borrowers and hence come into the market between 9.00 a.m. and 9.30 a.m. Toronto time.

6 For example, investment counsellors, who purchase large blocks, would resort to the smaller splits.

7 A separate form must be used for each maturity, similarly with DIALCOM.

8 Manitoba: tender Monday, issued Tuesday. British Columbia, Alberta, Saskatchewan, and Ontario: tender Tuesday, issued Wednesday. Quebec, New Brunswick and Newfoundland: tender Wednesday, issued Thursday.

9 It 'asks questions, but offers no opinions'.

10 Investment dealers may be asked to tender on behalf of customers. These are known as 'pre-tenders'.

11 Borrowing securities is not as common as in the past and is more usual in the bond market (especially at the longer end), though Treasury bills may be employed in putting up collateral for a like amount (but actual borrowing of Treasury bills to make delivery is not common); for this service, a borrower of securities pays a fee. Usually securities are borrowed (mostly by dealers) from the major chartered banks. Other lenders of securities would include life insurance companies, utilities such as Ontario Hydro, and corporates.

12 Initially, they were supposed to be based on a bona fide commercial transaction, but even then some operators maintained that the bankers' acceptance in Canada was not necessarily tied to specific commercial transactions and that it was rather similar to a commercial paper note, but with a bank guarantee.

13 There are also term deposit receipts; the chartered banks will usually buy back their own term deposit receipts, subject to a penalty determined by the keenness of the competition. Dealers come into the picture by standing prepared to advise on and to assist in placing funds in these ways.

14 Sometimes referred to as a bearer discount note.

15 Others post rates and invite applications.

16 The calculation period to run from mid-month to mid-month corresponding to two of the previous reserve averaging periods for chartered banks.

17 Say about 6.00 a.m.

18 This has now been done away with – in the early 1970s.

19 There are interest rate caps, floors, and collars. (A firm may purchase

an interest rate cap, and, if rates rise over the rate cap ceiling, the issuer will pay the firm the difference between the cap rate and the actual bankers' acceptance (BA) rate; declining rates will allow the firm to borrow at lower interest costs on its BA line. At the same time, a firm may sell a 'floor' to offset the cost of the cap; hence if interest rates fall, the firm will pay the purchaser of the cap the difference between the floor rate and the actual rate – this package is called a 'collar'.)

20 For information on investment dealers' inventories, see *Bank of Canada Reviews*, Table D.6.

21 But some companies do issue both bankers' acceptances and commercial paper.

22 Foreign-owned banks – as well as the Banque Canadienne Nationale – can also 'stamp' bankers' acceptances.

23 In recent years, swapped deposits have tended to become unbundled, with the investor putting his own transactions together from various parties.

24 Since major banks have acquired large investment dealers, the tendency has been for the swap desks to be moved into the bank and for the money market desk to be moved to the dealer.

25 See S. Sarpkaya: *The Money Market in Canada*, pp. 32ff.

26 Brokers tend to be used more when trading in money market instruments.

27 These are the so-called 'free credit balances'.

28 The direct clearers include eight chartered banks and five near-banks, which clear payment items directly through a settlement account held at the Bank of Canada. To qualify as a direct clearer, an institution must account for at least one half of 1 per cent of the total annual volume of payment items through the clearings.

29 Since April 1986, the government has placed any balances not needed to meet its immediate cash requirements on term deposit with the direct clearers. These deposits, which are allocated by auction, vary in term but are generally under 7 days.

30 Up to August 1989, the government's demand balances were allocated among the direct clearers based on each institution's share of Canadian dollar deposit liabilities. Since September 1989, and until bank cash reserve requirements were phased out (beginning in November 1991), the allocation shares were determined at an auction held prior to the beginning of each reserve averaging period.

31 See speech by John W. Crow, Governor of the Bank of Canada to the Toronto Money Market Association on 26 April 1989. See also speech by Governor Crow on 'Clearing and settlement of financial transactions: a perspective from the Bank of Canada' at the Treasury Management Association of Canada's Eighth Annual Cash and Treasury Management Conference, Toronto, Ontario, 7 November 1990, and Bank of Canada press release on 'Targets for reducing inflation and reaching price stability in Canada', 26 February 1991.

32 Governor John Crow has had a policy of disseminating information to the market place by means of the public speech. His appearances before

the House of Commons Finance Committee has also allowed him to articulate what at the time was current Bank policy.

33 Governor Crow reported an annual turnover in the money market of C\$ 1 trillion.

34 See *Bank of Canada Reviews*, Table G.6.

CHAPTER 10

1 See the Banking Ordinance, Chapter 155 of *Laws of Hong Kong* (reprint 1 July 1990). This has seen a number of amendments, the most material of which is the Banking (Amendment) (No. 2) Ordinance 1991.

2 See Banking Ordinance (as printed, pp. 91–2 and the Fourth Schedule, pp. 125–6).

3 These banks include some foreign banks operating in Hong Kong dollars.

4 Dealers have their morning meeting at 7.45 a.m.

5 See Government Secretariat, Economic Services Branch, *Hong Kong: First Quarter Economic Report 1991* (May 1991), pp. 38–9. See also *The 1991/92 Budget Speech by the Financial Secretary, moving the Second Reading of the Appropriation Bill, 1991*, as printed, pp. 9–10.

6 See The Director of the Office of the Exchange Fund on behalf of the Hong Kong Government, *Information Memorandum: Hong Kong Government Bond Programme for Tender on a Bid–Price Basis*, October 1991.

7 See *Financial Times*, 7/6/91.

8 See *Financial Times*, 10/1/91 and 26/6/91.

9 See *Financial Times* and *South China Morning Post*, 29/5/92.

CHAPTER 11

1 See also J. S G. Wilson, 'The business of banking in India' in R. S. Sayers (editor) *Banking in the British Commonwealth*, 1952, pp. 150–216; B. K. Madan, 'India' in W. F. Crick (editor) *Commonwealth Banking Systems*, 1965, pp. 186–242; J. S. G. Wilson, 'The Indian money market', in *Monetary Policy and the Development of Money Markets*, 1966, pp. 243–69; J. S. G. Wilson, 'Changing emphases in Indian banking – I: The structure; II: The business of banking', *The Banker* (London), October and November 1981; *Reserve Bank of India – Functions and Working*, fourth edition, 1983; 'Aspects of the black economy in India', *Report of a Study by the National Institute of Public Finance and Policy*, March 1985; *Report of the Committee to Review the Working of the Monetary System* (Chairman Sukhamoy Chakravarty), April 1985; *Reserve Bank of India: Report of the Working Group on The Money Market*, January 1987; and J. S. G. Wilson, 'The Indian money market', Banca Nazionale del Lavoro *Quarterly Review*, December 1987.

2 One lakh = 100,000; 1 crore = 100 Lakhs = 10 million.

CHAPTER 12

1 On this and related matters, see Monetary Authority of Singapore, *The Financial Structure of Singapore* (third revised edition 1989). The quotation is from p. 12.
2 For a survey of the earlier discount market, see J. S. G. Wilson on 'Singapore' in *Banking in the Far East: Structures and Sources of Finance* (edited by Anne Hendrie), *Financial Times Business Information*, 1986, pp. 284–7.
3 See Wilson, op. cit., p. 285.
4 Changes in these rates were usually initiated by the Association of Banks in consultation with the MAS.
5 For details, see *The Financial Structure of Singapore*, p. 70.
6 Such maturities may vary from time to time.
7 See Monetary Authority of Singapore, *Monthly Statistical Bulletins*, Tables III.1 and III.2.
8 Money brokers function as intermediaries between banks for the placement of currency deposits and in implementing FOREX transactions. Their role is to match the best buyer with the best seller. Through their worldwide communications network, they are able to link banks in Singapore with those in other major financial centres throughout the world. They help to create a more efficient market by disseminating current rate and price information and indeed news of anything relevant to the foreign exchange market. In July 1985, the eight money broking firms formed the Singapore Foreign Exchange and Money Brokers Association. Among its objectives are the provision of an efficient broking system in Singapore, and the promotion and maintenance of a high standard of professional conduct and ethics among its members. The brokers also have to adhere to guidelines laid down by the Singapore Foreign Exchange Market Committee. The Committee comprises senior personnel from MAS, banks and money broking firms in charge of foreign exchange and financial market operations.
9 ASEAN countries consist of Singapore, Malaysia, Indonesia, Thailand, the Philippines, and Brunei.
10 See Monetary Authority of Singapore, *Monthly Statistical Bulletins*, Table V.1B.
11 See ibid., Table V.1A.
12 See *The Financial Structure of Singapore*, pp. 57–8.
13 It is now subject to the 1986 Futures Trading Act administered by MAS. It covers *inter alia* the licensing of market participants, accounts and audit requirements, requirement of licencees to segregate customers' funds from the firm's own funds; and prohibition of fraudulent practices such as market manipulation and 'bucketing' (i.e. accepting customer orders without causing orders to be executed on an exchange in accordance with its rules). In line with the emphasis of MAS on self-regulation by market participants, SIMEX has been given the primary responsibility of regulating the daily operations of its members, MAS acting in an oversight capacity.
14 Under the gross margining system, a broking firm with customers

purchasing or selling futures had to place a margin with SIMEX in respect of each and every position. The margins relating to each position might not be offset against each other.

CHAPTER 13

1 For further background information, see Commission of Inquiry into the Monetary System and Monetary Policy in South Africa (the De Kock Commission), *The Monetary System and Monetary Policy in South Africa*, RP 70/1984, Government Printer, Pretoria, 1985. See also: H. B. Falkena, L. J. Fourie, and W. J. Kok (editors), *The Mechanics of the South African Financial System – Financial Institutions, Instruments and Markets*, second edition (1986) and third edition (1989); H. B. Falkena, W. J. Kok, and J. H. Meijer (editors), *The Dynamics of the South African Financial System – Financial Risk Management* (1987). Additional references include H. B. Falkena, L. J. Fourie, and W. J. Kok (editors): *The Mechanics of the South African Financial System*, third edition (1989); H. B. Falkena, W. J. Kok, and J. H. Meijer (editors): *Financial Risk Management in South Africa* (1989); H. B. Falkena and W. J. Kok (editors): *Financial Risk Management* (1991); J. H. Meijer, H. B. Falkena, and E. J. Van der Merwe (editors): *Financial Policy in South Africa* (1991); H. B. Falkena, W. J. Kok, C. W. Luüs, and G. E. Raine, *The Futures Market* (1989); H. B. Falkena, W. J. Kok, C. W. Luüs, and S. P. M. Yates, *The Options Market* (1989); W. J. Potgieter, H. B. Falkena, W. J. Kok, and M. C. C. van Ettinger (editors): *The Foreign Exchange Market* (1991); A. P. Faure, H. B. Falkena, W. J. Kok, and G. E. Raine (editors): *The Interest-bearing Securities Market* (1991); and I. Goodspeed, H. B. Falkena, P. Morgenrood, and R. K. Store (editors): *The Regulation of Financial Markets* (1991).

2 In January 1992, a further merger was planned between ABSA and Bankorp (a group comprising Trust Bank, Senbank, and Bankfin). See *Financial Times*, 30/1/92 and 26/2/92.

3 By 1955, the NFC felt sufficiently well established voluntarily to surrender these statutory privileges.

4 These were invested in Treasury bills and short-dated bonds. No private sector deposits were taken.

5 This has been due to a combination of circumstances – lower prices and the rise in costs, where South Africa has moved from being the world's lowest cost producer to the highest (with its share of non-communist world production falling from 70 per cent to 40 per cent), and with the possibility of the imminent closing of mines (though marginal mines are estimated to produce only about 15 per cent of the country's gold). The core of the problem is that the industry's costs are rising faster than its revenue. The outlook for catalysts like platinum (and related products rhodium and palladium), low-sulphur coal, and diamonds, however, are much more encouraging, also vanadium, chrome, and manganese. For further analysis, see *Financial Times Supplement on South Africa*, 11/6/90, p. 6.

6 Government departments that have to wait for new money to become available spend heavily at this time of year. There also tend to be seasonal salary increases in the public sector, some of them taking effect on 1 April.

7 Most of the large banks use seven reporting centres based on regional offices clearing with Reserve Bank branches.

8 Apart from cash, these would include Treasury bills, Land Bank bills, bankers' acceptances of deposit-taking institutions which are discountable at the Reserve Bank, government stocks with maturities of up to 3 years, and self-liquidating bills or promissory notes.

9 Corporates would include: the oil companies and industrial conglomerates; wheat, citrus, and dried fruit companies; the maize boards; and all companies with money market desks.

10 Smaller companies may pay a rate twenty-five basis points (one-quarter of a per cent) higher than would be charged to the large corporates.

11 In addition, there is also a kind of 'public sector inter-company market'. Within the vast public sector, there may be large borrowers of funds and at times lenders of funds, all between the constituent members of the public sector and without resort to financial intermediaries; this is also done through CPD deposits and withdrawals.

12 For further details, see H. B. Falkena *et al.*, *The Mechanics of the South African Financial System* (1986), pp. 433ff.

13 See ibid., pp. 53ff.

14 'Other assets' consist *inter alia* of loan levy stock, preference shares, and trade and industry bills.

15 There are six mining houses, of which Anglo-American Corporation is the largest. Depending on the cash flow situation, they may have sizeable amounts of short-term funds to invest. Discount houses also borrowed from insurance companies and pension funds. The last only put money out occasionally for a day or so, if flush with funds, but sometimes in large amounts.

16 See Table for 'Discount houses' in South African Reserve Bank *Quarterly Bulletins*. It should be noted that these were end-of-period figures.

17 For the record, in its statistics, the Reserve Bank continued for a time to produce separate figures for the assets and liabilities of discount houses, commercial banks, merchant banks, and general banks, as well as some figures for the Land and Agricultural Bank and other deposit-taking institutions (including mutual building societies). See Tables at S.6 to S.20 in South African Reserve Bank, *Quarterly Bulletin*, September 1991. The changeover in the Tables to 'deposit-taking institutions' was made in the December 1991 issue.

18 See Table for 'Ownership Distribution of Marketable Treasury Bills' in South African Reserve Bank *Quarterly Bulletins*.

19 For further details, see Falkena *et al.* (1986), pp. 234–6. Note that the Land Bank also issues debentures, usually for periods of between 1 and 3 years (see ibid., pp. 236–9).

20 For further details, see Falkena *et al.* (1986), pp. 203–7.

21 This would be for the finance of trade, which facility may be rolled over

regularly. Alternatively, there may be an overall financial package comprising bankers' acceptances, call loans, and an ordinary overdraft.

22 It is said that one does not see broken amounts very often, since usually banker's acceptance finance would be used in conjunction with an overdraft facility.

23 The definitions of these terms were included in the Regulations relating to the Deposit-taking Institutions Act.

24 See H. B. Falkena *et al.* (1986), p. 275. For a detailed survey of the subject in a South African context, see ibid., pp. 273–317. On Euromarkets, see ibid., pp. 344ff.

25 See *Government Gazette*, July 11 1990, No. 12617 and *Government Gazette*, November 30 1990, No. 12871.

26 See *Government Gazette*, No. 12871.

27 All deposit-taking institutions may now also use the discount window – after 1988 this included some of the building societies that had demutualized.

28 If a loan was made to a bank instead of a 'repo', the security would usually be a long-dated gilt.

29 Formerly, if there was a surplus in the market early in the day, the Reserve Bank might do a 'reverse repo' with a discount house for the purpose of 'mopping up'.

30 And, depending on how active the Reserve Bank is in the bond market, the structure of rates also.

31 For further information, see H. B. Falkena *et al.* (1987), pp. 193ff; see also ibid., pp. 183–4.

32 See Philip Gawith in *Financial Times*, 27/3/92.

Index

NOTE: The names of authors (also where appropriate of certain institutions) whose works are quoted, are allocated page references that relate to the Notes at the end of the book. Further, where the main mention in the text is as an acronym, this is indexed under the acronym itself.

Abbey National 10
Acceptance House/Accepting Houses 9, 18
Accepted rule of law 3
Accepting Bank for Industry 365
Access to information 2
Agents des marchés interbancaires 162n
Ahmedabad 338, 342
Aitken Campbell (Gilts) Limited 44n
Alberta 301n
Alcatel 181
Alexanders Discount plc 8
Allied Building Society 363
All-States Discount Limited 268
Amalgamated Banks of South Africa (ABSA) 363
Ames, A. E. & Company Limited 299n
Amsterdam 147
Anglo-American Corporation 356, 363n
L'appel d'offres 166, 167, 168, 169
Arbitrage 2, 15, 18, 106, 122, 137, 143, 144, 163, 244, 248, 252, 260, 276, 284, 355, 382; 'interest arbitrage' 276, 357
Arbitrageur 146

Artigiancassa 223
ASEAN (Association of South East Asian Nations) 358
Asian Currency Units (ACUs) 348–9, 355, 357–60
Asian dollar(s)/Market 142, 323, 332, 333–5, 349, 351, 356–60, 389–90; assets 359; currencies transacted 356, 358; 'gapping' operations 358; liabilities 358–9; maturities of Asian dollar credits 357, 358; securitisation 359; tax incentives 359–60
Associazione fra le Casse di Risparmio Italiane 222
Astley and Pearce 332
AT & T 137
Atlanta 107
Austraclear 282–3
Australia 5, 6, 323, 334, 355, 358, 360
Australian Bills of Exchange Act 285
Australian Discount Limited 268
Australian dollar, floating of 286, 293, 294, 295
Australian Loan Council 281
Australian Wheat Board 285
'Authorised dealers' (**Australia**)

268–9, 272n, 273, 277, 279,
280, 281, 283, 284, 293, 294,
295; 'gearing maximum'/
multiplier 269–70, 274, 291, 294
Automated Clearing and
Settlement System (ACSS) 315
Aziende di credito 221

Bagehot, Walter 388
Bahrain (Middle East) 143
Balance of payments deficits
(USA) 20
Banca Commerciale Italiana 221,
411
Banca Nazionale dell' Agricoltura
222
Banca Nazionale del Lavoro 221
Banco di Napoli 221
Banco di Roma (Banca di Roma)
221
Banco di Santo Spirito 222
Banche di credito ordinario 221
Banche d'interesse nazionale 221
Banche popolari co-operative 222,
235
Bangalore 338, 342
Bank Act (Canada) 298, 301
Bank cheque funds (Australia)
270, 272, 273, 275, 276
Bank Deutscher Länder 190
Banker, The (London) 406, 414
Bankers' acceptances 388;
Australia 282; Canada 302–3,
304, 310, 311; Italy 230; Japan
249, 265; London 18, 19, 73,
80–1; South Africa 376–7, 377,
379, 384, 385; USA 103, 114n,
128–31; *see also* Bills of
exchange
Bankers Trust 135, 136
Bankers Trust Commercial
Corporation 135
Bank Export Services Act 1982 129
Bankfin 363n
Bank for International Settlements
(BIS) 31n
Bank holding companies 132, 138
Banking Act: Germany 189n;
Singapore 348, 360

Banking Act 1987 (United
Kingdom) 98
Banking practice, conventions of 3
Bank lines 231, 256, 286, 305, 311;
committed 17; uncommitted 17
Bank of America 111
Bank of Canada 297ff, 418, 420,
421; agencies 298; and foreign
exchange 317–18; and money-
market dealers 299–300; and
Treasury bill tenders 300–1; as
fiscal agent 315, 318; dealer
limits at 297; drawdown/
redeposit technique 315–16;
information 318; interest rates
317–18, 319; intervention by
315–19; line of credit with 313,
315
Bank of China 321, 323, 331
Bank of East Asia 322
Bank of England 7–101 *passim*,
214, 217, 393, 395, 397, 398,
399, 400; and exposures 98–9;
and facilities at 2.30 p.m. 74–5,
85, 91; at 2.45 p.m. 74–5,
85–6; at 2.50 p.m. 87–8; and
gilt-edged market 76–7, 84; and
'repos' 83; assistance morning/
afternoon 82–3, 84–5; 'bands'
– for eligible bills 82; direct
assistance 74; evolution of
policy 89ff; Gilt-Edged and
Money Markets Division 46, 82;
'indirect assistance' 74;
intervention by 18, 20, 73–89;
in commercial bills 89–90; late
assistance 85, 86–7; 'mopping
up' 74, 88; prudential
supervision 91–101; relief of a
shortage 82–4, 89; screen
information 11n, 81–2, 84;
signals 85; 'special buyer'/
broker 19–20
Bank of France 156, 158, 159,
160, 162, 214, 216, 405, 406;
and *réserves obligatoires* 160;
intervention by 166–9; *taux
d'intervention* 169; '*taux
directeurs*' 168

Bank of India 343
Bank of Italy 222ff *passim*;
    Discount Department 238;
    discount window 239–40;
    'divorce' from Treasury 224;
    intervention by 238–40; use of
    broker 240
Bank of Japan 241ff *passim*, 412,
    413; credit lines with 249;
    information supplied 264;
    intervention by 264–6
Bank of Tokyo 140
Banking Ordinance (**Hong Kong**)
    320
Bankorp 363n
Bank rate 39, 74, 306, 316, 319,
    338, 374, 383, 384
'Bank swap' 308–9
Banque Française du Commerce
    Extérieur 159n
Banque d'Escompte 164, 165
Banque Morgan 164
Banque Nationale de Paris (BNP)
    159n, 164, 165, 166
Banque San Paolo 166
Banques de trésorerie 156, 163
Barclays 363
Barclays de Zoete Wedd Gilts
    Limited 44n, 71
Barclays de Zoete Wedd Securities
    Inc. 111
Baring Sterling Bonds 44n
Base rate(s) 74, 85, 91
Battellino, R. 414–15
Bayerische Hypotheken- und
    Wechsel-Bank 172
Bayerische Landesbank
    Girozentrale 172
Bayerische Vereinsbank 172
BCCHK Limited 320
Bearer Deposit Notes (BDNs)
    303–4, 312
Bear, Stearns & Co. Inc. 111
Becker, A. G. 133
Berlin 171, 172, 175
BHP (**Australia**) 276
'Big Bang' 42ff, 46
Bill Discount Market (**India**)
    340

Bill Discount Market (**Japan**) 242,
    243, 244, 245, 246–9, 260, 263,
    264
Billets de trésorerie 159, 170
Billets globaux de mobilisation
    167
Bills of Exchange 388; **Australia**
    269, 272, 273, 274, 276, 281–3;
    allonge 282, endorsement of
    281, futures 290, non-bank bill
    281, 282, secondary market 283,
    usances 282; **Germany** 179–80,
    trade bills 191; **India** 340, 341;
    Japan 241, 246–9; **London** 7, 8,
    18–20, 34, 55, 60, 97, 'bill
    mountain' 20, eligibility 19,
    finance bills 18n, fine bank bills
    19, trade paper 18n, 19, 34,
    388–9, samples of 19–20;
    Singapore 350, 351; **South
    Africa** 376–7
Board of Commissioners of
    Currency of Singapore 347
BOJ-NET 246n
Bolitho, J. G. 72
Bombay 1, 337, 338, 339, 342,
    344
Bons à moyen terme négociables
    (BMTN) 169–70
*Bons des institutions et sociétés
    financières* (BISF) 159
Bons du Trésor 157–8, 161, 162,
    164, 166, 167, 168; brokers 158;
    secondary market 158
Bons du Trésor à interêts annuels
    (BTAN) 157
Bons du Trésor à taux fixe (BTF)
    157, 158; auction 158
Bons du Trésor sur formules 157
Bordenave, P. L. 406
Boston 107
Boysson, H. de 406
Bretton Woods, collapse of 66
British Bankers Association 395
British Columbia 301n
British Government stocks *see*
    Gilt-Edged, Gilts
British Petroleum 16–17
BT Gilts Limited 44n

BT Securities Corporation 111
Budgetary deficit: **Germany** 215;
Italy 215; **United Kingdom** 52,
218
Budget surplus: **Australia** 280,
295, 296; **Japan** 265; **United
Kindom** 51
Building societies: **Australia** 273,
277, 279, 285, and financial
futures 290; **South Africa** 363,
368, 370, 372, 373, 374, 377,
378, 379; **United Kingdom** 8,
10, 14–15, 34, 55, 69, 217, and
CDs 24, 25–7, and Euro-bonds
15, and term loans 15, and
Treasury bills 30, mortgage
lending of 14, 15
Building Societies Association
(BSA) (**United Kingdom**) 14,
25–6, 394, 395
Building Societies Commission
(**United Kingdom**) 14
Bund 182–3; and futures 70, 183,
184
Bundesbank *see* Deutsche
Bundesbank
Bundesbank Act 178, 181, 190,
192, 199
Bundesobligationen 182
Bundesschatzanweisungen 182
Buoni Ordinari del Tesoro (BOTs)
224, 228, 229, 236, 237, 238;
auctions 224–6; 'belt' (*cintura*)
226; secondary market 229,
238–9; underwriting of 225
Buoni Tesoro Poliennali (BTPs)
227, 228, 238; secondary screen
market 227
Bureau of Public Debt (**USA**) 104
Burns Fry Ltd 299n
Busy season (**India**) 339
'Buy-backs' 267, 273, 298, 377
Buy-back brokers 267n

Caisses de crédit municipal 156
Caisse de Dépôts et Consignations
156, 161, 162–3, 164, 165
Caisse de Gestion Mobilière 164
Calcutta 1, 337, 338, 339, 342, 344

'Callable fixtures' (**United
Kingdom**) 8
Call loans: **Canada** 312, 313, 314;
South Africa 376n; **USA** 118
Call money: **Australia** 272, 273;
India 338, 339, 344–5; **Japan**
241, 242, 243, 247, 250, 263,
266; **Singapore** 360; **South
Africa** 368, 371, 387
Campbell, Katherine 408
Canada 5, 6
Canada Government Bond (CGB)
302, 310, 312
Canada Post 300
Canadian Bond Rating Service
(CBRS) 305
Canadian Depository for Securities
(CDS) 319
Canadian Payments Association
301
Canadian Wheat Board 300
Cantor Fitzgerald (Gilts) Limited
44n
Capital adequacy: **Australia** 270,
286; **France** 162; **India** (of
Multanis) 344; **Japan** 257;
United Kingdom 92, 93, 96;
USA 114, 119, 151
Capital base 93, 96, 97, 98–9,
270
Capital Investment Fund (**Hong
Kong**) 330
Capital Works Reserve Fund
(**Hong Kong**) 330
Carew, Edna 414, 416
Carroll McEntee & McGinley
Incorporated 111
'Cash loan' (**South Africa**) 369
Cash management bills (**USA**) 106
Cash management tenders (for
Canadian Treasury bills) 301
Cash ratio(s) 5, 382; **Canada** 5,
298
Cash reserve requirement (**South
Africa**) 382
Cash reserves (**India**) 337–8
*Casse di risparmio e monti di
credito su pegno di 1° categoria*
222

Casse rurali e artigiane e monti di credito su pegno de 2° categoria 222

Cater Allen Ltd 8

Cater Ryder & Co, Ltd 392

Cazenove Money Brokers 393

CEDEL (Centrale de Livraisons de Valeurs Mobilières) 31, 66

Central Bank Council (CBC) of Bundesbank 189, 191, 201–2, 203

Central Bank(s) 3, 4, 5, 30, 139, 206, 207, 216, 251–2, 267–8, 297, 301, 355, 359, 388; and central bank paper 296; and government balances 391; and interest rates 390; and signals 390; intervention by 390–1

Central Bank of India 343

Central Finance and Acceptance Corporation 365

Central Gilts Office (CGO), of United Kingdom 35, 54, 86

Central Money Markets Office (CMO), of United Kingdom 34–7

Central Provident Fund (CPF), of Singapore 353

Certificates of Deposit (CDs) (also Negotiable Certificates of Deposit) 389; and brokers 21, 24–5; forward markets/ contracts 21, 25n; tiered 4, 25; **Australia** 269, 272, 275, 283, 284–5, and forward market 285, and marginal adjustment 284, secondary market 284; **Canada** 303; **France** 157, 158–9, 161, 169–70; **Germany** 180–1; **Hong Kong** 327; **India** 342; **Italy** 223, 228, 229–30, 233; **Japan** 241, 242, 244, 248, 253–5, 261, 263, 264, 265, registered 255, 389, secondary market 253, 254, 255; **London** 7, 8, 10n, 12n, 13n, 14–15, 16, 17, 21n, 21–7, 34, 35, 36, 37, 97, dollar CDs 21, secondary market 25, 27, sterling CDs 24; **Singapore** 350,

351; **South Africa** 370, 371, 377–9, and stamp duty 379, secondary market 378–9; **USA** 103, 114n, 122, 123, 138–41, 144, 389, and brokers 140n, and dealers 139, 140, direct issue 140, 'hot money' 139, negotiable CDs 139–40, non-negotiable CDs 138, 139, maturities 140, retail CDs 139, secondary market 140, tiered 139, Yankee CDs 141

Certificates of Indebtedness (**USA**) 104

Certificati del Tesoro con Opzione (CTOs) 228, 238; as example of 'retractable bond' 228

Certificati di credito Tesoro (CCTs) 224, 226–7, 228, 229, 236, 238; secondary market 226–7, 229, 238

Chakravarty Report 421

Chartered banks (**Canada**) 5, 297, 298, 299, 300, 302, 303, 304, 306, 307, 308, 309, 311, 312

Chase Manhattan 136

Chase Securities, Inc. 111

Cheap money (**United Kingdom**) 38

Chemical Securities, Inc. 111

Chicago 1, 102, 103, 107, 120, 130, 133, 143, 144, 307, 332, 361

Chicago Board of Trade (CBOT) 66, 146, 148, 288, 310

Chicago Mercantile Exchange (CME) 66, 146, 147, 361

CHIPS (Clearing House Interbank Payments) 124, 126–7, 128

Chit funds (**India**) 337, 343

CIT 131

Citibank 21, 139, 363

Citicorp 135

Citicorp Securities Markets, Inc. 111

City banks (**Japan**) 241, 243n, 244, 246, 248, 249, 250; and NCDs 253; credit lines with Bank of Japan 249

City of London Options 72
Clearing banks: **London** 9, 24, 30,
54, 88, 137, 309; **Scotland** 9, 13,
54, 88, 137
'Clearing banks' **(USA)** 113, 117,
126
Cleaver, George and Pamela 392
Cleveland 107
Clive Discount Company Ltd 8n
Close, R. O. 400
'Club money' 79–80
Coles-Myer **(Australia)** 276
COMEX (Commodity Exchange,
New York) 289
Commercial banks: **South Africa**
363, 367, 368–9, 370, 373, 374,
377, 378, 379, 381, 382, 383;
USA 102, 103, 113, 117, 120,
141, 146, 149; and investment
portfolios 115, and trading
positions 115
Commercial paper 389; **Australia**
285–6; **Canada** 299n, 304–6,
309, 310, 311, 314; **France** 157,
159, 170; **Germany** 181–2;
Hong Kong 328; **India** 342; **Italy**
231; **Japan** 241, 242, 251,
256–7, 261, 263, 264, 265, 266;
Singapore 350, 351; **South
Africa** 380–1; **United Kingdom**
18, 34, 36, 55–64, 389 (*see also*
sterling commercial paper), and
Banking Act 1979 55, and
Banking Act 1987 59, and
Banking Act (Exempt
Transactions) Regulations 59,
and Companies Act 1989 59,
and Control of Borrowing
Order 56, conditions of issue
55–6, cost of issue 60, Euro-
market 55, 59, 60, guarantees
59, maturity 58, 60, placement
market 58, secondary market
58, tiered 4; **USA** 103, 114n,
123, 129, 131–8, 170, 389, and
financial companies 132, and
non-financial companies 132,
bank lines of credit 132, 133,
bank-related paper 132, cost

132–3, Discount Note 135,
placed direct 131, 132, placed
through dealers 131, 132,
133–4, 137, Master Notes 134,
maturities 133, ratings 133,
secondary market 134, 137,
'universal commercial paper'
132, unrated paper 137
Commerzbank 172, 184
Commissioner of Banking and
Monetary Affairs **(Hong Kong)**
320
Commodity brokers 69
Commodity futures 66
Commonwealth Government
securities 269, 270, 272, 273n,
274, 283, 295; auctions 279–80;
bonds 279–80; bond futures
280, 289, 290; 'reporting' bond
dealers 271, 280n, 292; reverse
bond tender 280, 295; secondary
market 271, 279, 280
Competition and Credit Control
(United Kingdom) 28, 39–40,
40n, 74, 76–8; demise of 91
Comptoir des Entrepreneurs 159
Comptroller of the Currency
(USA) 120, 125
Conseil National du Crédit 405
Continental Illinois (and related)
crises 1982–3 139
Control of Borrowing Order 56
Co-operative banks **(India)** 336–7,
338, 343
Corporation bills 87, 88, 90; *see
also* local authority bills
Corporation for Public Deposits
(CPD) **(South Africa)** 363, 366,
370, 374, 383; rate tender 383
Corporations, non-financial 4, 8,
10, 15, 16–18, 30, 57, 113, 133,
137, 139, 141, 146, 157, 158n,
159, 172, 173, 180, 229, 232,
250, 254, 255, 270, 272, 273,
274–5, 276, 279, 282, 284, 286,
287, 298, 300, 305, 306–7, 311,
312, 314, 353, 355, 364, 369,
372, 378, 379, 380–1, 389
Correspondent relationships 102,

120, 121, 122–3, 138, 149, 235, 246
Corrigan, E. Gerald 150, 405
CRA (Australia) 276
Craig, Malcolm 392
Crédit Agricole 156, 163, 164
Credit ceilings (Italy) 230
Crédit Commercial de France 164, 165n
Credit control 40, 76, 77
Credit co-operatives: France 156; Germany 171, 172
Crédit Foncier 156, 159, 161
Crédit Lyonnais 8, 159n, 164, 165, 166
Crédit National 156, 159, 161
Credito Italiano 221
Credit ratings 4, 57, 138, 159, 167, 168, 170, 342; Moody's 57, 137, 139; Standard & Poor 57, 137
Credit unions 102, 119, 121, 388
Credot, F.-J. 406
Crick, W. F. 421
Cross-currency swaps 148
'Crowding out' 106
Crowe, John W. 318n, 319, 418, 420
Crown corporations (Canada) 300
CRT Government Securities Ltd 111
CSFB (GILTS) Limited 44n
CSR (Australia) 276
Currency futures 66, 70, 146, 147, 260, 262, 287, 289, 332, 362
Currency options 70, 147, 262, 287
Currency reform 1948 (Germany) 178
Currency swaps 17, 144, 148, 236, 242, 258–9, 273, 276, 287, 323, 332–3, 356, 382

Daimler-Benz 181
Daiwa Europe (Gilts) Limited 44n
Daiwa Securities America Inc. 111
Dallas 107
Daylight overdrafts: Australia 271; Canada 299; USA 123–8

Day-to-day money: Canada 298, 299, 306, 312–13; Germany 174, 178, 207, 211
DAX (Deutscher Aktienindex) 183, 212
DBRS (Dominion Bond Rating Service); Canada 305
Dealers (money market, Canada) 297–300, 304, 305, 307, 309; see also Investment dealers, Canada
Dealing houses 3, 6; approval/recognition 3–4, 6
Dean Witter Reynolds Inc. 111
Debentures 380, 381
Debenture stock 266
Debt management: Australia 294–5; South Africa 385; United Kingdom 105; USA 104, 107, 109
Debt Register claims (Germany) 192, 193
De Kock Commission 423
Delhi 337, 338, 339, 342, 344
Denver 120
Départements d'outre mer 156
Department of Trade and Industry (United Kingdom) 69, 84
Deposit Insurance and Credit Guarantee Corporation (India) 341
Depository Institutions Deregulation and Monetary Control Act 1980 (also known as Monetary Control Act) 119
Deposits, large 180, 181, 285, 303; Australia 285; Germany 180–1, in foreign currency 327, 328
Deposit-taking Companies (DTCs) 320, 321–2, 323, 327, 332, 333
Deposit-taking Institutions Act (South Africa) 363; exemption from 381
Deregulation of money markets (Japan) 243, 247, 260–1
Deutsche Bank 172, 181, 184
Deutsche Bank Government Securities, Inc. 111
Deutsche Bundesbank 172, 175,

180–1, 182, 212–13, 214, 216, 220, 407, 408, 409, 410; and Landeszentralbanken 172; discount rate 191, 192, 193, 198, 200, 201, 203, 204; econometric model 188; 'fine-tuning' 199, 204–6, 207, 208; interest rate tender 197, 198, 199, 202, 203, 204, 208; intervention by 173, 176–7, 184–208, 217; lombard policy 190, 192–5, 197, 198; operating variables in money market 194; 'quick tender' 199–200, 201, 205, 208; quotas 191–2, 203, 208; rediscount policy 190, 191–2; refinancing policy 190–5, 197, 208; repurchase agreements 193, 197–204, 207, 208, 214, 217; signals 204, 207, 211; S.17 allocations 199, 204, 205, 208, 211; volume tender 197, 198, 200, 201, 202, 208

Deutsche Genossenschaftsbank 171, 172, 174, 184

Deutsche Terminbörse (DTB) 183–4; contracts 183, 184; DAX index 183; futures 183, 184; membership 184; options 183, 184

Developed banking and financial system 3

DIALCOM 300, 301

Dillon, Read & Co. Inc. 111

Direct assistance 74

Direct clearers (Canada) 306, 315–16; Government cash balances with 315

Discount and Finance House of India (DFHI) 338, 341, 345; refinance facility at Reserve Bank of India 341

Discount Corporation of New York 111

Discount houses: London 6, 7, 8–10, 13, 15, 16, 17n, 18, 19, 20, 21, 24, 25, 27, 30, 34, 36, 37–8, 41, 54, 69, 73–4, 75, 77, 82–4, 86–8, 89, 91–9, 391,

'additions' 92, 'adjusted total book' 92, 96, 99, and club money 79–80, and gilt-edged 77, and short bonds 38–9, assets 8, borrowings 8, 9, 11–12, capital base 93, 96, cartel 28, foreign currency assets 92, 'good money' 74, lenders to 9, money book 12n, multiplier(s) 7, 76, 91–2, 93, 96, 99, 'other currency' assets 92, ratios 39, 76, shareholders' funds 8, top hat 11, trading in futures markets 92, Treasury bills 8, 28, 30, underwriting of Treasury bill tender 28–30; Singapore 350–1, 353; South Africa 363, 365, 368, 369–73, 374, 375, 376, 377, 378, 379, 380, 383, 384, assets 370, bond dealings 365, borrowings 370–3, limits 372, multiplier 372, retailing 372, security 371, 372, traders in government securities 372–3

Discount House of South Africa Limited 369

Discount market (Singapore) 350

Discount rate: Australia 292; Germany 191, 192, 193, 198, 200, 201, 202, 203, 204, 207, 208, 214; Italy 239, 240; Japan 243, 256, 261

Discount windows: Hong Kong 335; Italy 239–40; London 75; South Africa 368, 383–4; USA 110

Donaldson, Lufkin & Jenrette Securities Corporation 111

Dotsey, Michael 414

Dresdner Bank 172, 184

Dual-capacity system 42

Dusseldorf 172, 175

Eastern Europe 334

Easy-money policy 41

Economic and Monetary Union (EMU) 213

Economic policy (**United Kingdom**) 215, 217–20
ECUs (European Currency Units) 31n, 159, 213, 233; bonds in 33; futures 166; Treasury bills in 31–3, 227
Editoriale Lavoro 411, 412
Edmonton 312
Effets privés 162, 167, 388
Effets privés éligibles 166, 168
Effets sous dossier 162
Emery, Robert F. 412, 413
Equalisation claims (**Germany**) 178
Equalisation of Burdens Fund 191
'Equilibrium' price 2
ERP Special Fund 176, 191
Escudo 216
Établissements de crédit 156, 167
Eurobrokers Inc. 119
Euroclear 31, 66
Euro-currencies 21, 143, 144, 241, 307
Euro-dollar market/Eurodollars 20, 21, 22–3, 122, 123, 129, 141–5, 159, 174, 245, 249, 273, 323, 356, 357, 362, 382n, 389–90; brokers 144; direct deals 144; Euro-commercial paper 59, 138; Euro-deposits 231; Eurodollar CDs 140n, 309; Euro-franc 159; Euro-lire CDs 230; Euro-Note(s) 55, 138; Euro-sterling 159; Euro-yen 260, 261, 262; limits 145; secondary market 309
EUROMOBILIARE 411
European Community (EC) 213
European Investment Bank 223
European Monetary System (EMS) 91, 212, 213, 214, 220
Exchange Banks' Association (now HKAB) 320–1
Exchange banks (**India**) 343
Exchange control 216; end of, in **Australia** 286; of capital movements 216; **South Africa** 385
Exchange Fund (**Hong Kong**) 321, 324, 325, 329, 331; assets 325,

329; certificates of indebtedness 321, 324; discount window 335; 'liquidity adjustment facility' 335; loans to 335; powers of office director 335; ultimate provider of liquidity 325
Exchange Fund Bills 327, 329, 335; and monetary policy 329; tender for 329
Exchange Rate Mechanism (ERM) 91, 212, 213, 214, 215, 216, 217, 218–20
Exchange (rate) risk 143–4, 147
Exchange settlement funds (**Australia**) 270, 272, 275
Expectations 2; FOREX rates 335; interest rates 89–90, 115, 163n, 173, 200, 228, 236, 279, 335, 378
Export Credit Insurance Corporation (**Hong Kong**) 322
Export credit paper 84
Export Credits Guarantee Department (ECGD) 84
Export Development Corporation (**Canada**) 300
Export economy 5
Export-Import Bank (**USA**) 118
Export-Import Bank of Japan 241

Factoring companies 222
Falkena, H. B. 423, 424, 425
Farm Credit Banks 122
Farm Credit System 118
Farmers' Home Adminstration 118, 125
FBA (Discount) Ltd 269
Federal Agencies (**USA**) 103, 117–18, 135, 153, 154–5; securities of 102–3, 114n, 125
Federal Appeals Court (**USA**) 136
Federal Banking Supervisory Office (**Germany**) 192
Federal Business Development Bank (**Canada**) 300
Federal Deposit Insurance Corporation (FDIC) (**USA**) 122, 125

Federal funds 103, 109, 112,
118–23, 135, 137, 138, 149,
172, 307, 387–8; and small
banks 120–1; and time
differences 120; brokers 114,
119–20; dealers 119, 122;
defined 118–19; origins 119;
overnight 122, 149; term 122
Federal Government (Germany)
177, 178, 185, 199, 206, 208,
209
Federal Home Loan Banks 118,
121, 122, 388
Federal Home Loan Mortgage
Corporation 118
Federal Housing Administration
118
Federal National Mortgage
Association 118
Federal Open Market Committee
(FOMC) (USA) 107–10;
directive 108, 109, 110
Federal Post Office (Germany)
176, 177, 178, 191, 196, 197,
206
Federal Railways (Germany) 177,
182, 191, 206
Federal Reserve Bank of New
York 107, 109, 114, 116, 126,
128, 130, 133, 150, 403, 404,
405; Market Reports Division
114
Federal Reserve Banks 103, 107,
127, 128
Federal Reserve Board (Board of
Governors of the Federal
Reserve System) 136, 401, 403,
404, 405
Federal Reserve System 102, 107,
113n, 117, 118–19, 124ff, 149,
172, 207; and bankers'
acceptances 128–9; and
consultation with the Treasury
107; as fiscal agent of the
Treasury 104
Fedwire 124, 125, 126, 128
FIBOR (Frankfurt Inter-Bank
Offered Rate) 182
Fidler, Stephen 398, 414

Finance bills (Japan) 241, 249,
251, 255–6, 263, 265; finance
bills 18n, 131, 282, 343
Finance Companies Act 1967
(Singapore) 350
Finance company(-ies) 222, 232,
267, 272, 304–5, 346–7, 349,
350, 351, 368
Finance Ministry: Bonn 216;
French 216
Finance paper (USA & Canada)
131, 303, 311
Financial futures 390; Australia
288–91, contracts 288, 289, 290,
'locals' 290; Canada 309–10;
Hong Kong 330–2; Japan
261–2; Singapore 356, 360–2,
'mutual offset' system 361,
'night shift' 356; United
Kingdom 66–73, 114n, and
management of bank balance
sheets 68, 69, 70, clearing
system 67, defined 66, exchange
traded 67, hedging 67–8,
liquidity 67, margin 67, 69
(initial margin 67, variation
margin 67), over the counter
(OTC) 67, trading 71; USA
145–8, clearing corporation
146, currency futures 146, 147,
DM futures contract 147,
Eurodollars 146, 148, exchange
rate risk 147, futures contract
145–6, interest rate futures 144,
145, liquidity 146, 147, options
146–7, US Treasury bonds 146
Financial packages, unbundling of
72–3
Financial Secretary (Hong Kong)
321, 330
Financial Services Act (United
Kingdom) 56
'Financing' paper (Germany) 177
Finland 213
FINTRACS (Financial
Transactions Recording and
Clearing System) 283
First Boston Corporation, The
111, 133

First Chicago Capital Markets,
Inc. 111
First National Bank (South
Africa) 363
First National City Bank of New
York 21, 139
Fixed deposits: Australia 267;
Singapore 349; South Africa 371
'Fixed term' money (Australia)
272
Floating debt 4
Floating Rate Notes (FRNs) 15n,
26, 65−6; maturities 65; 'quoted
margin' 65; sizes 65; trading 65,
66
Ford 305, 311
Ford, Douglas 332
Foreign banks: Australia 275;
Canada 303, 307, 311; France
164; Germany 170, 171, 175−6,
184; Hong Kong 323, 333; India
337, 340, 343; Italy 222, 236,
237; Japan 244, 248, 257, 258,
260, 263−4; London 81;
Singapore 348, 349, 351, 357;
USA 122, 129, 132, 137, 140−1
Foreign central banks 131
Foreign exchange (FOREX) 3;
Australia 275, 276, 286−8, 291,
authorised dealers 287, brokers
287, forward market 287,
intervention 288, 293, position
limits 288; Canada 317−18;
Germany, repurchase
agreements in 205−6, 211; Hong
Kong 326, 327, 332−5, brokers
332, dealers 332, no exchange
control 332, 334; India 342−3,
authorised dealers 343, brokers
342; Japan 258−9, 263n;
London 9, 10, 16−17, 21;
Singapore 355−6, 357, 360,
brokers 355, intervention
currency 356; South Africa 367,
381−2, 385
Foreign Exchange and Currency
Deposit Brokers Association 21
Foreign Exchange Association of
India 342

Foreign exchange swaps 198, 204,
205, 208, 354, 391
Forward Rate Agreements (FRAs)
18, 310
Fourchette de prix 158
Fourie, L. J. 423, 424
Four Seasons Communications
Bank 348
Frankfurt 172, 174−5, 183, 212,
307
French Banks' Association 165
French franc 216, 217
French Merchant Bank 363
Fry Mills Spence & Company
Limited 299n
Fuji Securities Inc. 111
Full licence banks (Singapore) 348,
349
Fully-drawn advance (Australia)
276, 281
Futures Trading Act 1986
(Singapore) 361n

Gaika yokin (Japan) 242
Garban Gilts Limited 44n
Garvin Bantel & Co. 119
Garvin GuyButler Corp. 119
Gawith, Philip 425
Gendreau, Brian 405
General banks (South Africa) 363,
368, 374, 382
General Insurance Corporation of
India (GIC) 339, 340, 341
Gensaki (Japan) 242, 243, 266,
389; and securities transaction
tax 242, 248, 251; bond dealers
250−1, 252; CD gensaki 248,
251, 253, 254, 263; itaku gensaki
251; jiko gensaki 251; overnight
251
Gensaki market 250−2
German Bund 70
Gerrard & National Ltd 8
Gerrard & National Securities
Limited 44n
Gerrard & Reid 8
Gillett Brothers Discount Company
Limited 392
Gilt-Edged (Gilts) 8, 9, 10, 35, 74;

and 'fallow' period 49; and
National Debt Commissioners
53; and recession (post-1990) 52;
conventionals 46, 47; convertibles
46; deficit financing 53; direct
sales 48, 53; funding programme
47, 48, 52, 53−4; index-linked
stocks 46, 47, 53n; methods of
issue 47−51; maturities 46;
overfunding 89; role of the
authorities 46ff; tender 46, 47,
51; tranche 47; 'tranchettes' 47,
48; underwriting by Bank of
England 47, 49
Gilt-Edged (South Africa) 379, 384
Gilt-Edged market (United
Kingdom) 37−54, 76−7; and
'Big Bang' 42−4, 52; and
budget surpluses 51−2; and
jobbing firms 42; auctions
47−51; Central Gilts Office 54;
Government broker 39, 46, 79;
secondary market 48, 49
Gilt-Edged market-makers 7−8,
36, 43−5, 44n, 49, 50, 51, 52,
54, 69, 99−100; 'back' book 45;
'front' book 45
Gilt-Edged Market-Makers
Association (GEMMA) 44
Giro institutions (including
Girozentralen): Germany 171,
172; postal giro 171, 172, 174
Glass-Steagal Act 135, 136
GMAC 131, 134, 305, 311
GNMA (Government National
Mortgage Association) 118,
146
Goldman, Sachs & Co. 111, 132,
133
Goldman Sachs Government
Securities (UK) Limited 44n
Goodson, H. F. 396
Goodspeed, I. 423
Government Account Series (USA)
104
Government Agencies (USA) 103,
104
Government Bonds 251, 252, 266,
341

Government broker (London) 39,
46, 79
Government-guaranteed bonds
(Japan) 251
Government Securities Act 1986
(USA) 116
Government securities (and
markets): Australia 267; France
163−4; Germany 206; Hong
Kong 330, 335; India 341; Italy
224−8; Japan 241; Singapore
348, 350, 351−3, auctions 353,
355, primary dealers 352, 353,
354, 'same-day dealers' 355,
secondary market 352, 355;
South Africa 370−1, 379;
United Kingdom see gilt-edged
market; USA (includes Treasury
bonds) 103−7, 114n, 117,
123−4, 125, 127, 146, 149, and
automation 151−2, and
'winner's curse' 152, 153, 154,
auctions 104, 105ns, 151−5;
Dutch auction 152, futures 146,
purchases by Fed for own or
customers' account 106
Government securities dealers
(USA) 111−16, 146, 390; and
'clearing bank' 113; and other
traders 114−15; bank dealers
112, 114, 390; funding desk
112−13; non-bank dealers 112,
113, 114, 390; positions 112,
113; size 114
Grand Cayman (Caribbean) 143
Grands établissements 156
'Graveyard shift' 149
Greenwell Montagu Gilt-Edged 8n,
44n, 53
Greenwich Capital Markets, Inc.
111
Gross National Product (GNP)
209
Guaranteed Investment Certificates
(GICs) 304, 312
Gulf War 52−3, 208

Halifax Building Society 10
Hamburg 172, 175

Hessische Landesbank Girozentrale 172
Hang Seng Bank 322
Hang Seng Stock Exchange Futures 331, 332
Harris Government Securities Inc. 111
Herstatt Bank failure 145
HIBOR (Hong Kong Inter-Bank Offered Rate) 328
Hills Independent Traders 72
HKAB Rules on Interest Rates and Deposit Charges 321
Hong Kong 142, 143, 148, 276, 307, 358
Hongkong and Shanghai Banking Corporation 321, 323, 324, 331; Government's banker 321, 324; note issue 321, 324–5, 326; quasi-central banking functions 321
Hong Kong Association of Banks (HKAB), formerly EBA 321, 325
Hong Kong Building and Loans Agency Ltd 322
Hong Kong dollar, exchange value 321, 325, 326, 329
Hong Kong Futures Exchange (formerly Hong Kong Commodity Exchange) 330, 331
Hong Kong Futures Guarantee Corporation 331
Hong Kong Government accounts 324
Hong Kong Government bonds 330, 335; entry into international market 330
Hong Kong Land 323
Hong Kong Stock Exchange 331
Hours of operation: Australia 272, 275, 276, 278, 291–2, 293; Canada 302, 306, 308, 312, 313, 315, 317, 318; France 158, 160–1, 167; Germany 173, 175–6; Hong Kong 323, 325, 326, 333, 335; India 338, 342–3; Italy 234, 238, 239, 240; Japan 245–6, 248, 264; South Africa

367, 369, 373, 374; USA 148–9
Howard, Donna 418
Hundi broker 343
Hundis (India) 343–4

IBIS (Inter Banken Informations System) 183
Icard, A. 406
ICCREA (Istituto di Credito delle Casse Rurali e Artigiane) 222, 235
ICCRI (Istituto di Credito delle Casse di Risparmio Italiane) 222
ICI (Imperial Chemical Industries) 16
ICI Finance 16
IMI (Istituto Mobiliare Italiano) 223, 236
Income and Corporation Taxes Act 1970 43
India: 'black money' 345; hundis 343–4; indigenous bankers 337, 343–4; moneylenders 337; 'social' control of banking 337
Indigenous bankers (India) 337, 343–4; hundi broker 343; hundis 343–4; limits 343, 344; multani shroff 343–4
Indirect assistance 74
Indonesia 323
Indosuez 164
Industrial Development Bank of India 345
Institute of Bankers 392, 396
Institutions financières specialisées (IFS) 157
Insurance companies 25, 36, 57, 69, 103, 106, 131, 133, 137, 146, 157, 241, 250, 283, 349, 363n, 368, 371, 377, 378
Integrity 3, 96, 174
Interbank (call) loan market 4, 9, 10, 137, 387, 388; brokers 12, 14, 160, 162, 237, 274; direct deals 12, 14, 16, 274; rates 13; Australia 275; Canada 306–8; France 157, 160–3, 167, 388; Germany 172–6, 388; Hong Kong 322–7, borrowers 323,

lenders 322, 323, money market dealing lines 322; **India** 337–9, 344–5, and brokers 345; **Italy** 232, 233–8, 388, call 237, overnight 236–7; **Japan** 242, 243–6, 248, 260, 263–4; **London** 9, 10, 12–13, 73; **Singapore** 350, 351; **South Africa** 364, 368–9, 383, 'grey market' 369
Interbank Discount House Limited 370
'Inter-bank participations' **(India)** 342
Inter-company market(s): **Australia** 276, 286; **India** 343, 345; **South Africa** 369
Inter-dealer brokers: **France** 158, 164; **London** 43, 44, 50, 52, 54; **USA** 116
Inter-dealer loans **(Australia)** 272
Interest-bearing deposits (IBDs) 181, 292
Interest equalisation tax **(USA)** 308
Interest rate cap 310n
Interest rate ceiling **(India)** 338
Interest rate collar 310n
Interest rate expectations 89–90, 115, 163n, 173, 200, 228, 236, 279, 335, 378
Interest rate floor 310n
Interest rate futures 144, 145–6, 332, 362
Interest rate swaps 17, 147–8, 310
Interest subsidies 223
International Banking Facilities (IBFs) 122, 143, 144
International paper **(Canada)** 308–9
Intra-day loans **(Japan)** 246, 263
Investment counsellors 300n
Investment dealers **(Canada)** 300, 301, 302, 307, 310–15; borrowings 312–14; inventory 310, 311–12, 314; margin accounts 314; off-street money 312; stock retailing 314
Investment funds 300

Investment trusts 25, 57, 244
IRI (Istituto per la Ricostruzione Industriale) 221
Irrationalities 2
Istituti di credito di diritto pubblico 221
Istituto Bancario Italiano 222
Istituto Bancario S. Paolo di Torino 221
Italy 213, 215–16; savings ratio 229

James Capel Gilts Limited 44n, 72
Japan 355, 358, 362
Japan Development Bank 241
Jardines 323
Jobbers (money market, **Canada**) 297–300
Johannesburg Stock Exchange, listing on 381
Juttner, D. J. 415

Kane, Daniel R. 395
Kansas City 107
Kidder, Peabody & Co. 111
King, W. T. C. (Wilfrid) 392, 397
King & Shaxson Ltd 8n
Kleinwort Benson Gilts Limited 44n, 72
Knight, Gary 332
Kobe 246
Kok, W. J. 423, 424, 425
Koko (finance corporations) 241
Konczaty, M. 406
Koppenhauer, G. D. 405
Korea 334
Krona (Danish) 216

Lamont, Norman 213
Land and Agricultural Bank (Land Bank) 363–4
Land Bank bills 370, 375–6, 379, 384, 385; debentures 370, 375n, 379; tender 375, 376; secondary market 376
Länder governments 177
Landeszentralbanken 172
Lanston, Aubrey G. & Co., Inc. 111
Lasser Marshall Inc. 119

LDMA (London Discount Market Association) 7, 8, 19, 28, 75, 76, 92
Leasing companies 222
Lee, P. J. (Peter) 395, 398–9
Lehman Brothers Gilts Limited 44n
Lehman Government Securities, Inc. 111, 133
Lender of last resort (and facilities) 5, 6, 7, 28, 75, 86–7, 113, 267, 268, 270, 293, 298, 325
Lending of securities 44–5, 113–14, 164, 271, 298, 302
Letter of credit 282, 376
Levesque Beaubien Inc. 299n
Lewis, M. K. 405
LIBID (London Inter-Bank Bid Rate) 64
LIBOR (London Inter-Bank Offered Rate) 64, 65, 133, 146, 148, 182, 358
Licensed banks (Hong Kong) 320, 332; merchant banking division 328
Licensed deposit-takers 8, 55, 56, 59, 78
Life assurance companies 4, 273n, 280, 281
Life insurance companies 302n, 305, 314, 377
Life Insurance Corporation (LIC) (India) 339, 340, 341, 345
LIFFE (London International Financial Futures Exchange) 18, 33, 66, 69–73, 97, 165, 166, 183, 184, 224n, 227, 289, 290, 362; Board of Exchange 70; contracts 70–1; geographic position 71, 72; 'locals' 69; Market Supervision Department 70; membership 69; merger with LTOM 71–2
Limits, unadvised or internal 388, 390; Australia 276, 282, 284; Canada 307–8, 313; Germany 174; Hong Kong 322; India 339; Italy 237; Japan 245, 253, 258;

London 10, 12, 18; Singapore 351; South Africa 368; USA 121
'Liquefiable assets' (Hong Kong) 320
Liquid assets 1, 3, 27, 283, 284, 367, 371, 375, 387
Liquidity: defined 1; in all other contexts, passim
Liquidity paper (Germany) 178, 196–7
Liquidity ratios 5; of building societies 14n, 15; of clearing (and other 'statistical') banks 78
Lira 213, 215, 217
Local Authority(ies) (United Kingdom) 8, 15, 21, 55; bills 8, 13, 16, 17, 34, 74, 83, 87; Bonds 18, 34; non-quota loans 34; quota loans 34; securities 33n, 33–4, 38
Local authority securities (Australia) 280–1
Local governments (USA) 103, 104, 113, 131
Lombard borrowing (Germany) 176, 190, 192–5, 197, 198, 199, 200, 202, 203, 204, 390
Lombard rate 200, 201, 202, 203, 204, 207, 208, 214
London 1, 2, 142, 143, 144, 148, 149, 158, 230, 276, 286, 307, 309, 332, 333, 342, 354
Long-Term Credit Bank of Japan 256
Long-term credit banks (Japan) 241, 243, 248
Los Angeles 102
LTOM (London Traded Options Market) 71–2
Luüs, C. W. 423
Luxembourg 227

Maastricht Treaty 213, 216, 220; French referendum 216
Mabon Nugent 119
Macfarlane, I. J. 414, 415
Madan, B. K. 421
Madras 337, 338, 339, 342, 344
Mainz 172, 175

Maisons de réescompte 156, 163, 164
Maisons de titres 156
Managing bank assets and liabilities: **Italy** 231; **Japan** 244
Manitoba 301n
Marché interbancaire 156–7
Marginal reserve requirements **(USA)** 21n
Maritime Administration **(USA)** 118
Maritimes **(Canada)** 312
Market-makers: **Australia** 271; **India** 338, 341; **Italy** 225; **Singapore** 352; **South Africa** 370–1, 377
Marshalls 332
Mass Transit Railway **(Hong Kong)** 328
MATIF (*Marché à Terme International de France*, formerly *Marché à Terme des Instruments Financiers*) 163, 165–6, 224n, 227; clearing house 165; contracts 165; ECU bond futures 166; members 165; Treasury bond future 165; stock index future 165
Maturities 2, 3; **Australia** 279, 282, 284, 285, 291; **Canada** 302, 303, 304, 305, 308, 311, 313; **Hong Kong** 322, 328, 329, 330; **India** 339; **Italy** 224–5, 227, 228, 229, 230; **Japan** 242, 247, 248, 256, 260, 261; **Singapore** 351; **South Africa** 368, 377, 378, 379; **United Kingdom** 89–90, 93, 97; **USA** 104–5, 106, 107
Meade, James 218–19
Mediocredito Centrale 223
Medium Term Financial Strategy 90–1
Medium-term notes 59
Meijer, J. H. (Jaap) 386, 423, 425
Melbourne 1, 267, 275n, 288
Merchant banks: **Australia** 272, 273, 275, 279, 281–2, 283, 284, 285, 286; **Hong Kong** 327, 328; **Italy** 222; **London** 27, 71, 309;

Singapore 349, 350, 351, 355, 357; **South Africa** 363, 370, 373, 374, 380, 382
Merck 137
Merrill Lynch 299n
Merrill Lynch Government Securities Inc. 111, 133
Meulendyke, Ann-Marie 400
MID (*Mercato telematico interbancario dei depositi*) 234, 237
Middle East 343, 356, 358
Midland Doherty Ltd 299n
Midland Montagu 57
Miller, Robert 398
Minimum Lending Rate (MLR) 74, 80, 89, 214, 215, 217; and 'unpublished band' 80
Minimum reserves (requirements): **Germany** 172, 173, 189–90, 201, 203, 207, 208; **India** 338–9; **Japan** 265; **Singapore** 347; **South Africa** 364, 367; **USA** 119
Mining houses **(South Africa)** 364, 368, 370, 371, 372, 376, 378, 379
Ministry of Finance **(Japan)** 253, 255, 256, 265
Minneapolis 107
Mobilisation paper **(Germany)** 178, 196–7
Monaco 156, 162
Monetarist Views, of the Bank of England 40, 90
Monetary Affairs Branch **(Hong Kong)** 321
Monetary aggregates 90, 185, 186–7, 209–11
Monetary authority 5
Monetary Authority of Singapore (MAS) 346ff *passim*, 422; exchange rate policy 347; monetary policy 347–8; open market operations 354
Monetary targeting 184–9, 209, 214, 216–17; definitions 185; 'corridor concept' 188–9, 204
Money brokers 387; **Australia** 274–5, 276; **Canada** 307, 314;

Germany 174, 387; **Hong Kong** 327; **India** 338, 345; **London** 9, 12, 14, 69, 71; **Singapore** 349, 350, 351, 355, 357; **South Africa** 368, 369, 371
Money centre banks **(USA)** 113, 120–1, 122, 136, 149; and call loans 113, 118; and 'lender of last resort' assistance 113, 149
Money management team 11, 173
Money market certificates **(Japan)** 253
'Money market corporations' **(Australia)** 272, 274, 295
Money market deposit accounts 138
Money-market funds 131, 137, 139, 141
Money markets: and competition 1–2; 'condominium' 1; cost of information 2–3; definition 1, 387, 391; imperfections 2; integration of 3, 101, 149; nature of the economy 3, 5–6; parallel markets 101; personalised credit relations 2; secondary markets 101; **Australia** 1, 267–96, official money market 268–71, 272, 276, 295, unofficial money market 268, 272, 273–4, 276, 295; **Canada** 1, 297–319; **France** 156–70, fixing of rates 161; **Germany** 171–220, as a 'hybrid' system 171, DM as reserve currency 189; **Hong Kong** 320–35; **India** 1, 336–45, busy season 339, public sector 336–7; **Italy** 221–40; **Japan** 1, 241–66; **London** 1, 7–101; **Singapore** 328, 346–62; **South Africa** 5, 363–86, origins of 364–6; **USA** 102–55, integration of 149
Money position: of banks, **Canada** 306–7, **France** 160–1, 163, **Germany** 173, **Hong Kong** 323–4, **India** 337–8, **Italy** 232, 233–4, **Japan** 245, **London** 10–11, **South Africa** 367, **USA**

122; money position: of corporates 16
Montreal 1, 147, 299, 308, 309, 310, 312
Montreal Stock Exchange 310
'Mopping up' (surpluses) 4, 9, 74, 88, 169, 202, 204, 205, 207, 211, 238, 245, 249, 265, 266, 291, 292, 294, 317, 325, 329, 338–9, 354, 366, 384, 385, 390
Morgan, J. P. 181, 184
Morgan Guaranty 181
Morgan, J. P. Securities Inc. 111, 135
Morgan Stanley & Co. Incorporated 111
Morgan, J. P. Sterling Securities Ltd 44n
Morgenrood, P. 423
Mortgage banks **(Germany)** 171, 172
Mortgage loan companies **(Canada)** 300
Mullens & Co. 46
Multani shroff **(India)** 343–4
Munich 172, 175
Mutual funds 131, 137, 157

Nagoya 245, 247, 249, 261, 263
Nakamoto, Michiyo 414
Nassau 143
National Bank for Agriculture and Rural Development (NABARD) **(India)** 340–1, 345
National Credit Union Administration 125
National Discount Company 8
National Discount House of South Africa Limited (NHD) 369–70
National Finance Corporation (NFC) **(South Africa)** 5, 6, 364–6, 369, 375
National Provincial Building Society 10
National Savings 217
Nationwide Anglia Building Society 10, 30
Nationwide Building Society 26
NatWest Gilts Limited 44n

'Near-banks' 14
Nedbank 363
NEDCOR 363
Nedperm Bank 363
Negotiable Certificates of Deposit
    (NCDs) *see* Certificates of
    Deposit (CDs)
Nesbitt Thomson Deacon Inc. 299n
Nesbitt Thomson Securities
    Limited 299n
New Brunswick 301n
Newfoundland 301n
New Orleans 120
New York 1, 2, 102, 119, 120,
    121, 130, 135, 143, 144, 148,
    149, 158, 276, 286, 288, 307,
    308, 332, 342, 354, 388, 390
New Zealand 5, 323, 334, 356
Nichols, Dorothy M. 403
Nidhis (India) 337, 343
Nikko Securities Co. International,
    Inc., The 111
Nolo contendere 151
Nomura Gilts Limited 44n
Nomura Securities International
    Inc. 111
Non-primary dealers (USA) 114-16
Noonan, Astley & Pearce, Inc. 119
N paper (*Nicht reguliert*) 177, 178
Norddeutsche Landesbank
    Girozentrale 172
Norin Chukin Bank 241, 243, 248
Note issue (Hong Kong) 324-5,
    326

Obligations assimilables du Trésor
    (OATs) 168
Offshore banking (Singapore) 350,
    357, 360
Offshore borrowing: Australia
    273, 276; Hong Kong 323
Offshore earnings 334
Offshore investors 277, 280
Offshore licence banks (Singapore)
    348, 349
Offshore loans 334
Offshore market: Japan 242,
    259-60; Singapore 357
Oil companies 16, 137, 314, 369n

Oil royalties 9
Oil traders 249
'Old boy network' 2, 351
OMF 165
Ontario 301n
Ontario Hydro 302n
Osaka 1, 245, 247, 249, 261, 262,
    263
Ottawa 300, 312
Open market operations 390;
    Australia 291, 293, 294, 295-6;
    France 166, 169; Germany 178,
    179, 196, 204, 206-8; Italy 232,
    240; Japan 247, 255, 265, 266;
    Singapore 354; South Africa 385;
    United Kingdom 80; USA 109
Open Market Sweden 165n
Opérateurs principaux du marché
    (OPMs) 167
Opérations de réméré (also
    réméré) 160, 168
Options 66-7, 68, 97-8, 114n,
    160, 165, 168, 227, 228, 261,
    262, 390; and management of
    bank balance sheets 68-9;
    clearing system 67; defined
    66-7; 'delta value' 97; hedging
    67-8; margin 67
Osaka 1, 245, 247, 249, 261, 262,
    263
Osugi, K. 414
Ottawa 300, 312
Over-certification charge (Canada)
    299
Overdraft 4, 10, 18, 60, 236, 276,
    281, 306, 314, 340, 369, 376ns;
    at Bank of England 11, 88
Overnight call rate: target (Japan)
    266
Overnight loans: Singapore 354;
    South Africa 371, 384
Overnight market 315, 317, 377
Overnight money 11, 12, 242,
    243, 246, 249, 257, 258, 272,
    273, 275, 276, 308, 312, 322,
    326, 335, 339, 351, 368, 369,
    371, 387, 389
Oversea-Chinese Banking
    Corporation (OCBC) 348

Overseas banks (London) 9

Pacific 334–5
Paine Webber Incorporated 111
PAR (Prime Assets Ratio)
   (Australia) 270, 272, 277n, 279
Parallel markets 101
Paribas 133, 159n, 164, 165
Parliament of Commonwealth of
   Australia 415
Payments system (Canada) 319
Pension (also *en pension*) 160,
   162, 166, 167, 168–9, 389;
   pension livrée 168; *pensions à 7
   jours* 168; *pensions à 5–10
   jours* 168, 169
Pension funds 4, 36, 57, 106, 117,
   131, 133, 139, 141, 146, 157,
   208, 314, 363n, 371, 377, 378
People's Republic of China 322,
   334
'Period' money: Germany 174;
   Hong Kong 322, 326; London
   11, 12–13; Singapore 351
Perth (Western Australia) 275n
Peseta (Spanish) 215
Philadelphia 107, 120, 147
Philip Hill Acceptance Company
   365
Phillips, Brian 395
Phillips, M. J. 415
Phillips, Patrick 397
Phillips Report 25
PIBOR (Paris Inter-Bank Offered
   Rate) 165
Pittsburg 120
P-note (Australia) 274, 275, 276,
   282, 283, 285–6; private
   placement of 286
Political stability 3
Polly Peck 64
Postal Service (USA) 118
Post Office: France 156; Japan
   241
Potgieter, W. J. 423
Potter Warburg Discount Limited
   269
Prebon Money Brokers Inc. 119
Price differentials 2

Primary dealers: France 163, 164,
   'non-competitive bids' 164;
   Singapore 352, 353, 355; USA
   102, 110, 111, 114, 115, 116,
   127, 128, future of 150ff
Primary distributors (Canada)
   299, 300, 301
Prime Rate: Singapore 352; USA
   148
Privatdiskont-AG 179–80, 192
PROMETEIA 234
Promissory note (PN): Australia
   283, 285–6; Japan 247–8;
   South Africa 379, 380
Province of British Columbia 299
Provincial Treasury Bill tenders
   (Canada) 301, 310
Prudential controls (United
   Kingdom) 91–101
Prudential Securities Incorporated
   112
PSBR (public sector borrowing
   requirement) 296
Public Debt Commissioners (South
   Africa) 366, 370
Public Investment Commissioners
   (PIC) (South Africa) 363, 366,
   374
Public sector banks (India) 336,
   337, 343, 345
Public sector deficit 206, 208
Public Works Loan Board
   (PWLB) 33–4
Punt, Irish 216
Purchase and Resale Agreements
   (PRAs) 298, 316; special PRAs
   316

Quebec 301n
Quebec Savings Bank Act 301
'Quick tender' (Germany)
   199–200, 201, 205, 208

Radcliffe Committee 396, 397
Raine, G. E. 423
Rand(s) 367, 385; commercial
   386; financial 386
RBC Dominion Securities Inc.
   299n

Real-time computer system 35, 128, 282–3
Receiver General for Canada 301, 307
Recession: in Japan 243; in United Kingdom 215, 217; in USA 219
Rediscount quotas (Germany) 179–80
Regional banks: Canada 307; France 156; Germany 171; Japan 241, 243, 244, 246, 248, 253
Regional Rural Bank Act 1975 336
Regional rural banks (India) 336, 337, 342
Registrar of Deposit-Taking Institutions (South Africa) 373
Regulation Q (USA) 20, 141
Reinhart, Vincent 155
Rémére 160, 168
Repurchase agreements (Repos) 389, 390; Australia 267, 269, 270, 276, 292, 293, 294, 295–6; Canada 305, 313, 314, 316–17; Germany 176, 179, 197–204; Hong Kong 335; India 341; Italy 231–3, 238–9; Japan 266; Singapore 354–5; South Africa 371, 372, 377, 379–80; United Kingdom 16, 83–4; USA 110–11, 113, 114n, 118, 123
Resale agreement 380
Reserve Bank of Australia 268ff passim, 415, 416, 417, 418; information, provision of 292, 294; intervention by 291–6; rediscounting with 271, 293; rediscount rate 292
Reserve Bank of India (RBI) 336–45 passim, 421; limits at 338; refinance facilities 338, 341; signals 341
Reserve requirements: Germany 181; Italy 229, 232, 233, 234–5, 236; Japan 266; USA 140, 141, 144
Restricted licence banks: Hong Kong 320; Singapore 348, 349, 357

Retail brokers (USA) 116, 117
Retail money 303
Reuters 65, 91, 164, 225, 238, 286n, 292, 342, 374
Reverse repos 9, 36, 110–11, 113, 231, 238, 266, 294, 354, 379, 384, 389, 390
Revolving fund of cash 3, 5, 6, 9, 387
Richardson Greenshields of Canada Ltd 299n
Richmond 107
Ridding, John 414
Rights of recourse 388
Risk(s) 2, 3, 114n, 125, 127, 128, 145, 148, 262, 273, 284, 287, 288, 299, 309–10, 319, 326, 333, 339, 342, 360, 378, 386, 388; and spectrum of rates 2; credit risk 96, 274; currency risk 287; forced sale risk 96, 97; payments system risk 128; position risk 96, 97; risk-taking 93; settlement risk 96, 97; systemic risk 124–5, 126
Risk coefficients (United Kingdom) 92, 94–5, 98, 100
RITS (Registry Information Transfer System) 283
Rothschild Australia Discount Limited 269
Roure, Francine 406
Royal Securities Limited 299n
Rupee (Indian), devaluation of 342
Rupee/Sterling rate 342

Sage Financial Services 363
St. Louis 107
Sale and repurchase agreements (SRAs) 242, 317; United Kingdom 9, 36; USA 110–11
Sale-purchase agreements (matched) 390
Salomon Brothers Inc. 112, 150; and trading scandal 150ff
Salomon Brothers UK Limited 44n
San Francisco 1, 102, 107, 130
Sanwa-BGK Securities Co., L. P. 112

Sapporo 246
Sarpkaya, S. 418, 420
Saskatchewan 301n
Savings and loan associations
  (USA) 106, 119, 121, 122, 137,
  388
Savings banks 106, 119, 121, 156,
  171, 172, 174, 222, 223, 235,
  272, 279, 281, 388
Savings bonds (USA) 104
Sayers, R. S. 392, 396, 398, 421
SBC Government Securities Inc.
  112
Scammell, W. M. 392
Schedule B banks (Canada) 307
Scheduled banks (India) 336, 337,
  338, 342
Schroders Australia Discount
  Limited 269
Scotia McLeod Inc. 299n
Screen brokers 116–17
Screen trading 1, 42, 183, 237,
  274, 379, 391
Seasonal influences/patterns 4, 5,
  9, 11, 16, 112, 172, 234, 235,
  244, 250, 265, 276, 307, 325–6,
  339, 366–7
Seasonal stringency 4
Seasonal Treasury notes
  (Australia) 268
SEC (Securities and Exchange
  Commission) (USA) 114, 115,
  131, 150, 405
Seccombe, Marshall & Campion
  plc 8n, 74
Sechold group 370
'Secondary' institutions 4
'Secondary' markets 101
Secretary of Monetary Affairs
  - (Hong Kong) 321
Securities Act 1933 131–2
Securities and Investment Board
  69–70
Securities Discount House Limited
  370
Securities houses (Japan) 244, 249,
  250–1, 252, 253, 255, 262, 263,
  266
Securities Industry Association 136

'See-saw effect' 90
Semi-government authorities
  (Australia) 283
Semi-government securities
  (Australia) 280–1, 291; and
  State banks 280; private
  placements 281
Senate Banking Committee 136
Senbank 363n
Shaw, E. R. 392
Shinkin 241, 244
Shinyo-kinko (shinkin) 241
Shinyo-kumiai 241
Shipbuilding paper 84
Shoko Chukin Bank 241
Short-dated bonds 4, 5, 38–9
Short Term Discount Limited 269
SIBOR (Singapore Inter-Bank
  Offered Rate) 358
SIMEX (Singapore International
  Monetary Exchange) 349,
  361–2; 'bucketing' 361n;
  contracts 362; gross margining
  system 361; incentives to
  development 361–2;
  membership 361
Singapore 142, 143, 148, 149,
  276, 307, 332–3; as an entrepot
  centre 346; exchange control,
  removal of 352, 357; floating of
  S$ 355
Singapore Foreign Exchange and
  Money Brokers Association
  355n
Singapore Foreign Exchange
  Market Committee 355n, 356
Single capacity trading 42
Small Business Administration
  (USA) 118
Smith Barney, Harris Upham &
  Co. 112
Smith New Court 71
'Smoothing out' operations 9, 74,
  205, 249, 294, 295, 325, 365
Société d'investissement à capital
  variable (SICAV) 159
Société Générale 159n, 164, 165,
  166
Sociétés financières 156

South Africa: balance of payments 386; debt standstill 386; gold production 366; seasonal factors 366–7
South African Permanent Building Society 363
South African Reserve Bank 363ff *passim*, 424; and interest rates 385; and managed floating 385; and Treasury bills 374; discount window 368, 383–4; exchange control 385; foreign desk 385; intervention by 382–6; open market operations 385; resort to repos 384
South America 334
South East Asia 334, 355
SPAN (standard portfolio analysis of risk) 67
Special buyer/broker (**United Kingdom**) 19–20, 74
Special call loans (**Canada**) 312, 313
Special credit institutions (**Italy**) 221, 222, 223, 230, 236
Special Deposit Scheme (**United Kingdom**) 78
Spécialistes en valeurs du Trésor 158n
SRD (Statutory Reserve Deposit) (**Australia**) 275n, 283
Stability and Growth Act 1967 (**Germany**) 178
Stals, Chris 386
Standard Bank of South Africa 363
Standard Chartered Bank 321, 323, 331; Government's banker 321, 324; quasi-central banking functions 321; note issue 321, 324–5, 326
Standard Chartered Perpetual 65
State Bank of India (SBI) 336, 337, 339, 343, 344–5
States (**USA**) 113, 131, 137
Statutory Liquidity Ratio (SLR): **India** 338, 341; **Singapore** 360
Sterling 214–15, 216–17, 218; devaluation of 215, 217

Sterling commercial paper 17, 37, 56, 57–64; and capital protection 57; and liquidity 57, 58; and recession 64; and yield pick-up 57; cost of issue 60; credit agency rating 57, 64; dealers 58, 64; dealing sizes 57; maturities 58, 60; unrated paper 64
Stigum, Marcia 400, 403, 404, 405
Stockbrokers 157, 165, 225, 267, 273n, 281
Stock exchange firms 69
Stock exchange money broker 13, 35n, 36, 44–5, 54, 87
Store, R. K. 423
Student Loan Marketing Association (**USA**) 118
Superannuation funds (**Australia**) 280
Supervision (**United Kingdom**) 91–101
Supreme Court (**USA**) 136
Swap operations 21, 144, 310, 312, 333, 367, 390; North-bound swap 314; South-bound swap 314; *see also* 'bank swap', cross-currency swap, currency swap, interest rate swap, and FOREX swap
Sweden 213
SWIFT (Society for Worldwide International Funds Transfer) 175
'Swing' shift 149
Swiss Bank Corporation 72
Switching transactions 41, 79, 84, 341
SYCOM (Sydney Computerised Overnight Market) 291
Sydney 1, 143, 267, 269, 275n, 287, 288
Sydney Futures Exchange 289–91; clearing house 289, 290; membership 289–90
Sydney Greasy Wool Futures Exchange 288
Sykes Memorial Lecture 399
Systemic risk 124–5, 126

System Open Market Account
(USA) 108, 109, 110

Tagesgeld 174
'Talk around': **Australia** 278;
    Canada 302
Tanshi houses 241, 243, 244, 245
    247, 248–9, 253–4, 255, 257,
    258, 263–4, 265–6; and Bank
    of Japan 263, 264; and intra-
    day loans 246, 263; as brokers
    263–4; collateral 244;
    commission 244, 247
Tap bills 256, 340, 341, 375, 388
Tap stocks 41, 47, 48, 77, 388
Tax payments/dates 9, 173, 174,
    199, 234, 264, 366, 371, 375,
    383, 391
Telecom Australia 281, 285
Telerate 65, 91, 164, 292
Tennessee Valley Authority 118
Terms of trade 3
Thailand 323
Thomson, Robert 414
TIFFE (Tokyo International
    Futures Exchange) 262
Time deposit receipts (TDRs) 304
Time deposits 139, 209, 237, 242,
    254, 285, 360; of building
    societies **(United Kingdom)** 15
Titres de créance négociables
    (TCNs) 169–70
Tokyo 1, 10, 142–3, 212, 245,
    246, 247, 249, 261, 262, 263,
    276, 288, 307, 332, 333, 334,
    356
Tokyo Dollar Call Market 242,
    257–60, 263
Toronto 1, 299, 308, 309, 312
Town Clearing 34, 82, 87, 88–9
Trade bill: **Australia** 283; **London**
    18n
Trade stock options 66
Trading banks **(Australia)** 267,
    270, 273, 277n, 279, 281, 283,
    286; and financial futures 290
Treasury bills, invention of 388;
    Australia 268, 277; **Canada** 297,
    300–2, 310, 312, 313, 315, 317,
318, 319, cash management
    tenders 301, payment for 301,
    retail demand 300, 'talk around'
    302, tender 297, 298, 300,
    310–11, secondary market 302;
    Germany 176, 177, 178, 179,
    interest rate tender 179,
    secondary market 179, volume
    tender 179; **India**, auctions 340,
    refinance facility for DFHI 341,
    rediscount 340, secondary
    market 340, 341, tap 340,
    3-month bills 340, 341, 182-day
    bills 340, 341; **Japan** 255–6,
    265; **Singapore** 347–8, 350, 351,
    353, 354, auctions 353, 355,
    maturities 353, primary dealers
    353, 'same-day dealers' 355,
    secondary market 353, 355;
    South Africa 373–5, 379, 384,
    385, administered rates 365,
    'little taps' 375, secondary
    market 375, special Treasury
    bills 375, 384–5, tender 365,
    374–5; **United Kingdom** 4, 5, 8,
    9, 10n, 13, 16, 18, 19n, 27–30,
    34, 35, 36, 73, 74, 80–1, 83, 87,
    89, 90, 388, 390, 'hot' bills 30,
    in ECUs 31–3, maturity 29,
    overseas interest 30, tender 28,
    syndicated bid 28, underwriting
    of tender 28–30, use of for
    'mopping up' 88; **USA** 103–6,
    109, 114n, 117, 118, 120,
    auctions 104, 105ns, 151,
    competitive 105, non-
    competitive 105
Treasury Bills Act 1877 29
Treasury bond futures 66, 165
Treasury discount paper **(Germany)**
    176, 177, 178, 198, 200
Treasury notes: **Australia** 268,
    271, 273, 277, 292, auctions
    277–9, 'talk around' 278, tap
    issues 277, underwriting 279;
    Singapore 353; **USA** 104, 106,
    114n, 117, 388
Trésor public 157
Treuhand **(Germany)** 181

Trust Bank 363n
Trust banks (Japan) 241, 243, 248, 250, 258
Trust companies 134, 137, 138, 300, 304, 305, 312, 314
Trust departments (of banks) 131, 133, 134, 137, 138, 141
Trust funds 378
Tschinkel, Sheila L. 401
Turnover tax (Germany) 181

UBS Phillips & Drew Gilts Limited 44n
UBS Securities Inc. 112
Unification (also reunification) of Germany 188, 192, 208, 211, 215, 217
Union Acceptances Limited 365
Union Bank of Calcutta 348
Union Building Society 363
Union Discount Company Ltd 8
Unit Trust of India (UTI) 339, 340, 341, 344, 345
Unit trusts 57, 157, 159, 378
'Universal' banks 173, 174
Usance promissory notes 340, 341
U-Schätze 176, 193, 196
US General Accounting Office 401, 402
US Treasury Bond Market 42
US west coast 286, 288

Vancouver 299, 308, 312
Van der Merwe, E. J. 423
Van Ettinger, C. C. 423
Velocity of circulation 185
Volksbanken 174
Volkskas 363
Volkswagen A.G. 182

Wagstyl, Stefan 414
Wall Street 331
Warburg, S. G., Akroyd, Rowe & Pitman, Mullens (Gilt-Edged) Ltd 8n, 44n, 71

Warburg, S. G. & Co., Inc. 112
Warehouse receipt 130
Washington Metropolitan Area Transit Authority 118
Watts, George S. 418
Ways and means advances 4
Wechsel 176, 179–80, 192, 388, 390
Westdeutsche Landes Bank Girozentrale 172
'Western accounts' (Canada) 299, 306, 308
Western Europe 358, 362
When-issued (WI): Canada 302; London 50; USA 106, 153–4
Wholesale money 139, 180, 303, 304, 307, 327–8, 378; London 11n, 13, 14, 15
Williams, Cooke, Lott & Kissack Limited 44n
Willis, Parker B. 402–3
Wilson, J. S. G. 392, 395, 396, 397, 398, 399, 400, 401, 403, 404, 405, 407, 414, 415, 416, 417, 418, 421, 422
Window dressing 79, 233, 235
Winnipeg 312, 332
Withholding tax: Australia 273n, 277, 280; Canada 308; Hong Kong 328, 334; Italy 228, 230; Japan 254, 258; Singapore 334, 359, 362; USA 308, 309
Wood Gundy Inc. 299n
Wood Gundy Limited 299n
Woolwich Building Society 10
World Bank 120, 135, 301

Yamaichi International (America), Inc. 112
Yates, S. P. M. 423

Zaitech (Japan) 256–7
Zenshiren Bank 243–4, 248
Zero cash policy 277n
Zero reserve requirements 306